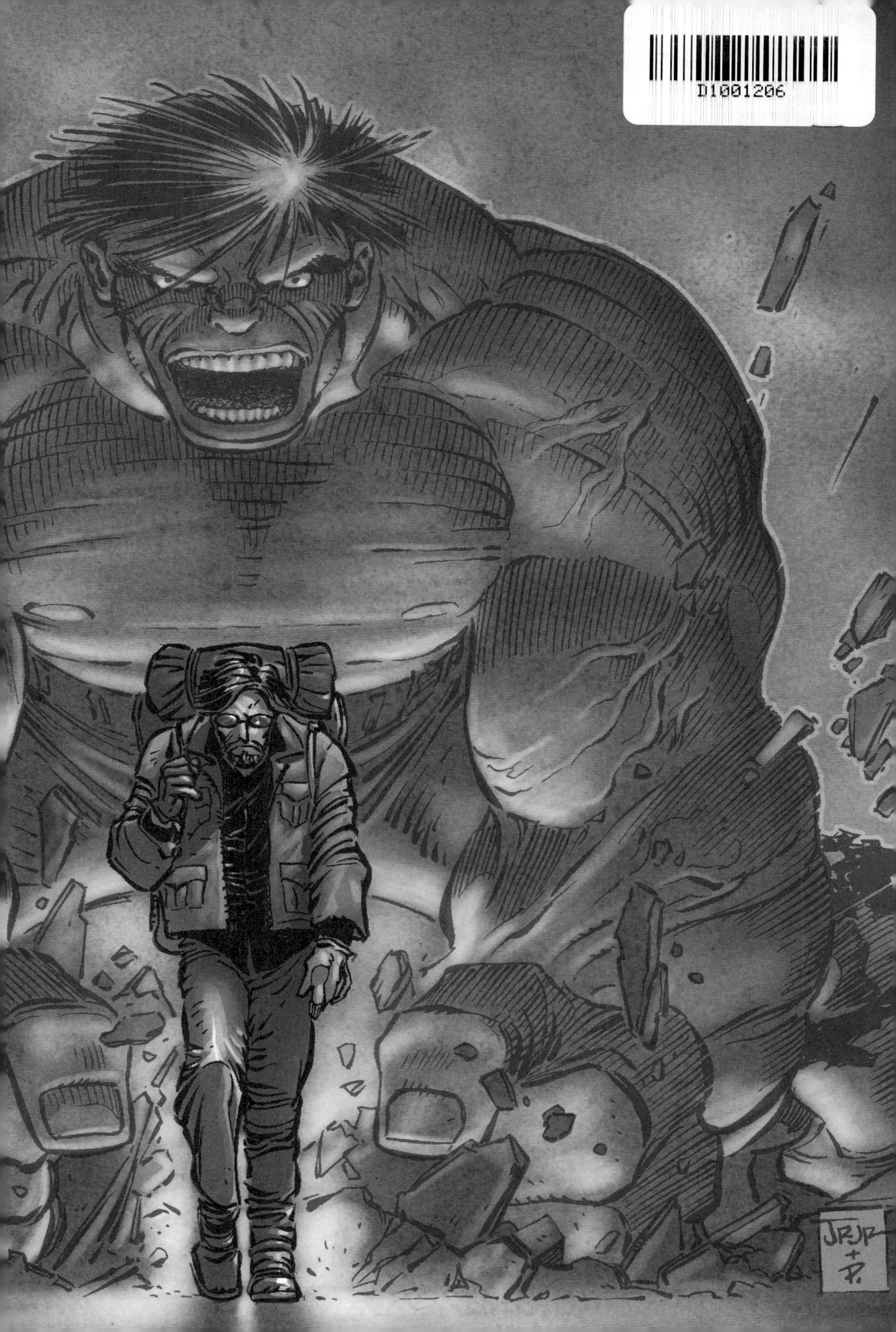

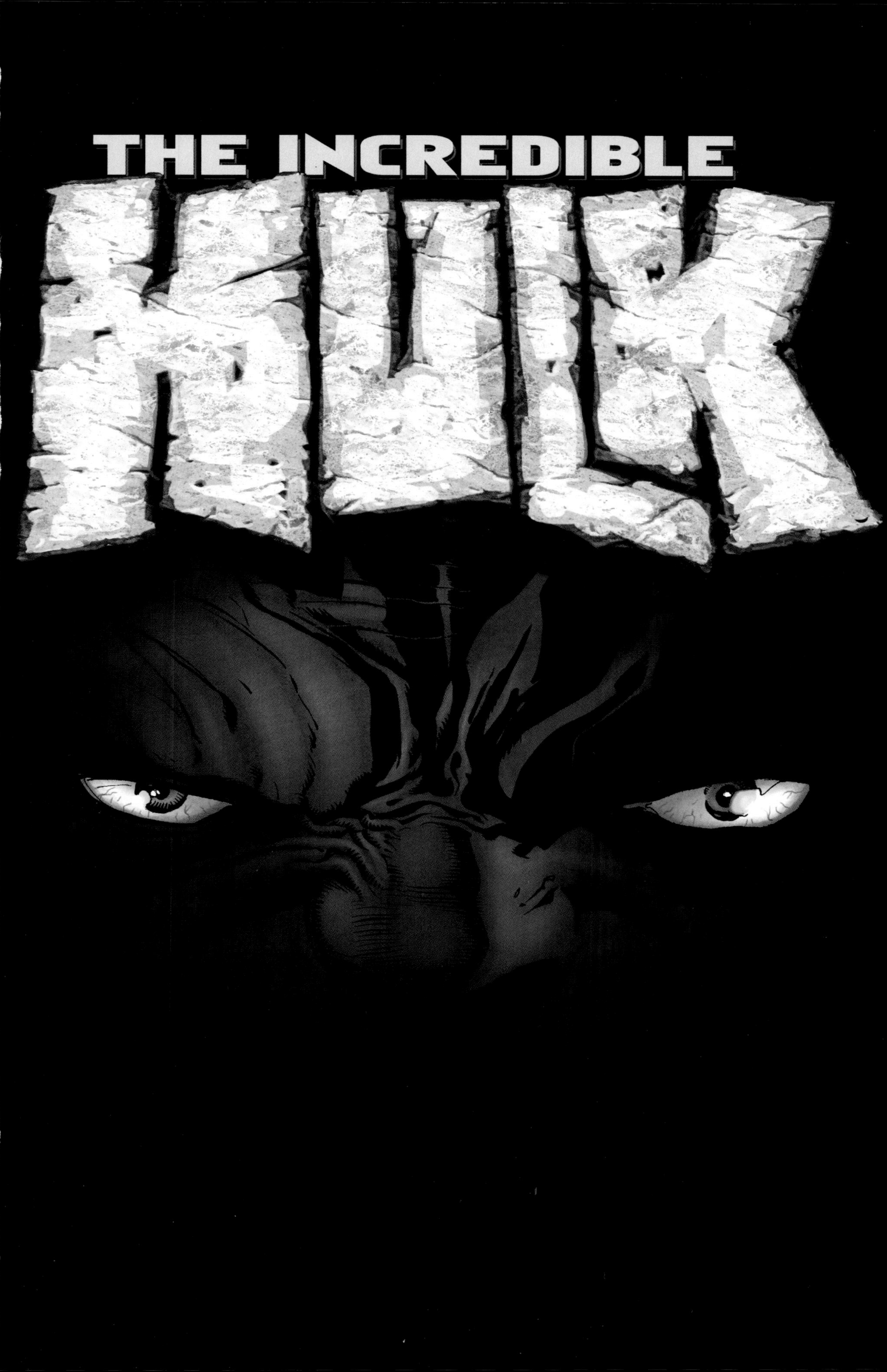
THE INCREDIBLE
HULK

MARVEL ENTERPRISES, INC.

CHIEF EXECUTIVE OFFICER
Peter Cuneo

CHIEF FINANCIAL OFFICER
Ken West

CHIEF CREATIVE OFFICER
Avi Arad

CHIEF INFORMATION OFFICER
Gui Karyo

PRESIDENT CEO, TOY BIZ
Alan Fine

EXECUTIVE V.P.-BUSINESS & LEGAL AFFAIRS
Allen Lipson

EXECUTIVE SALES V.P.-TOY BIZ
Ralph Lancelotti

V.P.-HUMAN RESOURCES
Mary Sprowls

ADVERTISING—PROMOTION—RETAIL SALES

EXECUTIVE VICE PRESIDENT/ CONSUMER PRODUCTS, PROMOTIONS & MEDIA SALES
Russell A. Brown

DIRECTOR OF ADVERTISING
Jeff Dunetz

TRADE BOOK SALES MANAGER
Jennifer Beemish

ADVERTISING SALES
Sara Beth Schrager

PUBLISHING GROUP

MANAGING EDITOR
David Bogart

PRODUCTION DIRECTOR
Dan Carr

DIRECTOR OF MANUFACTURING
Sangho Byun

SENIOR MARKETING COMMUNICATIONS MANAGER
Joseph Zerbo

MARKETING COMMUNICATIONS MANAGER
Bill Rosemann

PUBLISHING BUSINESS MANAGER
Chet Krayewski

SENIOR MANUFACTURING MANAGER
Fred Pagan

MANUFACTURING MANAGER
Christine Slusarz

MANUFACTURING REPRESENTATIVE
Stefano Perrone, Jr.

SPECIAL PROJECTS GROUP

EDITOR
Jeff Youngquist

PRODUCTION MANAGER
Johnny Greene

ART DIRECTOR
Matty Ryan

ASSISTANT EDITORS
Cory Sedlmeier
Jennifer Grünwald

BOOK DESIGNER
Patrick McGrath

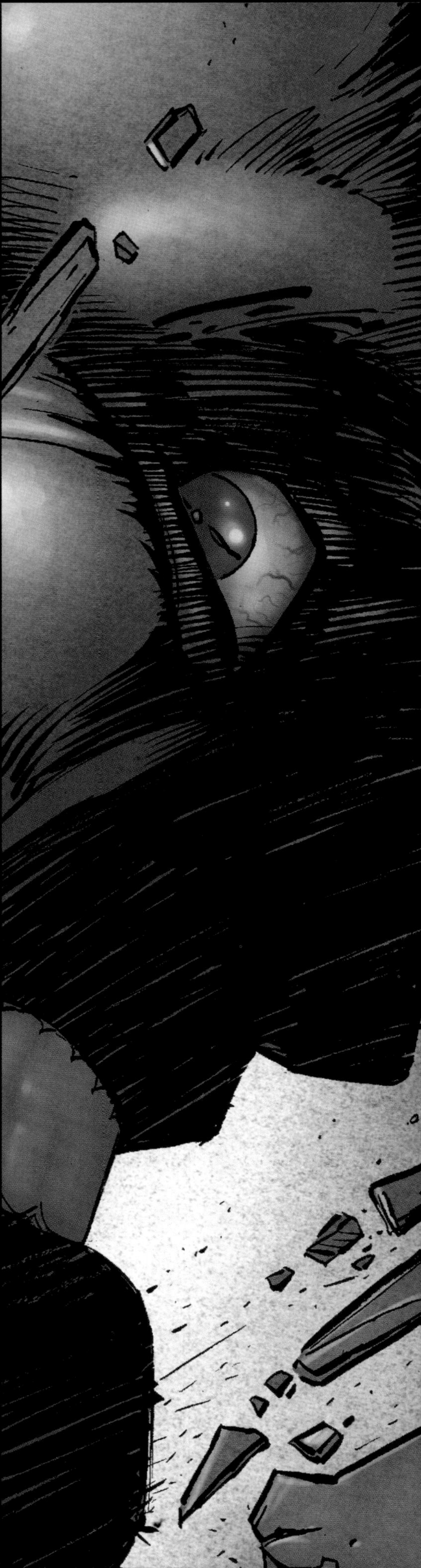

THE INCREDIBLE HULK

RETURN OF THE MONSTER
Incredible Hulk #34-39
writer: BRUCE JONES
pencils: JOHN ROMITA JR.
inks: TOM PALMER

BOILING POINT
Incredible Hulk #40-43
writer: BRUCE JONES
pencils: LEE WEEKS
inks: TOM PALMER

STARTLING STORIES: BANNER
writer: BRIAN AZZARELLO
artist: RICHARD CORBEN

colorist: STUDIO F
letters: RS & COMICRAFT'S WES ABBOTT

original editor: AXEL ALONSO
assistant editor: JOHN MIESEGAES
editor in chief: JOE QUESADA
president: BILL JEMAS

INCREDIBLE HULK VOL. 1. Contains material originally published in magazine form as INCREDIBLE HULK #34-43 and STARTLING STORIES: BANNER #1-4 . First printing 2002. ISBN# 0-7851-1022-4. Published by MARVEL COMICS, a division of MARVEL ENTERTAINMENT GROUP, INC. OFFICE OF PUBLICATION: 10 East 40th Street, New York, NY 10016. Copyright © 2001 and 2002 Marvel Characters, Inc. All rights reserved. $29.99 per copy in the U.S. and $48.00 in Canada (GST #R127032852); Canadian Agreement #40668537. All characters featured in this issue and the distinctive names and likenesses thereof, and all related indicia are trademarks of Marvel Characters, Inc. No similarity between any of the names, characters, persons, and/or institutions in this magazine with those of any living or dead person or institution is intended, and any such similarity which may exist is purely coincidental. **Printed in the U.S.A.** STAN LEE, Chairman Emeritus. For information regarding advertising in Marvel Comics or on Marvel.com, please contact Russell Brown, Executive Vice President, Consumer Products, Promotions and Media Sales at 212-576-8561 or rbrown@marvel.com

10 9 8 7 6 5 4 3 2 1

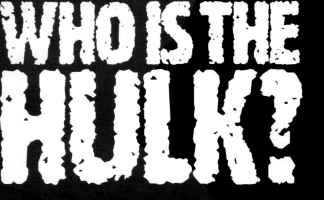

WHO IS THE HULK?

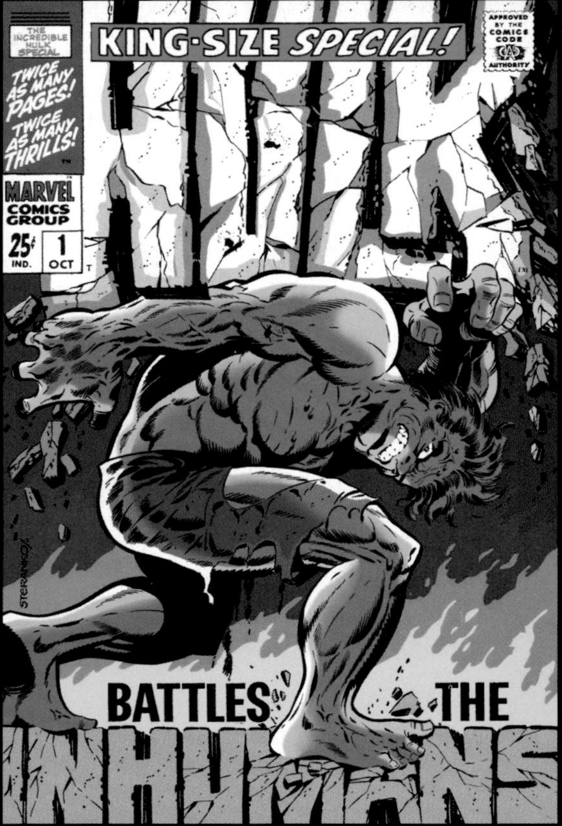
THE INCREDIBLE HULK SPECIAL
KING-SIZE SPECIAL!
TWICE AS MANY PAGES! TWICE AS MANY THRILLS!
MARVEL COMICS GROUP
25¢ IND.
1 OCT
APPROVED BY THE COMICS CODE AUTHORITY
STERANKO
BATTLES THE INHUMANS

***Hulk Special #1* cover by Jim Steranko, 1968.**

Like rock and roll and Ford Thunderbirds, he's been around in one form or another most of our lives. First the Stan Lee comic in the '60s, then the hit Bill Bixby TV series in the '70s, then bumper stickers and soda cups—and now an upcoming movie by Ang Lee, celebrated auteur of *Crouching Tiger, Hidden Dragon.*

But who *is* the Hulk?

A green mountain of rage, birthed within the psyche of Dr. Bruce Banner by a massive exposure to gamma rays? A genie freed from its bottle via the rising blood pressure of its reluctant host? The perfect id monster with the primitive temper of a 2-year-old and all the attendant lack of control, wrapped in an impossibly buff body Schwarzenegger would kill for? Or the 800-hundred-pound gorilla we all secretly wanted at our command to face down the playground bully?

Inarticulate, infuriated, destructive and seemingly unrepentant, the Hulk may be all the above and more… the repressed frustration and impotency of a nation mired in the Cold War… an island of security perhaps more keenly felt than ever in this new kind of battle.

When I was allowed the opportunity to write the Hulk, I found myself initially stymied by the sheer weight and omnipresence of that big green wall. I hammered, I struck, pounded and cursed…and the Hulk just laughed in my face: implacable, immutable, impenetrable.

Like the audience in Hitchcock's *Psycho* who lost their identifying protagonist in the death of Janet Leigh, I had nowhere to turn. And like the audience who turned

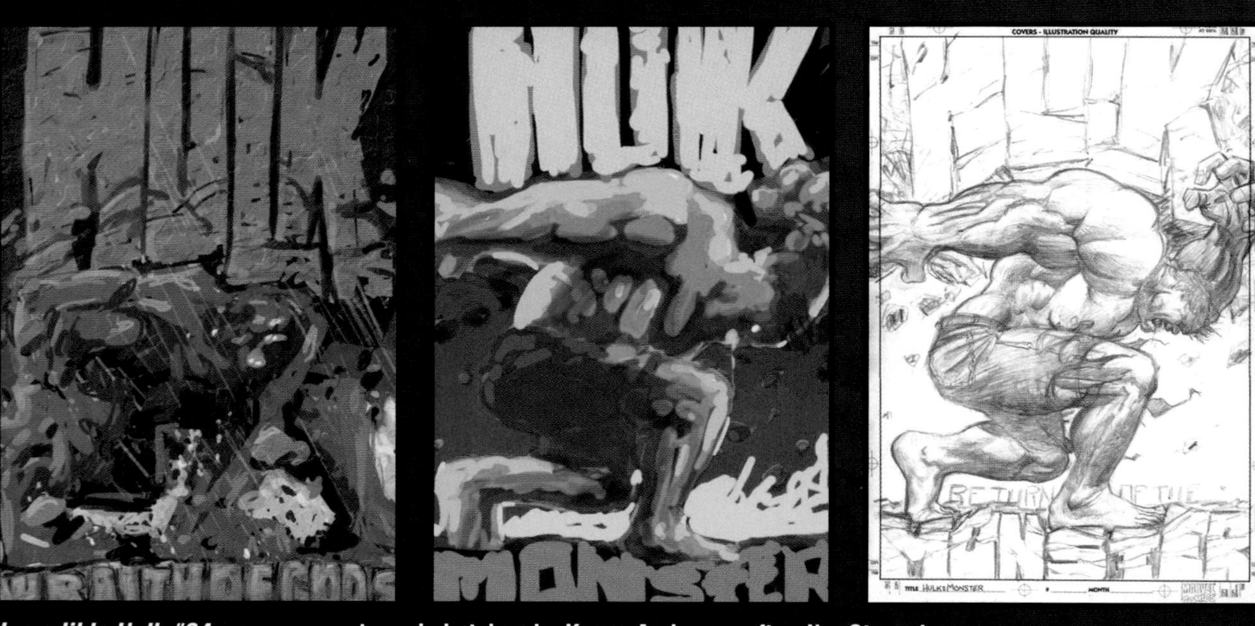
HULK
HULK
MONSTER
COVERS - ILLUSTRATION QUALITY
RETURN OF THE

***Incredible Hulk #34* cover concepts and sketches by Kaare Andrews, after Jim Steranko.**

o Norman Bates, I turned to the closest thing left standing: Bruce Banner.

And the more I looked, the more fascinated I became by his quiet, multi-layered alter ego—and the more certain I was I had the answer!

Not all of them, no. There are still many parts of the puzzle that don't fit, still much research and study to be done. But the path to understanding the Hulk, I was convinced, was through Banner.

Banner. The hapless/helpless guardian of his out-of-control calamity. Calm, intelligent, an everyman with an overweening conscience, he was not the Dr. Jekyll who willingly swallowed the potion to let out Hyde. Nor was he a Frankenstein who created his own Monster. Banner was a victim of circumstances, in the wrong place at the wrong time. And that's when the second epiphany hit me: I had assumed that Hulk had a clearly defined starting point: the advent of the gamma bomb explosion and Banner's exposure to it. But Banner had his own history long before that pivotal event. And if Hulk is in part an extension of Banner, perhaps we need to go even farther back than I'd anticipated.

Unlike Spider-Man or Daredevil, Banner doesn't spend his days as the Hulk-in-disguise. One of the most singular aspects of Banner's personality is his utter repugnance regarding his destructive counterpart—equaled only, perhaps, by the Hulk's hatred for Banner.

Norman Mailer once described people's fear of cancer as the body's ultimate betrayal. It seemed to me yet another metaphor for the Hulk. The illness not only grows stronger as it spreads, it performs the ultimate obscenity: It doesn't die.

Yet neither does it completely reign. Even the giant must sleep. Banner—and by extension the world—is at risk only during those times the good doctor's will fails him. When he loses his temper. When his anguish and fury is so great it will not be contained. Then must a terrible price be paid.

Terrible, yes. But isn't, in truth, such an indestructibly mindless force also strangely satisfying, seductively cathartic? Grudgingly compelling? "My big brother's gonna beat you up for that!" Only this time it isn't a bluff, this

time the playground bully knows a terror of his own...

What became increasingly fascinating for me was how Banner became more and more frustrated by his lack of control over the beast, which in turn only exacerbated an already bad thing—allowed the beast greater and greater access. A vicious and escalating cycle.

Anger-management classes were clearly out of the question. So what to do?

My Banner took a lead from my own inspiration: The path to the beast was through Banner, the road to containment was in his own mind. And the control of it. Yoga, self-hypnosis, the strengthening of will. For above all, Banner wants to be civilized, craves control over himself in a world in which he, like us, can control nothing else.

Just one problem: The Hulk doesn't happen to agree with this.

Which brings us back to the square-one dilemma: which really came first, the chicken or the egg? Did Hulk spring fully formed from Banner's personality, as Athena sprang from the forehead of Zeus? Or did Banner incubate him through years of daily living and suppression, shape him with the same fantasies of revenge and control we all share, and then, with the convenient horror of the Gamma Ray incident, let the monster loose, albeit unwillingly, to walk where Banner never dared walk before?

Or was it really "unwitting" at all…?

The plot, as they say, thickens.

The law says we are responsible for our actions. But what if that option were magically removed from out path?

What if you were Bruce Banner? And the Hulk was your ultimate nightmare, a kind of intermittent insanity that intruded on your most intimate moments, your most secret dreams? How would you handle yourself?

How would you handle the Hulk?

And perhaps most terrifying of all … how would he handle you?

Who is the Hulk?

Read on…

Bruce Jones
Septembe   002

INCREDIBLE HULK #34
Cover sketch by Kaare Andrews

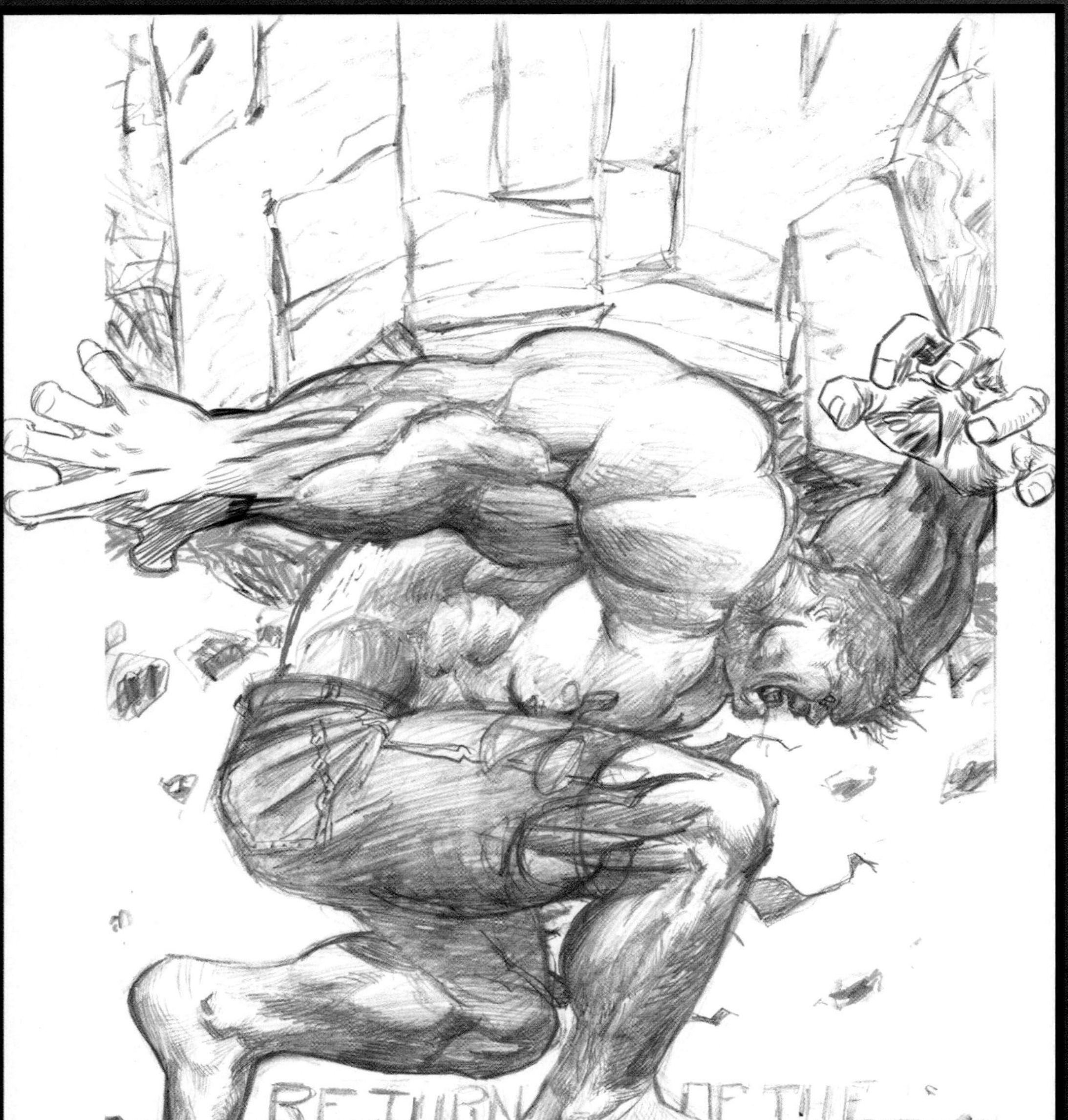

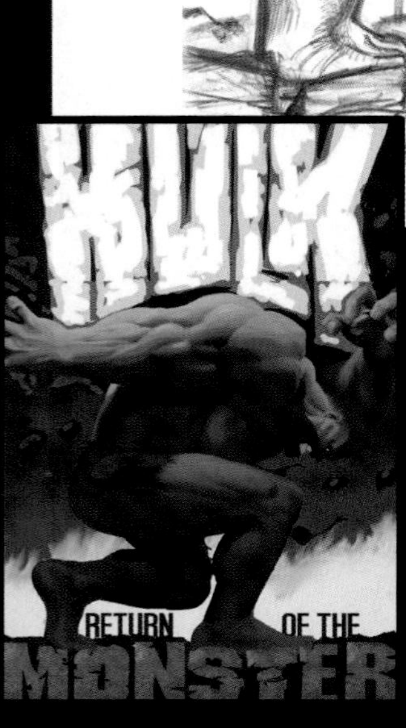
HULK
RETURN OF THE
MONSTER

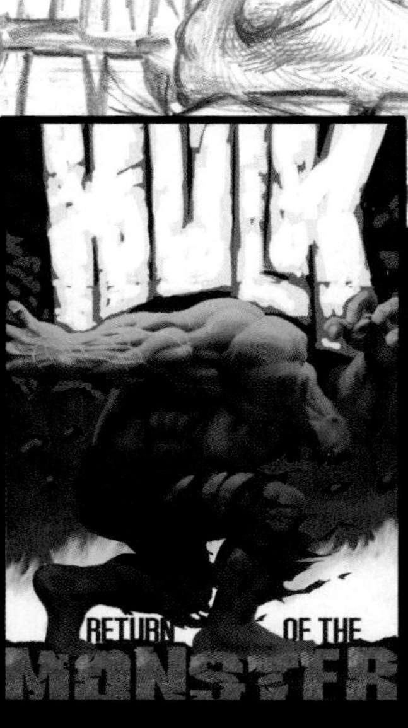
HULK
RETURN OF THE
MONSTER

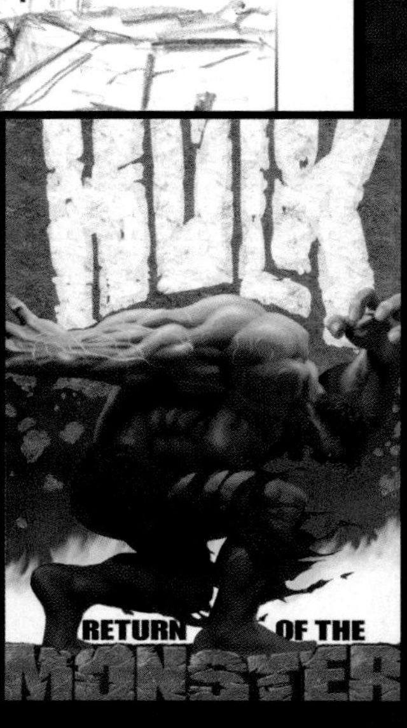
HULK
RETURN OF THE
MONSTER

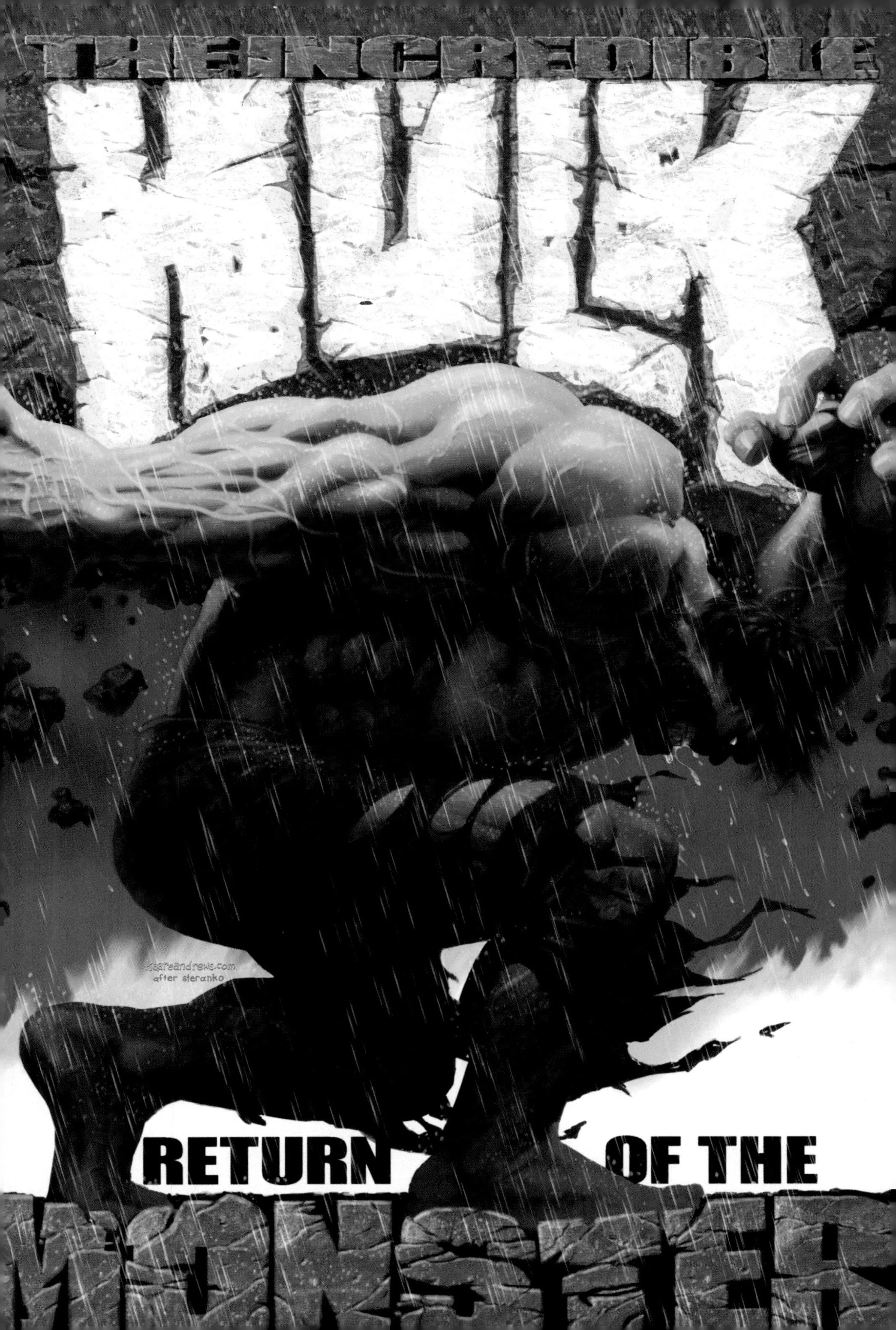
THE INCREDIBLE
HULK
kaareandrews.com
after steranko
RETURN OF THE
MONSTER

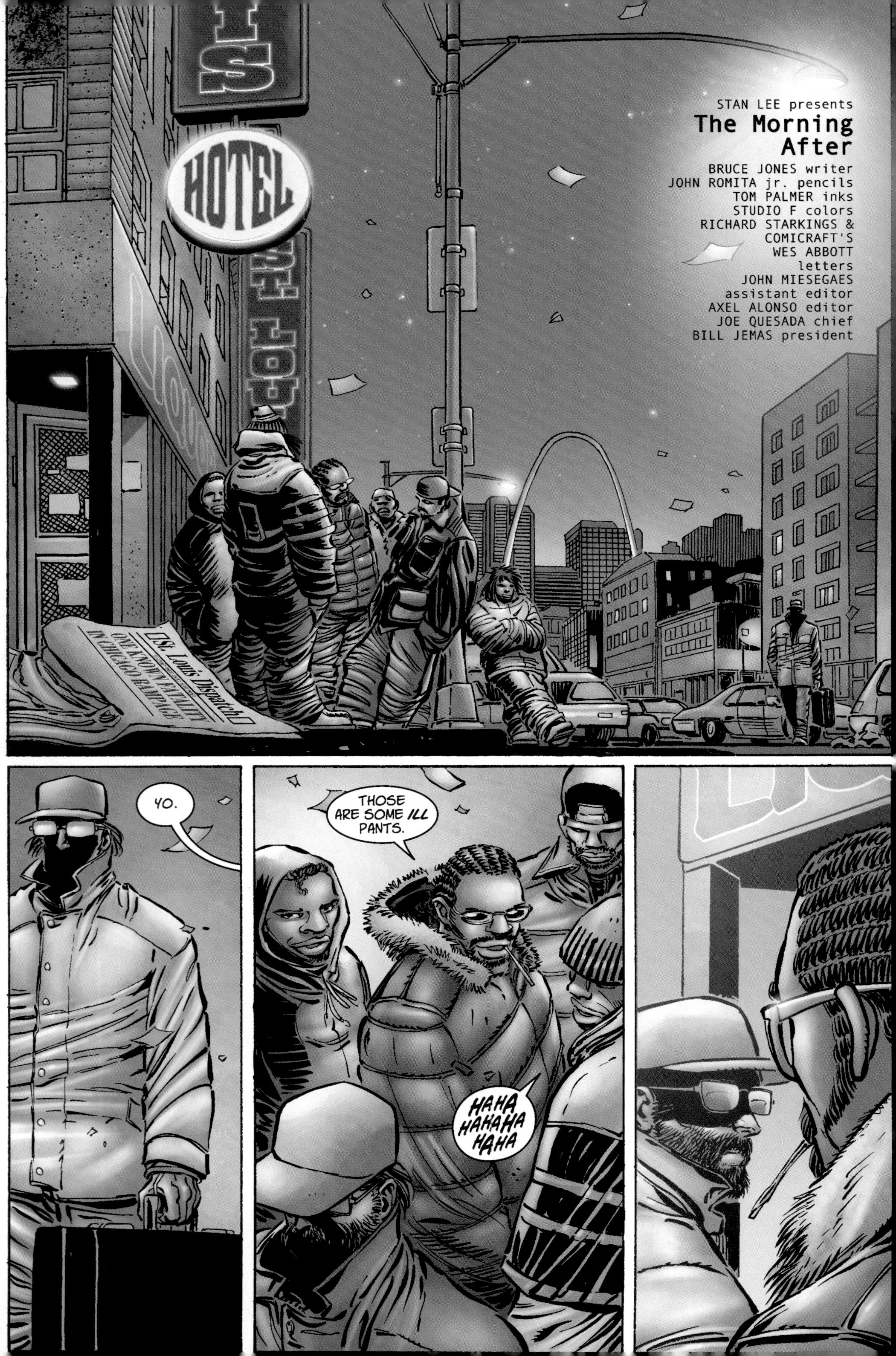
STAN LEE presents
The Morning After
BRUCE JONES writer
JOHN ROMITA jr. pencils
TOM PALMER inks
STUDIO F colors
RICHARD STARKINGS & COMICRAFT'S WES ABBOTT letters
JOHN MIESEGAES assistant editor
AXEL ALONSO editor
JOE QUESADA chief
BILL JEMAS president
HOTEL
St. Louis Dispatch
ONE KNOWN FATALITY IN CHICAGO RAMPAGE
YO.
THOSE ARE SOME ILL PANTS.
HAHA HAHAHA HAHA

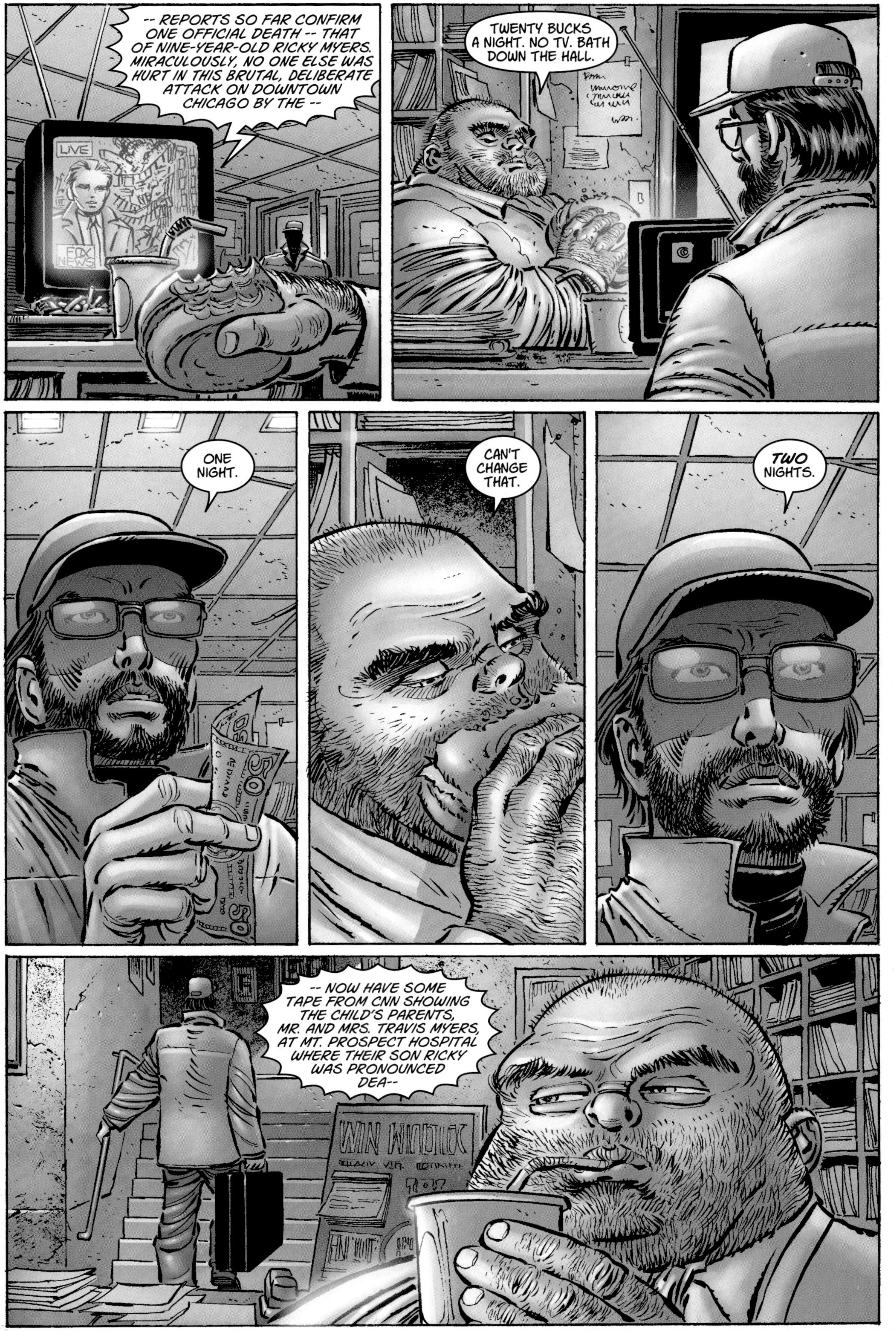
-- REPORTS SO FAR CONFIRM ONE OFFICIAL DEATH -- THAT OF NINE-YEAR-OLD RICKY MYERS. MIRACULOUSLY, NO ONE ELSE WAS HURT IN THIS BRUTAL, DELIBERATE ATTACK ON DOWNTOWN CHICAGO BY THE --
LIVE
FOX NEWS
TWENTY BUCKS A NIGHT. NO TV. BATH DOWN THE HALL.
ONE NIGHT.
CAN'T CHANGE THAT.
TWO NIGHTS.
-- NOW HAVE SOME TAPE FROM CNN SHOWING THE CHILD'S PARENTS, MR. AND MRS. TRAVIS MYERS, AT MT. PROSPECT HOSPITAL WHERE THEIR SON RICKY WAS PRONOUNCED DEA--

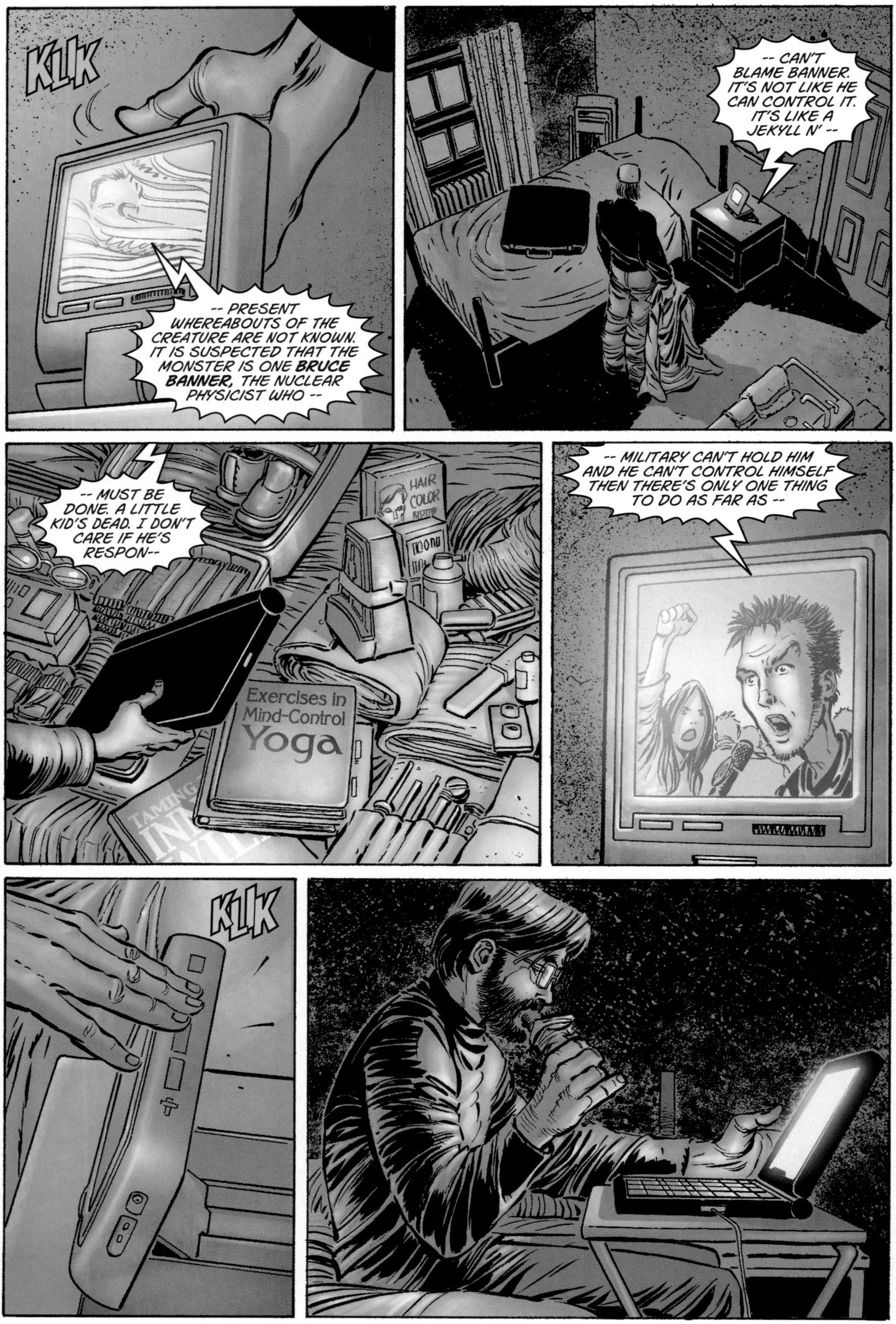
KLIK
-- PRESENT WHEREABOUTS OF THE CREATURE ARE NOT KNOWN. IT IS SUSPECTED THAT THE MONSTER IS ONE BRUCE BANNER, THE NUCLEAR PHYSICIST WHO --
-- CAN'T BLAME BANNER. IT'S NOT LIKE HE CAN CONTROL IT. IT'S LIKE A JEKYLL N' --
-- MUST BE DONE. A LITTLE KID'S DEAD. I DON'T CARE IF HE'S RESPON--
HAIR COLOR
Exercises in Mind-Control Yoga
-- MILITARY CAN'T HOLD HIM AND HE CAN'T CONTROL HIMSELF THEN THERE'S ONLY ONE THING TO DO AS FAR AS --
KLIK

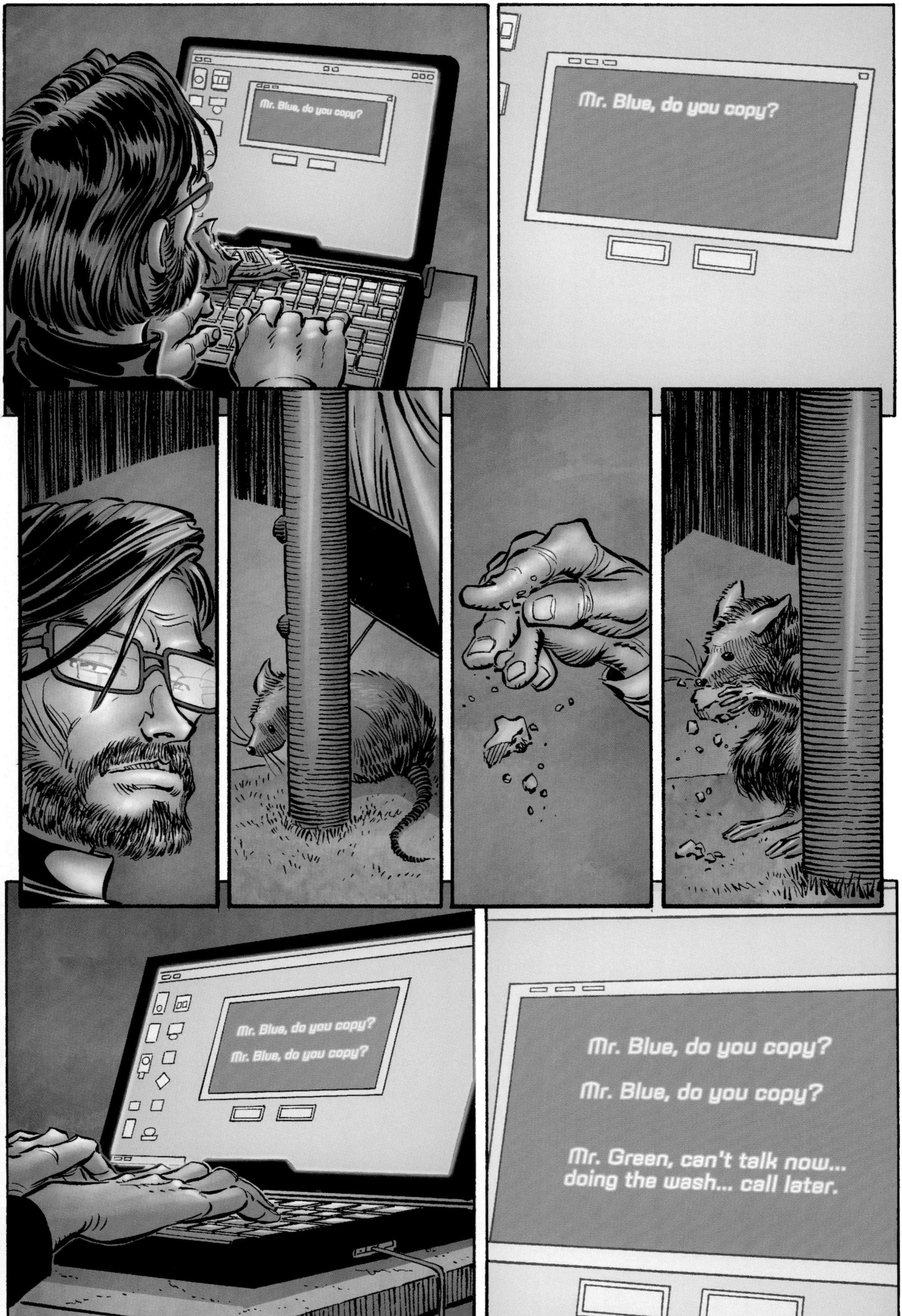
Mr. Blue, do you copy?
Mr. Blue, do you copy?
Mr. Blue, do you copy?
Mr. Blue, do you copy?
Mr. Blue, do you copy?
Mr. Blue, do you copy?
Mr. Blue, do you copy?
Mr. Green, can't talk now... doing the wash... call later.

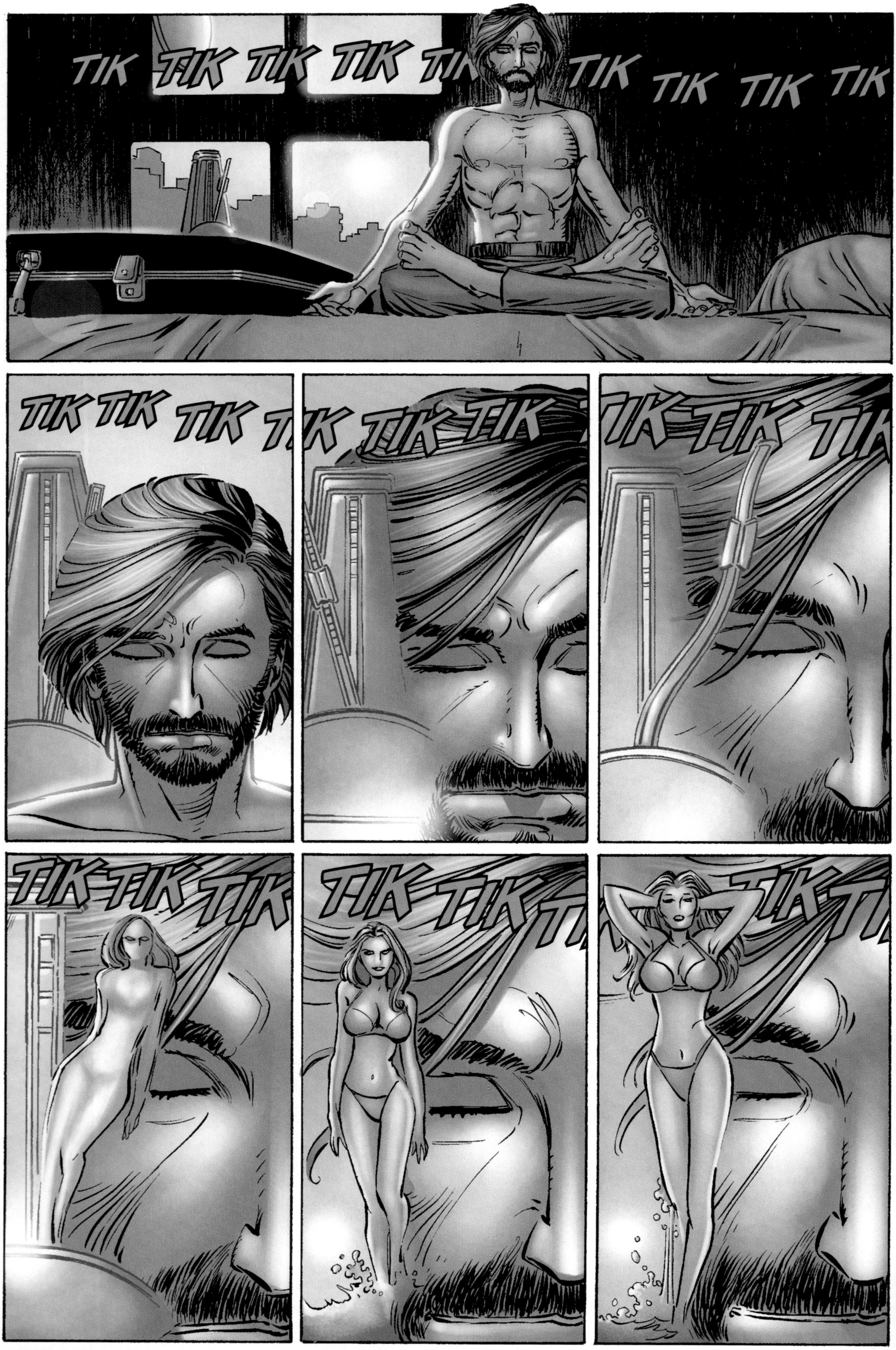
TIK TIK TIK TIK
TIK TIK TIK TIK
TIK TIK TIK
TIK TIK
TIK TIK TIK
TIK TIK TIK
TIK TIK
TIK TIK TIK
TIK

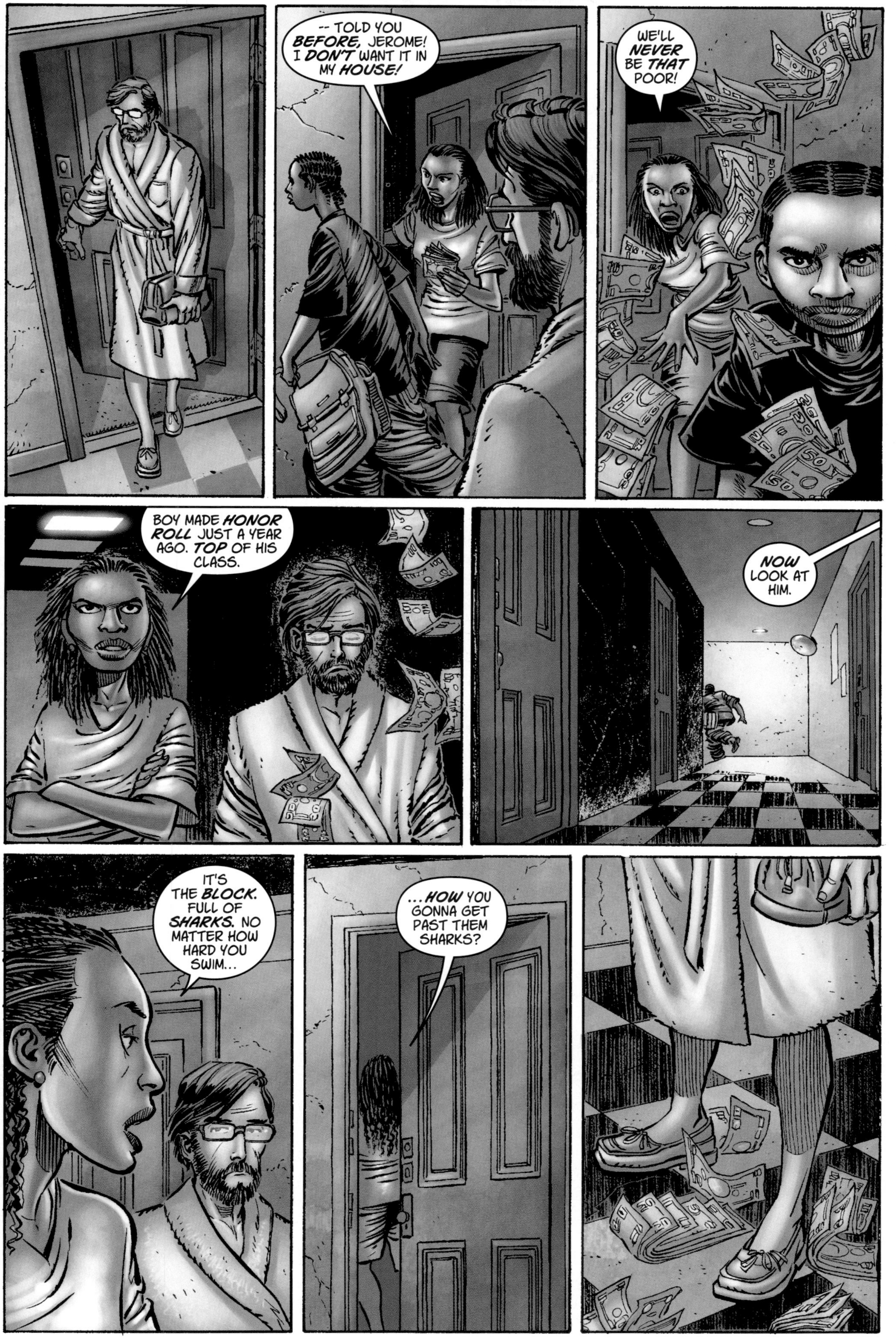
-- TOLD YOU BEFORE, JEROME! I DON'T WANT IT IN MY HOUSE!
WE'LL NEVER BE THAT POOR!
BOY MADE HONOR ROLL JUST A YEAR AGO. TOP OF HIS CLASS.
NOW LOOK AT HIM.
IT'S THE BLOCK. FULL OF SHARKS. NO MATTER HOW HARD YOU SWIM...
...HOW YOU GONNA GET PAST THEM SHARKS?

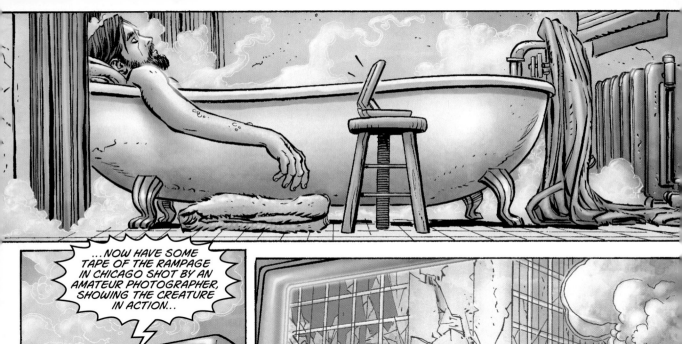

...NOW HAVE SOME TAPE OF THE RAMPAGE IN CHICAGO SHOT BY AN AMATEUR PHOTOGRAPHER, SHOWING THE CREATURE IN ACTION...

IF YOU SEE **THIS MAN**, DO **NOT** APPROACH. NOTIFY THE POLICE IMMEDIATELY BY DIALING THE 911 EMERGENCY NUMBER. THE SUSPECT IS NOW BELIEVED TO BE WEARING A **BEARD**.

REPEAT: DO NOT APPROACH!

EXPIRES 08-17-

ROBERT BRUCE BANNER
1205 MEOHFSVLKVENZNDI
SANTA FROHUDKRISA OEN

HAIR: BRN
HT: 5-09   WT: 1

Robert B.

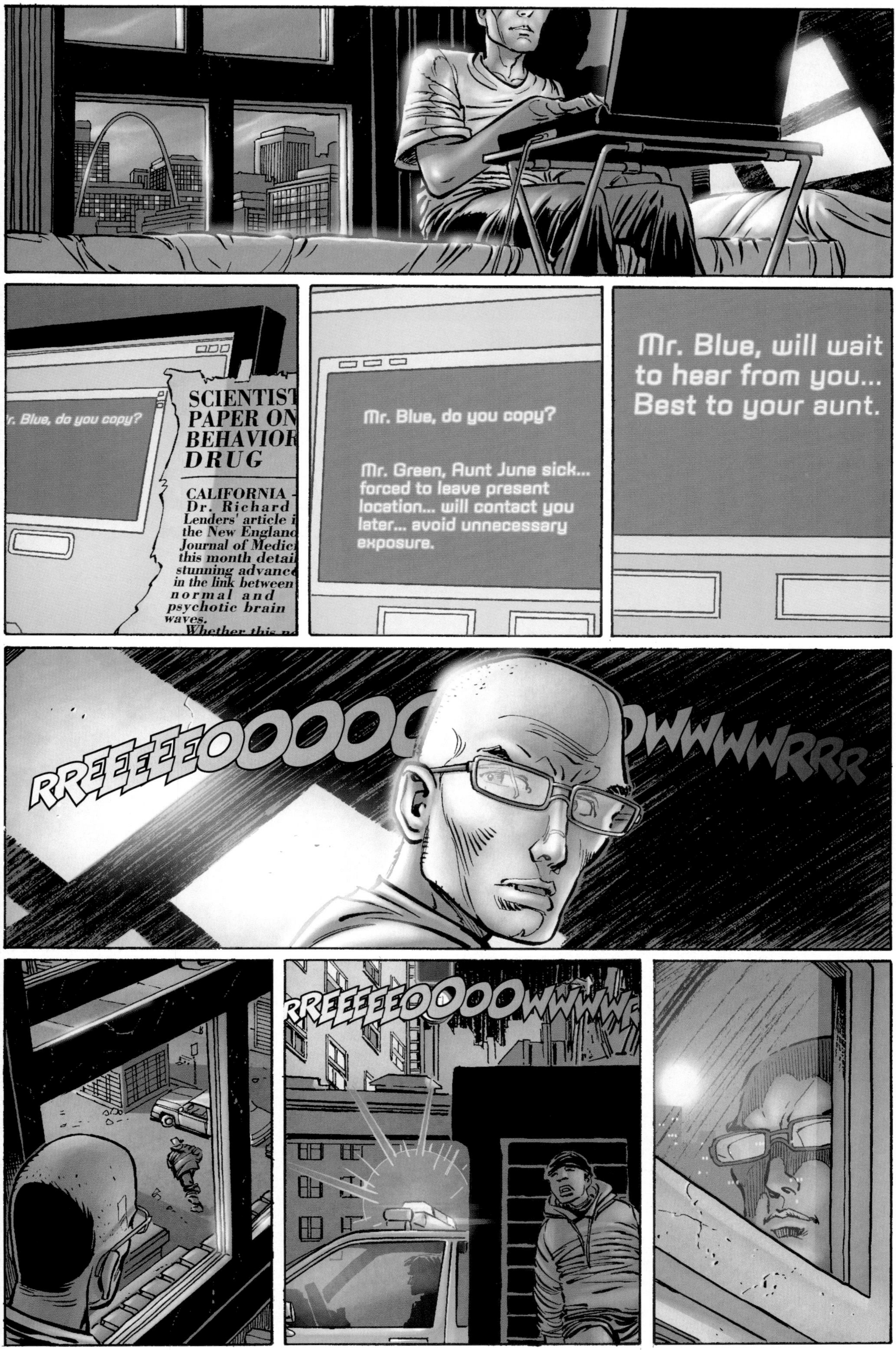
SCIENTIST
PAPER ON
BEHAVIOR
DRUG
CALIFORNIA -
Dr. Richard
Lenders' article i
the New England
Journal of Medic
this month detail
stunning advanc
in the link between
normal and
psychotic brain
waves.
r. Blue, do you copy?
Mr. Blue, do you copy?
Mr. Green, Aunt June sick... forced to leave present location... will contact you later... avoid unnecessary exposure.
Mr. Blue, will wait to hear from you... Best to your aunt.
RREEEEEOOOOOO
OWWWWRRR
RREEEEEOOOOOWWWW

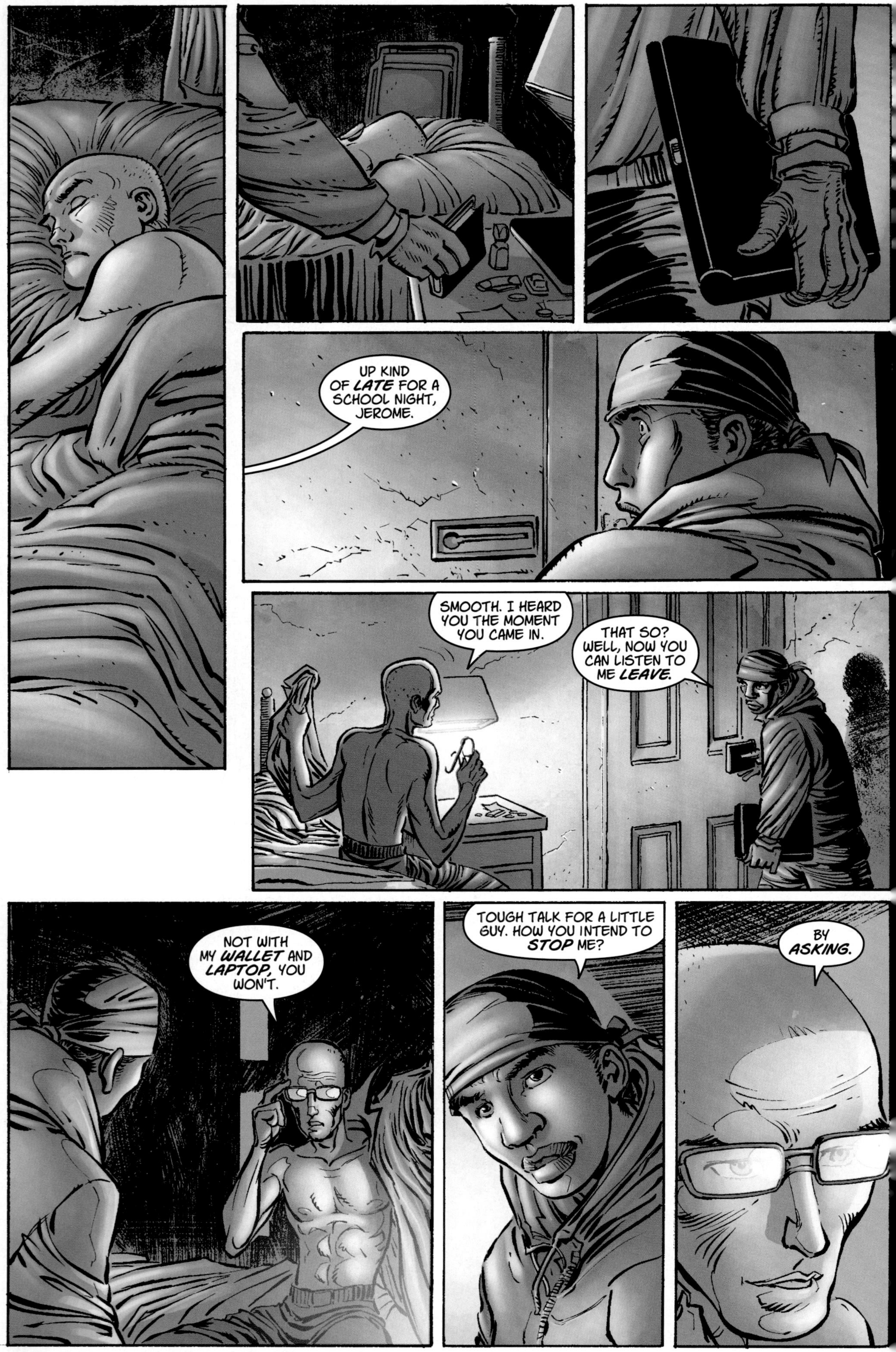
UP KIND OF LATE FOR A SCHOOL NIGHT, JEROME.
SMOOTH. I HEARD YOU THE MOMENT YOU CAME IN.
THAT SO? WELL, NOW YOU CAN LISTEN TO ME LEAVE.
NOT WITH MY WALLET AND LAPTOP, YOU WON'T.
TOUGH TALK FOR A LITTLE GUY. HOW YOU INTEND TO STOP ME?
BY ASKING.

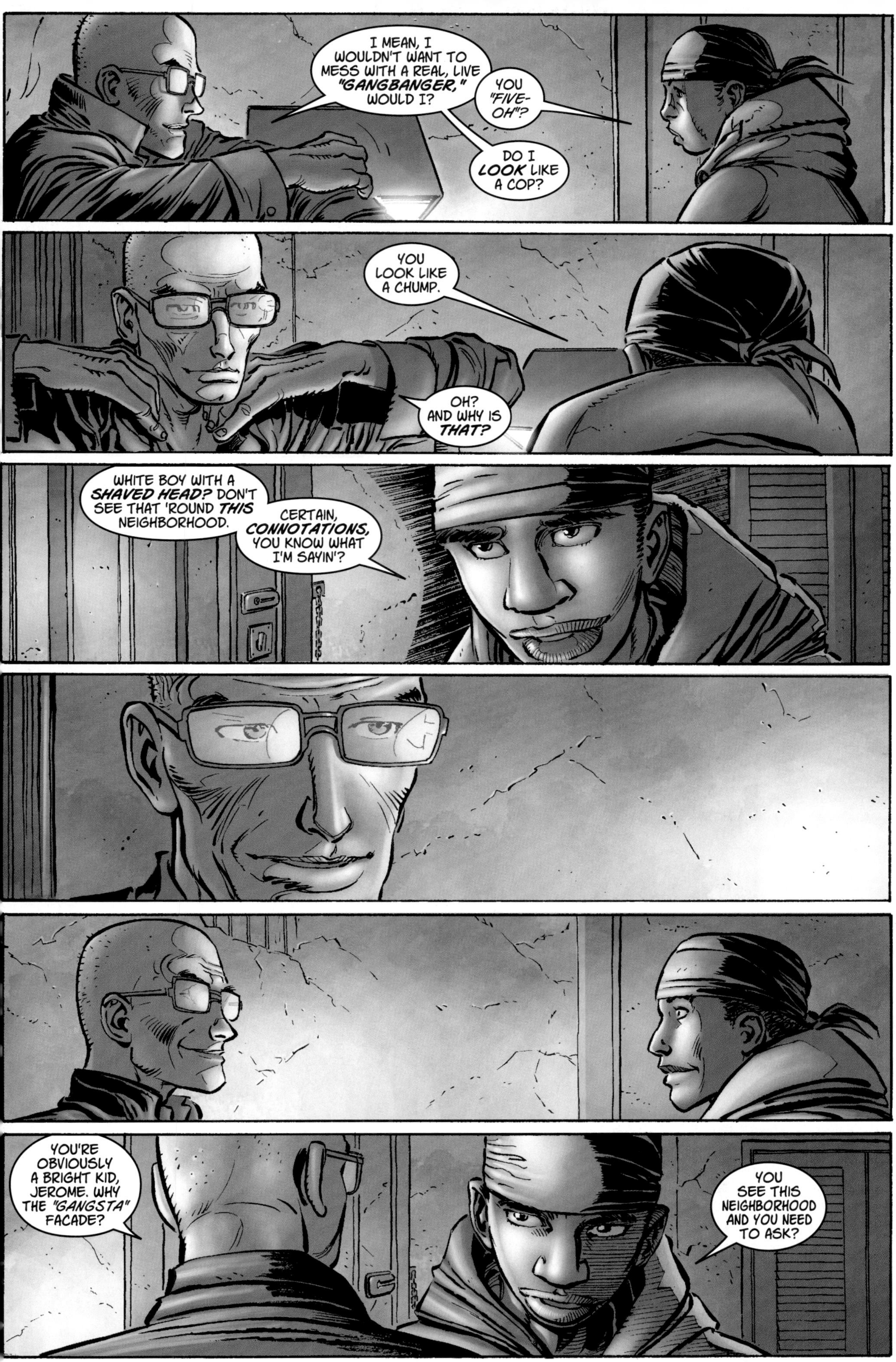
I MEAN, I WOULDN'T WANT TO MESS WITH A REAL, LIVE "GANGBANGER," WOULD I?
YOU "FIVE-OH"?
DO I LOOK LIKE A COP?
YOU LOOK LIKE A CHUMP.
OH? AND WHY IS THAT?
WHITE BOY WITH A SHAVED HEAD? DON'T SEE THAT 'ROUND THIS NEIGHBORHOOD.
CERTAIN, CONNOTATIONS, YOU KNOW WHAT I'M SAYIN'?
YOU'RE OBVIOUSLY A BRIGHT KID, JEROME. WHY THE "GANGSTA" FACADE?
YOU SEE THIS NEIGHBORHOOD AND YOU NEED TO ASK?

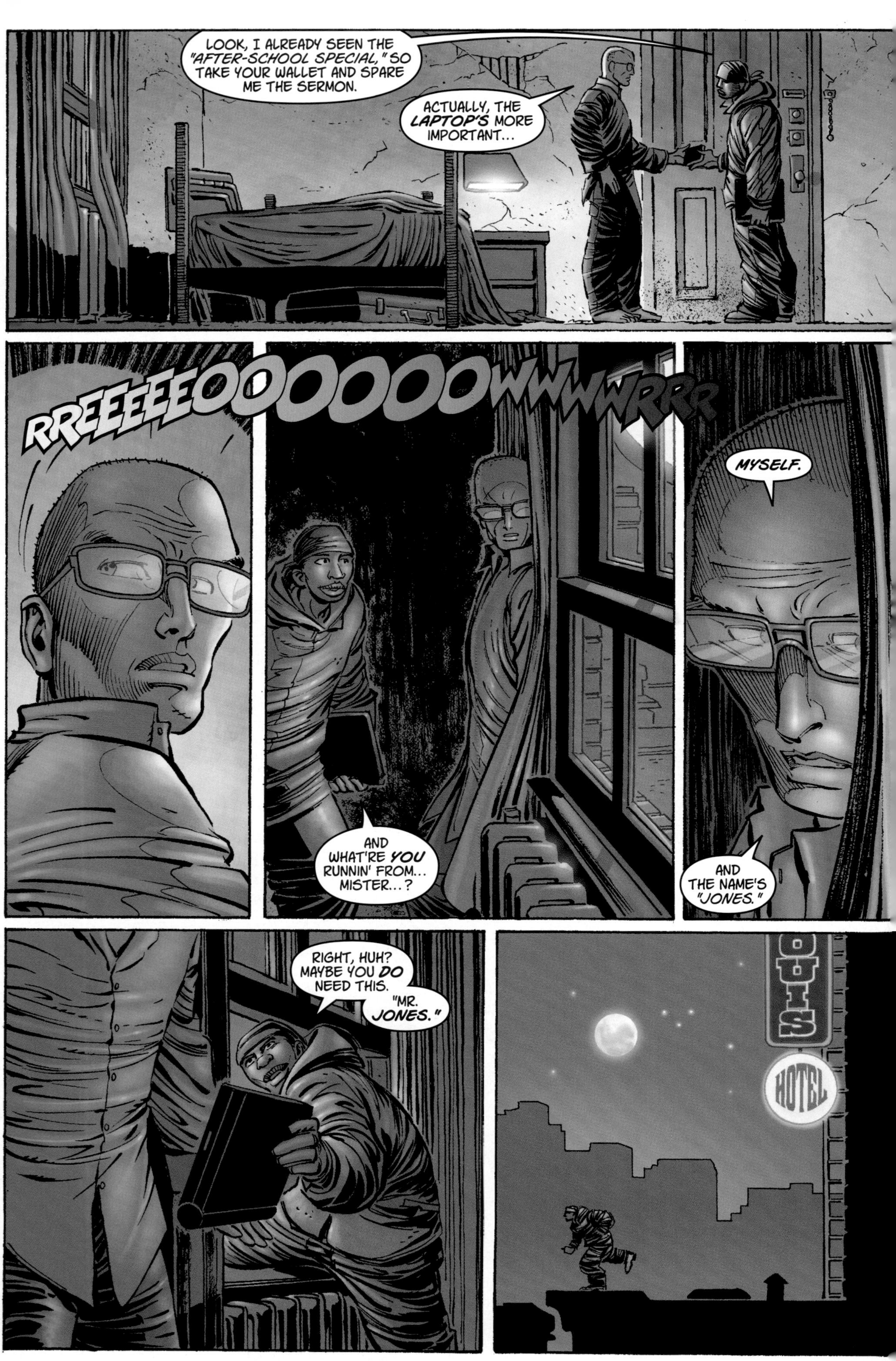

LOOK, I ALREADY SEEN THE "AFTER-SCHOOL SPECIAL," SO TAKE YOUR WALLET AND SPARE ME THE SERMON.
ACTUALLY, THE LAPTOP'S MORE IMPORTANT...
RREEEEEOOOOOOOOWWWWRRR
AND WHAT'RE YOU RUNNIN' FROM... MISTER...?
MYSELF.
AND THE NAME'S "JONES."
RIGHT, HUH? MAYBE YOU DO NEED THIS.
"MR. JONES."
OUIS
HOTEL

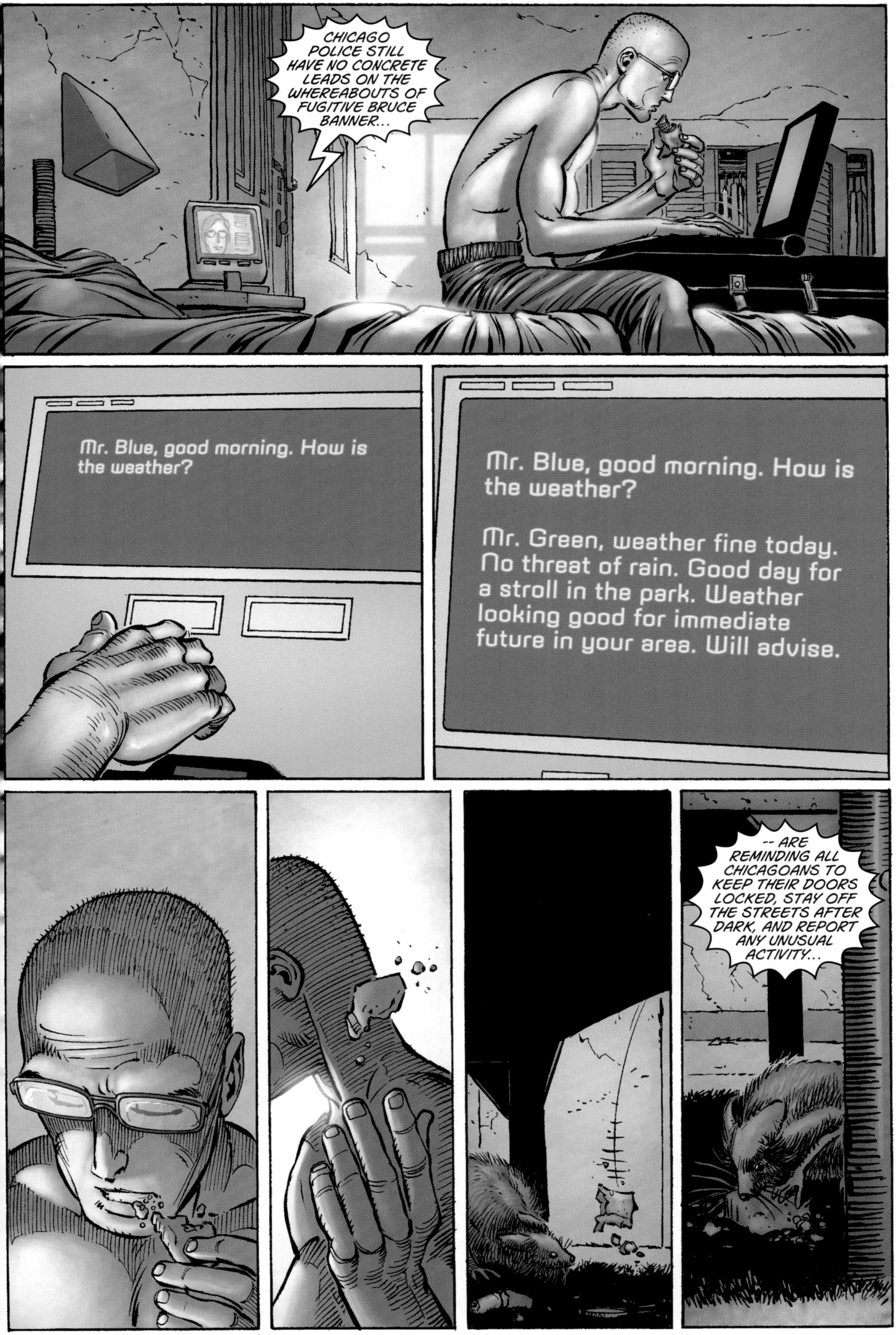
CHICAGO POLICE STILL HAVE NO CONCRETE LEADS ON THE WHEREABOUTS OF FUGITIVE BRUCE BANNER...
Mr. Blue, good morning. How is the weather?
Mr. Blue, good morning. How is the weather?
Mr. Green, weather fine today. No threat of rain. Good day for a stroll in the park. Weather looking good for immediate future in your area. Will advise.
-- ARE REMINDING ALL CHICAGOANS TO KEEP THEIR DOORS LOCKED, STAY OFF THE STREETS AFTER DARK, AND REPORT ANY UNUSUAL ACTIVITY...

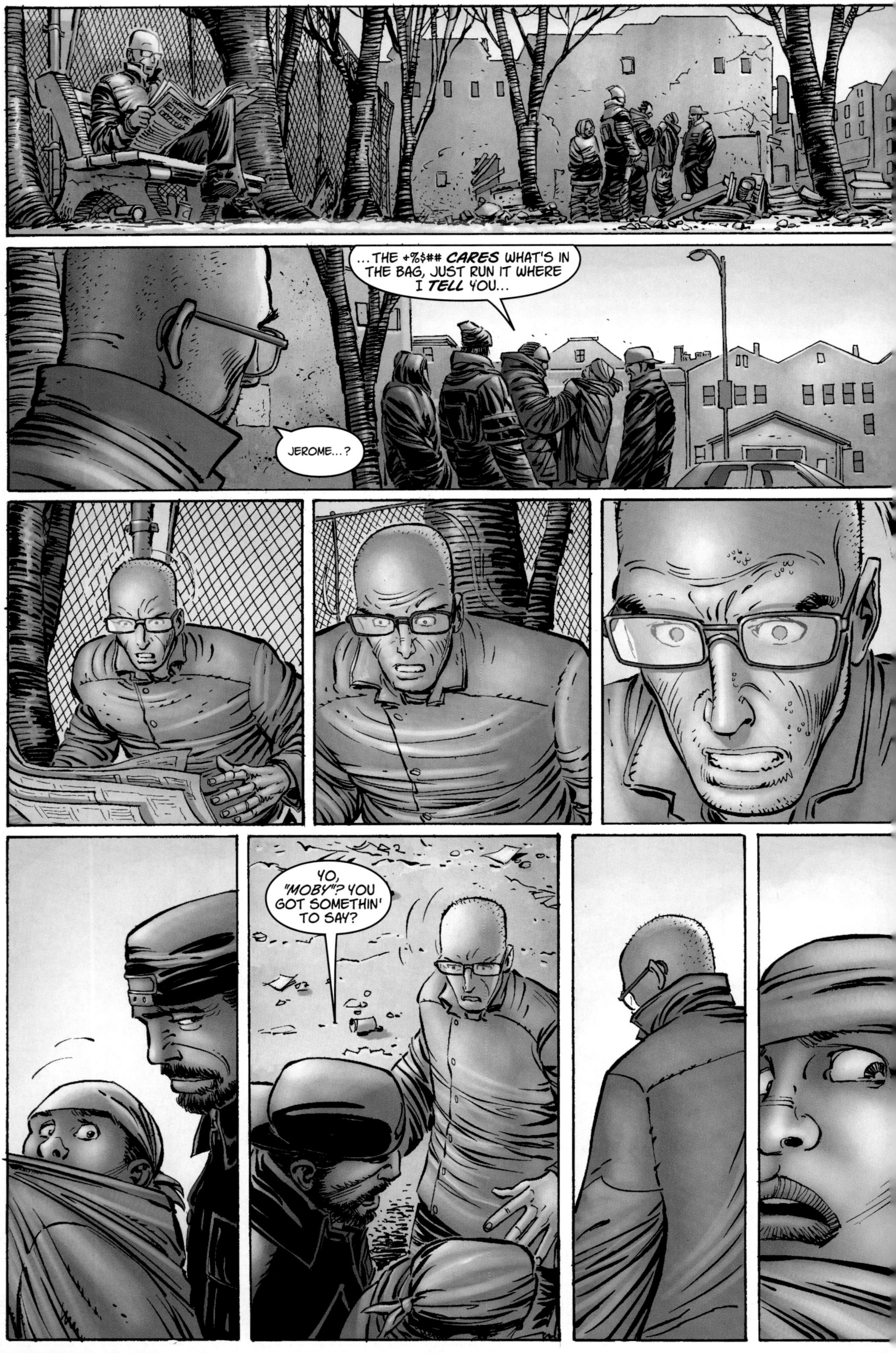
...THE +%$## CARES WHAT'S IN THE BAG, JUST RUN IT WHERE I TELL YOU...
JEROME...?
YO, "MOBY"? YOU GOT SOMETHIN' TO SAY?

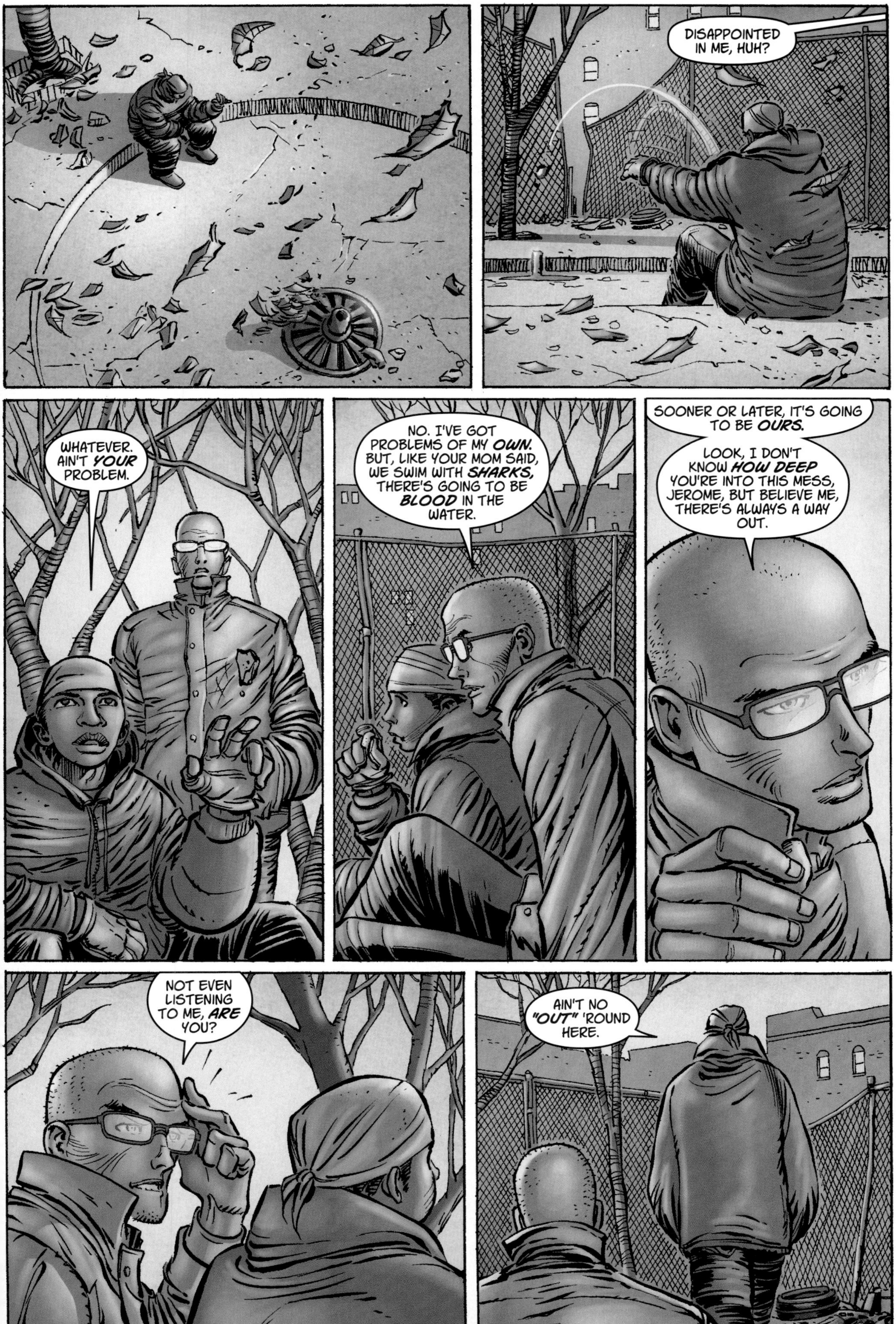
DISAPPOINTED IN ME, HUH?
WHATEVER. AIN'T YOUR PROBLEM.
NO. I'VE GOT PROBLEMS OF MY OWN. BUT, LIKE YOUR MOM SAID, WE SWIM WITH SHARKS, THERE'S GOING TO BE BLOOD IN THE WATER.
SOONER OR LATER, IT'S GOING TO BE OURS.
LOOK, I DON'T KNOW HOW DEEP YOU'RE INTO THIS MESS, JEROME, BUT BELIEVE ME, THERE'S ALWAYS A WAY OUT.
NOT EVEN LISTENING TO ME, ARE YOU?
AIN'T NO "OUT" 'ROUND HERE.

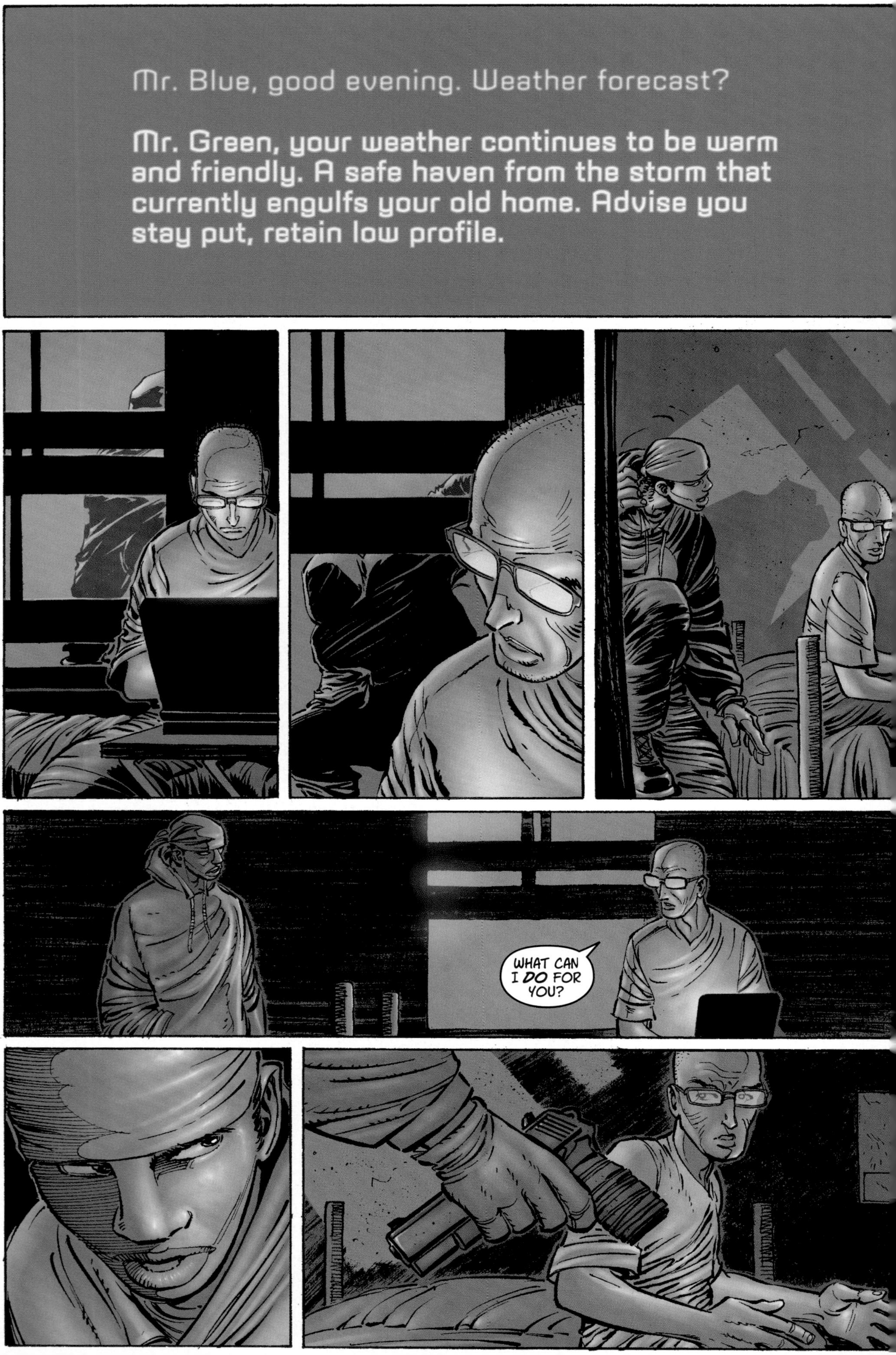
Mr. Blue, good evening. Weather forecast?
Mr. Green, your weather continues to be warm and friendly. A safe haven from the storm that currently engulfs your old home. Advise you stay put, retain low profile.
WHAT CAN I DO FOR YOU?

"JUICE." POWER. THAT'S WHAT LIFE'S ALL ABOUT, ISN'T IT-- WHO HOLDS IT?

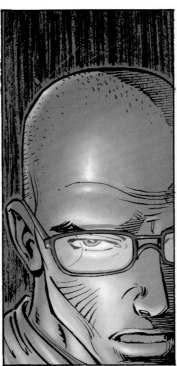

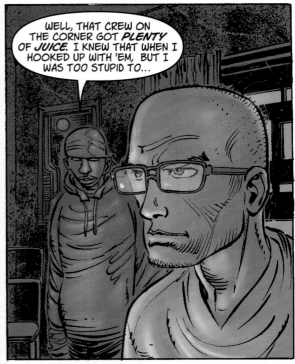

WELL, THAT CREW ON THE CORNER GOT PLENTY OF JUICE. I KNEW THAT WHEN I HOOKED UP WITH 'EM, BUT I WAS TOO STUPID TO...

I WAS TOO STUPID.

WHATEVER. I'M IN. DEEP. TOO LATE TO SWEAT ABOUT IT.

IS IT NOW?

WHAT?! YOU THINK I CAN JUST WALK AWAY FROM THE GAME? PICK UP AN' LEAVE?

YOU TELL ME.

YOU NEED ME TO SPELL IT OUT FOR YOU? "MR. JONES," YOU BEST GO BACK WHERE YOU CAME FROM.

I CAN'T.

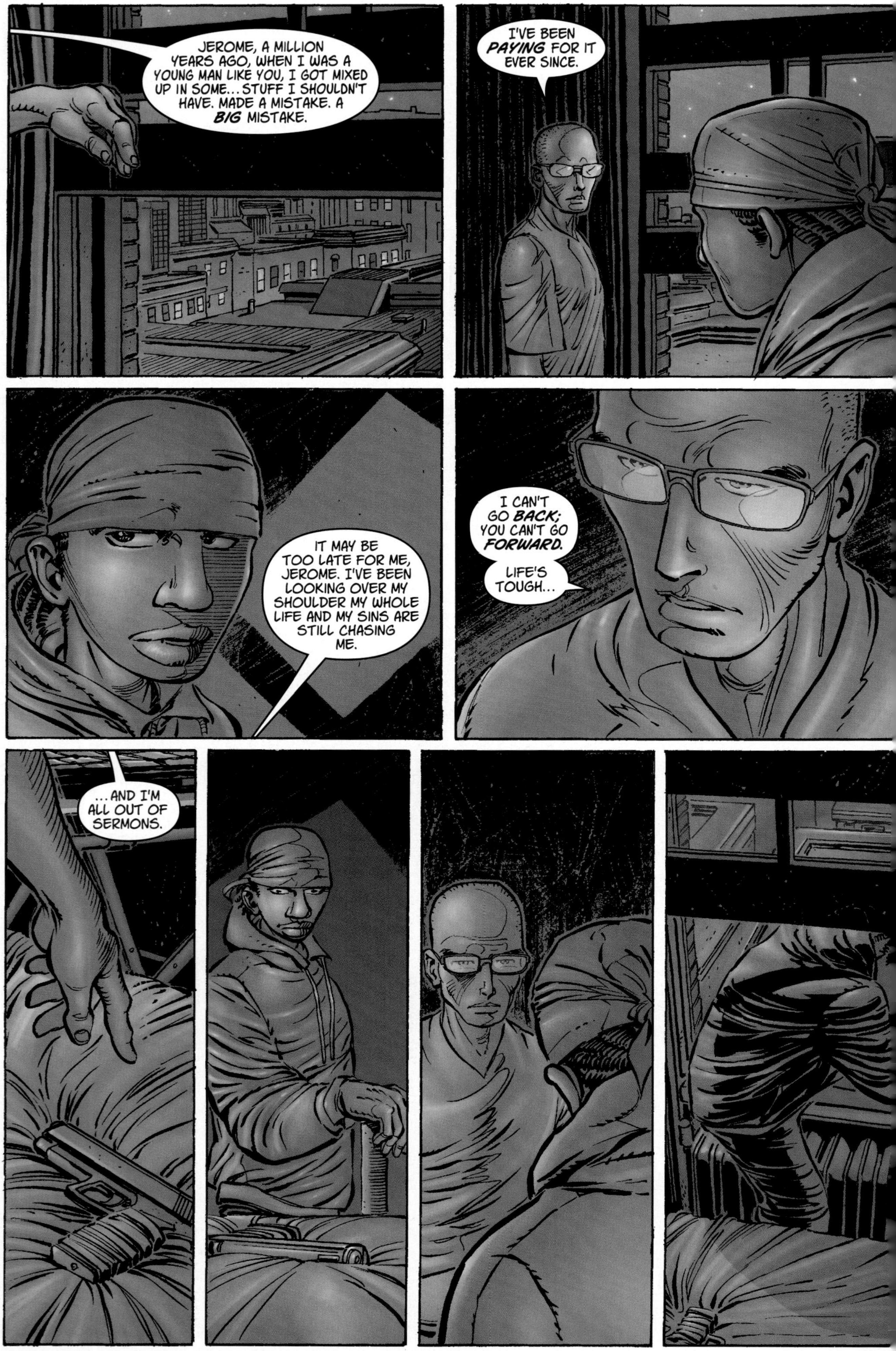
JEROME, A MILLION YEARS AGO, WHEN I WAS A YOUNG MAN LIKE YOU, I GOT MIXED UP IN SOME... STUFF I SHOULDN'T HAVE. MADE A MISTAKE. A BIG MISTAKE.
I'VE BEEN PAYING FOR IT EVER SINCE.
IT MAY BE TOO LATE FOR ME, JEROME. I'VE BEEN LOOKING OVER MY SHOULDER MY WHOLE LIFE AND MY SINS ARE STILL CHASING ME.
I CAN'T GO BACK; YOU CAN'T GO FORWARD.
LIFE'S TOUGH...
...AND I'M ALL OUT OF SERMONS.

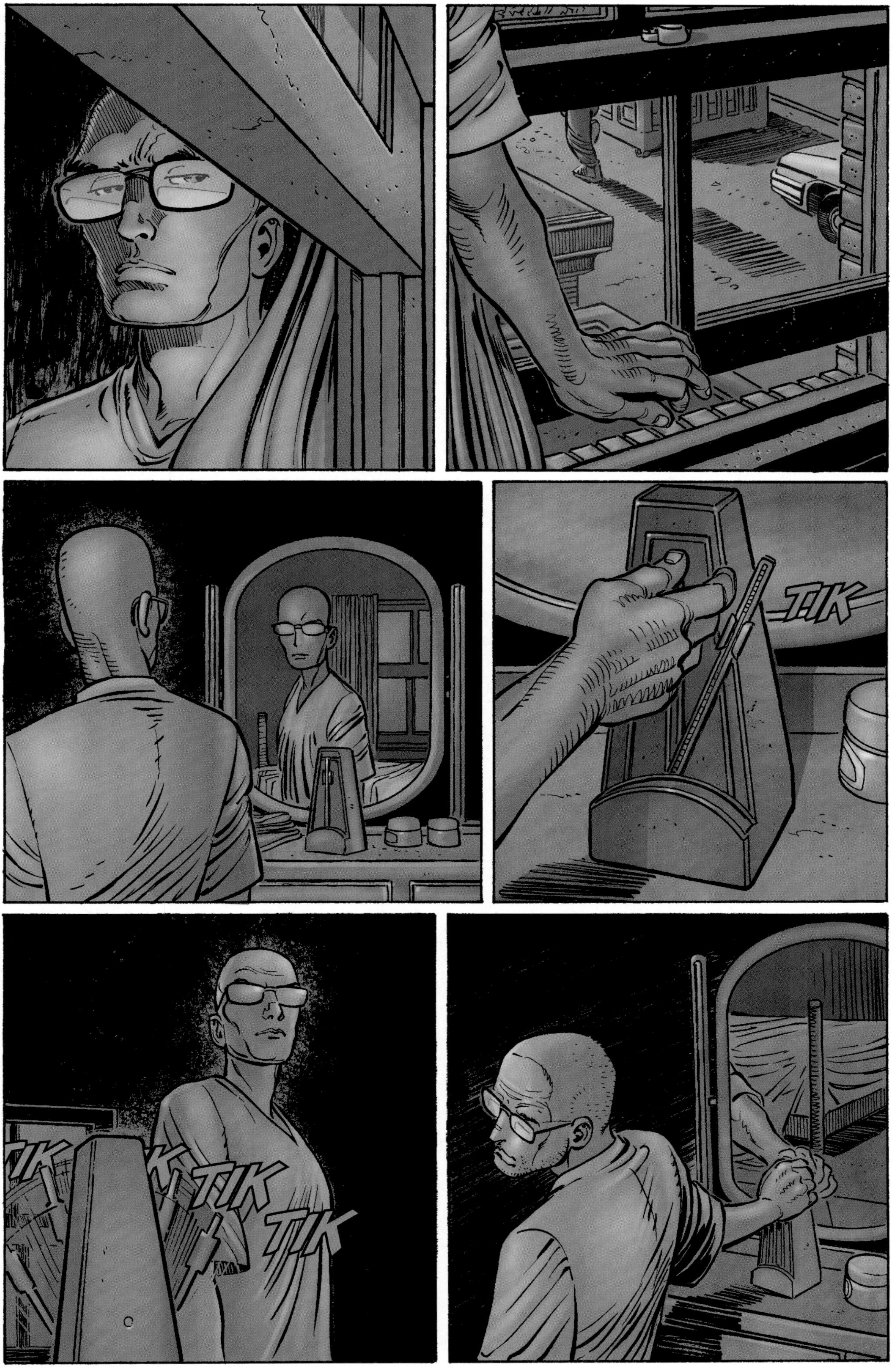
TIK
TIK
TIK

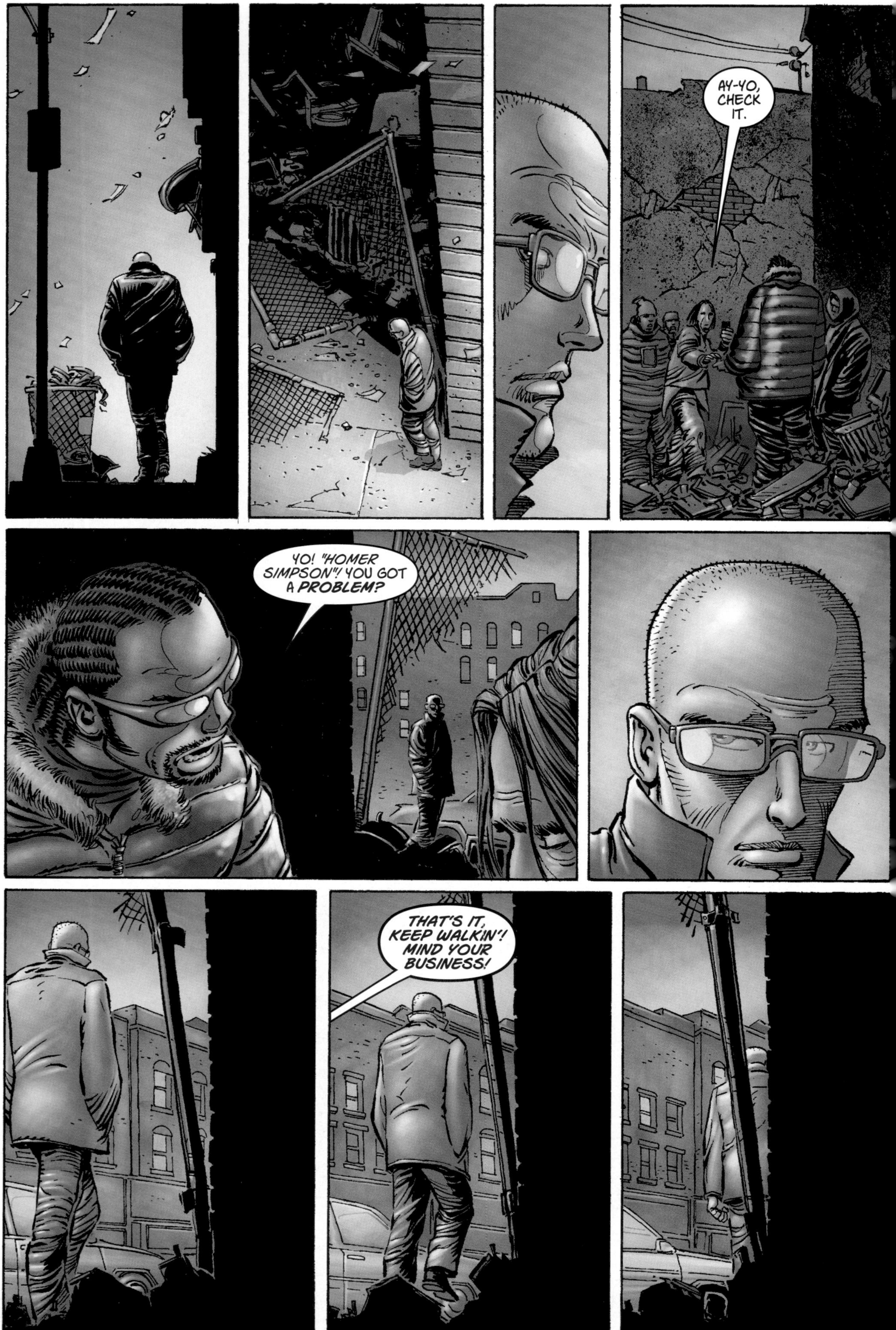
AY-YO, CHECK IT.
YO! "HOMER SIMPSON"! YOU GOT A PROBLEM?
THAT'S IT, KEEP WALKIN'! MIND YOUR BUSINESS!

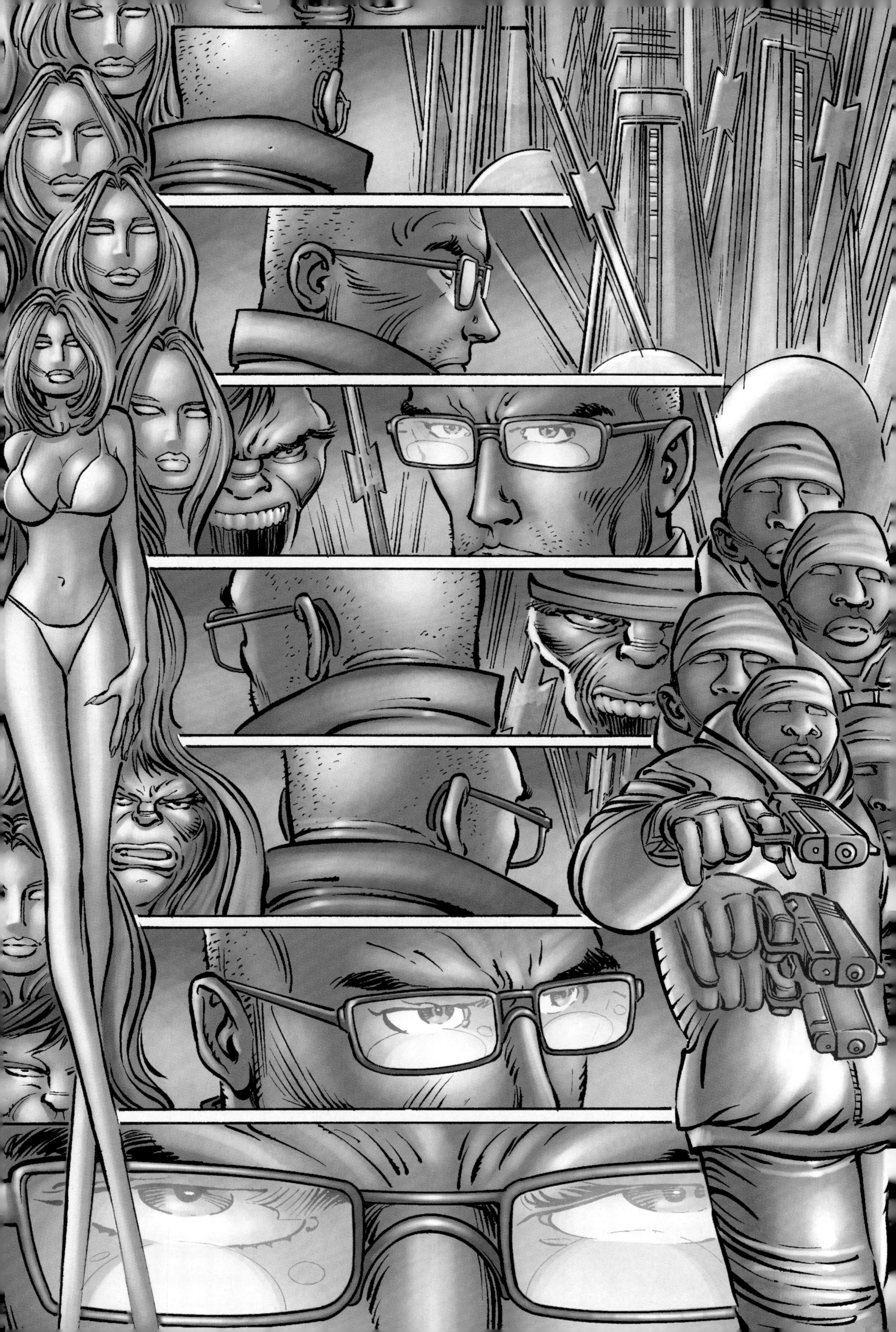

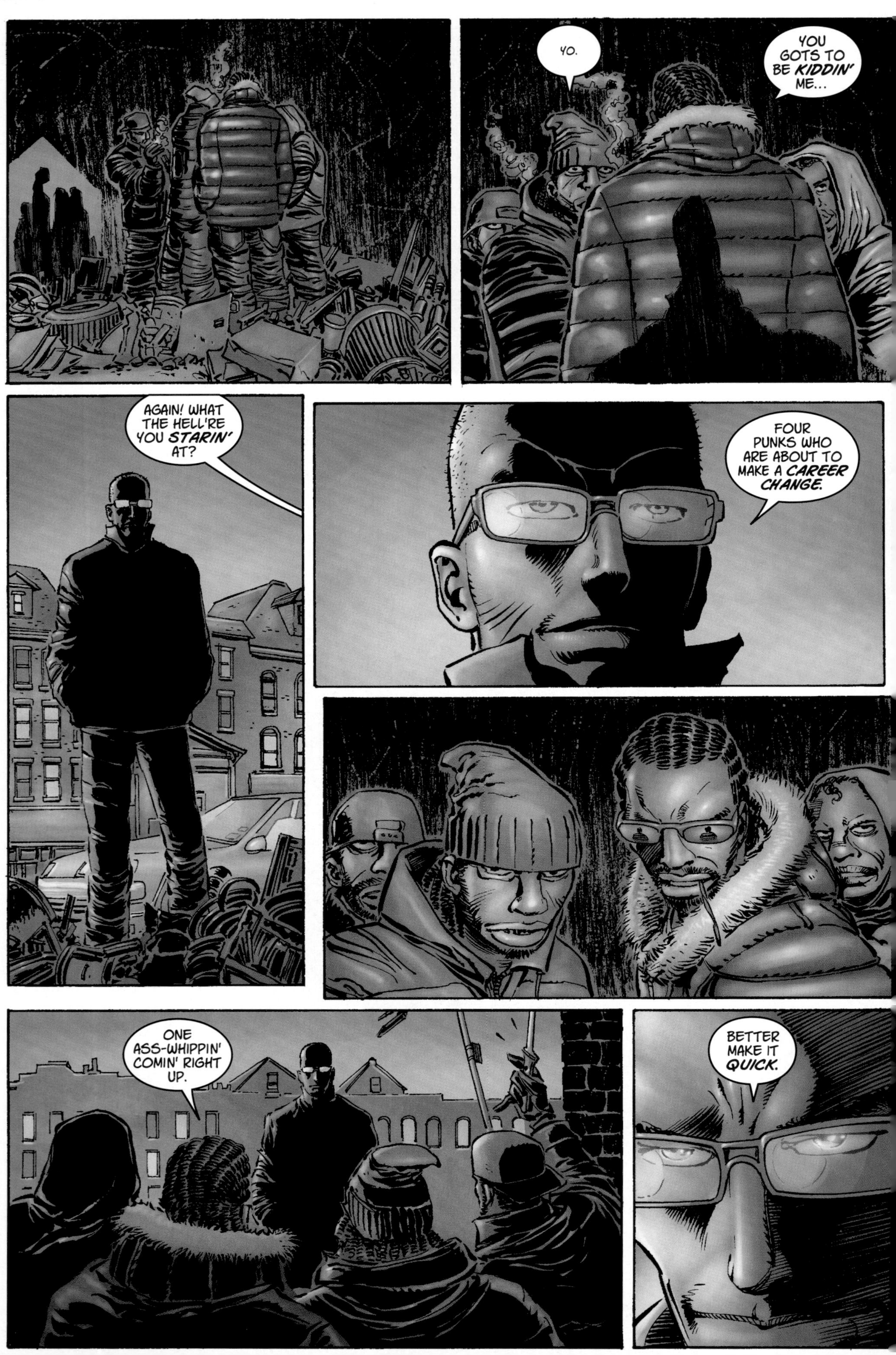
YO.
YOU GOTS TO BE KIDDIN' ME...
AGAIN! WHAT THE HELL'RE YOU STARIN' AT?
FOUR PUNKS WHO ARE ABOUT TO MAKE A CAREER CHANGE.
ONE ASS-WHIPPIN' COMIN' RIGHT UP.
BETTER MAKE IT QUICK.

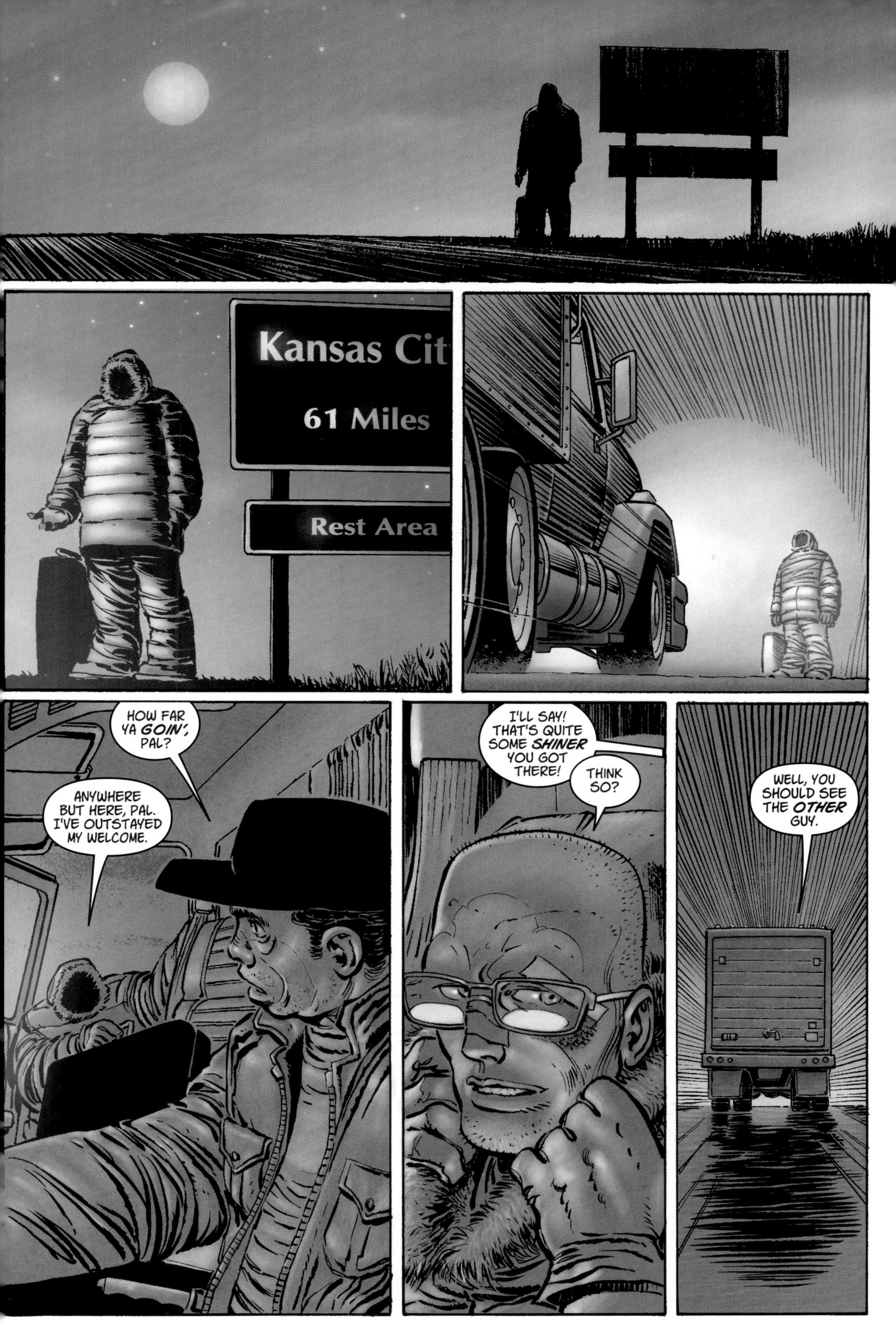
Kansas City
61 Miles
Rest Area
HOW FAR YA GOIN', PAL?
ANYWHERE BUT HERE, PAL. I'VE OUTSTAYED MY WELCOME.
I'LL SAY! THAT'S QUITE SOME SHINER YOU GOT THERE!
THINK SO?
WELL, YOU SHOULD SEE THE OTHER GUY.

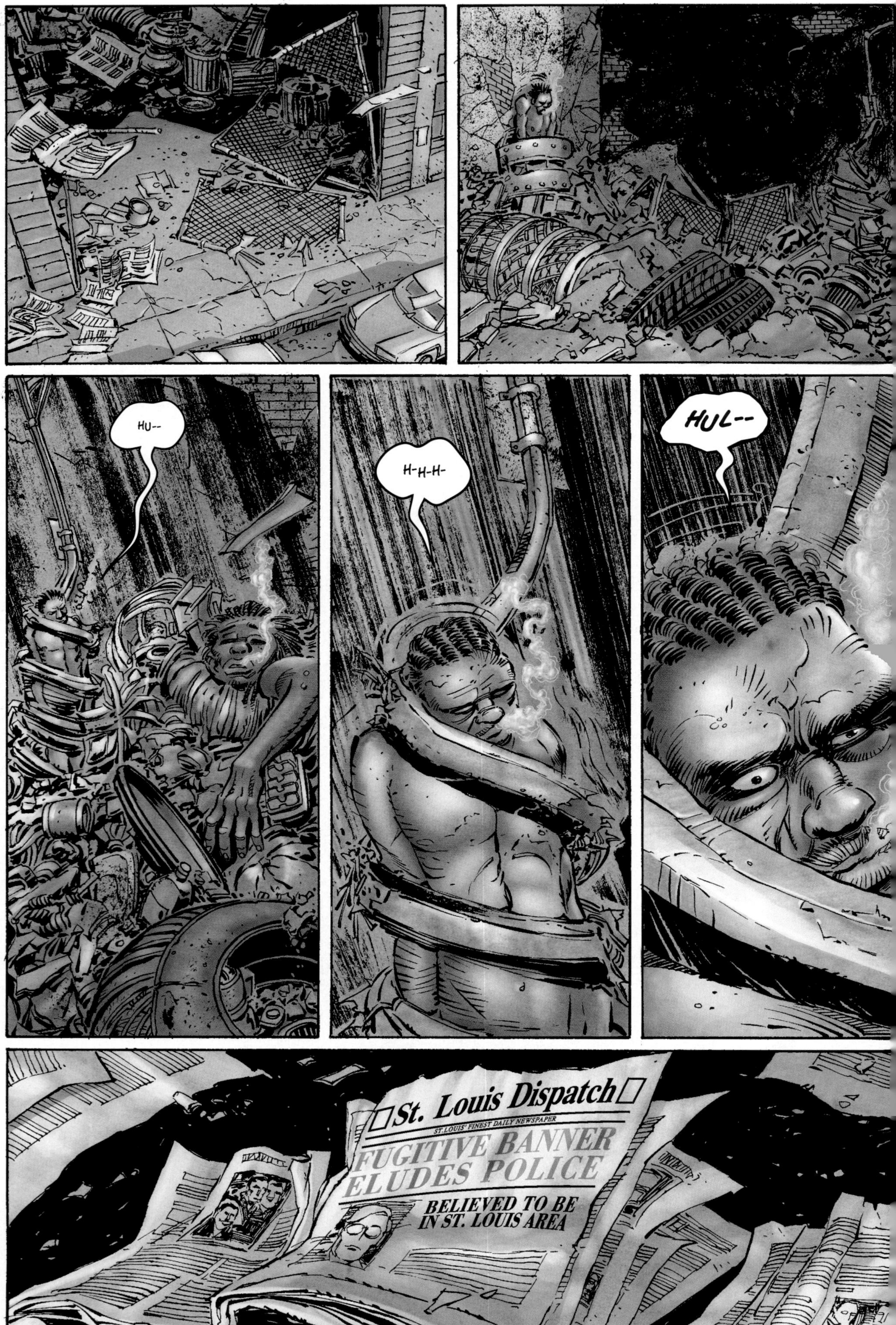
HU--
H-H-H-
HUL--
St. Louis Dispatch
ST. LOUIS' FINEST DAILY NEWSPAPER
FUGITIVE BANNER ELUDES POLICE
BELIEVED TO BE IN ST. LOUIS AREA

INCREDIBLE HULK #35
Cover sketch by Kaare Andrews

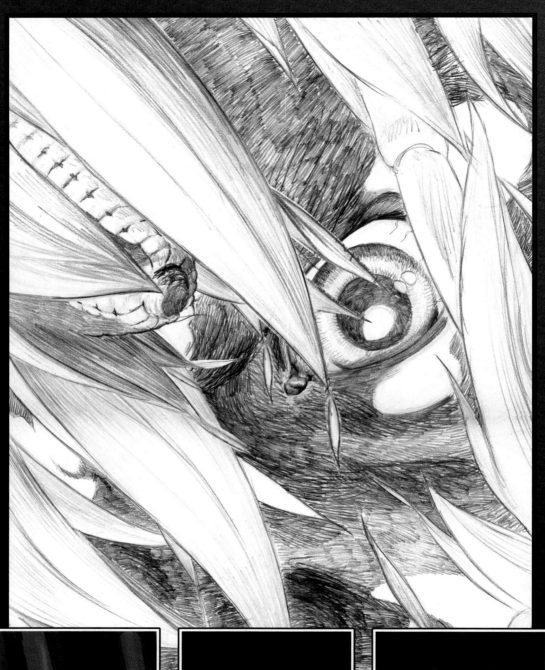

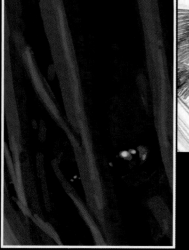

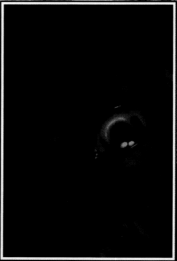

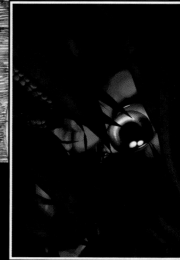

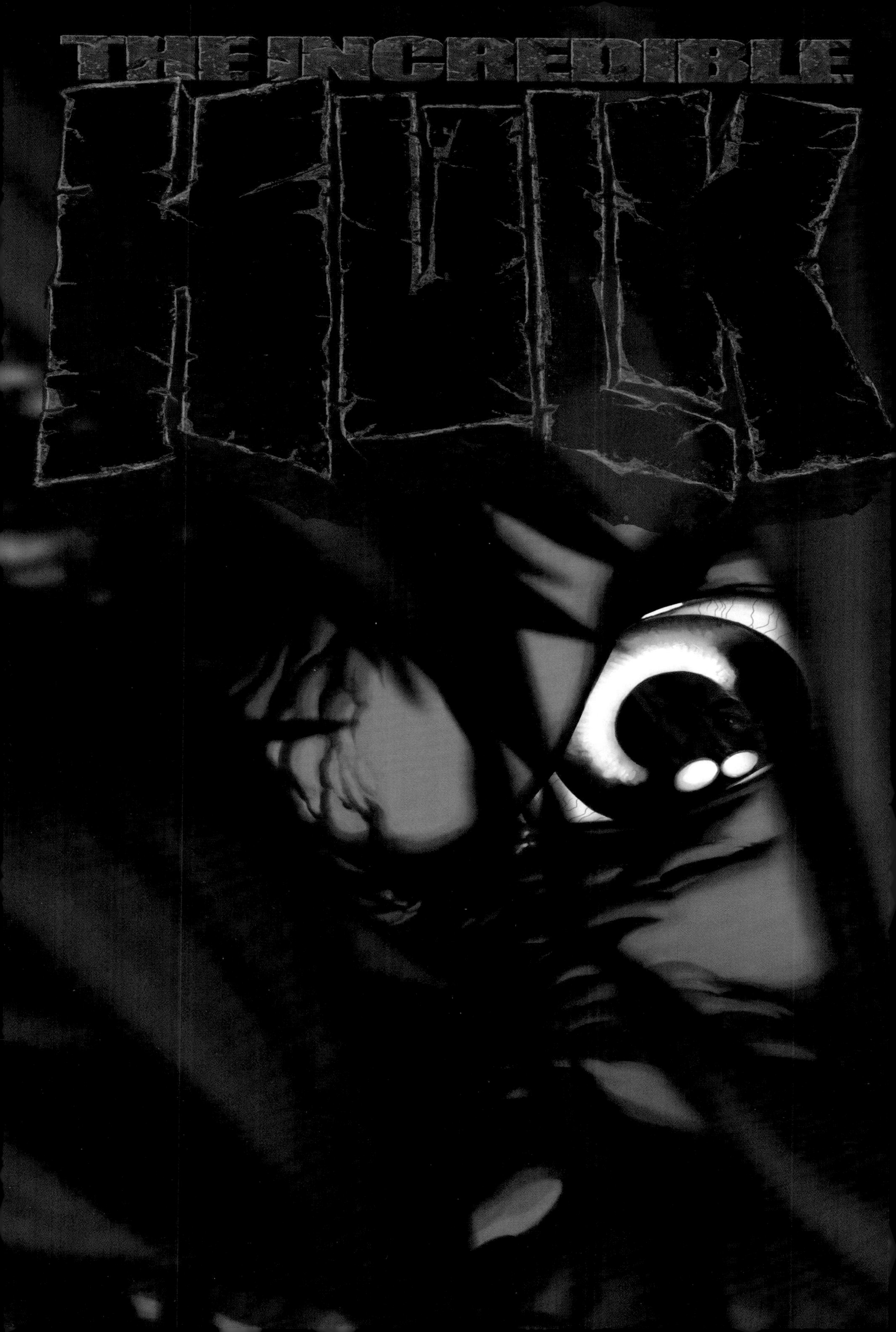
THE INCREDIBLE
HULK

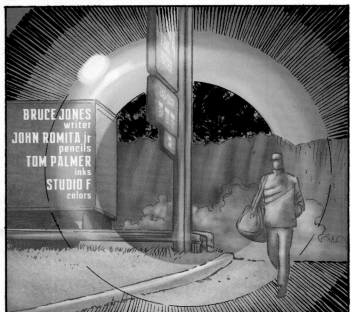

STAN LEE PRESENTS
SILENT RUNNING
Wanda's
DINER & REST STOP
FOOD • GAS
Regular 1.31
Premium 1.35
Super 1.45
OPEN 24HRS
SPEED LIMIT 45
SAVE! $$$
Air Conditioned
Wanda's DINER & REST STOP
BRUCE JONES
writer
JOHN ROMITA jr
pencils
TOM PALMER
inks
STUDIO F
colors
AMERICA
LOVE IT
OR LEAVE IT

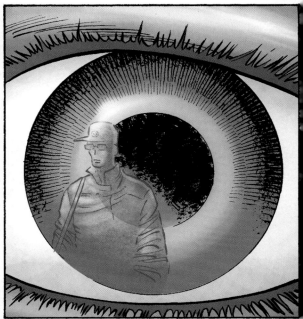

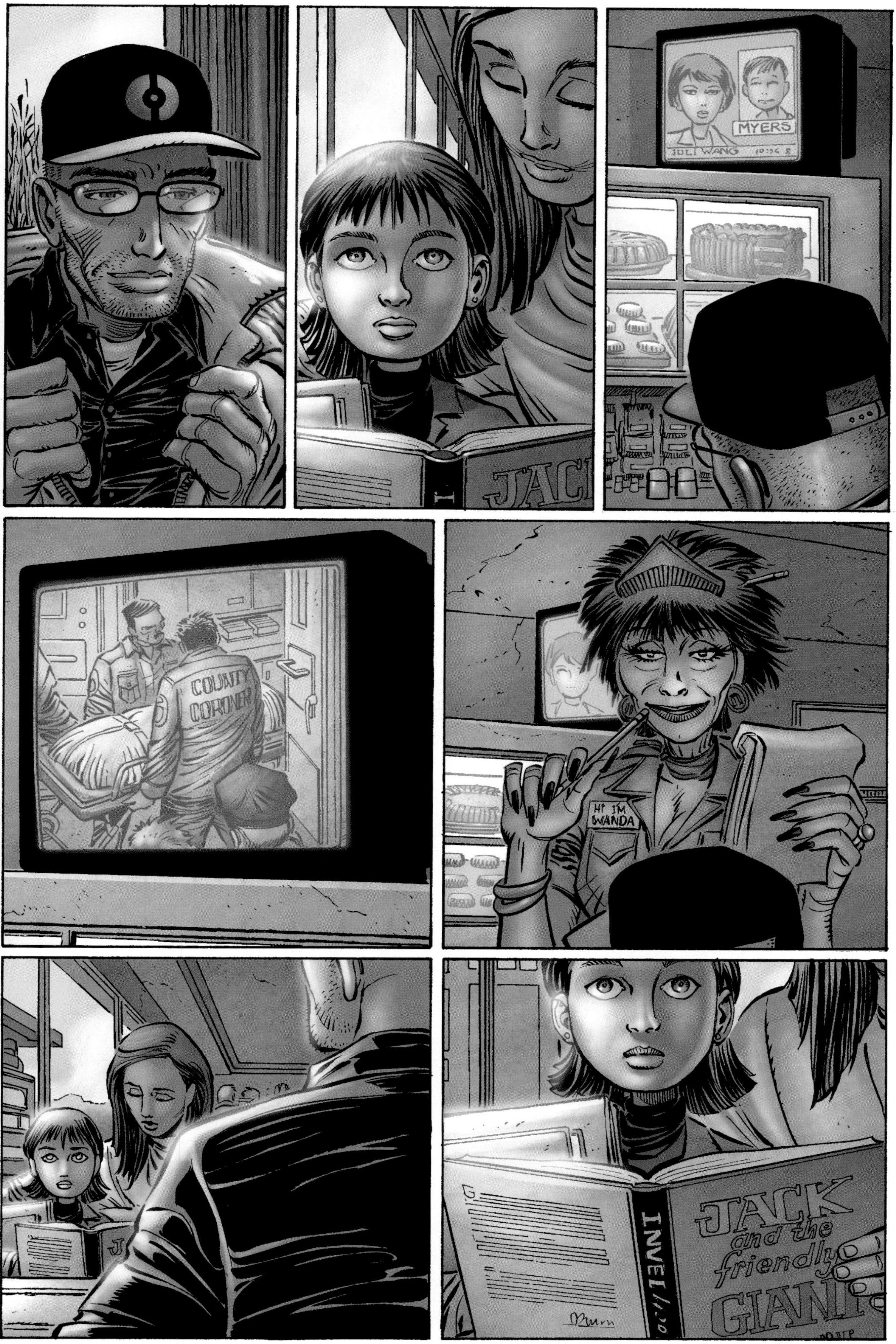
MYERS
JULI WANG
COUNTY CORONER
HI I'M WANDA
JACK and the friendly

RESTROO

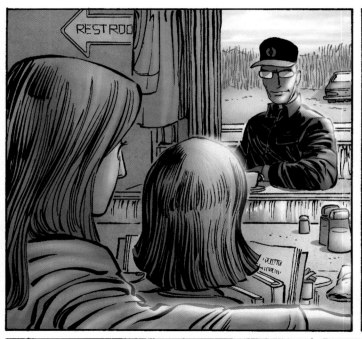

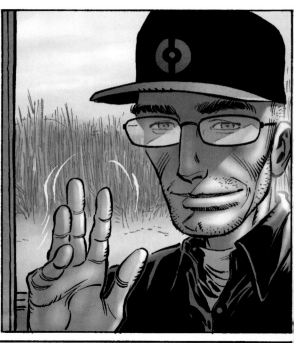

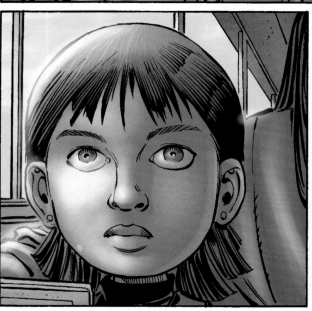

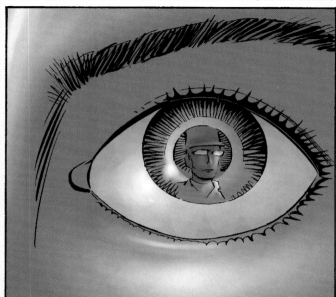

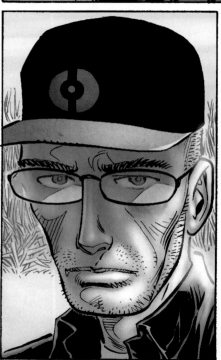

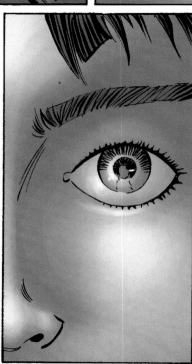

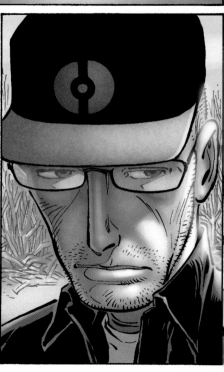

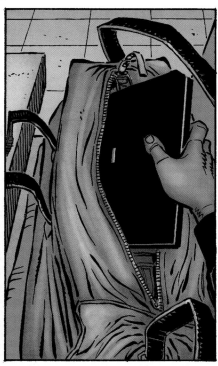

Mr. Blue,
Request weather report.

SEND   CANCEL

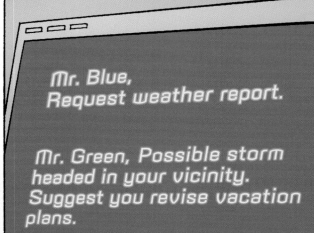

Mr. Blue,
Request weather report.

Mr. Green, Possible storm headed in your vicinity. Suggest you revise vacation plans.

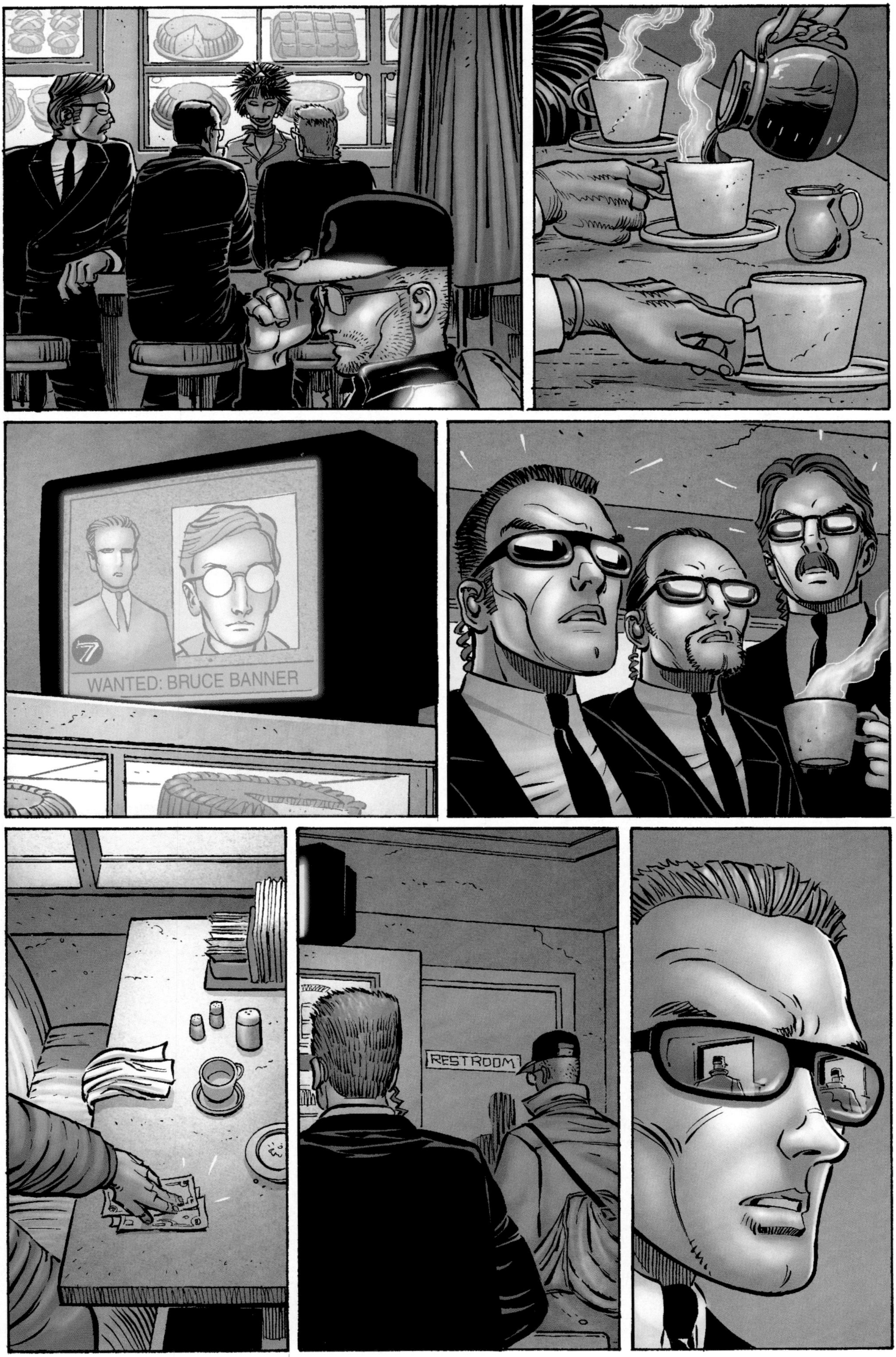
WANTED: BRUCE BANNER
RESTROOM

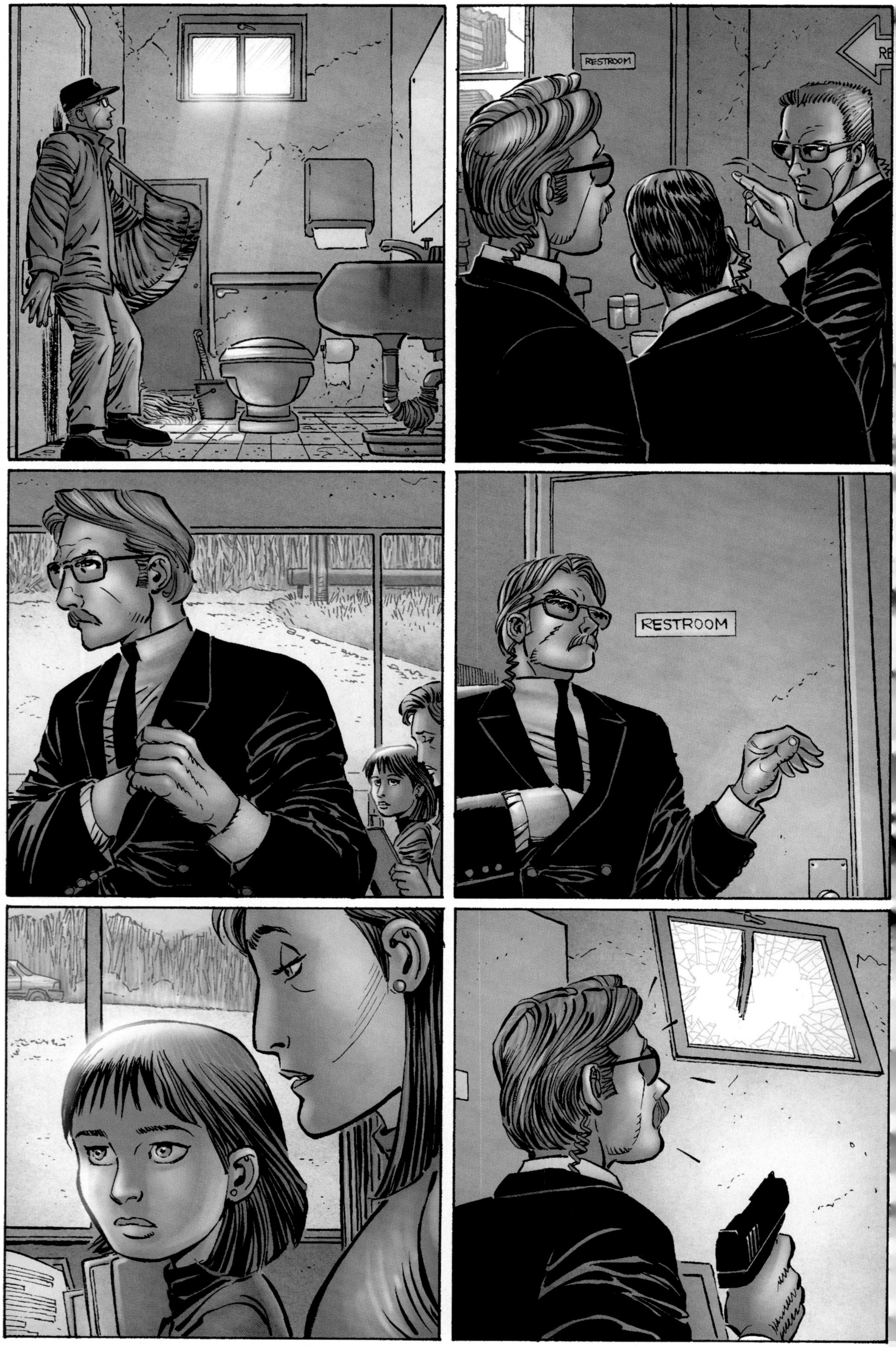
RESTROOM
RESTROOM

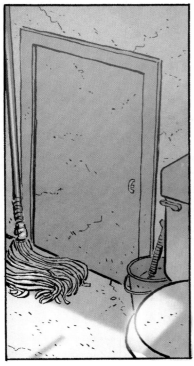
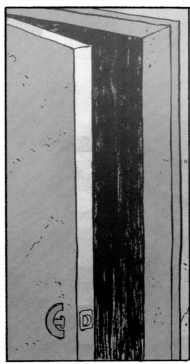

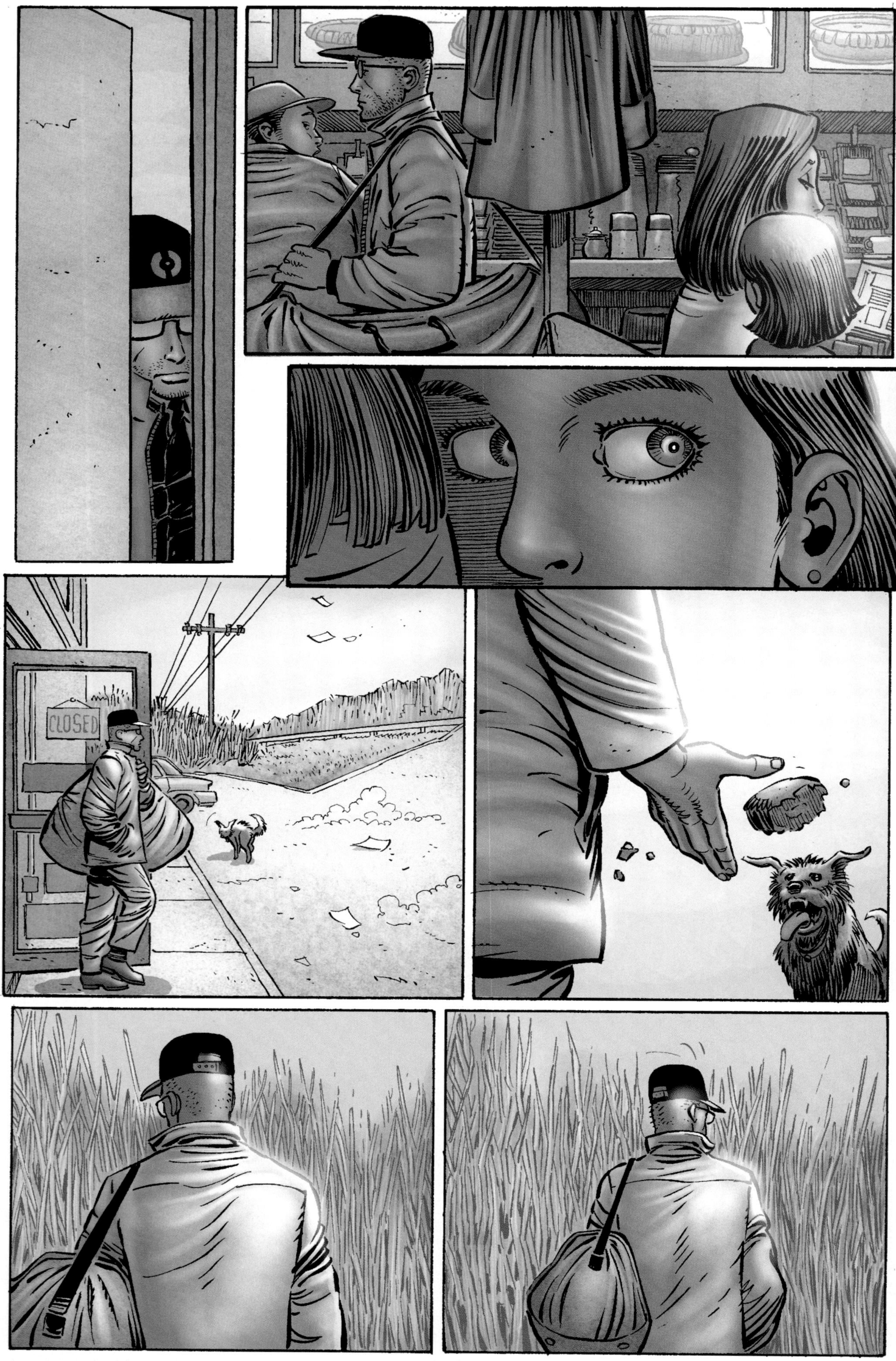
CLOSED

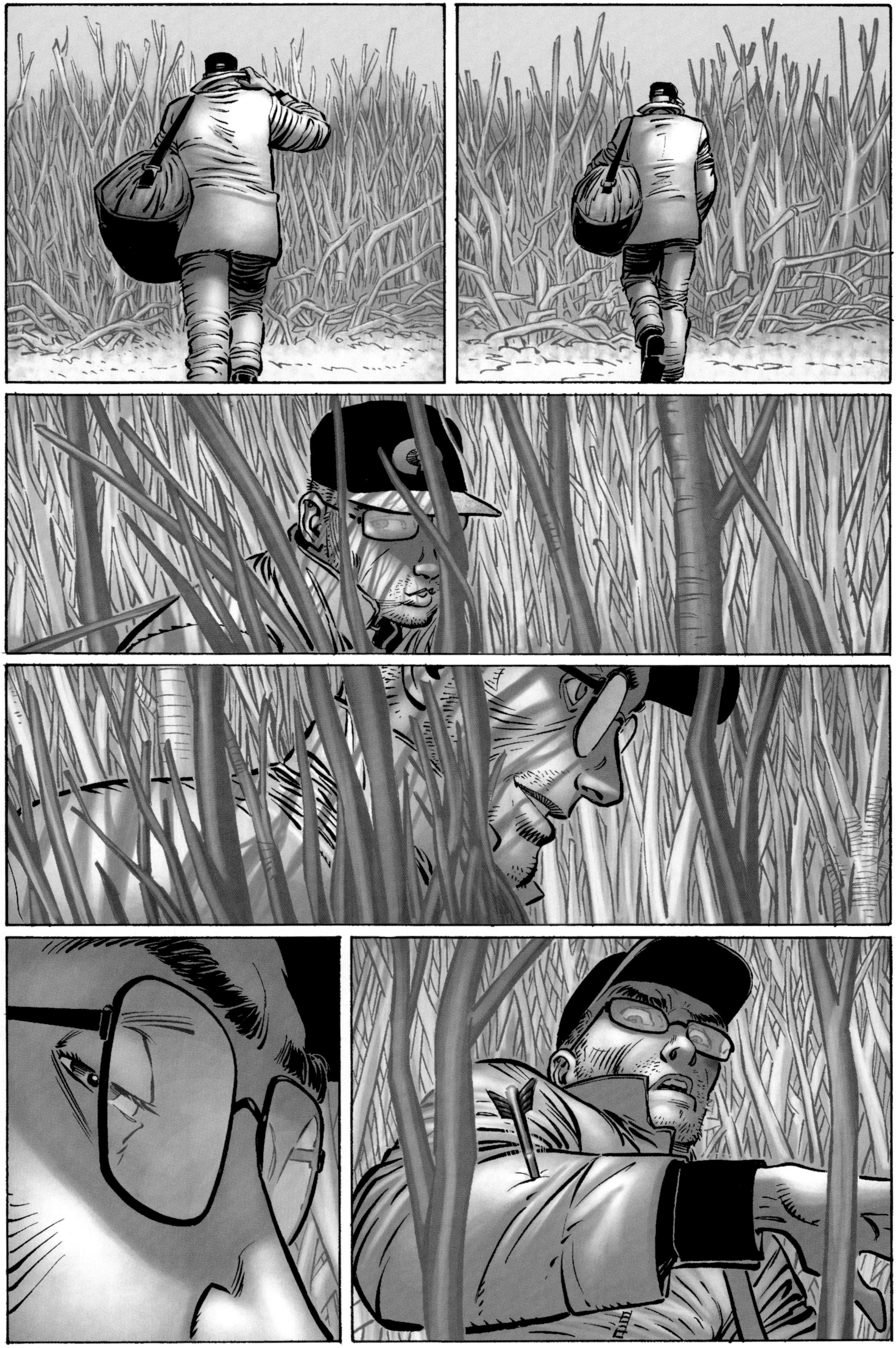

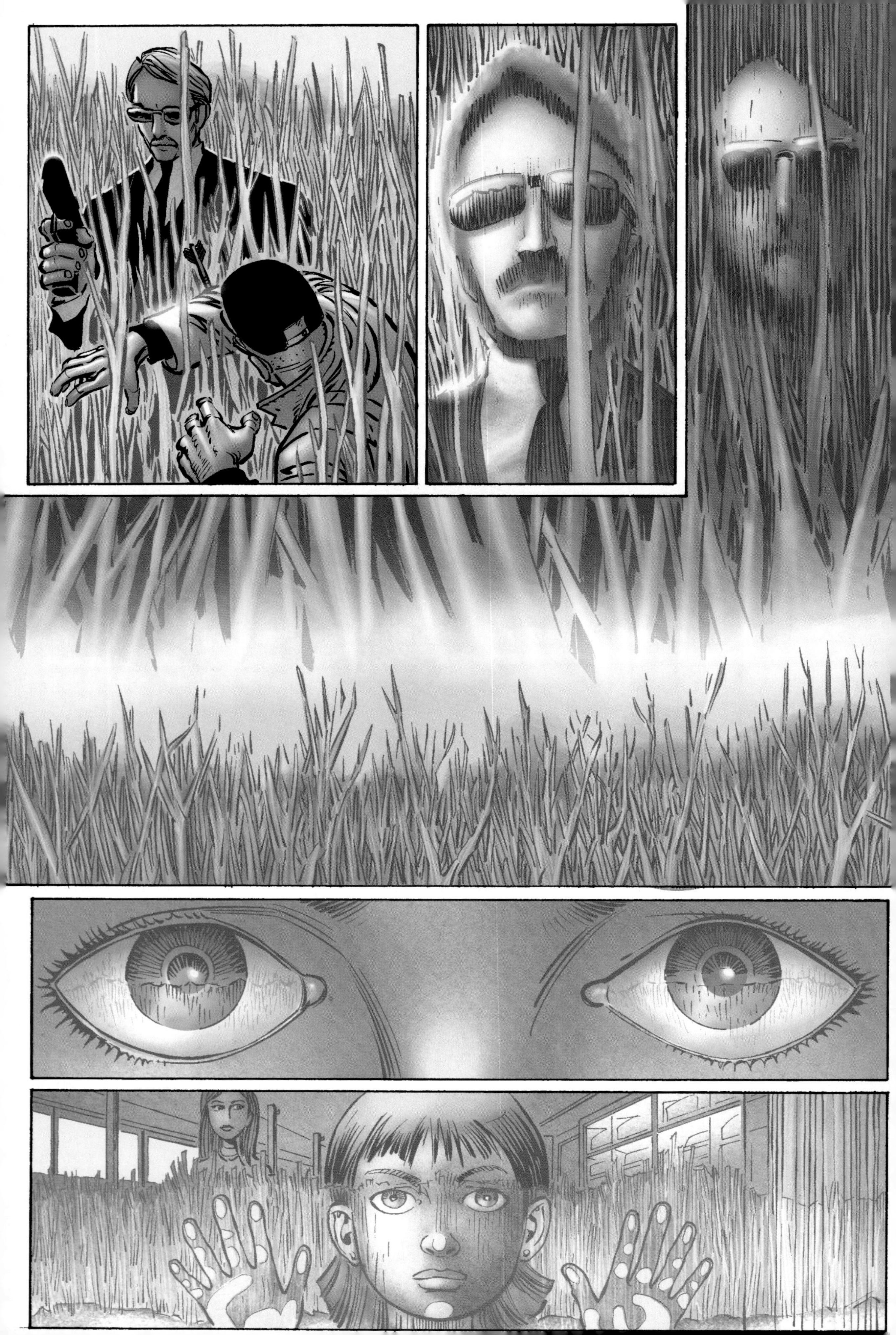

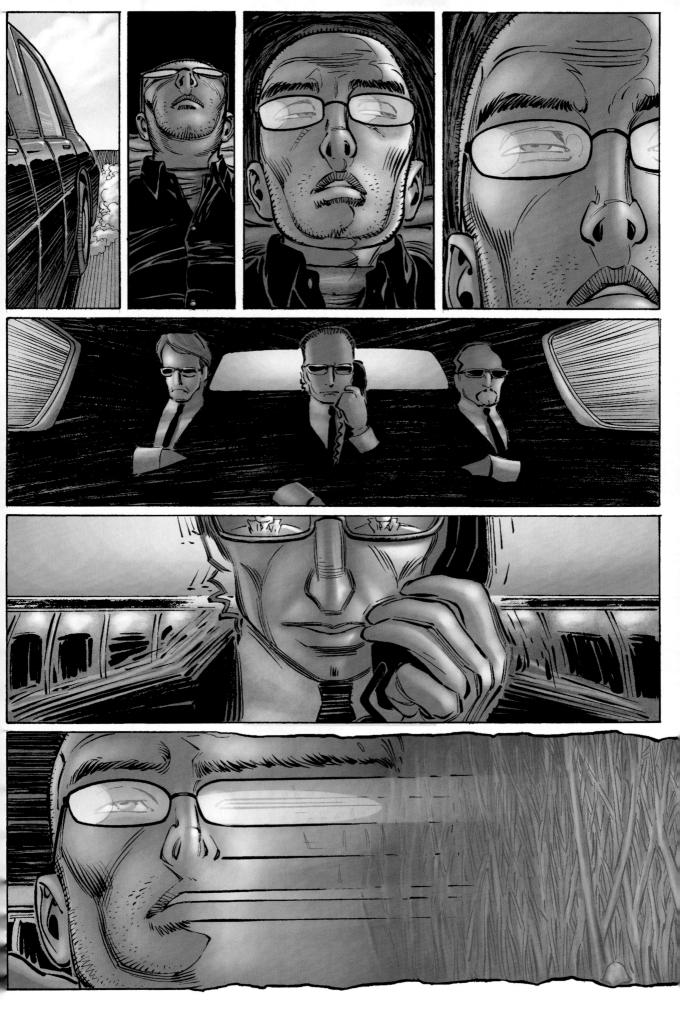

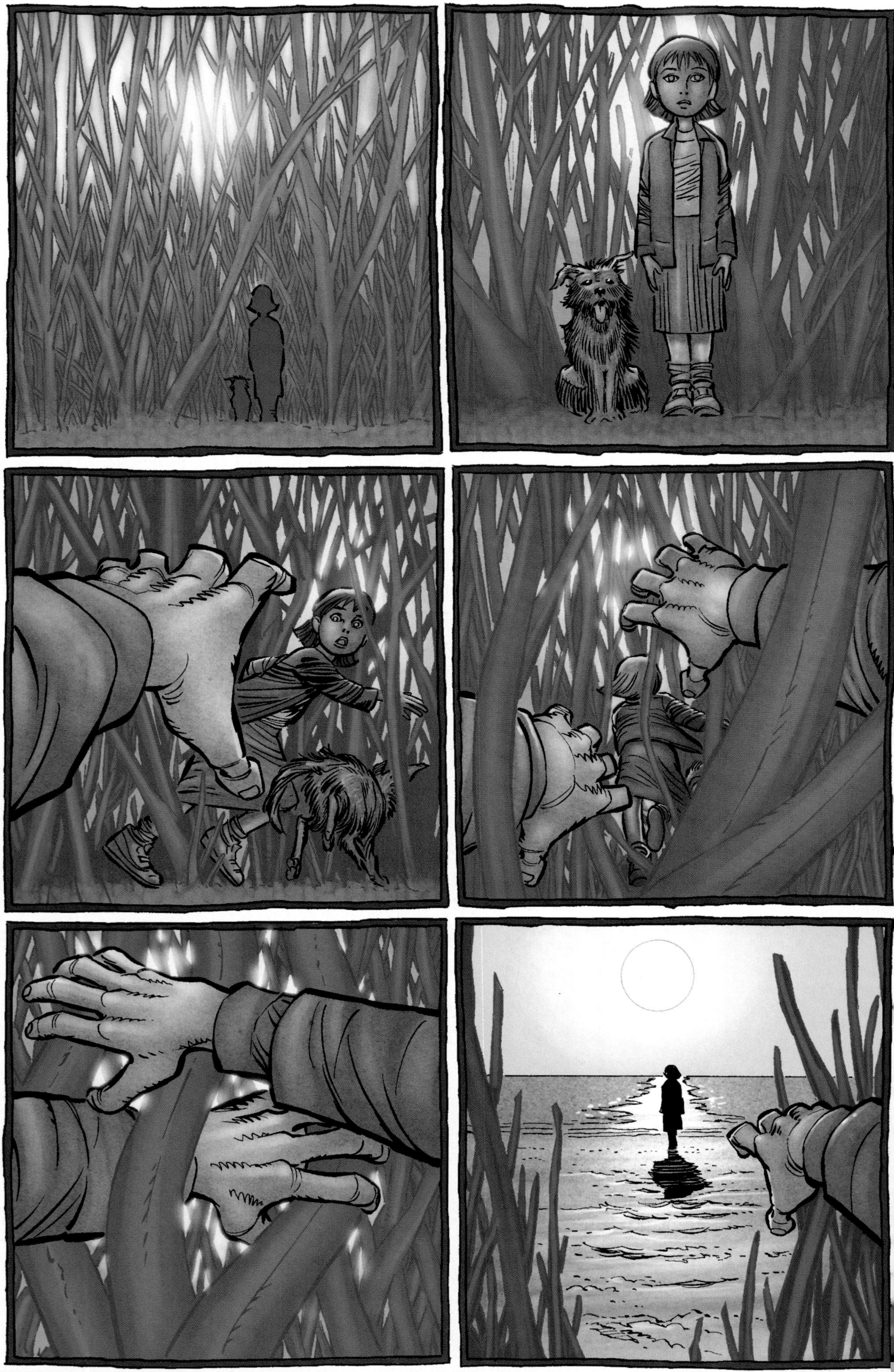

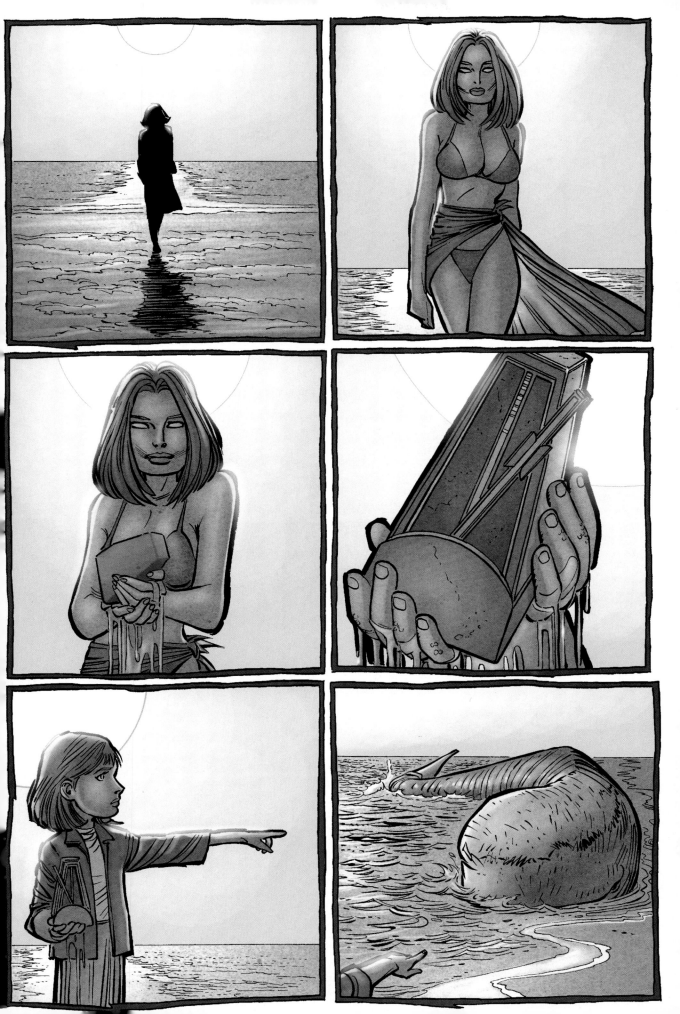

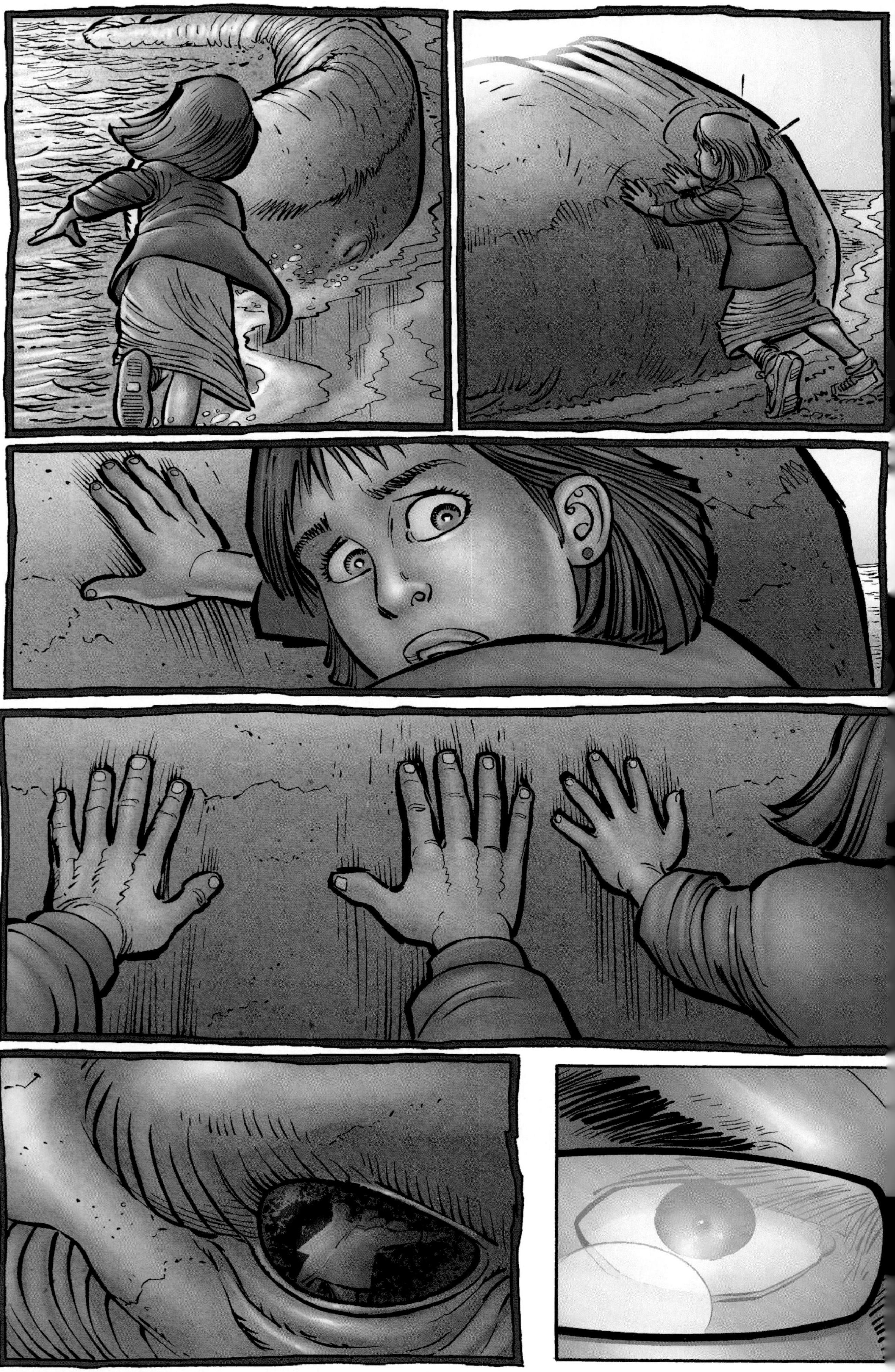

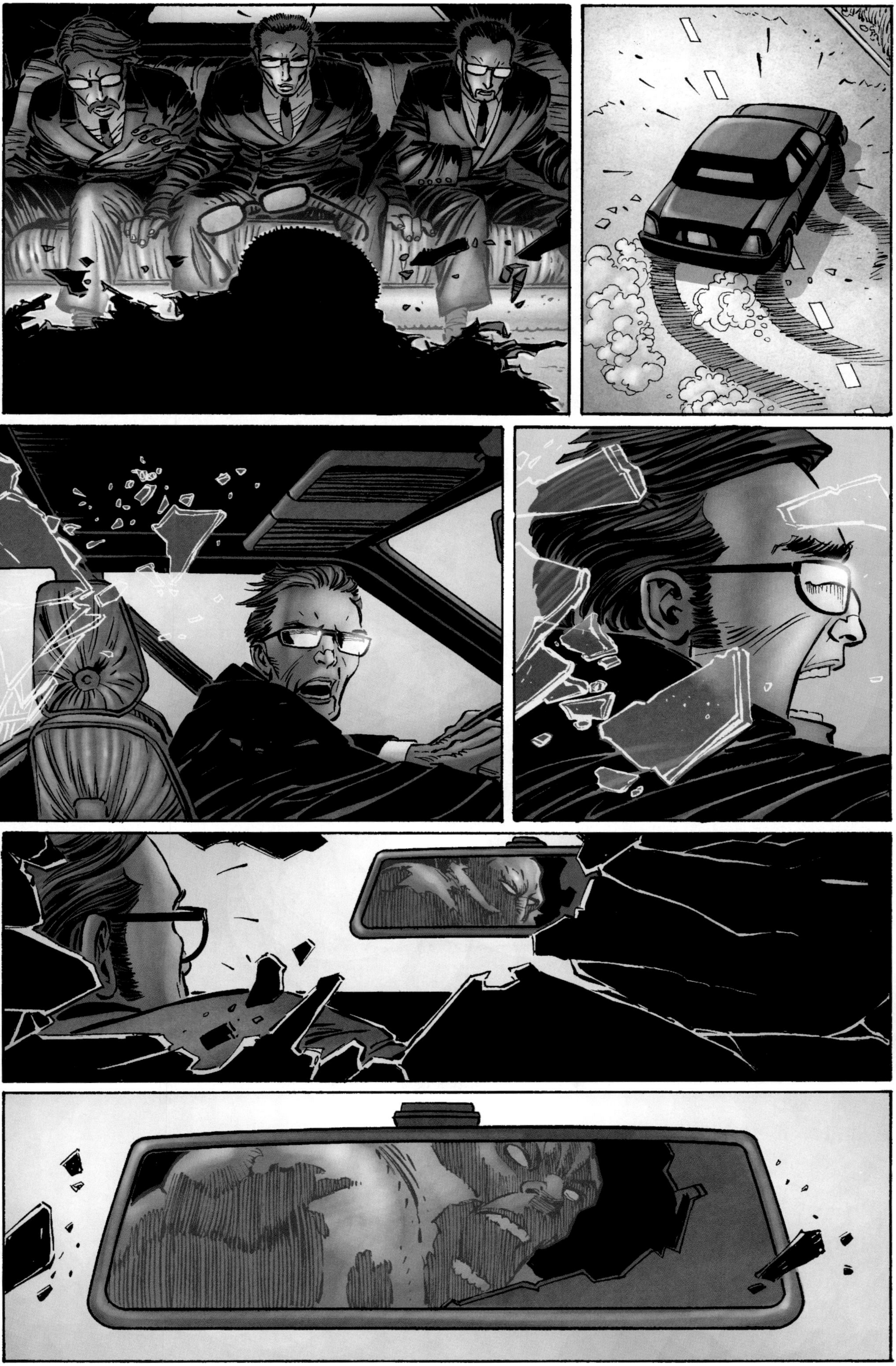

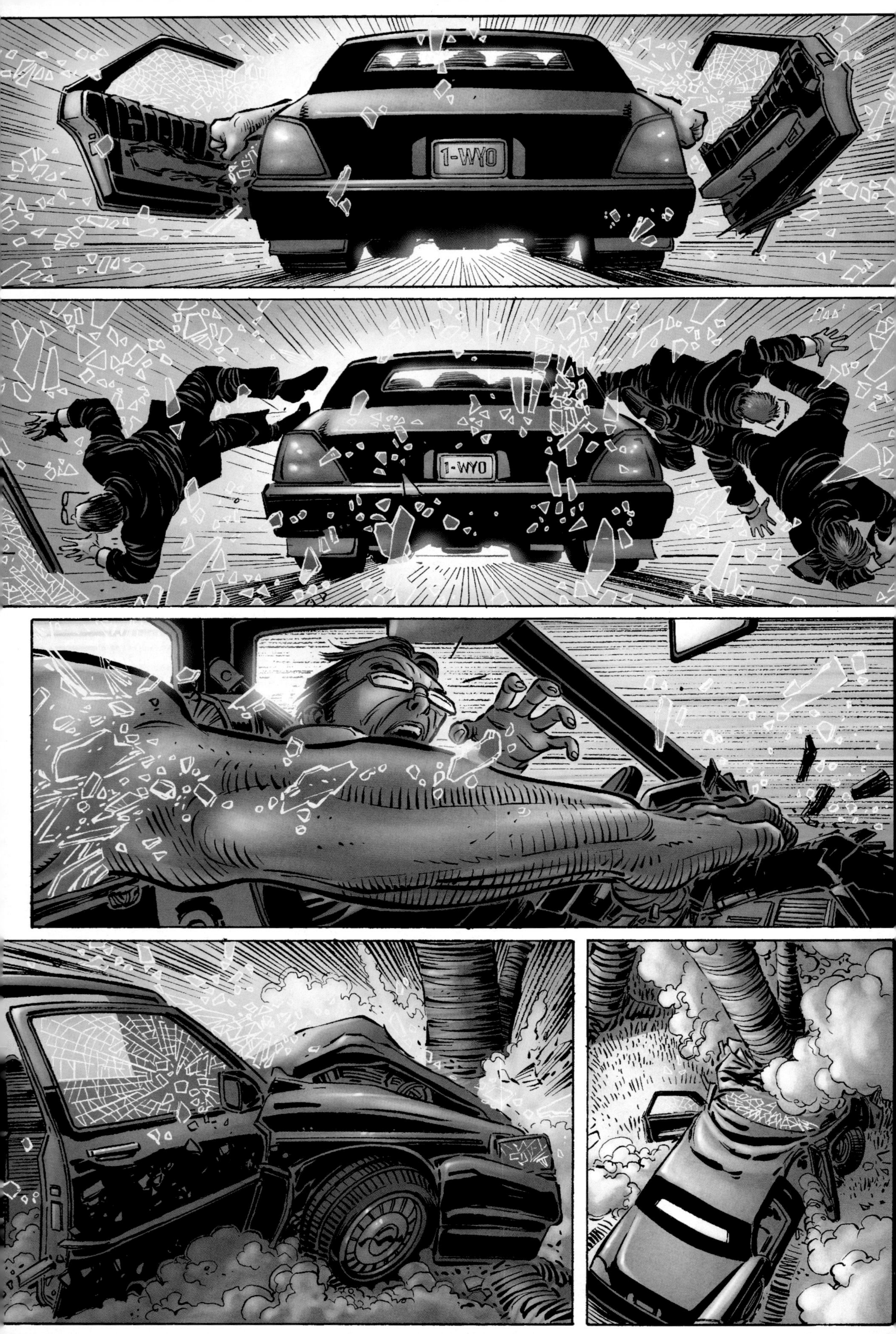
1-WYO
1-WYO

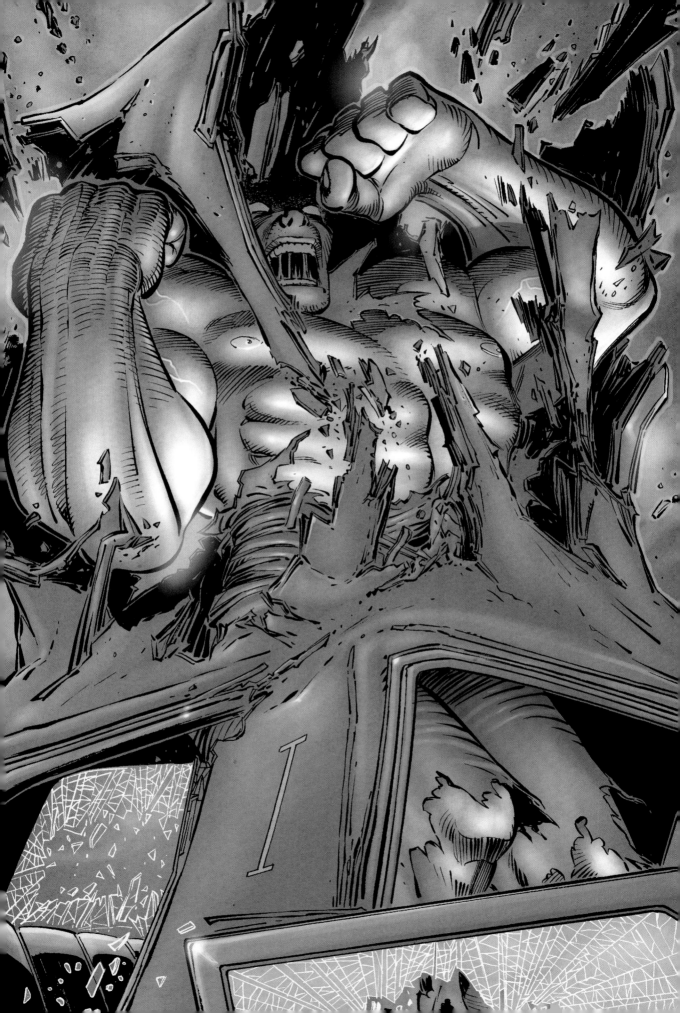

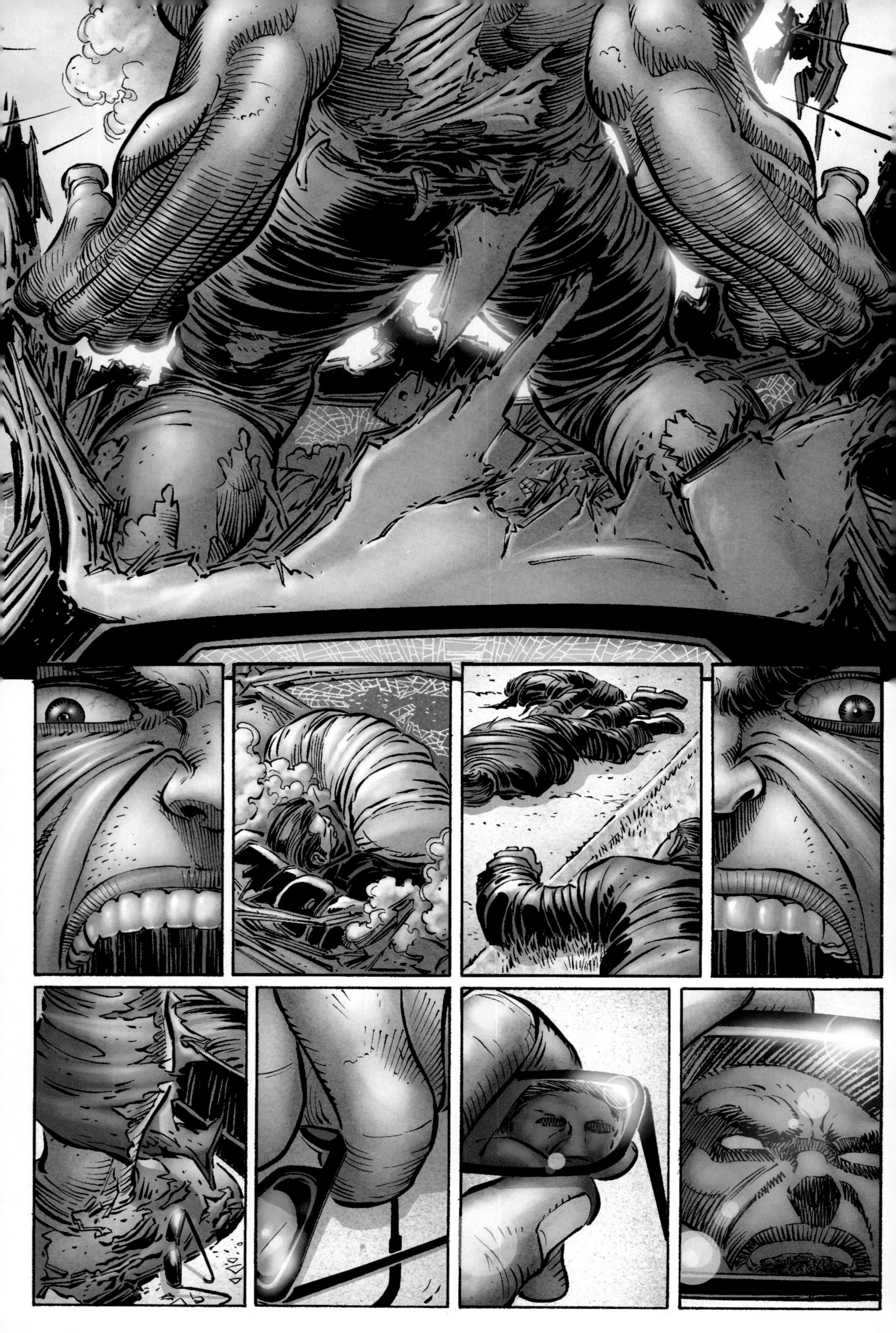

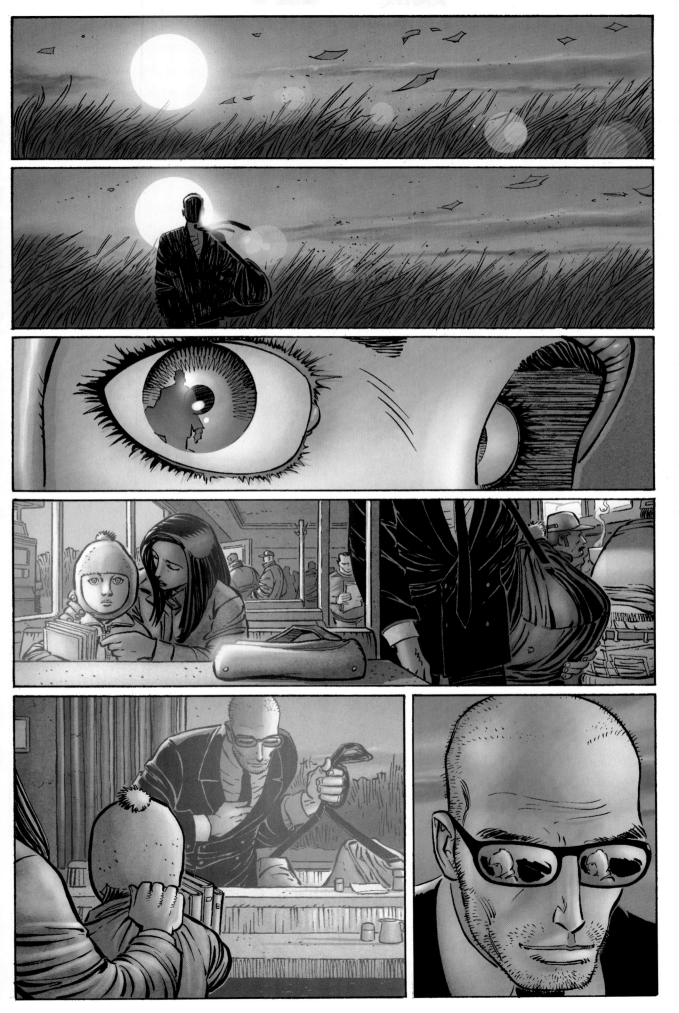

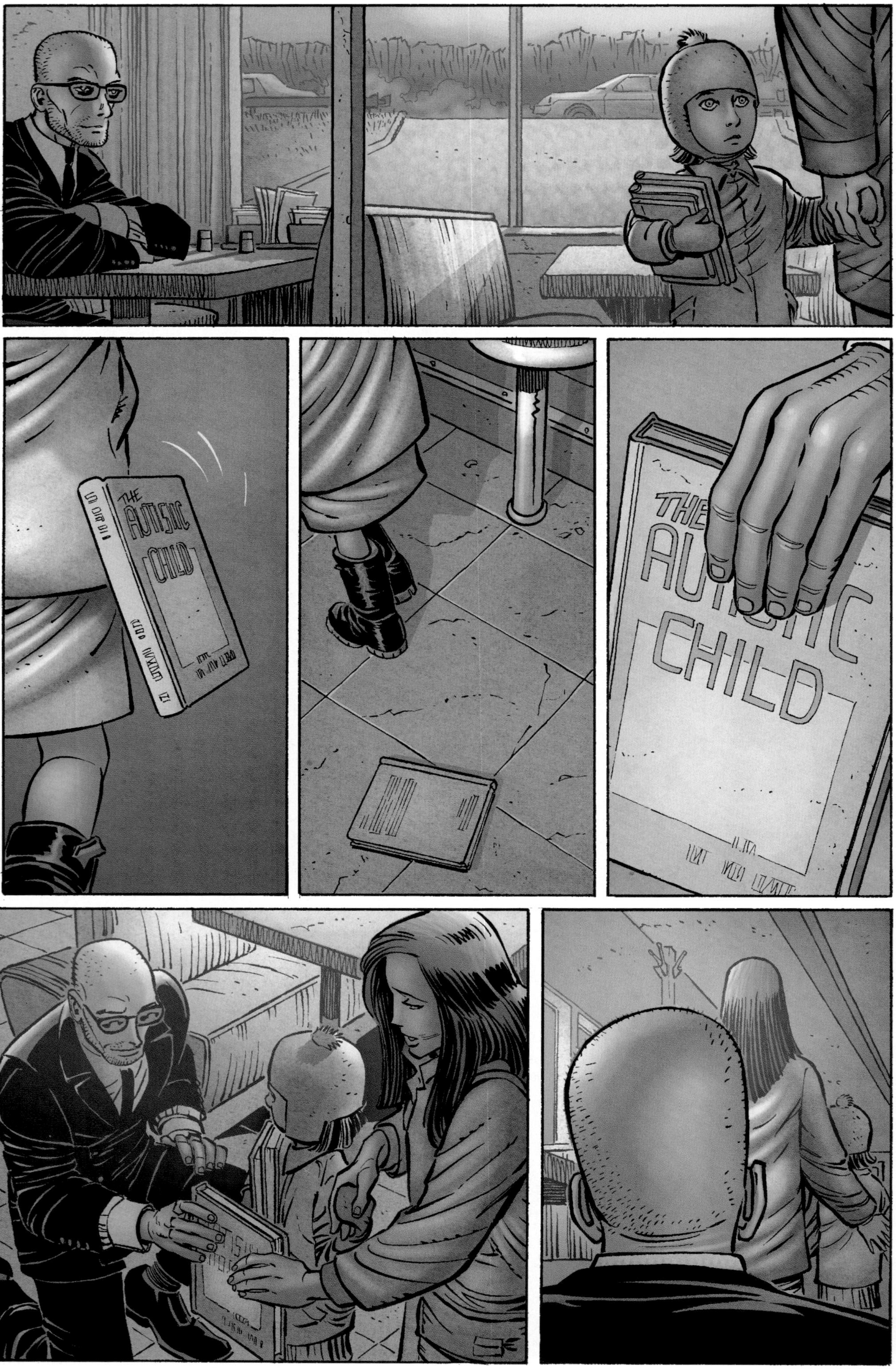
THE AUTISTIC CHILD
THE
CHILD

BWEN'S
WANDA'S DOGGIE BAG

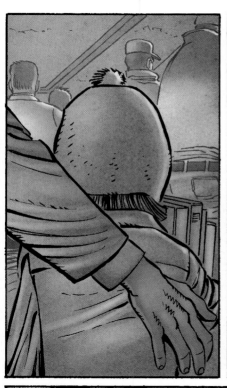

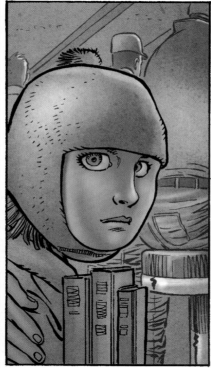

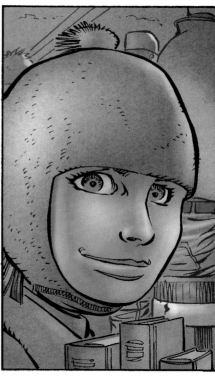

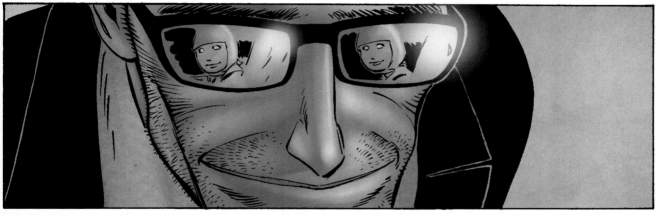

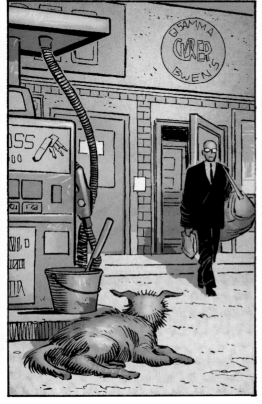

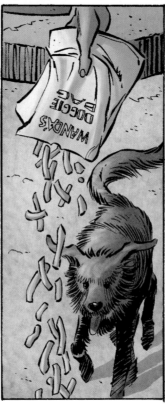

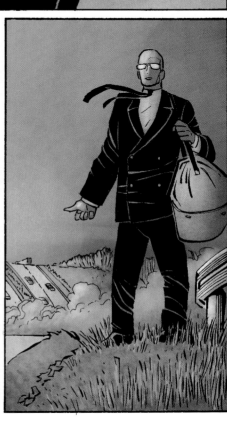

INCREDIBLE HULK #36
Cover sketch by Kaare Andrews

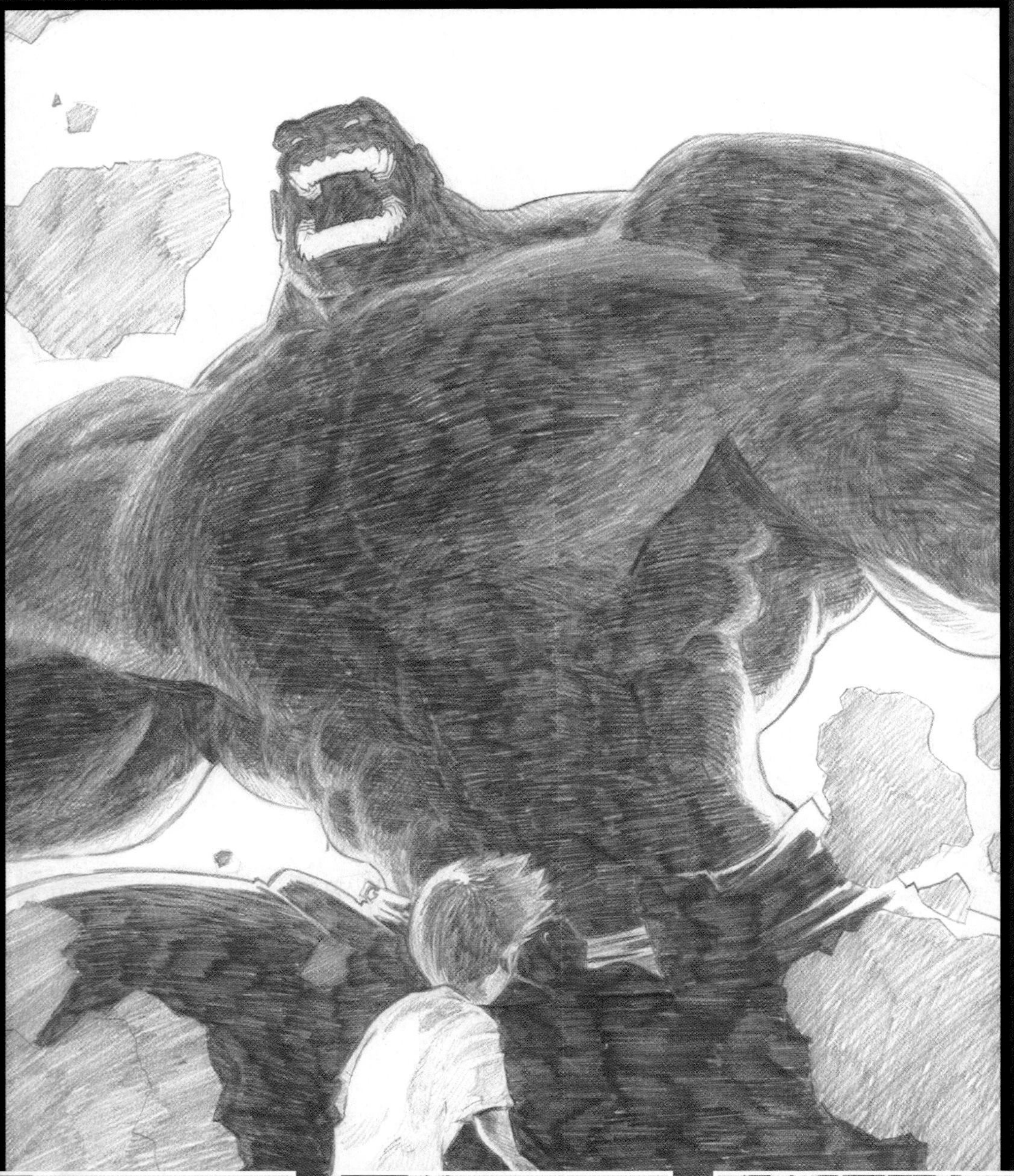

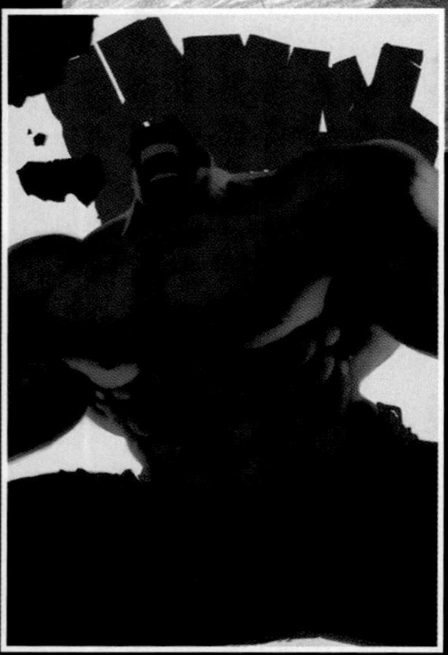

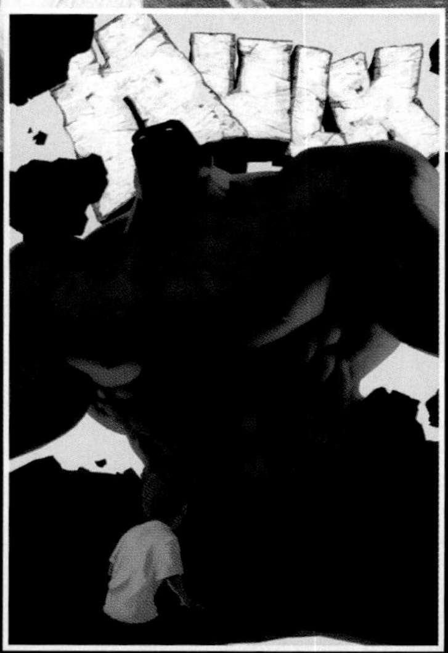

HULK

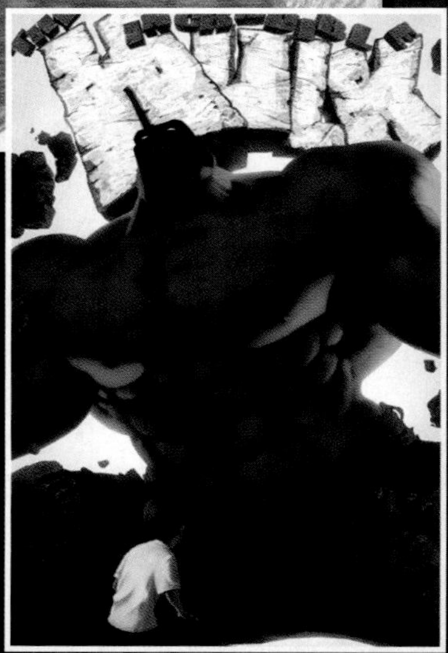

HULK

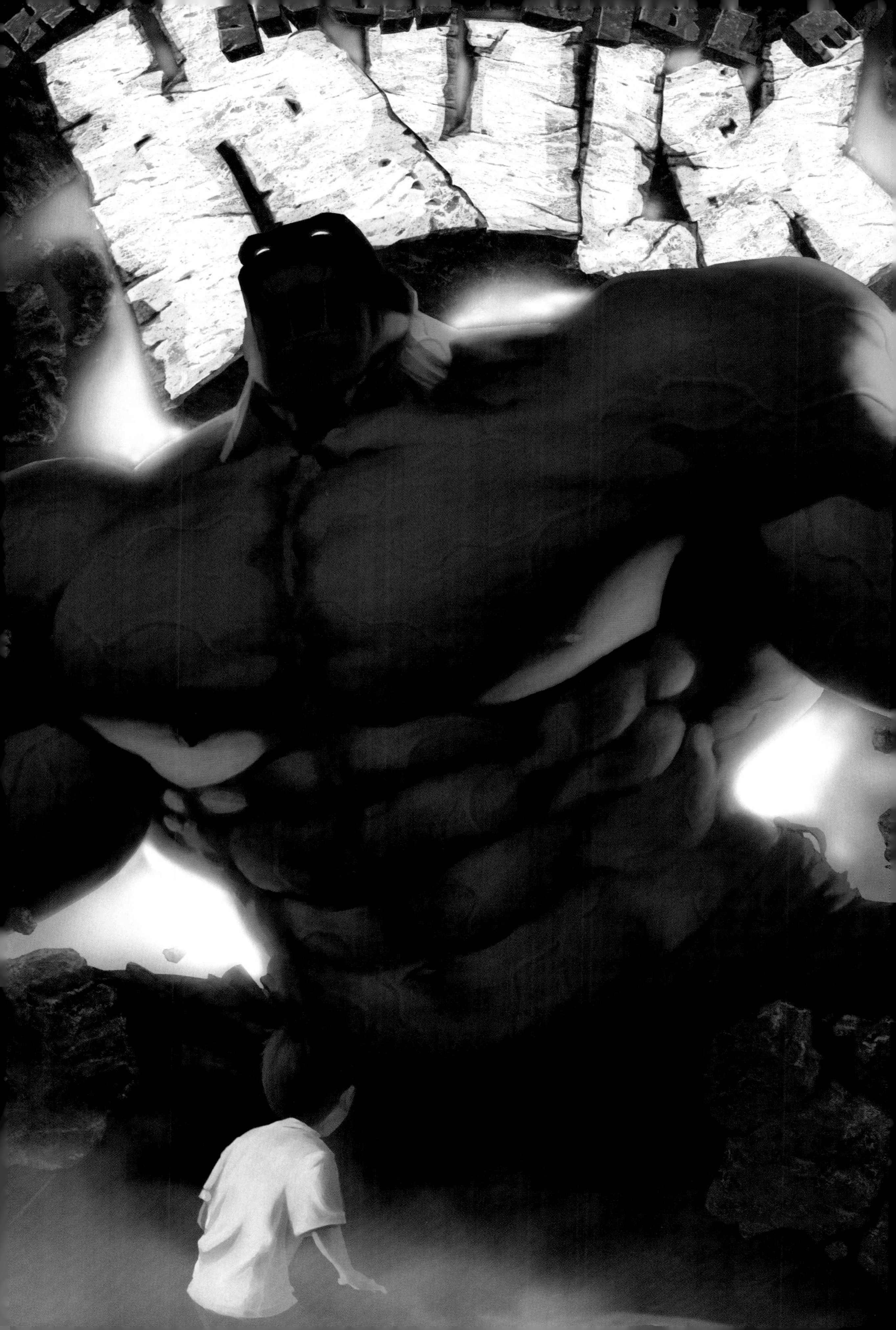
HULK

-- EXACT *LOCATION* OF THE CREATURE STILL UNKNOWN AT THIS TIME.

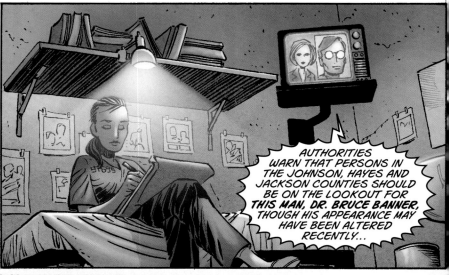

AUTHORITIES WARN THAT PERSONS IN THE JOHNSON, HAYES AND JACKSON COUNTIES SHOULD BE ON THE LOOKOUT FOR THIS MAN, DR. BRUCE BANNER, THOUGH HIS APPEARANCE MAY HAVE BEEN ALTERED RECENTLY...

WE HAVE FOOTAGE NOW OF THE CHICAGO INCIDENT WHERE LITTLE RICKY MYERS LOST HIS LIFE DURING THE MONSTER'S RAMPAGE...

CHANNEL 6 WARNS THE FOLLOWING CONTAINS GRAPHIC MATERIAL AND MAY NOT BE SUITABLE FOR YOUNGER VIEWERS...

ALMOST TIME, MISS VERDUGO. ANY *LAST* REQUEST?

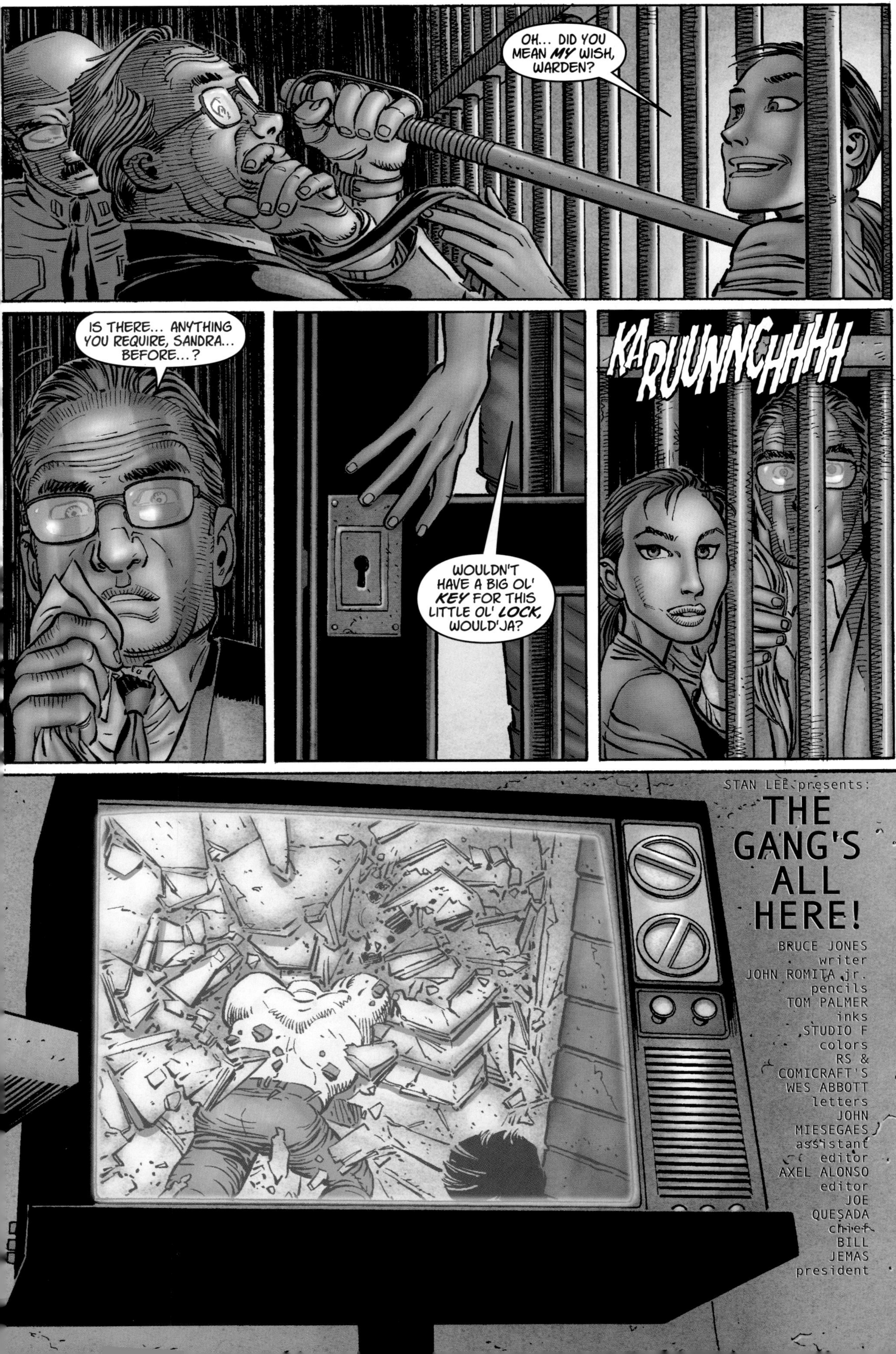
OH... DID YOU MEAN MY WISH, WARDEN?
IS THERE... ANYTHING YOU REQUIRE, SANDRA... BEFORE...?
WOULDN'T HAVE A BIG OL' KEY FOR THIS LITTLE OL' LOCK, WOULD'JA?
KARUUNNCHHHH
STAN LEE presents:
THE GANG'S ALL HERE!
BRUCE JONES writer
JOHN ROMITA jr. pencils
TOM PALMER inks
STUDIO F colors
RS & COMICRAFT'S WES ABBOTT letters
JOHN MIESEGAES assistant editor
AXEL ALONSO editor
JOE QUESADA chief
BILL JEMAS president

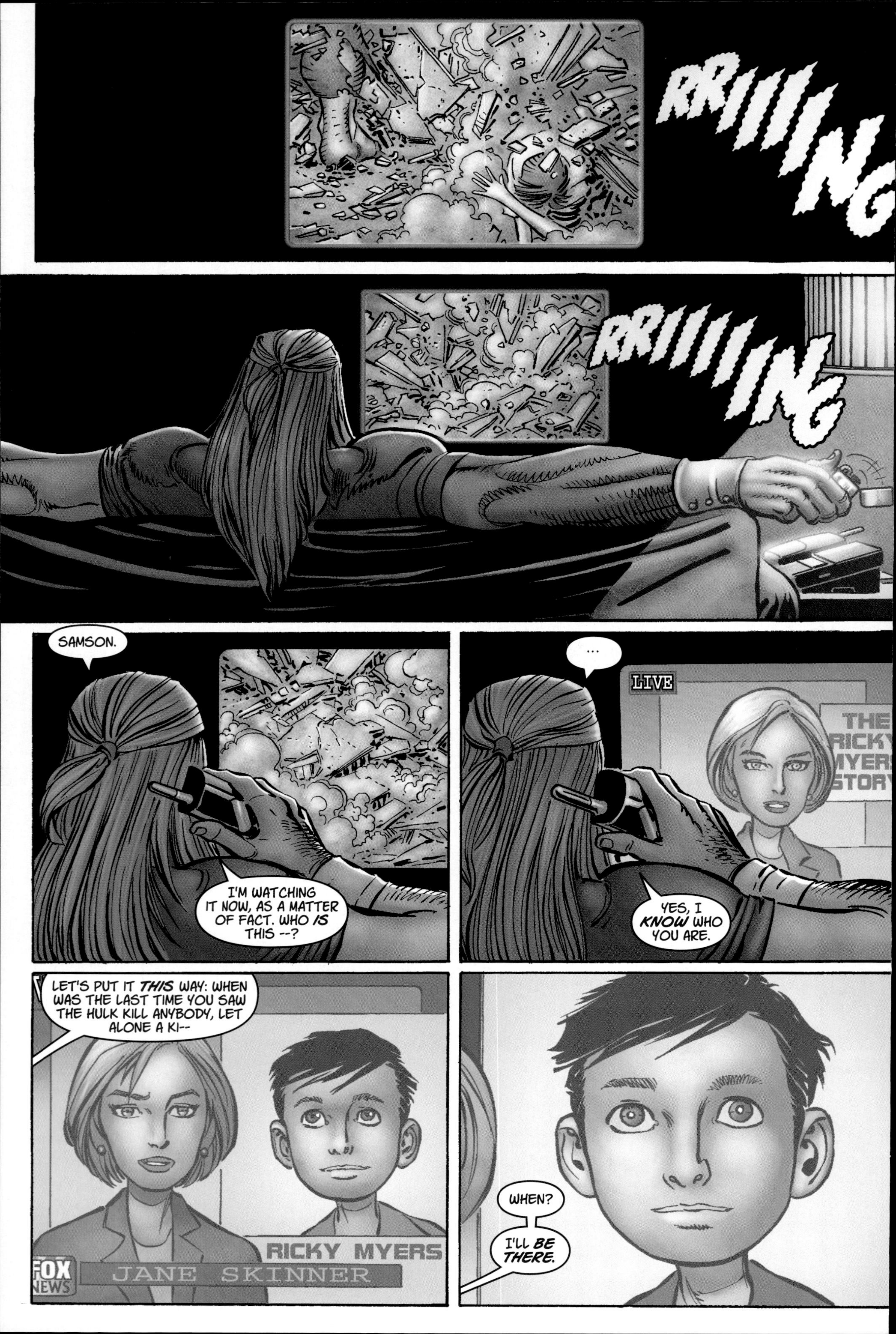
RRIIIING
RRIIIING
SAMSON.
I'M WATCHING IT NOW, AS A MATTER OF FACT. WHO *IS* THIS --?
...
LIVE
THE RICKY MYERS STORY
YES, I *KNOW* WHO YOU ARE.
LET'S PUT IT *THIS* WAY: WHEN WAS THE LAST TIME YOU SAW THE HULK KILL ANYBODY, LET ALONE A KI--
RICKY MYERS
FOX NEWS
JANE SKINNER
WHEN?
I'LL *BE THERE.*

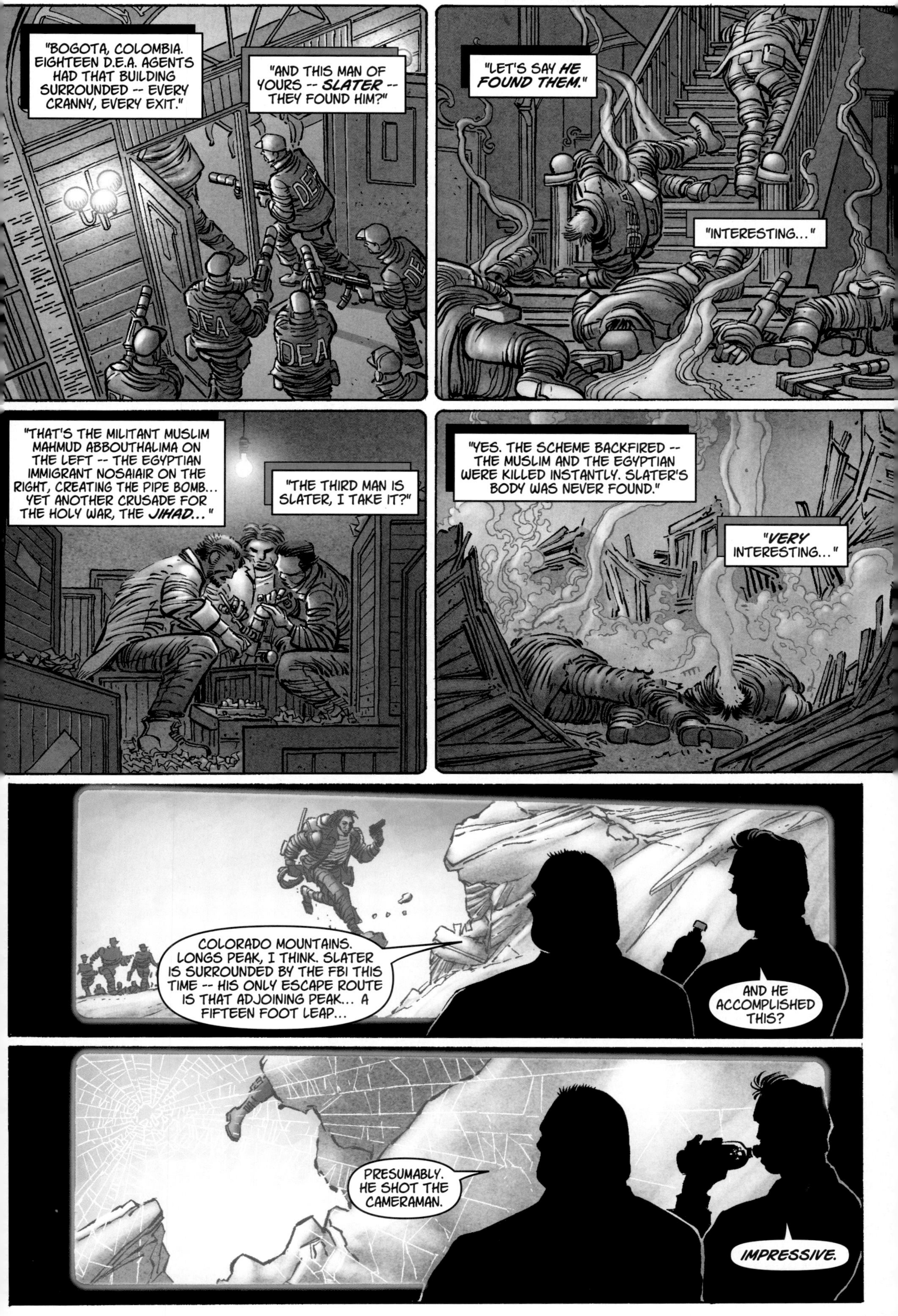
"BOGOTA, COLOMBIA. EIGHTEEN D.E.A. AGENTS HAD THAT BUILDING SURROUNDED -- EVERY CRANNY, EVERY EXIT."
"AND THIS MAN OF YOURS -- SLATER -- THEY FOUND HIM?"
DEA
"LET'S SAY HE FOUND THEM."
"INTERESTING..."
"THAT'S THE MILITANT MUSLIM MAHMUD ABBOUTHALIMA ON THE LEFT -- THE EGYPTIAN IMMIGRANT NOSAIAIR ON THE RIGHT, CREATING THE PIPE BOMB... YET ANOTHER CRUSADE FOR THE HOLY WAR, THE JIHAD..."
"THE THIRD MAN IS SLATER, I TAKE IT?"
"YES. THE SCHEME BACKFIRED -- THE MUSLIM AND THE EGYPTIAN WERE KILLED INSTANTLY. SLATER'S BODY WAS NEVER FOUND."
"VERY INTERESTING..."
COLORADO MOUNTAINS. LONGS PEAK, I THINK. SLATER IS SURROUNDED BY THE FBI THIS TIME -- HIS ONLY ESCAPE ROUTE IS THAT ADJOINING PEAK... A FIFTEEN FOOT LEAP...
AND HE ACCOMPLISHED THIS?
PRESUMABLY. HE SHOT THE CAMERAMAN.
IMPRESSIVE.

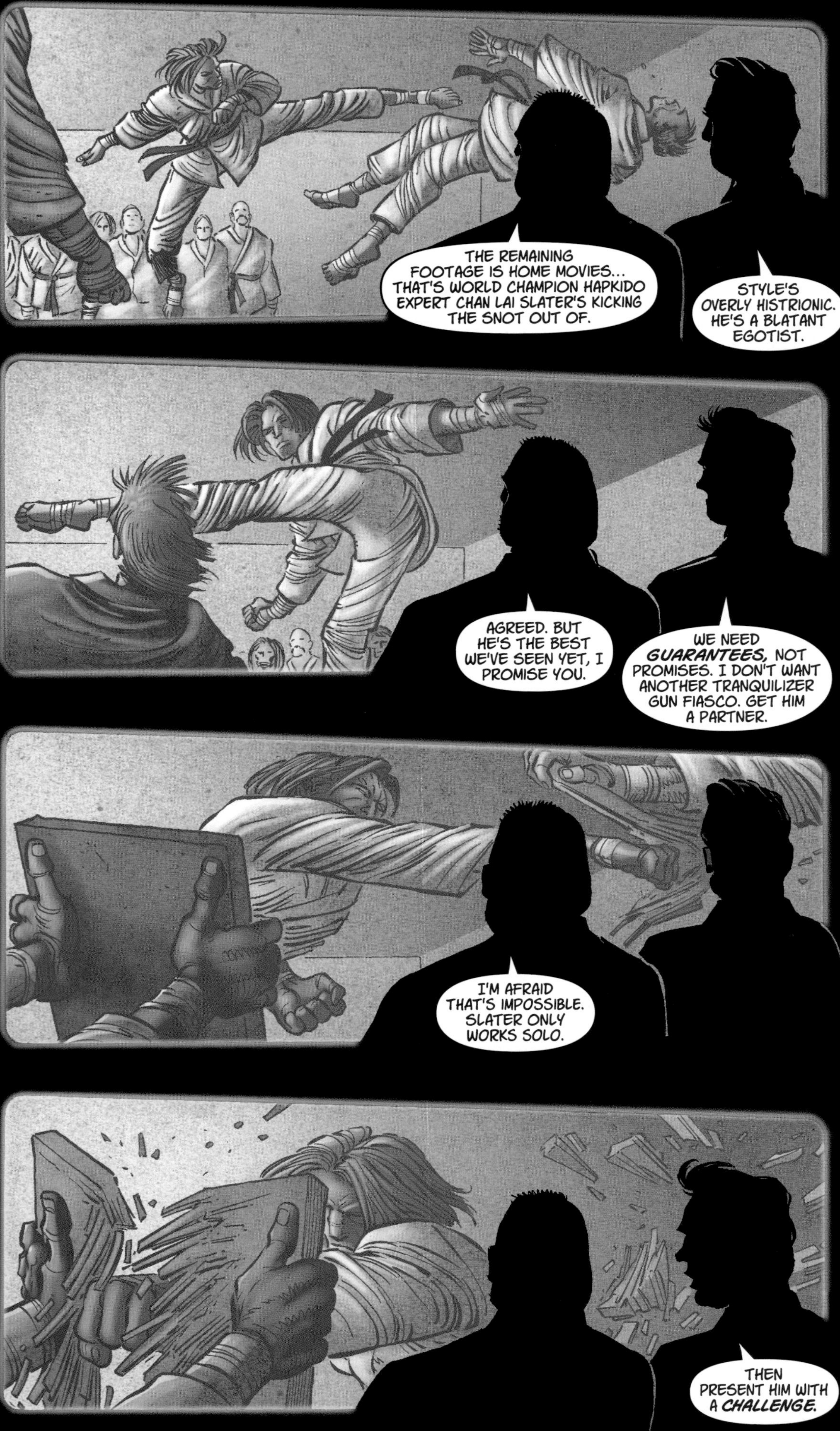
THE REMAINING FOOTAGE IS HOME MOVIES... THAT'S WORLD CHAMPION HAPKIDO EXPERT CHAN LAI SLATER'S KICKING THE SNOT OUT OF.
STYLE'S OVERLY HISTRIONIC. HE'S A BLATANT EGOTIST.
AGREED. BUT HE'S THE BEST WE'VE SEEN YET, I PROMISE YOU.
WE NEED *GUARANTEES,* NOT PROMISES. I DON'T WANT ANOTHER TRANQUILIZER GUN FIASCO. GET HIM A PARTNER.
I'M AFRAID THAT'S IMPOSSIBLE. SLATER ONLY WORKS SOLO.
THEN PRESENT HIM WITH A *CHALLENGE.*

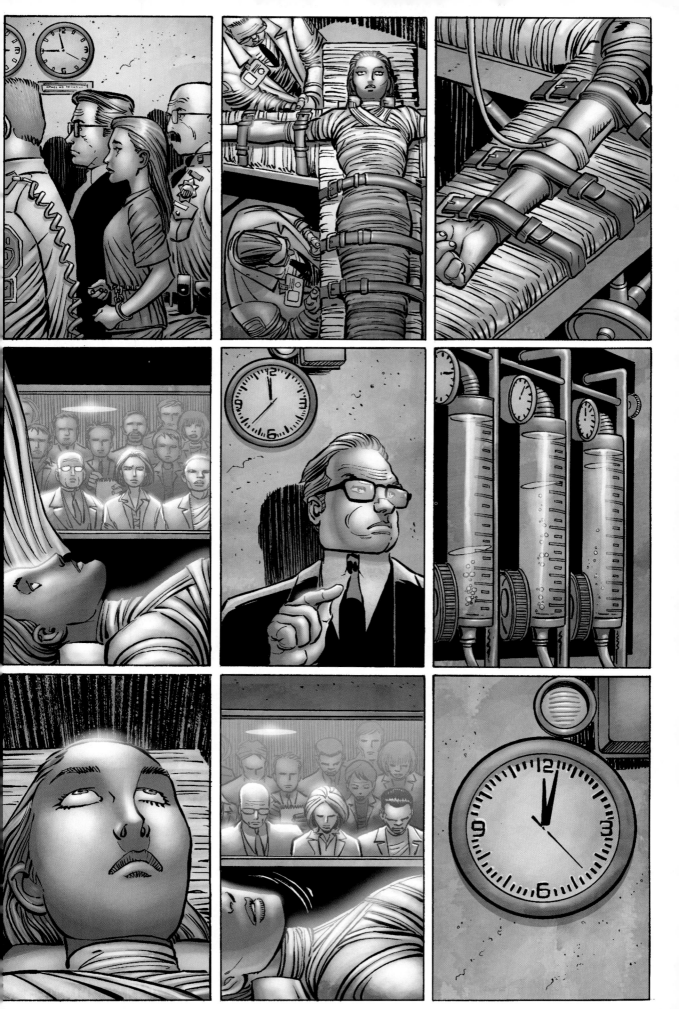

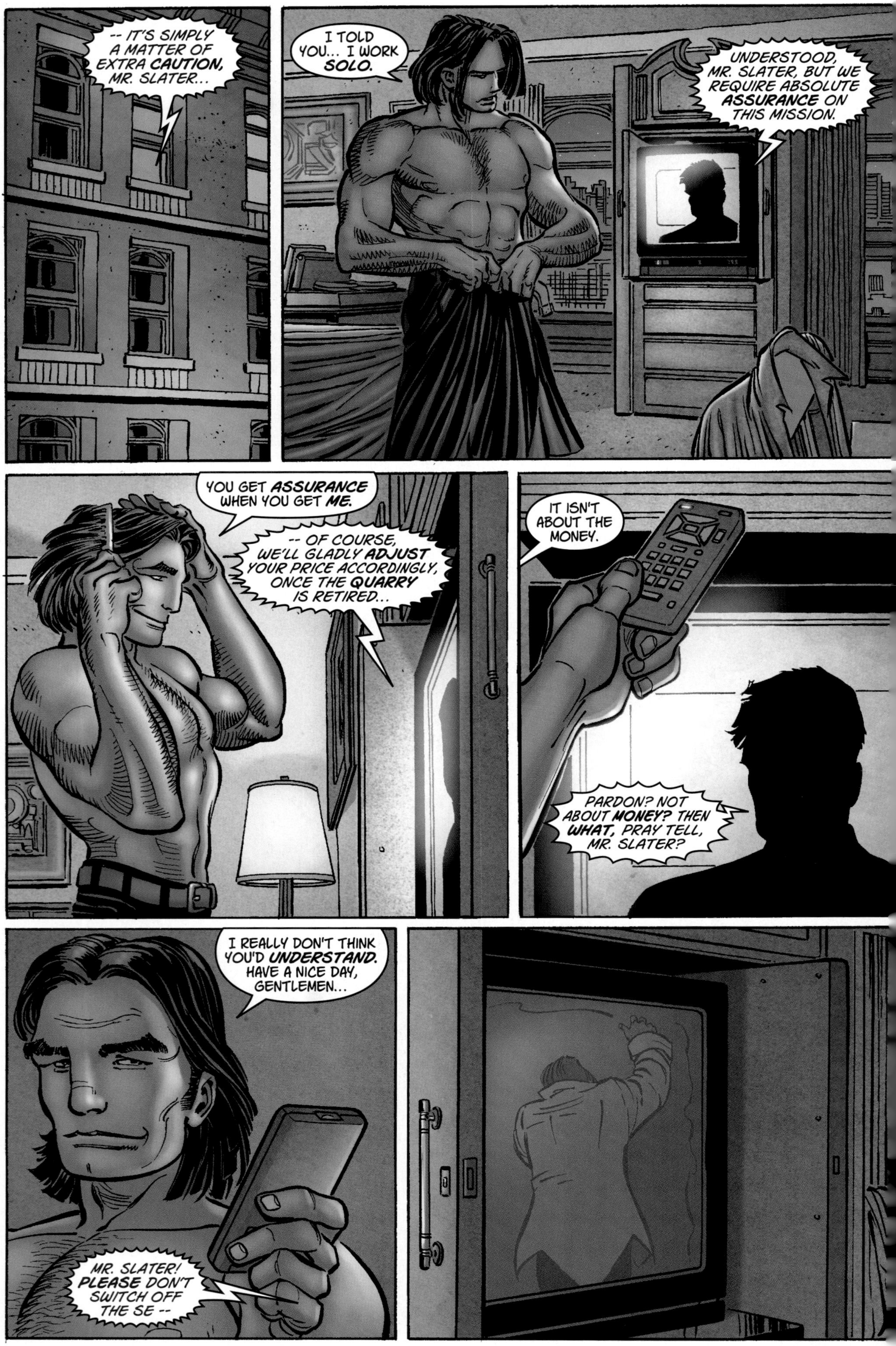
-- IT'S SIMPLY A MATTER OF EXTRA CAUTION, MR. SLATER...
I TOLD YOU... I WORK SOLO.
UNDERSTOOD, MR. SLATER, BUT WE REQUIRE ABSOLUTE ASSURANCE ON THIS MISSION.
YOU GET ASSURANCE WHEN YOU GET ME.
-- OF COURSE, WE'LL GLADLY ADJUST YOUR PRICE ACCORDINGLY, ONCE THE QUARRY IS RETIRED...
IT ISN'T ABOUT THE MONEY.
PARDON? NOT ABOUT MONEY? THEN WHAT, PRAY TELL, MR. SLATER?
I REALLY DON'T THINK YOU'D UNDERSTAND. HAVE A NICE DAY, GENTLEMEN...
MR. SLATER! PLEASE DON'T SWITCH OFF THE SE --

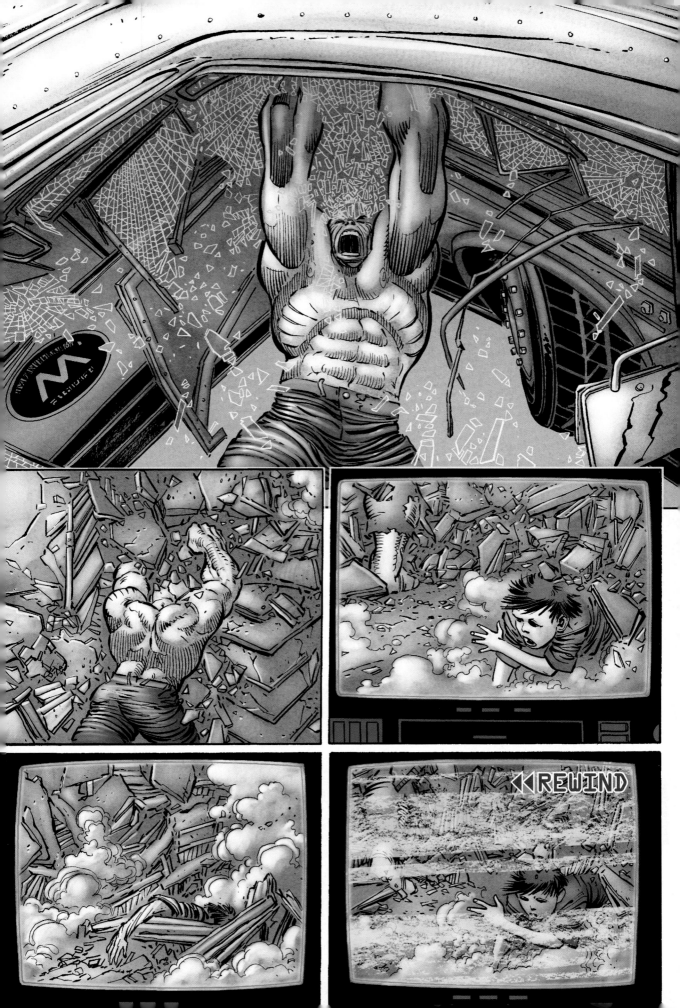

REWIND

GOD...
TELL ME I DIDN'T DO THAT...
TELL ME I WON'T SPEND THE REST OF MY LIFE SEEING THAT!

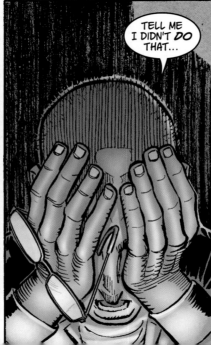

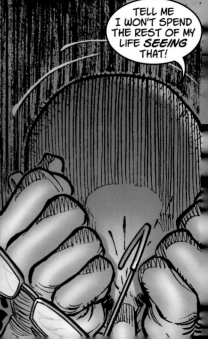

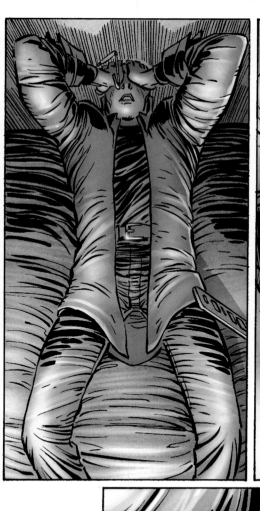

Mr. Green,
Advise you amend current
itinerary. Two very strong fronts
moving your way. Hot and cold
air masses. Extremely volatile.

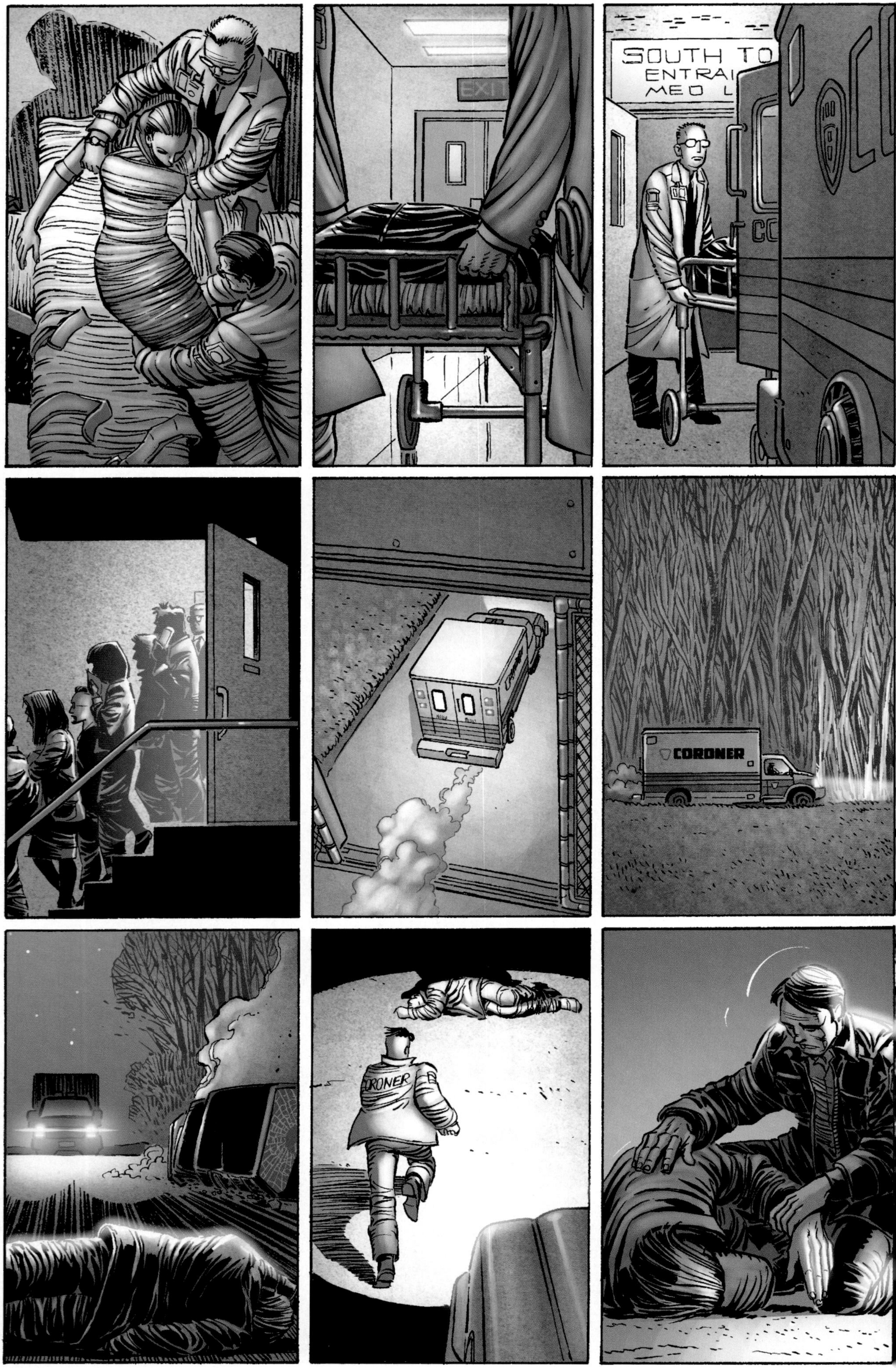
SOUTH TO
EXIT
CORONER
CORONER

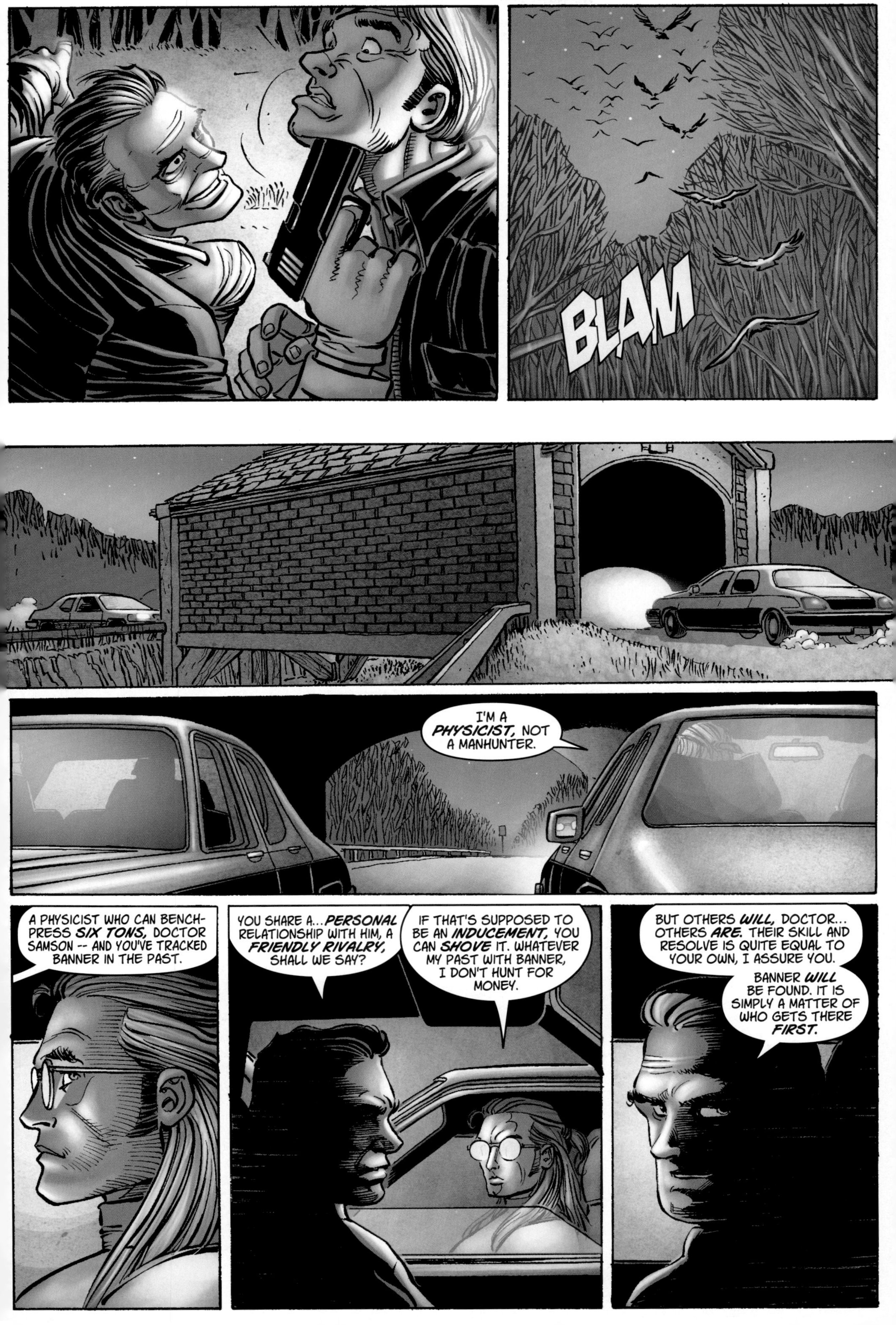

BLAM
I'M A PHYSICIST, NOT A MANHUNTER.
A PHYSICIST WHO CAN BENCH-PRESS SIX TONS, DOCTOR SAMSON -- AND YOU'VE TRACKED BANNER IN THE PAST.
YOU SHARE A...PERSONAL RELATIONSHIP WITH HIM, A FRIENDLY RIVALRY, SHALL WE SAY?
IF THAT'S SUPPOSED TO BE AN INDUCEMENT, YOU CAN SHOVE IT. WHATEVER MY PAST WITH BANNER, I DON'T HUNT FOR MONEY.
BUT OTHERS WILL, DOCTOR... OTHERS ARE. THEIR SKILL AND RESOLVE IS QUITE EQUAL TO YOUR OWN, I ASSURE YOU.
BANNER WILL BE FOUND. IT IS SIMPLY A MATTER OF WHO GETS THERE FIRST.

I WOULDN'T MAKE BANK ON THAT. BANNER'S A COOL HEAD...*ALWAYS* IN CONTROL.

INDEED?

WOULD YOU CARE TO TELL LITTLE RICKY MYERS' *MOTHER* THAT, DOCTOR? WE HAVE HER NUMBER.

YOU HAVE TWENTY-FOUR HOURS TO DECIDE, DOCTOR. TIME IS OF THE *ESSENCE*.

CLICK

CIGARETTE, DOCTOR?

I QUIT. IT'S A *REMINDER*.

RIGHT.

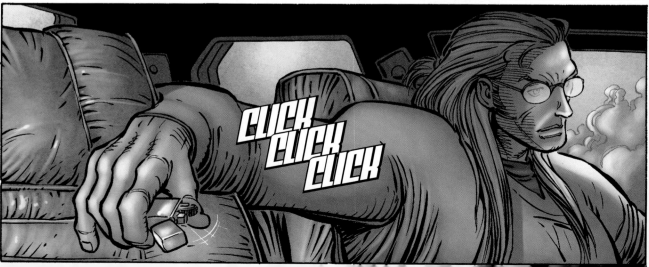

CLICK CLICK CLICK

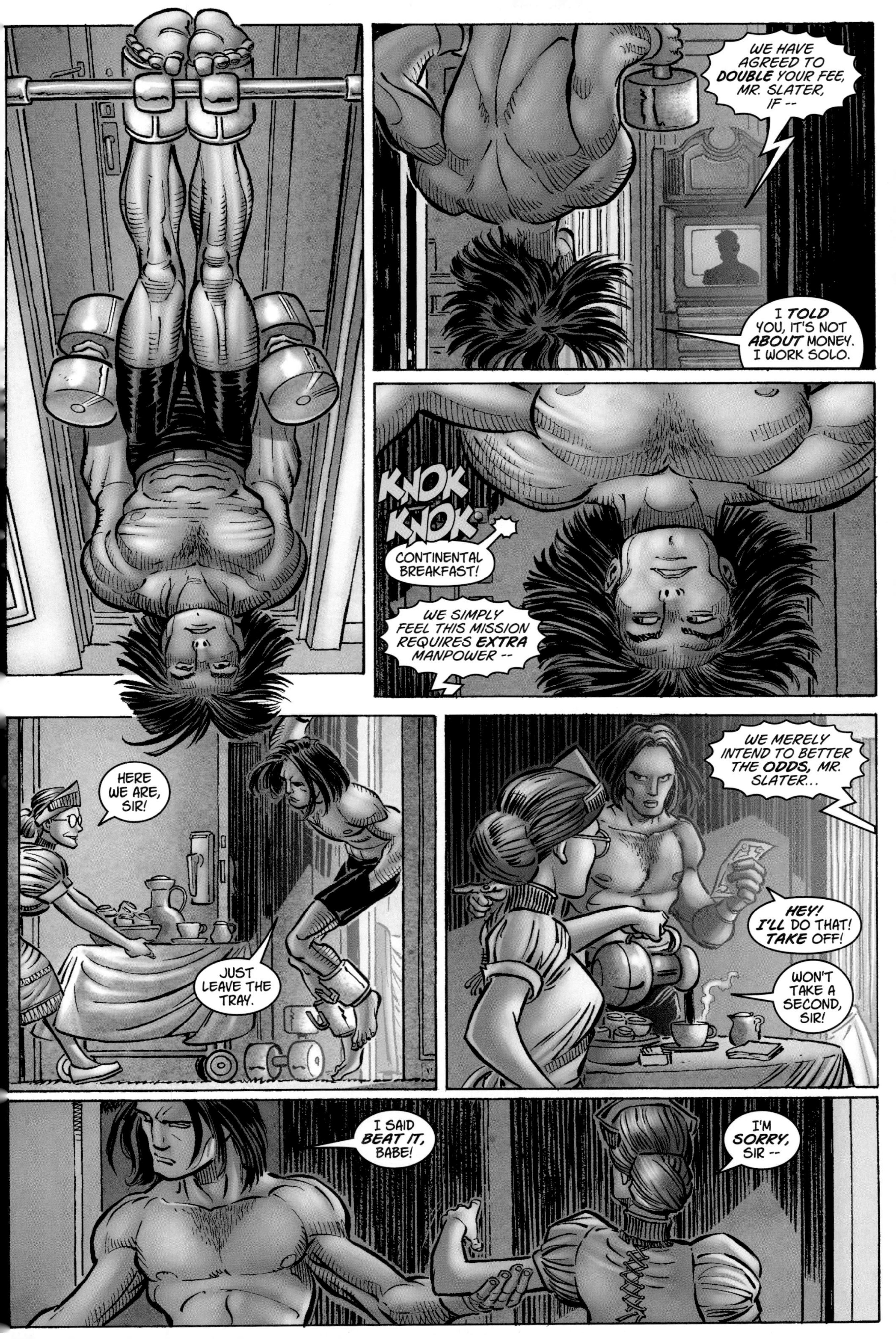

WE HAVE AGREED TO DOUBLE YOUR FEE, MR. SLATER, IF --
I TOLD YOU, IT'S NOT ABOUT MONEY. I WORK SOLO.
KNOK KNOK
CONTINENTAL BREAKFAST!
WE SIMPLY FEEL THIS MISSION REQUIRES EXTRA MANPOWER --
HERE WE ARE, SIR!
JUST LEAVE THE TRAY.
WE MERELY INTEND TO BETTER THE ODDS, MR. SLATER...
HEY! I'LL DO THAT! TAKE OFF!
WON'T TAKE A SECOND, SIR!
I SAID BEAT IT, BABE!
I'M SORRY, SIR --

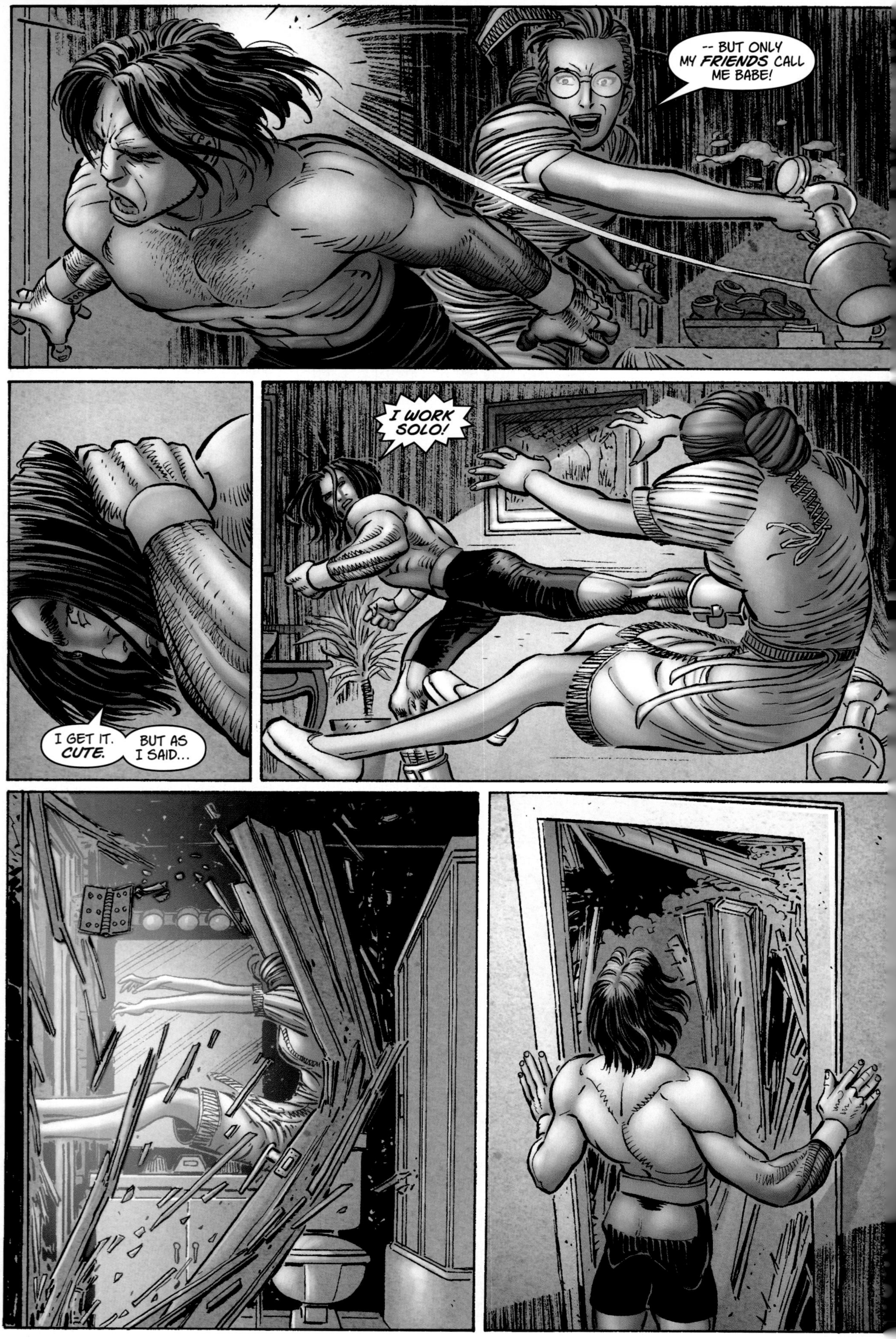

-- BUT ONLY MY FRIENDS CALL ME BABE!
I GET IT. CUTE.
BUT AS I SAID...
I WORK SOLO!

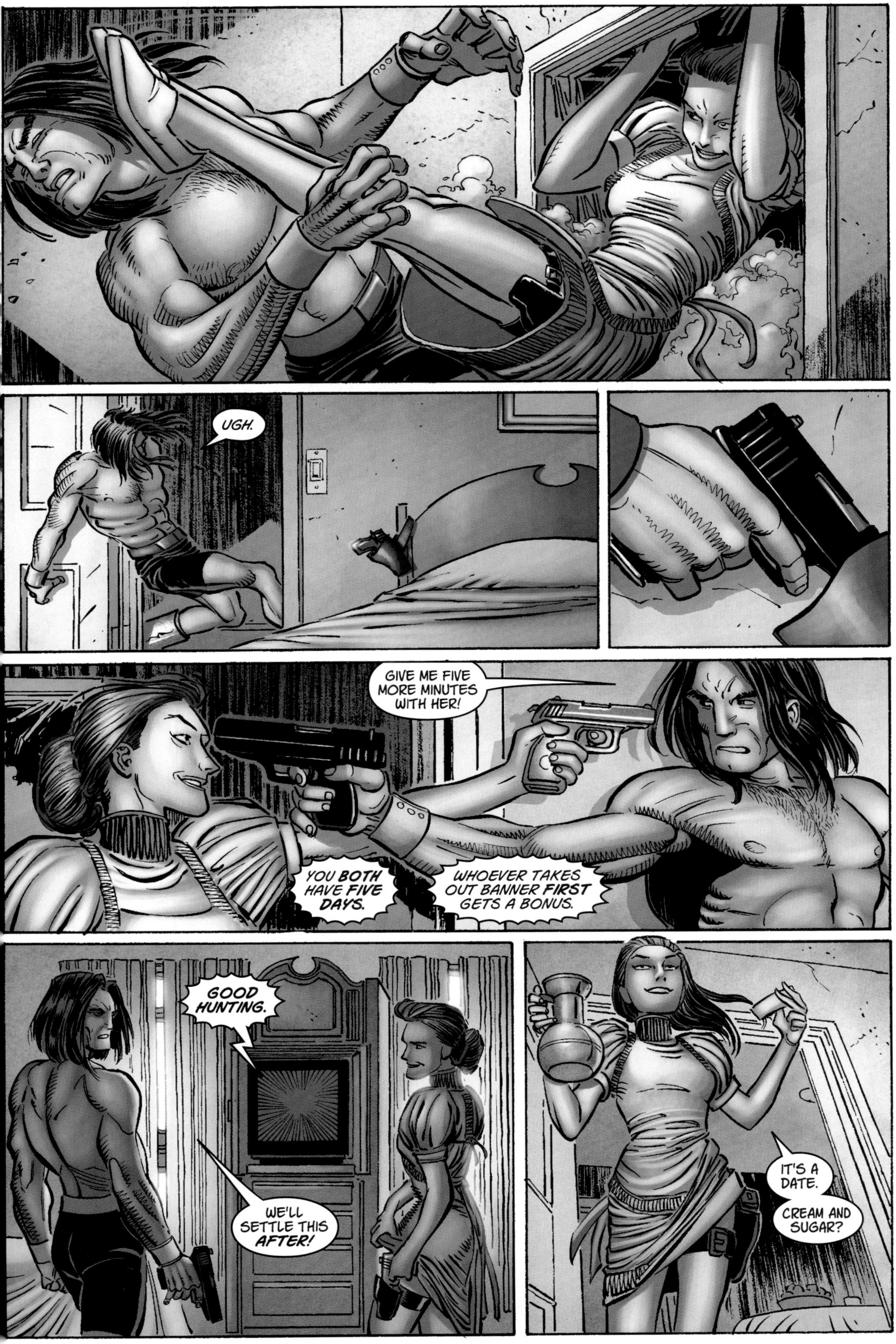
UGH.
GIVE ME FIVE MORE MINUTES WITH HER!
YOU BOTH HAVE FIVE DAYS.
WHOEVER TAKES OUT BANNER FIRST GETS A BONUS.
GOOD HUNTING.
WE'LL SETTLE THIS AFTER!
IT'S A DATE.
CREAM AND SUGAR?

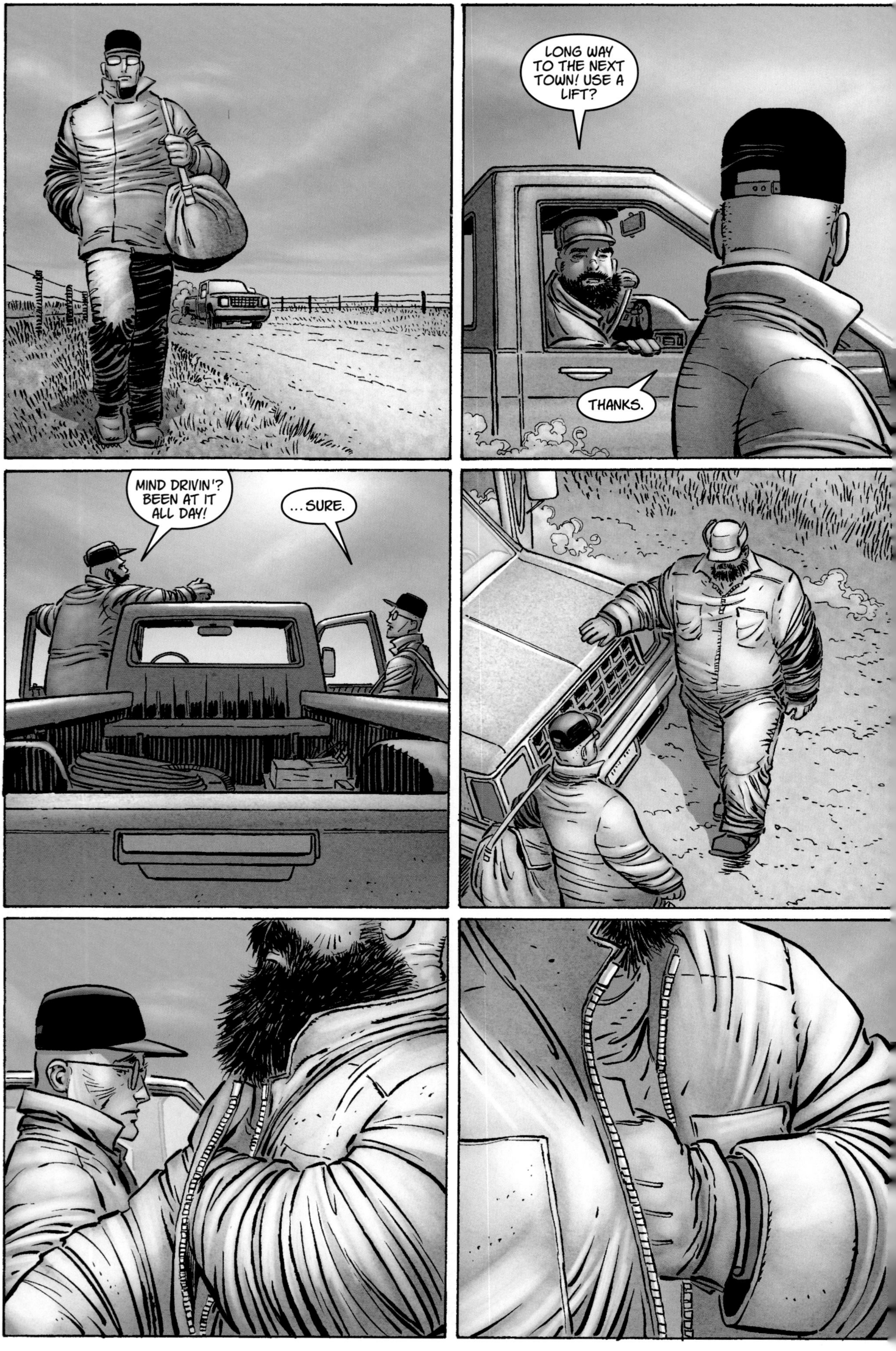
LONG WAY TO THE NEXT TOWN! USE A LIFT?
THANKS.
MIND DRIVIN'? BEEN AT IT ALL DAY!
...SURE.

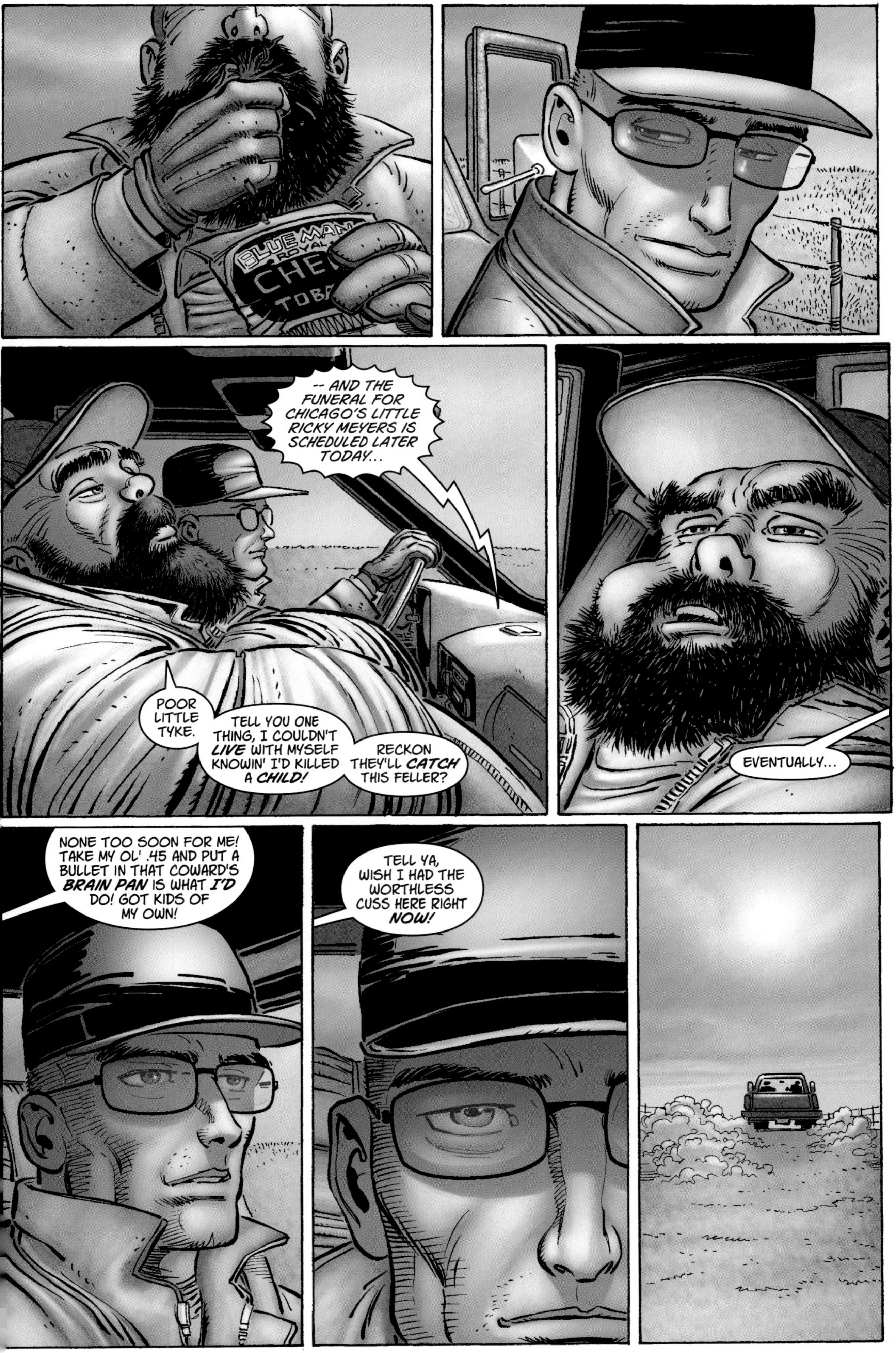
BLUE MAN
-- AND THE FUNERAL FOR CHICAGO'S LITTLE RICKY MEYERS IS SCHEDULED LATER TODAY...
POOR LITTLE TYKE.
TELL YOU ONE THING, I COULDN'T LIVE WITH MYSELF KNOWIN' I'D KILLED A CHILD!
RECKON THEY'LL CATCH THIS FELLER?
EVENTUALLY...
NONE TOO SOON FOR ME! TAKE MY OL' .45 AND PUT A BULLET IN THAT COWARD'S BRAIN PAN IS WHAT I'D DO! GOT KIDS OF MY OWN!
TELL YA, WISH I HAD THE WORTHLESS CUSS HERE RIGHT NOW!

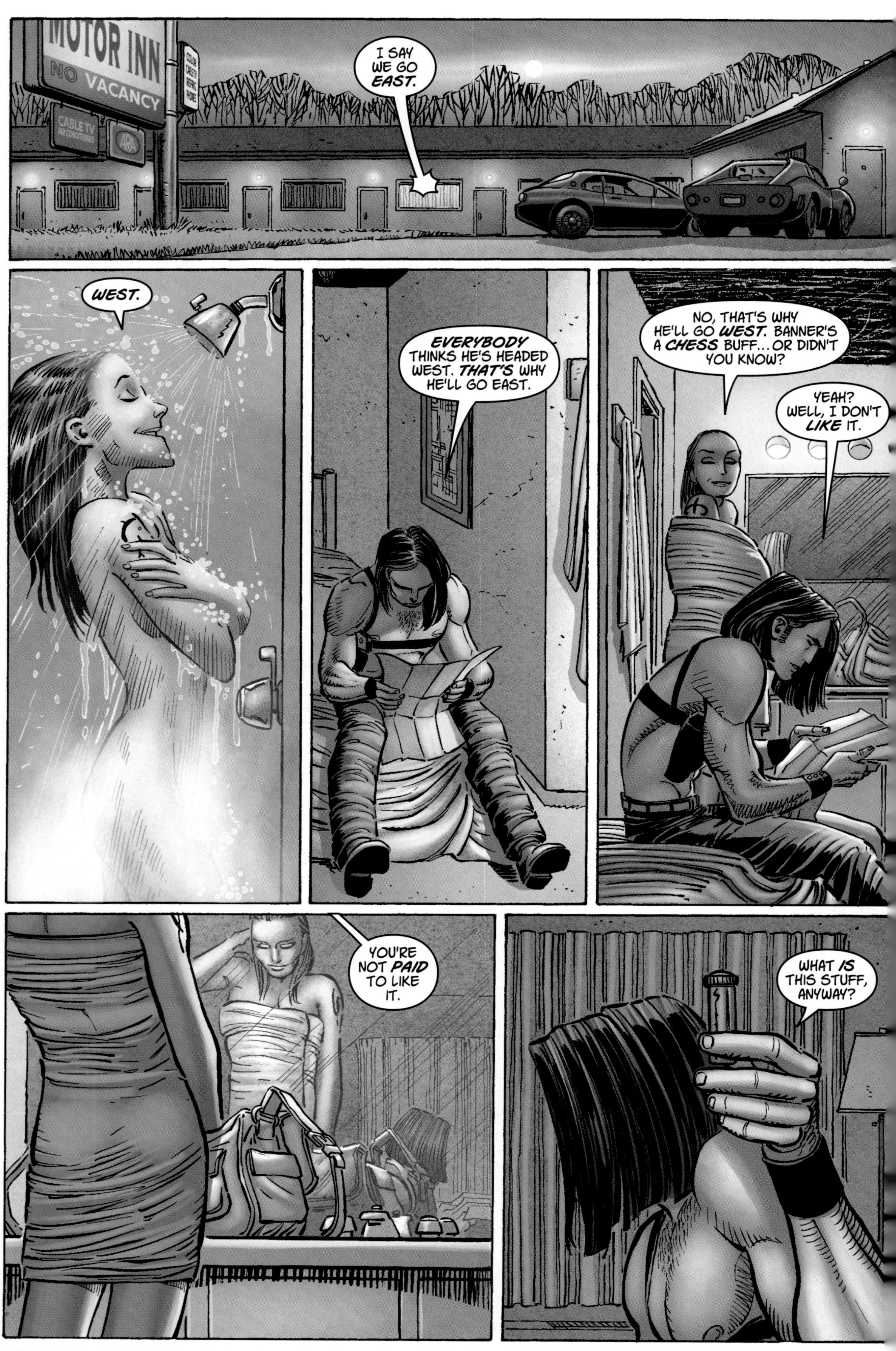
MOTOR INN
NO VACANCY
CABLE TV
I SAY WE GO EAST.
WEST.
EVERYBODY THINKS HE'S HEADED WEST. THAT'S WHY HE'LL GO EAST.
NO, THAT'S WHY HE'LL GO WEST. BANNER'S A CHESS BUFF... OR DIDN'T YOU KNOW?
YEAH? WELL, I DON'T LIKE IT.
YOU'RE NOT PAID TO LIKE IT.
WHAT IS THIS STUFF, ANYWAY?

DON'T *SCREW AROUND* WITH THAT!

GIVE!

AFTER YOU TELL ME...

TRANQUILIZER DARTS FAILED BECAUSE SEDATIVES ATTACK THE *MOTOR SYSTEM* --

-- WHICH WORKED FINE WITH BANNER...*NOT SO FINE* WITH THE HULK.

WHERE'D YOU STEAL IT?

GIFT FROM A SOUTH AMERICAN GENTLEMAN... GRATEFUL EMPLOYER.

GEE... I WONDER HOW YOU *PAID* FOR IT?

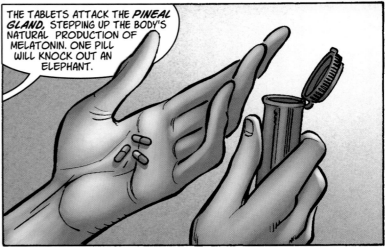

THE TABLETS ATTACK THE *PINEAL GLAND,* STEPPING UP THE BODY'S NATURAL PRODUCTION OF MELATONIN. ONE PILL WILL KNOCK OUT AN ELEPHANT.

THE BEAUTY IS, IT'S *GRADUAL.*

SLOW AND NATURAL.

THE VICTIM DOESN'T SEE IT COMING.

LIKE A *KNIFE* IN THE *BACK*.

THUNK

WONDERED WHERE THAT GOT TO.

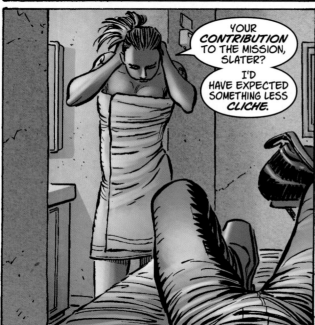

YOUR *CONTRIBUTION* TO THE MISSION, SLATER?

I'D HAVE EXPECTED SOMETHING LESS *CLICHE*.

LIKE YOUR LITTLE *SLEEPING AIDS?*

TELL ME, PRINCESS. HOW DO WE PERSUADE BANNER TO *INGEST* THESE MAGIC PILLS?

MISDIRECTION, SLATER... AVERTING THE ENEMY'S ATTENTION AT *PRECISELY* THE RIGHT MOMENT...

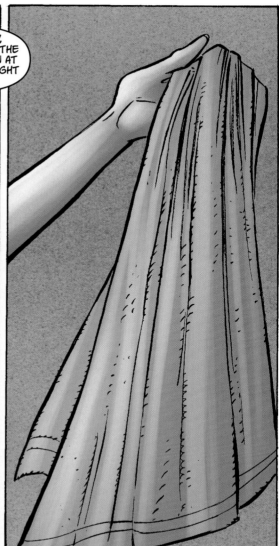

MY CONTRIBUTION!

INCREDIBLE HULK #37
Cover renderings by Kaare Andrews

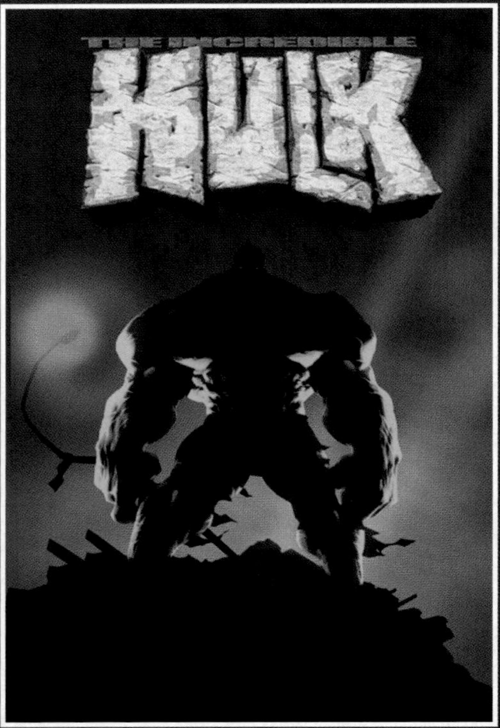
THE INCREDIBLE
HULK

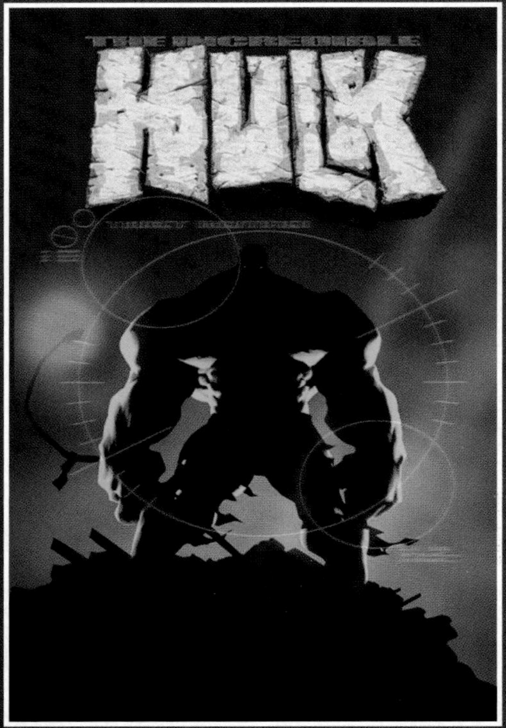
THE INCREDIBLE
HULK

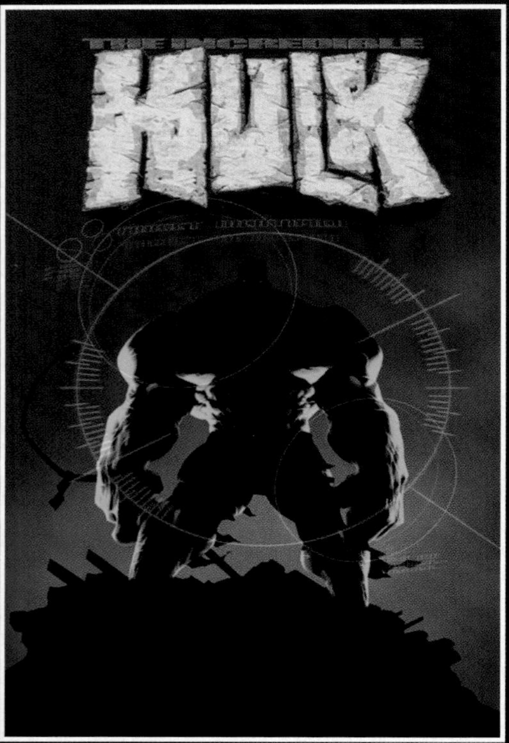
THE INCREDIBLE
HULK

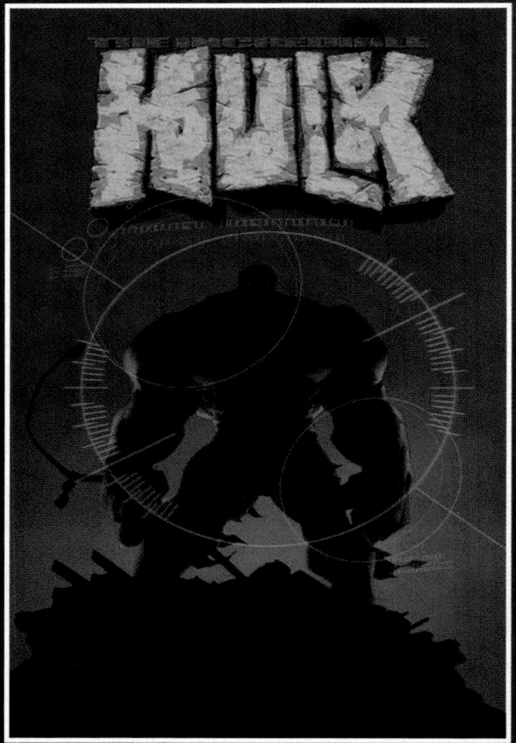
THE INCREDIBLE
HULK

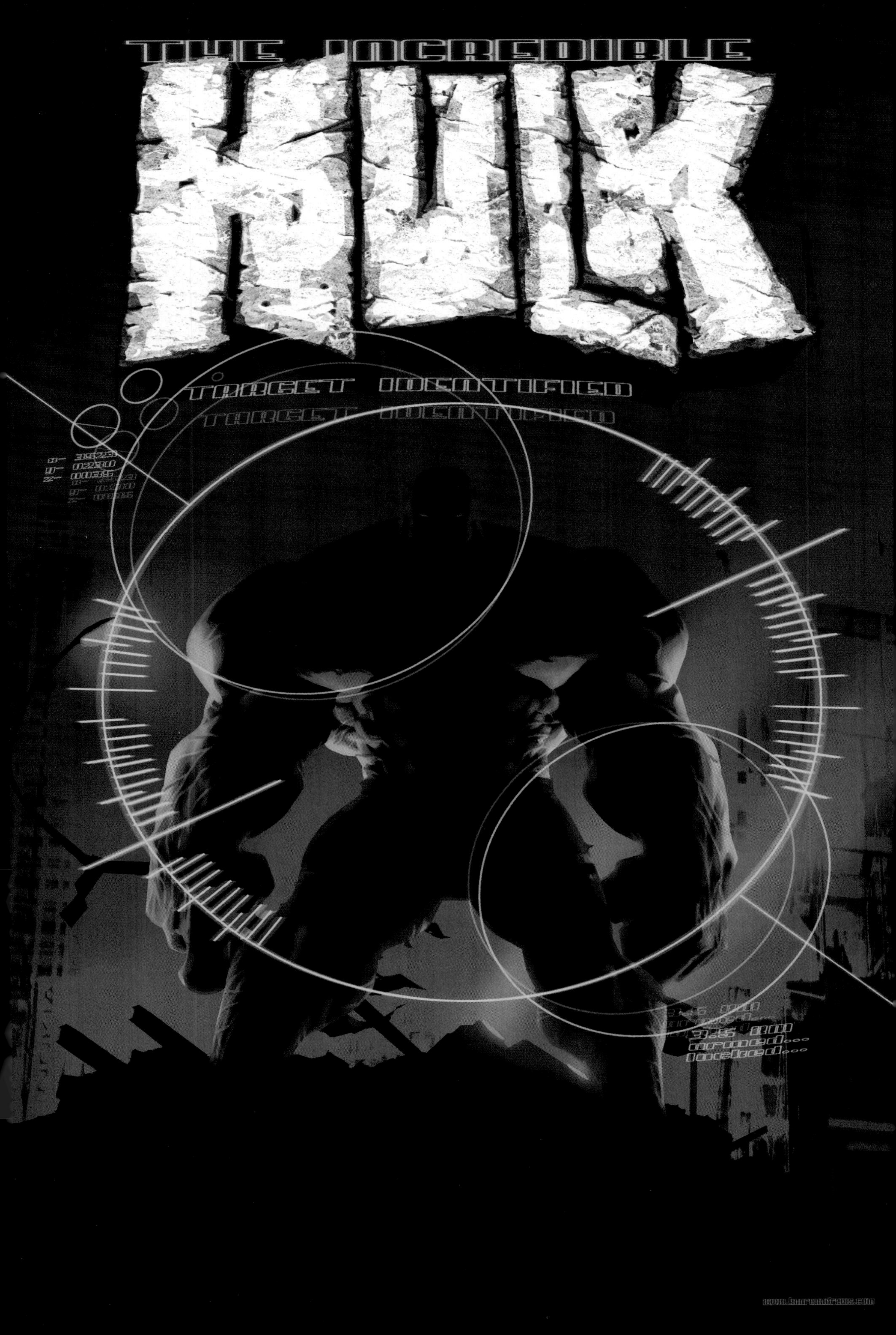
THE INCREDIBLE
HULK
TARGET IDENTIFIED
3.5 km
armed...
locked...

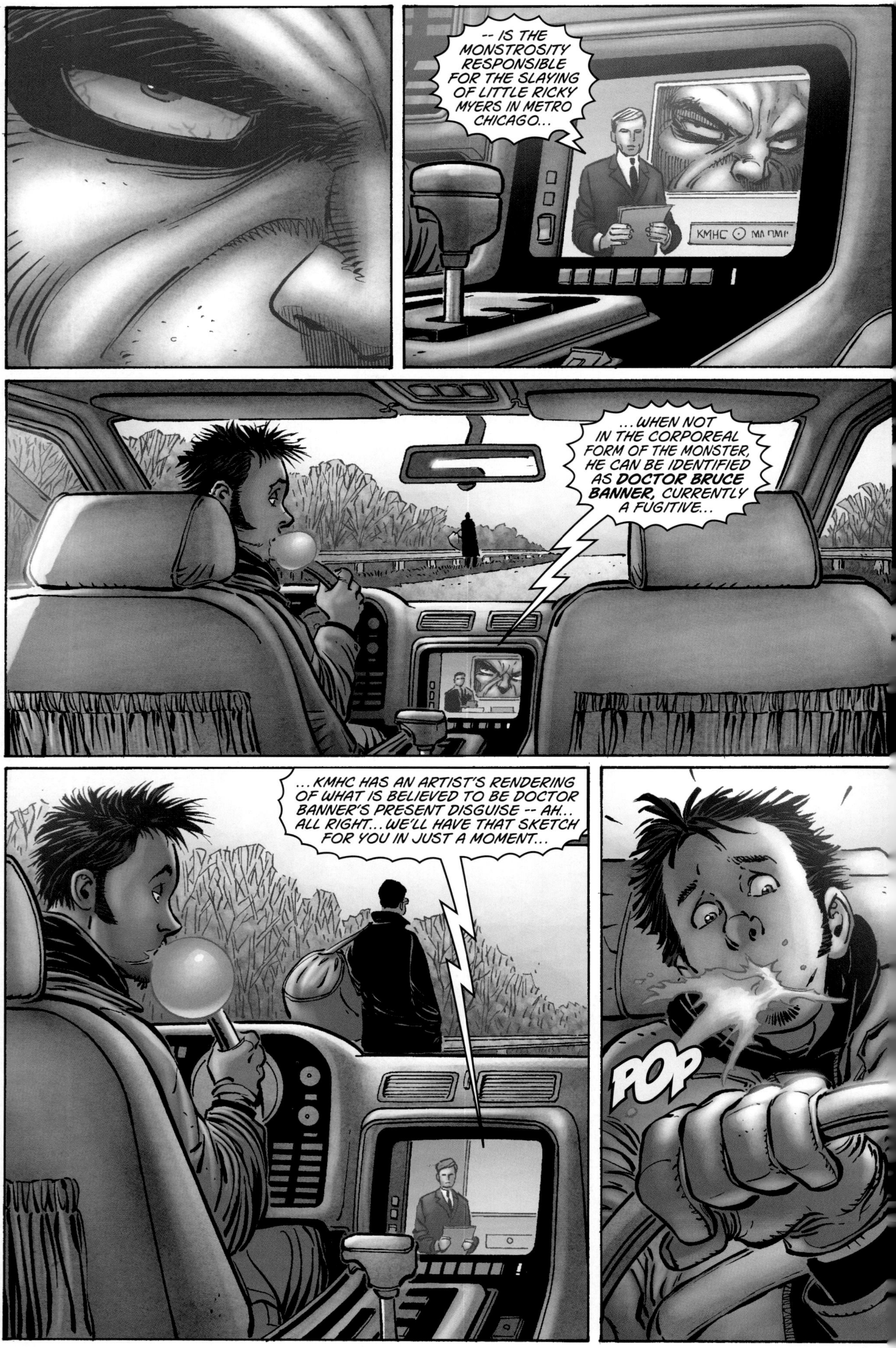
-- IS THE MONSTROSITY RESPONSIBLE FOR THE SLAYING OF LITTLE RICKY MYERS IN METRO CHICAGO...
KMHC
...WHEN NOT IN THE CORPOREAL FORM OF THE MONSTER, HE CAN BE IDENTIFIED AS **DOCTOR BRUCE BANNER,** CURRENTLY A FUGITIVE...
...KMHC HAS AN ARTIST'S RENDERING OF WHAT IS BELIEVED TO BE DOCTOR BANNER'S PRESENT DISGUISE -- AH... ALL RIGHT... WE'LL HAVE THAT SKETCH FOR YOU IN JUST A MOMENT...
POP

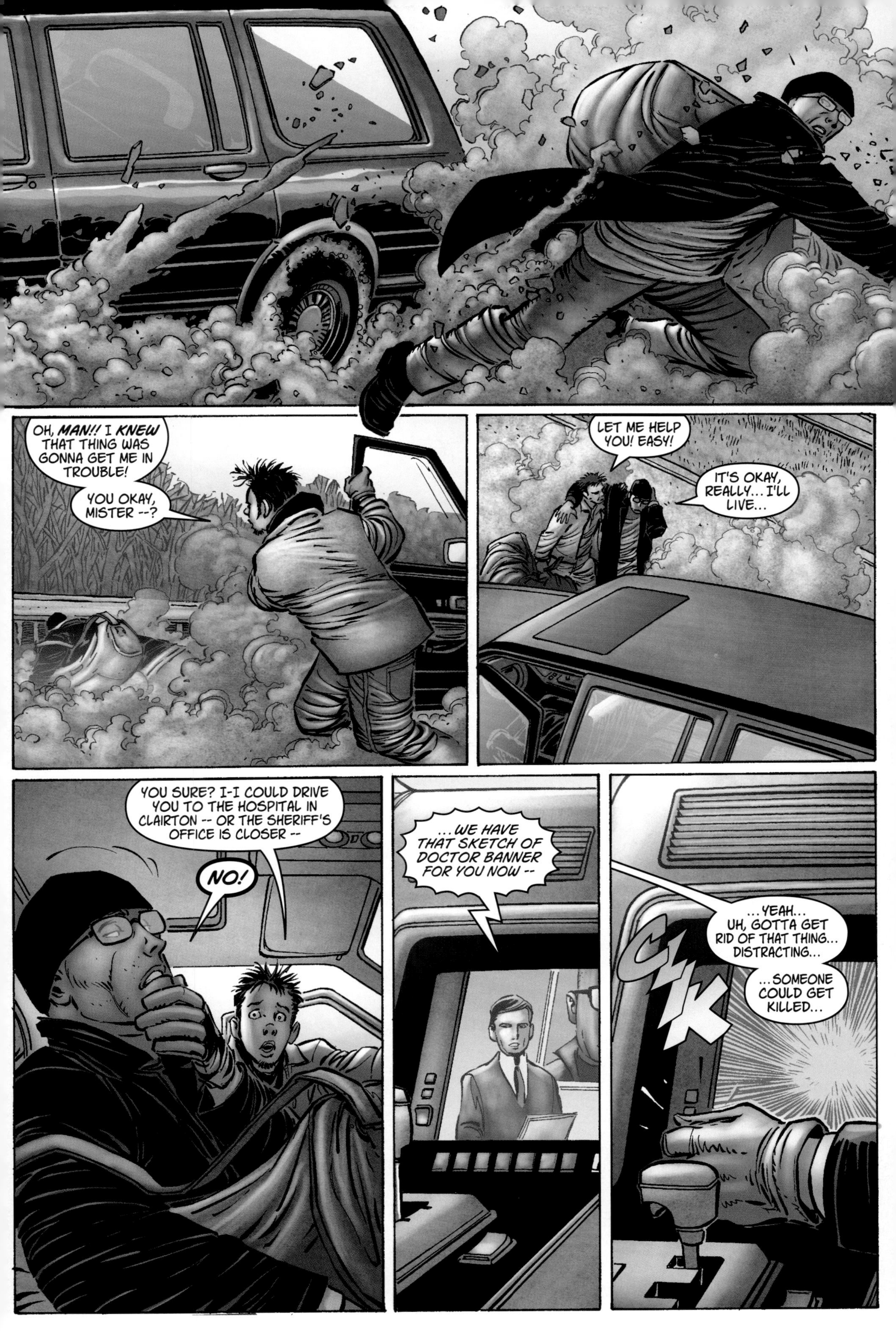
OH, MAN!! I KNEW THAT THING WAS GONNA GET ME IN TROUBLE!
YOU OKAY, MISTER --?
LET ME HELP YOU! EASY!
IT'S OKAY, REALLY... I'LL LIVE...
YOU SURE? I-I COULD DRIVE YOU TO THE HOSPITAL IN CLAIRTON -- OR THE SHERIFF'S OFFICE IS CLOSER --
NO!
...WE HAVE THAT SKETCH OF DOCTOR BANNER FOR YOU NOW --
CLIK
...YEAH... UH, GOTTA GET RID OF THAT THING... DISTRACTING...
...SOMEONE COULD GET KILLED...

KEESHH

MAYBE THIS WASN'T SUCH A HOT IDEA...

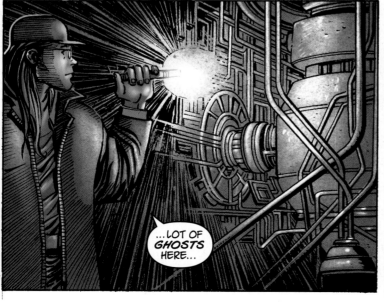

...LOT OF GHOSTS HERE...

MORE POWERFUL THAN THE HULK?

BIZARRE CATHEXIS-RAY CONVERTS BOOKISH PSYCHIATRIST INTO MODERN-DAY SAMSON!

The same brilliantly engineered machinery employed to save the life of Betty Ross has apparently turned Dr. Leonard Samson...

...LOT OF MEMORIES...

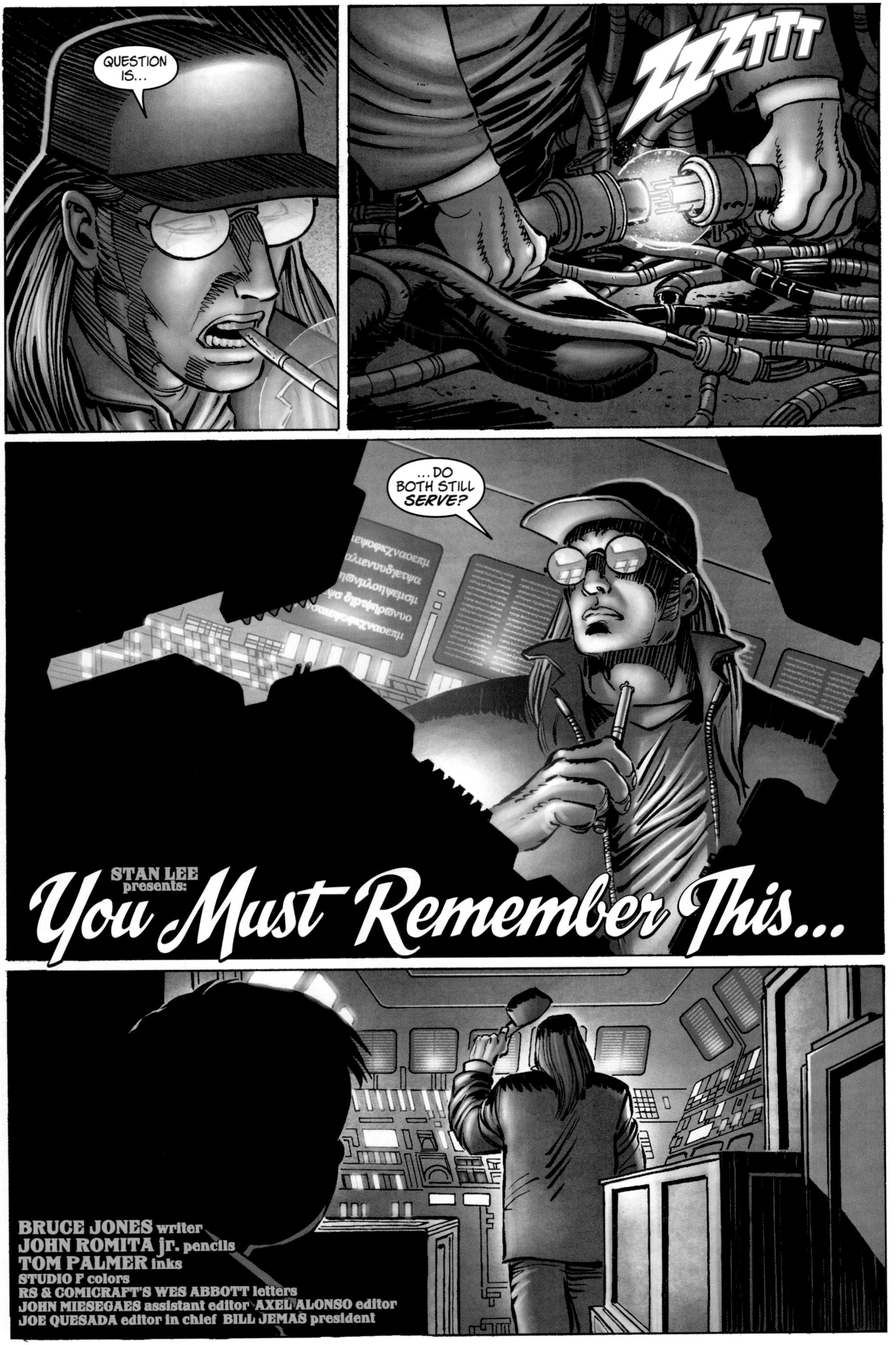
QUESTION IS...
ZZZTTT
...DO BOTH STILL SERVE?
STAN LEE presents:
You Must Remember This...
BRUCE JONES writer
JOHN ROMITA jr. pencils
TOM PALMER inks
STUDIO F colors
RS & COMICRAFT'S WES ABBOTT letters
JOHN MIESEGAES assistant editor AXEL ALONSO editor
JOE QUESADA editor in chief BILL JEMAS president

BLAM
LITTLE EARLY FOR TARGET PRACTICE, ISN'T IT, SLATER?
YOU MY PARTNER ON THIS GIG, OR MY *WIFE?*
BLAM
BLAM
AMBIDEXTROUS.
YOU OCCASIONALLY WEAR *SOMETHING* OTHER THAN A TOWEL?
DONE SOME OF MY BEST WORK IN A TOWEL.
NOT SO FAR YOU HAVEN'T.
BLAM
FRIENDLY LITTLE WAGER, MS. VERDUGO. YOU HIT DEAD CENTER AND I GET BREAKFAST! THERE'S ONE ROUND LEFT!

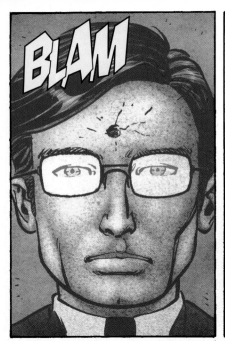

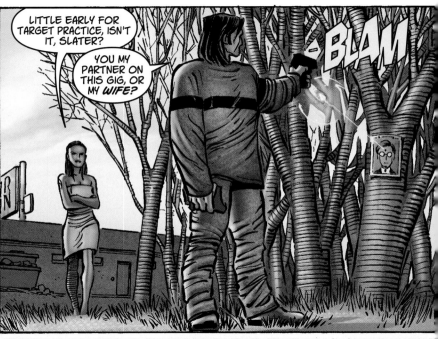

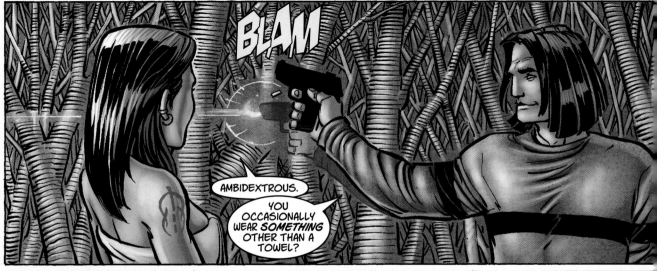

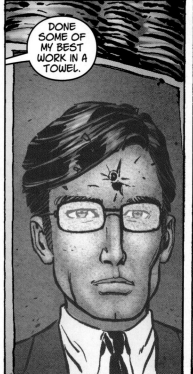

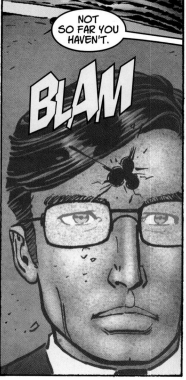

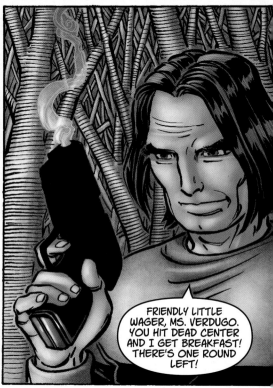

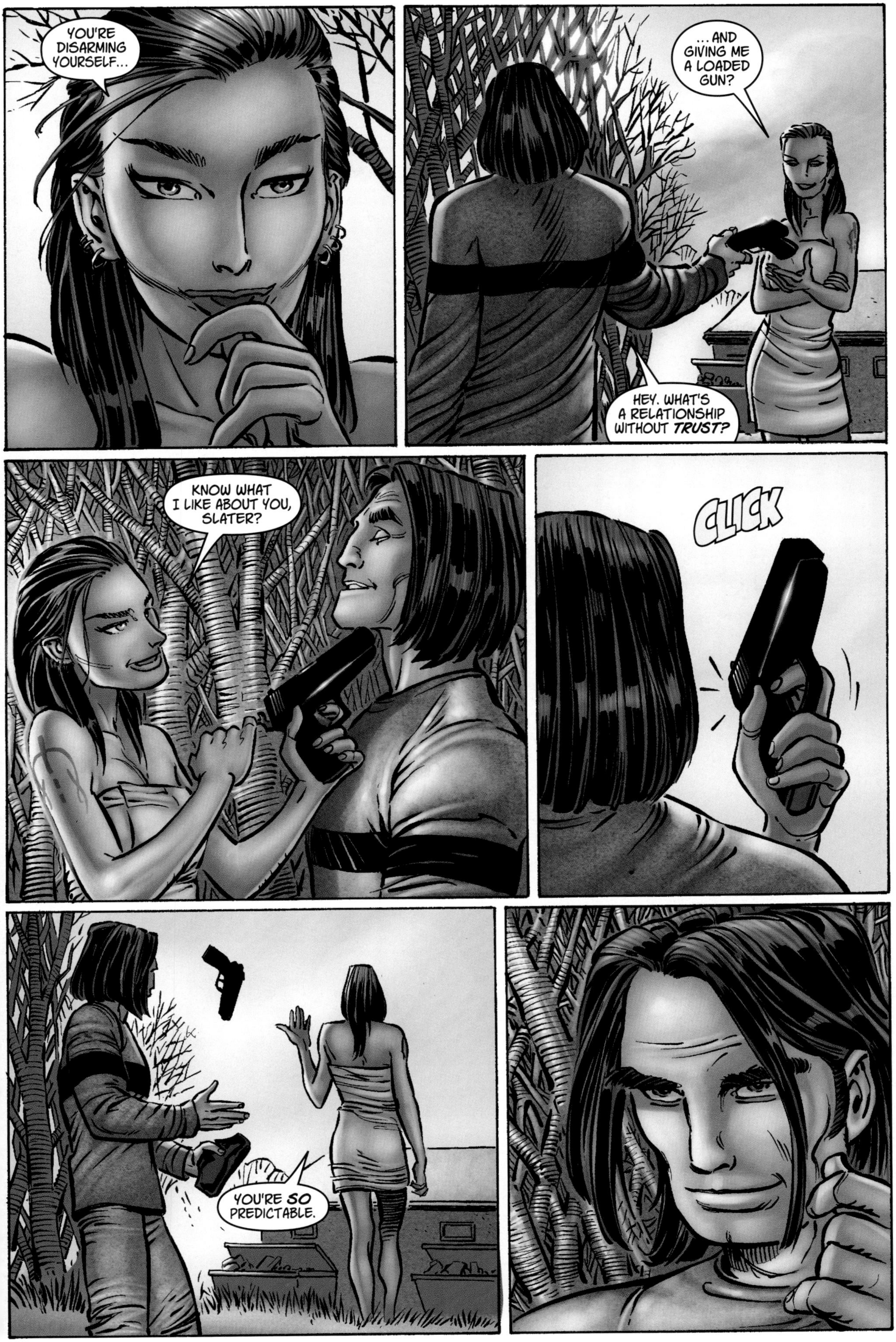
YOU'RE DISARMING YOURSELF...
...AND GIVING ME A LOADED GUN?
HEY. WHAT'S A RELATIONSHIP WITHOUT TRUST?
KNOW WHAT I LIKE ABOUT YOU, SLATER?
CLICK
YOU'RE SO PREDICTABLE.

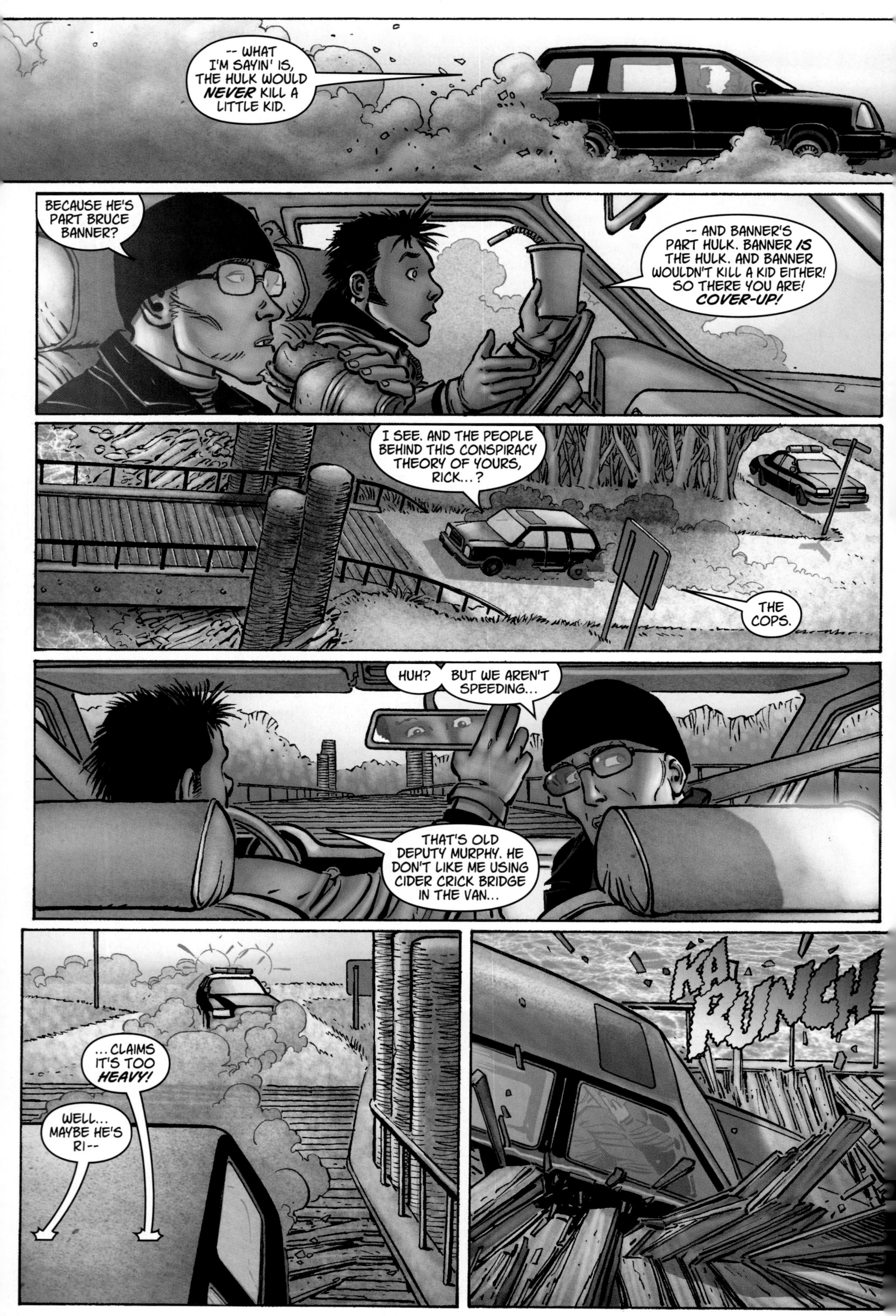
-- WHAT I'M SAYIN' IS, THE HULK WOULD NEVER KILL A LITTLE KID.
BECAUSE HE'S PART BRUCE BANNER?
-- AND BANNER'S PART HULK. BANNER IS THE HULK. AND BANNER WOULDN'T KILL A KID EITHER! SO THERE YOU ARE! COVER-UP!
I SEE. AND THE PEOPLE BEHIND THIS CONSPIRACY THEORY OF YOURS, RICK...?
THE COPS.
HUH?
BUT WE AREN'T SPEEDING...
THAT'S OLD DEPUTY MURPHY. HE DON'T LIKE ME USING CIDER CRICK BRIDGE IN THE VAN...
...CLAIMS IT'S TOO HEAVY!
WELL... MAYBE HE'S RI--
KA RUNCH

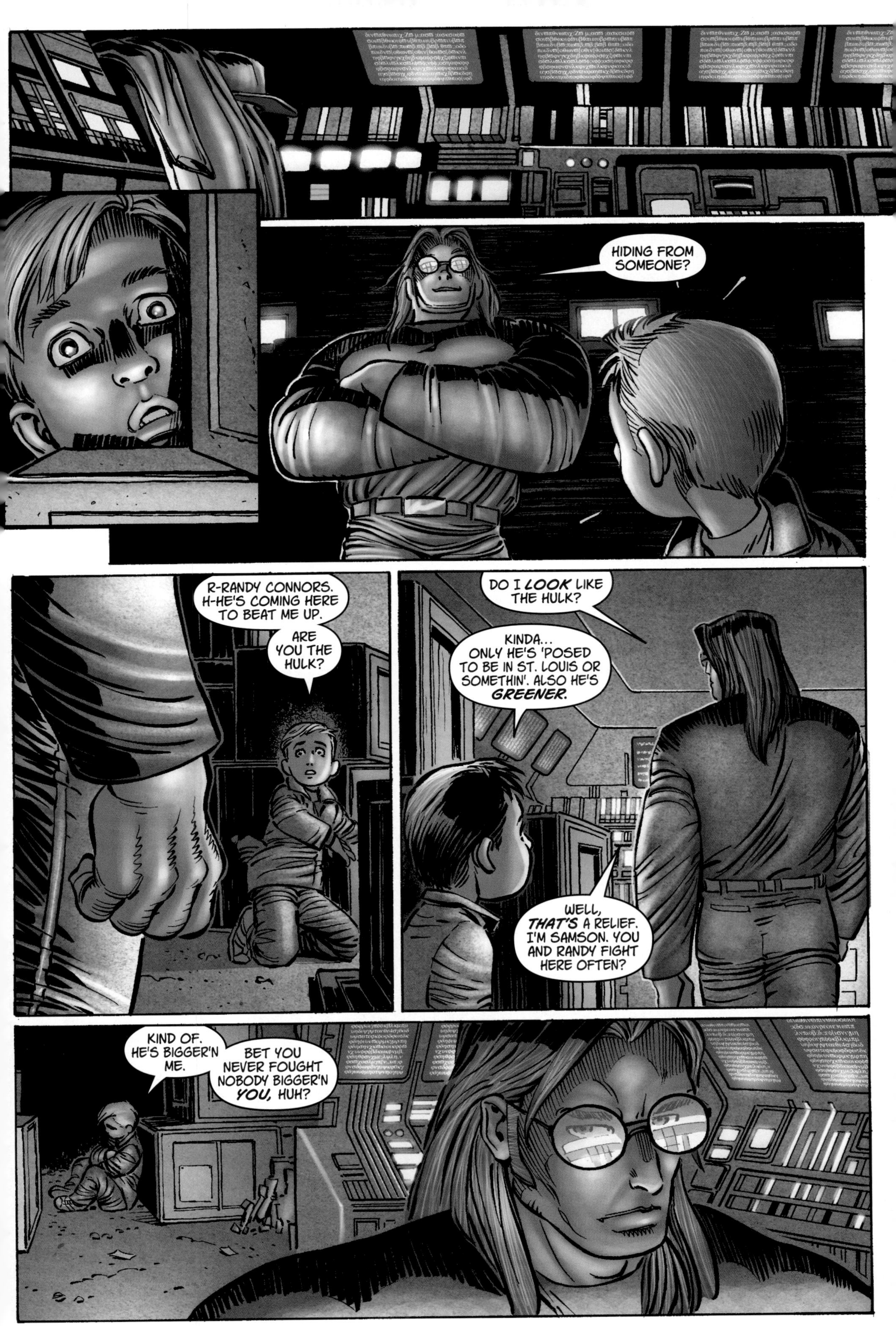
HIDING FROM SOMEONE?
R-RANDY CONNORS. H-HE'S COMING HERE TO BEAT ME UP.
ARE YOU THE HULK?
DO I LOOK LIKE THE HULK?
KINDA... ONLY HE'S 'POSED TO BE IN ST. LOUIS OR SOMETHIN'. ALSO HE'S GREENER.
WELL, THAT'S A RELIEF. I'M SAMSON. YOU AND RANDY FIGHT HERE OFTEN?
KIND OF. HE'S BIGGER'N ME.
BET YOU NEVER FOUGHT NOBODY BIGGER'N YOU, HUH?

ONCE OR TWICE.

WHY DO YOU KEEP FIGHTING RANDY... IF YOU KEEP LOSING?

HE CALLED ME A COWARD. BEAT ME UP. IN FRONT OF MY GIRLFRIEND.

BET *YOU* NEVER HAD *THAT* HAPPEN.

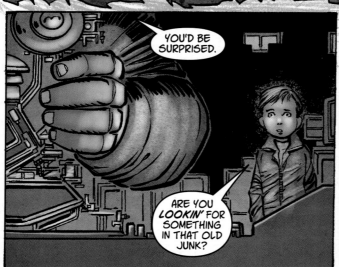

YOU'D BE SURPRISED.

ARE YOU *LOOKIN'* FOR SOMETHING IN THAT OLD JUNK?

YOU COULD SAY THAT... LOOKING FOR SOMEONE I USED TO *KNOW* PRETTY WELL...

...OR HIS *RESIDUE*, ANYWAY.

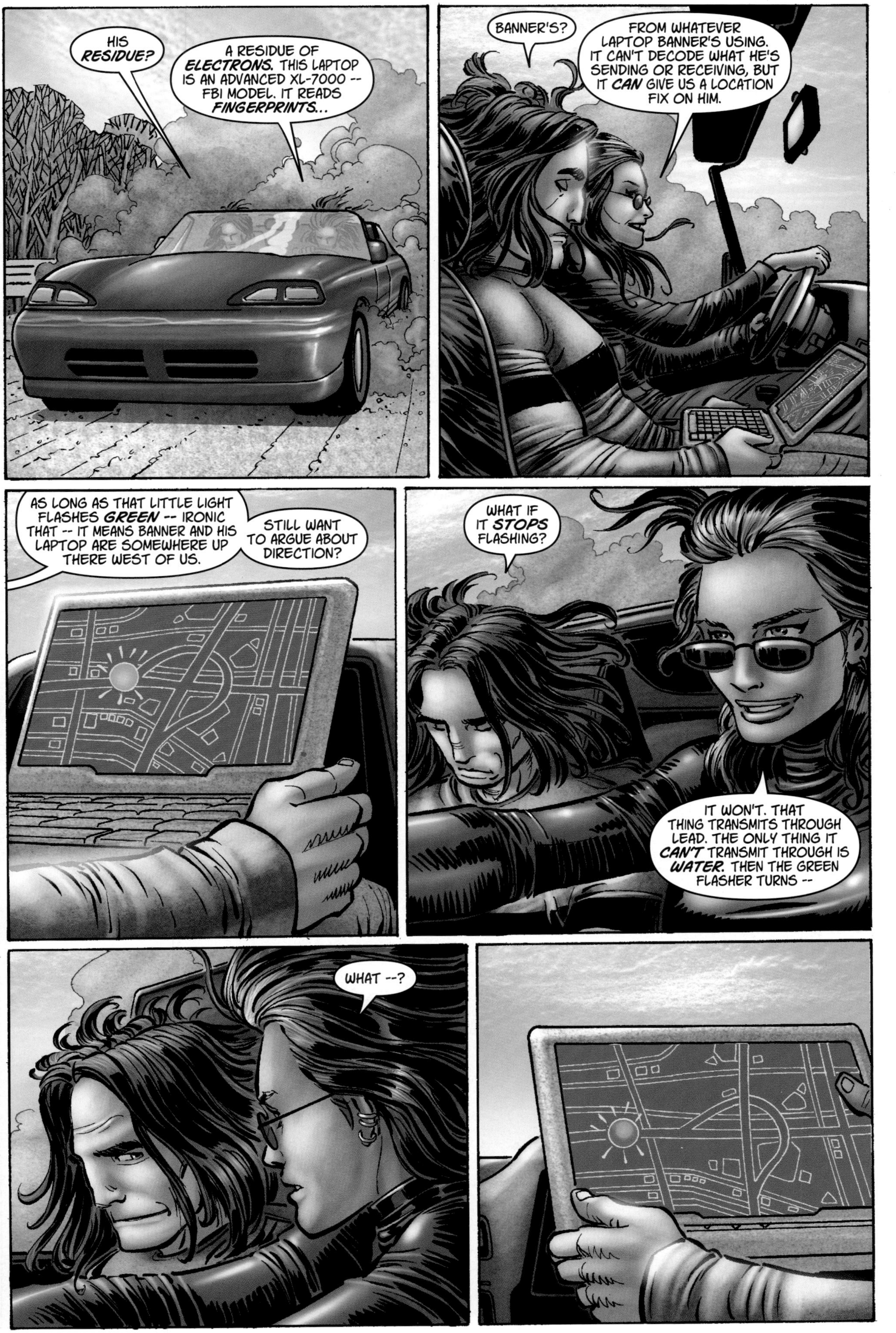
HIS RESIDUE?
A RESIDUE OF ELECTRONS. THIS LAPTOP IS AN ADVANCED XL-7000 -- FBI MODEL. IT READS FINGERPRINTS...
BANNER'S?
FROM WHATEVER LAPTOP BANNER'S USING. IT CAN'T DECODE WHAT HE'S SENDING OR RECEIVING, BUT IT CAN GIVE US A LOCATION FIX ON HIM.
AS LONG AS THAT LITTLE LIGHT FLASHES GREEN -- IRONIC THAT -- IT MEANS BANNER AND HIS LAPTOP ARE SOMEWHERE UP THERE WEST OF US.
STILL WANT TO ARGUE ABOUT DIRECTION?
WHAT IF IT STOPS FLASHING?
IT WON'T. THAT THING TRANSMITS THROUGH LEAD. THE ONLY THING IT CAN'T TRANSMIT THROUGH IS WATER. THEN THE GREEN FLASHER TURNS --
WHAT --?

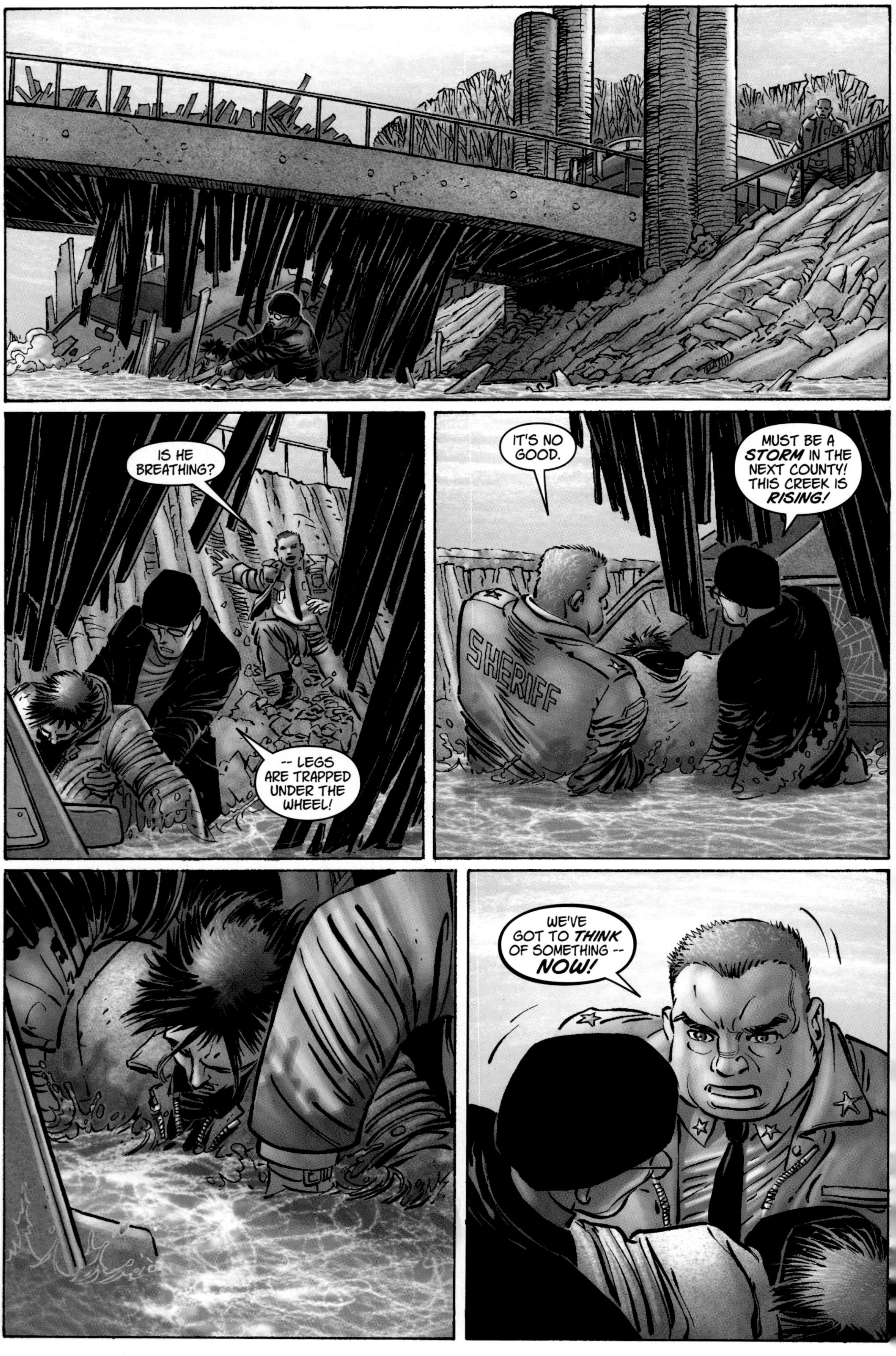
IS HE BREATHING?
-- LEGS ARE TRAPPED UNDER THE WHEEL!
IT'S NO GOOD.
MUST BE A STORM IN THE NEXT COUNTY! THIS CREEK IS RISING!
SHERIFF
WE'VE GOT TO THINK OF SOMETHING -- NOW!

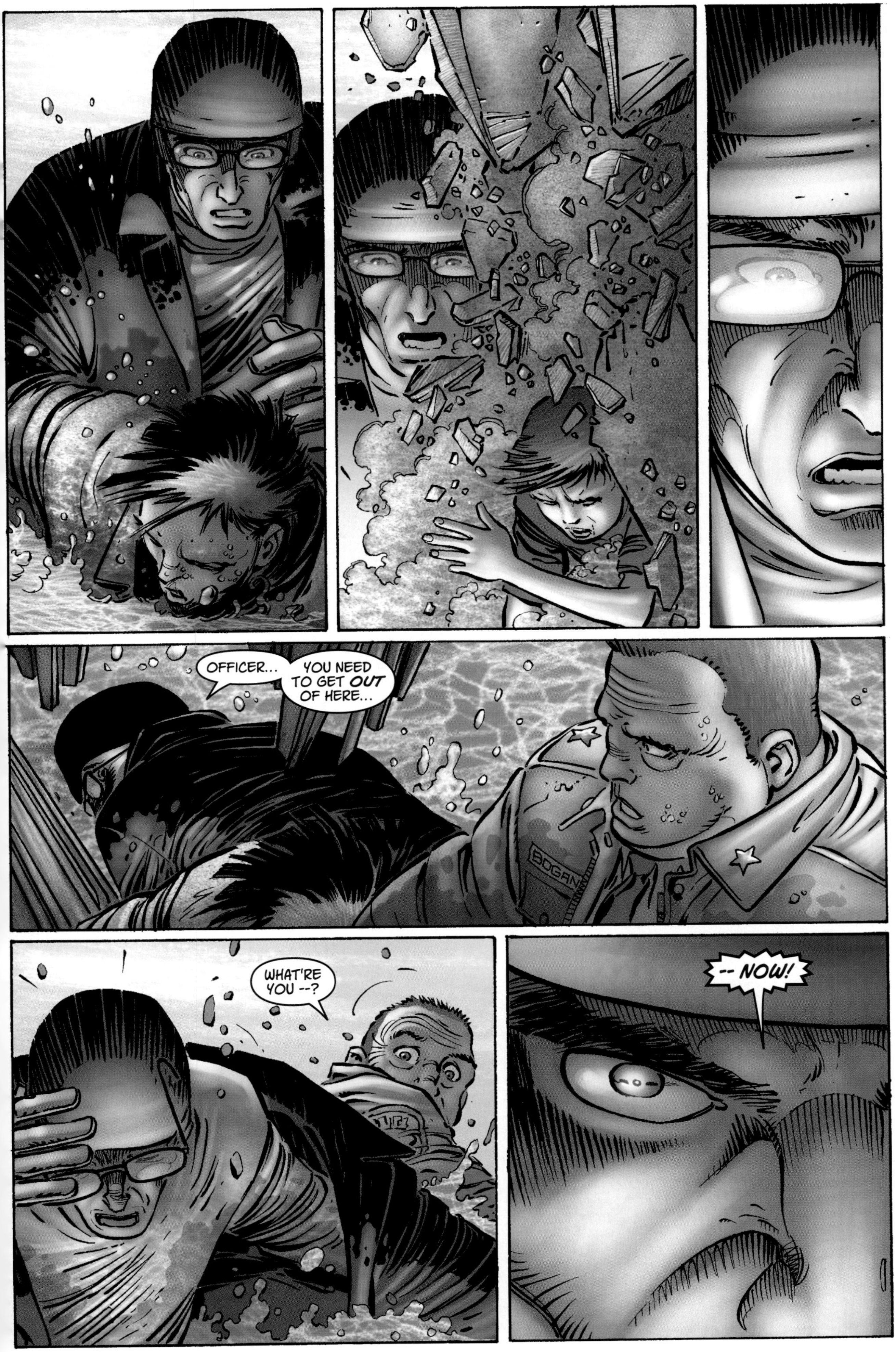
OFFICER...
YOU NEED TO GET OUT OF HERE...
BOGAN
WHAT'RE YOU --?
-- NOW!

-- FROM THIS VIAL WE TAKE A SAMPLE OF MY FRIEND'S *BLOOD*... AND FROM THAT WE EXTRACT HIS *DNA*...

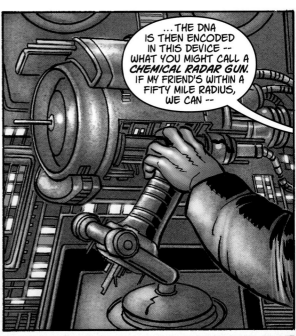

... THE DNA IS THEN ENCODED IN THIS DEVICE -- WHAT YOU MIGHT CALL A *CHEMICAL RADAR GUN*. IF MY FRIEND'S WITHIN A FIFTY MILE RADIUS, WE CAN --

-- HMM. NOT HELPING MUCH WITH YOUR *RANDY* PROBLEM, RIGHT, KEVIN?

HERE COMES MY BEATING *NOW*...

YOU KNOW, KEVIN... THIS *FRIEND* OF MINE, HE WAS PRETTY SAVVY...

... IN FACT, HE *KNEW* THE HULK, PERSONALLY...

THAT'S RIGHT. AND THE HULK TOLD HIM ONCE, "YA KNOW, LOT O' PEOPLE THINK I'M A *BULLY*, AND THAT TICKS ME OFF! I AIN'T A BULLY!

"IT'S JUST THAT OCCASIONALLY, WELL, I LOSE MY TEMPER."

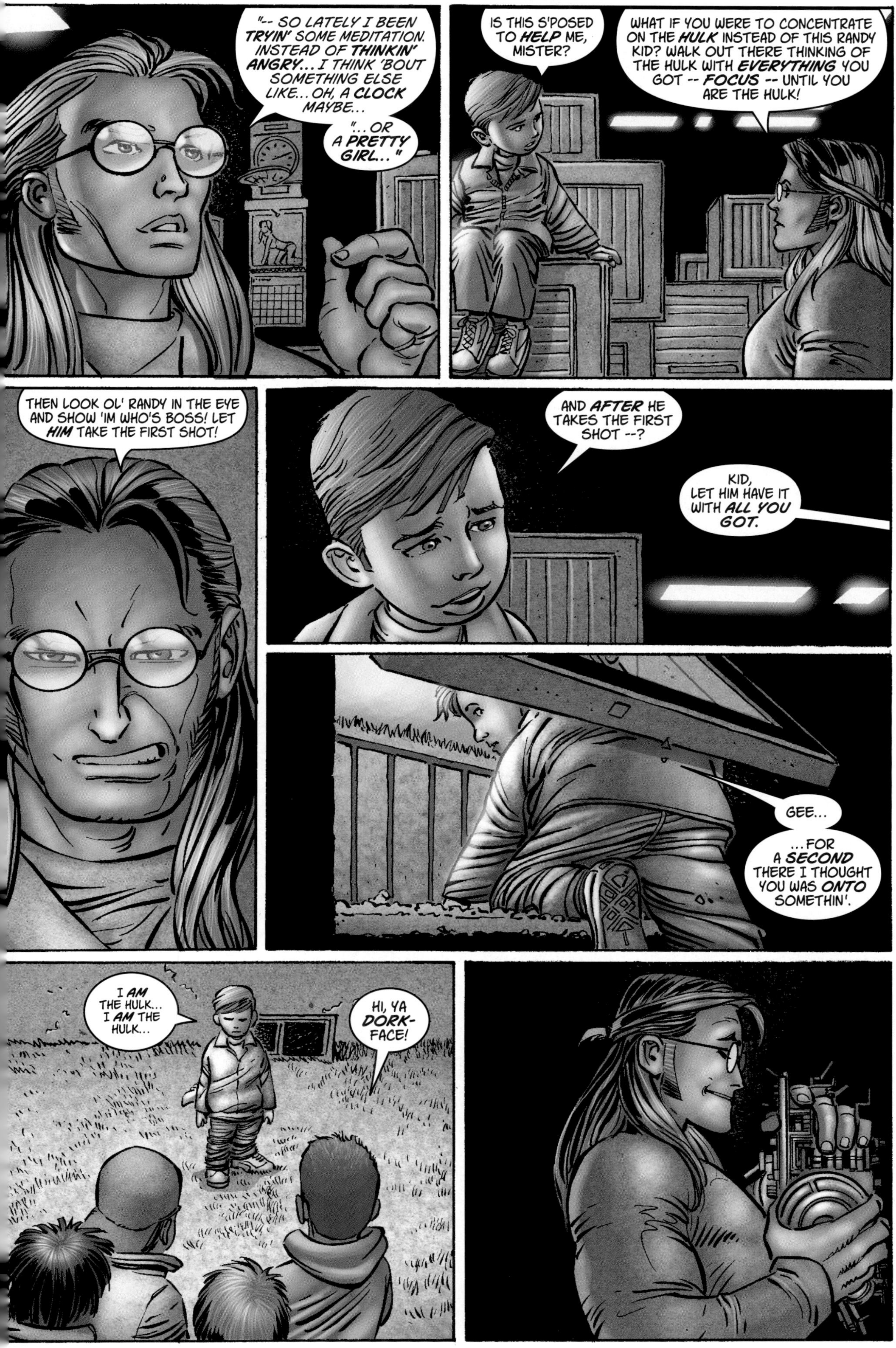
"-- SO LATELY I BEEN TRYIN' SOME MEDITATION. INSTEAD OF THINKIN' ANGRY... I THINK 'BOUT SOMETHING ELSE LIKE... OH, A CLOCK MAYBE...
"... OR A PRETTY GIRL..."
IS THIS S'POSED TO HELP ME, MISTER?
WHAT IF YOU WERE TO CONCENTRATE ON THE HULK INSTEAD OF THIS RANDY KID? WALK OUT THERE THINKING OF THE HULK WITH EVERYTHING YOU GOT -- FOCUS -- UNTIL YOU ARE THE HULK!
THEN LOOK OL' RANDY IN THE EYE AND SHOW 'IM WHO'S BOSS! LET HIM TAKE THE FIRST SHOT!
AND AFTER HE TAKES THE FIRST SHOT --?
KID, LET HIM HAVE IT WITH ALL YOU GOT.
GEE...
...FOR A SECOND THERE I THOUGHT YOU WAS ONTO SOMETHIN'.
I AM THE HULK... I AM THE HULK...
HI, YA DORK-FACE!

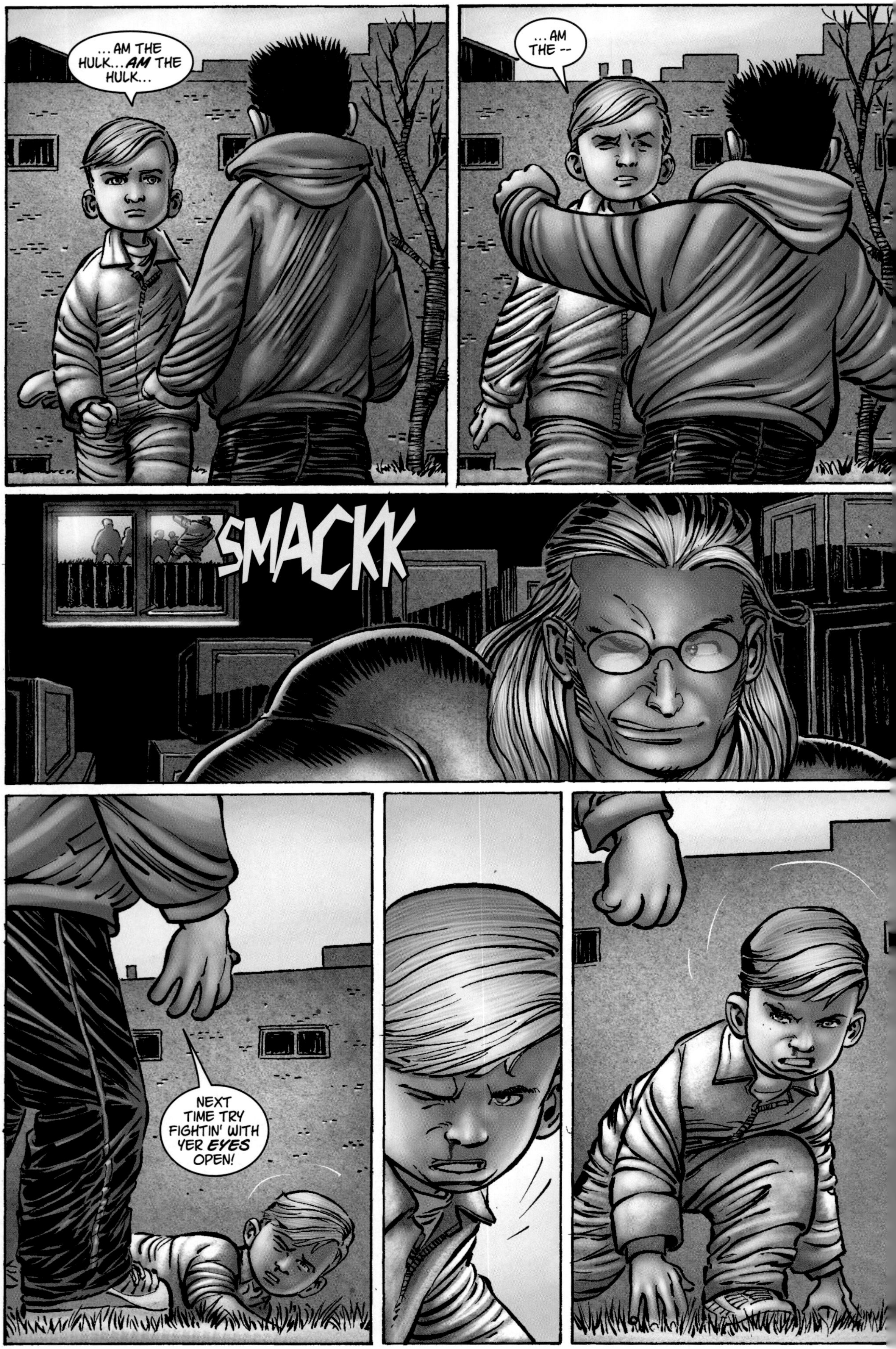
...AM THE HULK...AM THE HULK...
...AM THE --
SMACKK
NEXT TIME TRY FIGHTIN' WITH YER EYES OPEN!

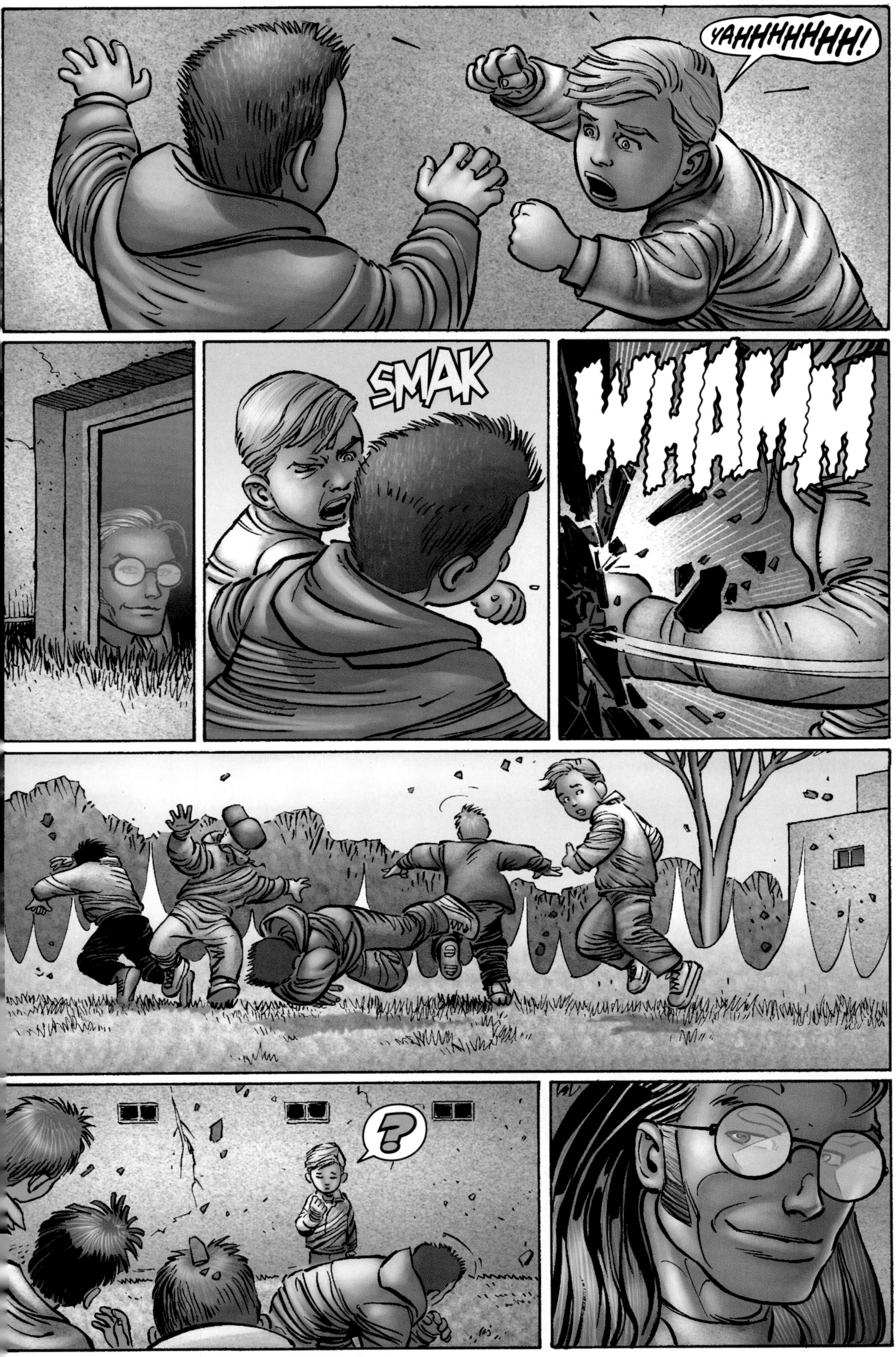
YAHHHHHHH!
SMAK
WHAMM
?

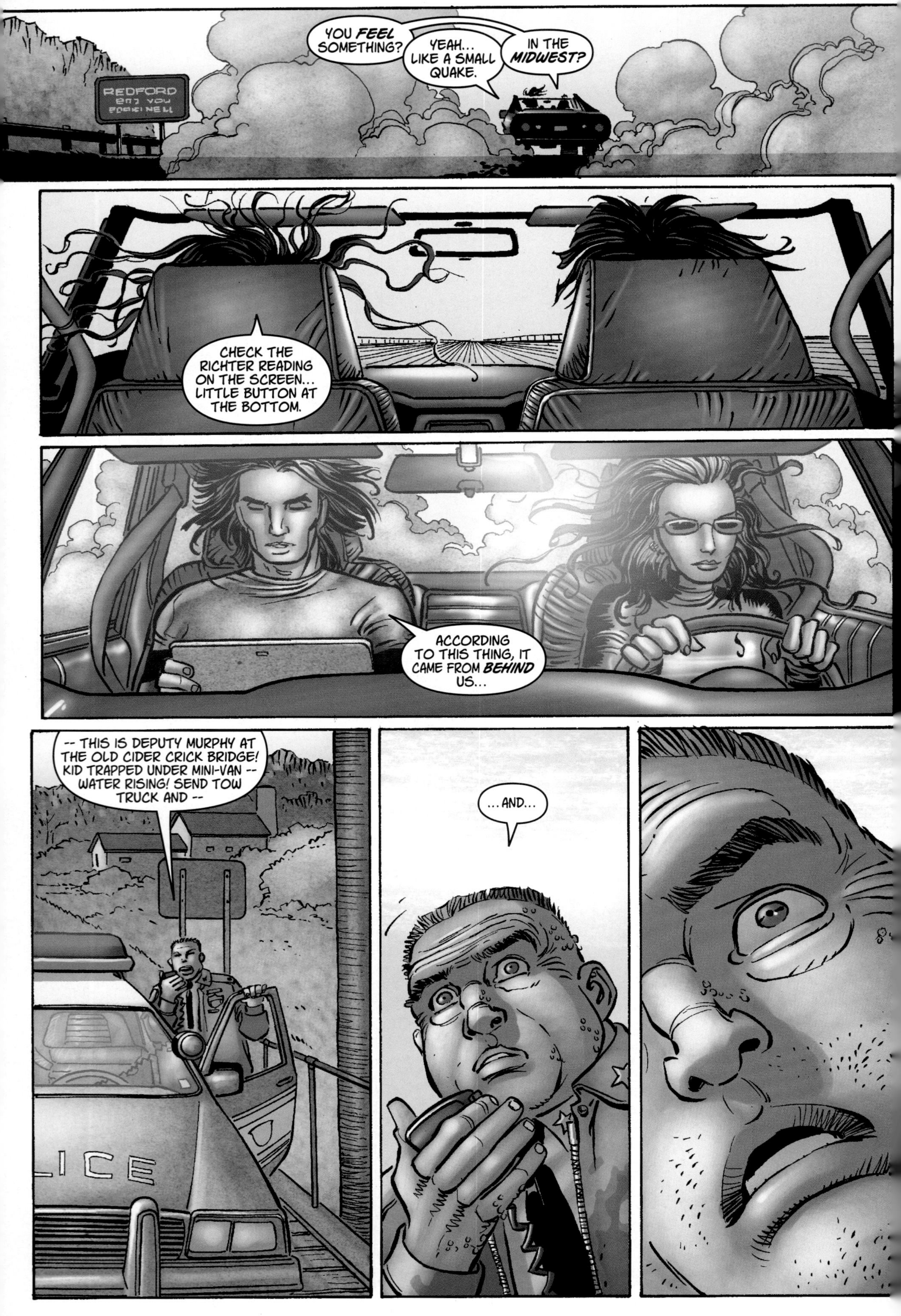
REDFORD
YOU *FEEL* SOMETHING?
YEAH... LIKE A SMALL QUAKE.
IN THE *MIDWEST?*
CHECK THE RICHTER READING ON THE SCREEN... LITTLE BUTTON AT THE BOTTOM.
ACCORDING TO THIS THING, IT CAME FROM *BEHIND* US...
-- THIS IS DEPUTY MURPHY AT THE OLD CIDER CRICK BRIDGE! KID TRAPPED UNDER MINI-VAN -- WATER RISING! SEND TOW TRUCK AND --
...AND...
LICE

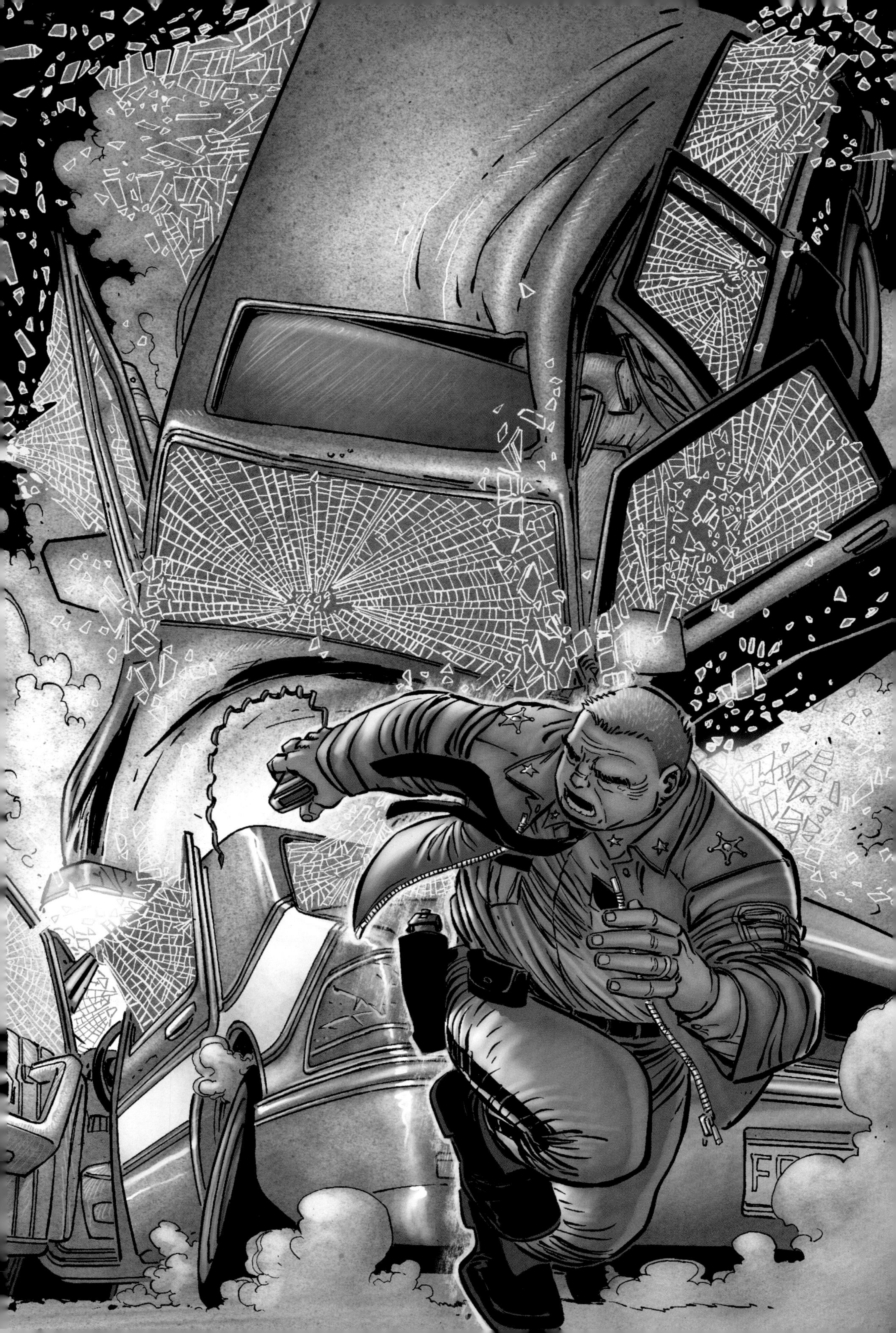

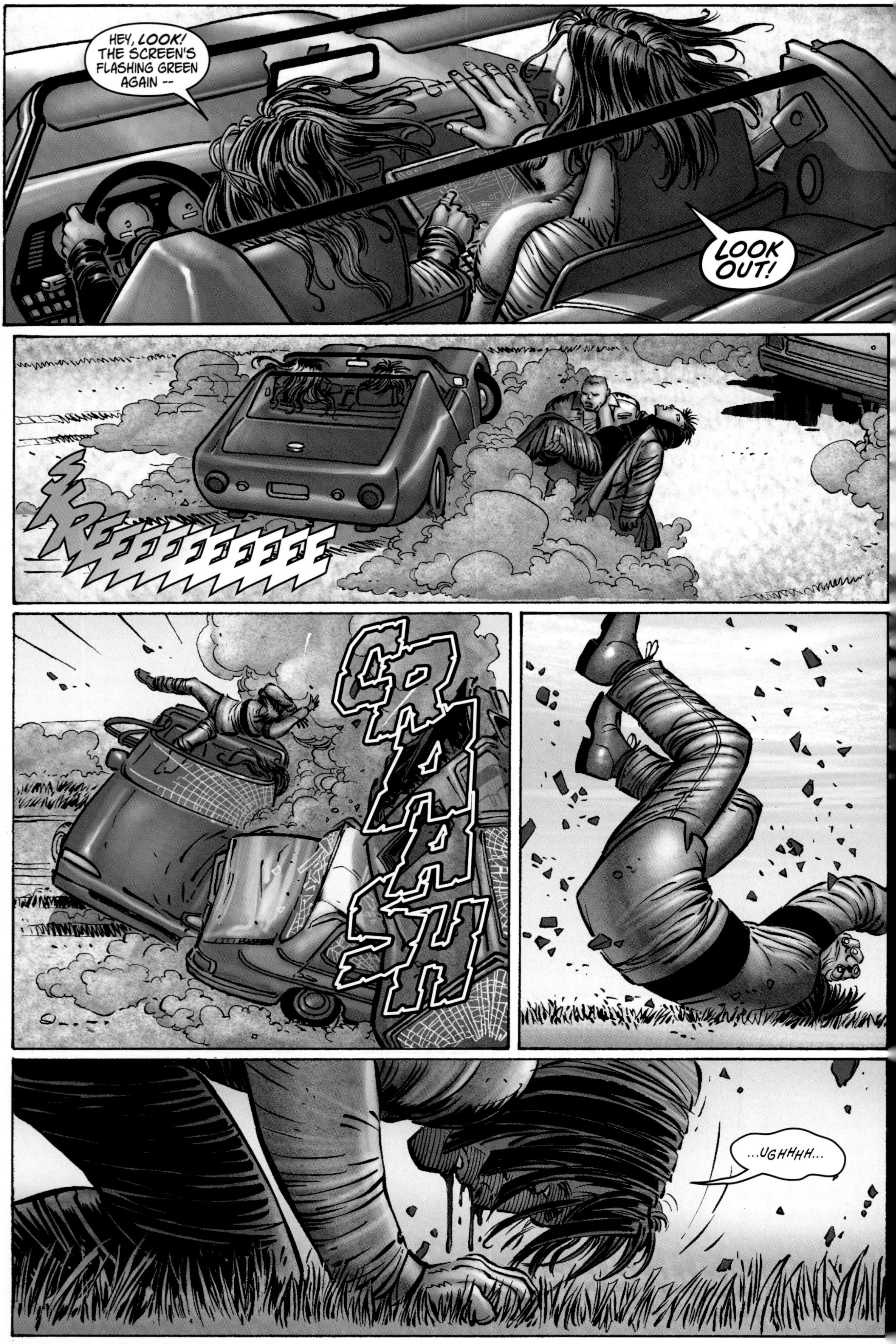

HEY, LOOK! THE SCREEN'S FLASHING GREEN AGAIN --
LOOK OUT!
SKREEEEEEEEEEE
CRASH
...UGHHHH...

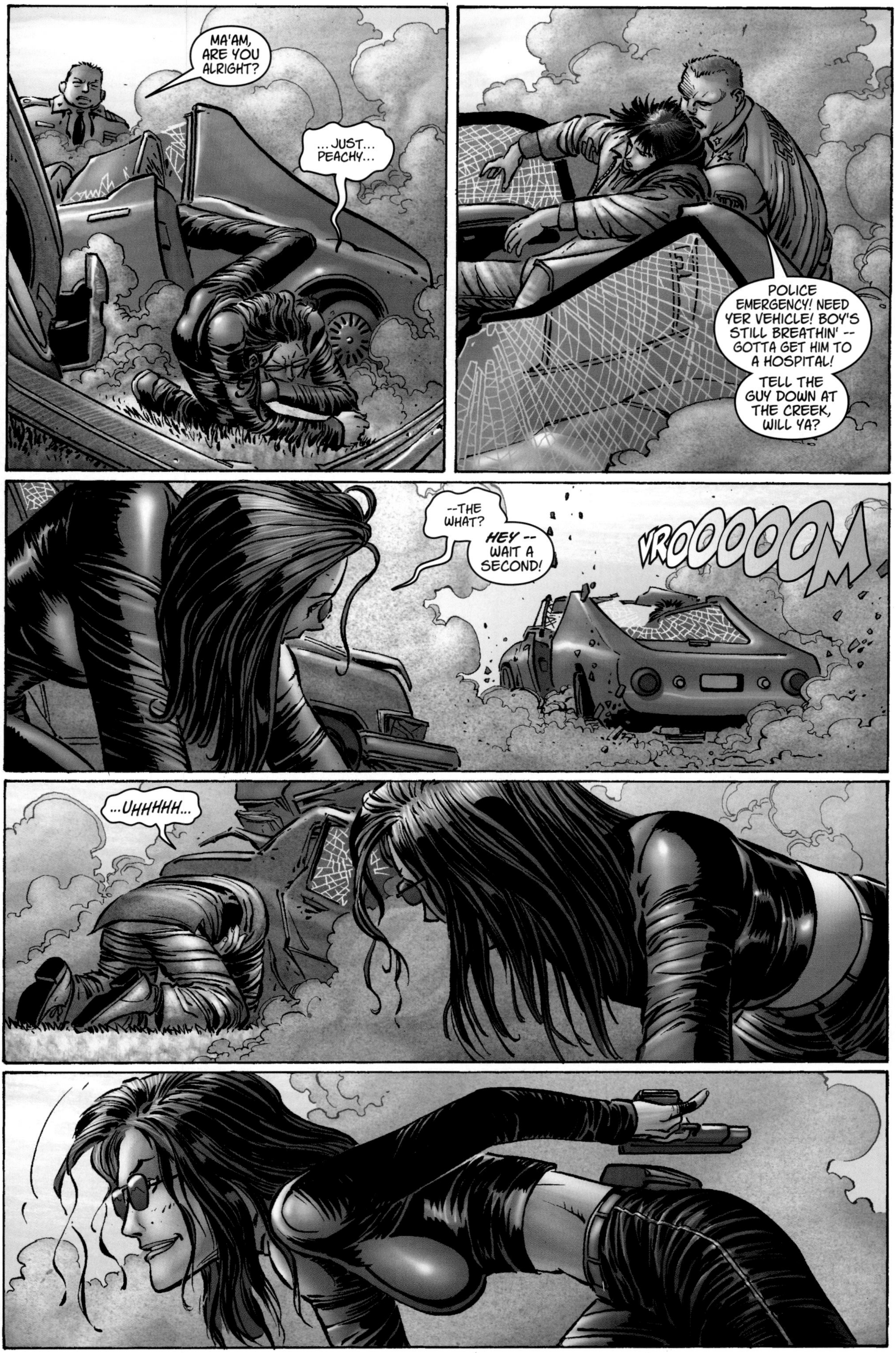
MA'AM, ARE YOU ALRIGHT?
...JUST... PEACHY...
POLICE EMERGENCY! NEED YER VEHICLE! BOY'S STILL BREATHIN' -- GOTTA GET HIM TO A HOSPITAL!
TELL THE GUY DOWN AT THE CREEK, WILL YA?
--THE WHAT?
HEY -- WAIT A SECOND!
VROOOOOOM
...UHHHHH...

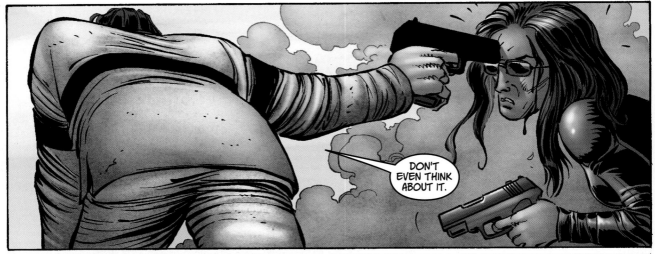

DON'T EVEN THINK ABOUT IT.

"LET ME LEAD," SHE SAYS... "GO WEST," SHE SAYS...

SHUT THE HELL UP!

"THE WOODS ARE LOVELY, DARK AND DEEP...

"...BUT I HAVE PROMISES TO KEEP...

"...AND MILES TO GO BEFORE I SLEEP...

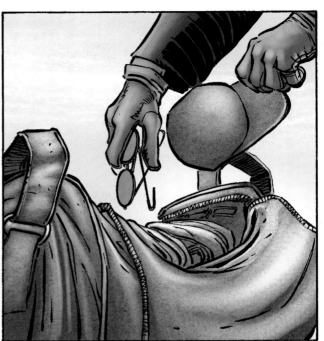

"...AND MILES TO GO BEFORE I SLEEP..."

INCREDIBLE HULK #38
Cover sketch by Kaare Andrews

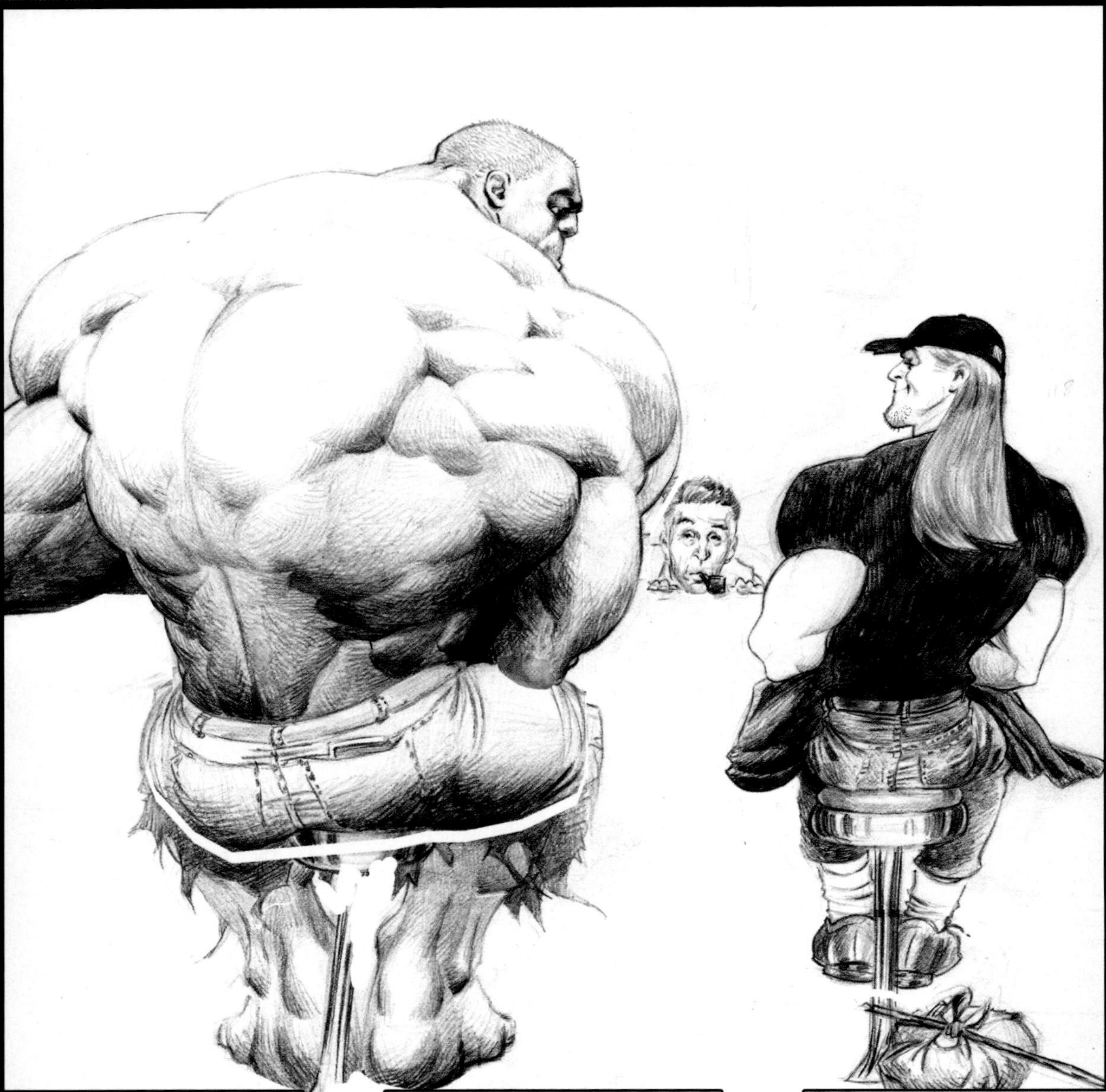

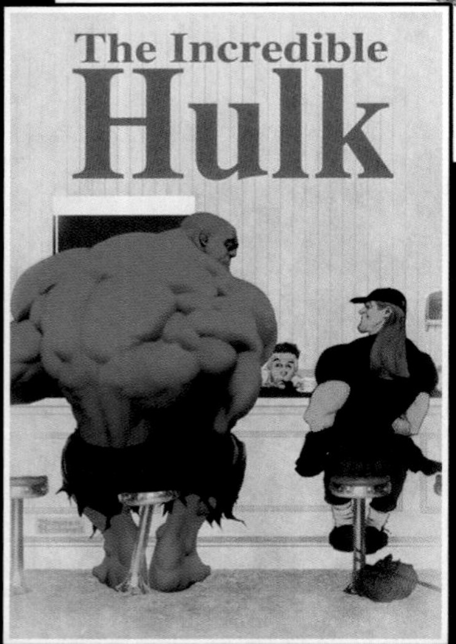
The Incredible
Hulk

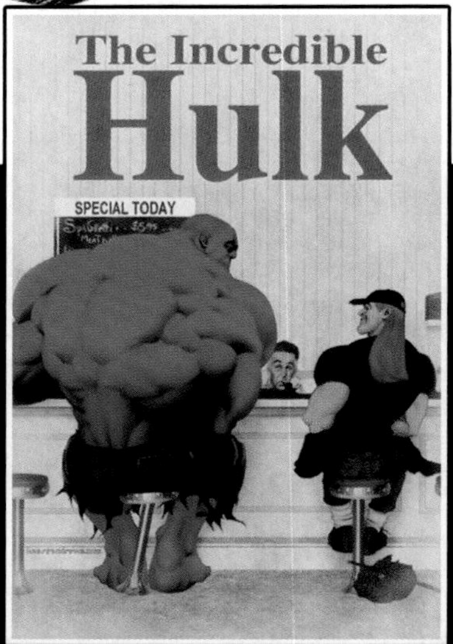
The Incredible
Hulk
SPECIAL TODAY

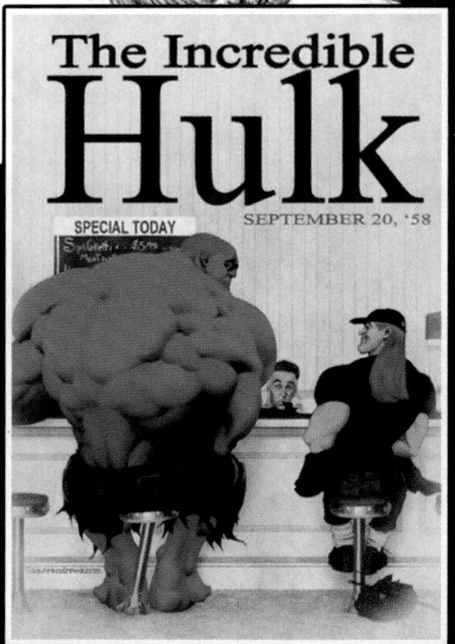
The Incredible
Hulk
SPECIAL TODAY
SEPTEMBER 20, '58

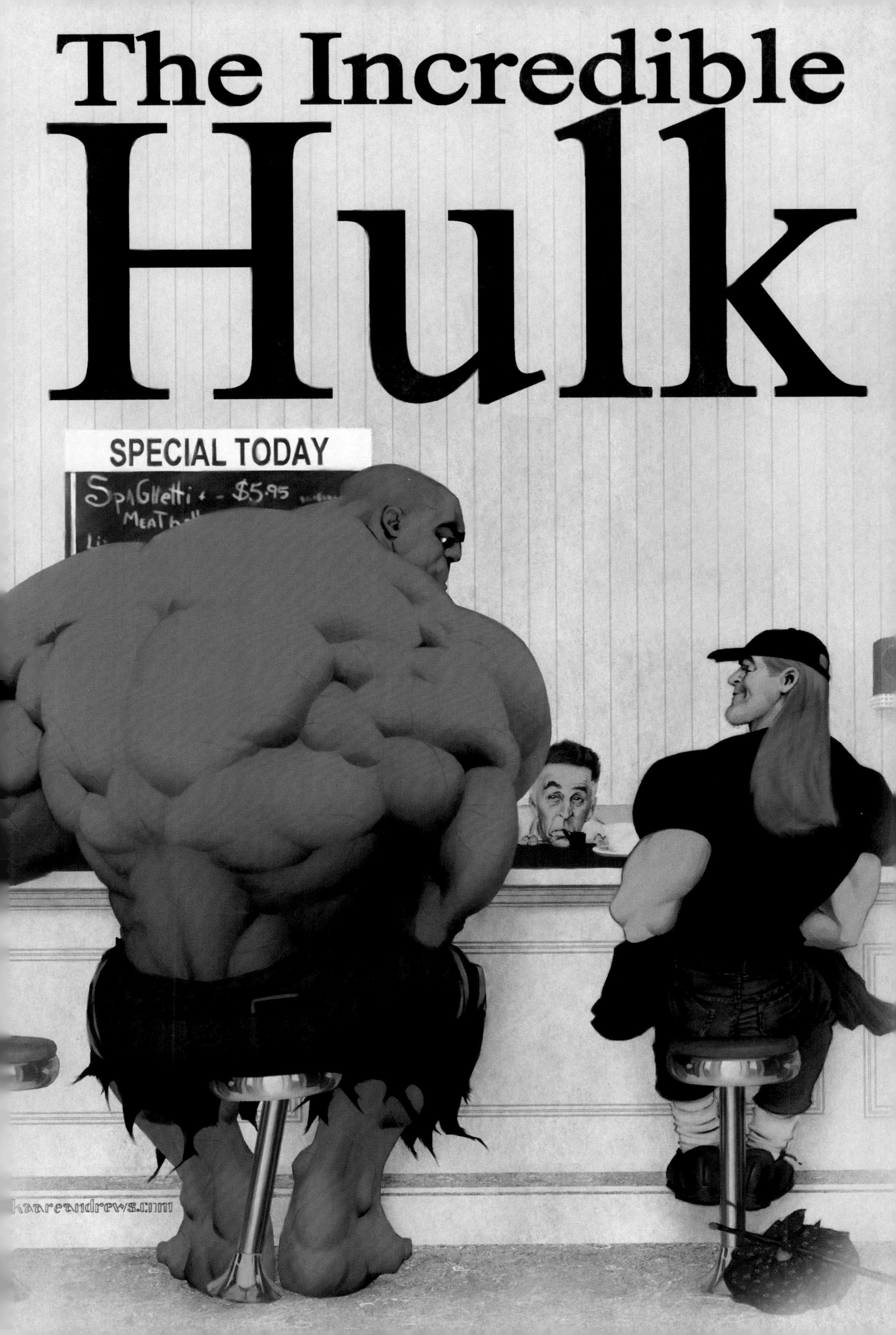

The Incredible
Hulk
SPECIAL TODAY
SpaGHetti - $5.95
kaareandrews.com

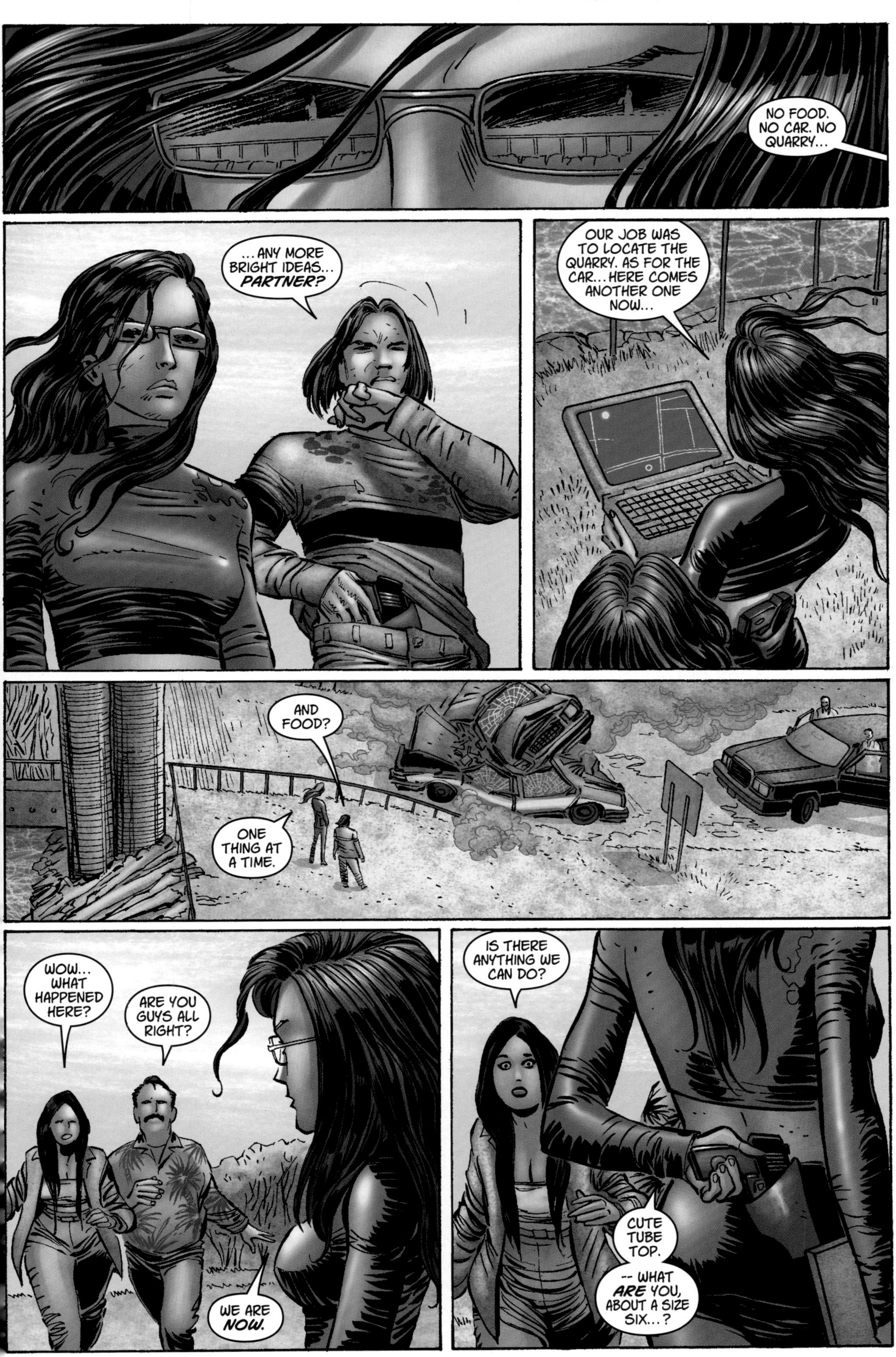
NO FOOD. NO CAR. NO QUARRY...
...ANY MORE BRIGHT IDEAS... *PARTNER?*
OUR JOB WAS TO LOCATE THE QUARRY. AS FOR THE CAR... HERE COMES ANOTHER ONE NOW...
AND FOOD?
ONE THING AT A TIME.
WOW... WHAT HAPPENED HERE?
ARE YOU GUYS ALL RIGHT?
WE ARE *NOW.*
IS THERE ANYTHING WE CAN DO?
CUTE TUBE TOP.
-- WHAT *ARE* YOU, ABOUT A SIZE SIX...?

ACCORDING TO YOUR HIGH-TECH ARSENAL HERE, BANNER'S RIGHT OVER THAT NEXT HILL. TURN LEFT AND WE'LL OVERTAKE HIM.

KANCAC

I SAID LEFT! WHAT THE HELL ARE YOU DOING?!

STICKING TO PLAN.

THE HELL WITH THE PLAN! WE'RE IN THE MIDDLE OF NOWHERE! HE'S ALL ALONE!

HE'S NEVER ALONE! OR HAVE YOU FORGOTTEN?

SEE THAT RED DOT? THAT'S A DINER. THE ONLY DINER FOR THE NEXT HUNDRED MILES!

BANNER WILL WALK RIGHT INTO IT IF HE KEEPS ON HIS PRESENT COURSE. AND WE'LL BE THERE AHEAD OF HIM.

-- WITH OUR LITTLE "COCKTAIL."

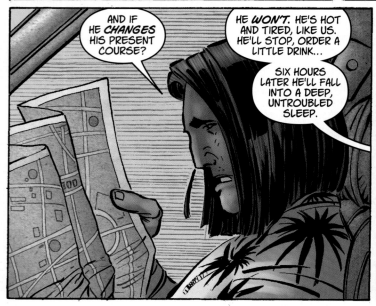

AND IF HE CHANGES HIS PRESENT COURSE?

HE WON'T. HE'S HOT AND TIRED, LIKE US. HE'LL STOP, ORDER A LITTLE DRINK...

SIX HOURS LATER HE'LL FALL INTO A DEEP, UNTROUBLED SLEEP.

THAT'S WHEN WE MOVE.

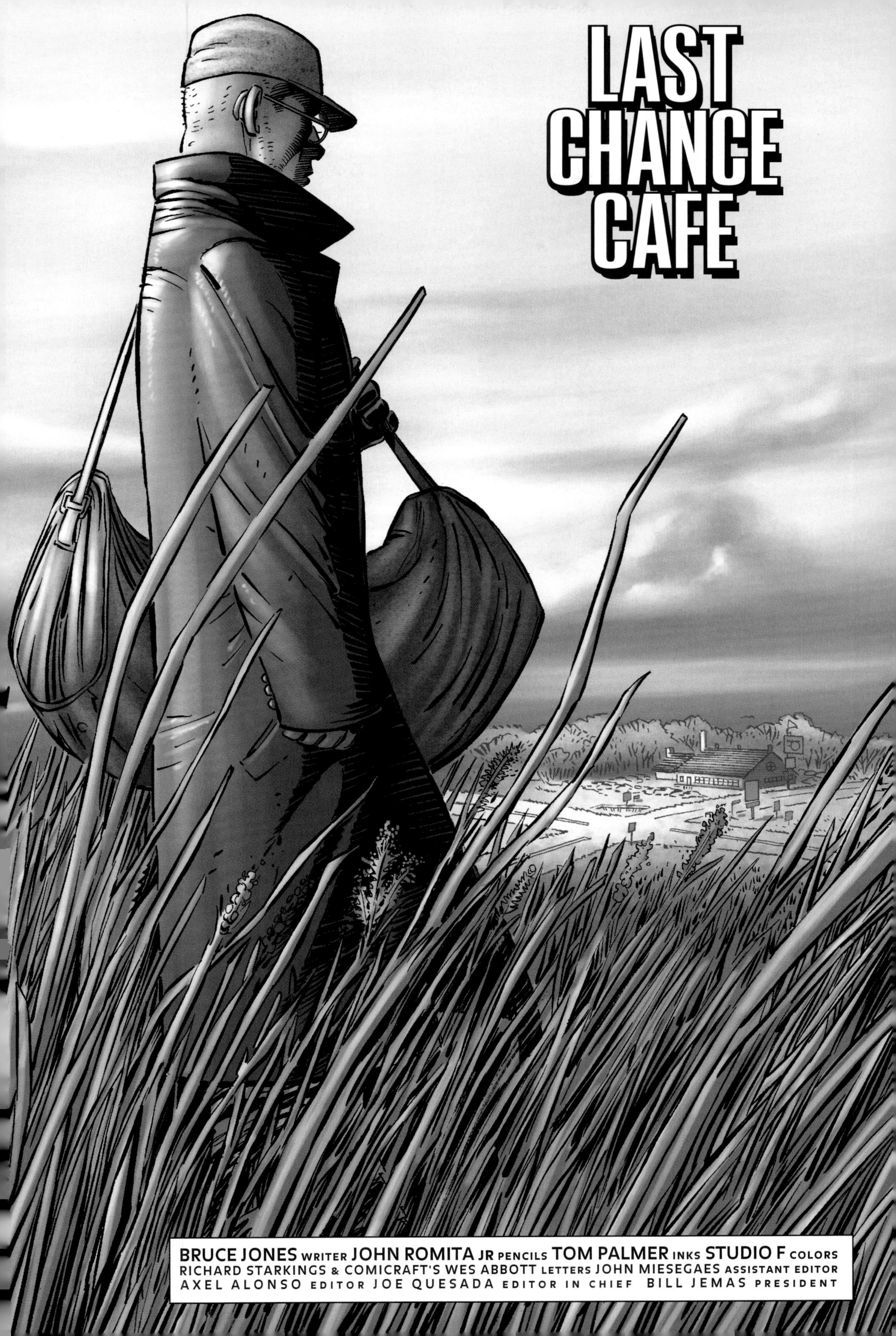
LAST CHANCE CAFE

BRUCE JONES WRITER JOHN ROMITA JR PENCILS TOM PALMER INKS STUDIO F COLORS
RICHARD STARKINGS & COMICRAFT'S WES ABBOTT LETTERS JOHN MIESEGAES ASSISTANT EDITOR
AXEL ALONSO EDITOR JOE QUESADA EDITOR IN CHIEF BILL JEMAS PRESIDENT

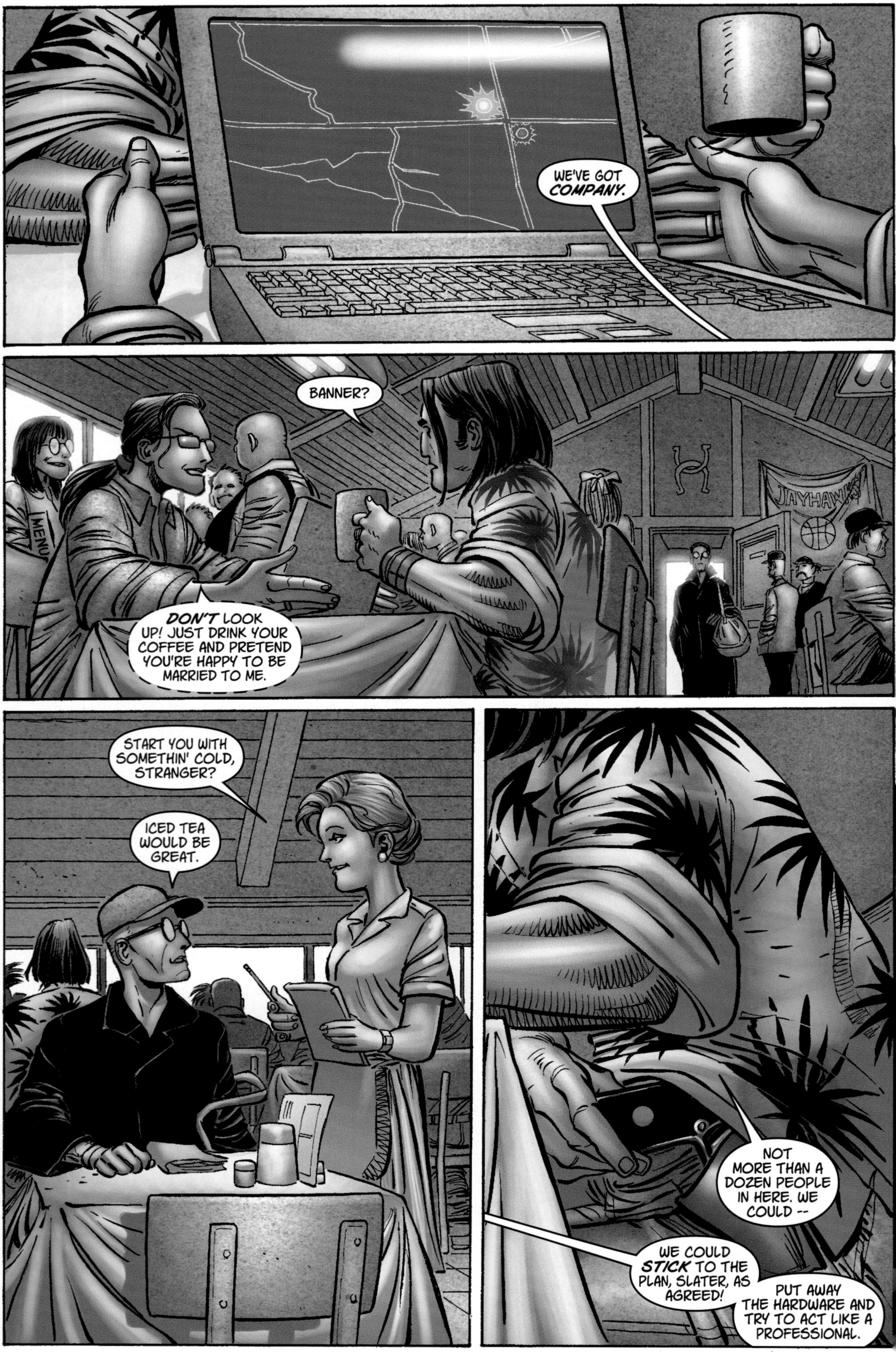
WE'VE GOT COMPANY.
BANNER?
DON'T LOOK UP! JUST DRINK YOUR COFFEE AND PRETEND YOU'RE HAPPY TO BE MARRIED TO ME.
JAYHAWKS
MENU
START YOU WITH SOMETHIN' COLD, STRANGER?
ICED TEA WOULD BE GREAT.
NOT MORE THAN A DOZEN PEOPLE IN HERE. WE COULD --
WE COULD STICK TO THE PLAN, SLATER, AS AGREED!
PUT AWAY THE HARDWARE AND TRY TO ACT LIKE A PROFESSIONAL.

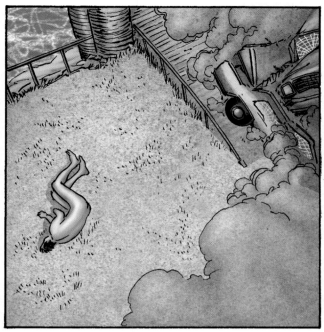

THIS THE PLACE, BOB?

WHERE'S THAT GUY WITH THE DUFFEL BAG WHO FREED THE KID IN THE CRICK?

AND WHERE'S THE COUPLE WHOSE CAR I BORROWED?

-- AND WHO'S *THIS* GUY?

BOB --?

-- HERE'S *ANOTHER ONE!*

WHAT THE DING-DONG BLAZES *HAPPENED* OUT HERE?

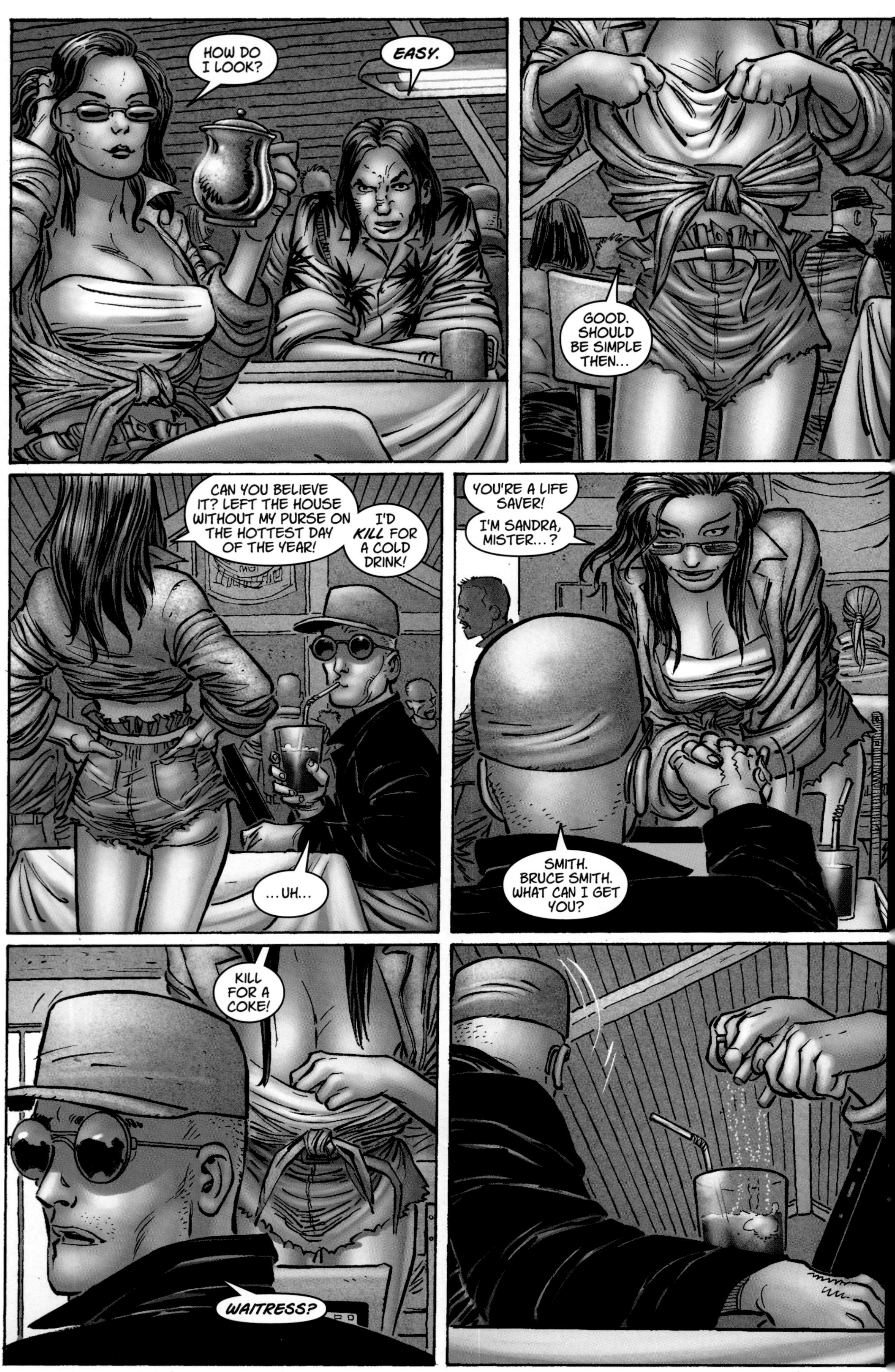
HOW DO I LOOK?
EASY.
GOOD. SHOULD BE SIMPLE THEN...
CAN YOU BELIEVE IT? LEFT THE HOUSE WITHOUT MY PURSE ON THE HOTTEST DAY OF THE YEAR!
I'D KILL FOR A COLD DRINK!
...UH...
YOU'RE A LIFE SAVER!
I'M SANDRA, MISTER...?
SMITH. BRUCE SMITH. WHAT CAN I GET YOU?
KILL FOR A COKE!
WAITRESS?

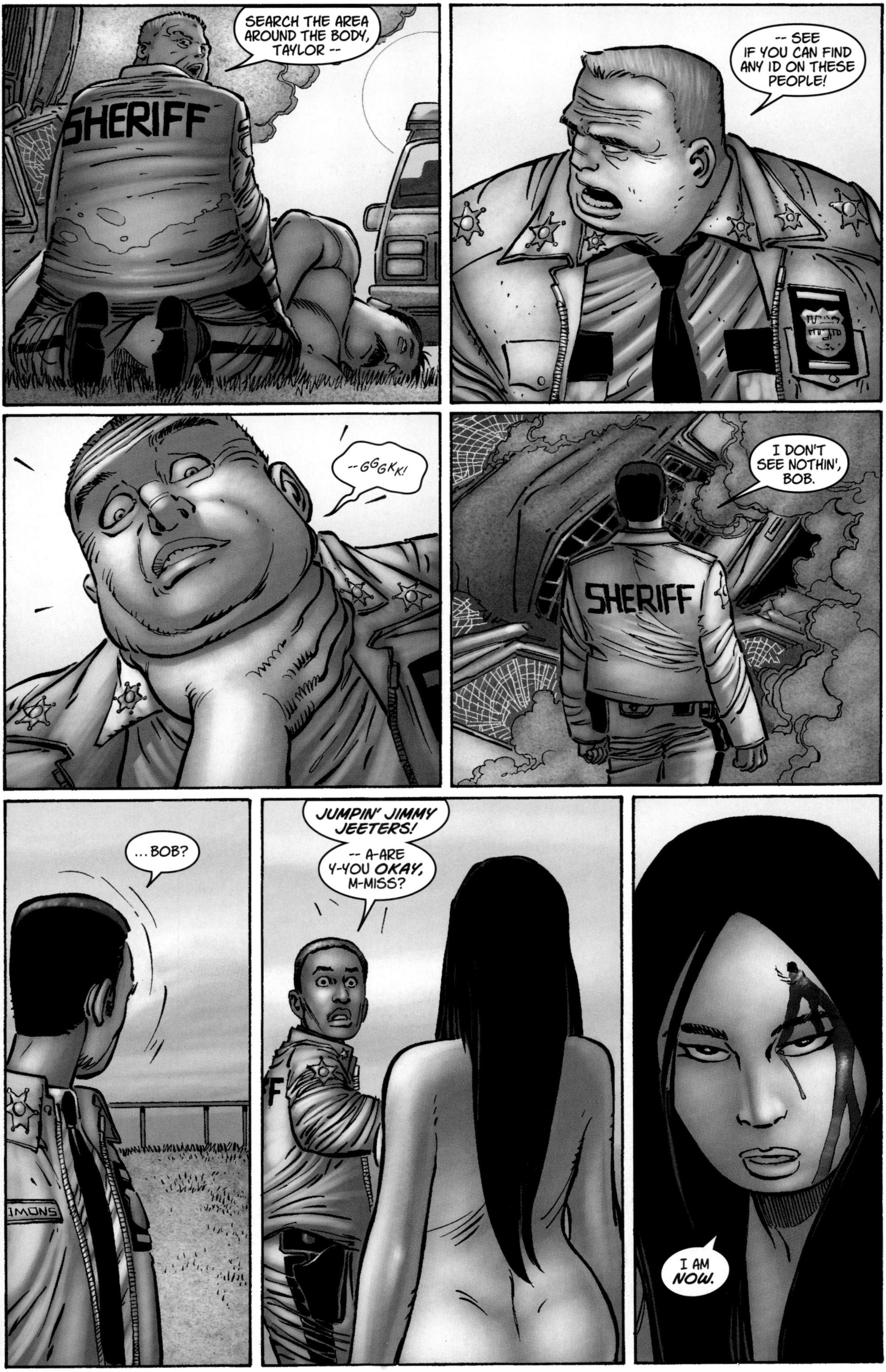
SEARCH THE AREA AROUND THE BODY, TAYLOR --
SHERIFF
-- SEE IF YOU CAN FIND ANY ID ON THESE PEOPLE!
--GGGKK!
I DON'T SEE NOTHIN', BOB.
SHERIFF
...BOB?
JUMPIN' JIMMY JEETERS!
-- A-ARE Y-YOU OKAY, M-MISS?
I AM NOW.

YOU FOLKS READY TO ORDER?

CHEESEBURGER AND FRIES.

I'M GOOD, THANKS.

TO *COOL WEATHER!*

DRINK TO THAT.

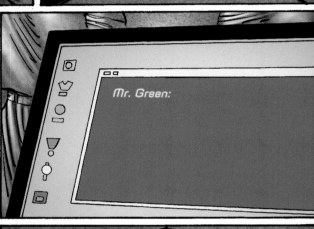

Mr. Green:

EXCUSE ME...

SURE.

Mr. Green: Present location unhealthy. Suggest you vacate at earliest convenience.

-- Mr. Blue

REPLY

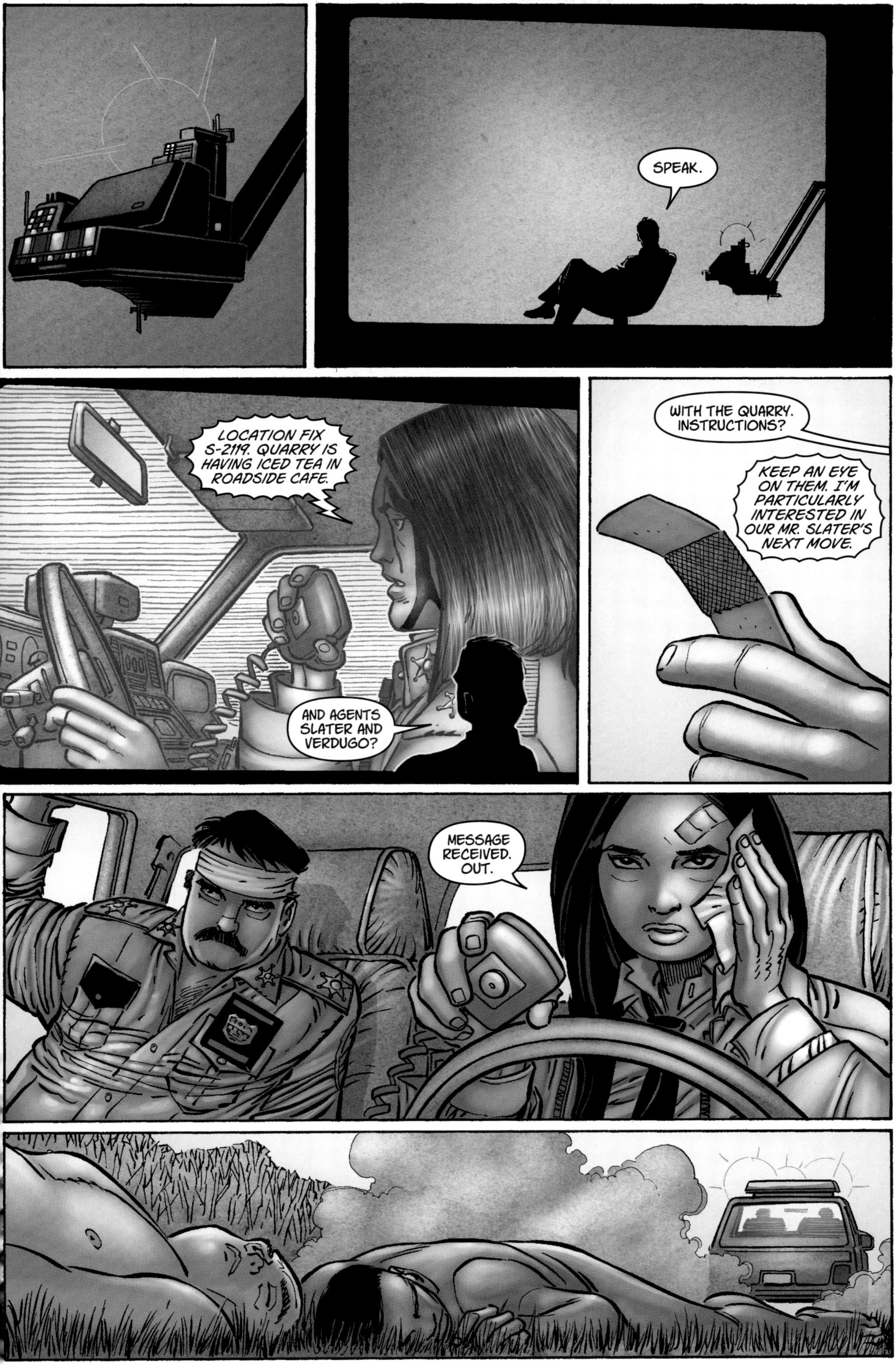
SPEAK.
LOCATION FIX S-2119. QUARRY IS HAVING ICED TEA IN ROADSIDE CAFE.
AND AGENTS SLATER AND VERDUGO?
WITH THE QUARRY. INSTRUCTIONS?
KEEP AN EYE ON THEM. I'M PARTICULARLY INTERESTED IN OUR MR. SLATER'S NEXT MOVE.
MESSAGE RECEIVED. OUT.

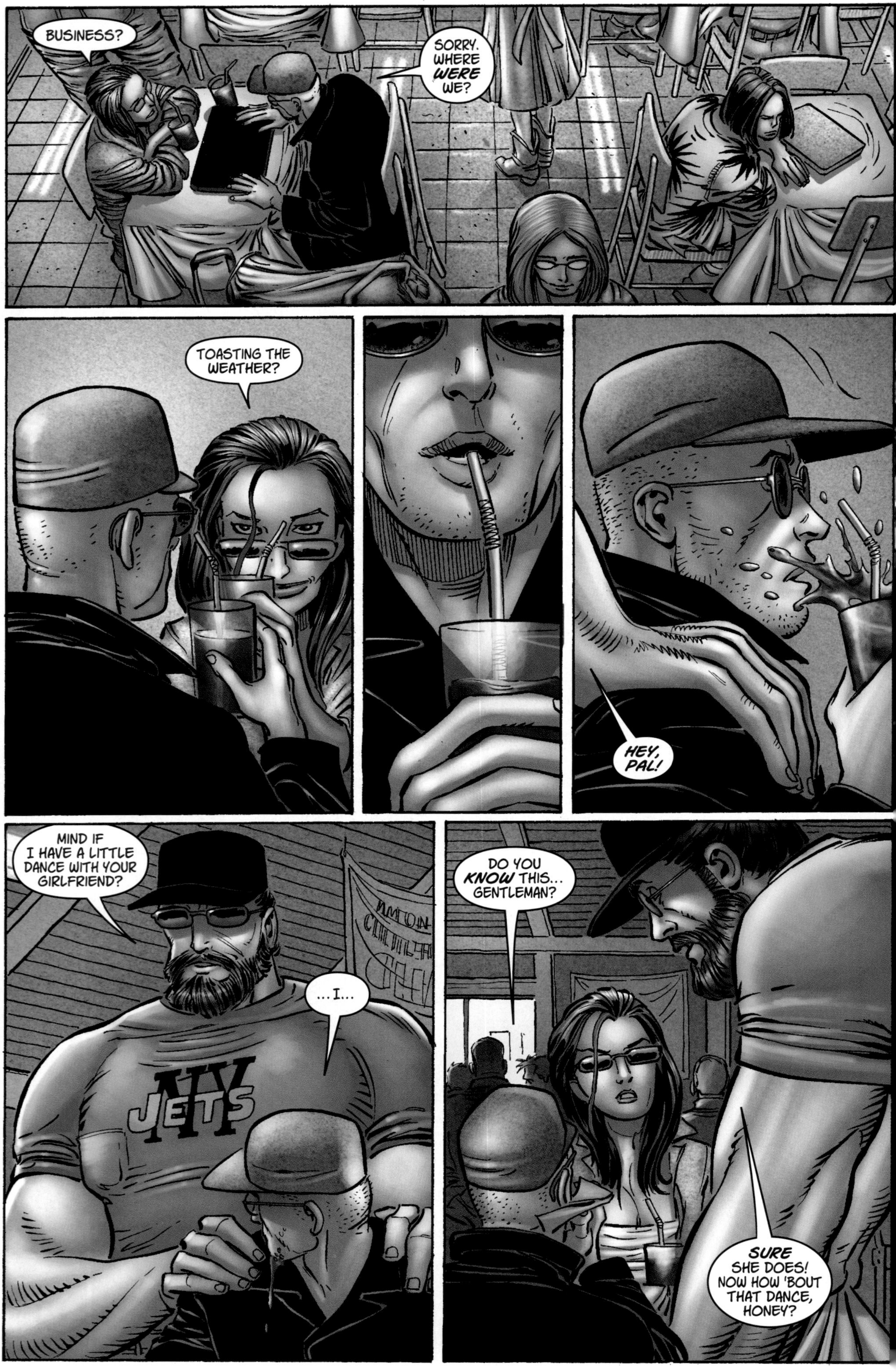
BUSINESS?
SORRY. WHERE WERE WE?
TOASTING THE WEATHER?
HEY, PAL!
MIND IF I HAVE A LITTLE DANCE WITH YOUR GIRLFRIEND?
...I...
NY JETS
DO YOU KNOW THIS... GENTLEMAN?
SURE SHE DOES! NOW HOW 'BOUT THAT DANCE, HONEY?

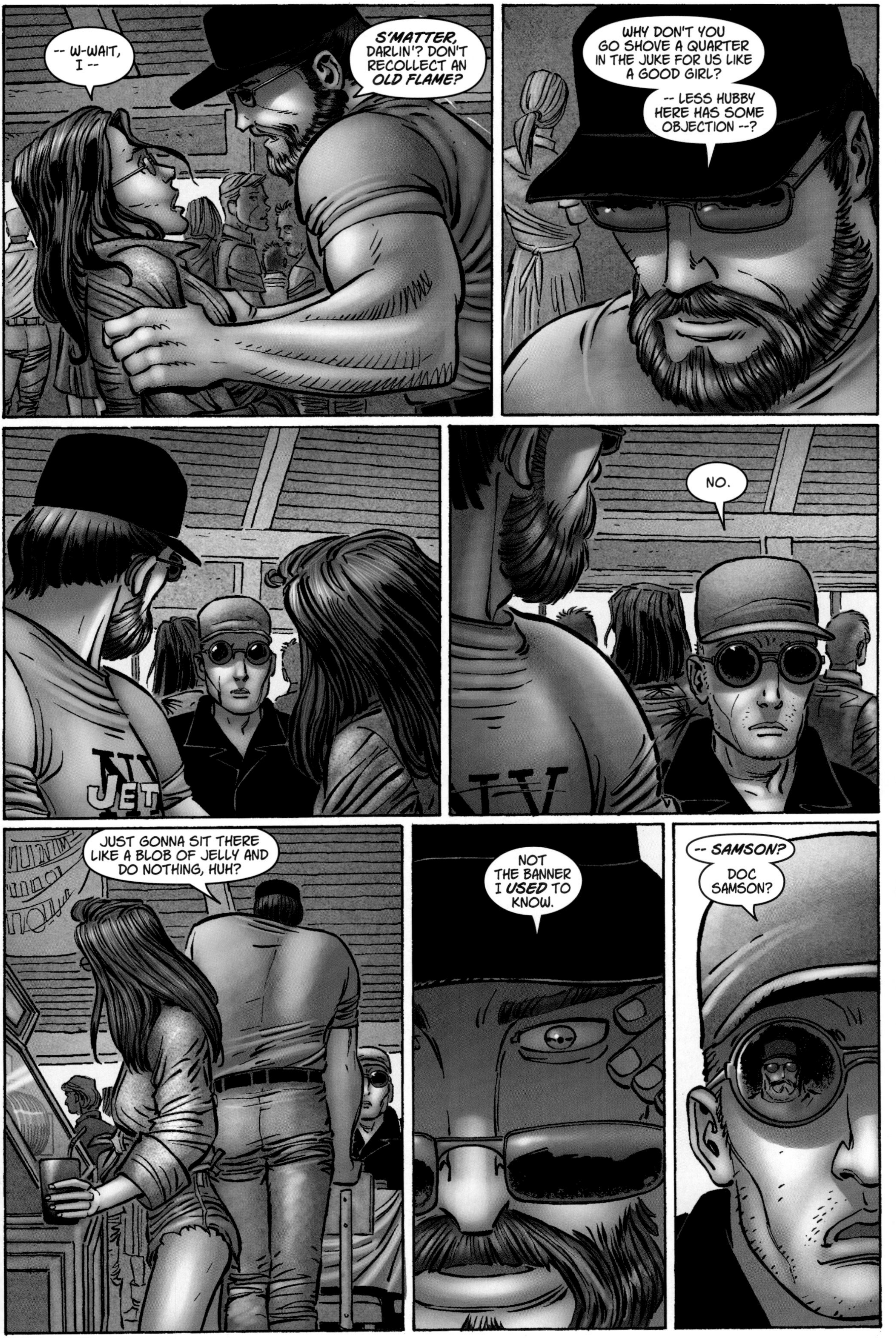
-- W-WAIT, I --
S'MATTER, DARLIN'? DON'T RECOLLECT AN OLD FLAME?
WHY DON'T YOU GO SHOVE A QUARTER IN THE JUKE FOR US LIKE A GOOD GIRL?
-- LESS HUBBY HERE HAS SOME OBJECTION --?
JET
NO.
JUST GONNA SIT THERE LIKE A BLOB OF JELLY AND DO NOTHING, HUH?
NOT THE BANNER I USED TO KNOW.
-- SAMSON?
DOC SAMSON?

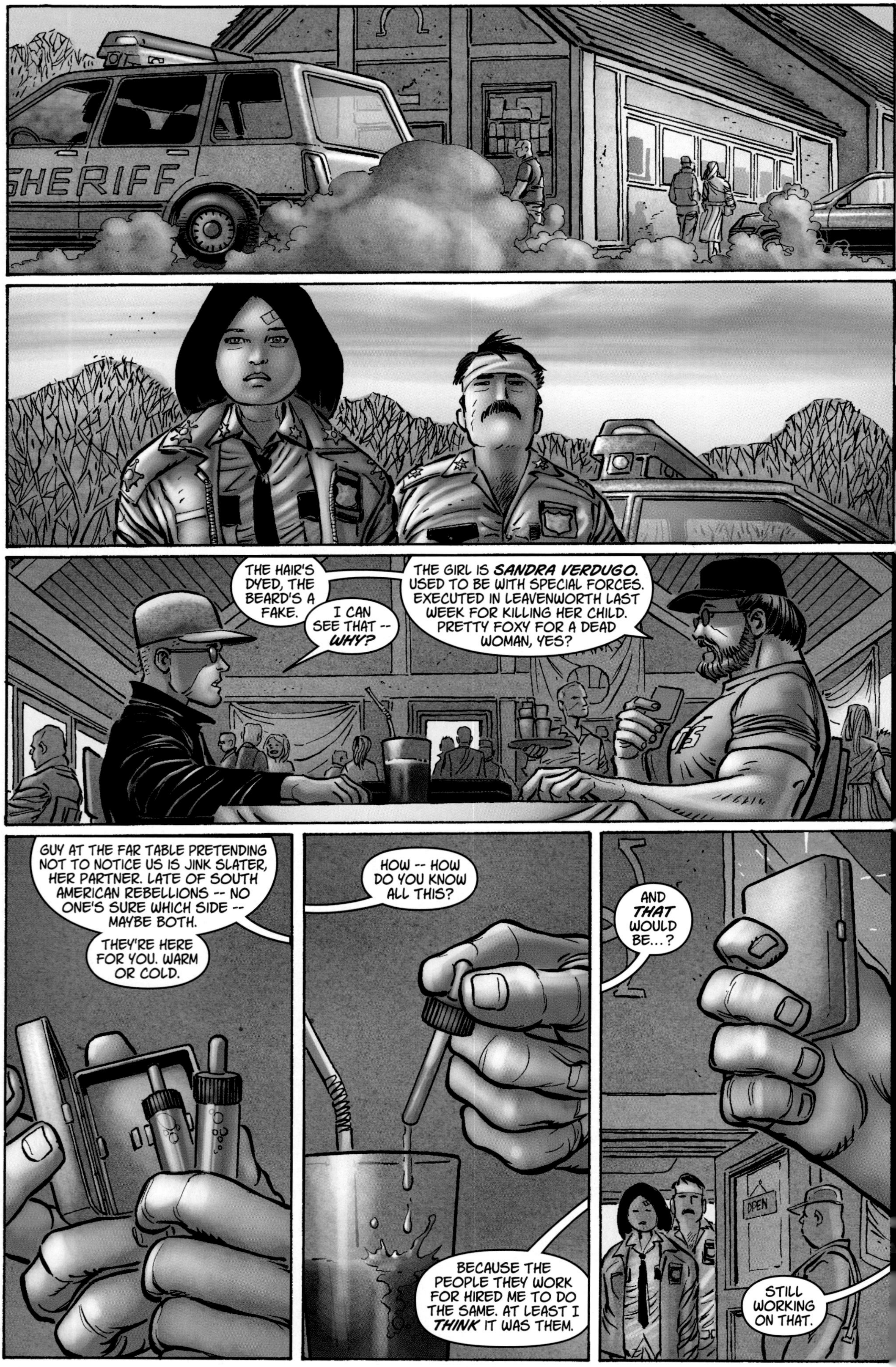
SHERIFF
THE HAIR'S DYED, THE BEARD'S A FAKE.
I CAN SEE THAT -- WHY?
THE GIRL IS SANDRA VERDUGO. USED TO BE WITH SPECIAL FORCES. EXECUTED IN LEAVENWORTH LAST WEEK FOR KILLING HER CHILD. PRETTY FOXY FOR A DEAD WOMAN, YES?
GUY AT THE FAR TABLE PRETENDING NOT TO NOTICE US IS JINK SLATER, HER PARTNER. LATE OF SOUTH AMERICAN REBELLIONS -- NO ONE'S SURE WHICH SIDE -- MAYBE BOTH.
THEY'RE HERE FOR YOU. WARM OR COLD.
HOW -- HOW DO YOU KNOW ALL THIS?
BECAUSE THE PEOPLE THEY WORK FOR HIRED ME TO DO THE SAME. AT LEAST I THINK IT WAS THEM.
AND THAT WOULD BE...?
OPEN
STILL WORKING ON THAT.

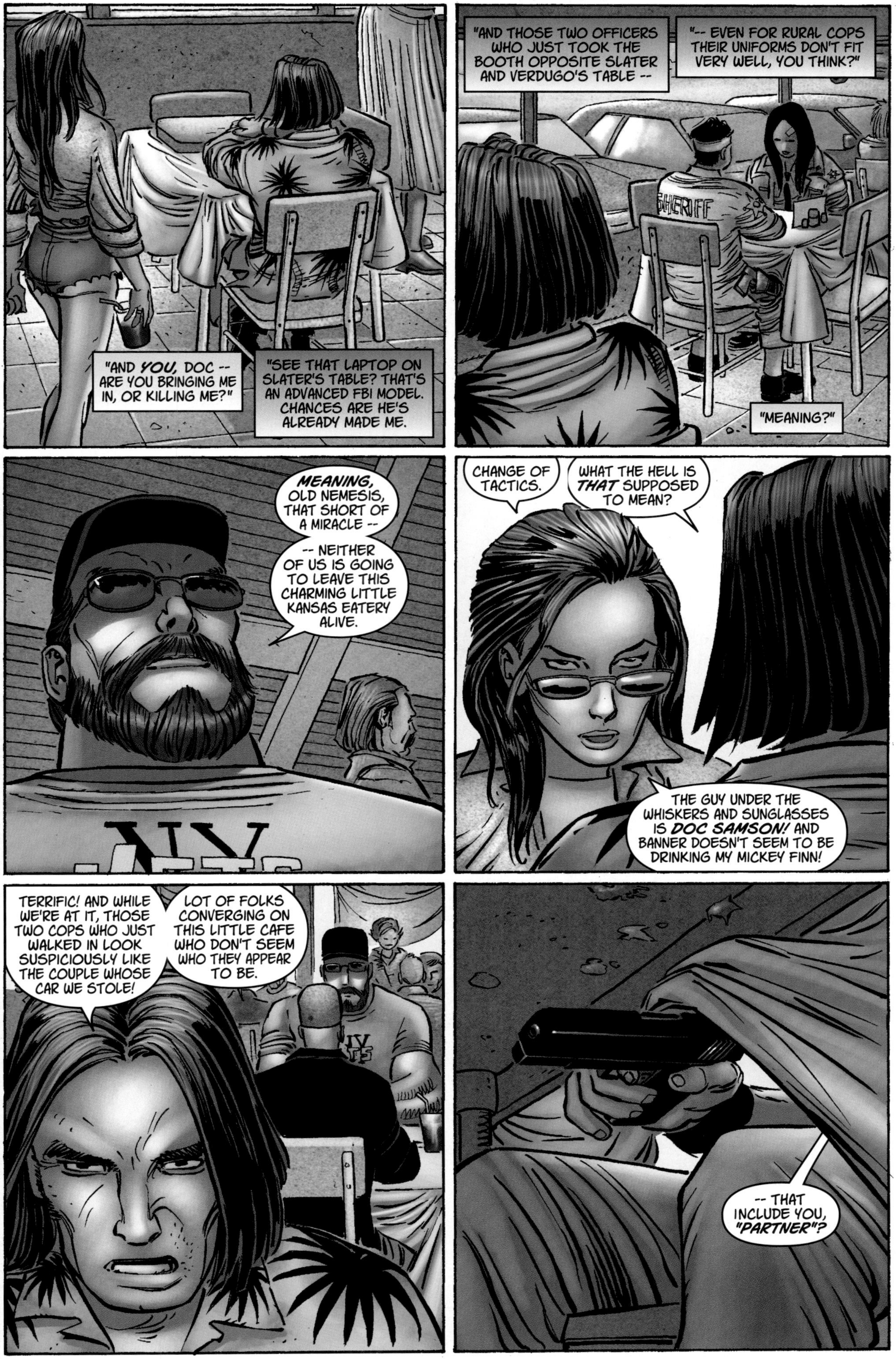
"AND YOU, DOC -- ARE YOU BRINGING ME IN, OR KILLING ME?"
"SEE THAT LAPTOP ON SLATER'S TABLE? THAT'S AN ADVANCED FBI MODEL. CHANCES ARE HE'S ALREADY MADE ME.
"AND THOSE TWO OFFICERS WHO JUST TOOK THE BOOTH OPPOSITE SLATER AND VERDUGO'S TABLE --
"-- EVEN FOR RURAL COPS THEIR UNIFORMS DON'T FIT VERY WELL, YOU THINK?"
SHERIFF
"MEANING?"
MEANING, OLD NEMESIS, THAT SHORT OF A MIRACLE --
-- NEITHER OF US IS GOING TO LEAVE THIS CHARMING LITTLE KANSAS EATERY ALIVE.
CHANGE OF TACTICS.
WHAT THE HELL IS THAT SUPPOSED TO MEAN?
THE GUY UNDER THE WHISKERS AND SUNGLASSES IS DOC SAMSON! AND BANNER DOESN'T SEEM TO BE DRINKING MY MICKEY FINN!
TERRIFIC! AND WHILE WE'RE AT IT, THOSE TWO COPS WHO JUST WALKED IN LOOK SUSPICIOUSLY LIKE THE COUPLE WHOSE CAR WE STOLE!
LOT OF FOLKS CONVERGING ON THIS LITTLE CAFE WHO DON'T SEEM WHO THEY APPEAR TO BE.
-- THAT INCLUDE YOU, "PARTNER"?

I WARNED YOU ABOUT SLATER.

SLATER AND VERDUGO ARE MOOT AT PRESENT -- IT'S BANNER'S REACTIONS WE'RE INTERESTED IN NOW.

SINCE WHEN ARE YOU AFRAID OF *NORMS*, DOC? UNLESS THEY'VE GOT AN ATOM BOMB IN THEIR BACKPACK, I'D SAY THEY'VE GOT A TALL ORDER IN FRONT OF THEM.

WHAT THEY'VE GOT IS TEN TIMES WORSE, *TRUST* ME.

SO WHAT'S THE *PLAN,* DOC?

DEPENDS. YOU KEPT YOUR TEMPER ADMIRABLY DURING MY LITTLE STRUGGLE WITH THE VERDUGO WOMAN. CAN YOU LOSE IT JUST AS EASILY?

IT DOESN'T WORK LIKE THAT, DOC. IT'S NOT A FAUCET I CAN TURN ON AND OFF WITHOUT A REASON.

THEN LET'S *GIVE* IT ONE...

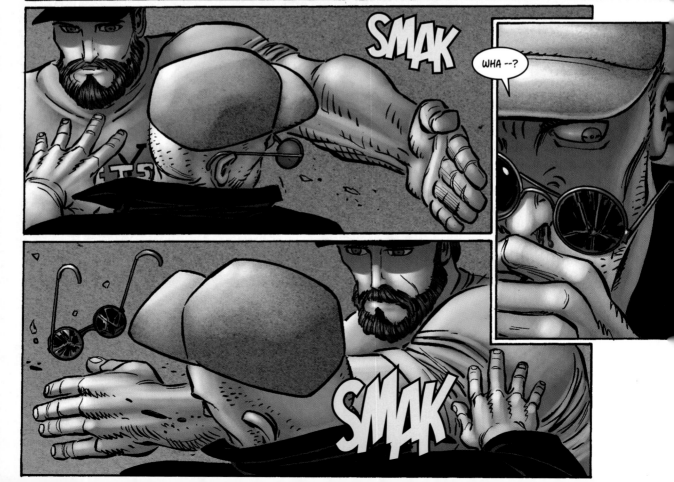

SMAK

WHA --?

SMAK

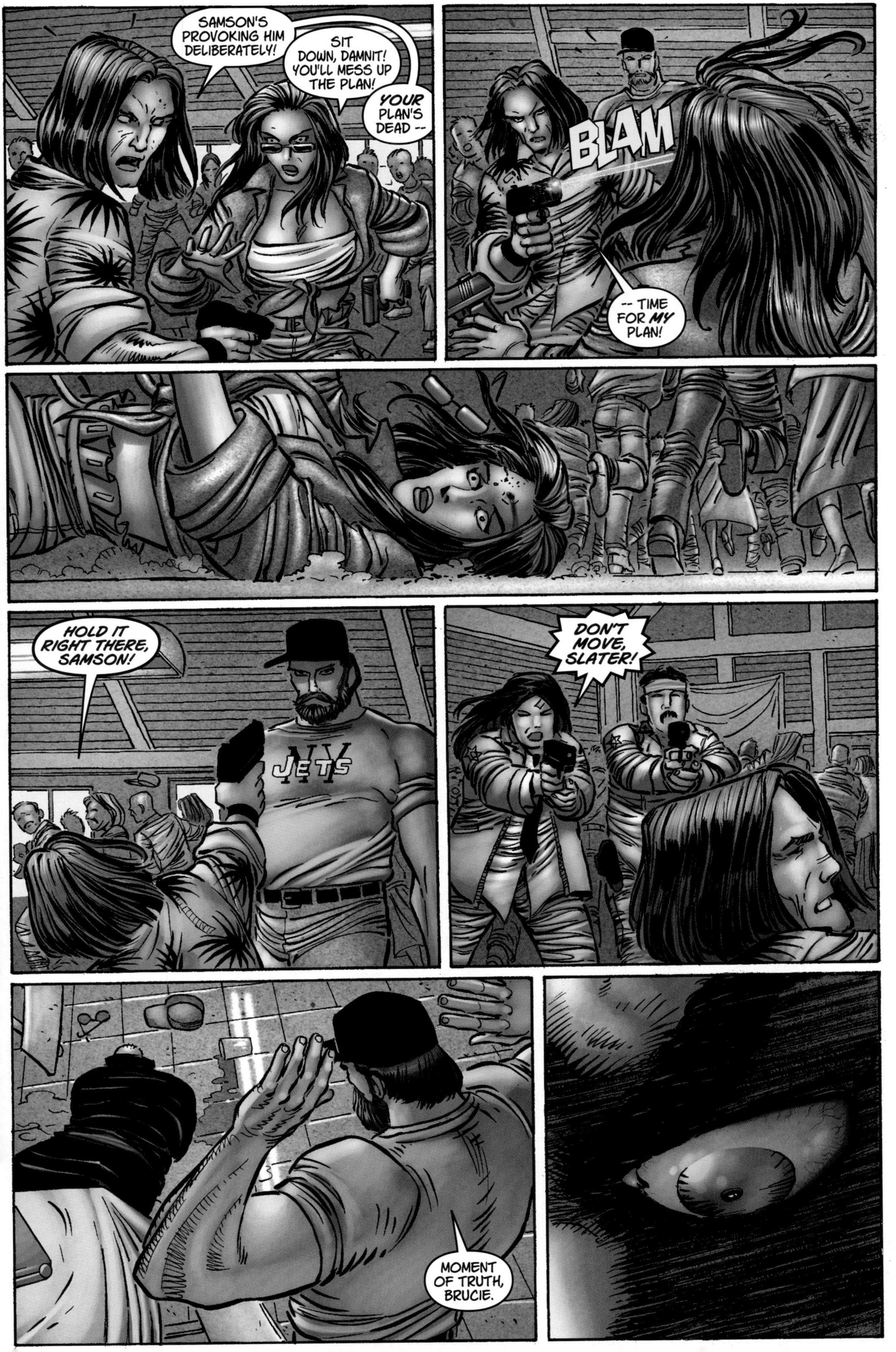
SAMSON'S PROVOKING HIM DELIBERATELY!
SIT DOWN, DAMNIT! YOU'LL MESS UP THE PLAN!
YOUR PLAN'S DEAD --
BLAM
-- TIME FOR MY PLAN!
HOLD IT RIGHT THERE, SAMSON!
NY JETS
DON'T MOVE, SLATER!
MOMENT OF TRUTH, BRUCIE.

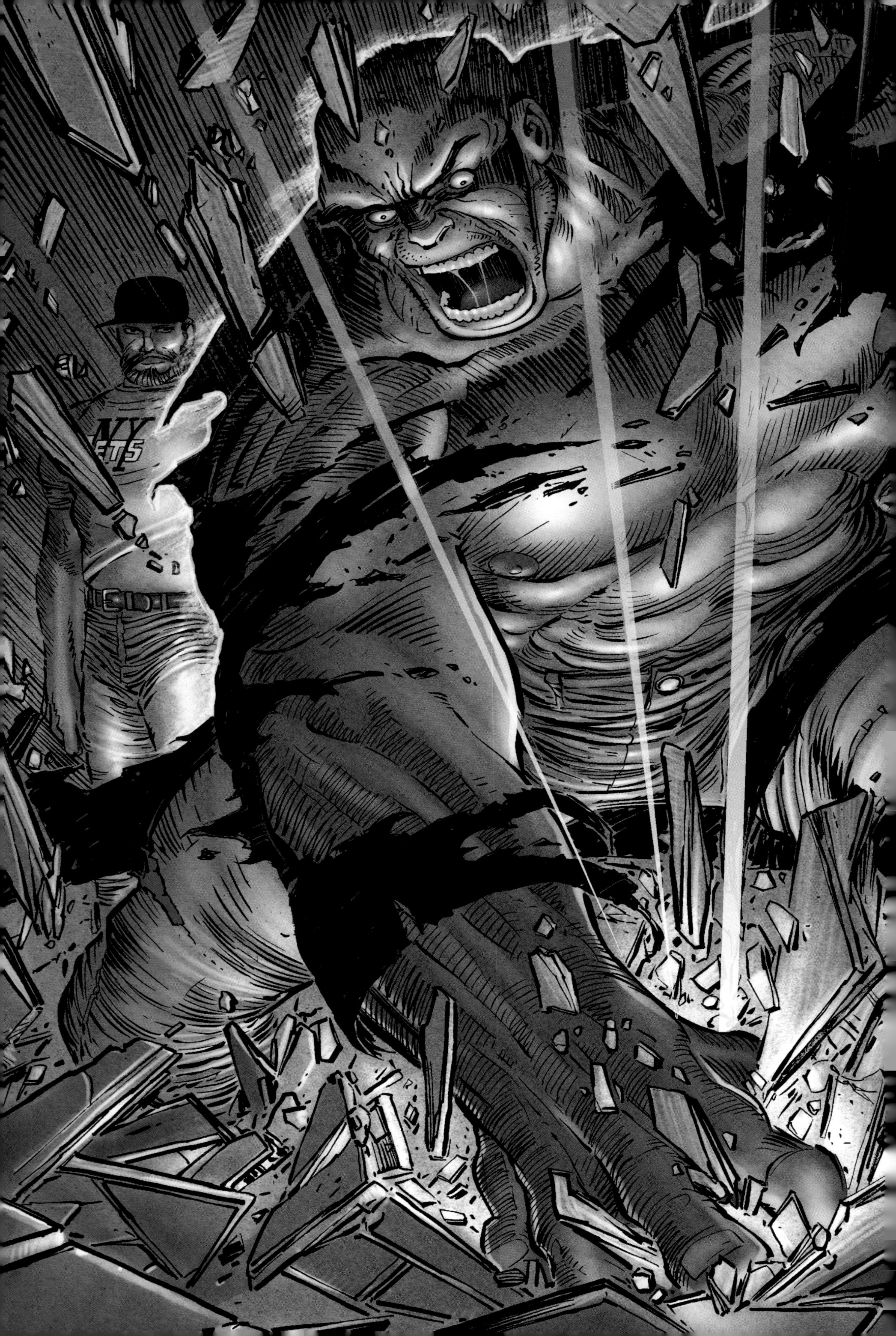
NY
ETS

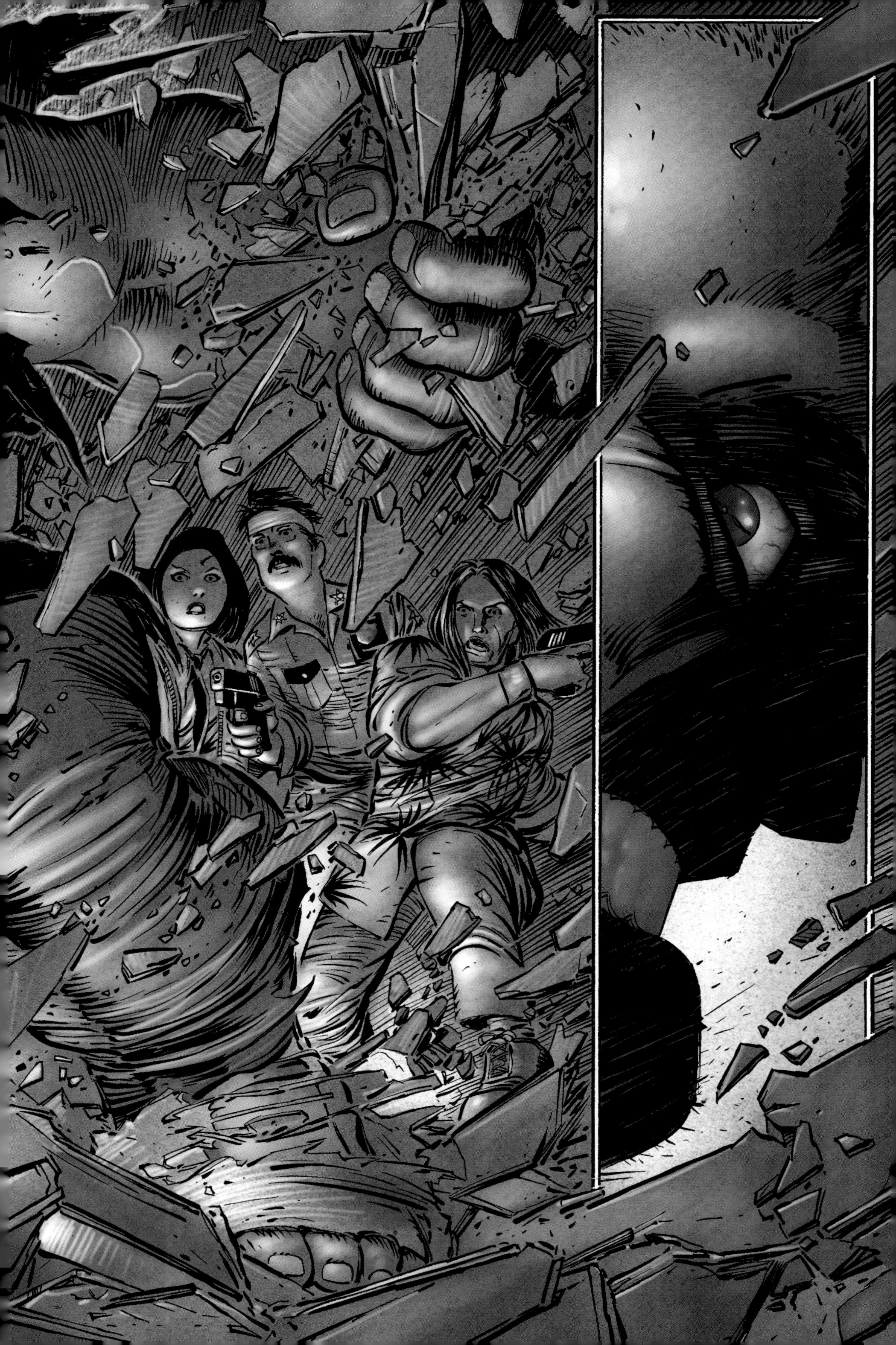

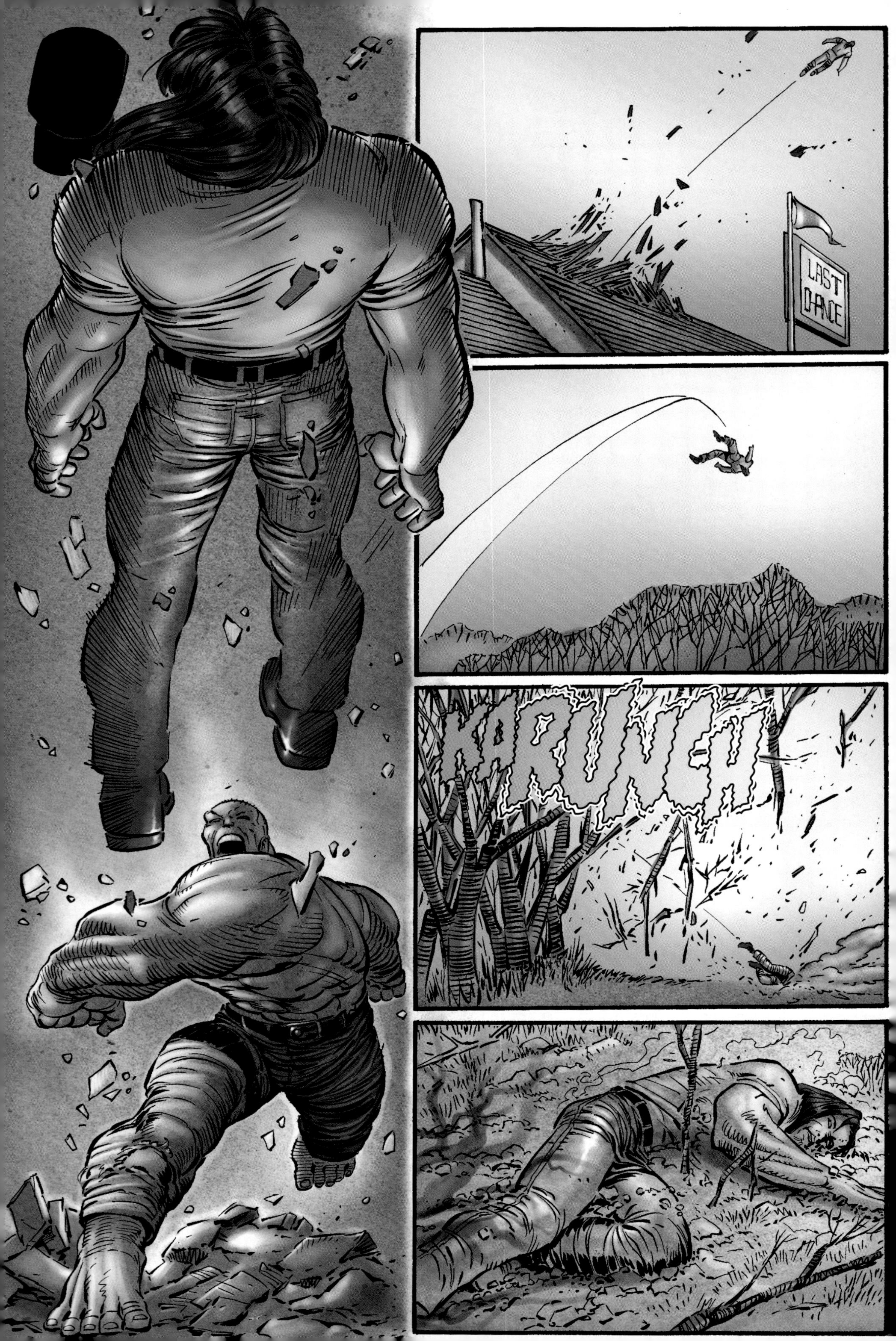
LAST CHANCE
KARUNCH

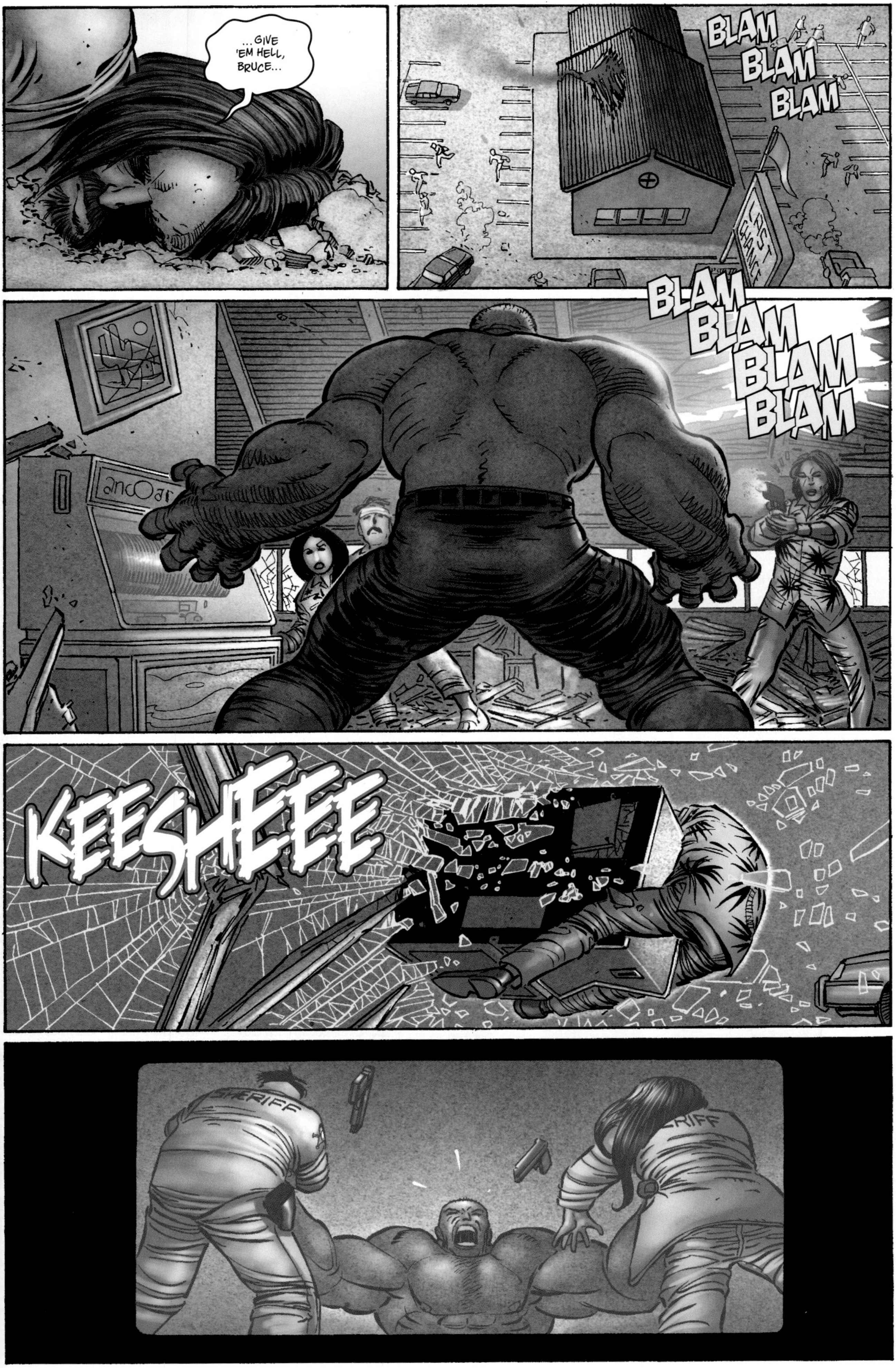
...GIVE 'EM HELL, BRUCE...
BLAM BLAM BLAM
LAST CHANCE
BLAM BLAM BLAM BLAM
KEESHEEE

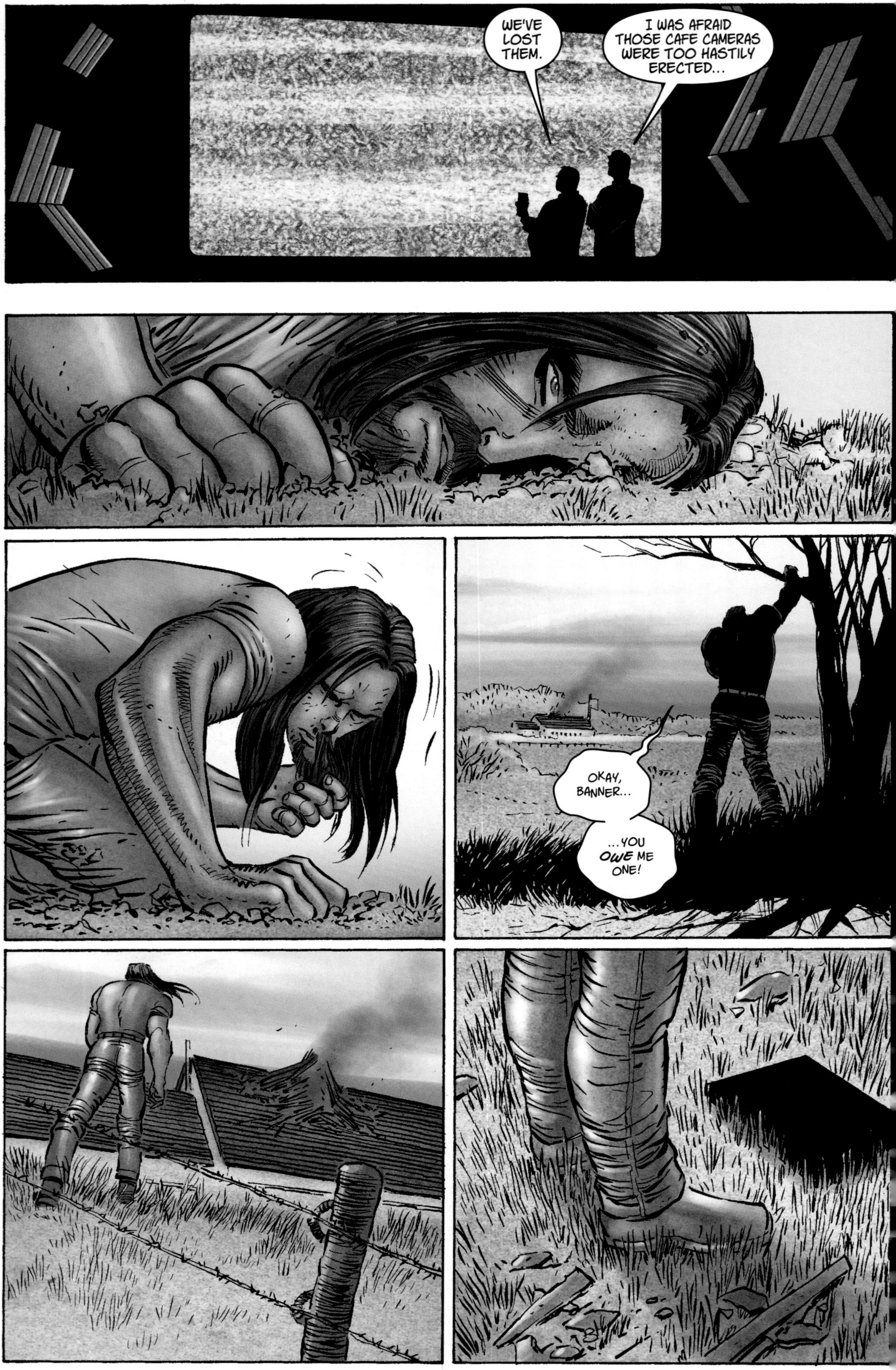
WE'VE LOST THEM.
I WAS AFRAID THOSE CAFE CAMERAS WERE TOO HASTILY ERECTED...
OKAY, BANNER...
...YOU OWE ME ONE!

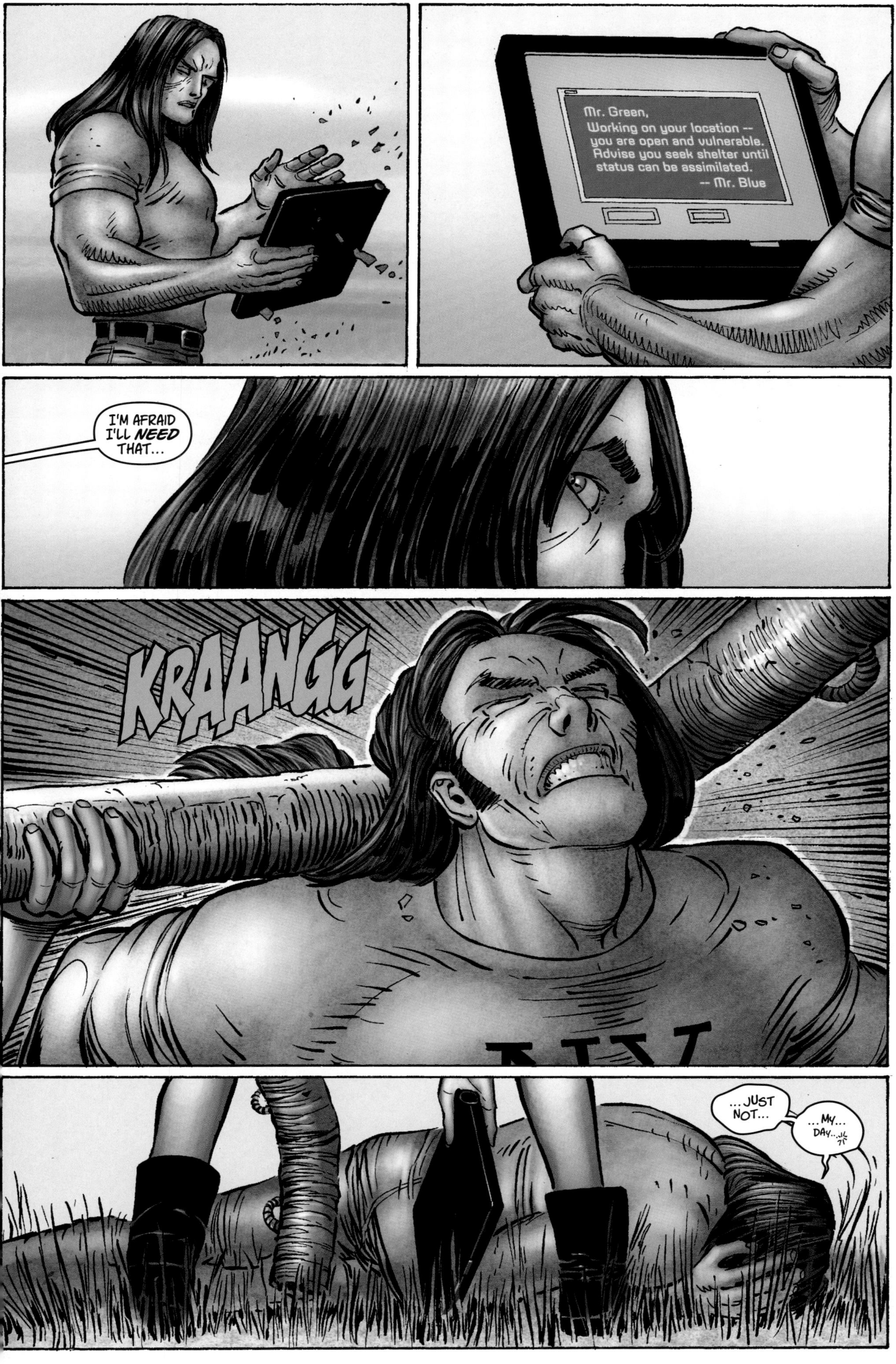

Mr. Green,
Working on your location -- you are open and vulnerable. Advise you seek shelter until status can be assimilated.
-- Mr. Blue
I'M AFRAID I'LL *NEED* THAT...
KRAANGG
...JUST NOT...
...MY... DAY...

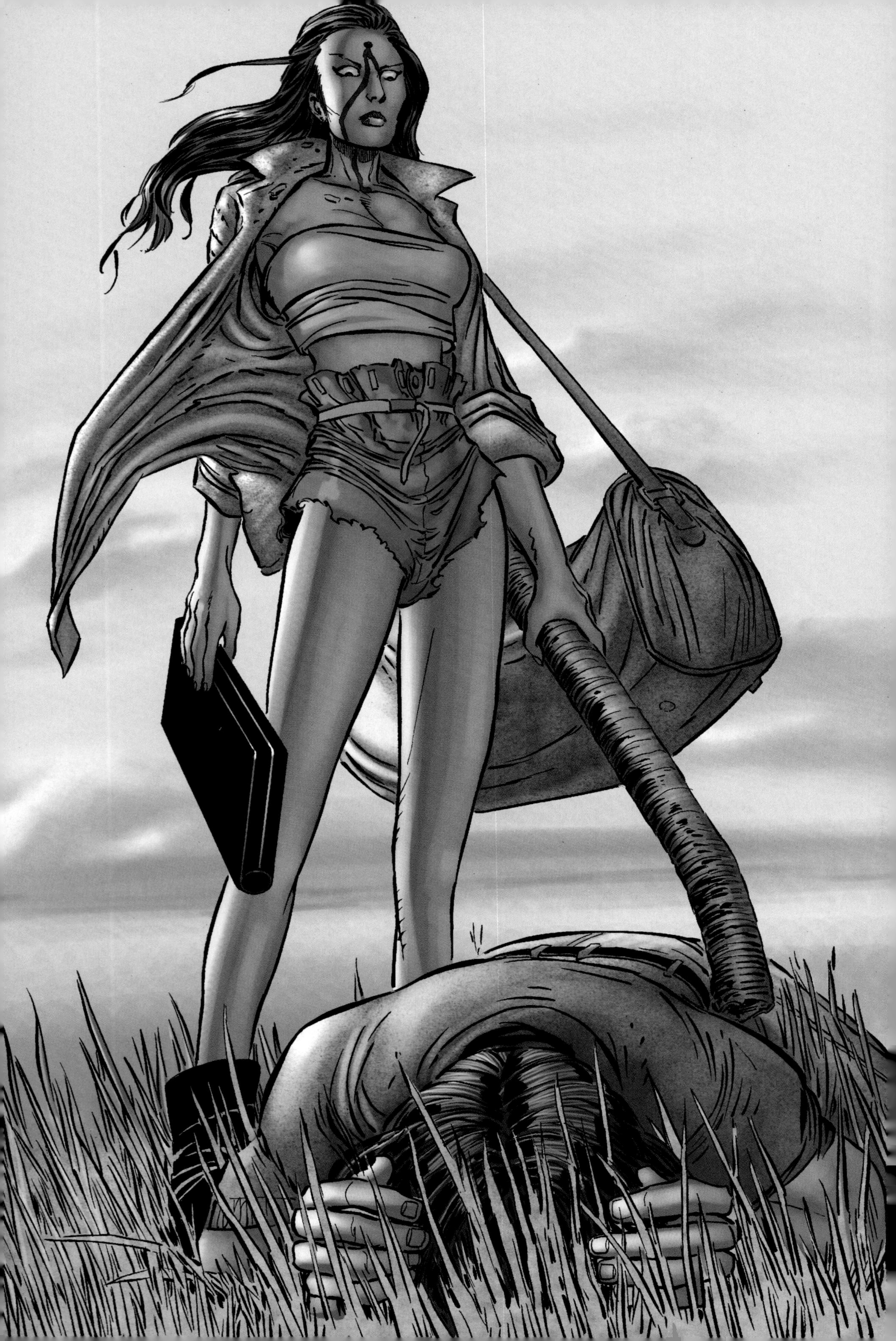

INCREDIBLE HULK #39
Cover sketch by Kaare Andrews

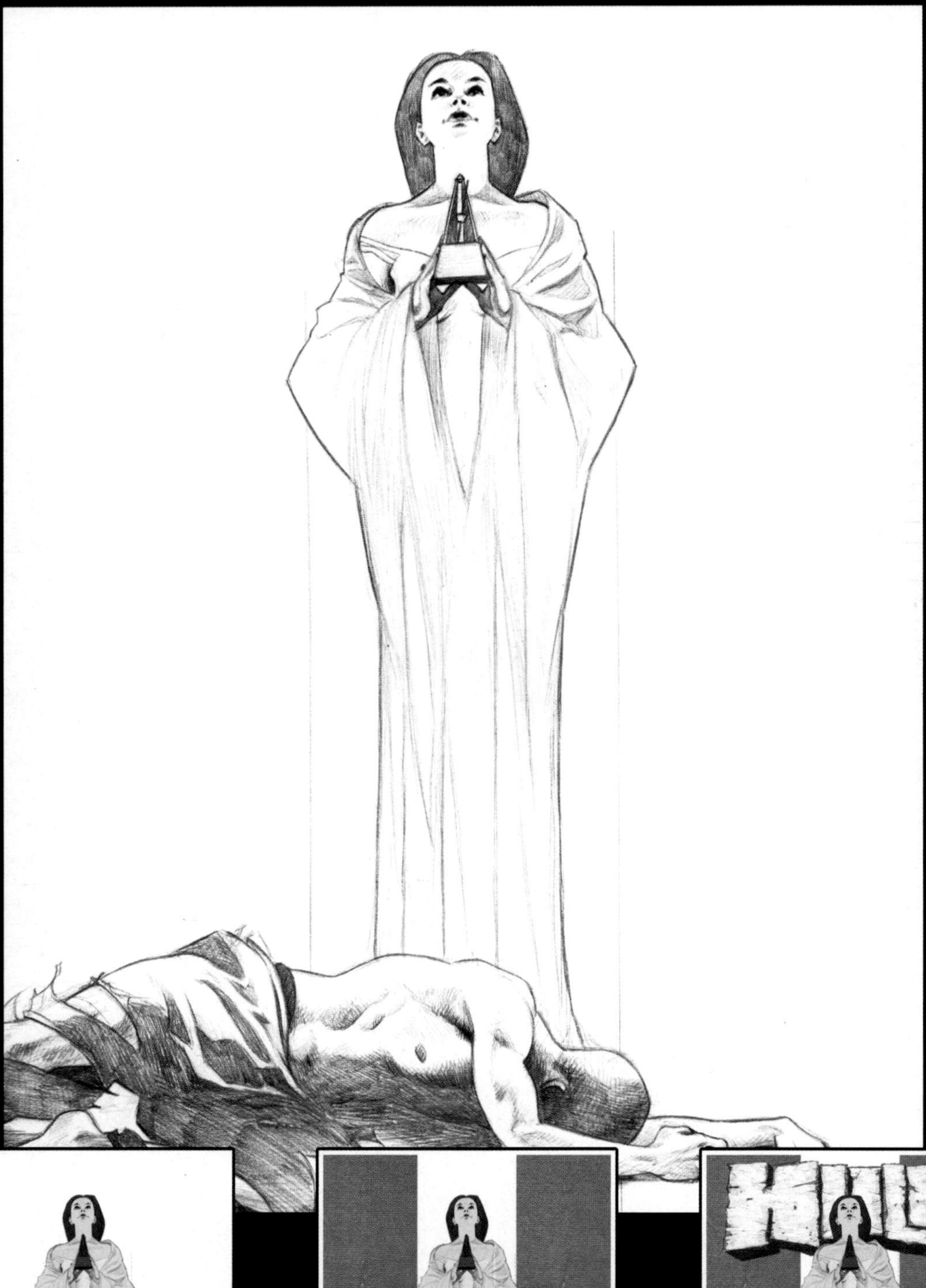

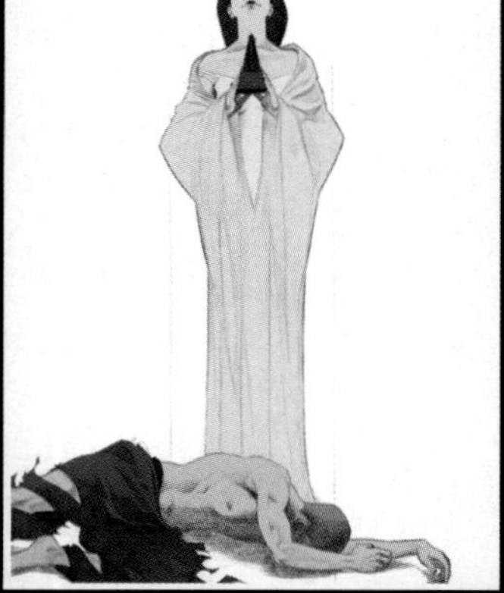

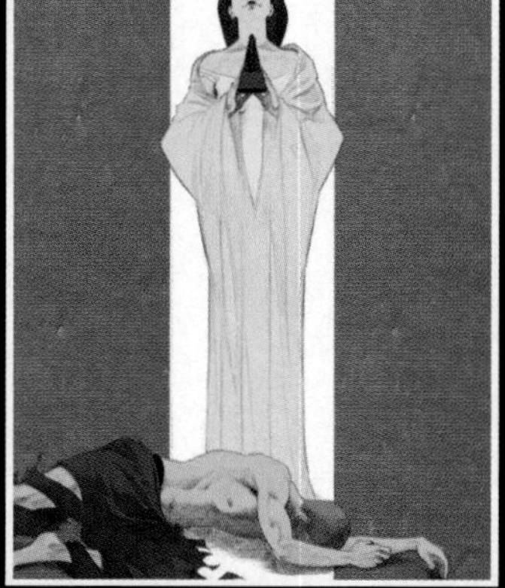

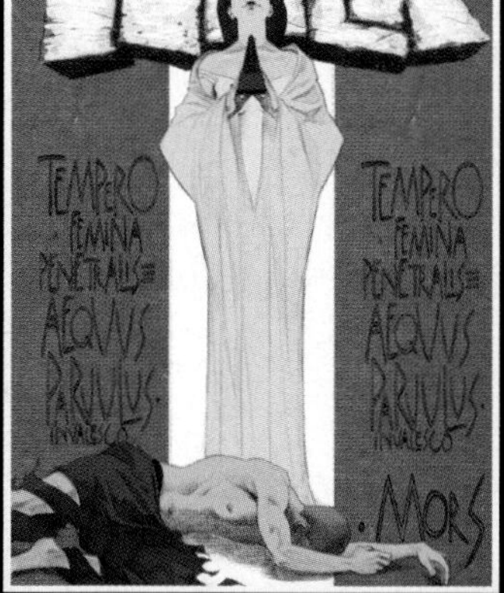
HULK
TEMPERO FEMINA PENETRALIS AEQVVS PARVLVS
TEMPERO FEMINA PENETRALIS AEQVVS PARVLVS
MORS

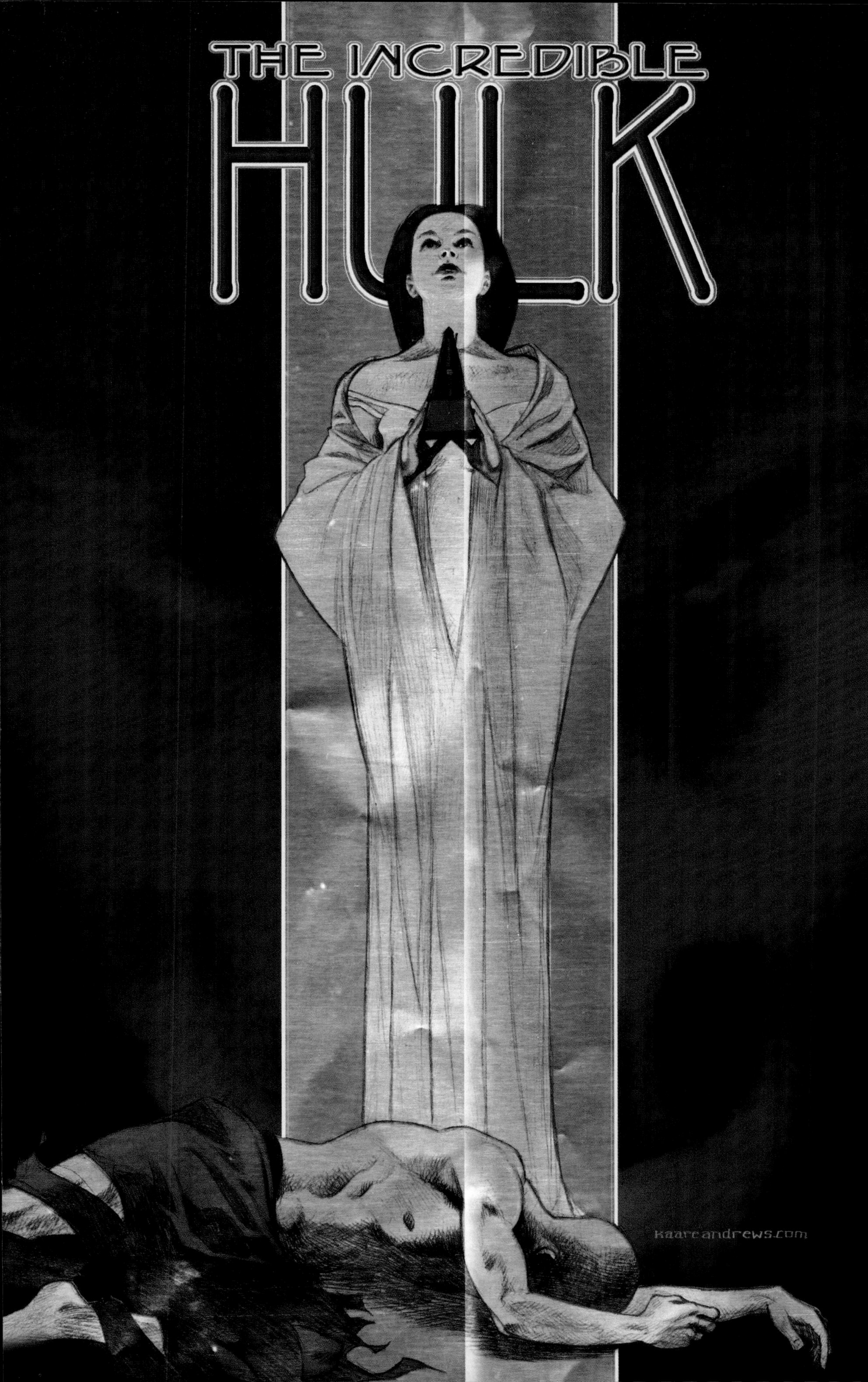
THE INCREDIBLE
HULK
kaareandrews.com

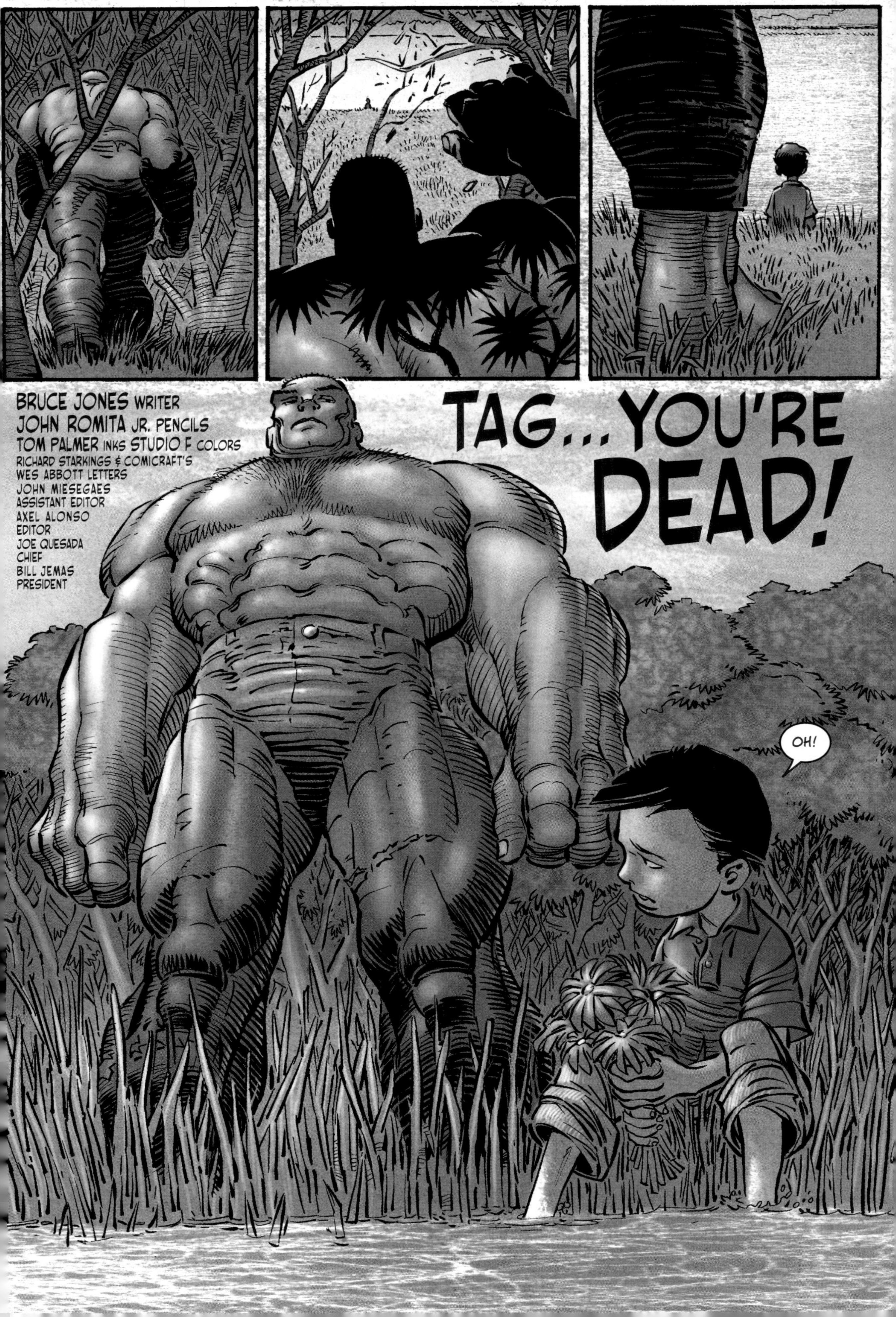
TAG... YOU'RE DEAD!
BRUCE JONES WRITER
JOHN ROMITA JR. PENCILS
TOM PALMER INKS STUDIO F COLORS
RICHARD STARKINGS & COMICRAFT'S
WES ABBOTT LETTERS
JOHN MIESEGAES
ASSISTANT EDITOR
AXEL ALONSO
EDITOR
JOE QUESADA
CHIEF
BILL JEMAS
PRESIDENT
OH!

MY NAME'S *RICKY.* ARE YOU A FRIEND OF MY *MOTHER'S?*

SHE'S NOT HOME JUST NOW. WOULD YOU LIKE TO *PLAY?*

HERE...

I CAN MAKE A BOAT -- *LOOK!*

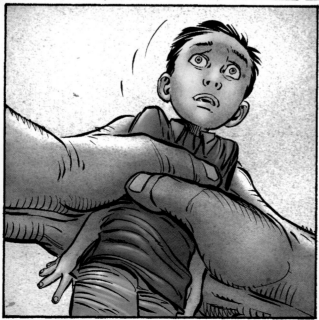

EEEEEEEEE!

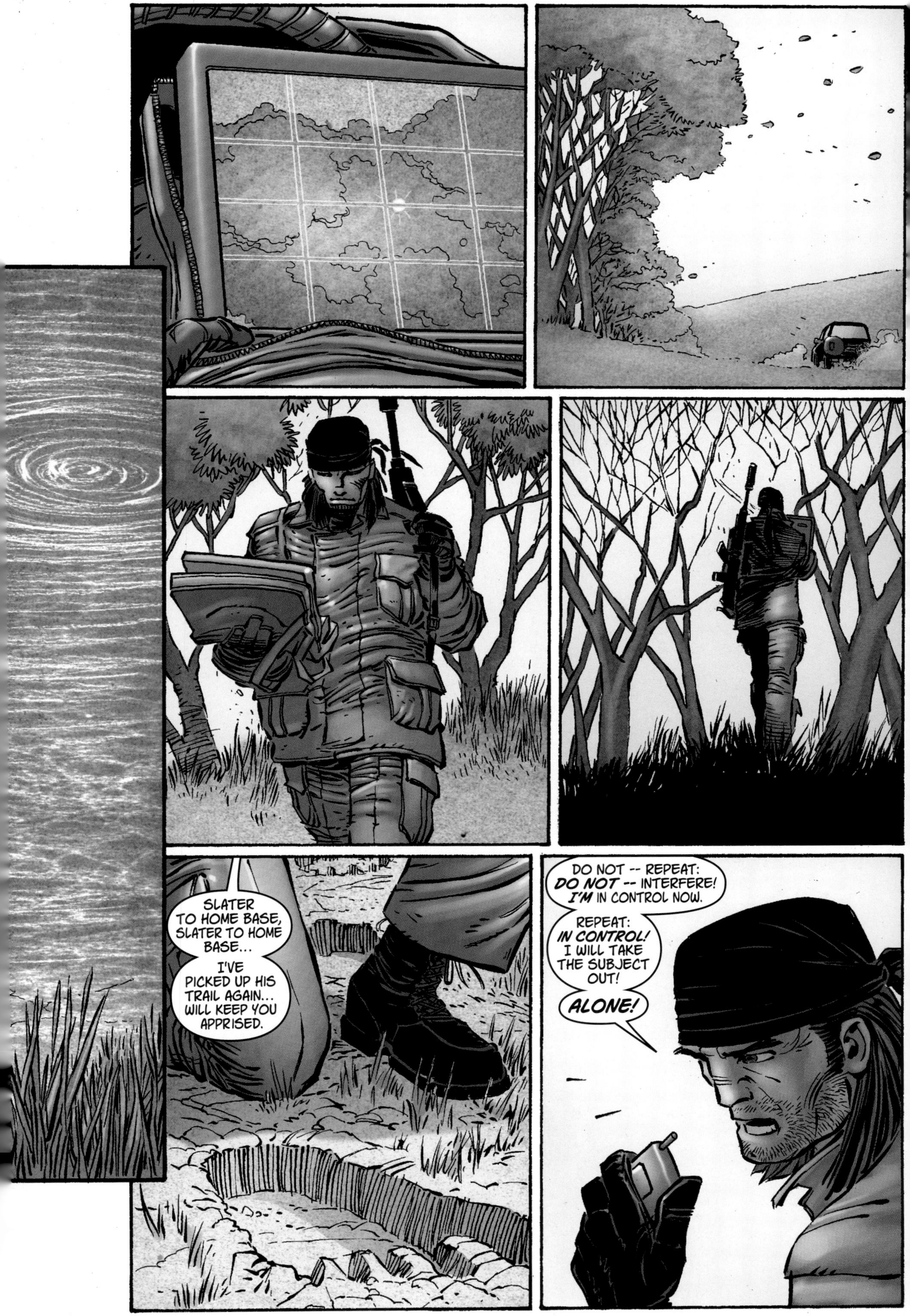
SLATER TO HOME BASE, SLATER TO HOME BASE...
I'VE PICKED UP HIS TRAIL AGAIN... WILL KEEP YOU APPRISED.
DO NOT -- REPEAT: DO NOT -- INTERFERE! I'M IN CONTROL NOW.
REPEAT: IN CONTROL! I WILL TAKE THE SUBJECT OUT!
ALONE!

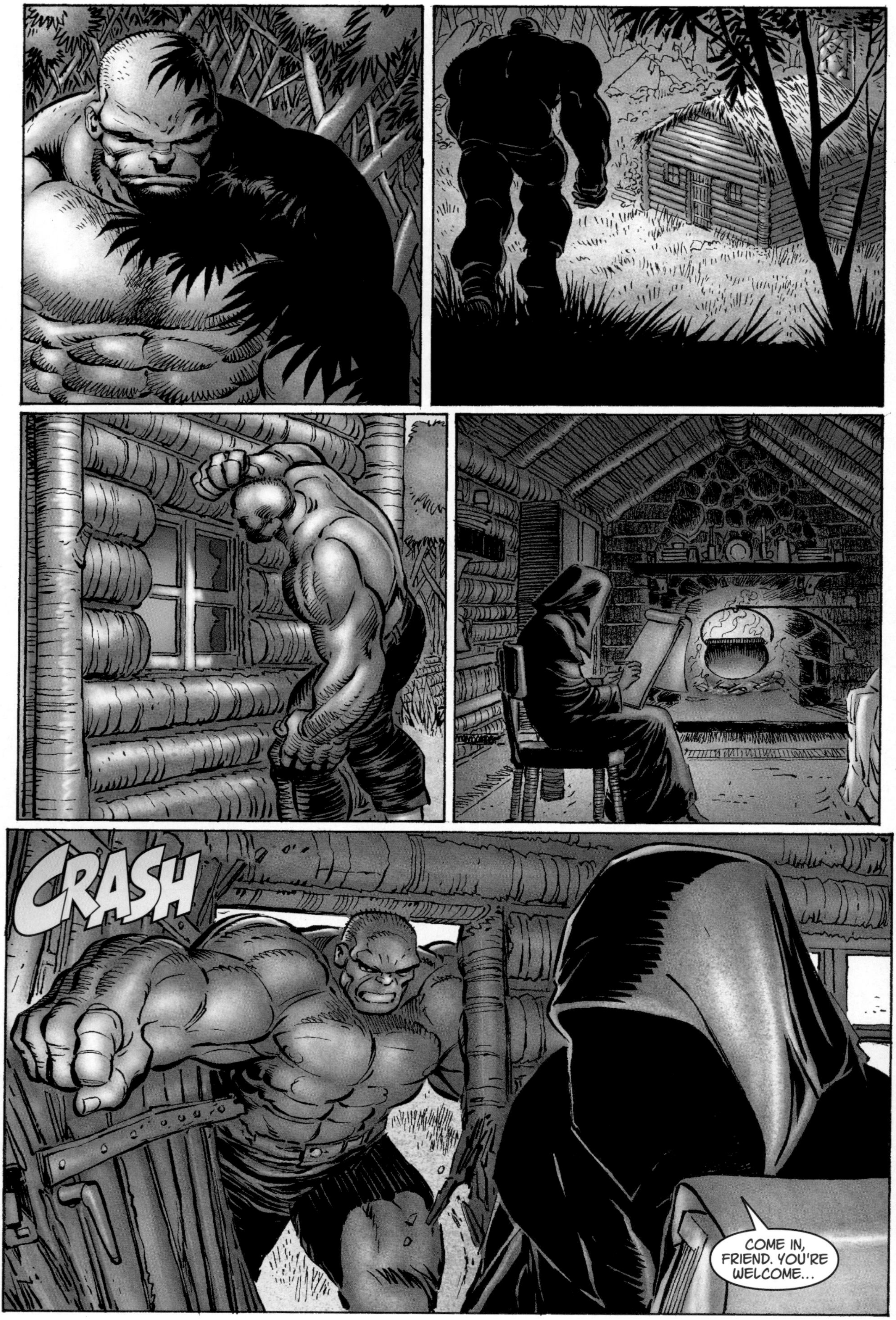
CRASH
COME IN, FRIEND. YOU'RE WELCOME...

STAY A WHILE. REST.

I'LL GET YOU SOMETHING TO EAT.

RELAX.

NO ONE'S GOING TO HURT YOU HERE...

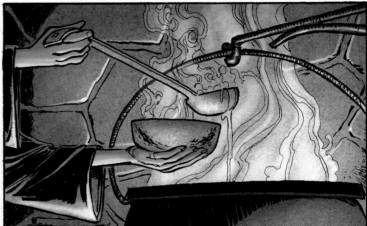

SIT.

EAT.

IT'S ALL RIGHT... IT'S ONLY STEW...

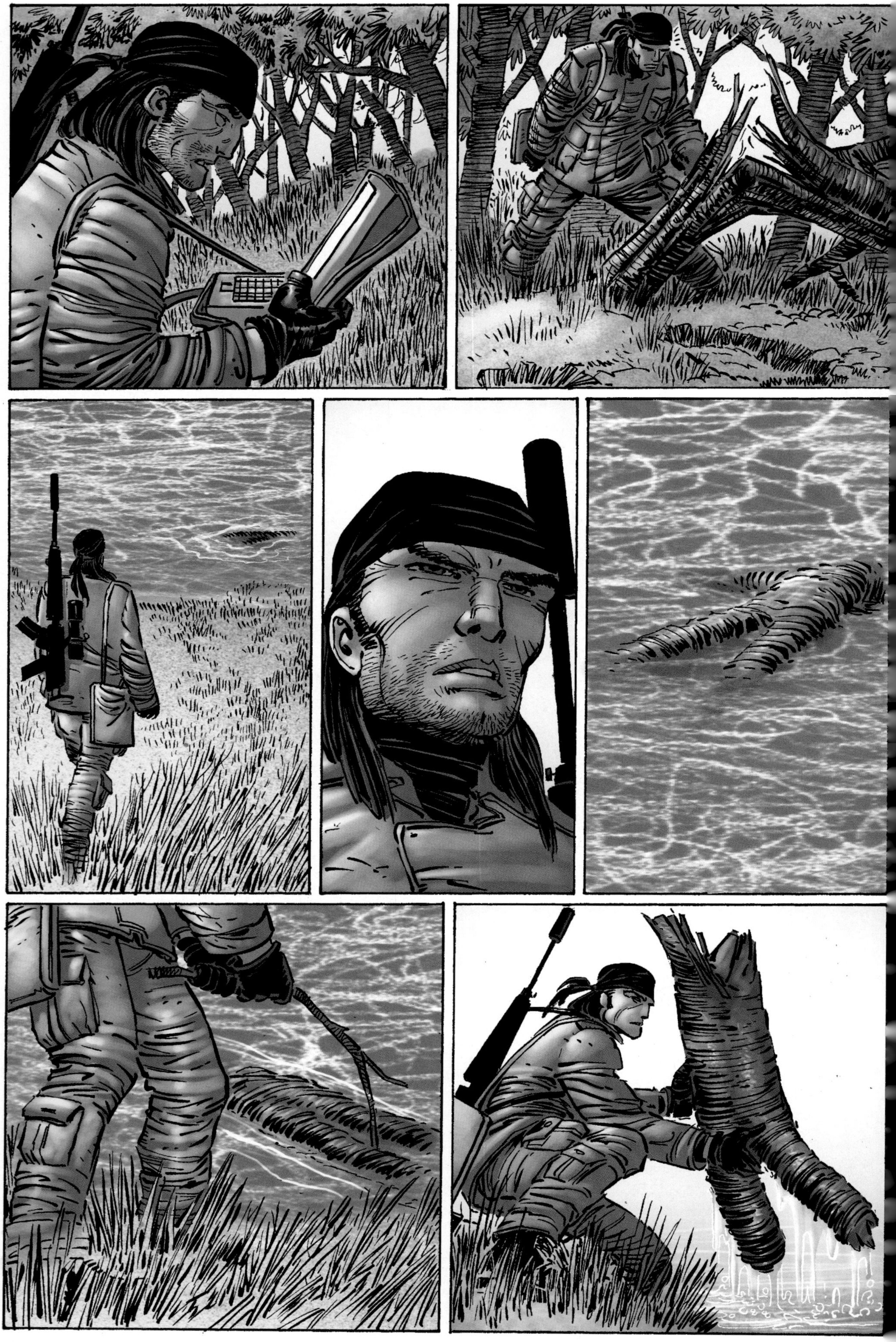

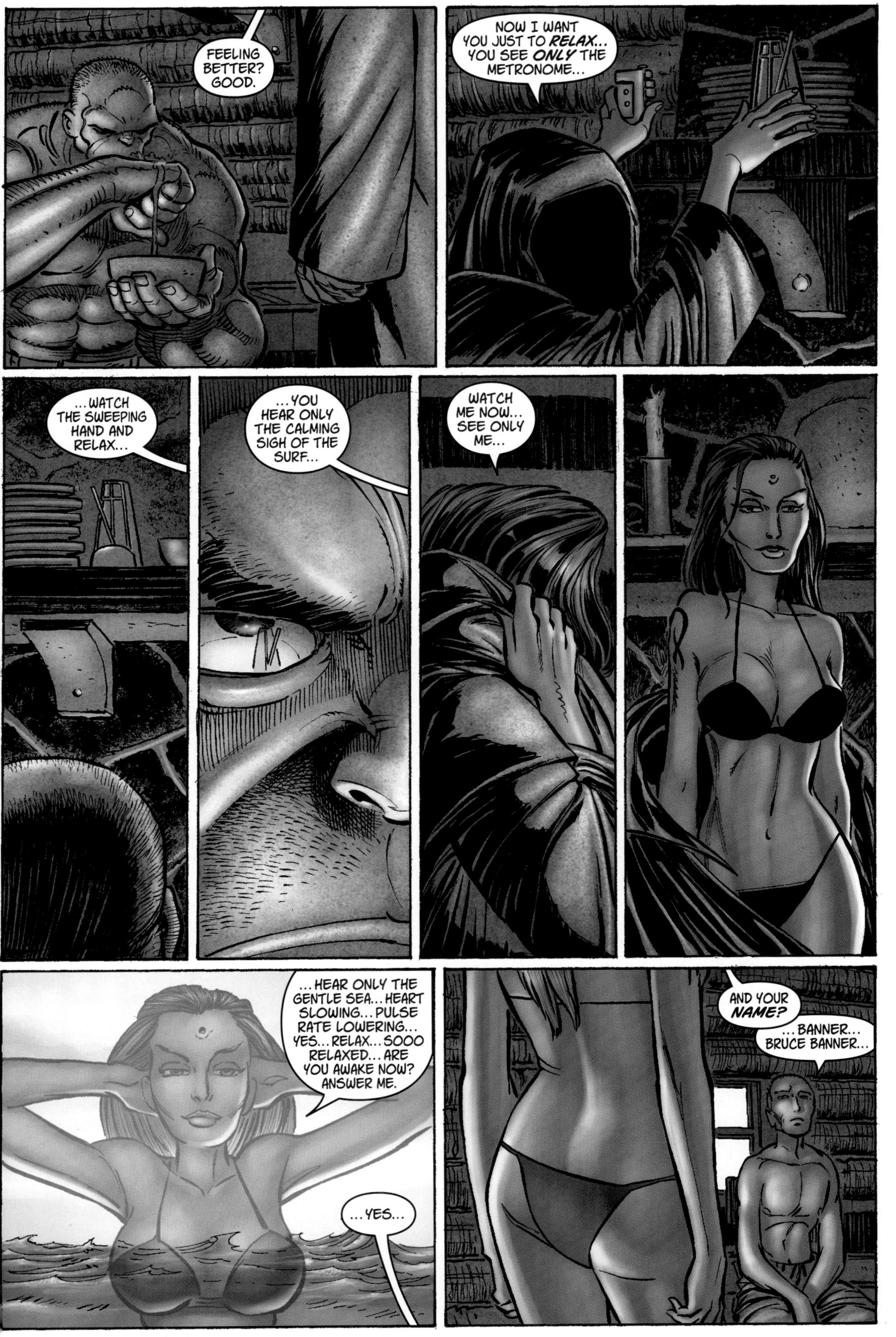
FEELING BETTER? GOOD.
NOW I WANT YOU JUST TO RELAX... YOU SEE ONLY THE METRONOME...
...WATCH THE SWEEPING HAND AND RELAX...
...YOU HEAR ONLY THE CALMING SIGH OF THE SURF...
WATCH ME NOW... SEE ONLY ME...
...HEAR ONLY THE GENTLE SEA... HEART SLOWING... PULSE RATE LOWERING... YES... RELAX... SOOO RELAXED... ARE YOU AWAKE NOW? ANSWER ME.
...YES...
AND YOUR NAME?
...BANNER... BRUCE BANNER...

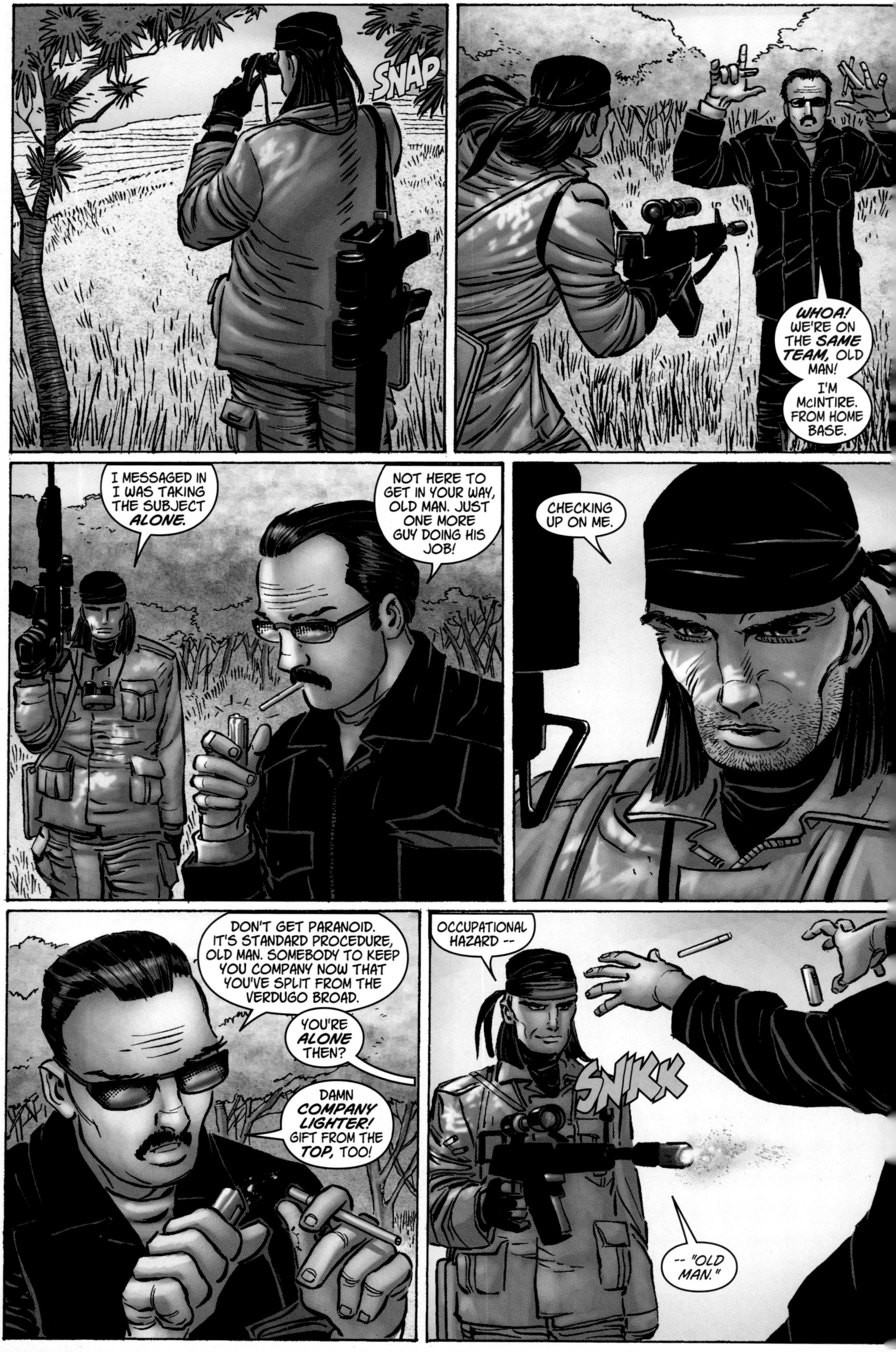
SNAP
WHOA! WE'RE ON THE SAME TEAM, OLD MAN!
I'M McINTIRE. FROM HOME BASE.
I MESSAGED IN I WAS TAKING THE SUBJECT ALONE.
NOT HERE TO GET IN YOUR WAY, OLD MAN. JUST ONE MORE GUY DOING HIS JOB!
CHECKING UP ON ME.
DON'T GET PARANOID. IT'S STANDARD PROCEDURE, OLD MAN. SOMEBODY TO KEEP YOU COMPANY NOW THAT YOU'VE SPLIT FROM THE VERDUGO BROAD.
YOU'RE ALONE THEN?
DAMN COMPANY LIGHTER! GIFT FROM THE TOP, TOO!
OCCUPATIONAL HAZARD --
SNIKK
-- "OLD MAN."

YOU'RE THE WOMAN FROM THE DINER... THE ONE SAMSON WARNED ME ABOUT...

HOW DID YOU KNOW ABOUT MY PERSONAL MEDITATION TECHNIQUES?

I KNOW *EVERYTHING* ABOUT YOU. THAT'S AN ASSASSIN'S *JOB*.

WHERE'S YOUR PARTNER? *SLATER* -- THAT HIS NAME?

PROBABLY *CLOSER* THAN EITHER OF US WANTS.

RELAX. IT'S *JUST* SCOTCH.

NOT THE STUFF YOU PUT IN MY *ICED TEA* AT THE DINER?

I HAD NO GUARANTEE YOU'D DRINK THAT. SO I SLIPPED YOU A LITTLE SOMETHING *BEFOREHAND*, JUST TO BE SURE...

SPIKED RING. WE SHOOK HANDS, REMEMBER, JUST BEFORE I SAT DOWN? NOT ENOUGH TO KNOCK YOU OUT... JUST MAKE YOU WALK IN YOUR SLEEP A BIT... MAKE YOU EASIER TO TRACK.

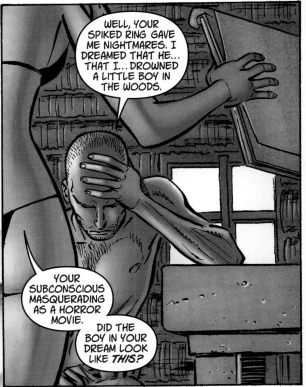

WELL, YOUR SPIKED RING GAVE ME NIGHTMARES. I DREAMED THAT HE... THAT I...DROWNED A LITTLE BOY IN THE WOODS.

YOUR SUBCONSCIOUS MASQUERADING AS A HORROR MOVIE.

DID THE BOY IN YOUR DREAM LOOK LIKE *THIS?*

YES. *RICKY MYERS.* THE KID WHO DIED IN THE CHICAGO BUILDING COLLAPSE. HOW DID YOU KNOW?

HE'S MY *SON.*

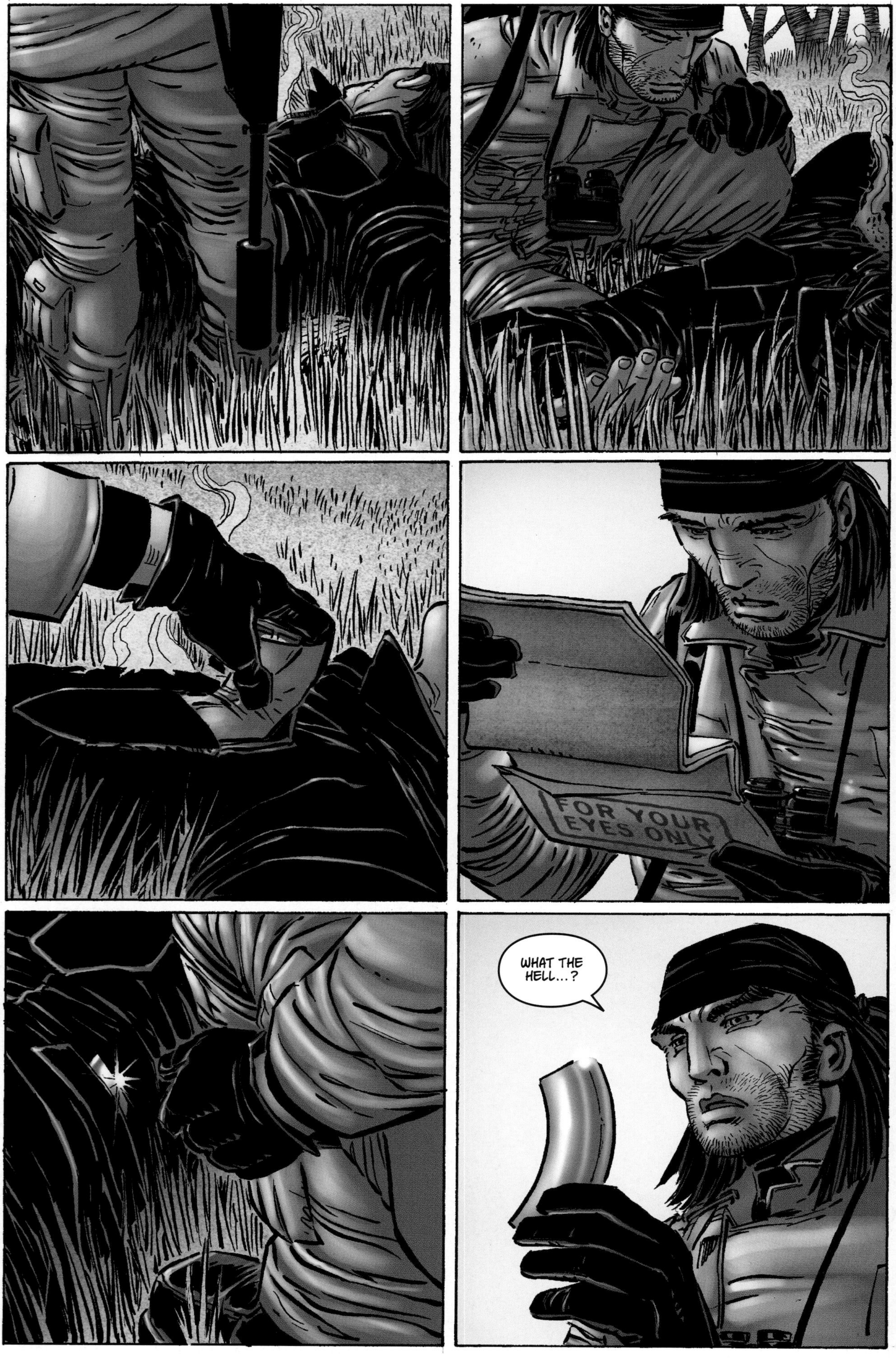
FOR YOUR EYES ONLY
WHAT THE HELL...?

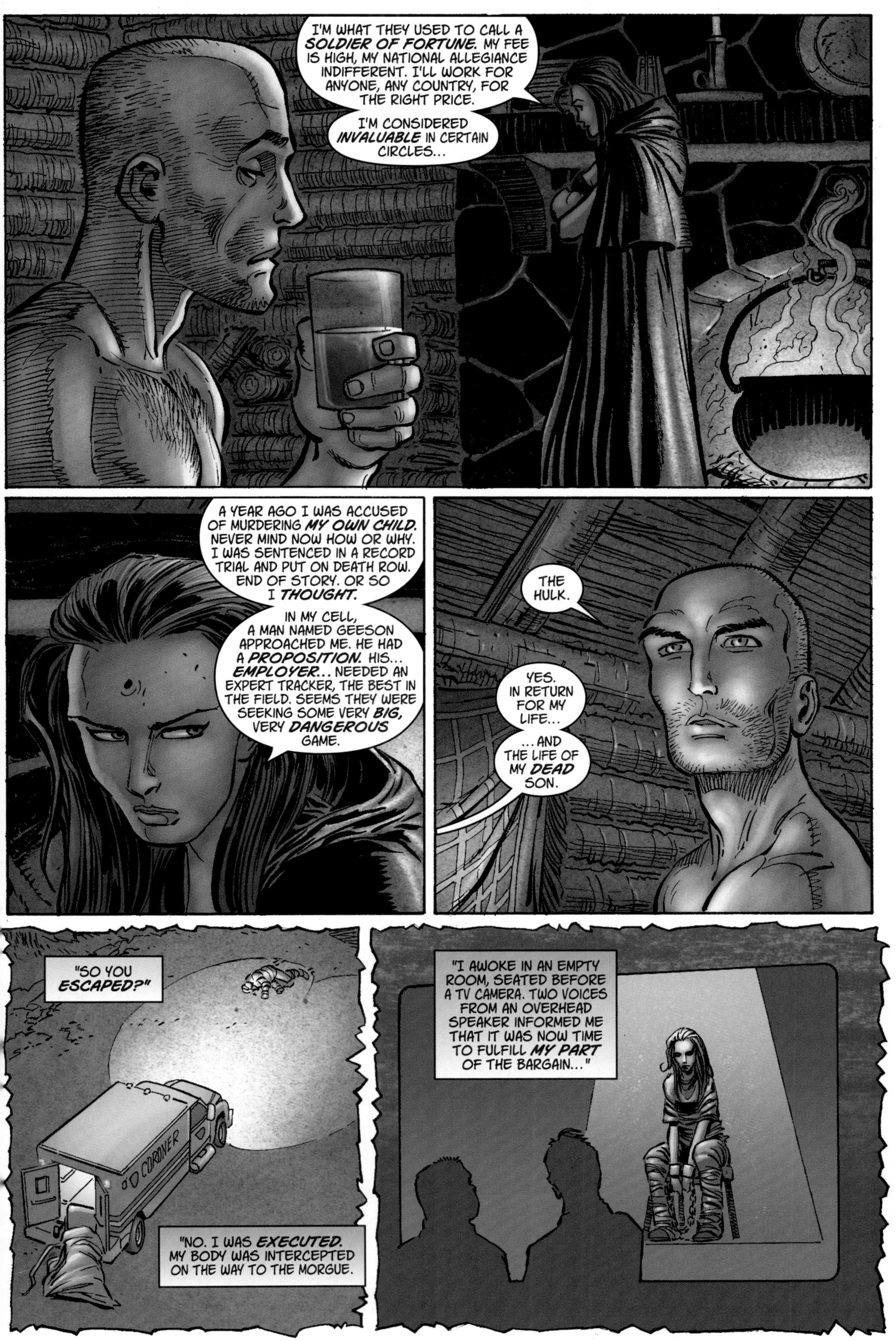
I'M WHAT THEY USED TO CALL A SOLDIER OF FORTUNE. MY FEE IS HIGH, MY NATIONAL ALLEGIANCE INDIFFERENT. I'LL WORK FOR ANYONE, ANY COUNTRY, FOR THE RIGHT PRICE.
I'M CONSIDERED INVALUABLE IN CERTAIN CIRCLES...
A YEAR AGO I WAS ACCUSED OF MURDERING MY OWN CHILD. NEVER MIND NOW HOW OR WHY. I WAS SENTENCED IN A RECORD TRIAL AND PUT ON DEATH ROW. END OF STORY. OR SO I THOUGHT.
IN MY CELL, A MAN NAMED GEESON APPROACHED ME. HE HAD A PROPOSITION. HIS... EMPLOYER... NEEDED AN EXPERT TRACKER, THE BEST IN THE FIELD. SEEMS THEY WERE SEEKING SOME VERY BIG, VERY DANGEROUS GAME.
THE HULK.
YES. IN RETURN FOR MY LIFE...
...AND THE LIFE OF MY DEAD SON.
"SO YOU ESCAPED?"
CORONER
"NO. I WAS EXECUTED. MY BODY WAS INTERCEPTED ON THE WAY TO THE MORGUE.
"I AWOKE IN AN EMPTY ROOM, SEATED BEFORE A TV CAMERA. TWO VOICES FROM AN OVERHEAD SPEAKER INFORMED ME THAT IT WAS NOW TIME TO FULFILL MY PART OF THE BARGAIN..."

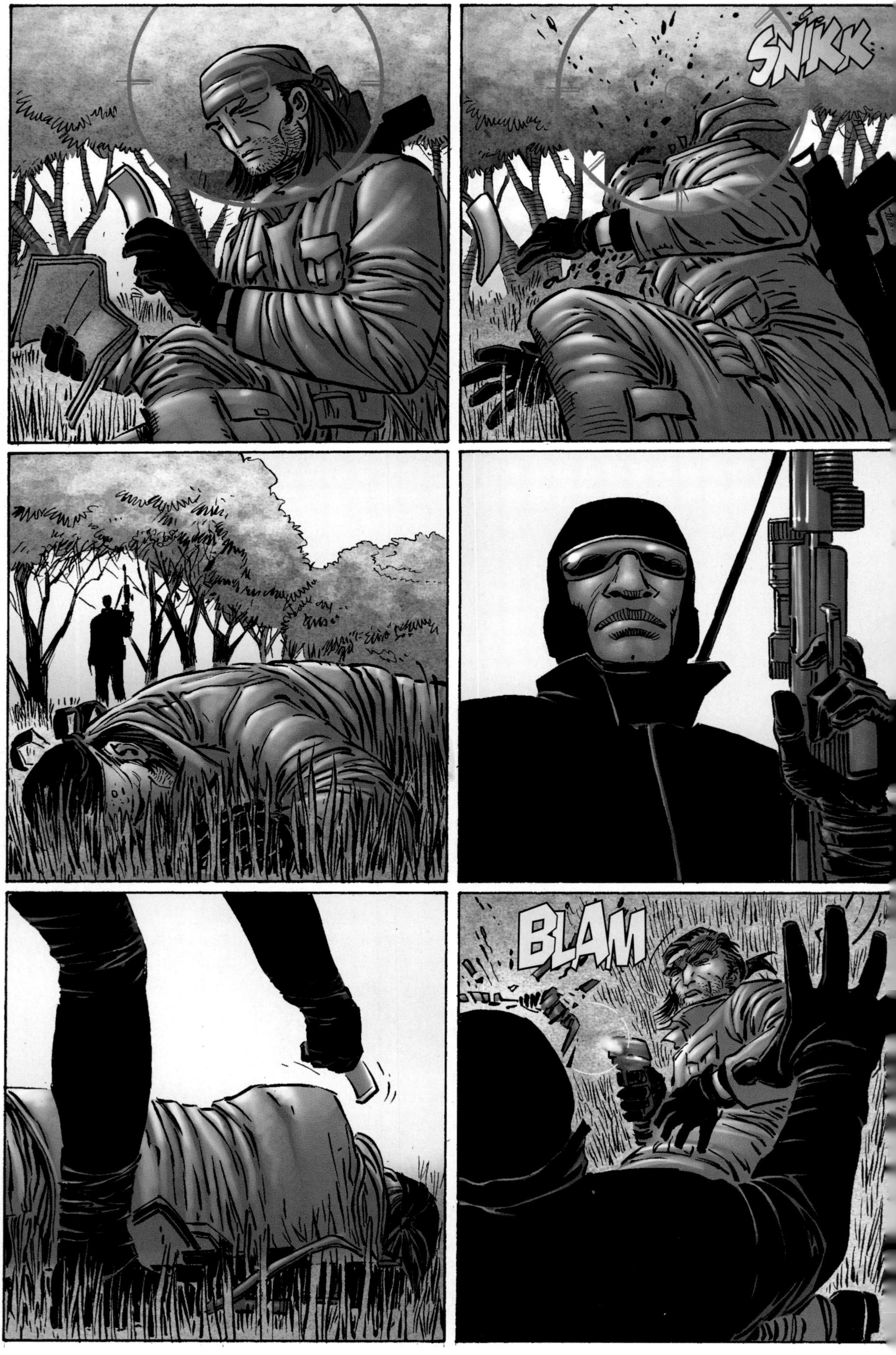
SNIKK
BLAM

AND WHO *ARE* THESE PEOPLE WHO WANT ME SO BAD? WHERE ARE *THEY* FROM?

I HAVE *NO* IDEA. ALL I WANT IS MY CHILD BACK.

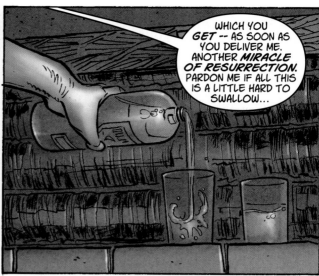

WHICH YOU *GET* -- AS SOON AS YOU DELIVER ME. ANOTHER *MIRACLE OF RESURRECTION.* PARDON ME IF ALL THIS IS A LITTLE HARD TO SWALLOW...

YOU SAW SLATER SHOOT ME AT THE DINER...YOU CAN SEE THE BULLET HOLE IN MY HEAD. DO I *LOOK* DEAD?

FRANKLY --

OKAY, BUT DO I *SOUND* DEAD?

THEY MEAN TO *HAVE* YOU, MR. BANNER, WHETHER *I* DO THE JOB OR NOT.

WHAT EXACTLY IS IT THEY *WANT* FROM ME?

NOT FROM YOU. FROM THE *HULK.*

I'VE ONLY BEEN ABLE TO PIECE TOGETHER SCRAPS OF IT. BUT IF THEY CAN BRING *DEAD PEOPLE* BACK TO LIFE... I'D RATHER NOT CONTEMPLATE THEIR PLANS FOR THE HULK, WOULD *YOU?*

YOU'VE *SEEN* THEIR OPERATION?

ONLY THE *DARK ROOM.* I WAS TAKEN BLINDFOLDED FROM THEIR HEADQUARTERS AND PUT TOGETHER WITH SLATER. WE WERE PART OF AN *ELITE TEAM,* HIRED TO HUNT YOU DOWN. NEITHER OF US WAS TOLD THE LOCATION OF HOME BASE.

THE FIRST NIGHT OUT, I WAS UNPACKING IN OUR MOTEL AND FOUND A LITTLE SURPRISE AMONG MY UNDERTHINGS...

A *COMPUTER DISC?* WHO PUT IT THERE?

I HAVE NO IDEA. BUT IT TOOK ME OVER SEVENTY HOURS TO FIGURE OUT HOW TO DECIPHER THE ENCRYPTION.

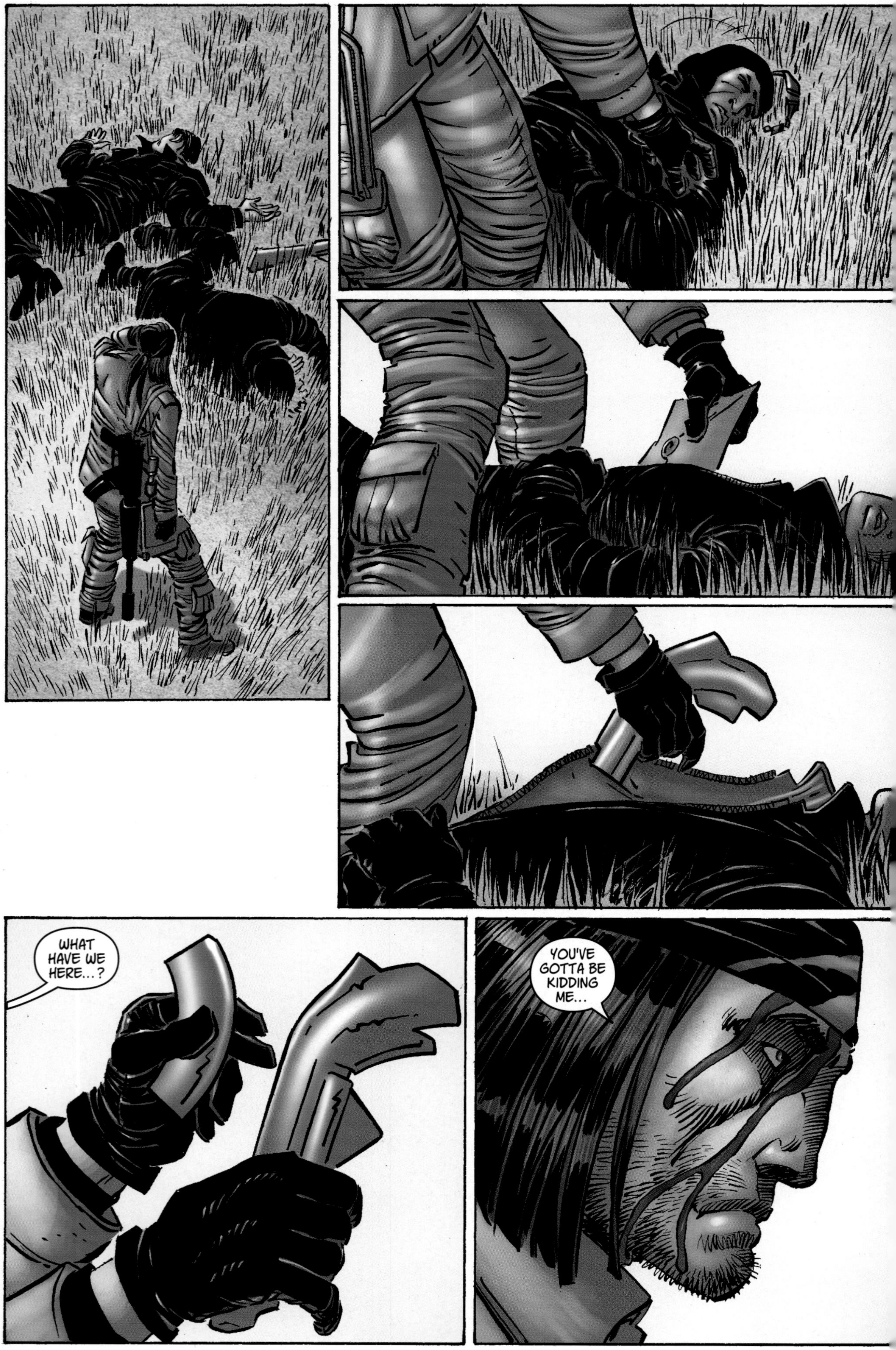
WHAT HAVE WE HERE...?
YOU'VE GOTTA BE KIDDING ME...

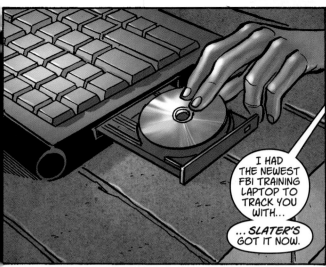

I HAD THE NEWEST FBI TRAINING LAPTOP TO TRACK YOU WITH...

...SLATER'S GOT IT NOW.

WE'LL JUST HAVE TO HOPE YOUR LITTLE NUMBER HERE IS UP TO THE TASK.

THERE'S JUST ONE TINY *PROBLEM* BEFORE I BEGIN...

WHICH IS?

SLATER'S LAPTOP IS *KEYED* TO THIS DISC. IF I'M ABLE TO BRING IT UP... WHATEVER WE SEE, *HE'LL* SEE.

AND THAT WILL *DOUBLE* HIS CAPACITY TO *TRACK* US.

DO IT. I CAN HANDLE SLATER.

I ADMIRE YOUR CONFIDENCE... EVEN IF IT'S *MISPLACED.* SLATER'S THE BEST KILLER IN THE BUSINESS. NEXT TO *ME.*

OKAY... THE BALL'S IN MOTION...

TOUCHDOWN...

...THE CROWD GOES WILD.

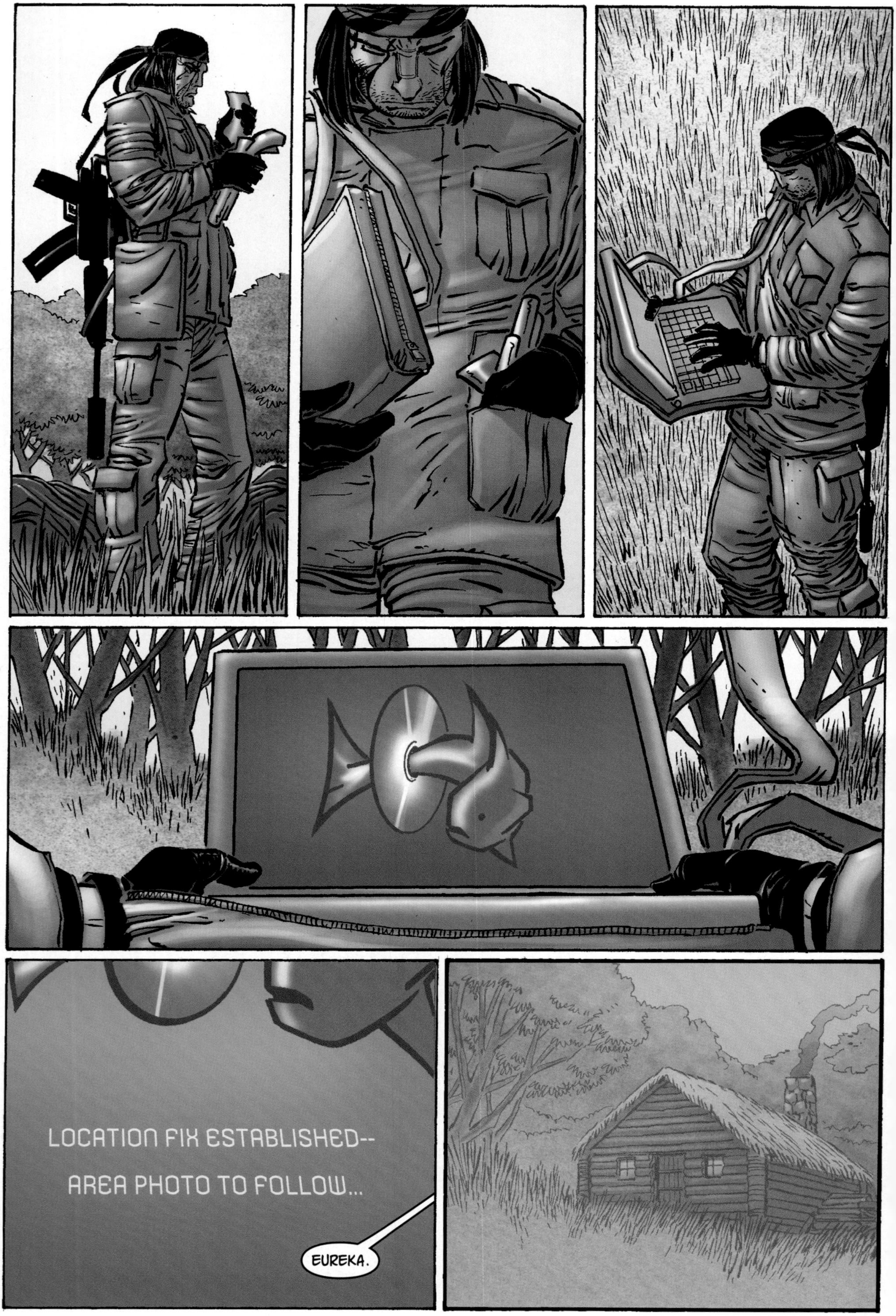
LOCATION FIX ESTABLISHED--
AREA PHOTO TO FOLLOW...
EUREKA.

WHO'S *THIS* GUY?

THAT'S *COLESON*... ONE OF THE AGENTS WORKING FOR THE SAME PEOPLE THAT HIRED ME.

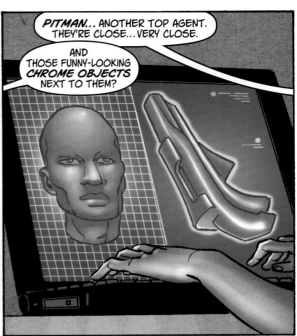

PITMAN... ANOTHER TOP AGENT. THEY'RE CLOSE... VERY CLOSE.

AND THOSE FUNNY-LOOKING *CHROME* OBJECTS NEXT TO THEM?

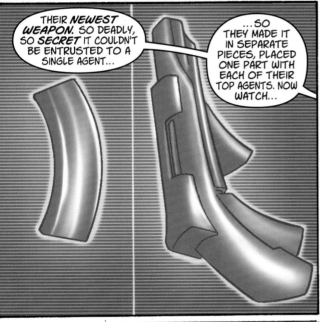

THEIR *NEWEST* WEAPON. SO DEADLY, SO *SECRET* IT COULDN'T BE ENTRUSTED TO A SINGLE AGENT...

...SO THEY MADE IT IN SEPARATE PIECES, PLACED ONE PART WITH EACH OF THEIR TOP AGENTS. NOW WATCH...

A *GUN*.

WHAT'S IT *DO*?

MOSQUITO--3X217 PROTOTYPE-- TOP SECRET.

KILLS HULKS, I IMAGINE... OR DROPS THEM IN THEIR TRACKS, ANYWAY.

FOR YOUR EYES ONLY

WHICH MAKES YOU AND SLATER *OBSOLETE*.

WE WERE OBSOLETE FROM THE *BEGINNING*. IT WAS ALWAYS ABOUT WHO COULD GET TO YOU FIRST. SLATER AND I WERE JUST ADDED INSURANCE.

THEY LIED TO US. THE SAME WAY THEY LIED TO THE MEDIA WITH THAT FAKED NEWS FOOTAGE OF RICKY DYING IN CHICAGO.

YOU'RE GOING TO HELP ME GET MY SON BACK. MAYBE THEY HAVE HIM AT HOME BASE, MAYBE HE'S BEING KEPT SOMEWHERE ELSE.

BUT ONCE THEY'VE GOT THE HULK, MY SON BECOMES DISPOSABLE. I CAN'T LET THAT HAPPEN. *WON'T* LET THAT HAPPEN.

SO I'M THE RANSOM. RICKY FOR THE HULK. *THAT* THE STORY?

NOT QUITE...

EIGHT YEARS AGO, I WAS RUNNING GUNS FOR A SMALL ARGENTINE FACTION -- DOESN'T MATTER WHICH.

I MET AN AMERICAN BUSINESSMAN THERE DURING THE REBELLION. WE HAD AN *AFFAIR*...

THE RESULT: RICKY.

THE REBELLION WAS PUT DOWN IN THREE WEEKS. I LEFT ARGENTINA BEFORE MY FIRST TRIMESTER. I NEVER TOLD THE FATHER ABOUT RICKY... HAVEN'T SEEN HIM SINCE. NOT UNTIL *YESTERDAY*...

DOC SAMSON.

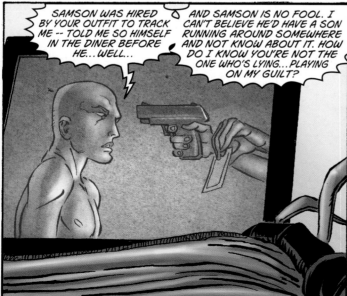

SAMSON WAS HIRED BY YOUR OUTFIT TO TRACK ME -- TOLD ME SO HIMSELF IN THE DINER BEFORE HE...WELL...

AND SAMSON IS NO FOOL. I CAN'T BELIEVE HE'D HAVE A SON RUNNING AROUND SOMEWHERE AND NOT KNOW ABOUT IT. HOW DO I KNOW YOU'RE NOT THE ONE WHO'S LYING...PLAYING ON MY GUILT?

SO MANY QUESTIONS... SO LITTLE TIME...

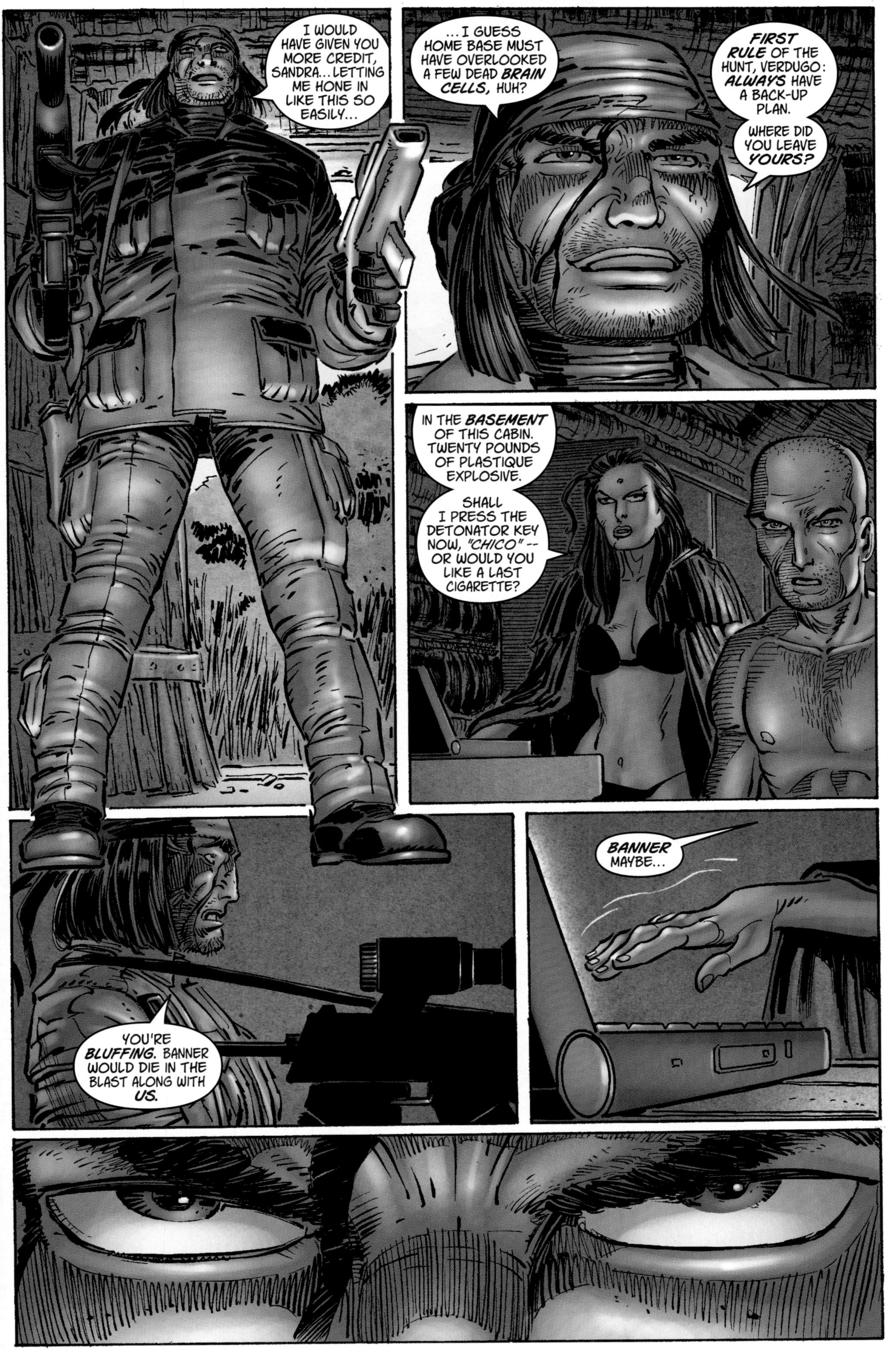
I WOULD HAVE GIVEN YOU MORE CREDIT, SANDRA... LETTING ME HONE IN LIKE THIS SO EASILY...
...I GUESS HOME BASE MUST HAVE OVERLOOKED A FEW DEAD BRAIN CELLS, HUH?
FIRST RULE OF THE HUNT, VERDUGO: ALWAYS HAVE A BACK-UP PLAN.
WHERE DID YOU LEAVE YOURS?
IN THE BASEMENT OF THIS CABIN. TWENTY POUNDS OF PLASTIQUE EXPLOSIVE.
SHALL I PRESS THE DETONATOR KEY NOW, "CHICO" -- OR WOULD YOU LIKE A LAST CIGARETTE?
YOU'RE BLUFFING. BANNER WOULD DIE IN THE BLAST ALONG WITH US.
BANNER MAYBE...

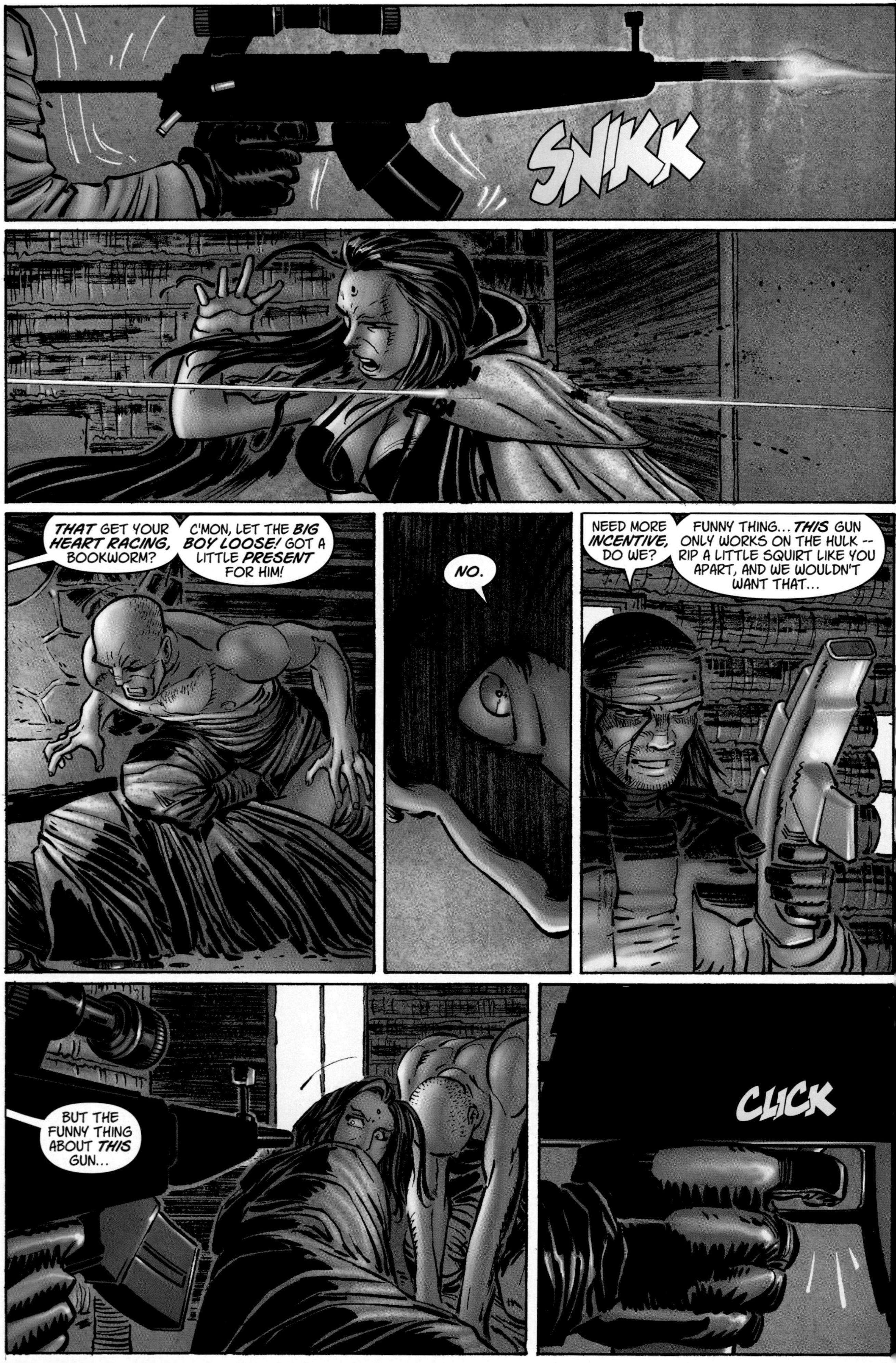
SNIKK
THAT GET YOUR HEART RACING, BOOKWORM?
C'MON, LET THE BIG BOY LOOSE! GOT A LITTLE PRESENT FOR HIM!
NO.
NEED MORE INCENTIVE, DO WE?
FUNNY THING... THIS GUN ONLY WORKS ON THE HULK -- RIP A LITTLE SQUIRT LIKE YOU APART, AND WE WOULDN'T WANT THAT...
BUT THE FUNNY THING ABOUT THIS GUN...
CLICK

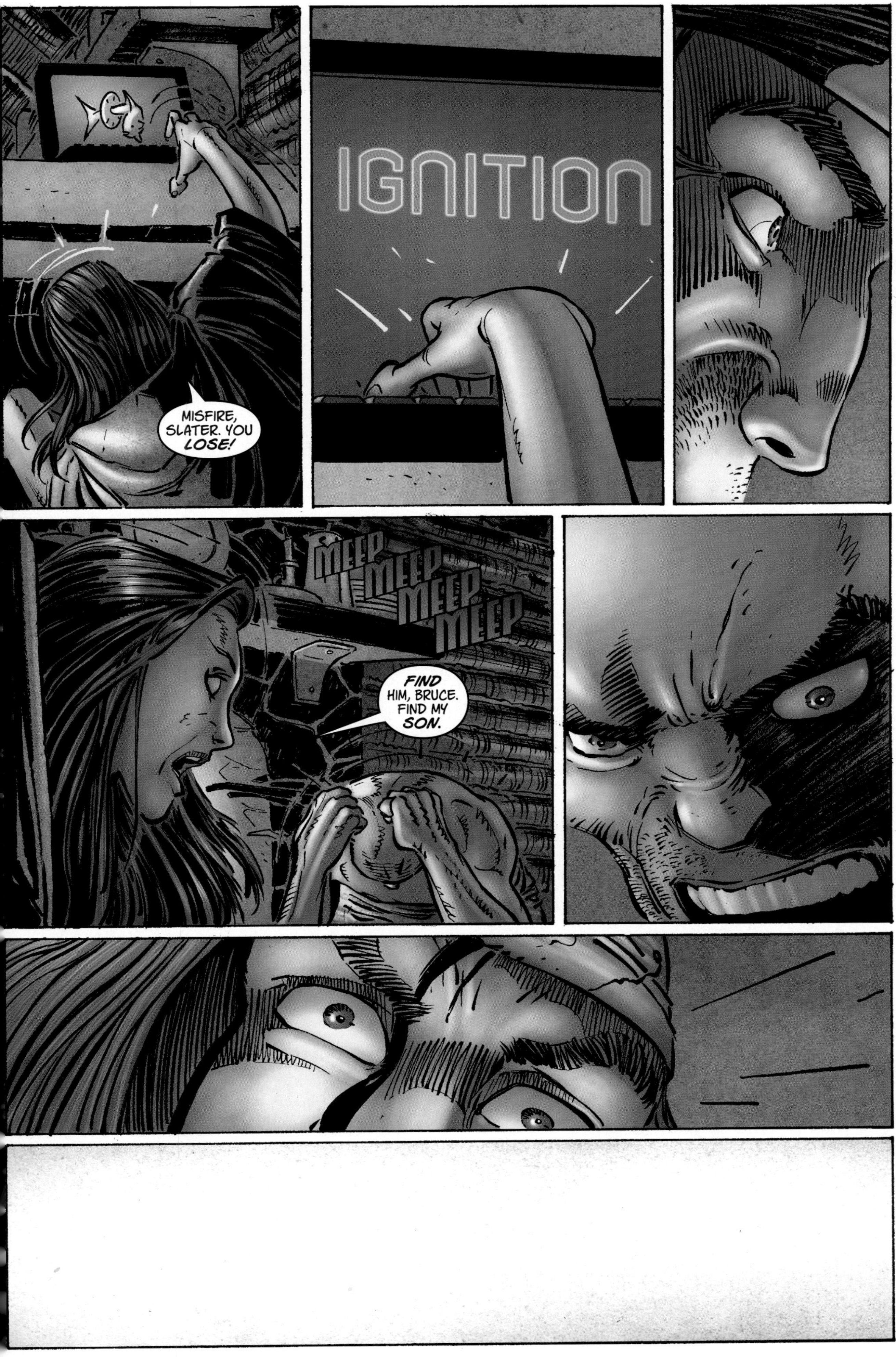
MISFIRE, SLATER. YOU LOSE!
IGNITION
MEEP MEEP MEEP MEEP
FIND HIM, BRUCE. FIND MY SON.

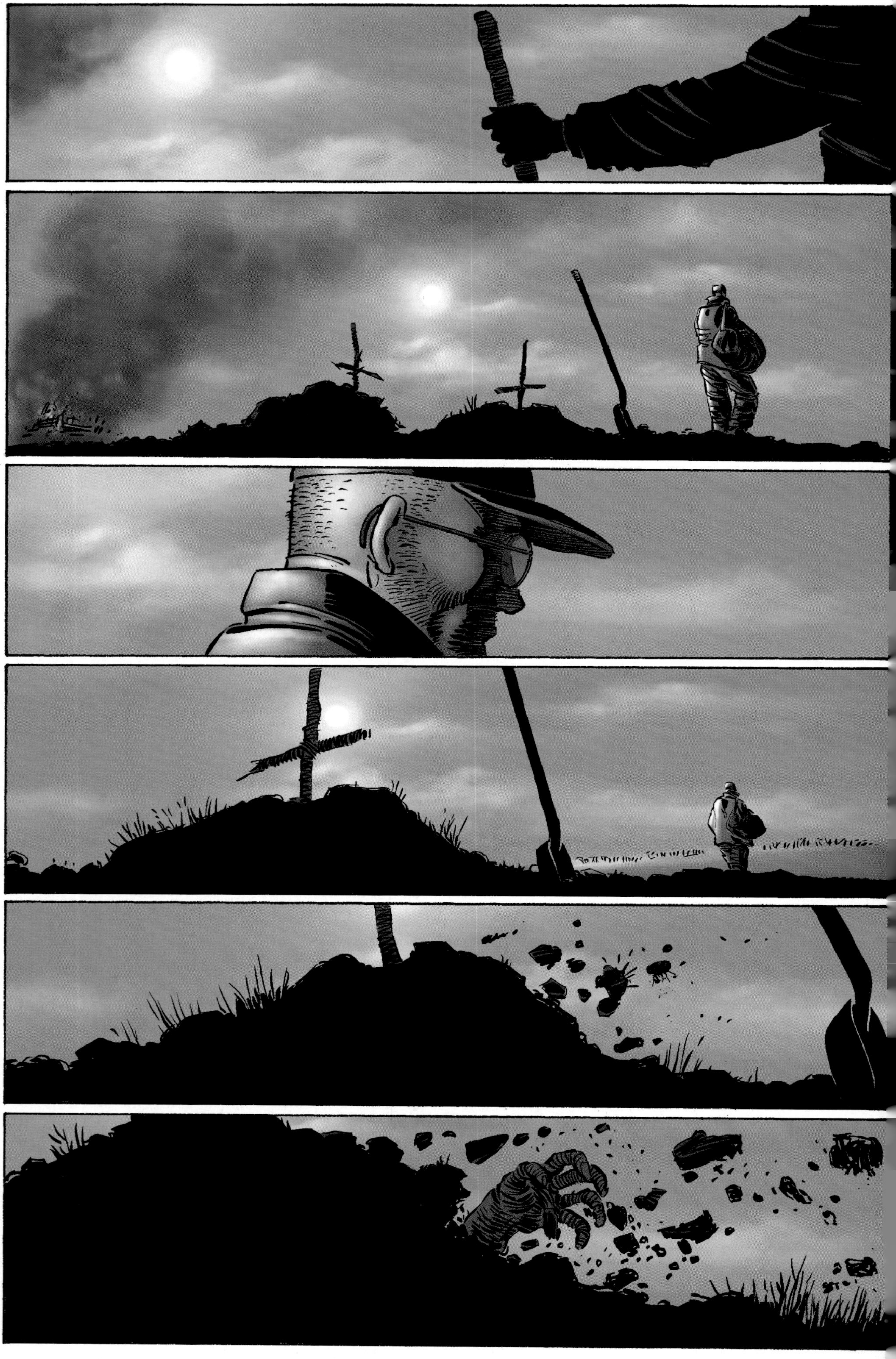

INCREDIBLE HULK #40
Cover sketch by Kaare Andrews

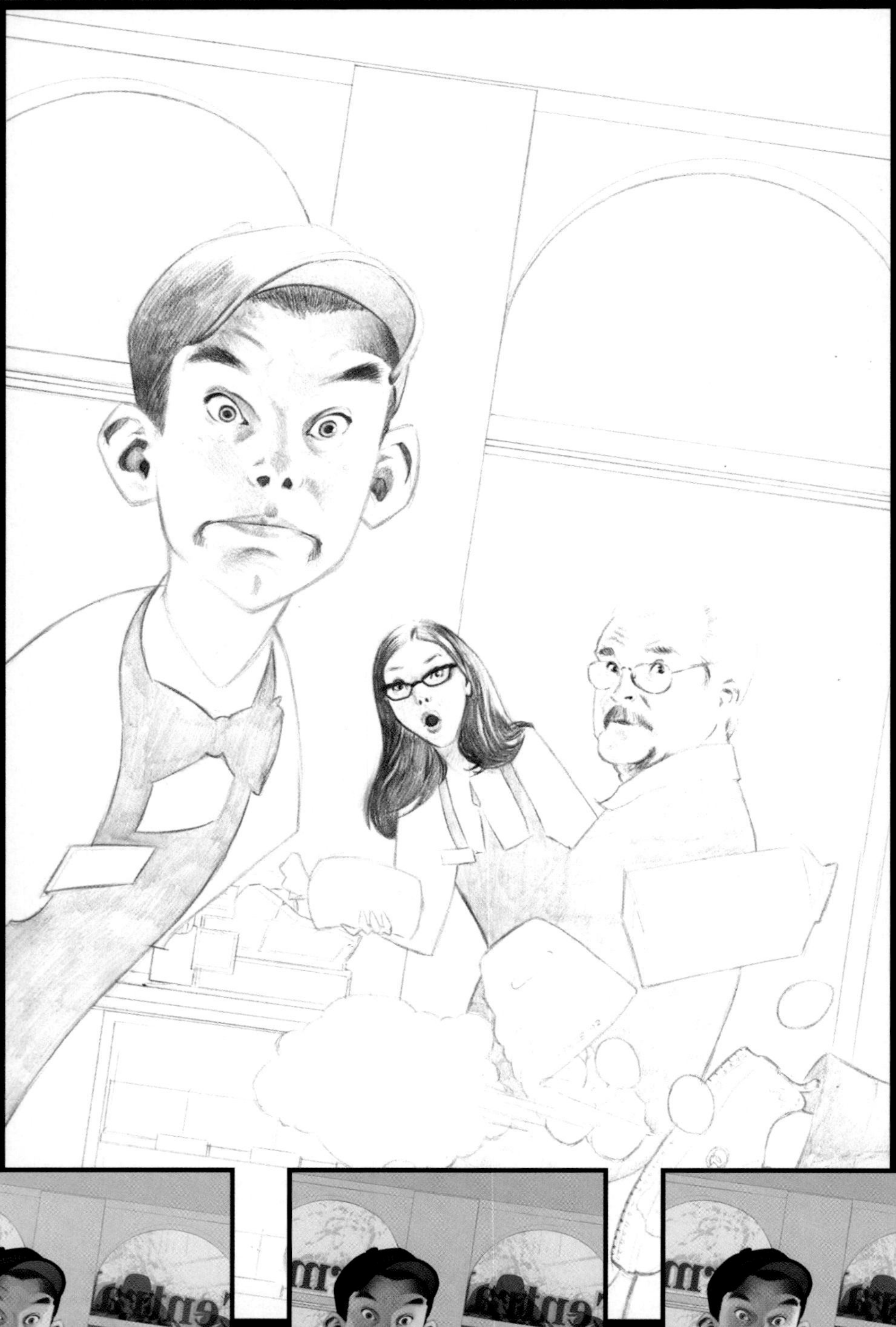

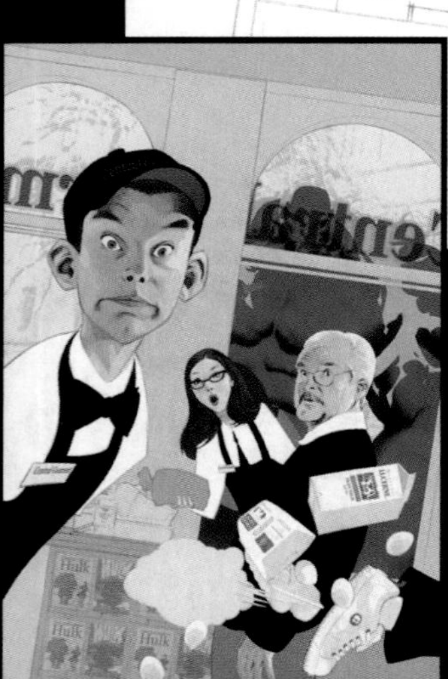

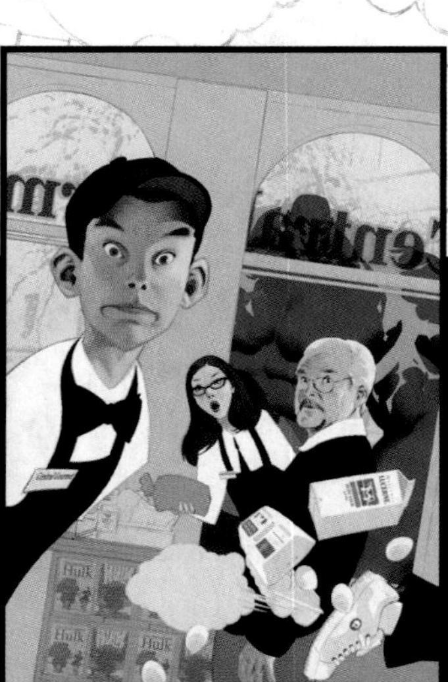

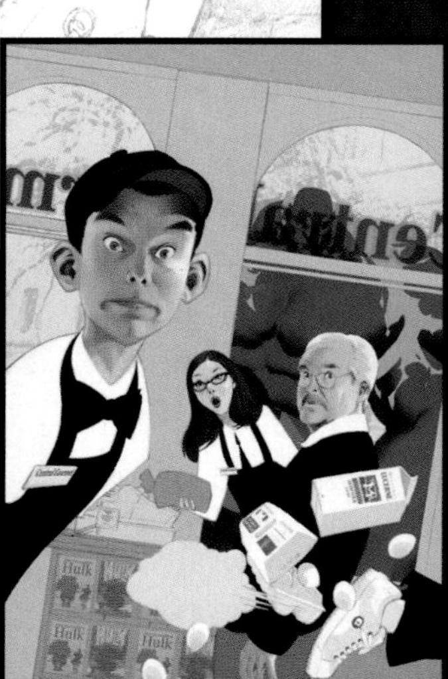

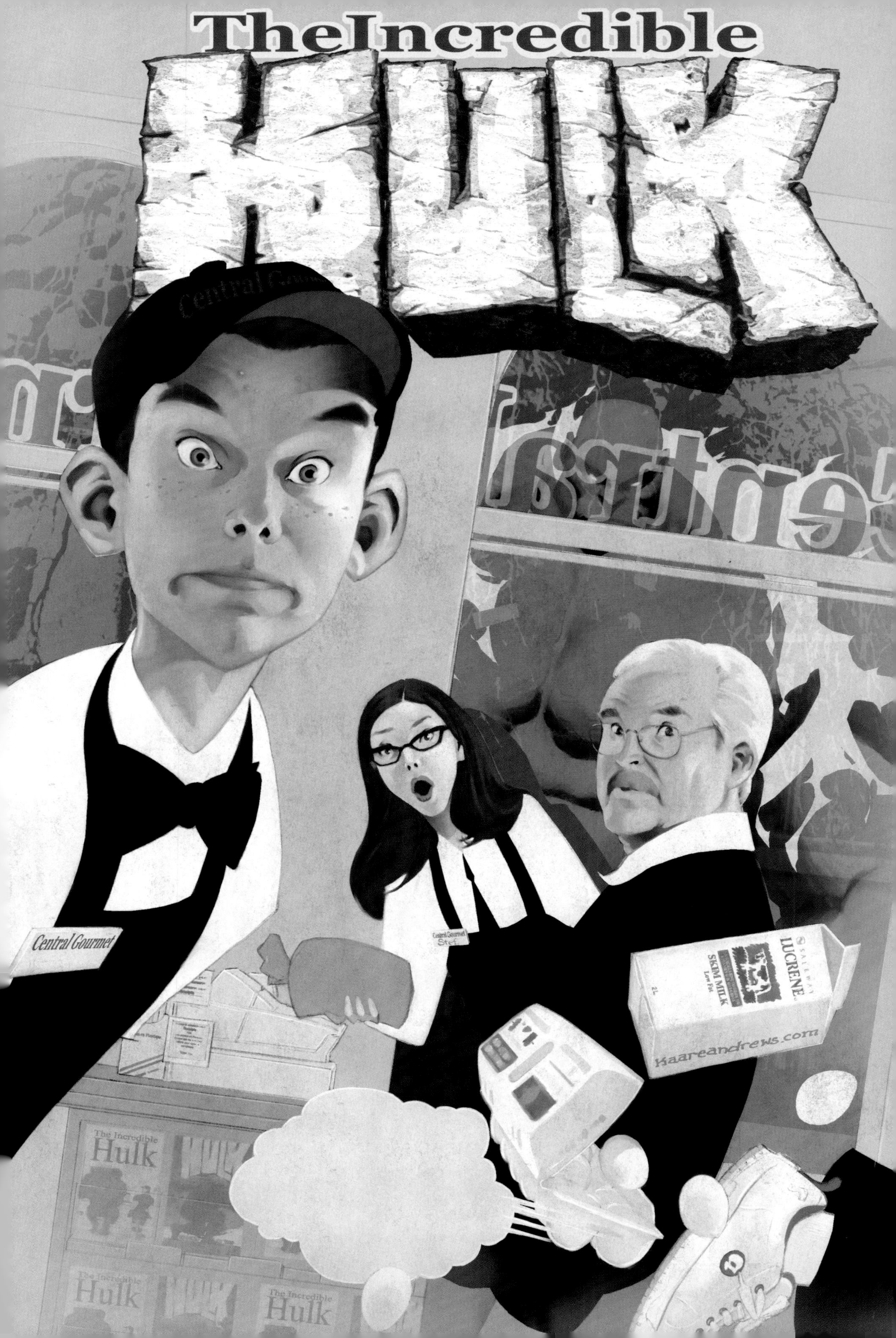

The Incredible
HULK
Central Gourmet
Central Gourmet
Stef
LUCERNE
SKIM MILK
2L
Kaareandrews.com
The Incredible
Hulk
The Incredible
Hulk
The Incredible
Hulk

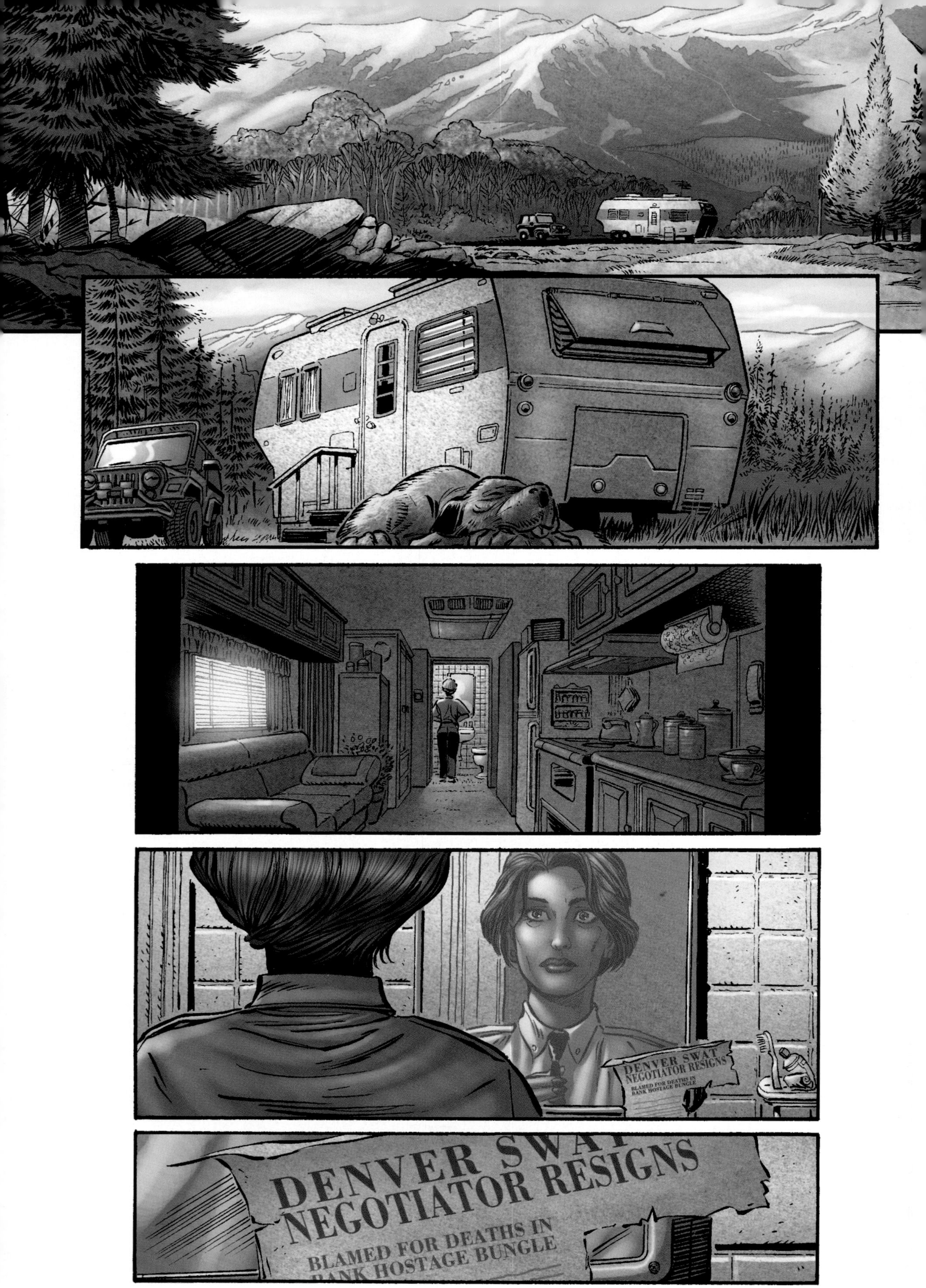
DENVER SWAT
NEGOTIATOR RESIGNS
BLAMED FOR DEATHS IN
BANK HOSTAGE BUNGLE
DENVER SWAT
NEGOTIATOR RESIGNS
BLAMED FOR DEATHS IN
HOSTAGE BUNGLE

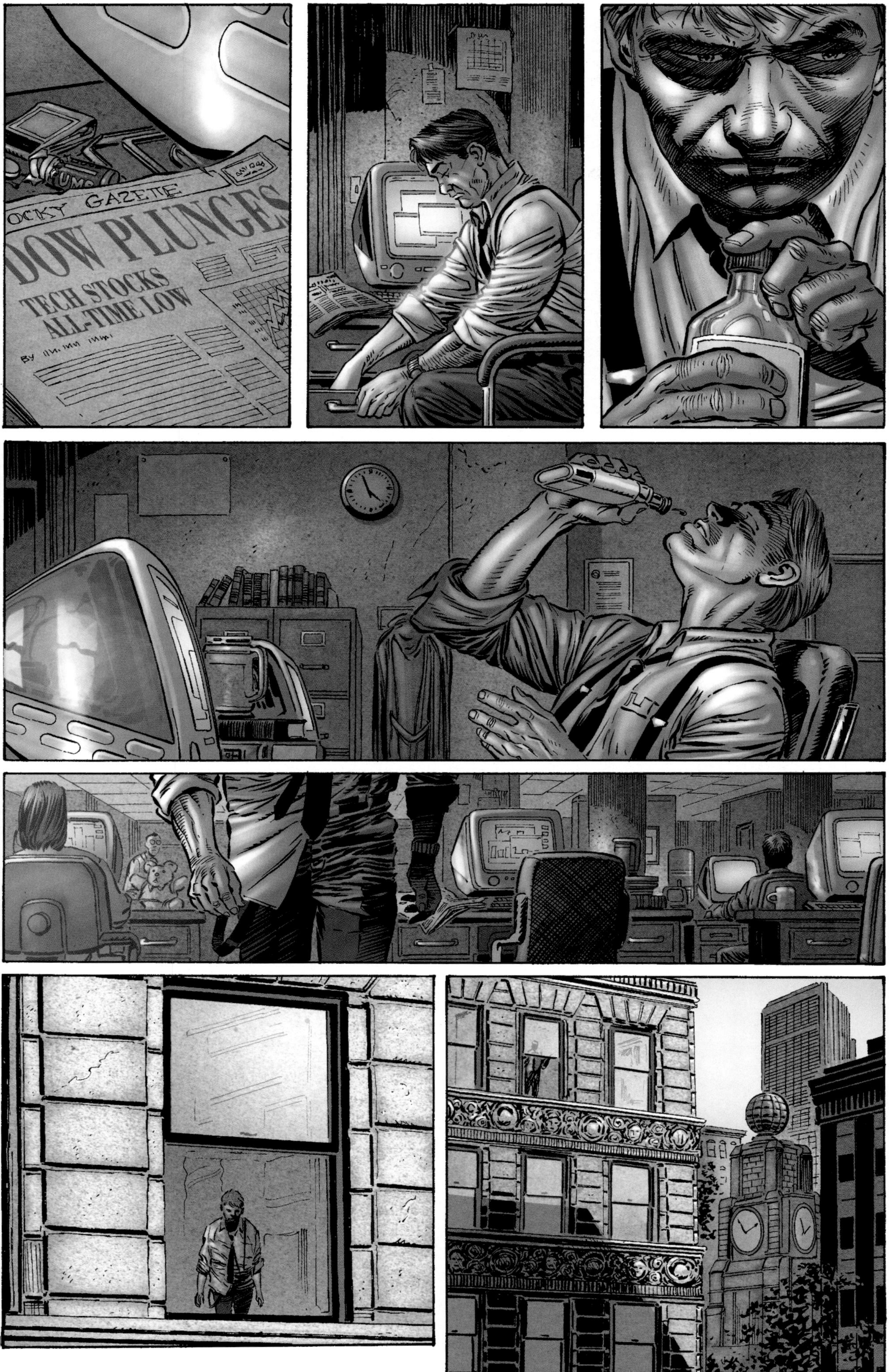
DOW PLUNGES
TECH STOCKS
ALL-TIME LOW

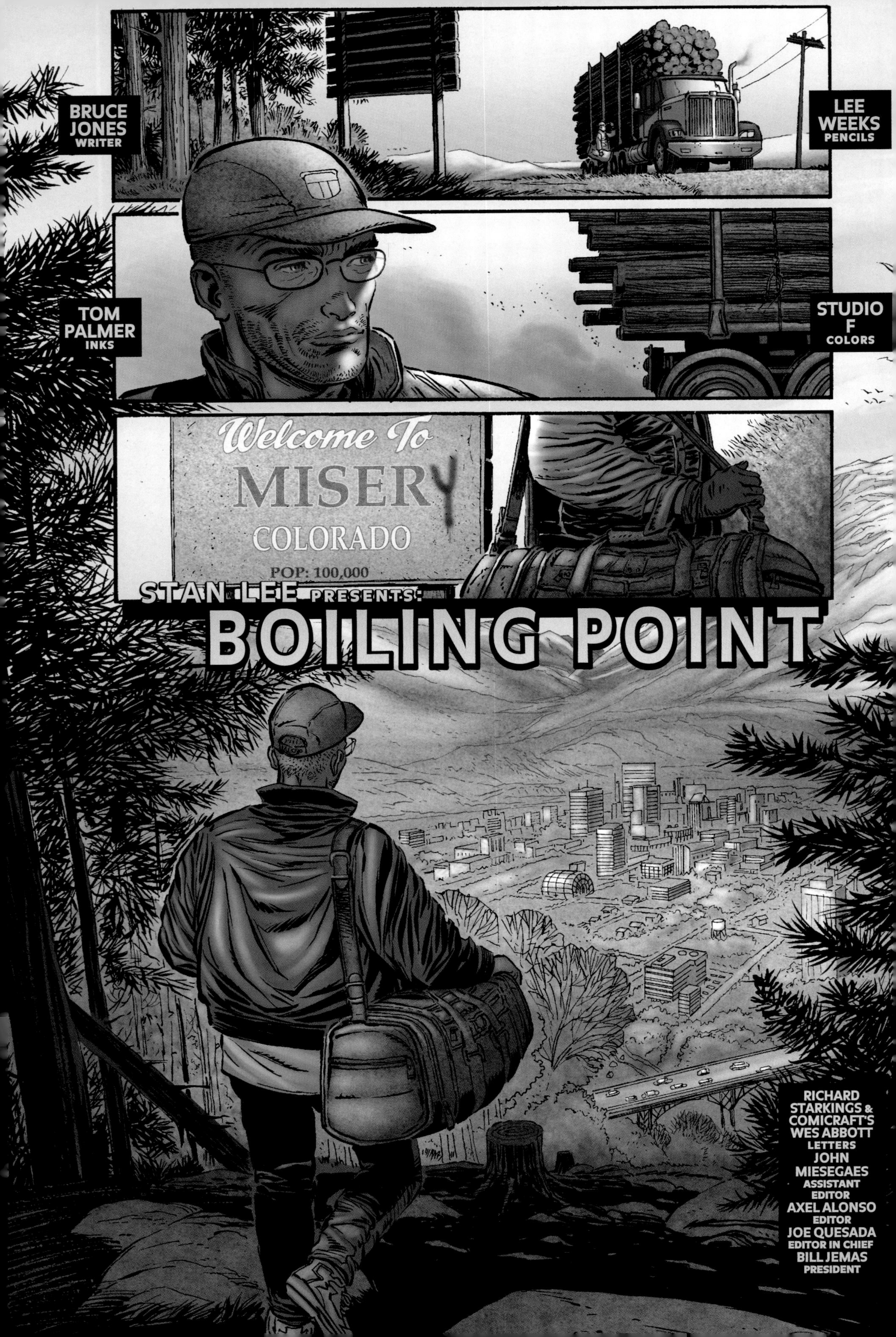
BRUCE JONES WRITER
LEE WEEKS PENCILS
TOM PALMER INKS
STUDIO F COLORS
Welcome To
MISERY
COLORADO
POP: 100,000
STAN LEE PRESENTS:
BOILING POINT
RICHARD STARKINGS & COMICRAFT'S WES ABBOTT LETTERS
JOHN MIESEGAES ASSISTANT EDITOR
AXEL ALONSO EDITOR
JOE QUESADA EDITOR IN CHIEF
BILL JEMAS PRESIDENT

DPD

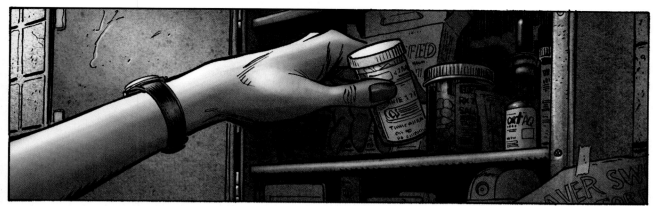

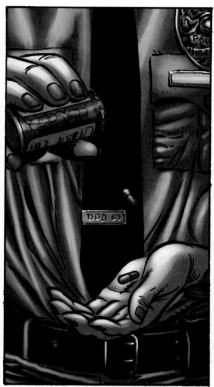

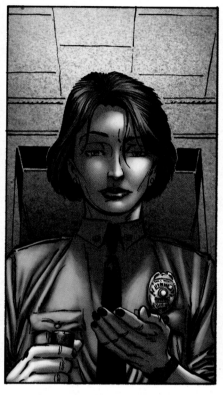

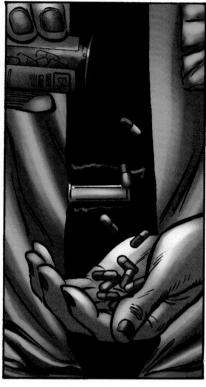

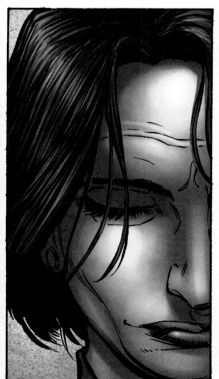

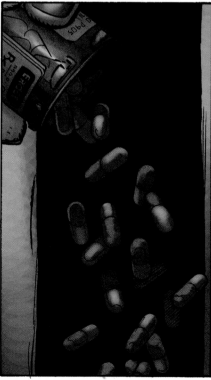

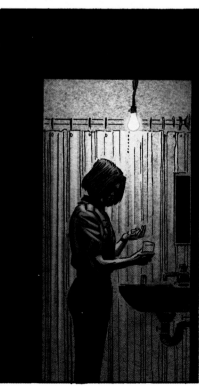

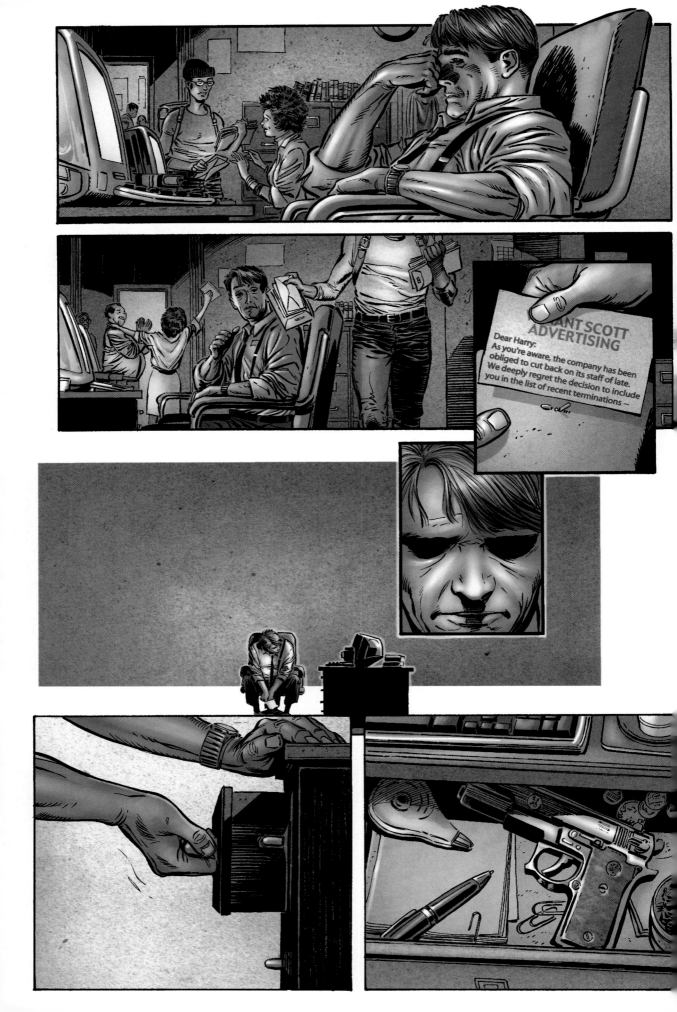

GRANT SCOTT
ADVERTISING

Dear Harry:
As you're aware, the company has been obliged to cut back on its staff of late. We deeply regret the decision to include you in the list of recent terminations —

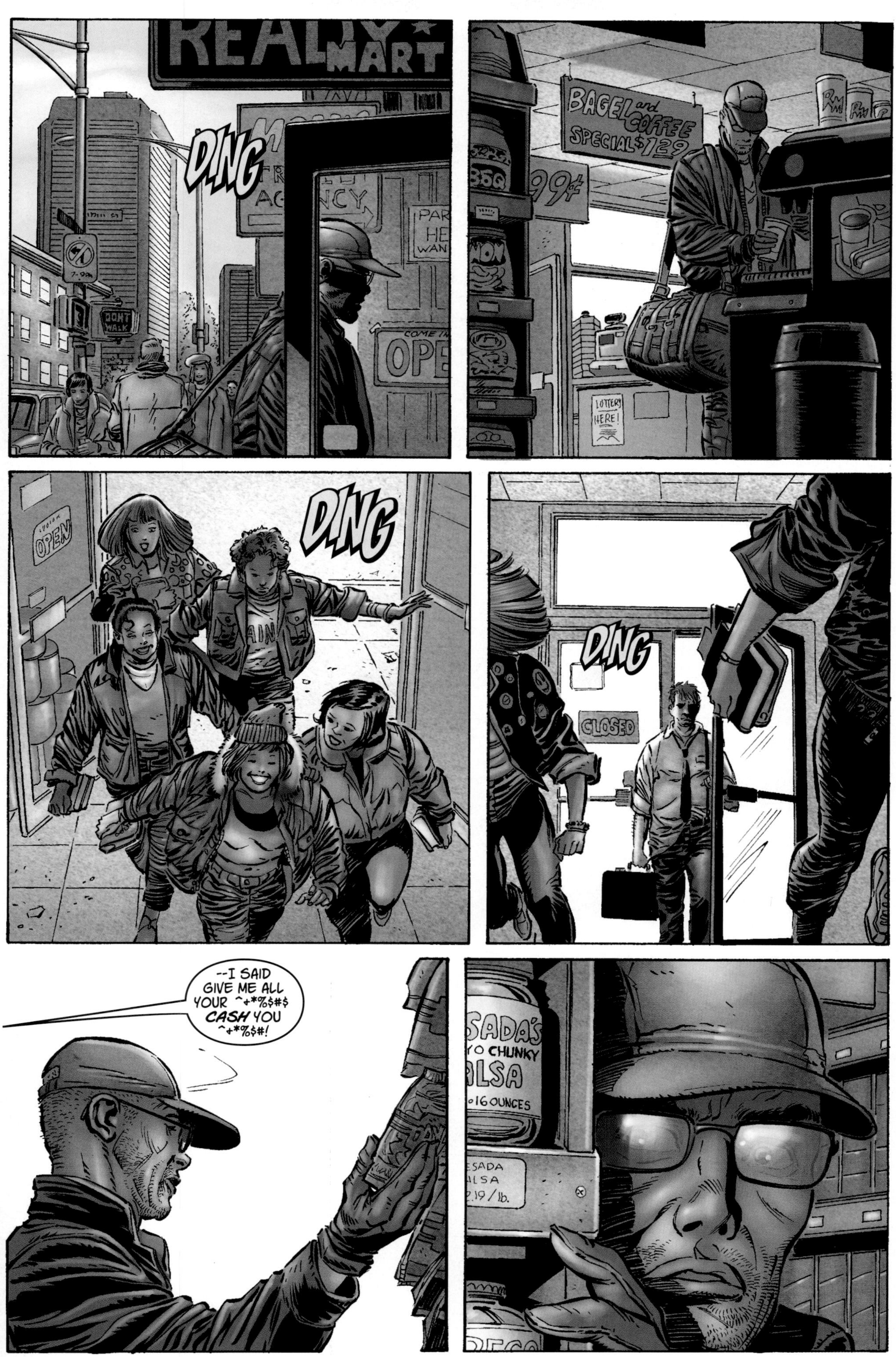
READY MART
DING
AGENCY
COME IN
OPEN
BAGEL and COFFEE SPECIAL $1.29
99¢
LOTTERY HERE!
DING
OPEN
DING
CLOSED
--I SAID GIVE ME ALL YOUR ^+*%$#$ CASH YOU ^+*%$#!
CHUNKY
16 OUNCES
2.19 / lb.

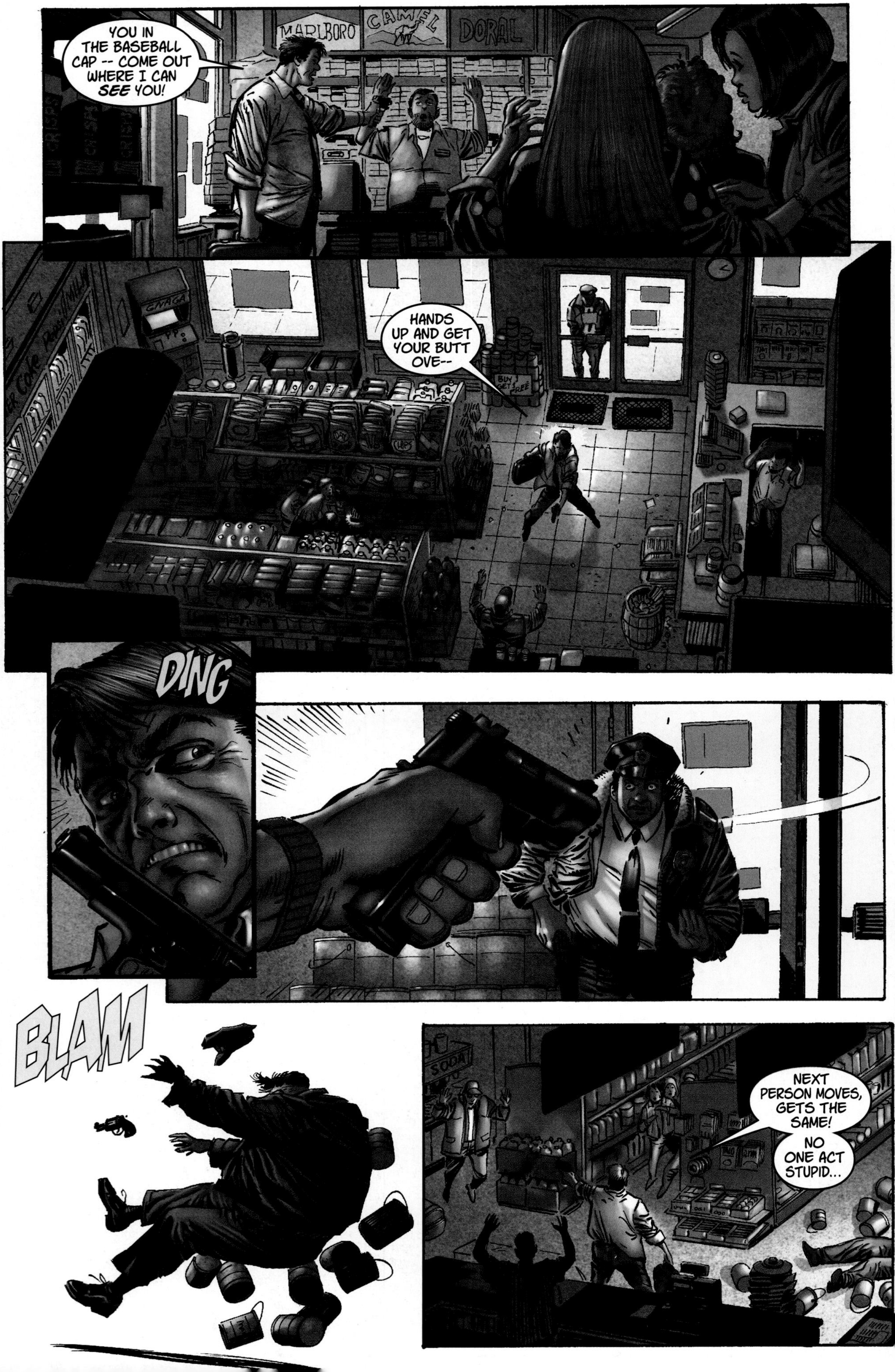
MARLBORO
CAMEL
DORAL
YOU IN THE BASEBALL CAP -- COME OUT WHERE I CAN *SEE* YOU!
HANDS UP AND GET YOUR BUTT OVE--
DING
BLAM
NEXT PERSON MOVES, GETS THE SAME!
NO ONE ACT STUPID...

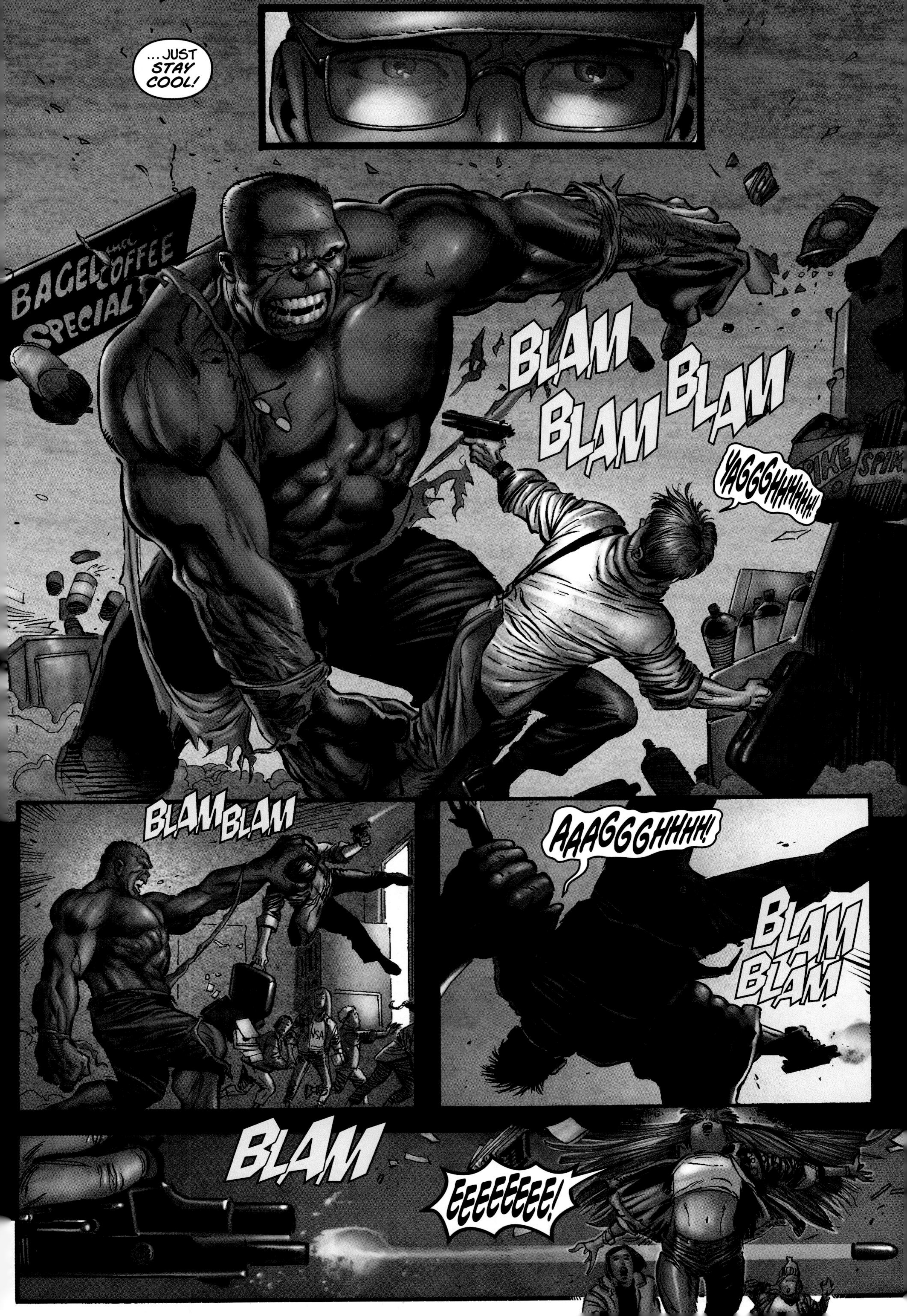

...JUST STAY COOL!
BAGEL and COFFEE SPECIAL
BLAM BLAM BLAM BLAM
YAGGGHHHHH!
BLAMBLAM
AAAGGGHHHH!
BLAM BLAM
BLAM
EEEEEEEE!

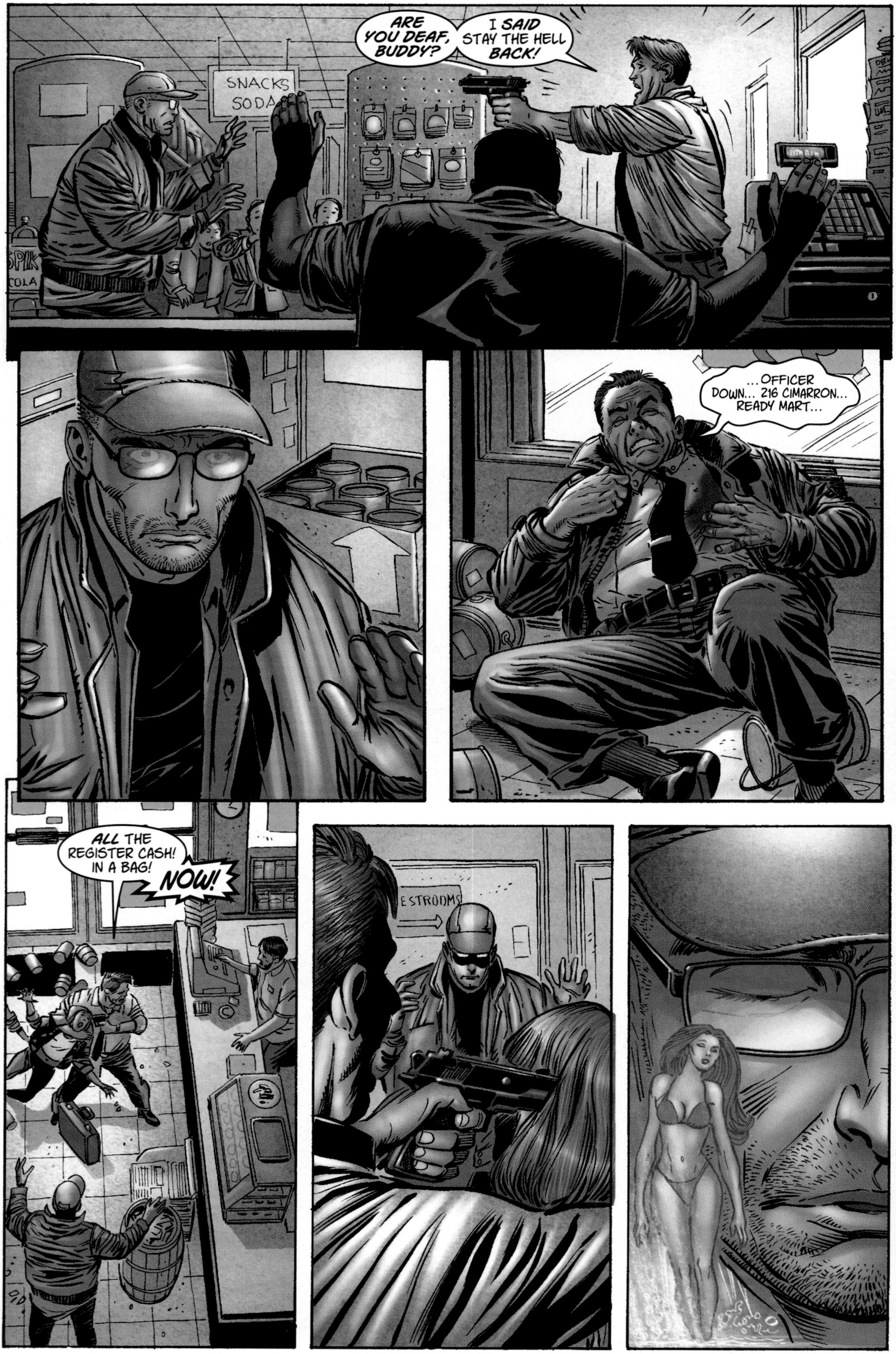
ARE YOU DEAF, BUDDY?
I SAID STAY THE HELL BACK!
SNACKS SODA
SPIK COLA
...OFFICER DOWN... 216 CIMARRON... READY MART...
ALL THE REGISTER CASH! IN A BAG!
NOW!
ESTROOMS

RIIIIINNNGG
RIIIIINNNGG

RIIIIINNNGG

...YEAH...

WHERE --?

GIMME *TEN* MINUTES!

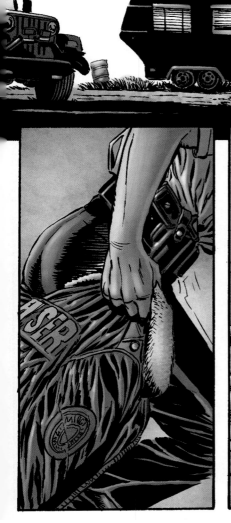

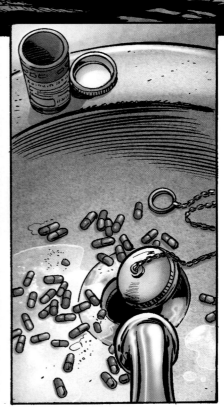

DENVER SWAT NEGOTIATOR RESIGNS
BLAMED FOR DEATHS IN BANK HOSTAGE BUNGLE

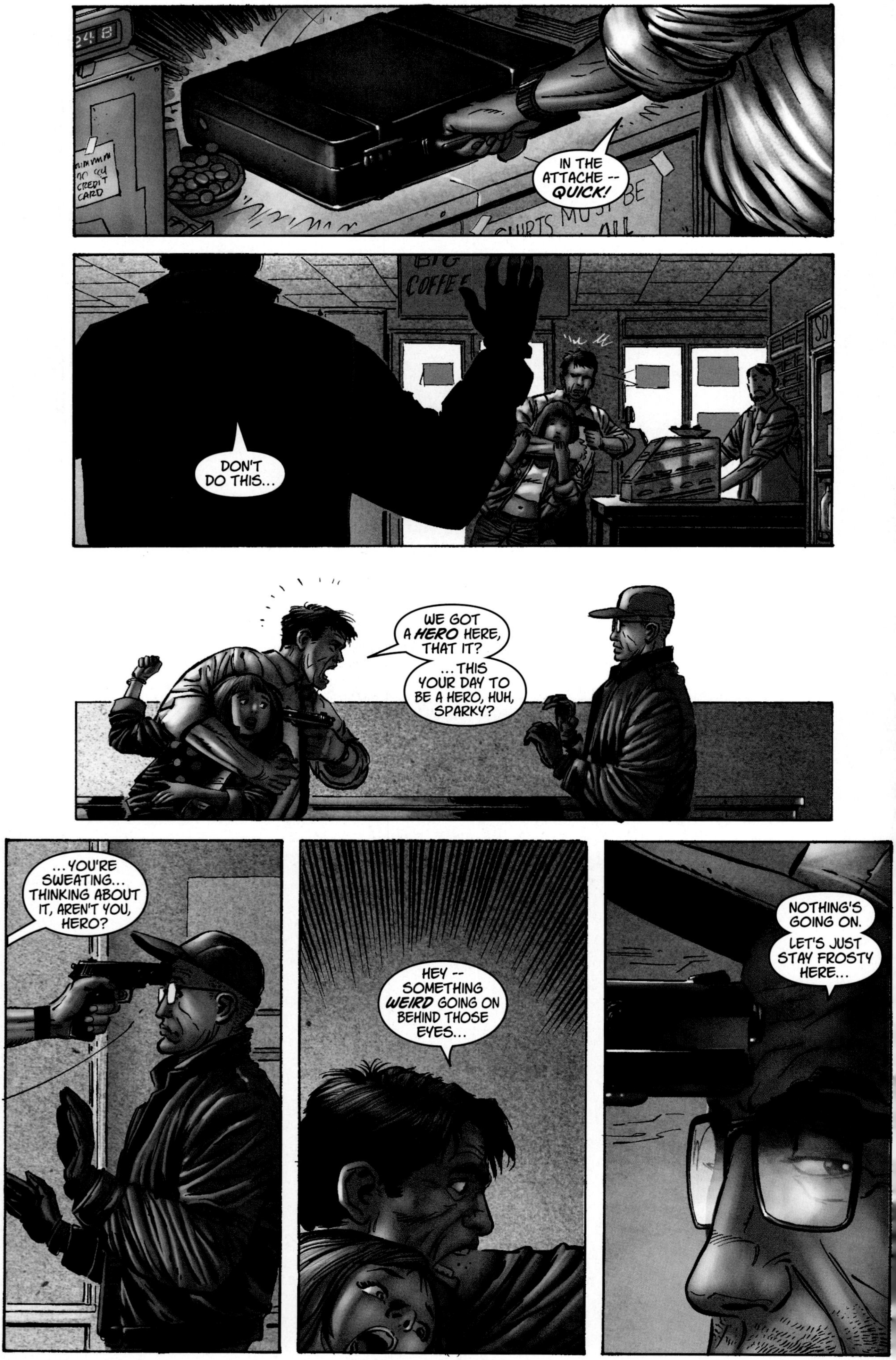
IN THE ATTACHE -- **QUICK!**
DON'T DO THIS...
WE GOT A **HERO** HERE, THAT IT?
...THIS YOUR DAY TO BE A HERO, HUH, SPARKY?
...YOU'RE SWEATING... THINKING ABOUT IT, AREN'T YOU, HERO?
HEY -- SOMETHING **WEIRD** GOING ON BEHIND THOSE EYES...
NOTHING'S GOING ON.
LET'S JUST STAY FROSTY HERE...

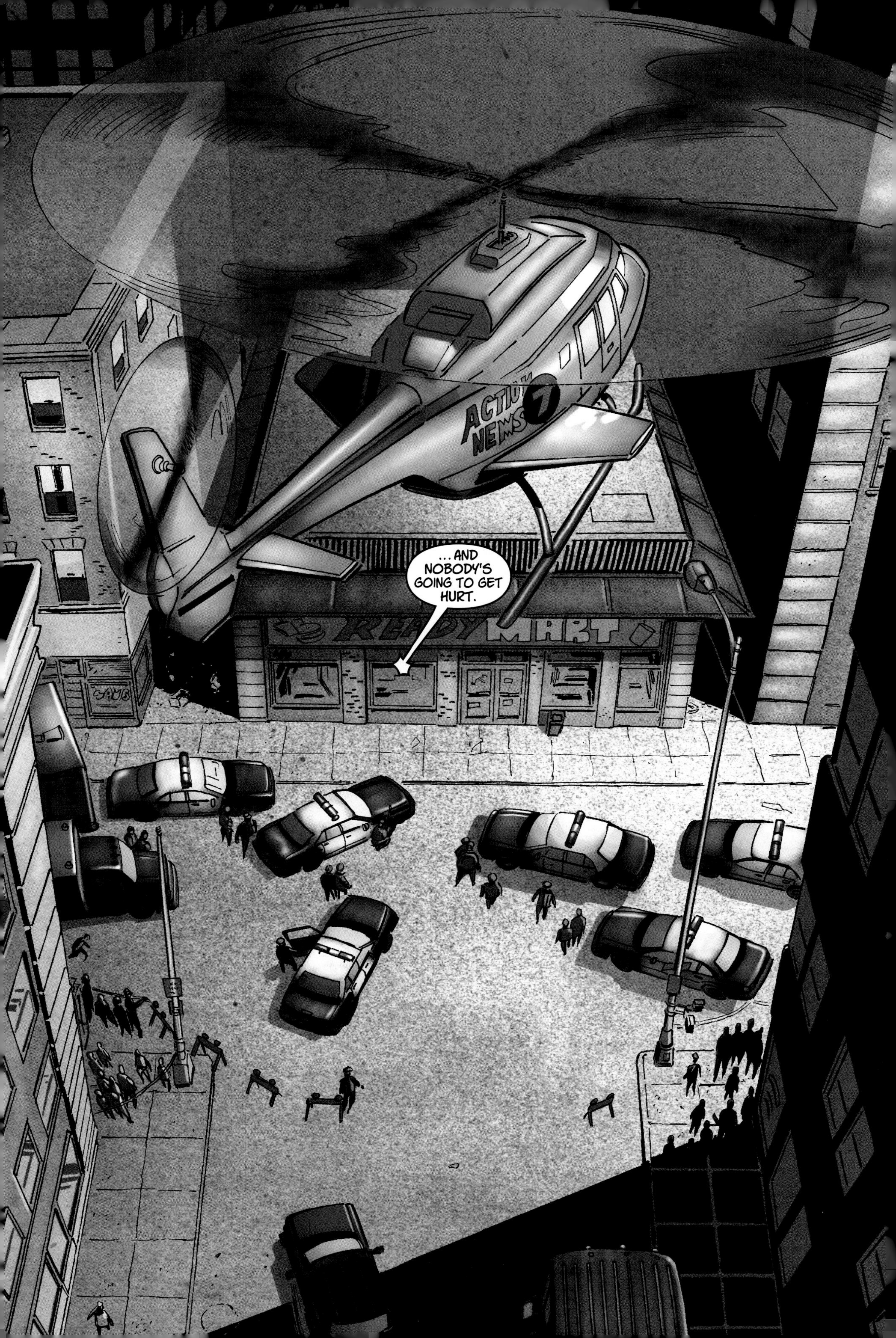
...AND NOBODY'S GOING TO GET HURT.
ACTION NEWS 7
READY MART

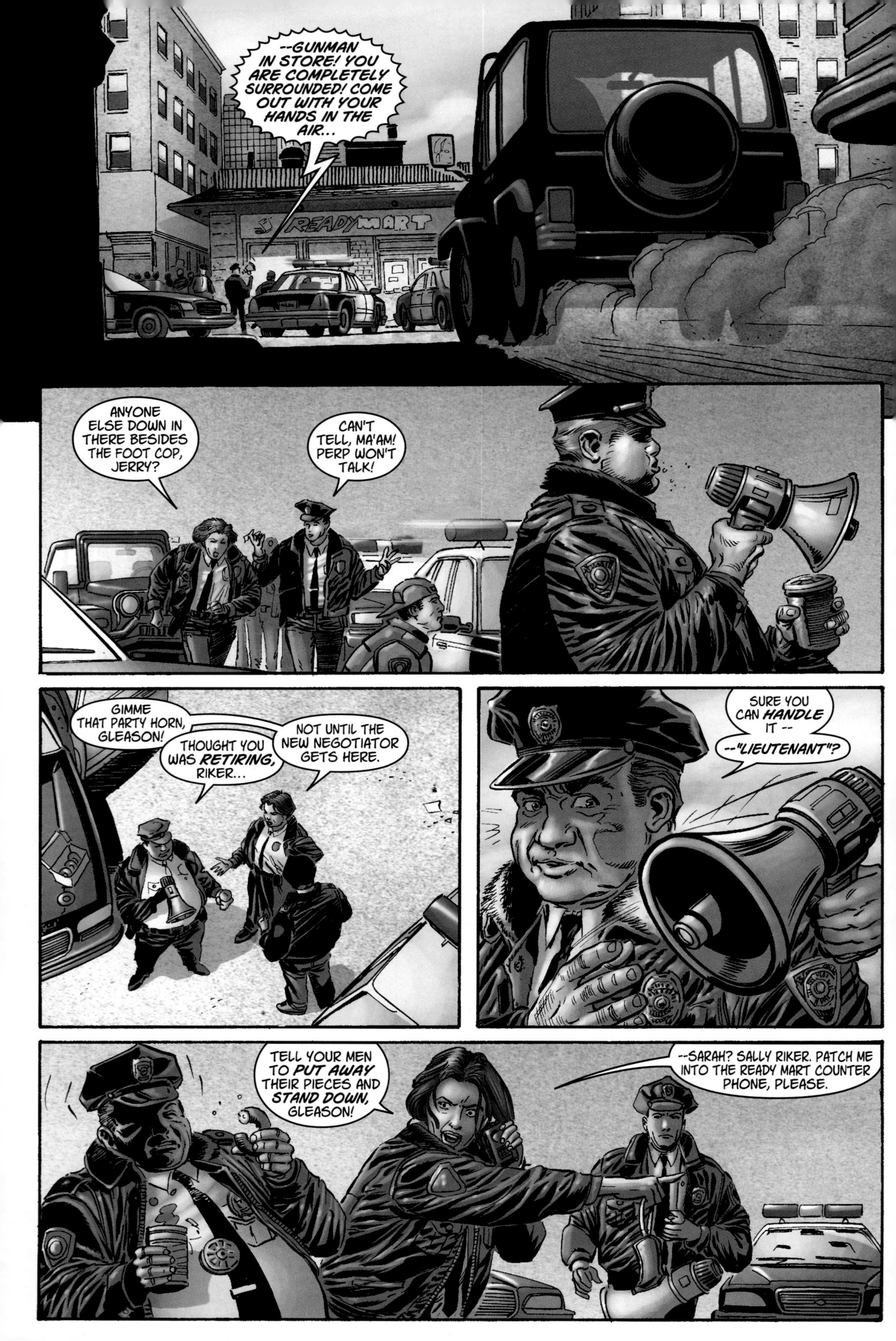
--GUNMAN IN STORE! YOU ARE COMPLETELY SURROUNDED! COME OUT WITH YOUR HANDS IN THE AIR...
READY MART
ANYONE ELSE DOWN IN THERE BESIDES THE FOOT COP, JERRY?
CAN'T TELL, MA'AM! PERP WON'T TALK!
GIMME THAT PARTY HORN, GLEASON!
THOUGHT YOU WAS RETIRING, RIKER...
NOT UNTIL THE NEW NEGOTIATOR GETS HERE.
SURE YOU CAN HANDLE IT --
--"LIEUTENANT"?
TELL YOUR MEN TO PUT AWAY THEIR PIECES AND STAND DOWN, GLEASON!
--SARAH? SALLY RIKER. PATCH ME INTO THE READY MART COUNTER PHONE, PLEASE.

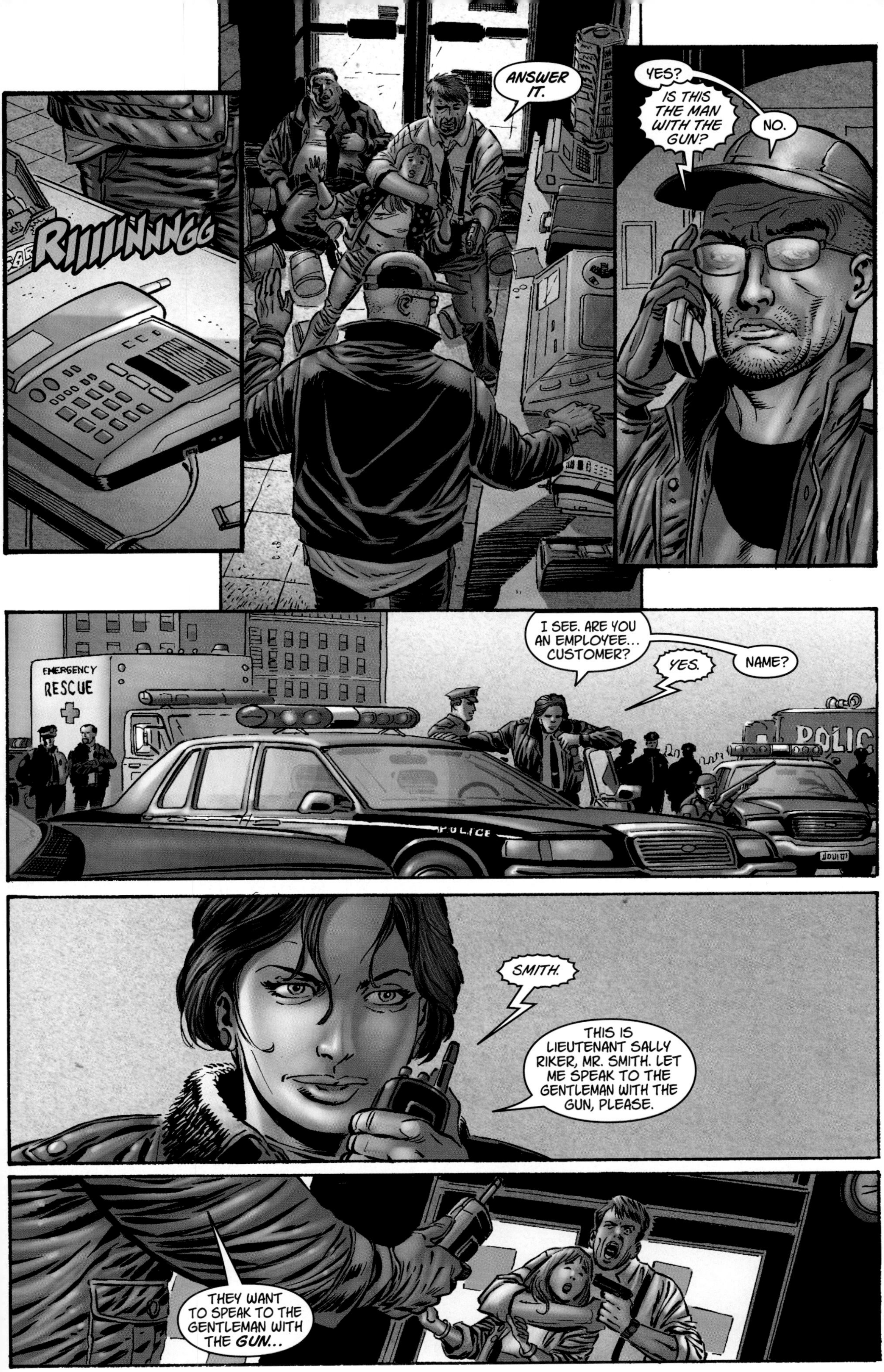
RIIIINNNGG
ANSWER IT.
YES?
IS THIS THE MAN WITH THE GUN?
NO.
I SEE. ARE YOU AN EMPLOYEE... CUSTOMER?
YES.
NAME?
EMERGENCY RESCUE
POLICE
SMITH.
THIS IS LIEUTENANT SALLY RIKER, MR. SMITH. LET ME SPEAK TO THE GENTLEMAN WITH THE GUN, PLEASE.
THEY WANT TO SPEAK TO THE GENTLEMAN WITH THE GUN...

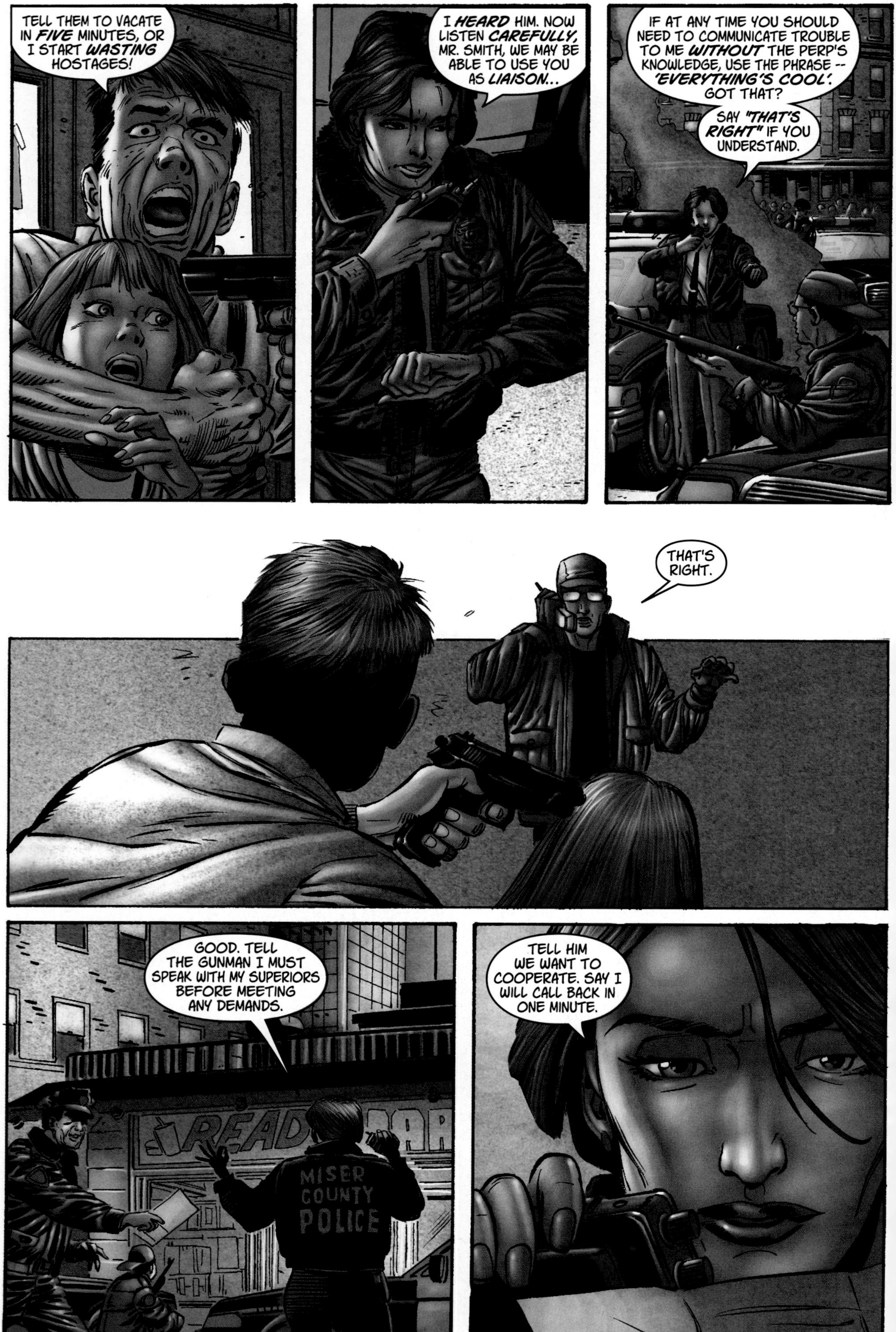
TELL THEM TO VACATE IN FIVE MINUTES, OR I START WASTING HOSTAGES!
I HEARD HIM. NOW LISTEN CAREFULLY, MR. SMITH, WE MAY BE ABLE TO USE YOU AS LIAISON...
IF AT ANY TIME YOU SHOULD NEED TO COMMUNICATE TROUBLE TO ME WITHOUT THE PERP'S KNOWLEDGE, USE THE PHRASE -- 'EVERYTHING'S COOL'. GOT THAT?
SAY "THAT'S RIGHT" IF YOU UNDERSTAND.
THAT'S RIGHT.
GOOD. TELL THE GUNMAN I MUST SPEAK WITH MY SUPERIORS BEFORE MEETING ANY DEMANDS.
MISER COUNTY POLICE
TELL HIM WE WANT TO COOPERATE. SAY I WILL CALL BACK IN ONE MINUTE.

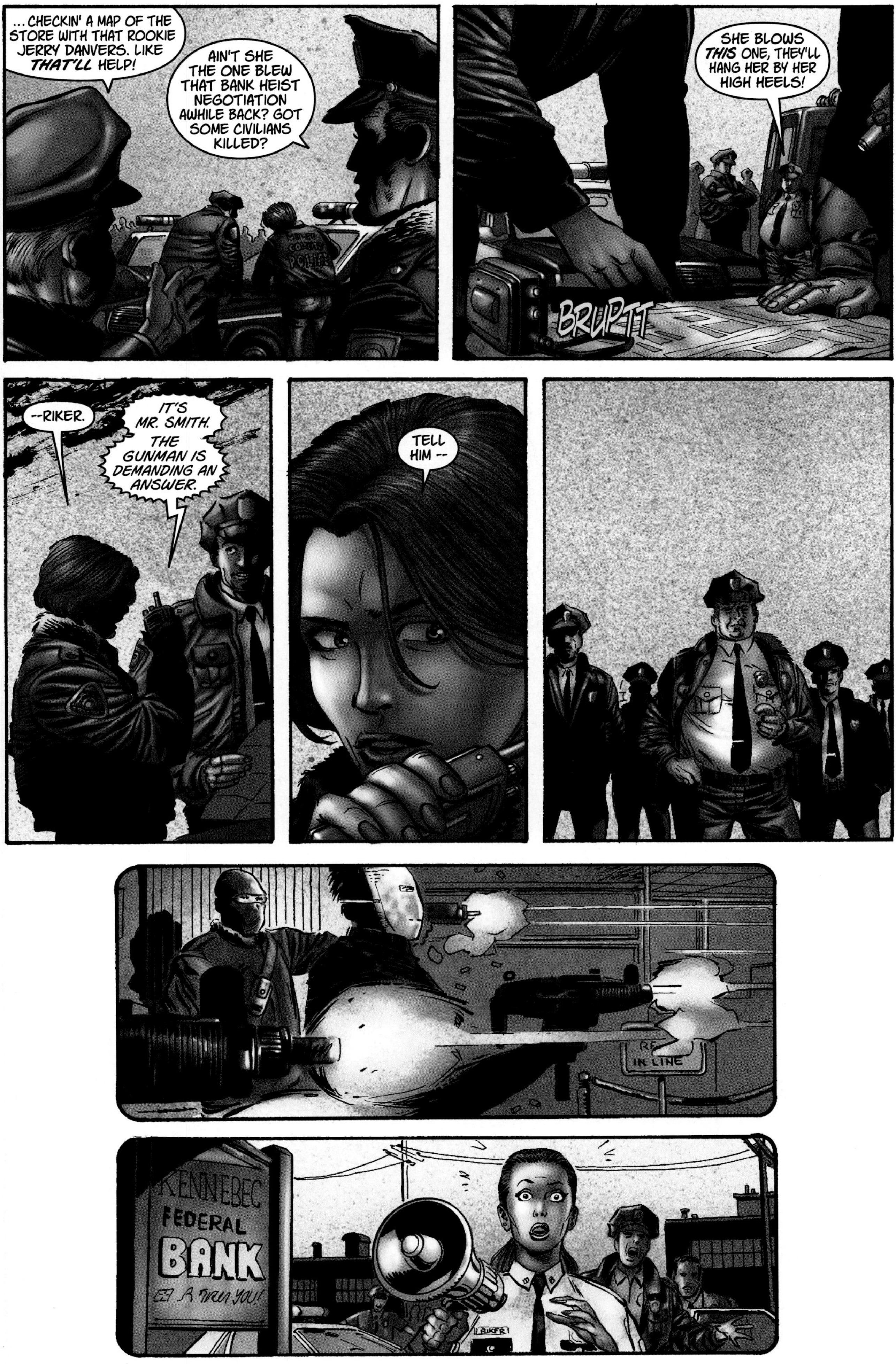

...CHECKIN' A MAP OF THE STORE WITH THAT ROOKIE JERRY DANVERS. LIKE *THAT'LL* HELP!
AIN'T SHE THE ONE BLEW THAT BANK HEIST NEGOTIATION AWHILE BACK? GOT SOME CIVILIANS KILLED?
SHE BLOWS *THIS* ONE, THEY'LL HANG HER BY HER HIGH HEELS!
BRUPTT
--RIKER.
IT'S MR. SMITH. THE GUNMAN IS DEMANDING AN ANSWER.
TELL HIM --
IN LINE
KENNEBEC
FEDERAL
BANK
RIKER

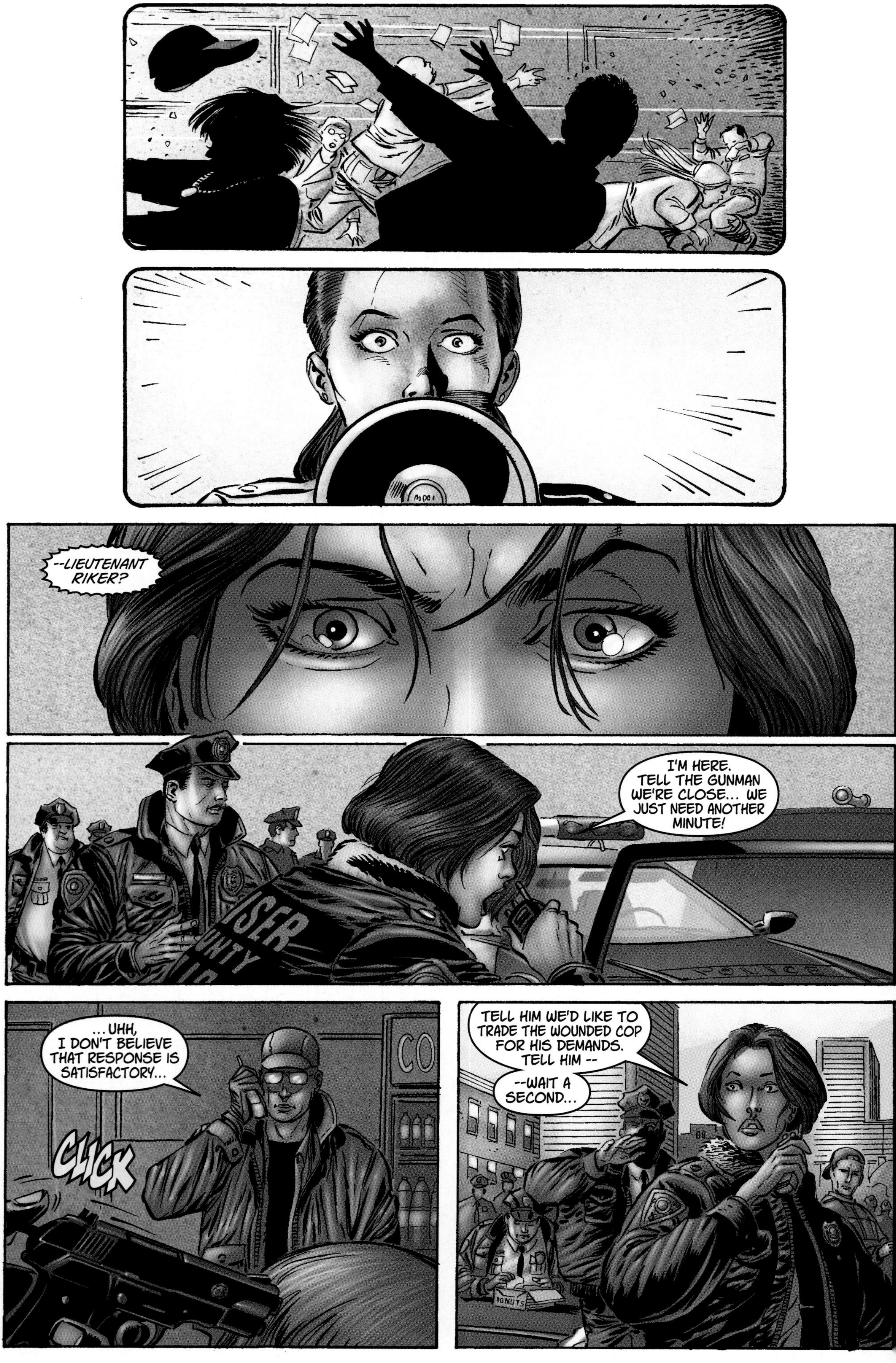
--LIEUTENANT RIKER?
I'M HERE. TELL THE GUNMAN WE'RE CLOSE... WE JUST NEED ANOTHER MINUTE!
...UHH, I DON'T BELIEVE THAT RESPONSE IS SATISFACTORY...
CLICK
TELL HIM WE'D LIKE TO TRADE THE WOUNDED COP FOR HIS DEMANDS. TELL HIM --
--WAIT A SECOND...

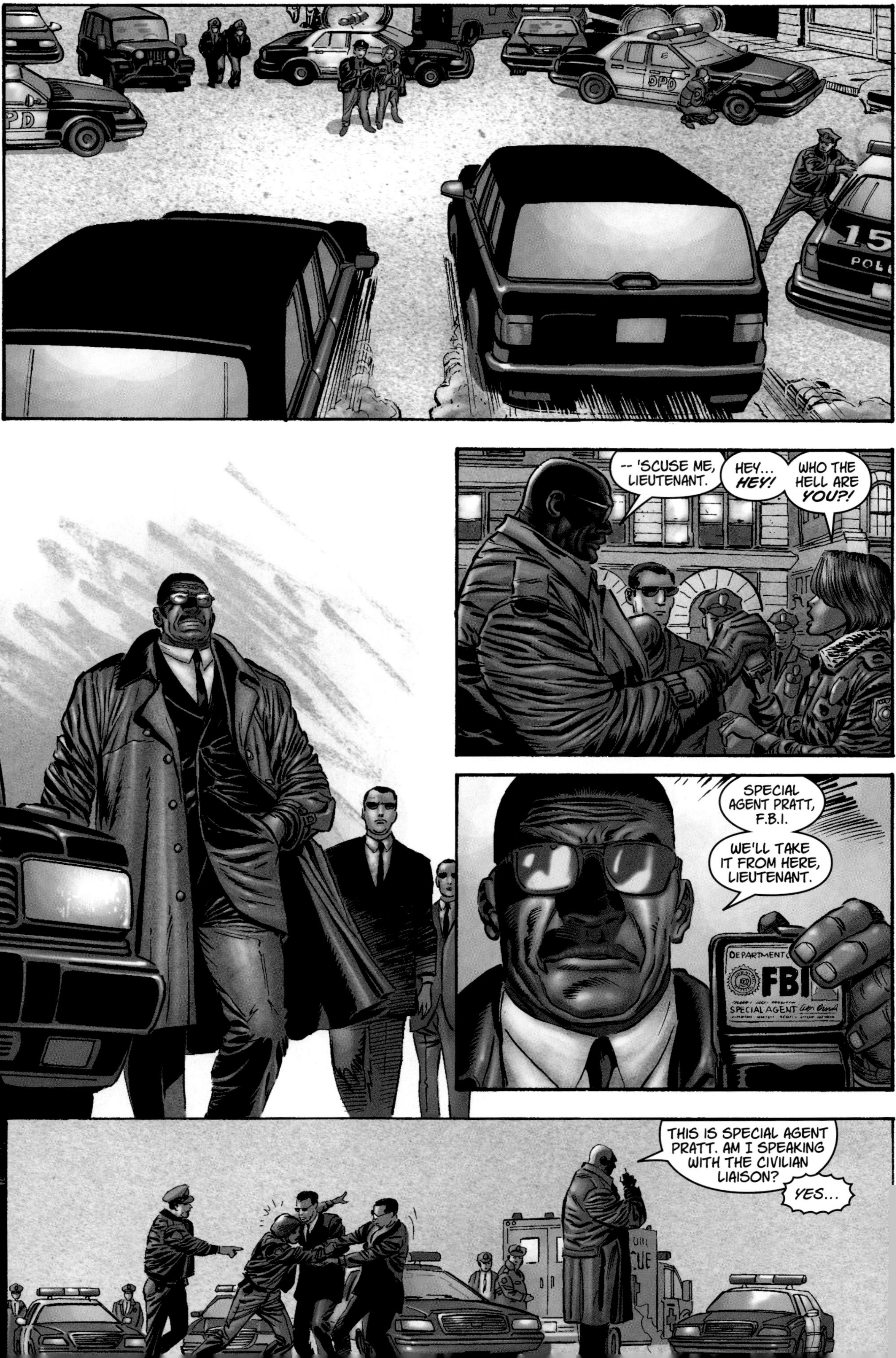
-- 'SCUSE ME, LIEUTENANT.
HEY... *HEY!*
WHO THE HELL ARE *YOU?!*
SPECIAL AGENT PRATT, F.B.I.
WE'LL TAKE IT FROM HERE, LIEUTENANT.
FBI
SPECIAL AGENT
THIS IS SPECIAL AGENT PRATT. AM I SPEAKING WITH THE CIVILIAN LIAISON?
YES...

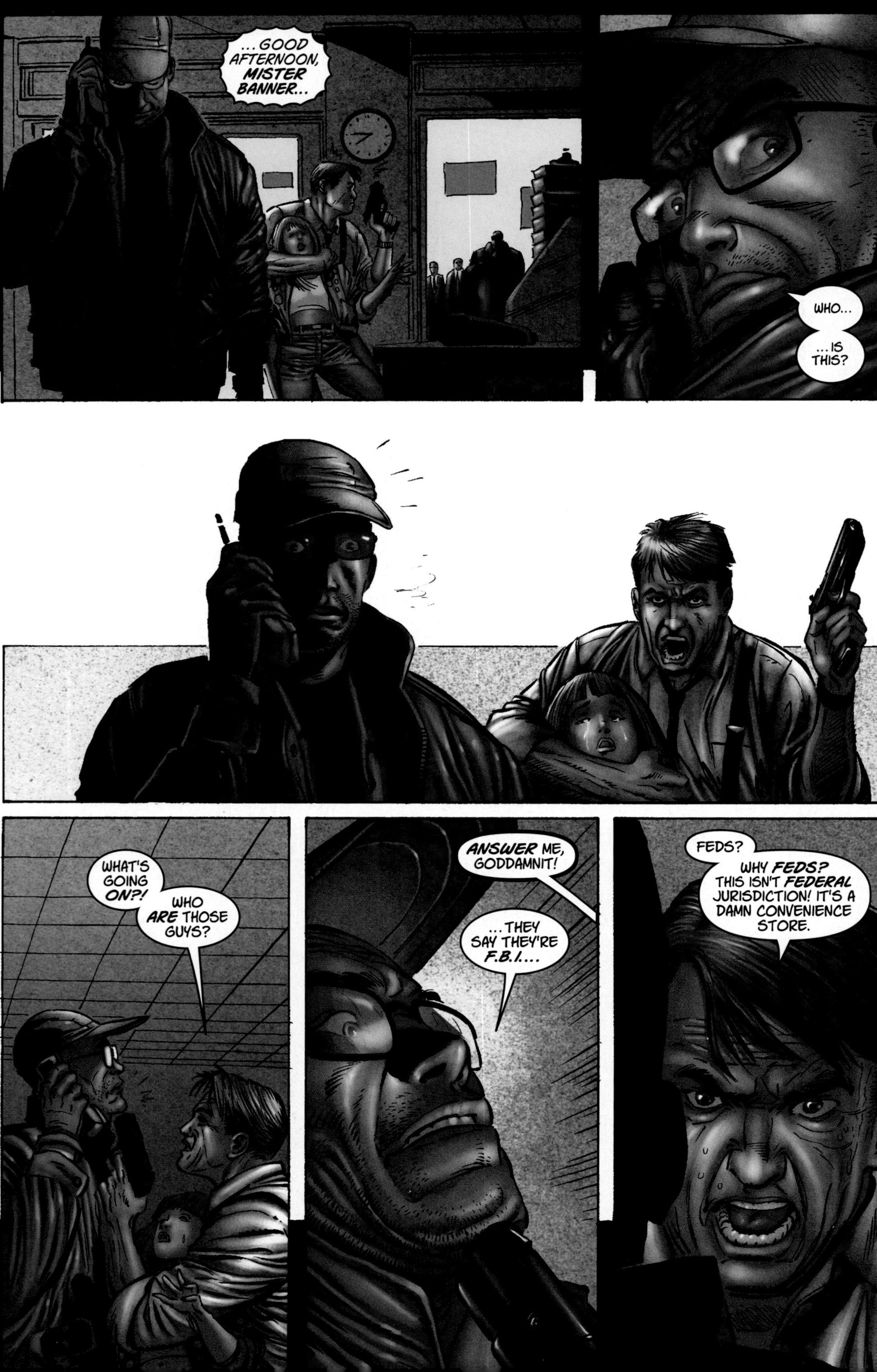
...GOOD AFTERNOON, MISTER BANNER...
WHO...
...IS THIS?
WHAT'S GOING ON?!
WHO ARE THOSE GUYS?
ANSWER ME, GODDAMNIT!
...THEY SAY THEY'RE F.B.I....
FEDS?
WHY FEDS? THIS ISN'T FEDERAL JURISDICTION! IT'S A DAMN CONVENIENCE STORE.

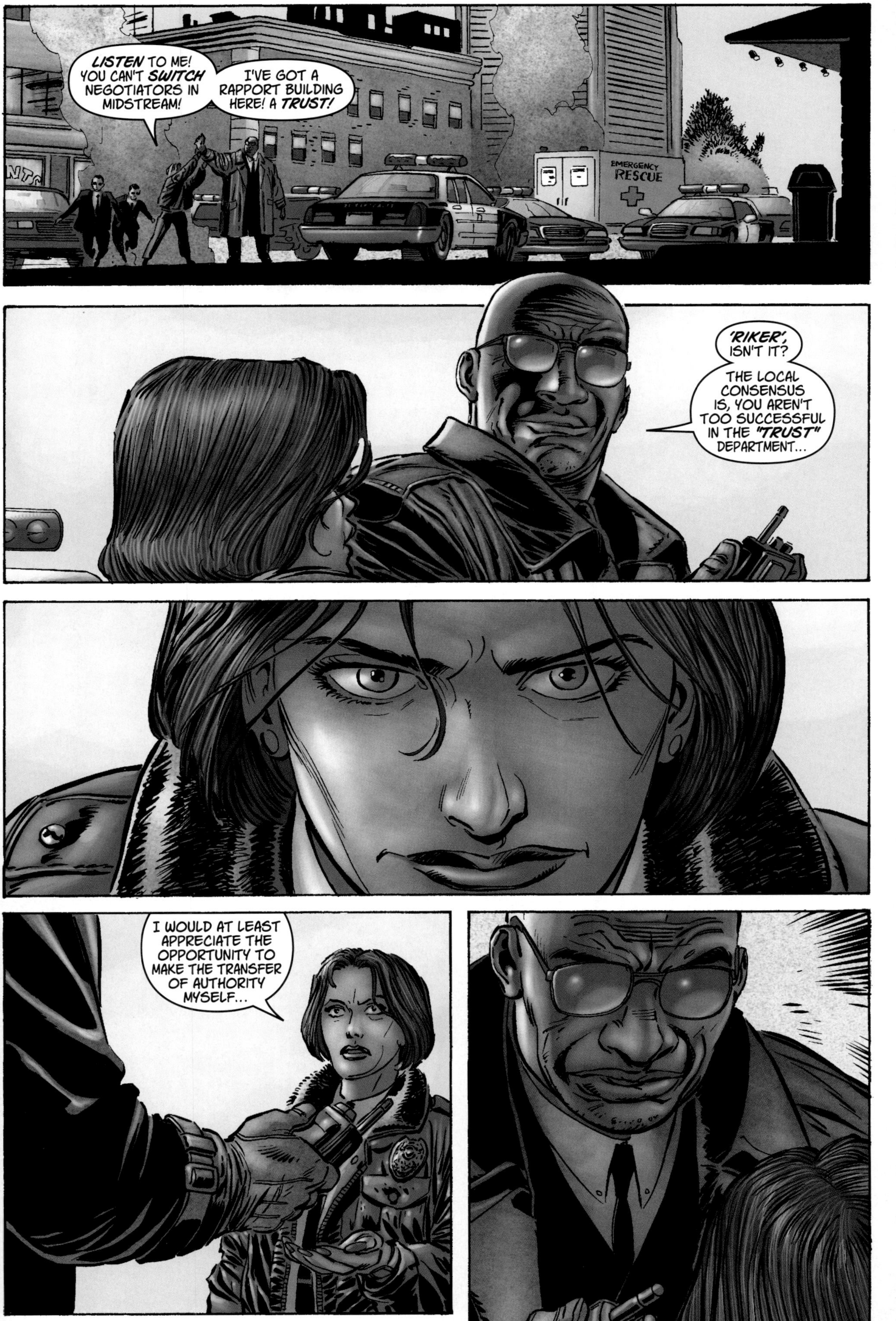
LISTEN TO ME! YOU CAN'T SWITCH NEGOTIATORS IN MIDSTREAM!
I'VE GOT A RAPPORT BUILDING HERE! A TRUST!
EMERGENCY RESCUE
'RIKER', ISN'T IT?
THE LOCAL CONSENSUS IS, YOU AREN'T TOO SUCCESSFUL IN THE "TRUST" DEPARTMENT...
I WOULD AT LEAST APPRECIATE THE OPPORTUNITY TO MAKE THE TRANSFER OF AUTHORITY MYSELF...

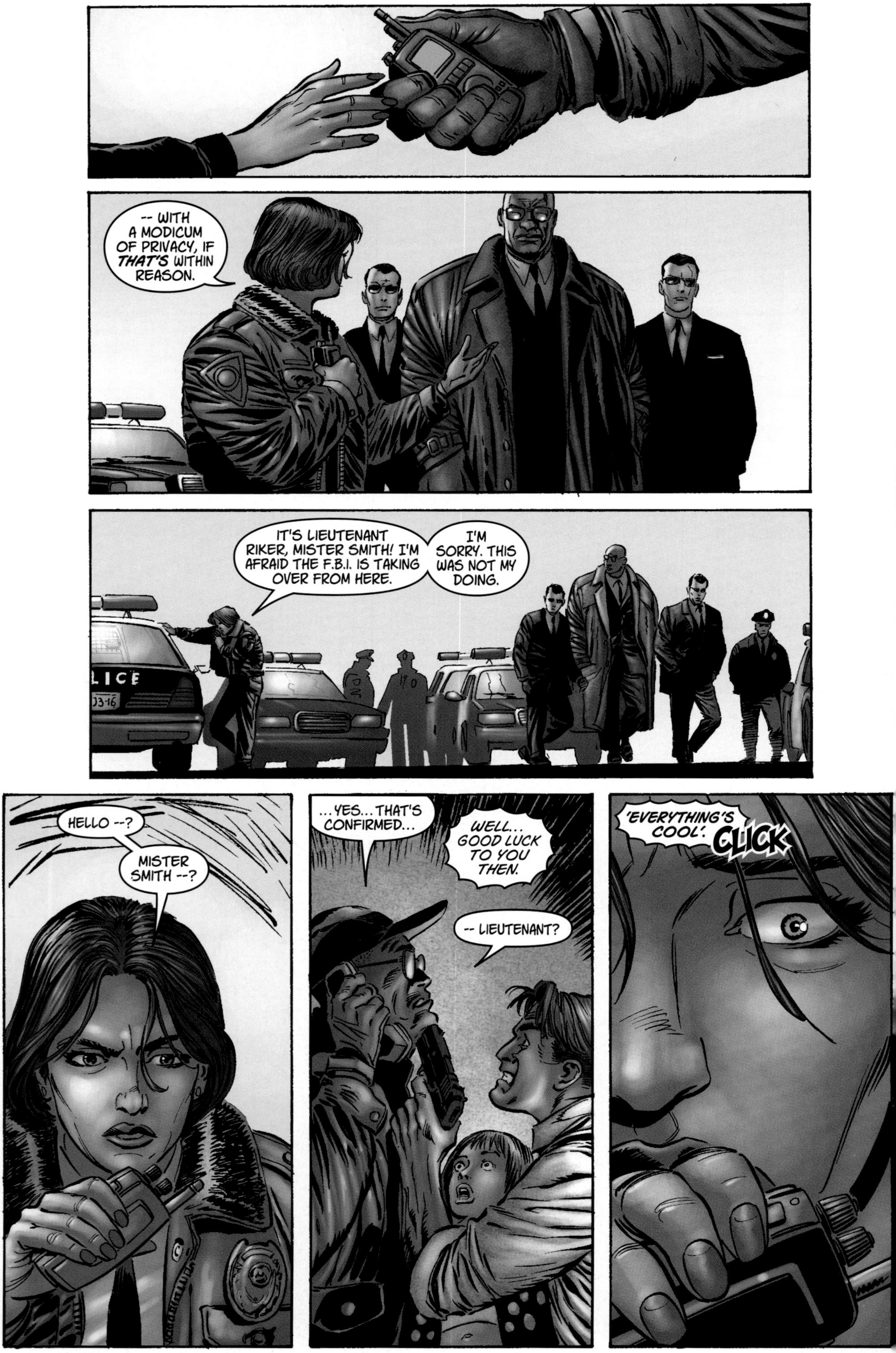
-- WITH A MODICUM OF PRIVACY, IF *THAT'S* WITHIN REASON.
IT'S LIEUTENANT RIKER, MISTER SMITH! I'M AFRAID THE F.B.I. IS TAKING OVER FROM HERE.
I'M SORRY. THIS WAS NOT MY DOING.
POLICE
HELLO --?
MISTER SMITH --?
...YES... THAT'S CONFIRMED...
WELL... GOOD LUCK TO YOU THEN.
-- LIEUTENANT?
'EVERYTHING'S COOL'.
CLICK

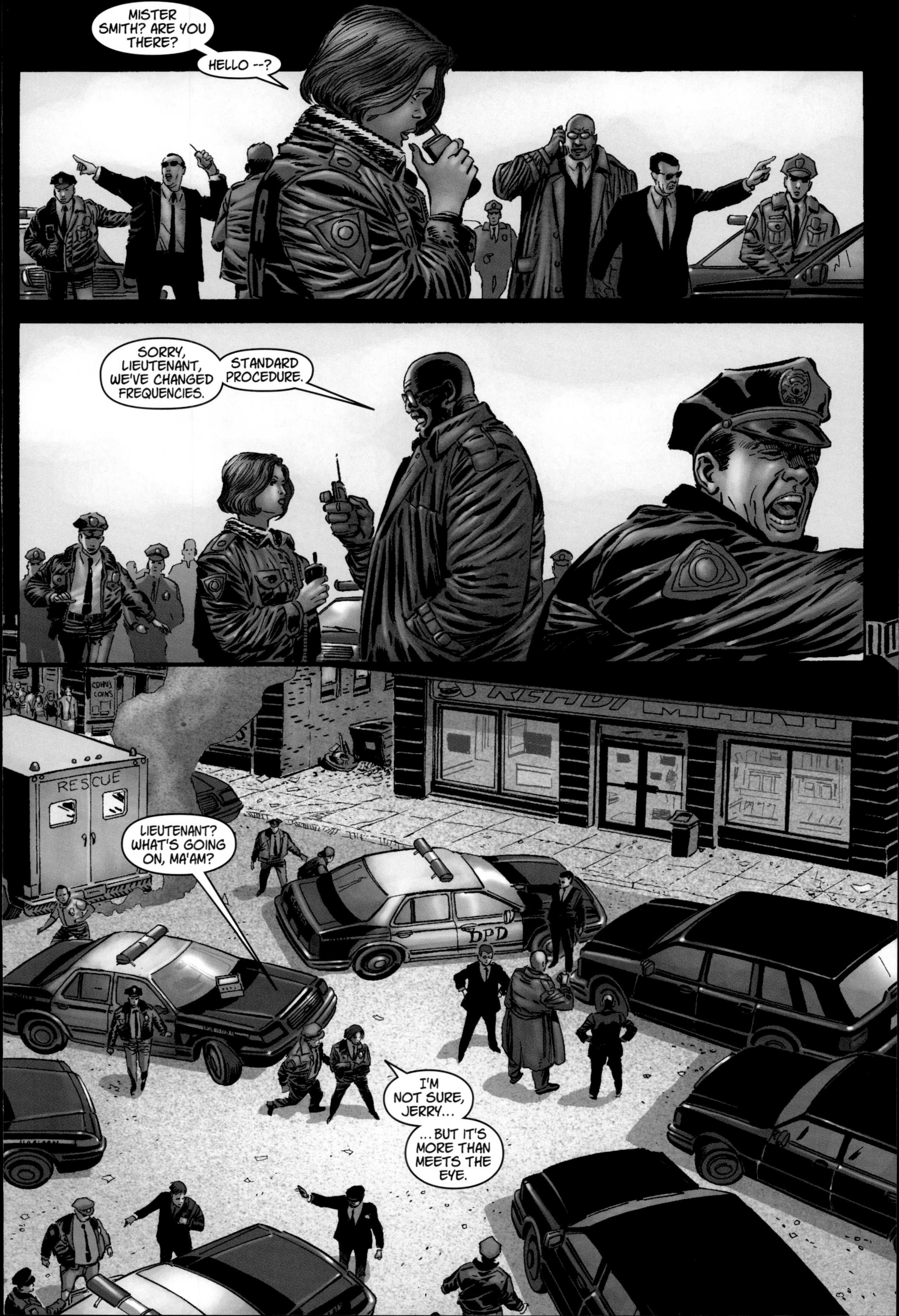
MISTER SMITH? ARE YOU THERE?
HELLO --?
SORRY, LIEUTENANT, WE'VE CHANGED FREQUENCIES.
STANDARD PROCEDURE.
LIEUTENANT? WHAT'S GOING ON, MA'AM?
RESCUE
DPD
I'M NOT SURE, JERRY...
...BUT IT'S MORE THAN MEETS THE EYE.

INCREDIBLE HULK #41
Cover sketch by Kaare Andrews

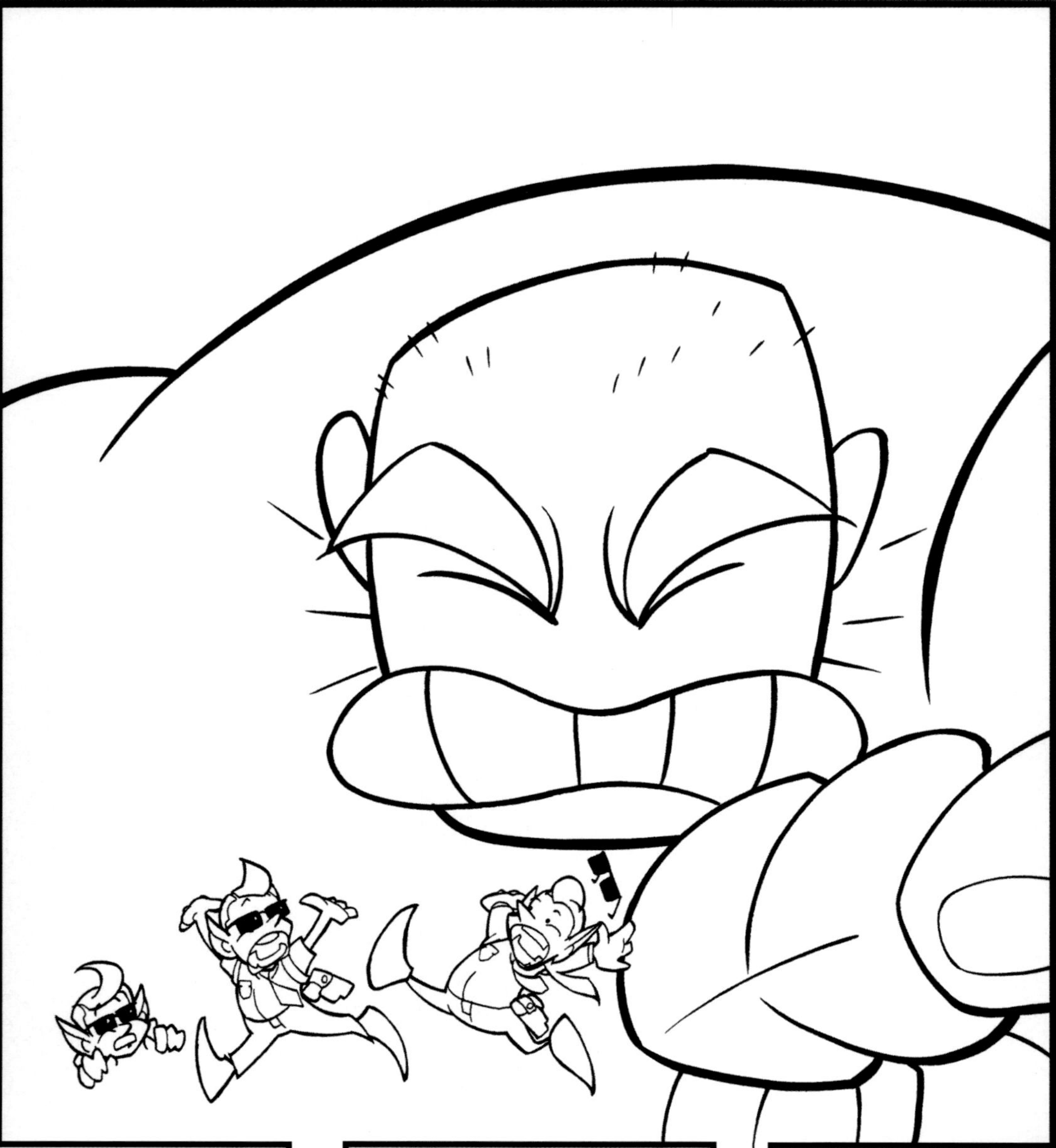

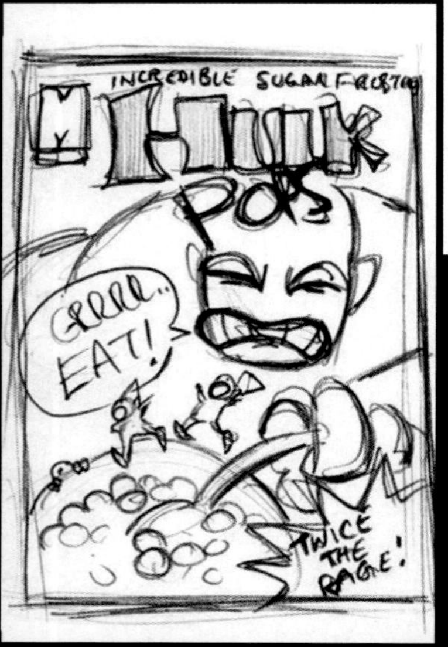
INCREDIBLE SUGAR FROSTED
HULK
POPS
GRRR... EAT!
TWICE THE RAGE!

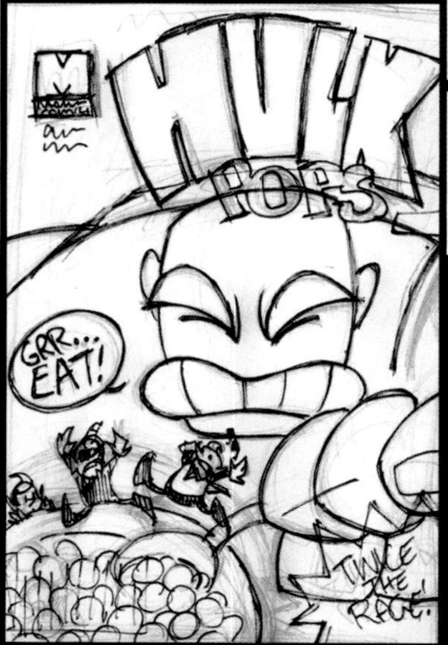
HULK
POPS
GRR... EAT!
TWICE THE RAGE

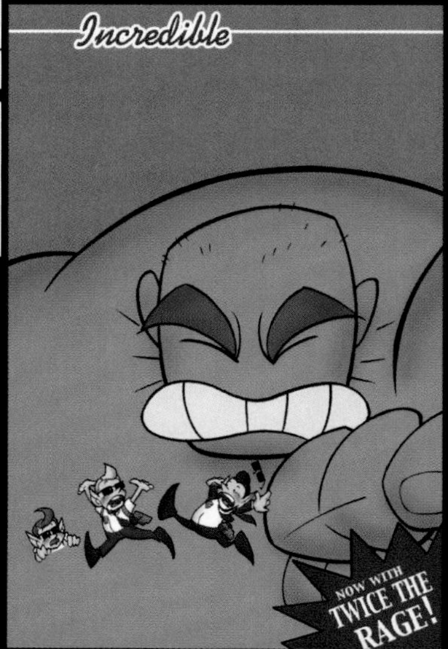
Incredible
NOW WITH TWICE THE RAGE!

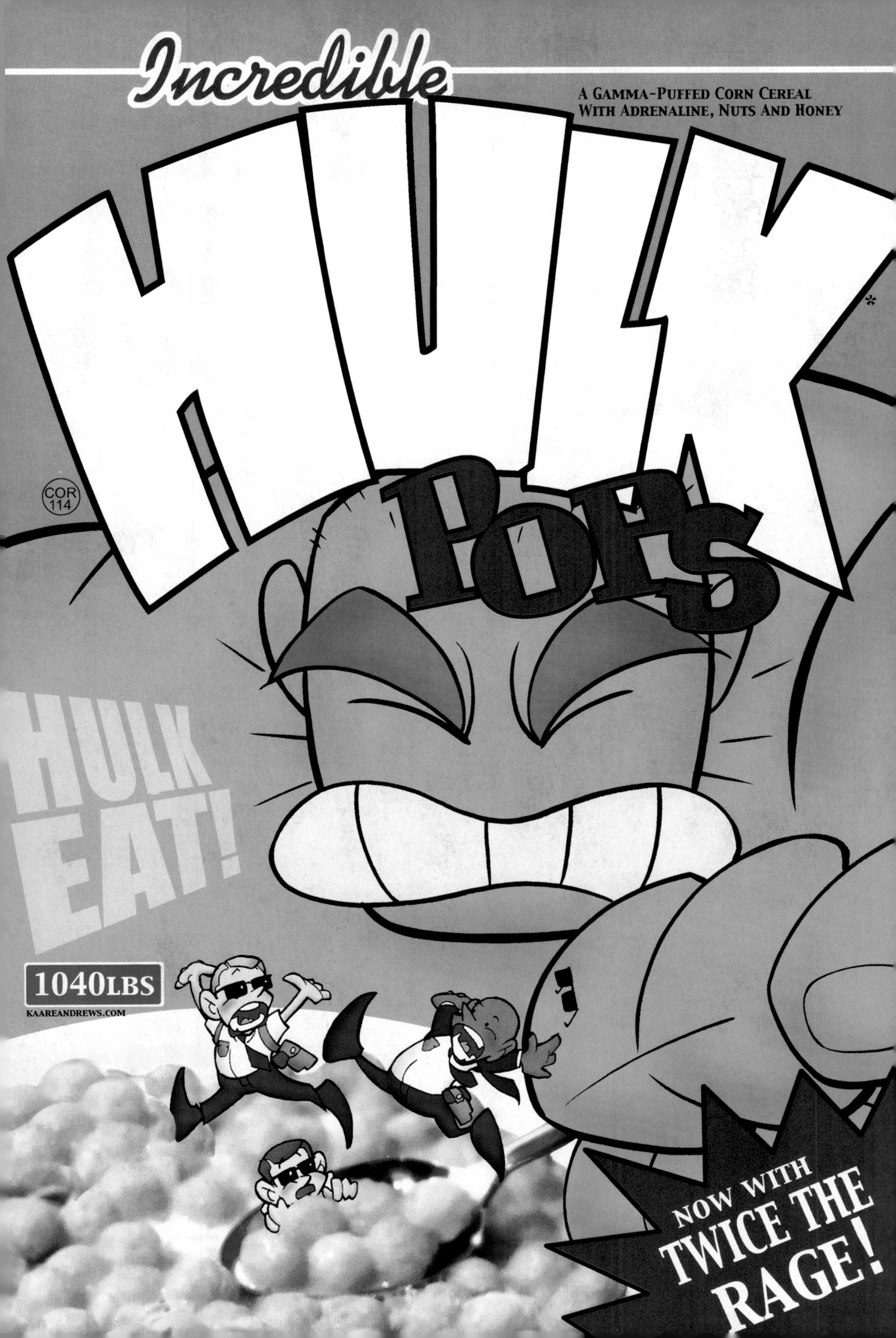

Incredible
A GAMMA-PUFFED CORN CEREAL
WITH ADRENALINE, NUTS AND HONEY
HULK*
POPS
COR 114
HULK EAT!
1040LBS
KAAREANDREWS.COM
NOW WITH
TWICE THE
RAGE!

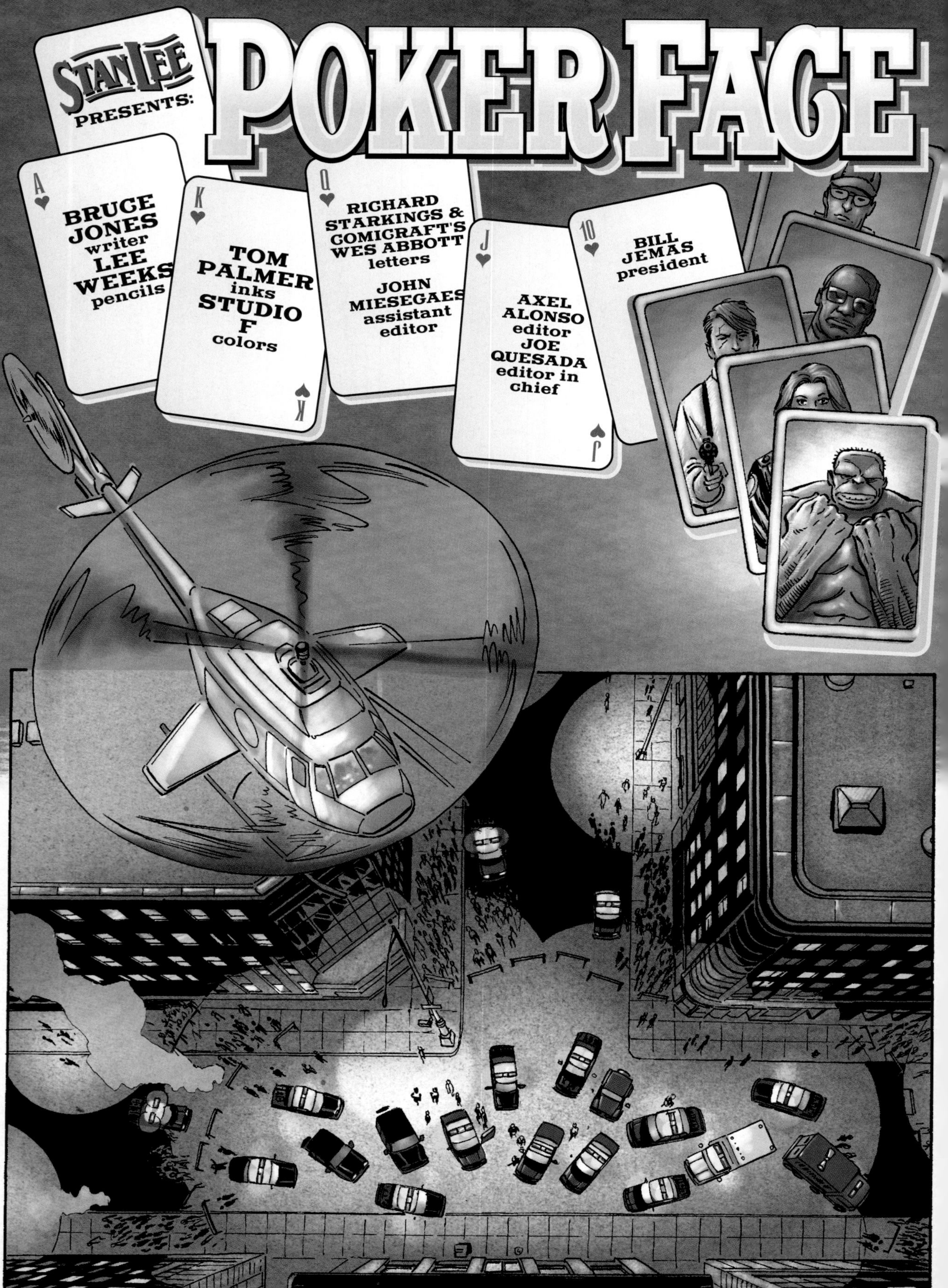

STAN LEE PRESENTS:
POKER FACE
A
BRUCE JONES writer
LEE WEEKS pencils
K
TOM PALMER inks
STUDIO F colors
Q
RICHARD STARKINGS & COMICRAFT'S WES ABBOTT letters
JOHN MIESEGAES assistant editor
J
AXEL ALONSO editor
JOE QUESADA editor in chief
10
BILL JEMAS president

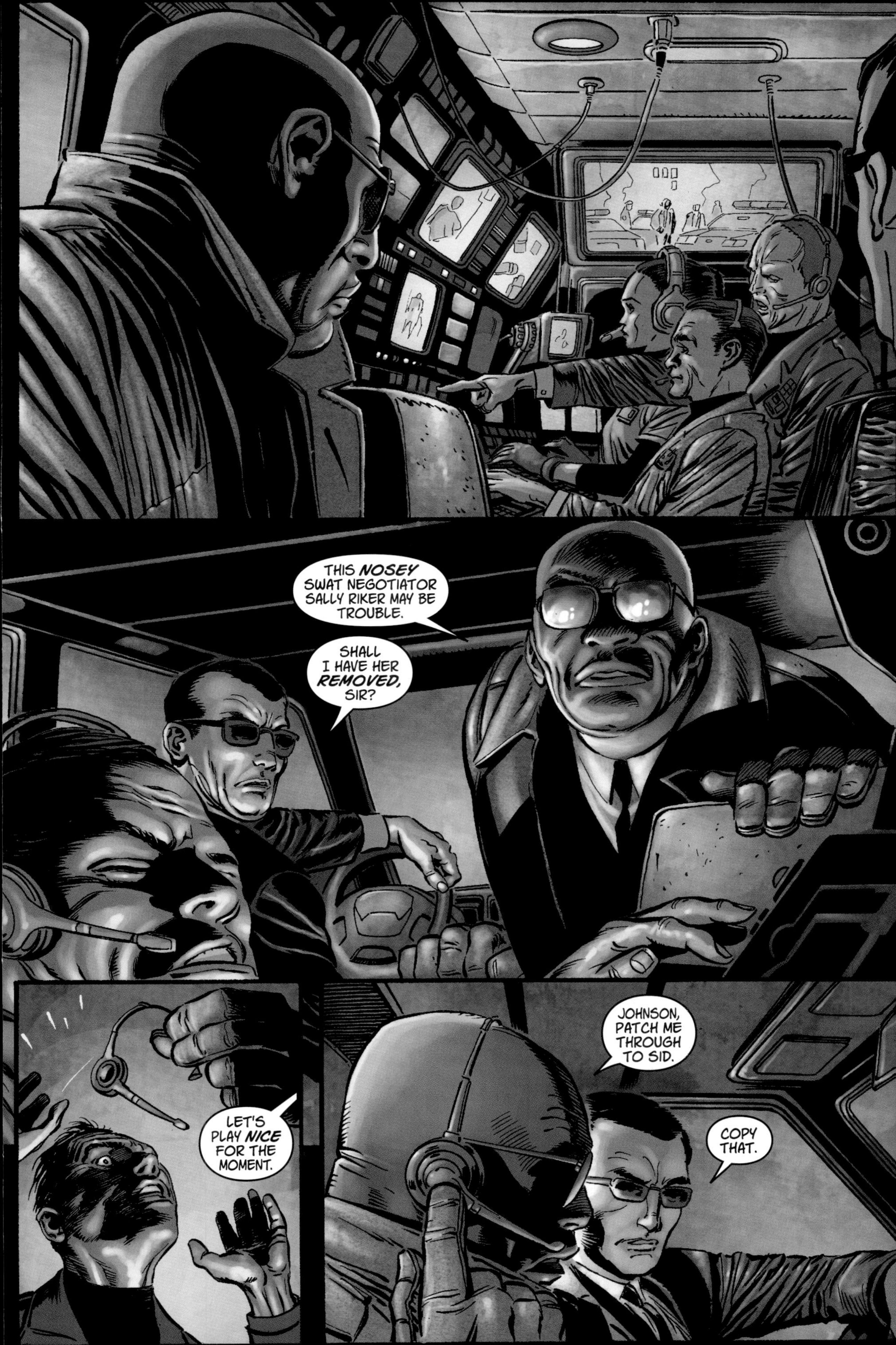
THIS NOSEY SWAT NEGOTIATOR SALLY RIKER MAY BE TROUBLE.
SHALL I HAVE HER REMOVED, SIR?
LET'S PLAY NICE FOR THE MOMENT.
JOHNSON, PATCH ME THROUGH TO SID.
COPY THAT.

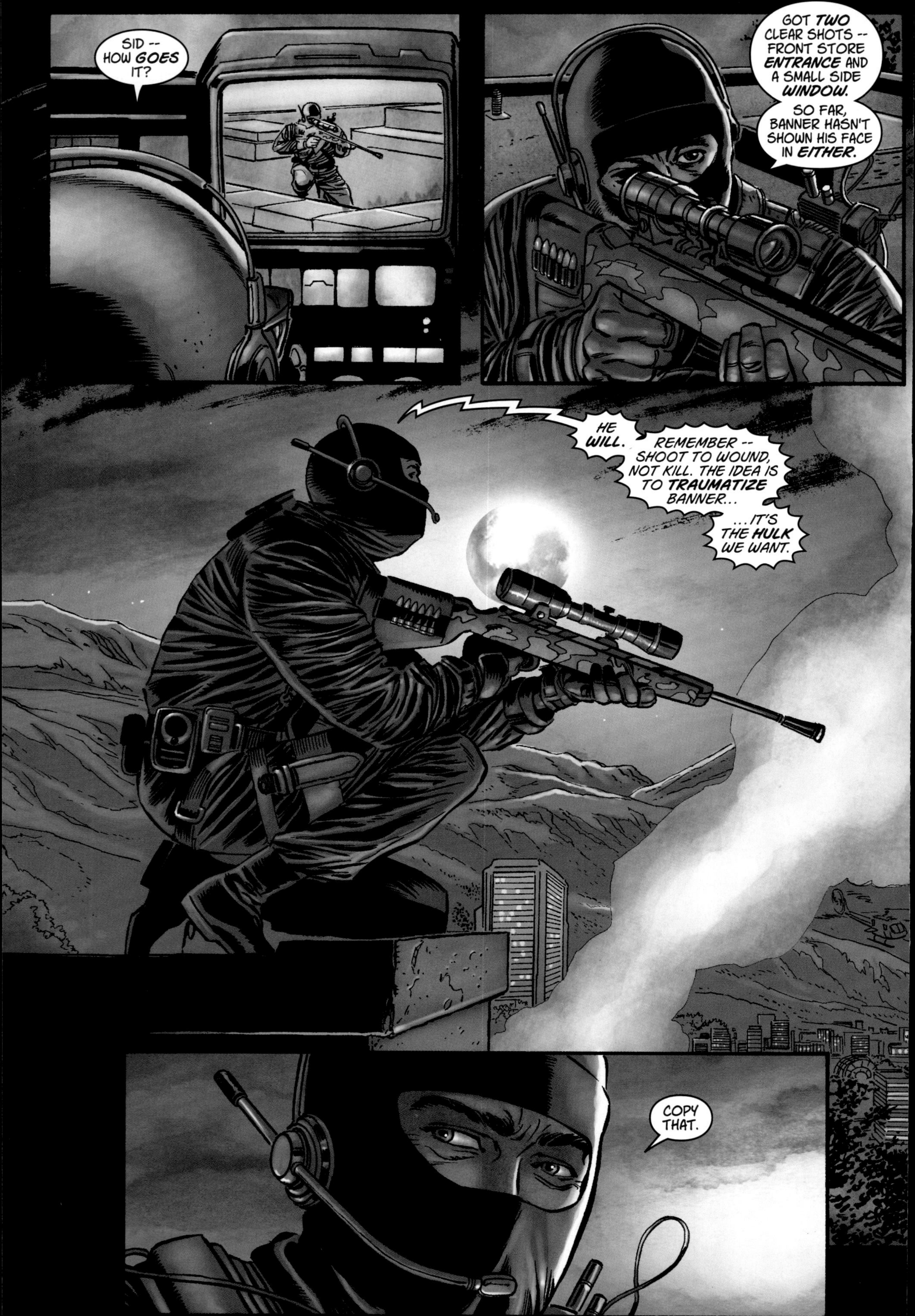
SID -- HOW GOES IT?
GOT TWO CLEAR SHOTS -- FRONT STORE ENTRANCE AND A SMALL SIDE WINDOW.
SO FAR, BANNER HASN'T SHOWN HIS FACE IN EITHER.
HE WILL.
REMEMBER -- SHOOT TO WOUND, NOT KILL. THE IDEA IS TO TRAUMATIZE BANNER...
...IT'S THE HULK WE WANT.
COPY THAT.

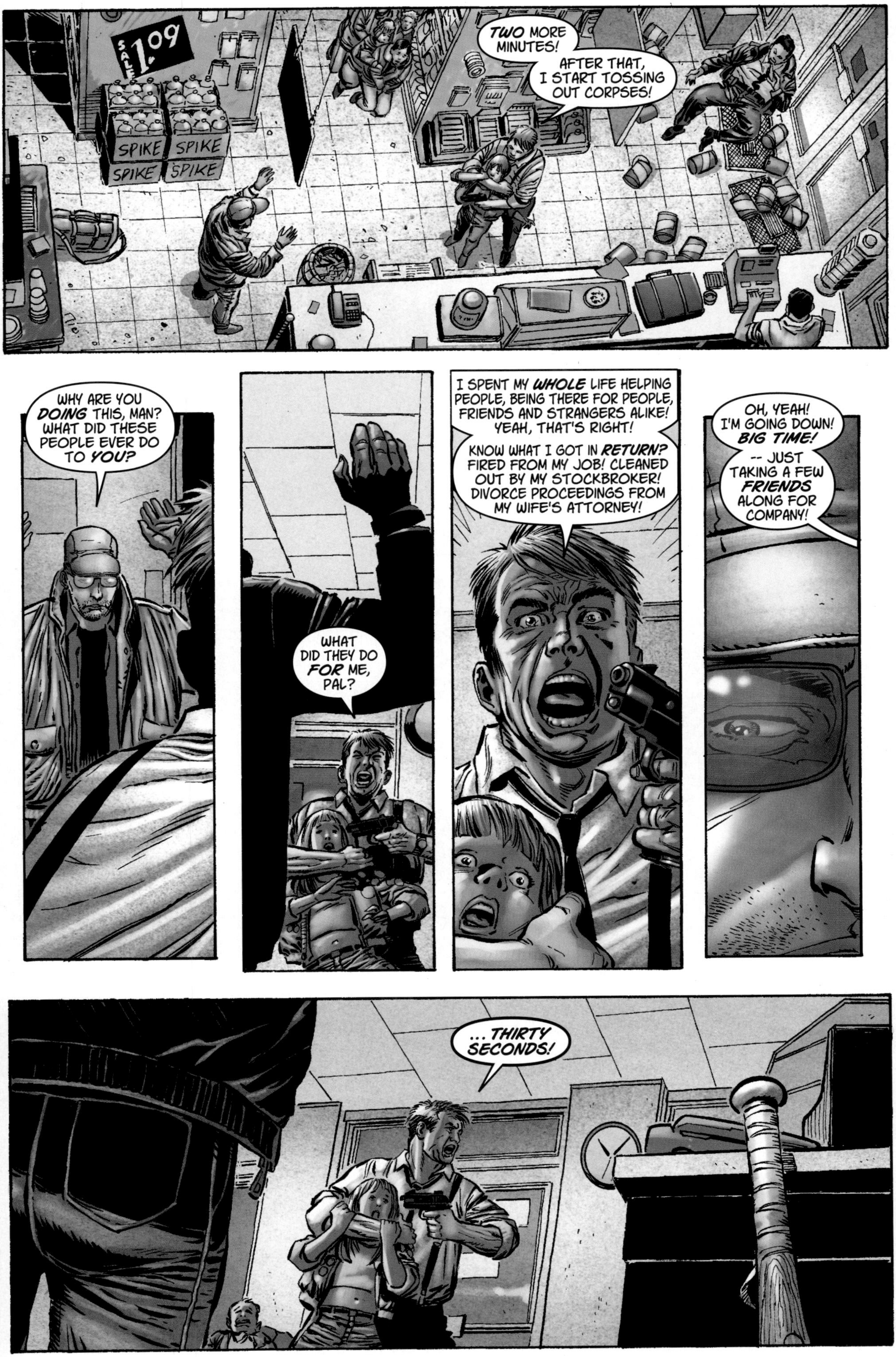
SALE 1.09
SPIKE SPIKE SPIKE SPIKE
TWO MORE MINUTES!
AFTER THAT, I START TOSSING OUT CORPSES!
WHY ARE YOU DOING THIS, MAN? WHAT DID THESE PEOPLE EVER DO TO YOU?
WHAT DID THEY DO FOR ME, PAL?
I SPENT MY WHOLE LIFE HELPING PEOPLE, BEING THERE FOR PEOPLE, FRIENDS AND STRANGERS ALIKE! YEAH, THAT'S RIGHT!
KNOW WHAT I GOT IN RETURN? FIRED FROM MY JOB! CLEANED OUT BY MY STOCKBROKER! DIVORCE PROCEEDINGS FROM MY WIFE'S ATTORNEY!
OH, YEAH! I'M GOING DOWN! BIG TIME!
-- JUST TAKING A FEW FRIENDS ALONG FOR COMPANY!
...THIRTY SECONDS!

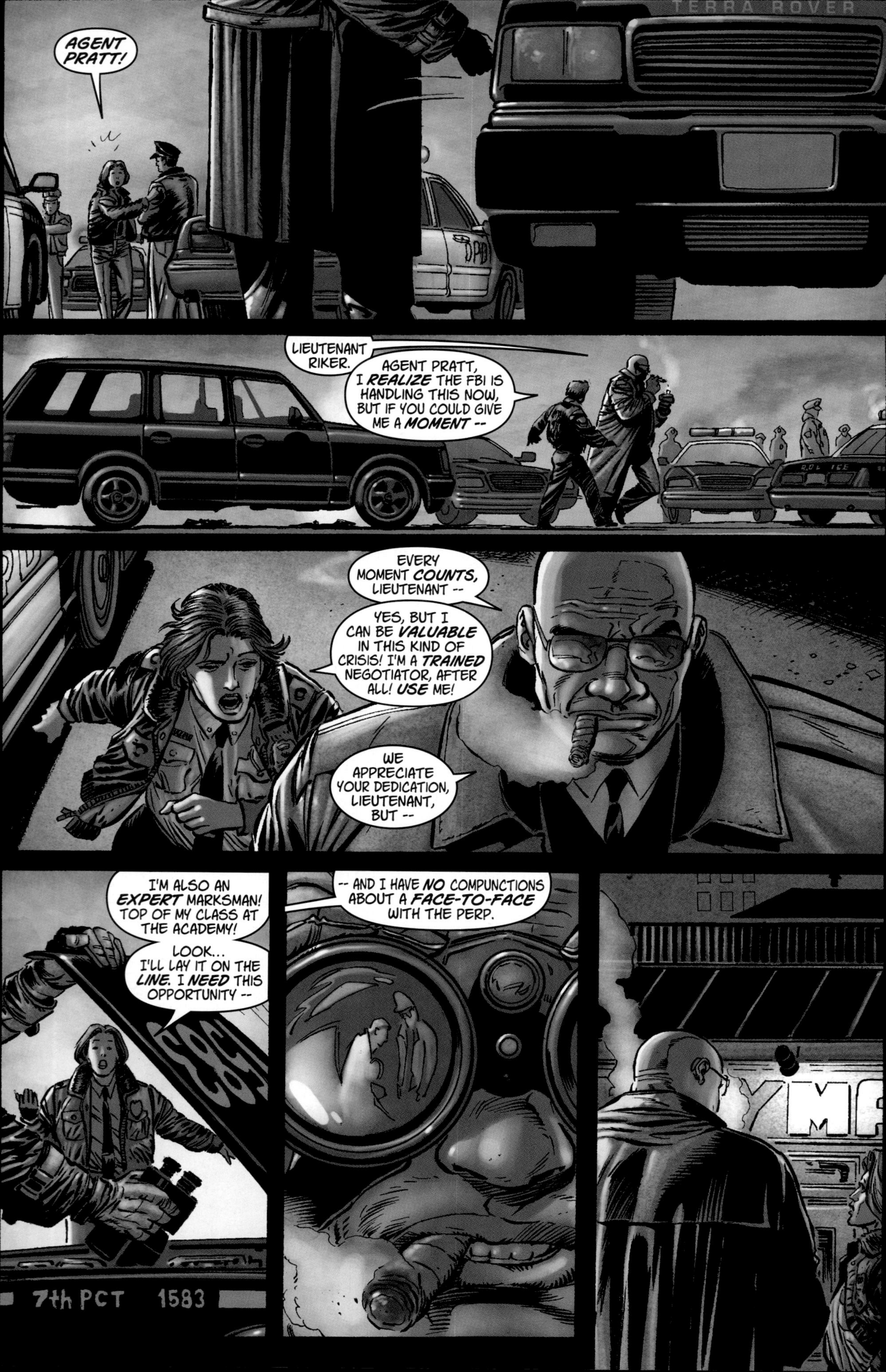
TERRA ROVER
AGENT PRATT!
DPD
LIEUTENANT RIKER.
AGENT PRATT, I REALIZE THE FBI IS HANDLING THIS NOW, BUT IF YOU COULD GIVE ME A MOMENT --
EVERY MOMENT COUNTS, LIEUTENANT --
YES, BUT I CAN BE VALUABLE IN THIS KIND OF CRISIS! I'M A TRAINED NEGOTIATOR, AFTER ALL! USE ME!
WE APPRECIATE YOUR DEDICATION, LIEUTENANT, BUT --
I'M ALSO AN EXPERT MARKSMAN! TOP OF MY CLASS AT THE ACADEMY!
LOOK... I'LL LAY IT ON THE LINE. I NEED THIS OPPORTUNITY --
7th PCT 1583
-- AND I HAVE NO COMPUNCTIONS ABOUT A FACE-TO-FACE WITH THE PERP.

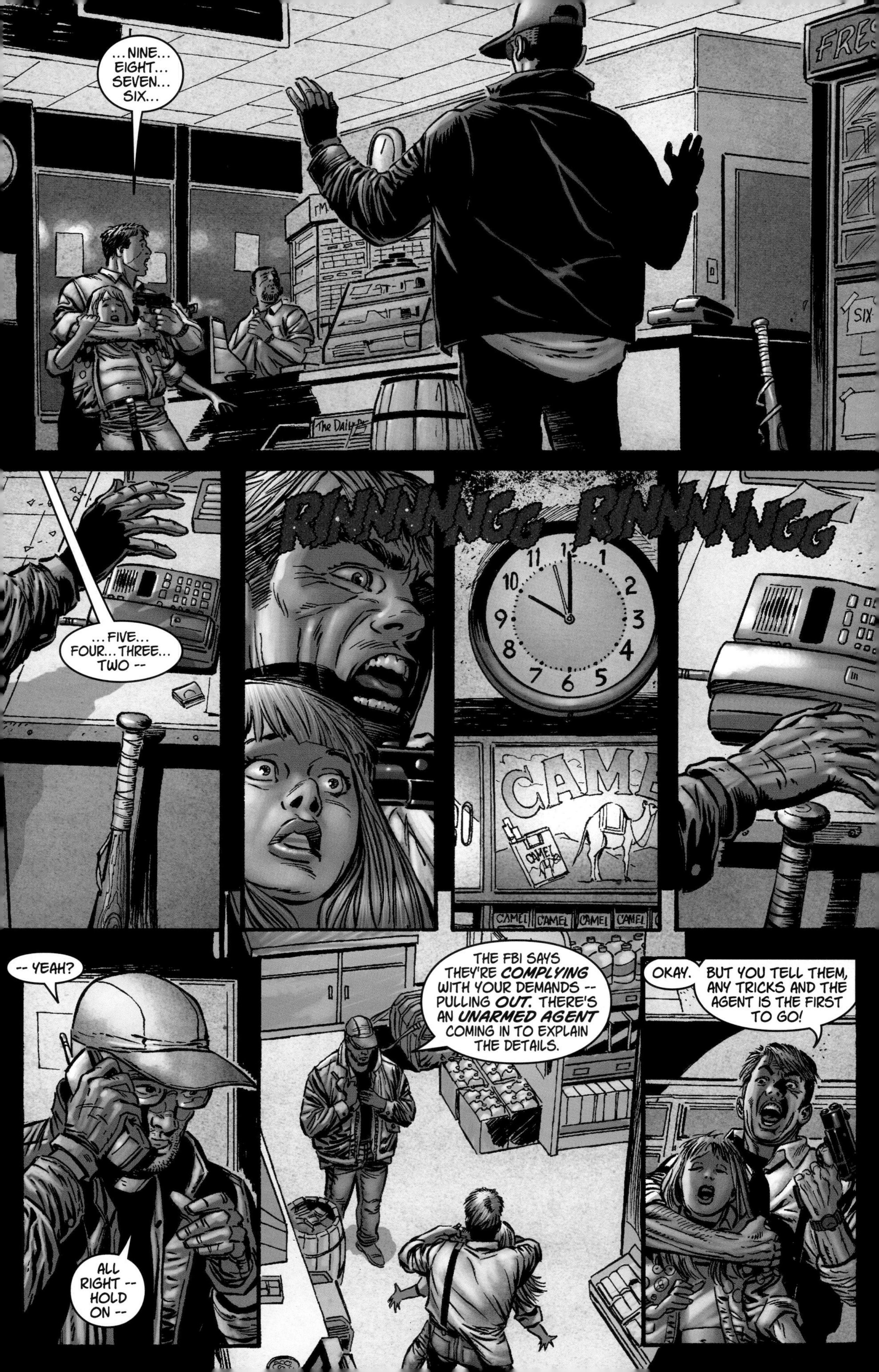
...NINE... EIGHT... SEVEN... SIX...
...FIVE... FOUR... THREE... TWO --
RINNNNNGG RINNNNNGG
-- YEAH?
ALL RIGHT -- HOLD ON --
THE FBI SAYS THEY'RE COMPLYING WITH YOUR DEMANDS -- PULLING OUT. THERE'S AN UNARMED AGENT COMING IN TO EXPLAIN THE DETAILS.
OKAY.
BUT YOU TELL THEM, ANY TRICKS AND THE AGENT IS THE FIRST TO GO!

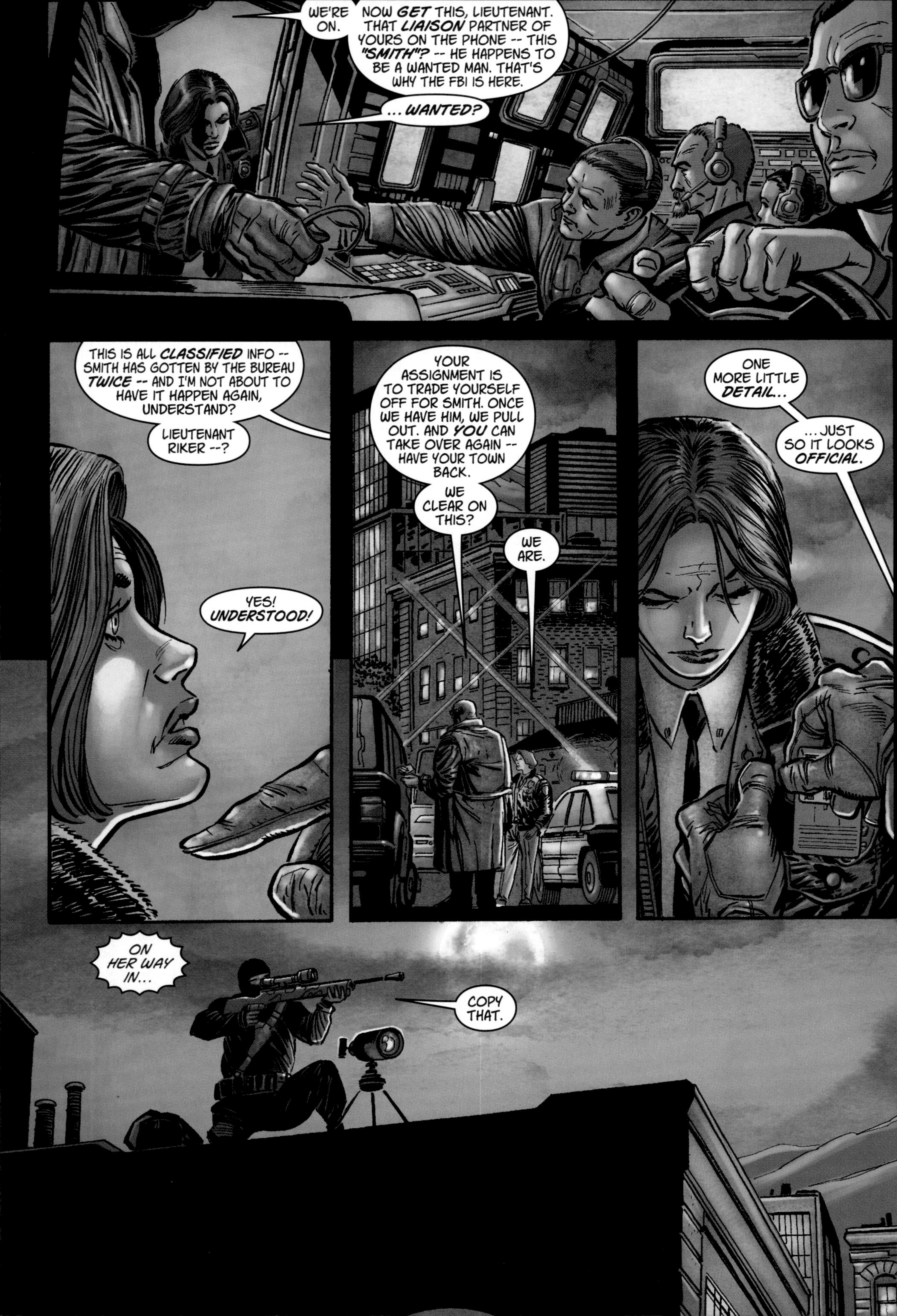
WE'RE ON.
NOW GET THIS, LIEUTENANT. THAT LIAISON PARTNER OF YOURS ON THE PHONE -- THIS "SMITH"? -- HE HAPPENS TO BE A WANTED MAN. THAT'S WHY THE FBI IS HERE.
...WANTED?
THIS IS ALL CLASSIFIED INFO -- SMITH HAS GOTTEN BY THE BUREAU TWICE -- AND I'M NOT ABOUT TO HAVE IT HAPPEN AGAIN, UNDERSTAND?
LIEUTENANT RIKER --?
YES! UNDERSTOOD!
YOUR ASSIGNMENT IS TO TRADE YOURSELF OFF FOR SMITH. ONCE WE HAVE HIM, WE PULL OUT. AND YOU CAN TAKE OVER AGAIN -- HAVE YOUR TOWN BACK.
WE CLEAR ON THIS?
WE ARE.
ONE MORE LITTLE DETAIL...
...JUST SO IT LOOKS OFFICIAL.
ON HER WAY IN...
COPY THAT.

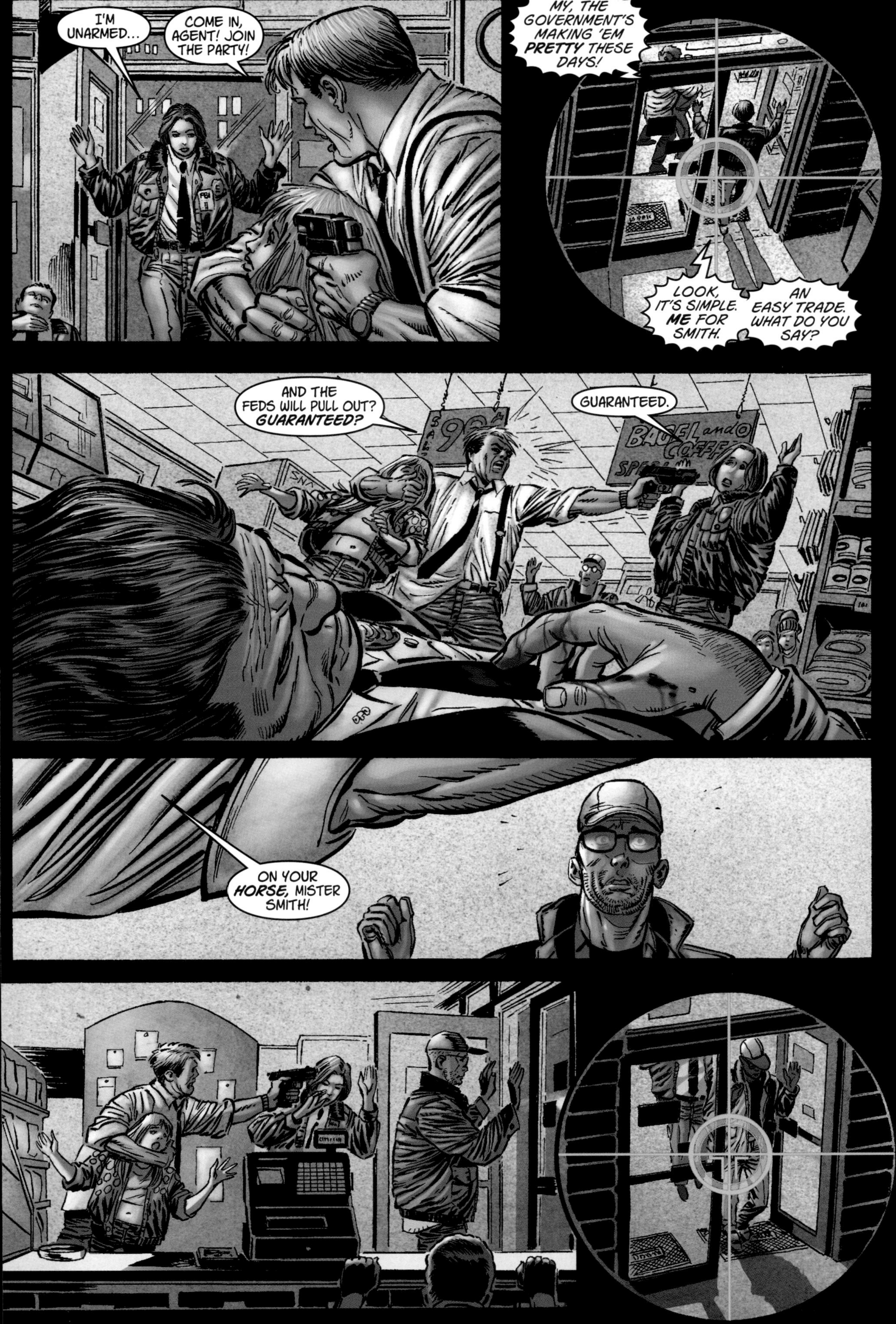
I'M UNARMED...
COME IN, AGENT! JOIN THE PARTY!
MY, THE GOVERNMENT'S MAKING 'EM PRETTY THESE DAYS!
LOOK, IT'S SIMPLE. ME FOR SMITH.
AN EASY TRADE. WHAT DO YOU SAY?
AND THE FEDS WILL PULL OUT? GUARANTEED?
GUARANTEED.
BAGEL and COFFEE
ON YOUR HORSE, MISTER SMITH!

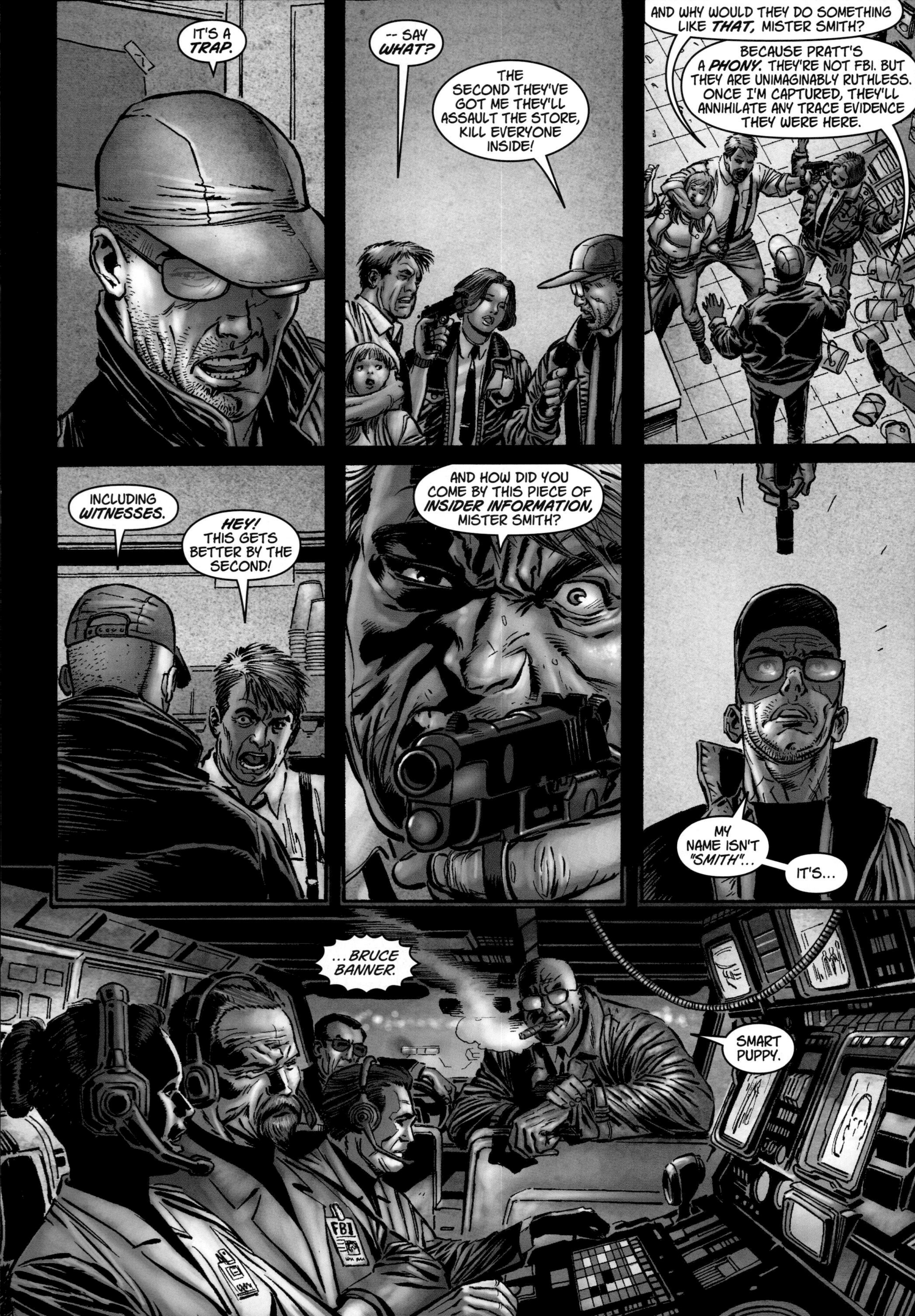
IT'S A *TRAP*.
-- SAY *WHAT?*
THE SECOND THEY'VE GOT ME THEY'LL ASSAULT THE STORE, KILL EVERYONE INSIDE!
AND WHY WOULD THEY DO SOMETHING LIKE *THAT,* MISTER SMITH?
BECAUSE PRATT'S A *PHONY*. THEY'RE NOT FBI. BUT THEY ARE UNIMAGINABLY RUTHLESS. ONCE I'M CAPTURED, THEY'LL ANNIHILATE ANY TRACE EVIDENCE THEY WERE HERE.
INCLUDING *WITNESSES*.
HEY! THIS GETS BETTER BY THE SECOND!
AND HOW DID YOU COME BY THIS PIECE OF *INSIDER INFORMATION,* MISTER SMITH?
MY NAME ISN'T "SMITH"...
IT'S...
...BRUCE BANNER.
SMART PUPPY.
FBI

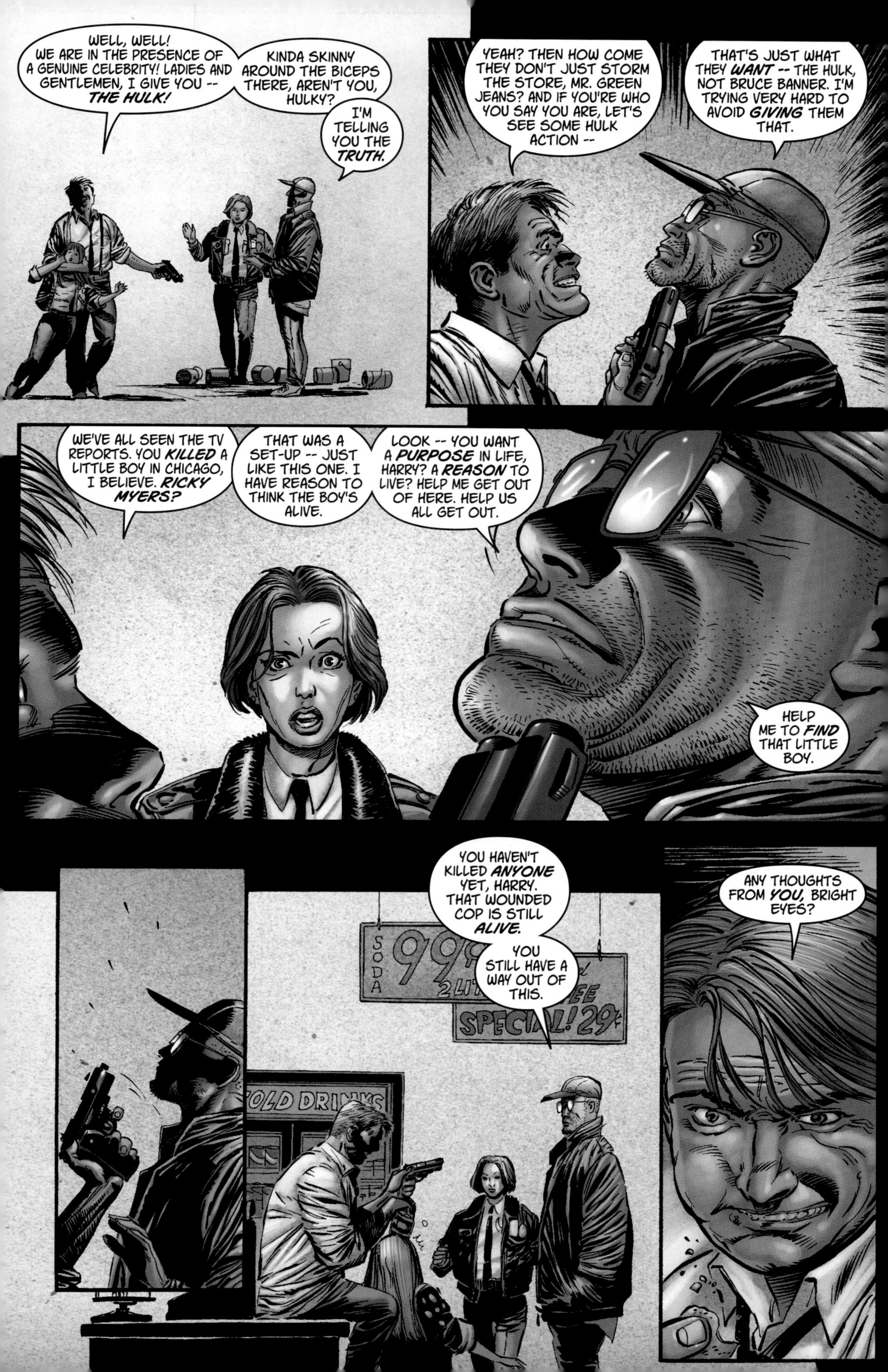
WELL, WELL! WE ARE IN THE PRESENCE OF A GENUINE CELEBRITY! LADIES AND GENTLEMEN, I GIVE YOU -- THE HULK!
KINDA SKINNY AROUND THE BICEPS THERE, AREN'T YOU, HULKY?
I'M TELLING YOU THE TRUTH.
YEAH? THEN HOW COME THEY DON'T JUST STORM THE STORE, MR. GREEN JEANS? AND IF YOU'RE WHO YOU SAY YOU ARE, LET'S SEE SOME HULK ACTION --
THAT'S JUST WHAT THEY WANT -- THE HULK, NOT BRUCE BANNER. I'M TRYING VERY HARD TO AVOID GIVING THEM THAT.
WE'VE ALL SEEN THE TV REPORTS. YOU KILLED A LITTLE BOY IN CHICAGO, I BELIEVE. RICKY MYERS?
THAT WAS A SET-UP -- JUST LIKE THIS ONE. I HAVE REASON TO THINK THE BOY'S ALIVE.
LOOK -- YOU WANT A PURPOSE IN LIFE, HARRY? A REASON TO LIVE? HELP ME GET OUT OF HERE. HELP US ALL GET OUT.
HELP ME TO FIND THAT LITTLE BOY.
YOU HAVEN'T KILLED ANYONE YET, HARRY. THAT WOUNDED COP IS STILL ALIVE.
YOU STILL HAVE A WAY OUT OF THIS.
SODA
SPECIAL! 29¢
COLD DRINKS
ANY THOUGHTS FROM YOU, BRIGHT EYES?

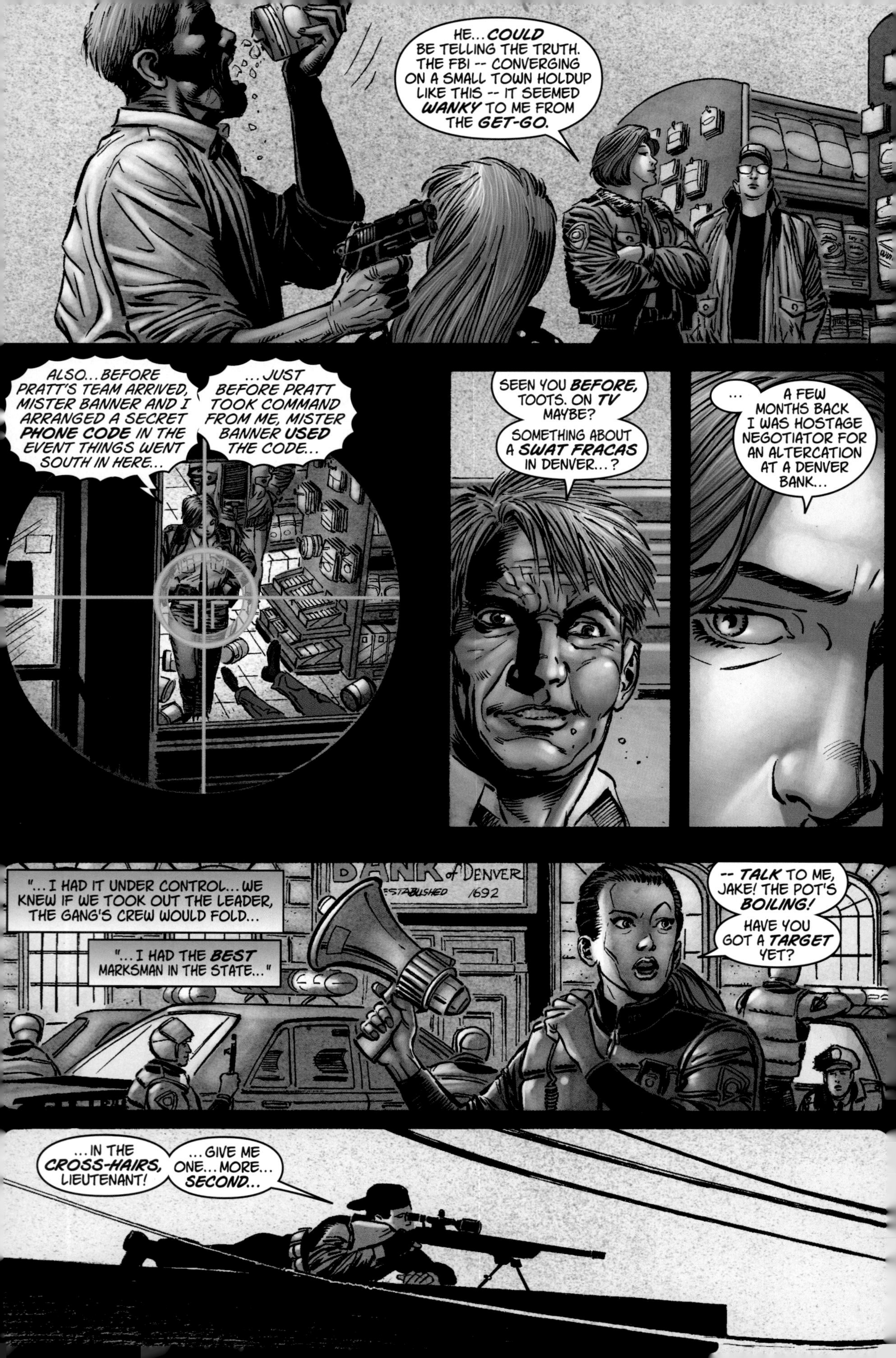
HE... COULD BE TELLING THE TRUTH. THE FBI -- CONVERGING ON A SMALL TOWN HOLDUP LIKE THIS -- IT SEEMED WANKY TO ME FROM THE GET-GO.
ALSO... BEFORE PRATT'S TEAM ARRIVED, MISTER BANNER AND I ARRANGED A SECRET PHONE CODE IN THE EVENT THINGS WENT SOUTH IN HERE...
... JUST BEFORE PRATT TOOK COMMAND FROM ME, MISTER BANNER USED THE CODE...
SEEN YOU BEFORE, TOOTS. ON TV MAYBE?
SOMETHING ABOUT A SWAT FRACAS IN DENVER...?
...
A FEW MONTHS BACK I WAS HOSTAGE NEGOTIATOR FOR AN ALTERCATION AT A DENVER BANK...
"... I HAD IT UNDER CONTROL... WE KNEW IF WE TOOK OUT THE LEADER, THE GANG'S CREW WOULD FOLD...
"... I HAD THE BEST MARKSMAN IN THE STATE..."
BANK of DENVER
ESTABLISHED 1692
-- TALK TO ME, JAKE! THE POT'S BOILING!
HAVE YOU GOT A TARGET YET?
... IN THE CROSS-HAIRS, LIEUTENANT!
... GIVE ME ONE... MORE... SECOND...

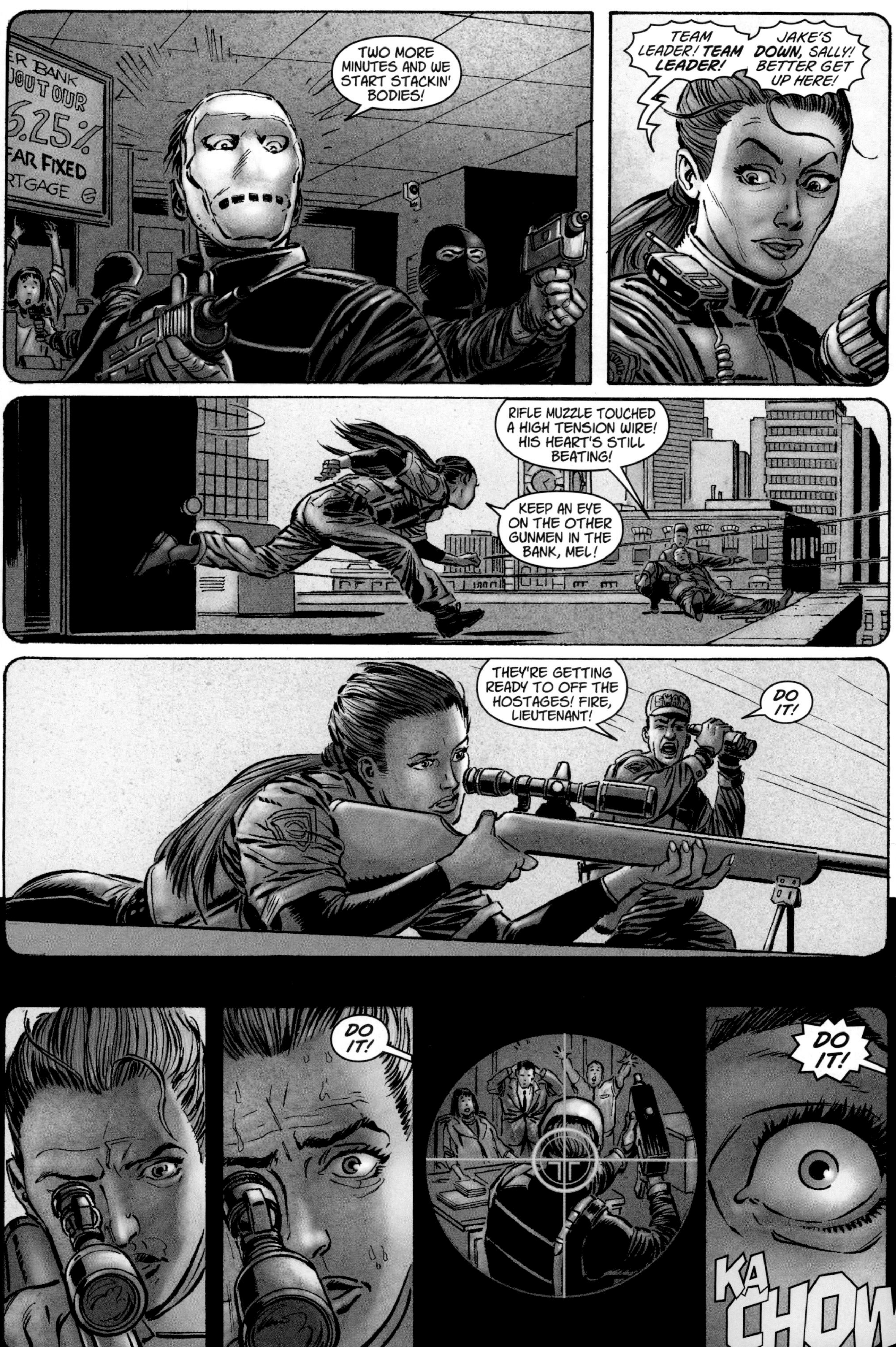
TWO MORE MINUTES AND WE START STACKIN' BODIES!
TEAM LEADER! **TEAM LEADER!**
JAKE'S **DOWN,** SALLY! BETTER GET UP HERE!
RIFLE MUZZLE TOUCHED A HIGH TENSION WIRE! HIS HEART'S STILL BEATING!
KEEP AN EYE ON THE OTHER GUNMEN IN THE BANK, MEL!
THEY'RE GETTING READY TO OFF THE HOSTAGES! FIRE, LIEUTENANT!
DO IT!
DO IT!
DO IT!
KA CHOW

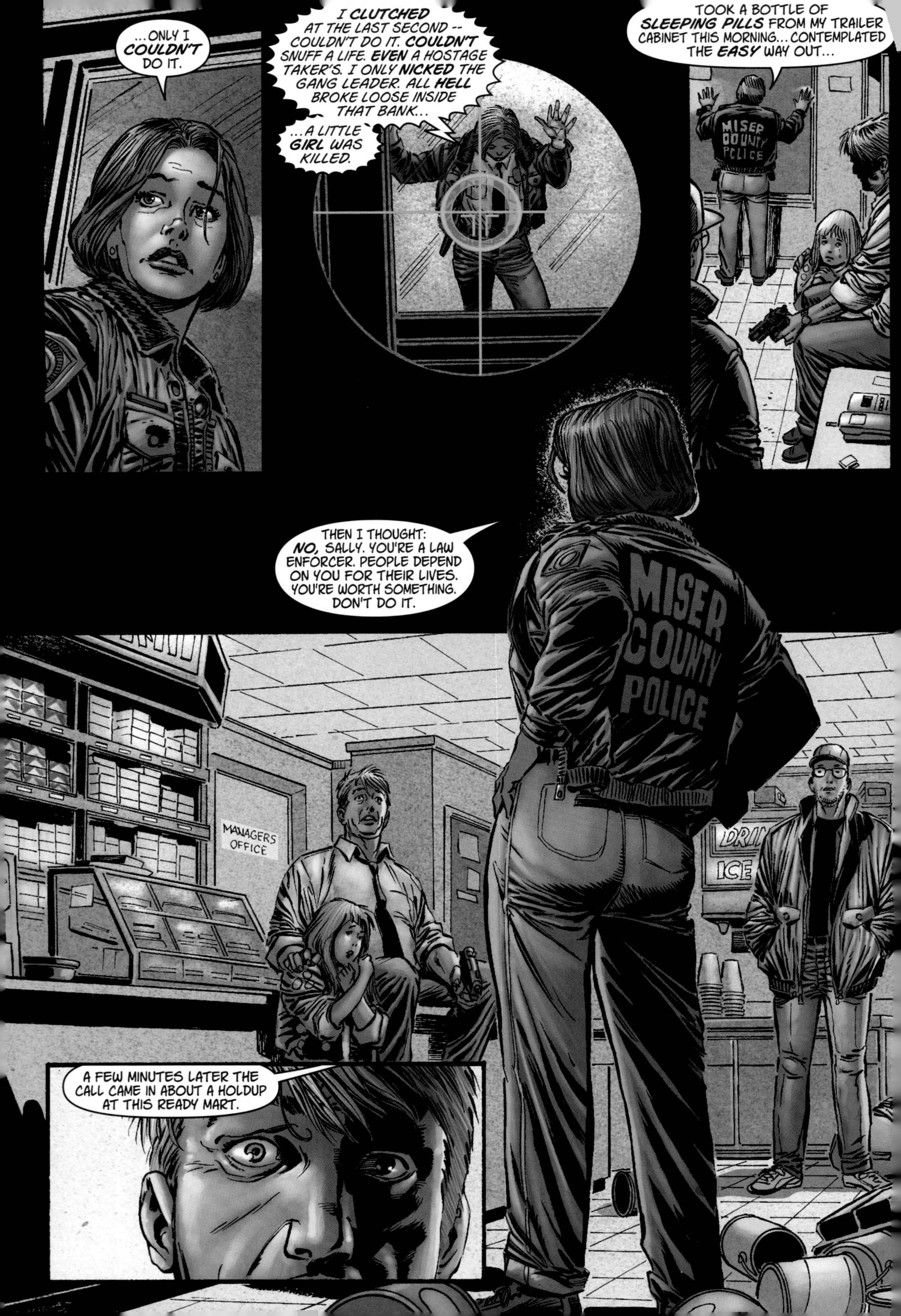
...ONLY I COULDN'T DO IT.
I CLUTCHED AT THE LAST SECOND -- COULDN'T DO IT. COULDN'T SNUFF A LIFE. EVEN A HOSTAGE TAKER'S. I ONLY NICKED THE GANG LEADER. ALL HELL BROKE LOOSE INSIDE THAT BANK...
...A LITTLE GIRL WAS KILLED.
TOOK A BOTTLE OF SLEEPING PILLS FROM MY TRAILER CABINET THIS MORNING... CONTEMPLATED THE EASY WAY OUT...
MISER COUNTY POLICE
THEN I THOUGHT: NO, SALLY. YOU'RE A LAW ENFORCER. PEOPLE DEPEND ON YOU FOR THEIR LIVES. YOU'RE WORTH SOMETHING. DON'T DO IT.
MISER COUNTY POLICE
MANAGERS OFFICE
ICE
A FEW MINUTES LATER THE CALL CAME IN ABOUT A HOLDUP AT THIS READY MART.

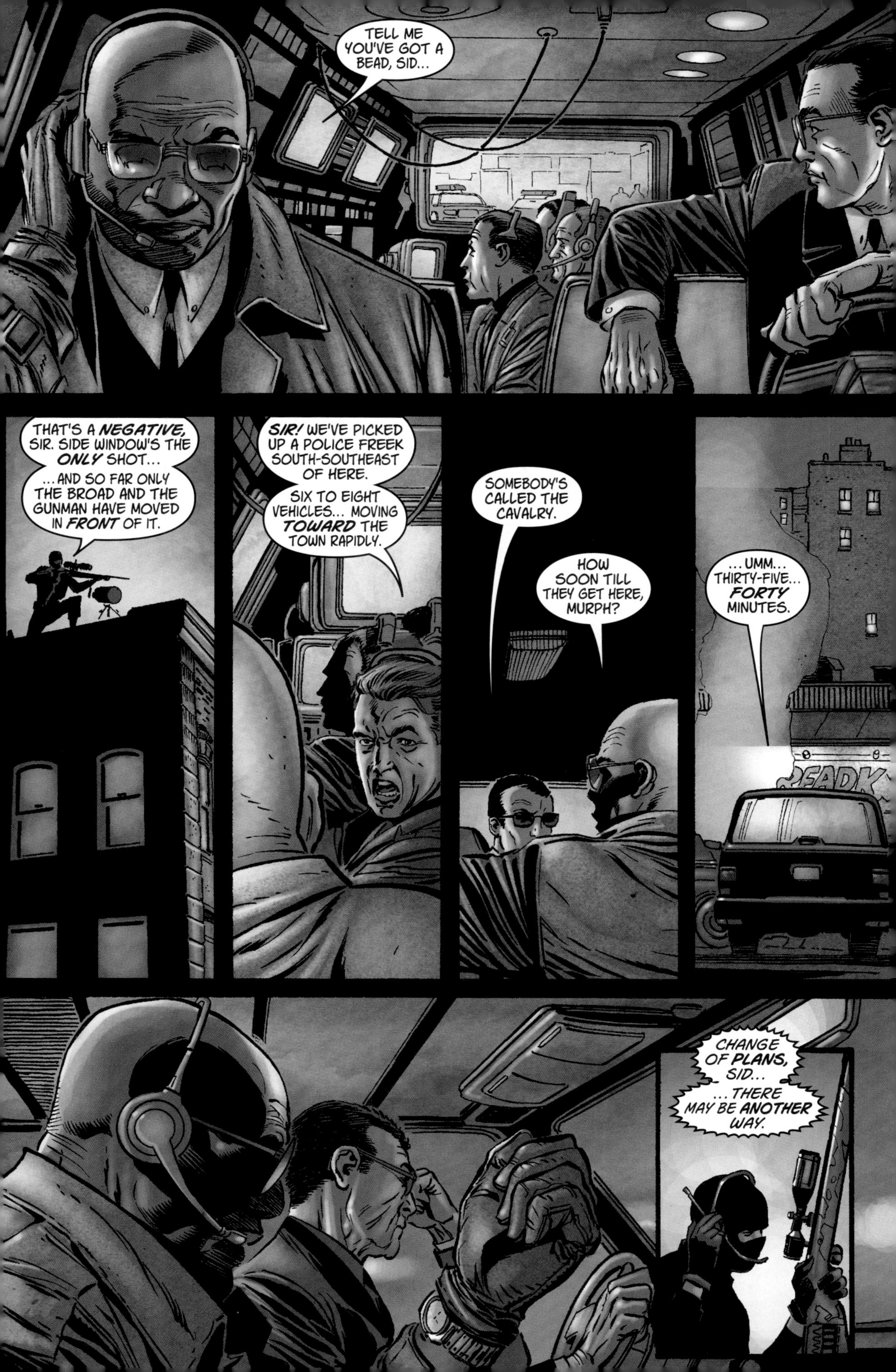
TELL ME YOU'VE GOT A BEAD, SID...
THAT'S A NEGATIVE, SIR. SIDE WINDOW'S THE ONLY SHOT...
...AND SO FAR ONLY THE BROAD AND THE GUNMAN HAVE MOVED IN FRONT OF IT.
SIR! WE'VE PICKED UP A POLICE FREEK SOUTH-SOUTHEAST OF HERE.
SIX TO EIGHT VEHICLES... MOVING TOWARD THE TOWN RAPIDLY.
SOMEBODY'S CALLED THE CAVALRY.
HOW SOON TILL THEY GET HERE, MURPH?
...UMM... THIRTY-FIVE... FORTY MINUTES.
CHANGE OF PLANS, SID...
...THERE MAY BE ANOTHER WAY.

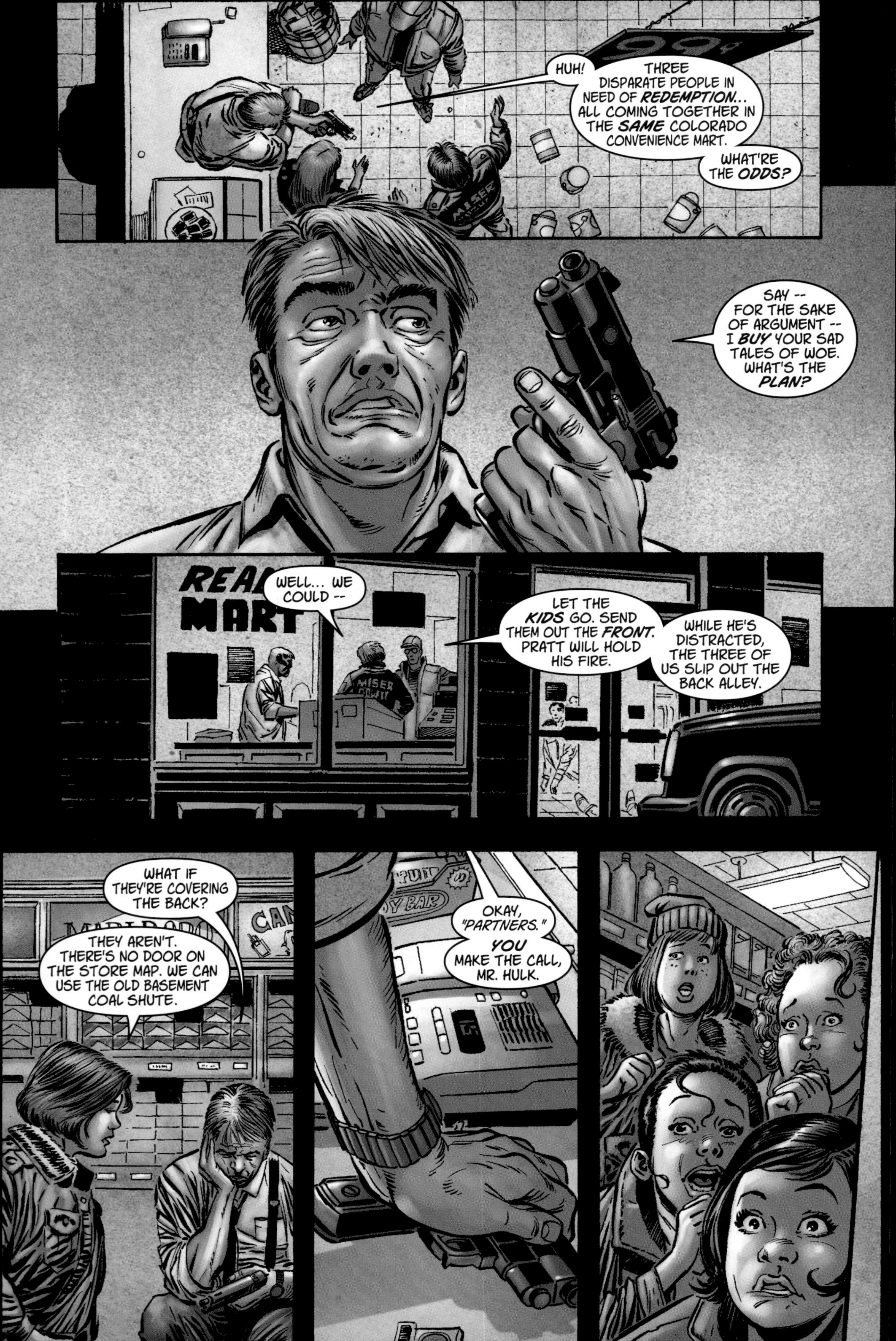
HUH!
THREE DISPARATE PEOPLE IN NEED OF REDEMPTION... ALL COMING TOGETHER IN THE SAME COLORADO CONVENIENCE MART.
WHAT'RE THE ODDS?
SAY -- FOR THE SAKE OF ARGUMENT -- I BUY YOUR SAD TALES OF WOE. WHAT'S THE PLAN?
REAL MART
WELL... WE COULD --
LET THE KIDS GO. SEND THEM OUT THE FRONT. PRATT WILL HOLD HIS FIRE.
WHILE HE'S DISTRACTED, THE THREE OF US SLIP OUT THE BACK ALLEY.
WHAT IF THEY'RE COVERING THE BACK?
THEY AREN'T. THERE'S NO DOOR ON THE STORE MAP. WE CAN USE THE OLD BASEMENT COAL SHUTE.
OKAY, "PARTNERS." YOU MAKE THE CALL, MR. HULK.

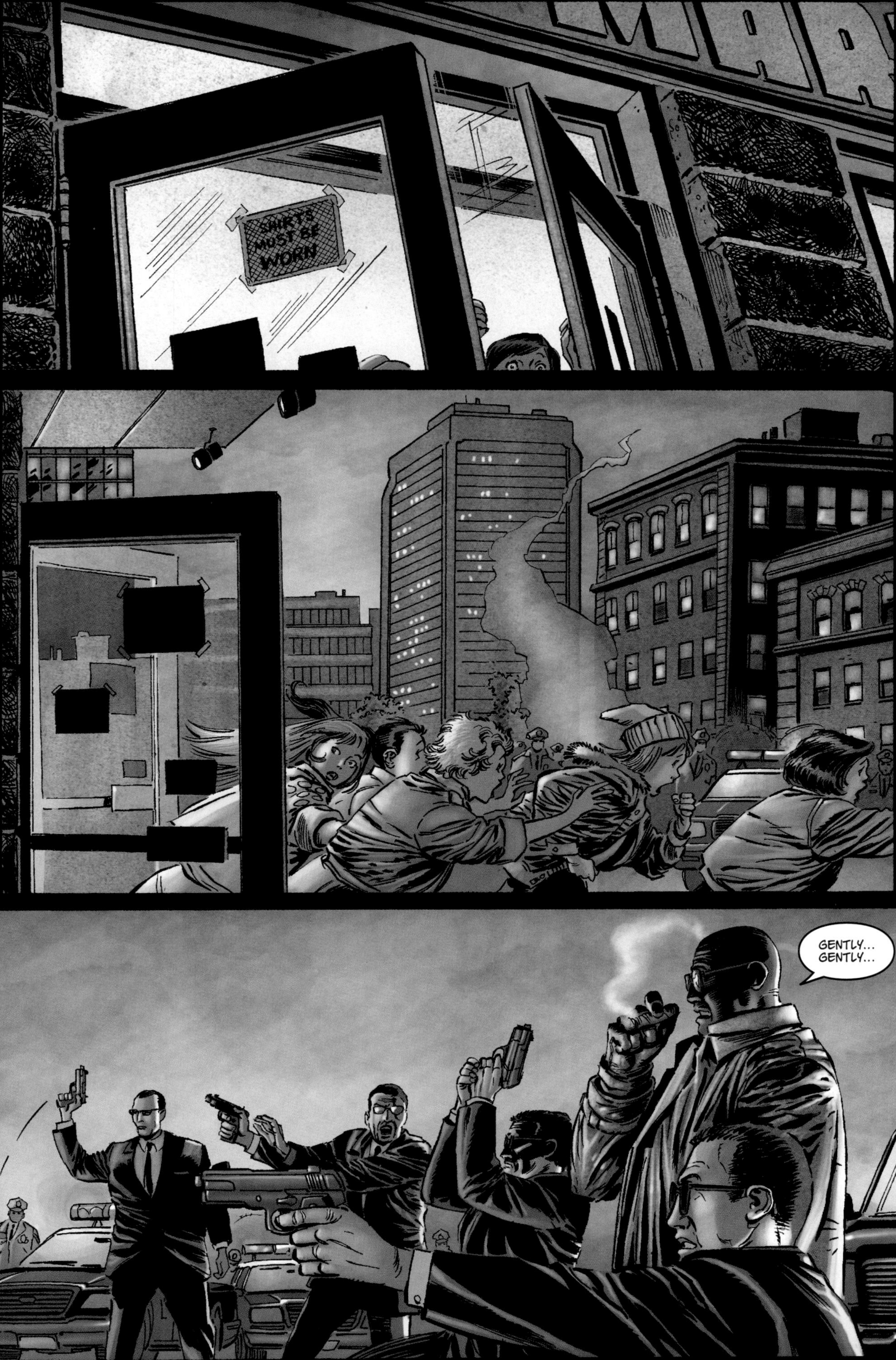
SHIRTS MUST BE WORN
GENTLY... GENTLY...

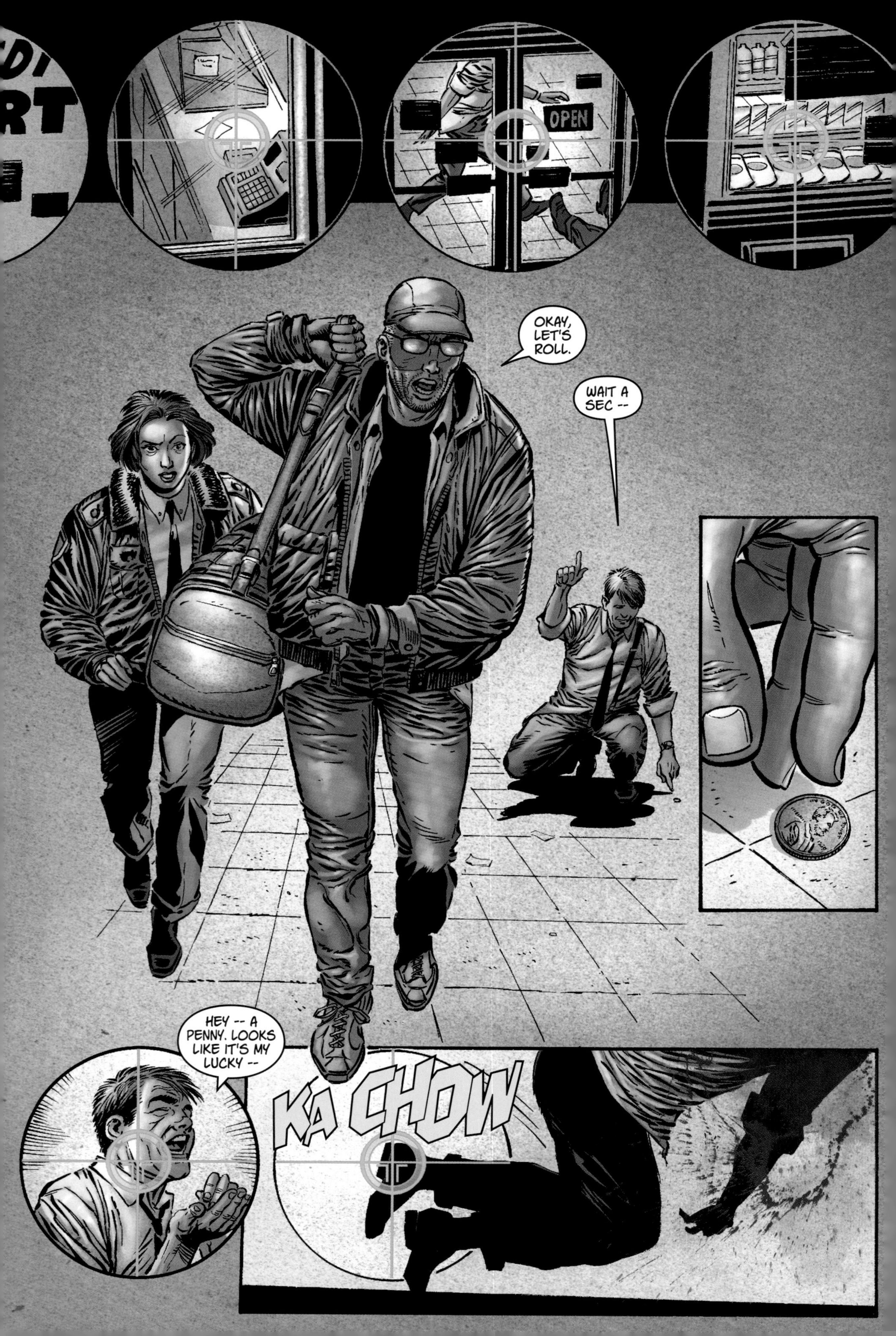

OPEN
OKAY, LET'S ROLL.
WAIT A SEC --
HEY -- A PENNY. LOOKS LIKE IT'S MY LUCKY --
KA CHOW

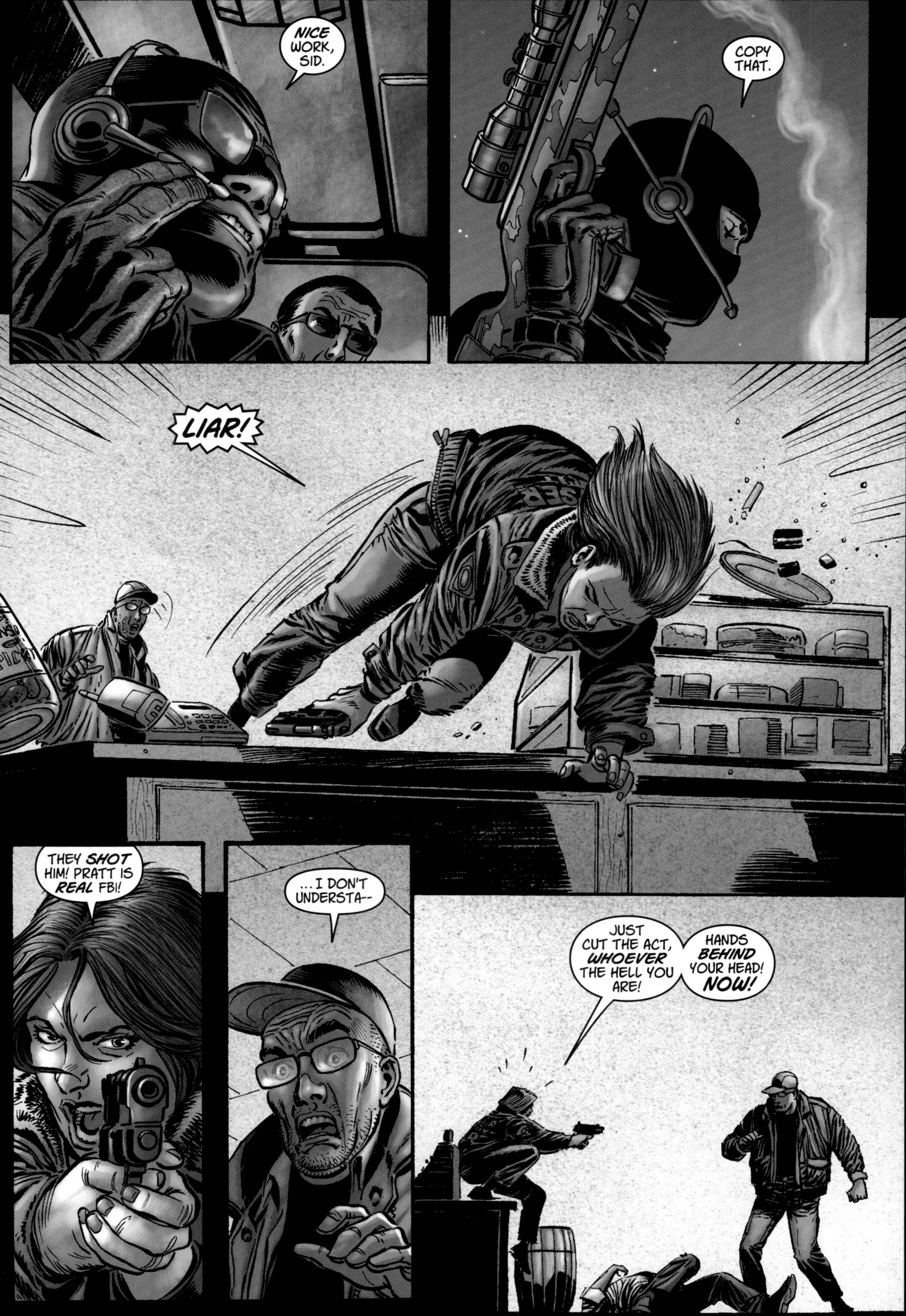
NICE WORK, SID.
COPY THAT.
LIAR!
THEY SHOT HIM! PRATT IS REAL FBI!
...I DON'T UNDERSTA--
JUST CUT THE ACT, WHOEVER THE HELL YOU ARE!
HANDS BEHIND YOUR HEAD! NOW!

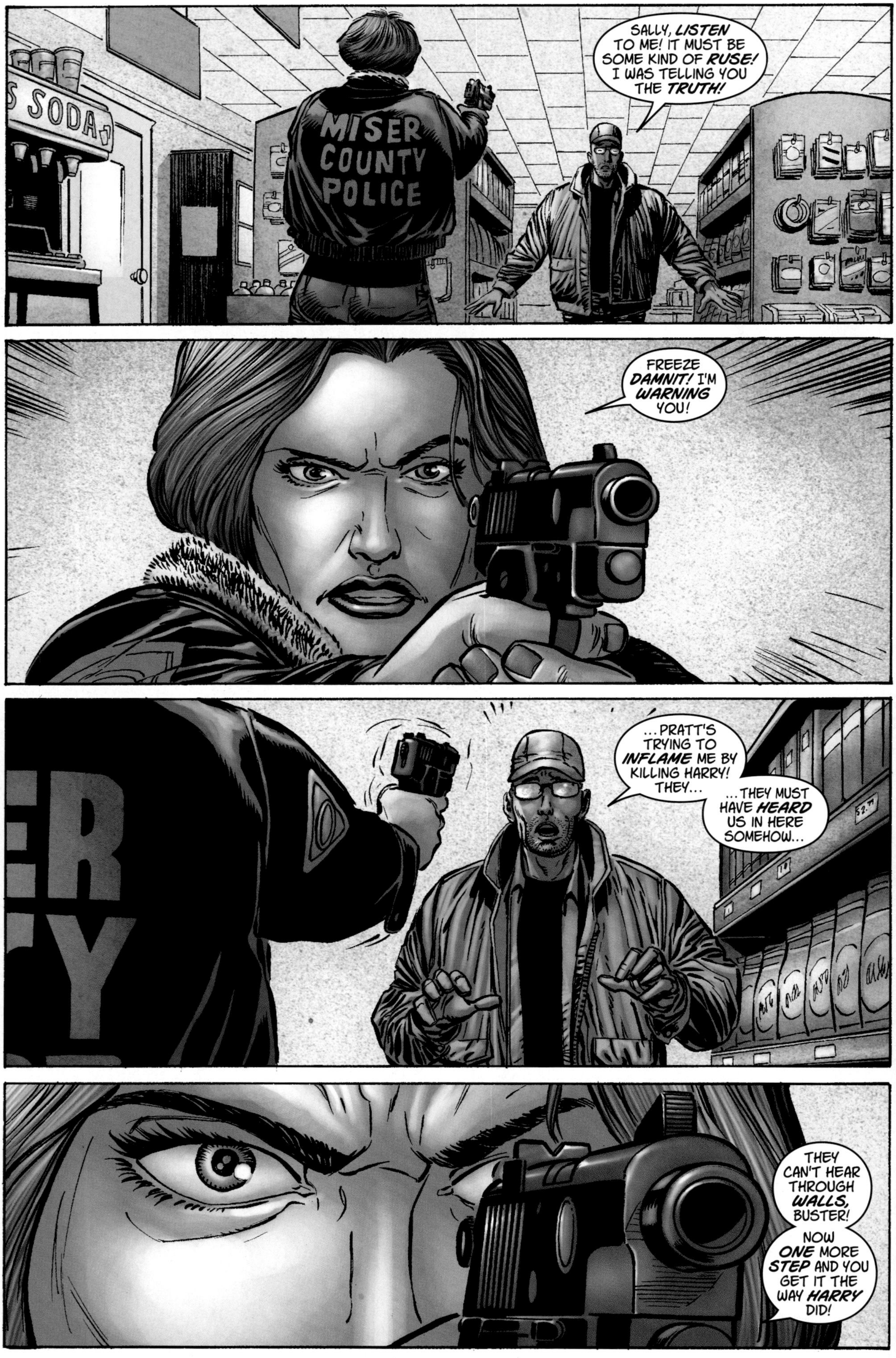
MISER COUNTY POLICE
SODA
SALLY, LISTEN TO ME! IT MUST BE SOME KIND OF RUSE! I WAS TELLING YOU THE TRUTH!
FREEZE DAMNIT! I'M WARNING YOU!
...PRATT'S TRYING TO INFLAME ME BY KILLING HARRY! THEY...
...THEY MUST HAVE HEARD US IN HERE SOMEHOW...
THEY CAN'T HEAR THROUGH WALLS, BUSTER!
NOW ONE MORE STEP AND YOU GET IT THE WAY HARRY DID!

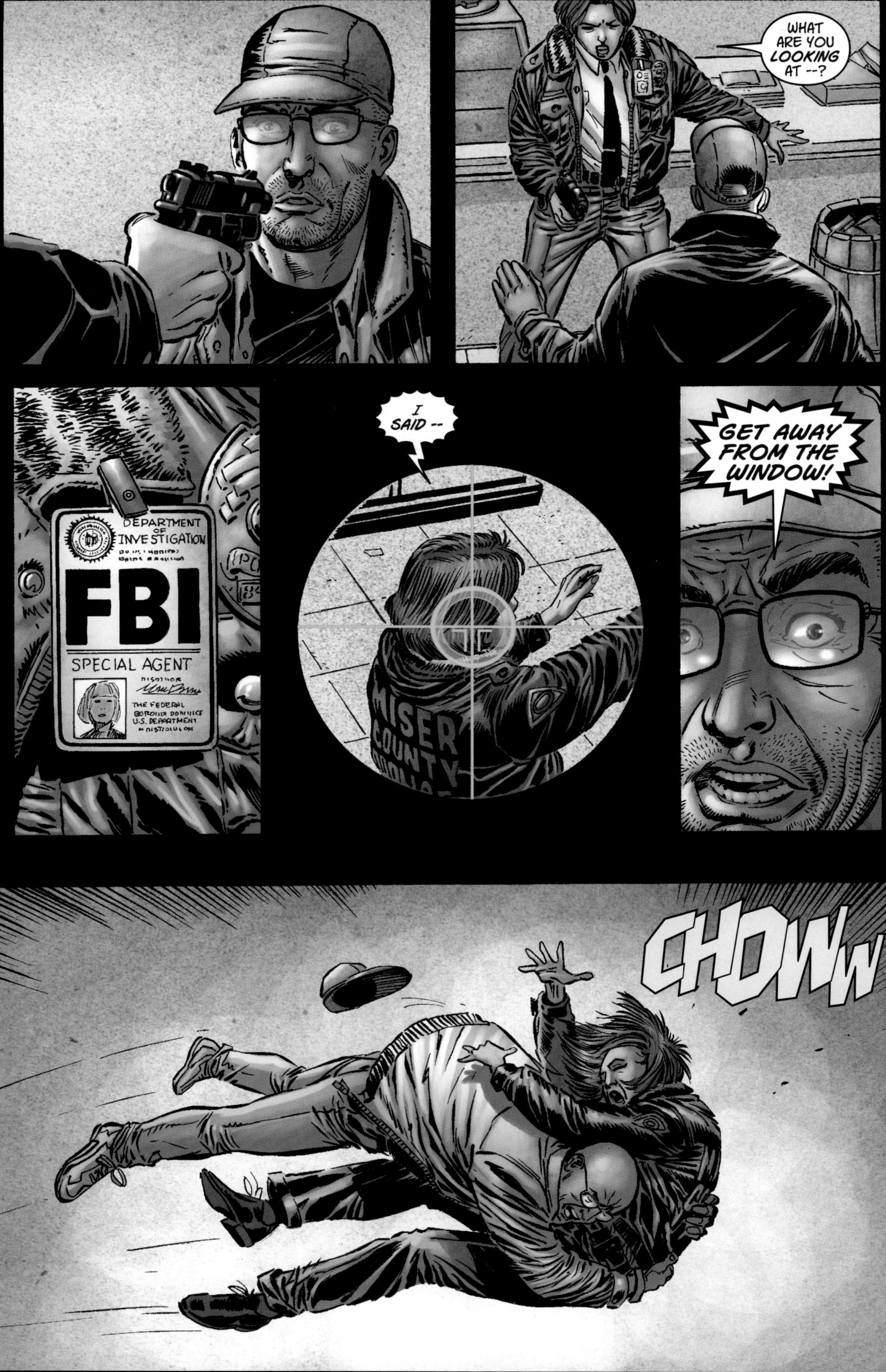
WHAT ARE YOU LOOKING AT --?
DEPARTMENT OF INVESTIGATION
FBI
SPECIAL AGENT
I SAID --
MISER COUNTY
GET AWAY FROM THE WINDOW!
CHOWW

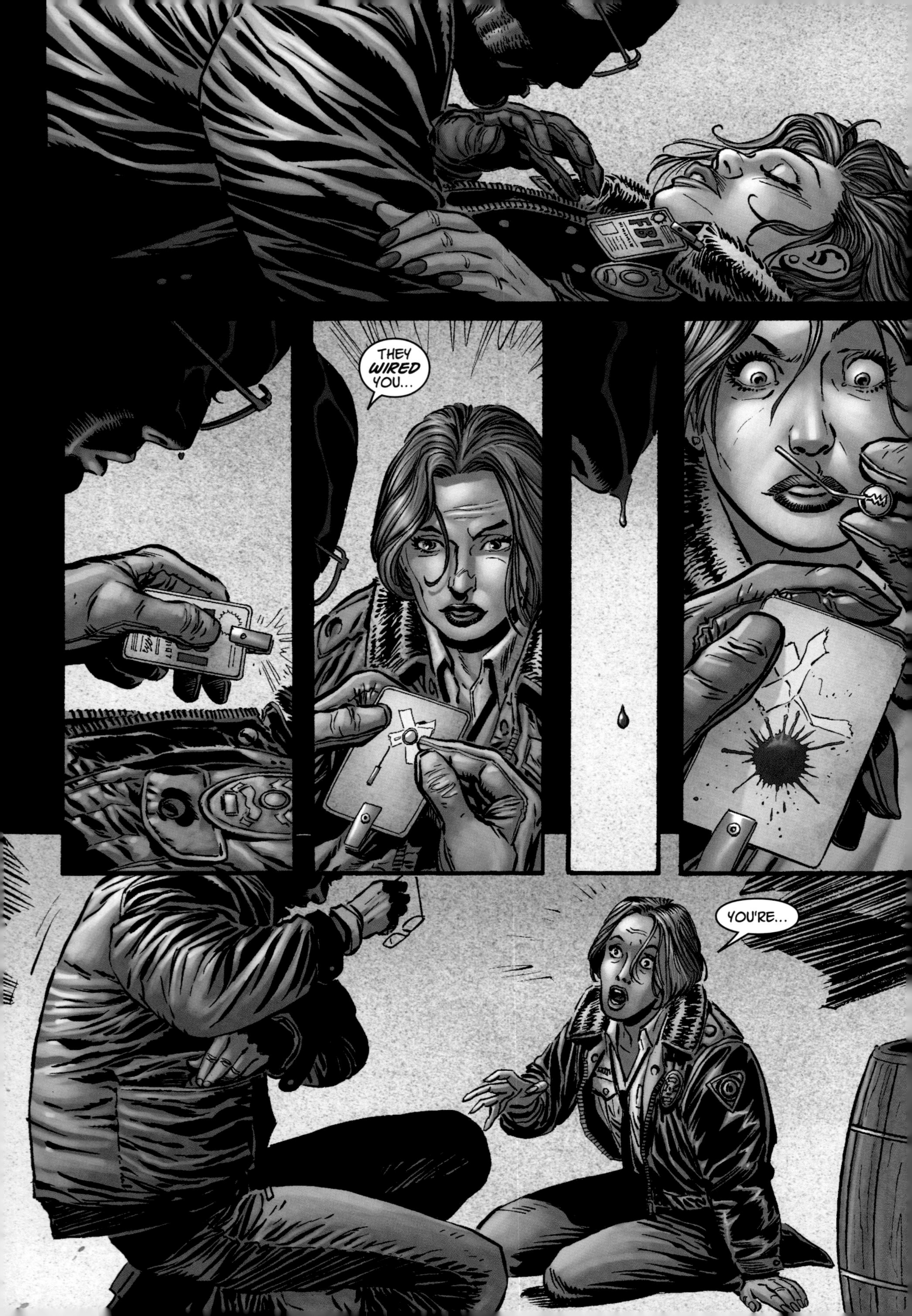
THEY *WIRED* YOU...
YOU'RE...

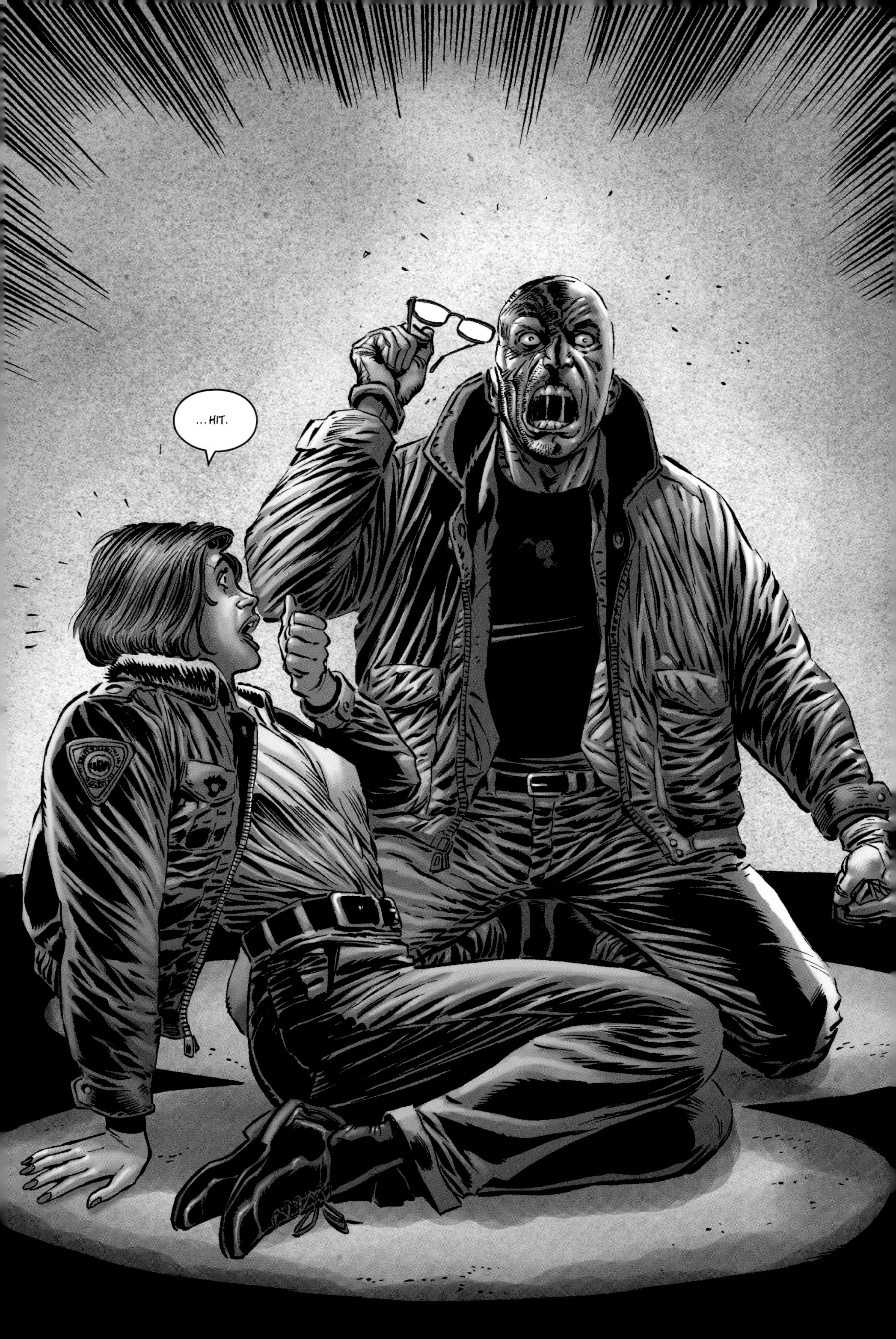
...HIT.

INCREDIBLE HULK #42
Cover by Kaare Andrews

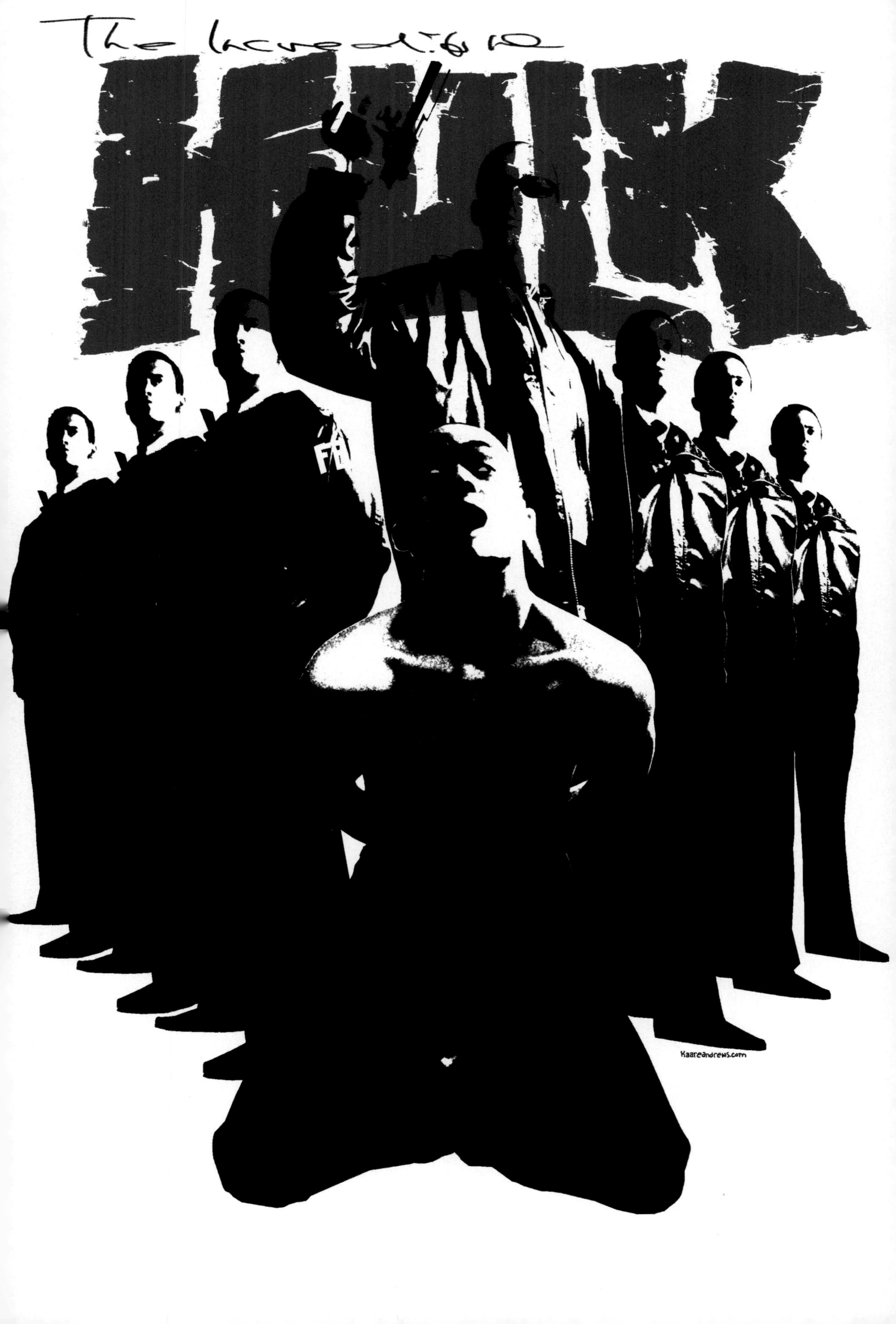
The Incredible
HULK
FBI
Kaareandrews.com

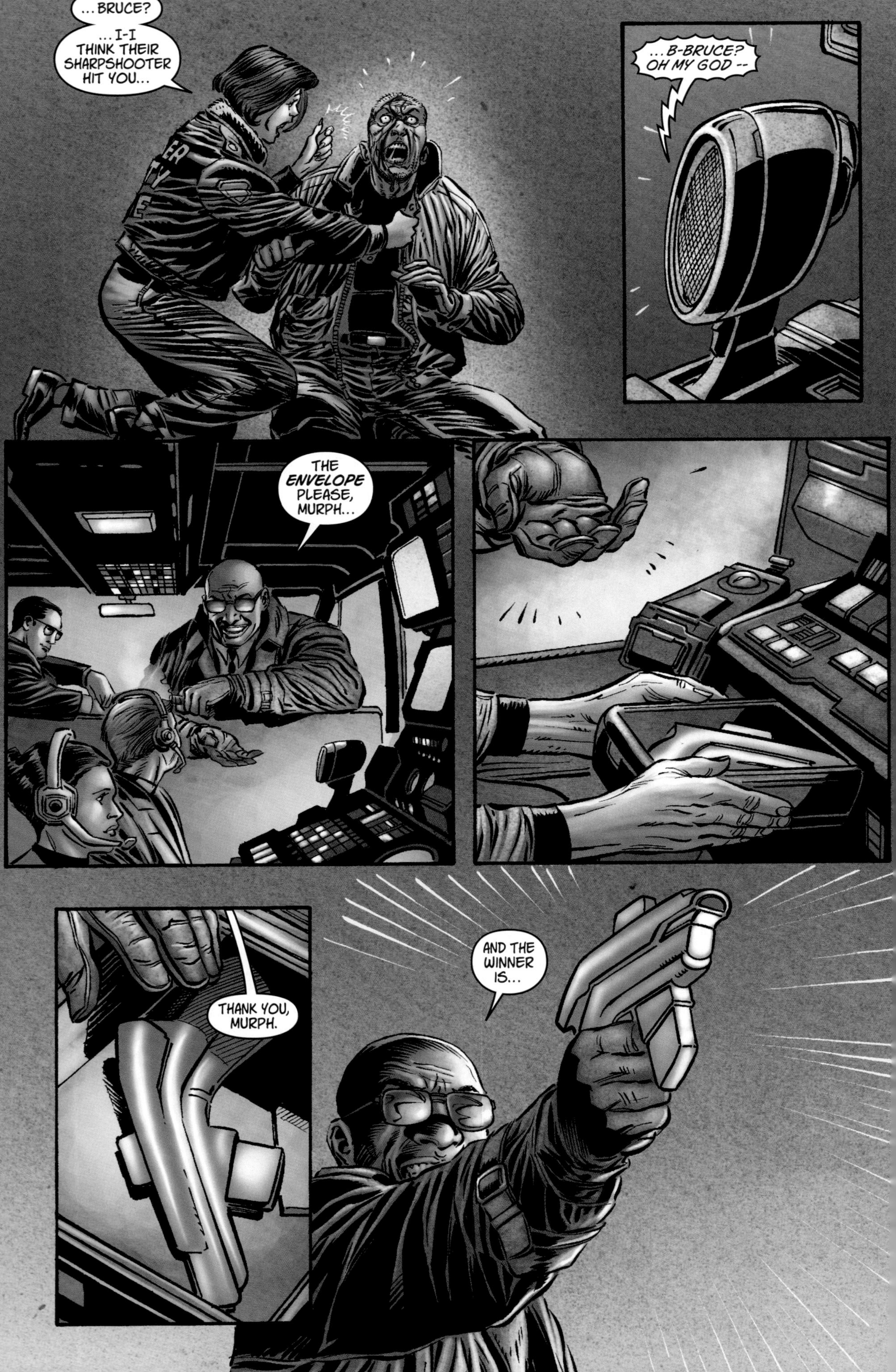
...BRUCE?
...I-I THINK THEIR SHARPSHOOTER HIT YOU...
...B-BRUCE? OH MY GOD --
THE ENVELOPE PLEASE, MURPH...
THANK YOU, MURPH.
AND THE WINNER IS...

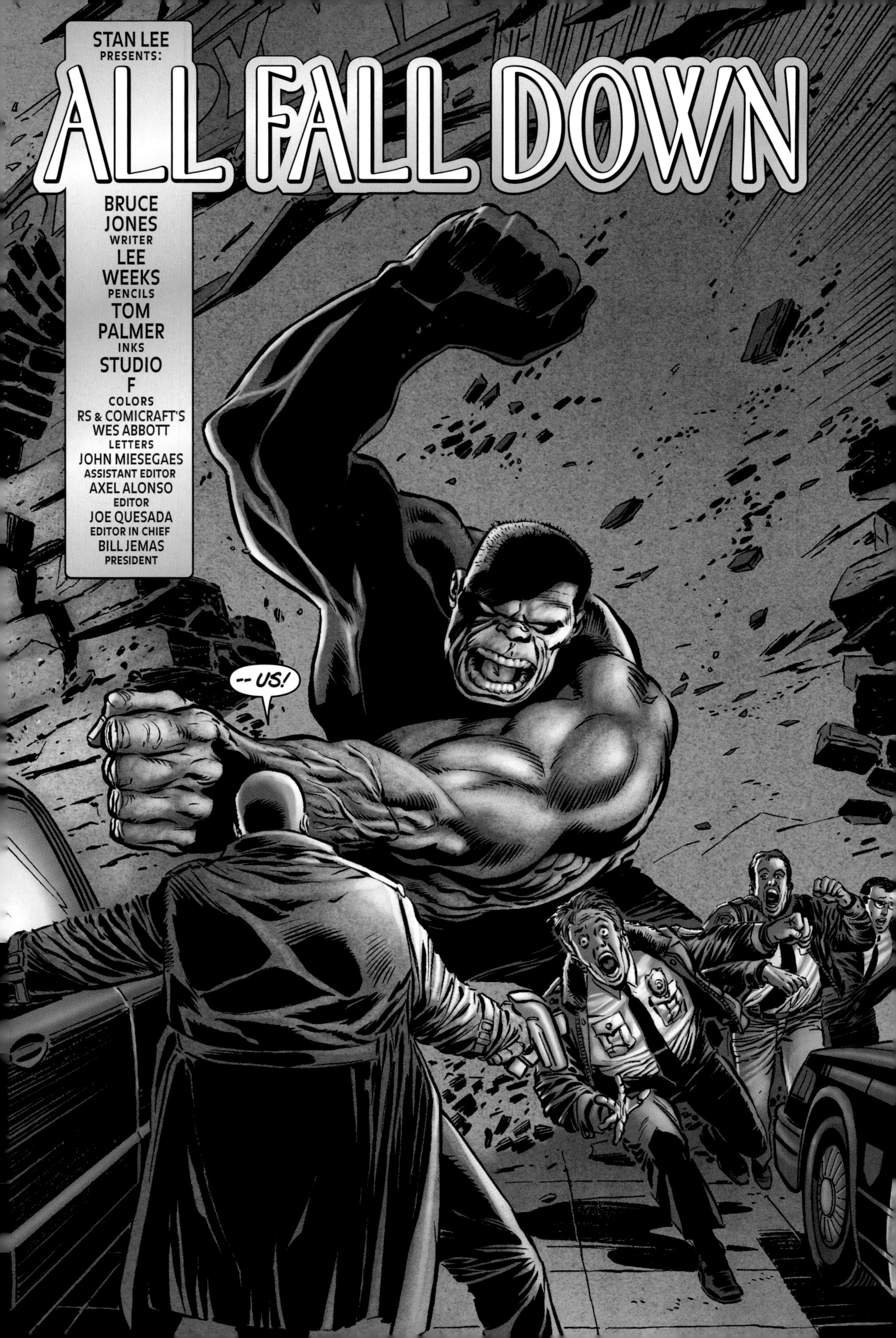
STAN LEE PRESENTS:
ALL FALL DOWN
BRUCE JONES WRITER
LEE WEEKS PENCILS
TOM PALMER INKS
STUDIO F COLORS
RS & COMICRAFT'S WES ABBOTT LETTERS
JOHN MIESEGAES ASSISTANT EDITOR
AXEL ALONSO EDITOR
JOE QUESADA EDITOR IN CHIEF
BILL JEMAS PRESIDENT
-- US!

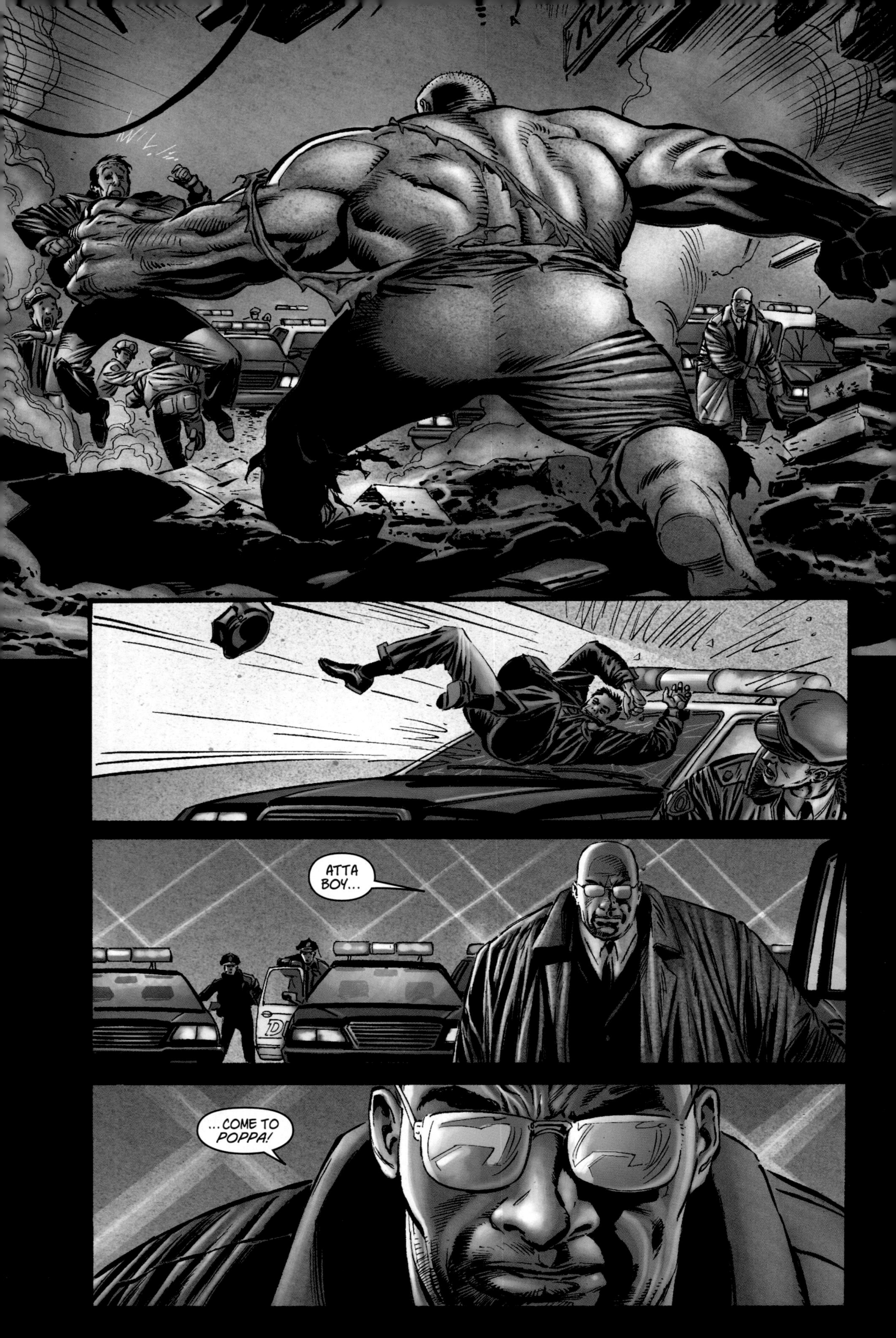
ATTA BOY...
...COME TO POPPA!

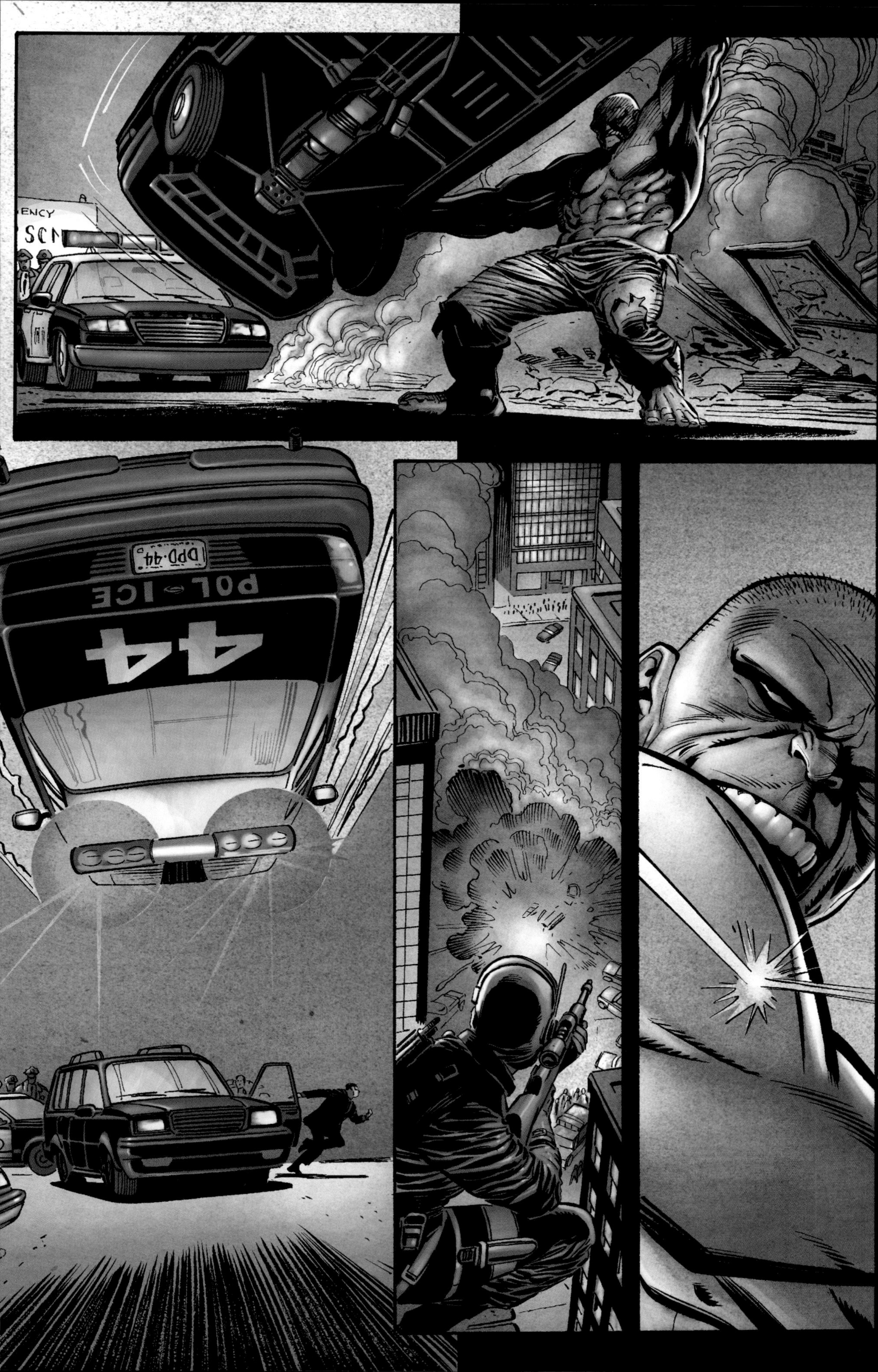
ENCY
DPD-44
POL ICE
44

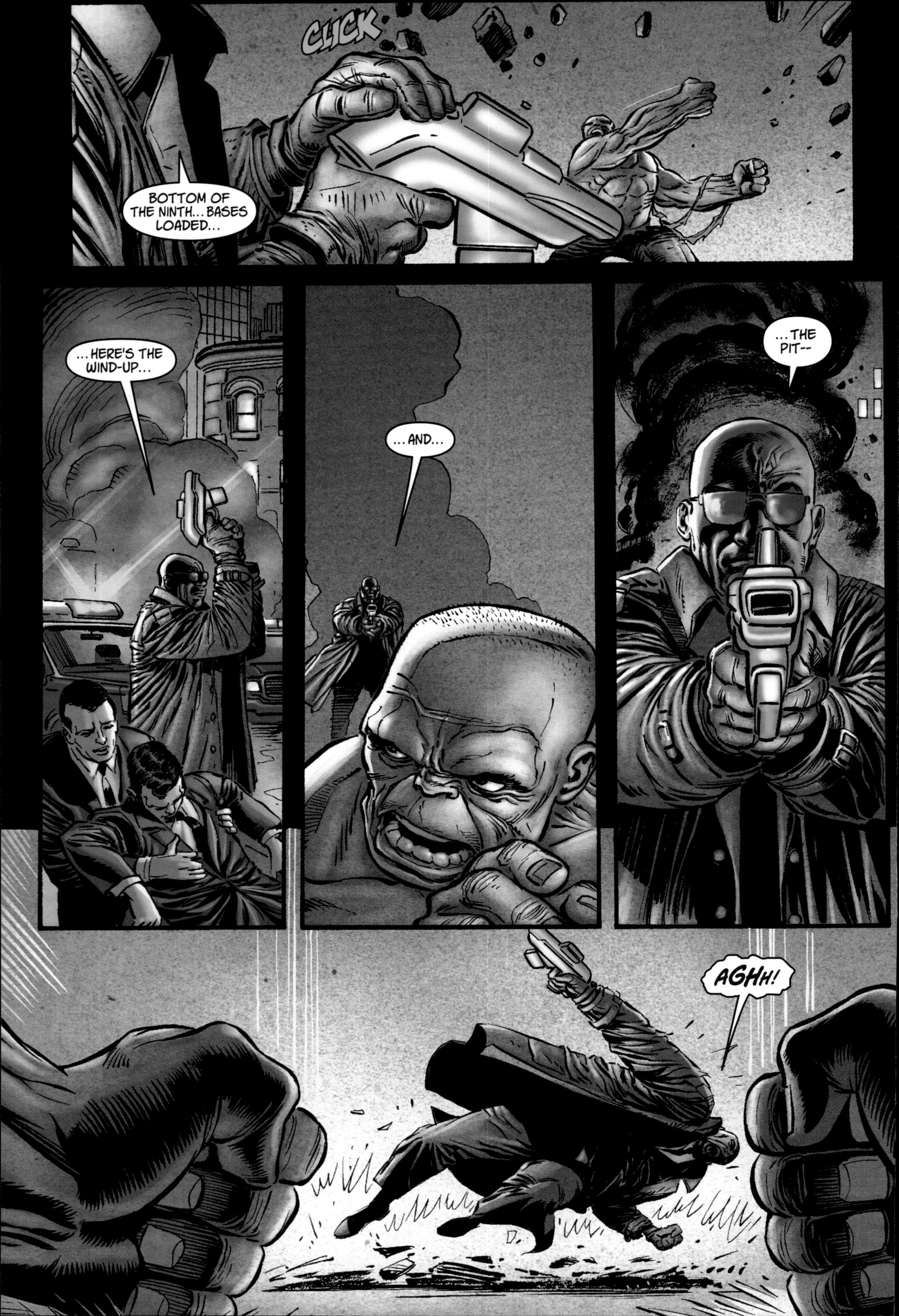
CLICK
BOTTOM OF THE NINTH... BASES LOADED...
...HERE'S THE WIND-UP...
...AND...
...THE PIT--
AGHH!

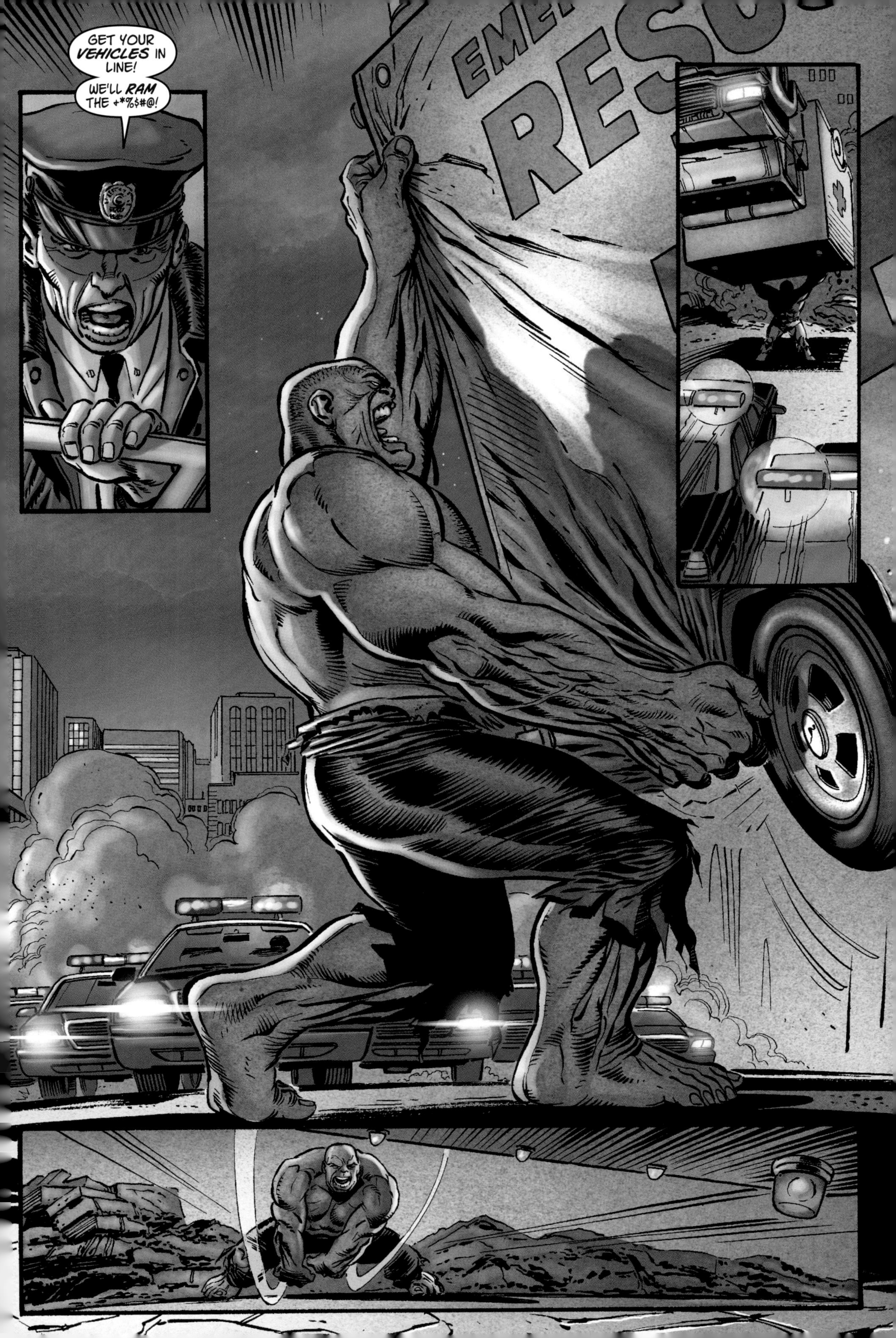
GET YOUR VEHICLES IN LINE!
WE'LL RAM THE +*%$#@!
EME
RESC

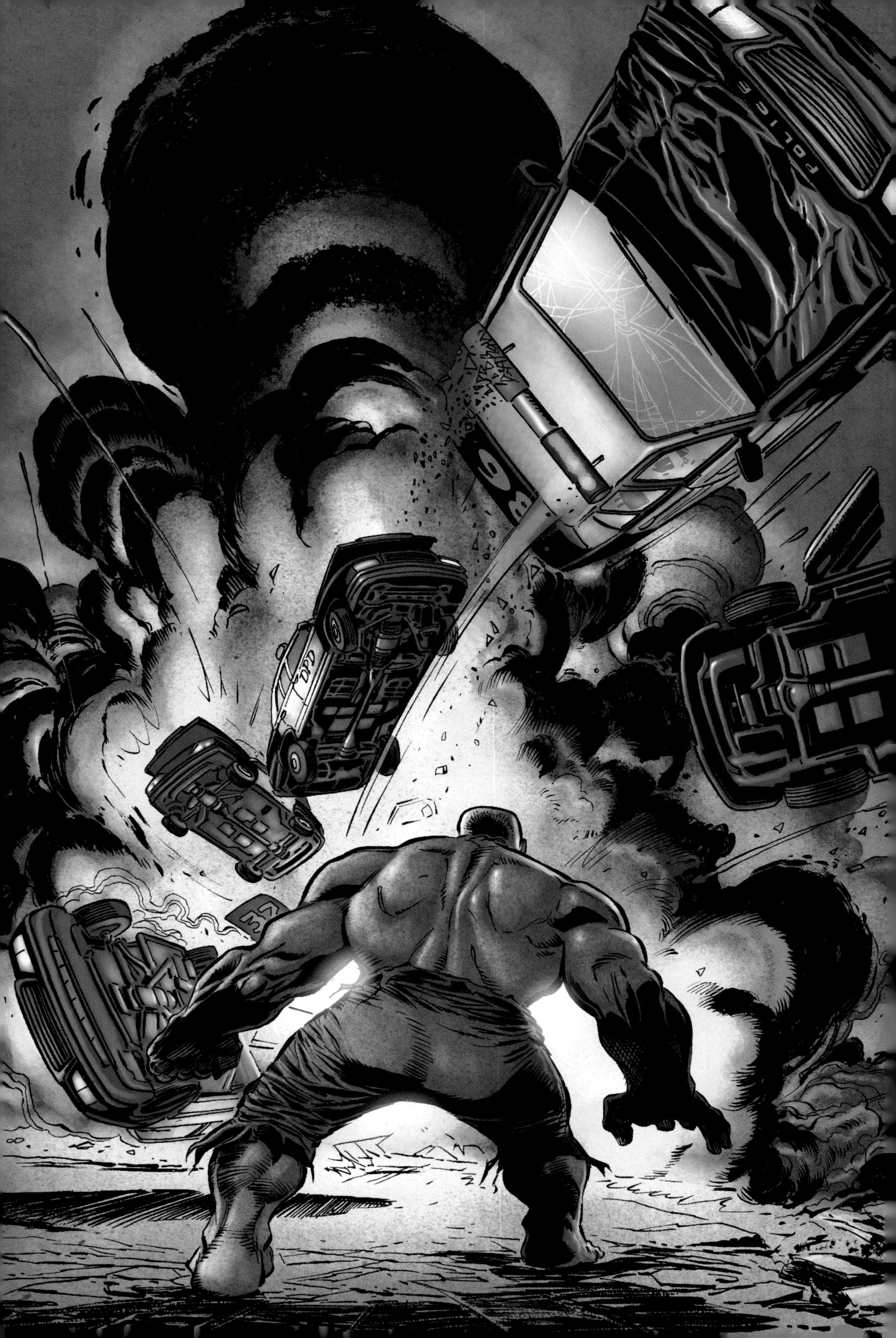
POLICE
DPD

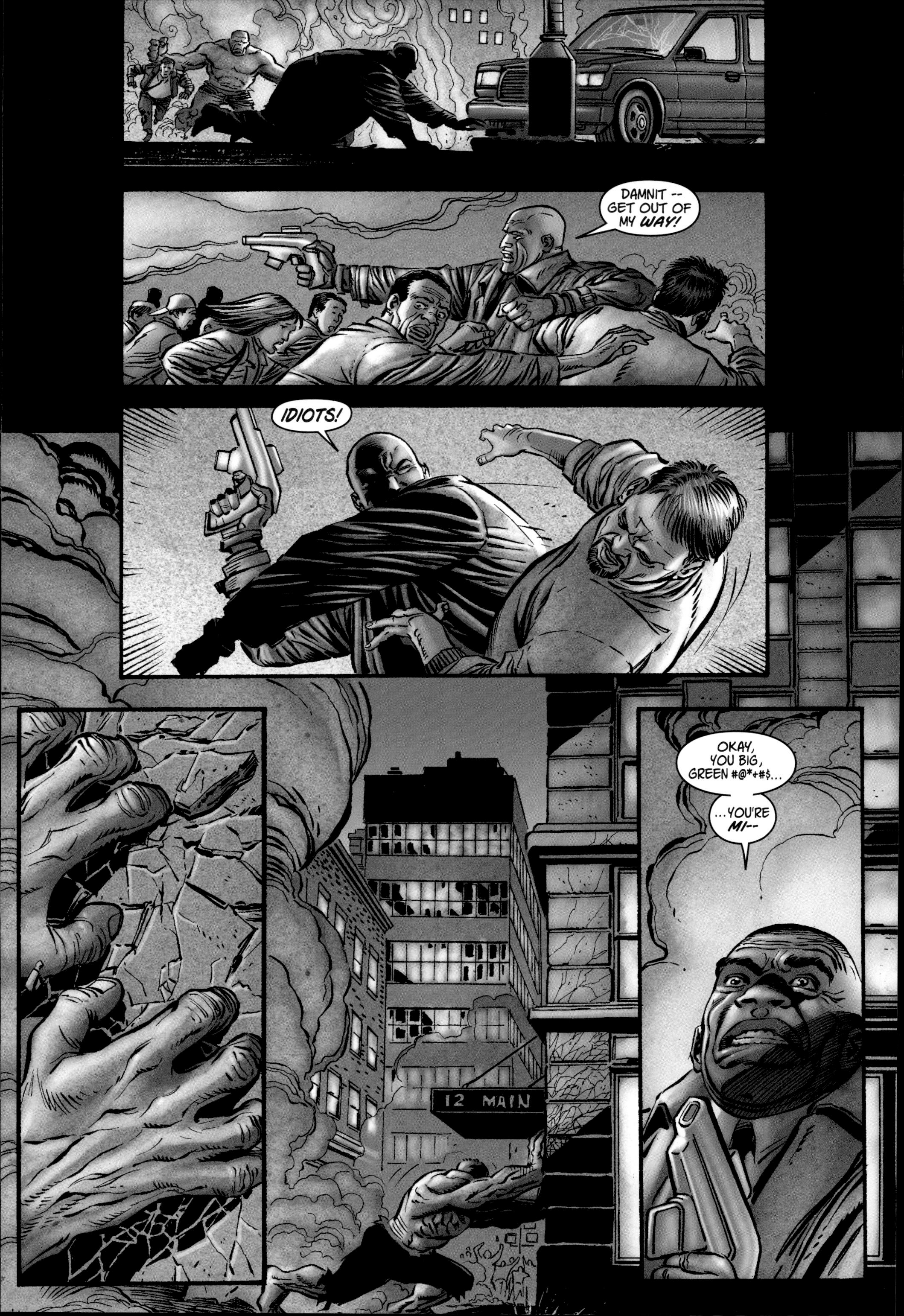
DAMNIT -- GET OUT OF MY WAY!
IDIOTS!
12 MAIN
OKAY, YOU BIG, GREEN #@*+#$...
...YOU'RE MI--

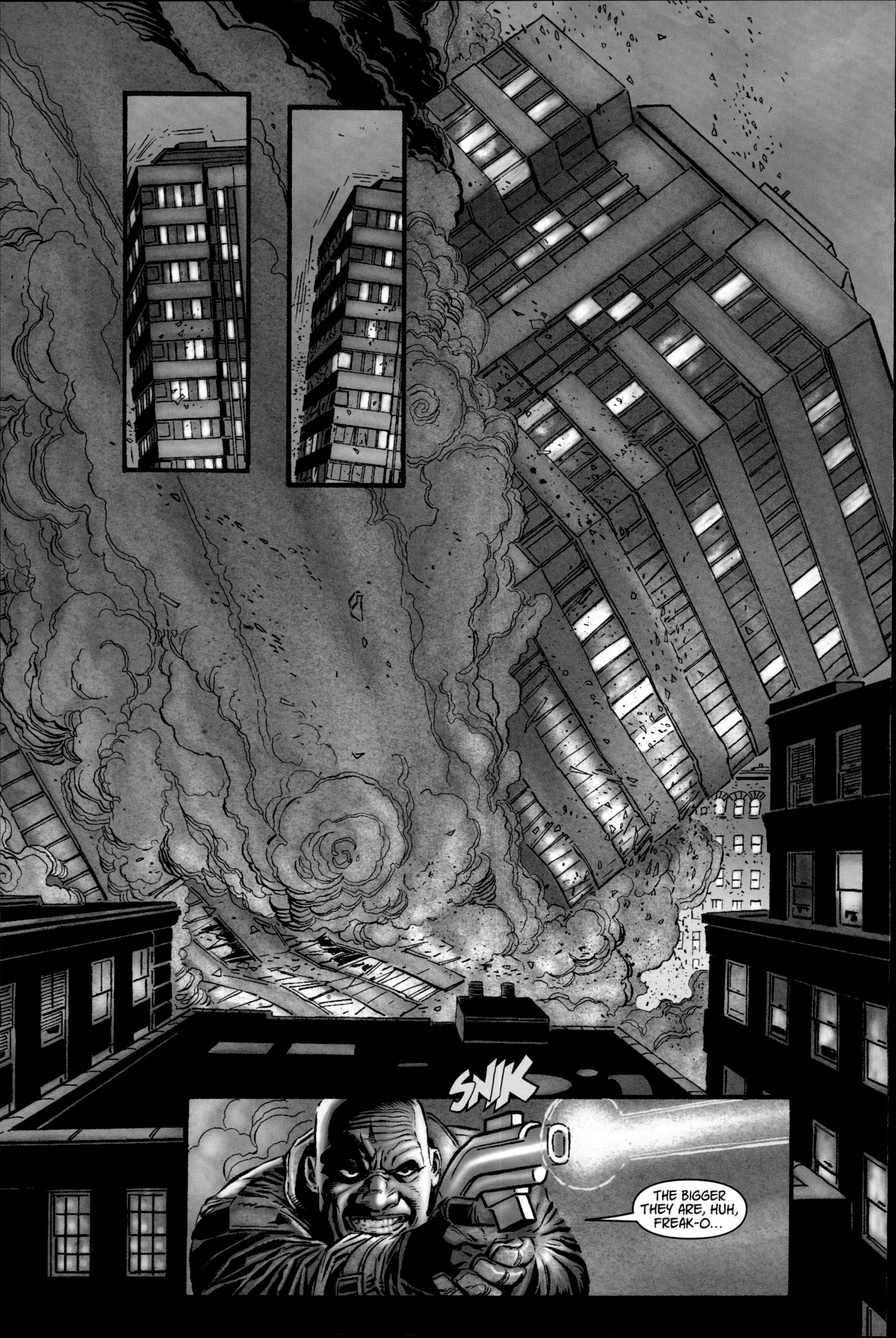
SNIK
THE BIGGER THEY ARE, HUH, FREAK-O...

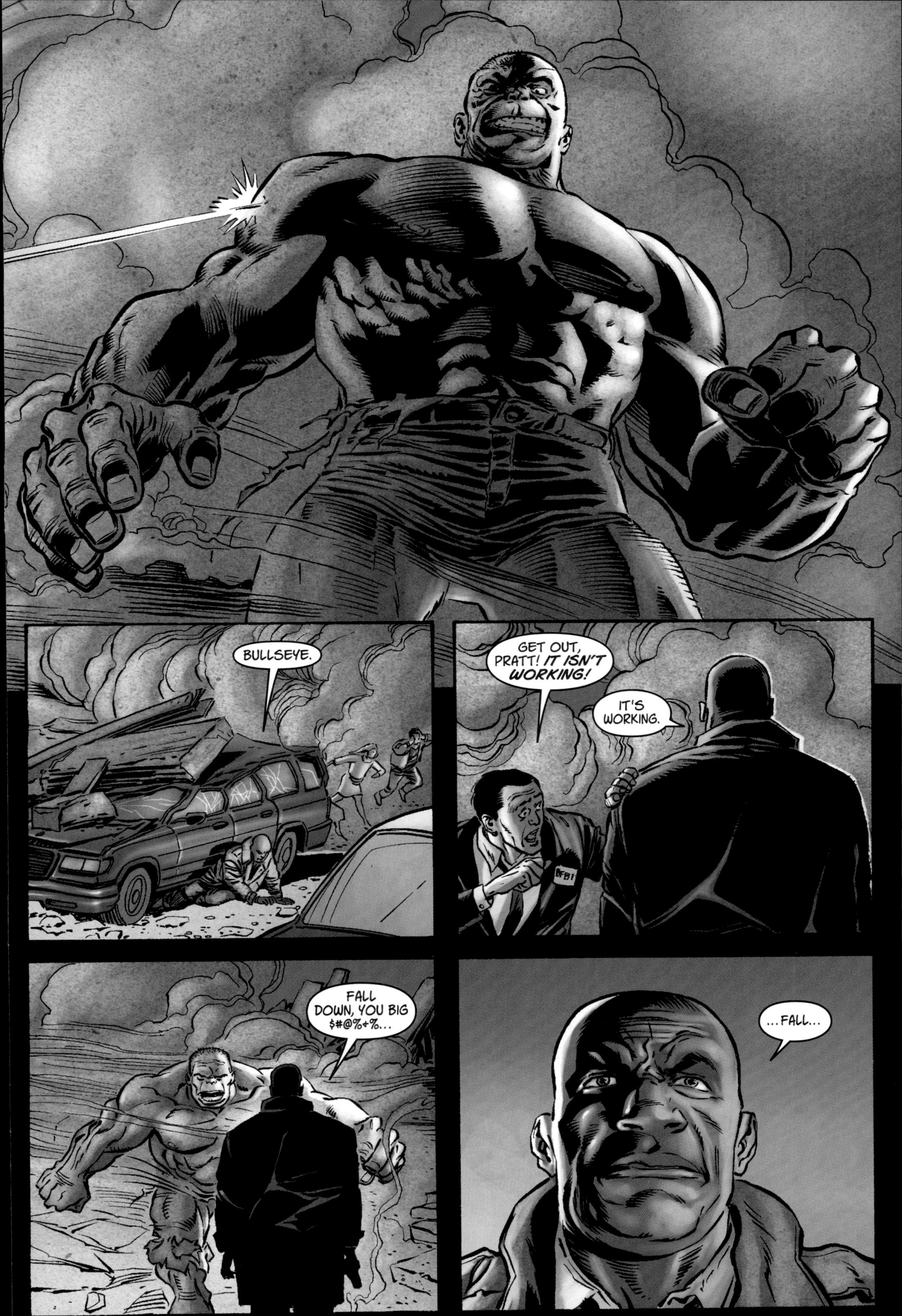
BULLSEYE.
GET OUT, PRATT! *IT ISN'T WORKING!*
IT'S WORKING.
FALL DOWN, YOU BIG $#@%+%...
...FALL...

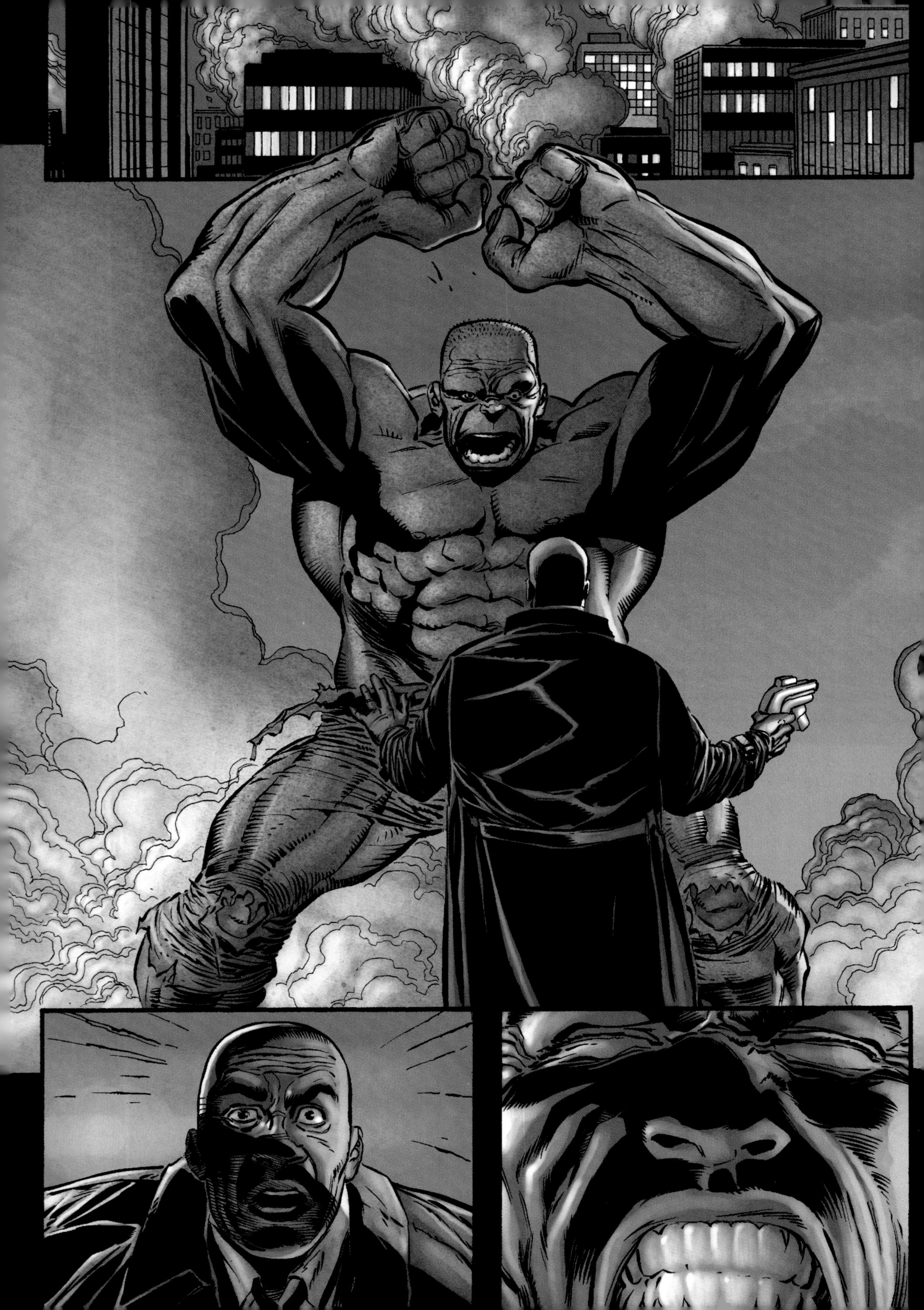

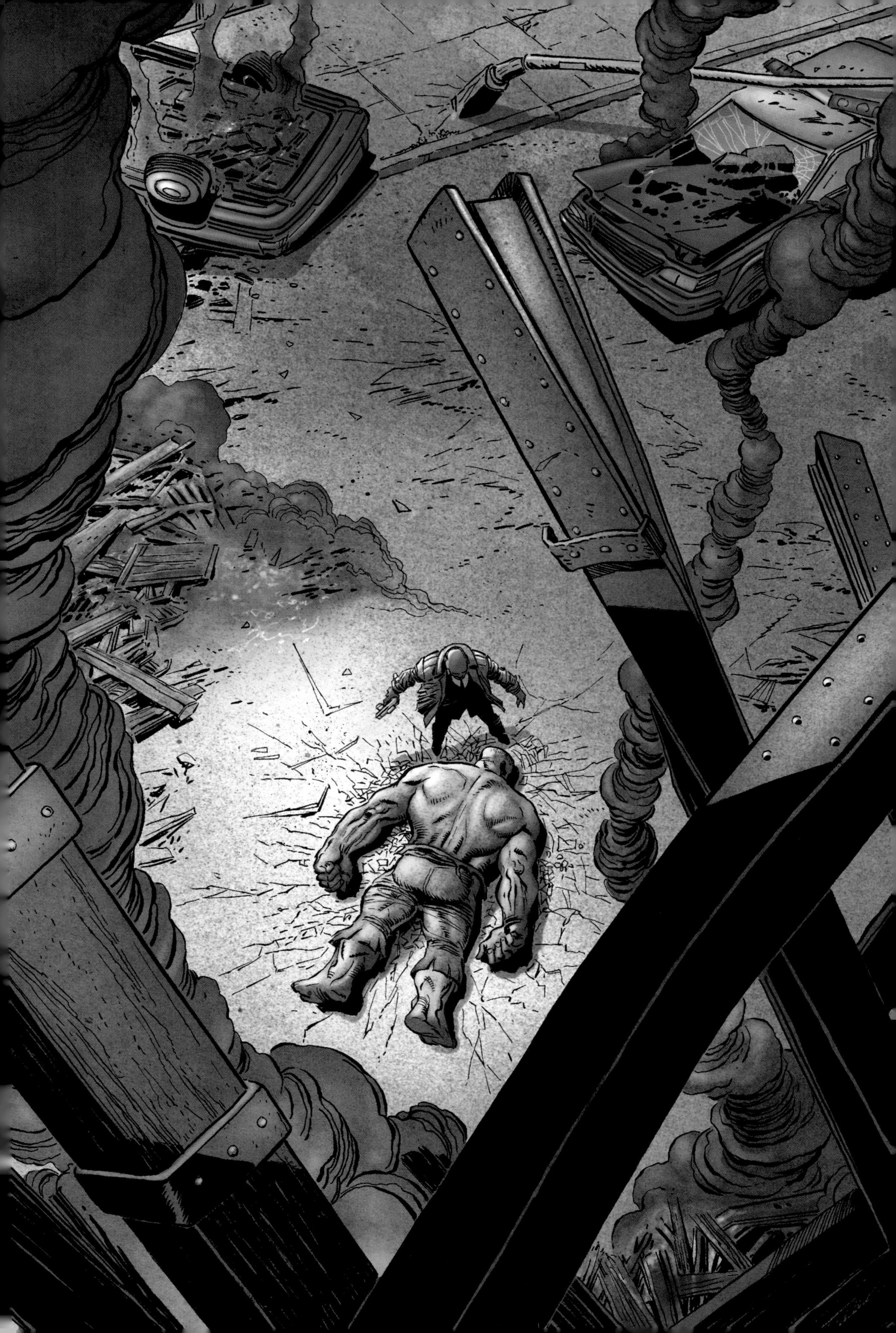

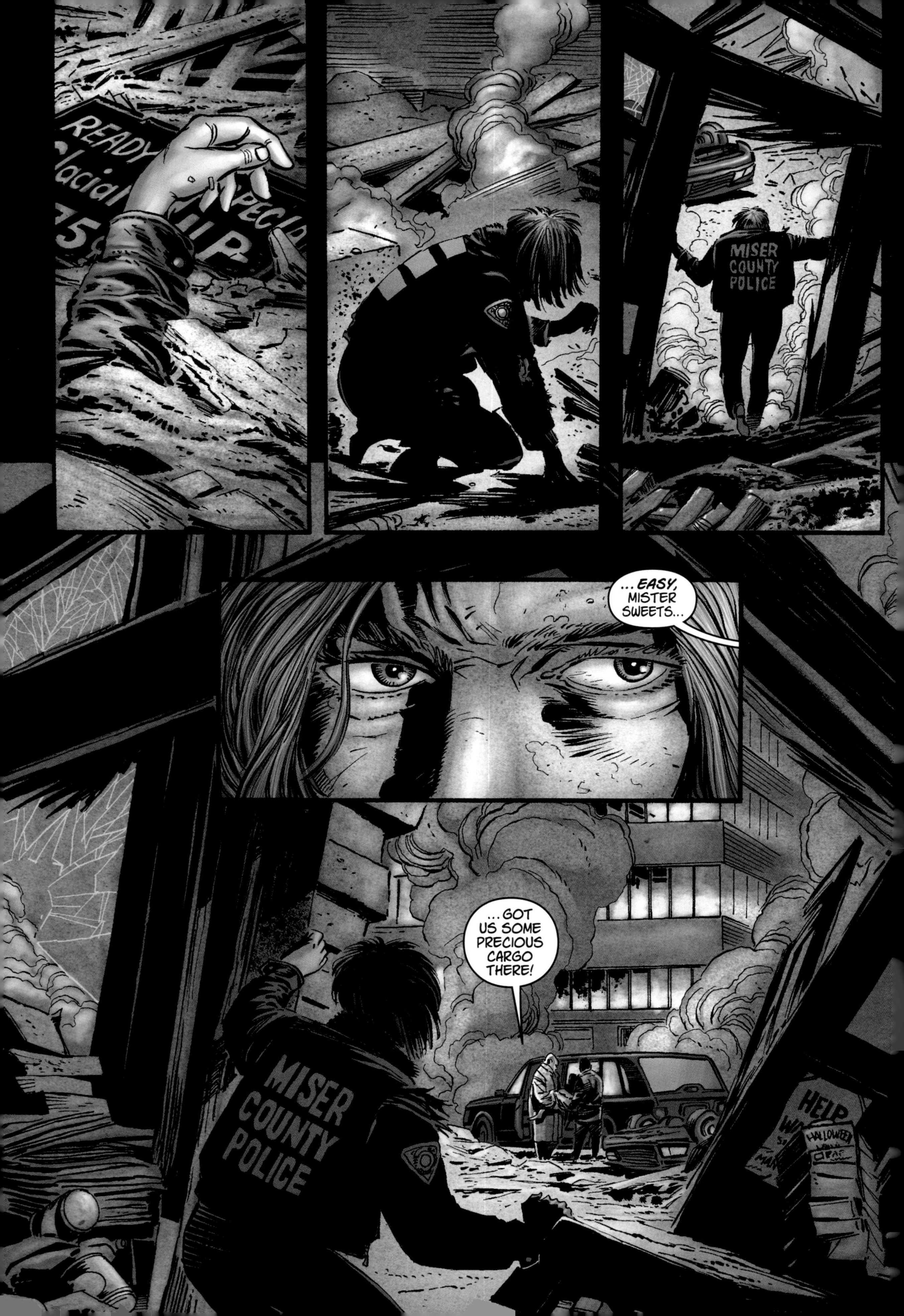
READY
Glacial
SPECIA
75¢
MISER COUNTY POLICE
...EASY, MISTER SWEETS...
...GOT US SOME PRECIOUS CARGO THERE!
MISER COUNTY POLICE
HELP
HALLOWEEN

I'LL HAVE THAT *SYRINGE-DART* NOW, IF YOU PLEASE, MISTER SWEETS!

I DON'T GET IT. WHY DO WE STILL NEED BANNER?

WE GOT HIS BLOOD. THE MISSION'S COMPLETE, RIGHT?

"GOD SAVE THEE, ANCIENT MARINER! FROM THE FIENDS THAT PLAGUE THEE THUS! WHY LOOK'ST THOU SO?"--WITH MY CROSS-BOW I SHOT THE ALBATROSS.

HUH?

COLERIDGE, MISTER SWEETS. "RIME OF THE ANCIENT MARINER."

BUT *WHY* WOULD THE MARINER KILL AN ANIMAL OLD SAILORS CONSIDERED A SIGN OF HOPE? ANSWER ME THAT.

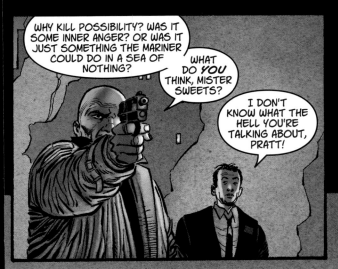

WHY KILL POSSIBILITY? WAS IT SOME INNER ANGER? OR WAS IT JUST SOMETHING THE MARINER COULD DO IN A SEA OF NOTHING?

WHAT DO *YOU* THINK, MISTER SWEETS?

I DON'T KNOW WHAT THE HELL YOU'RE TALKING ABOUT, PRATT!

...THOUGHT NOT.

BLAMM

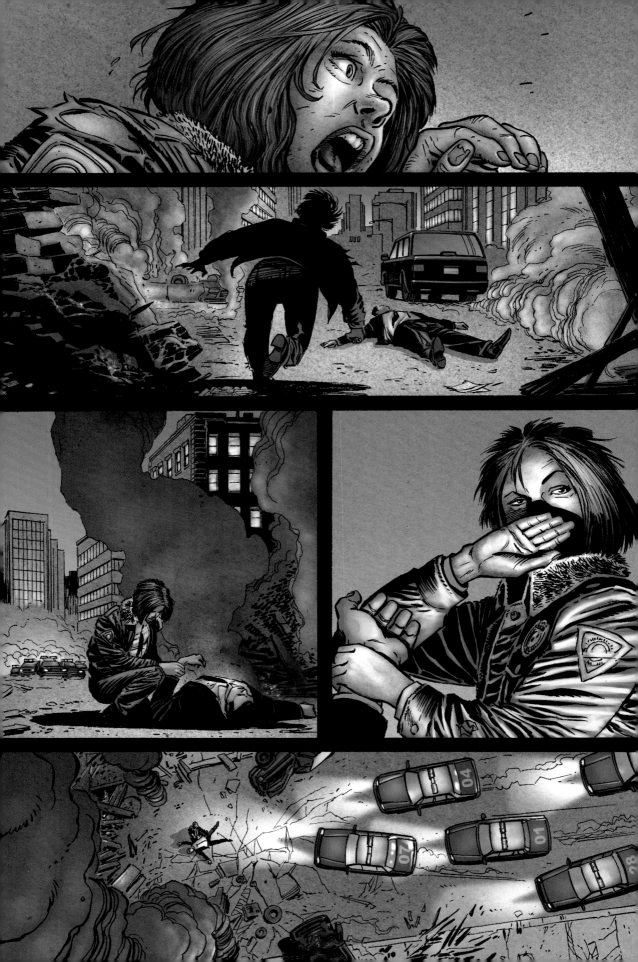

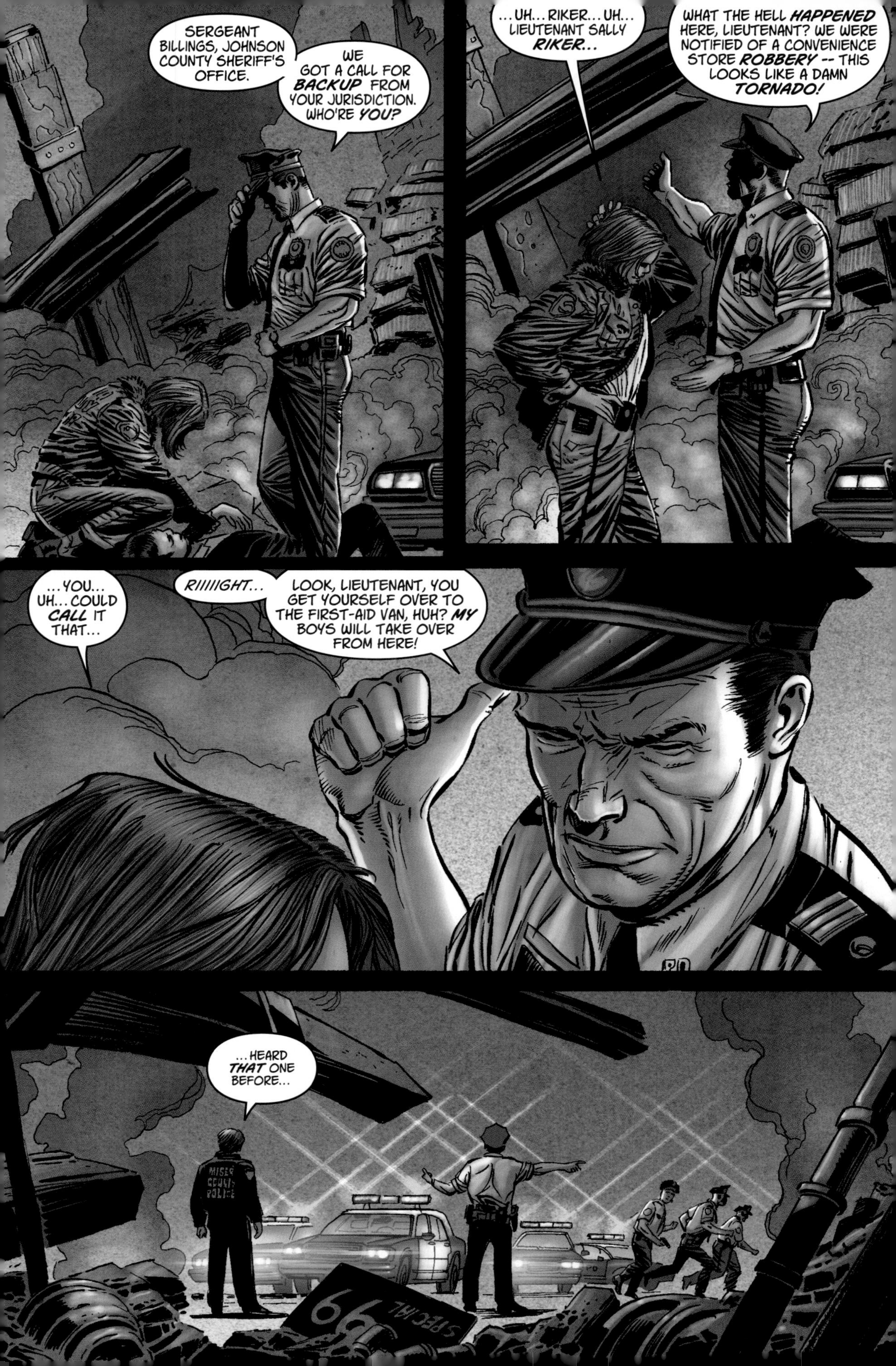
SERGEANT BILLINGS, JOHNSON COUNTY SHERIFF'S OFFICE.
WE GOT A CALL FOR BACKUP FROM YOUR JURISDICTION. WHO'RE YOU?
...UH...RIKER...UH... LIEUTENANT SALLY RIKER...
WHAT THE HELL HAPPENED HERE, LIEUTENANT? WE WERE NOTIFIED OF A CONVENIENCE STORE ROBBERY -- THIS LOOKS LIKE A DAMN TORNADO!
...YOU... UH...COULD CALL IT THAT...
RIIIIIGHT...
LOOK, LIEUTENANT, YOU GET YOURSELF OVER TO THE FIRST-AID VAN, HUH? MY BOYS WILL TAKE OVER FROM HERE!
...HEARD THAT ONE BEFORE...
SPECIAL 99

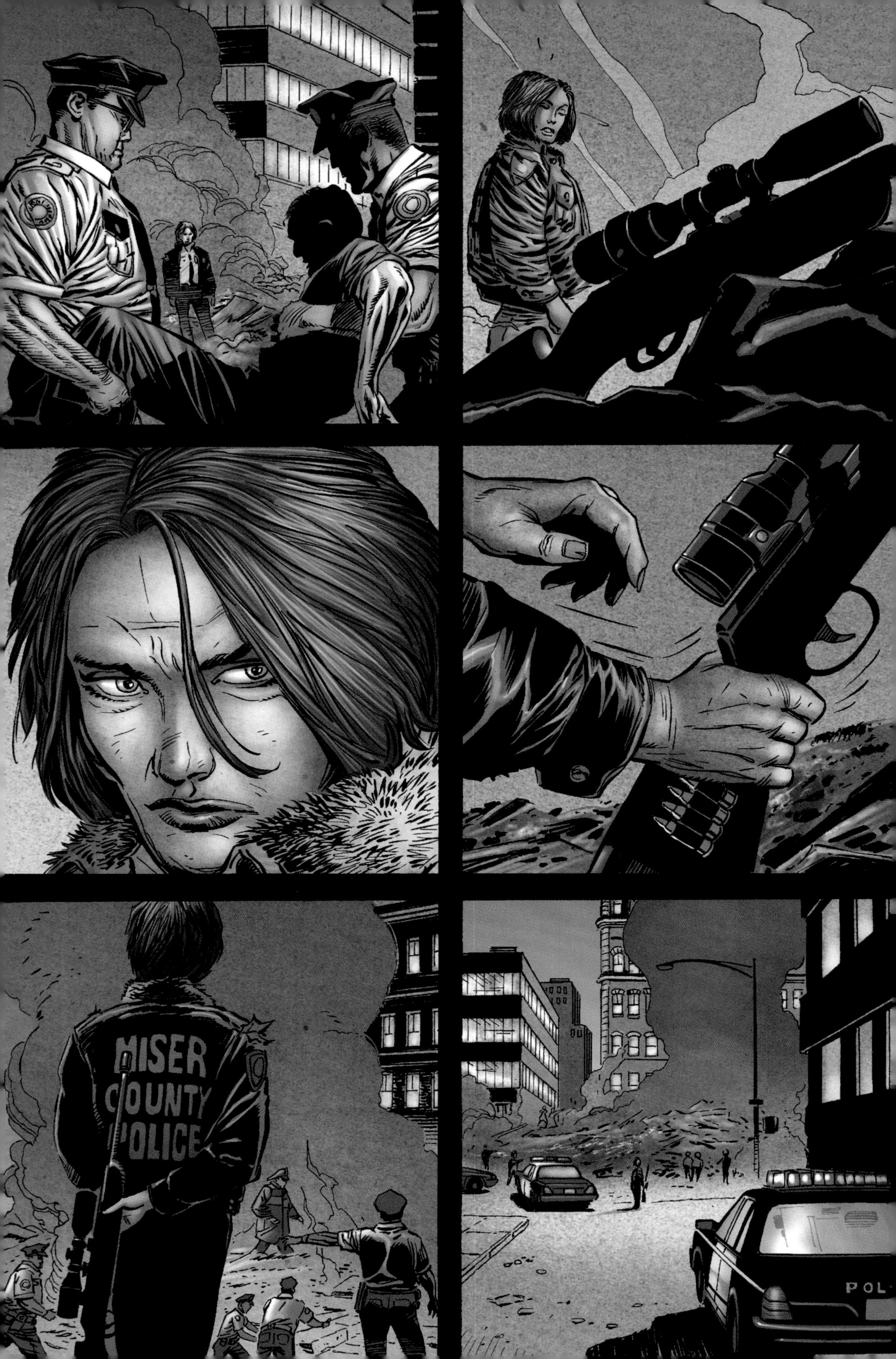
MISER
COUNTY
POLICE
POL

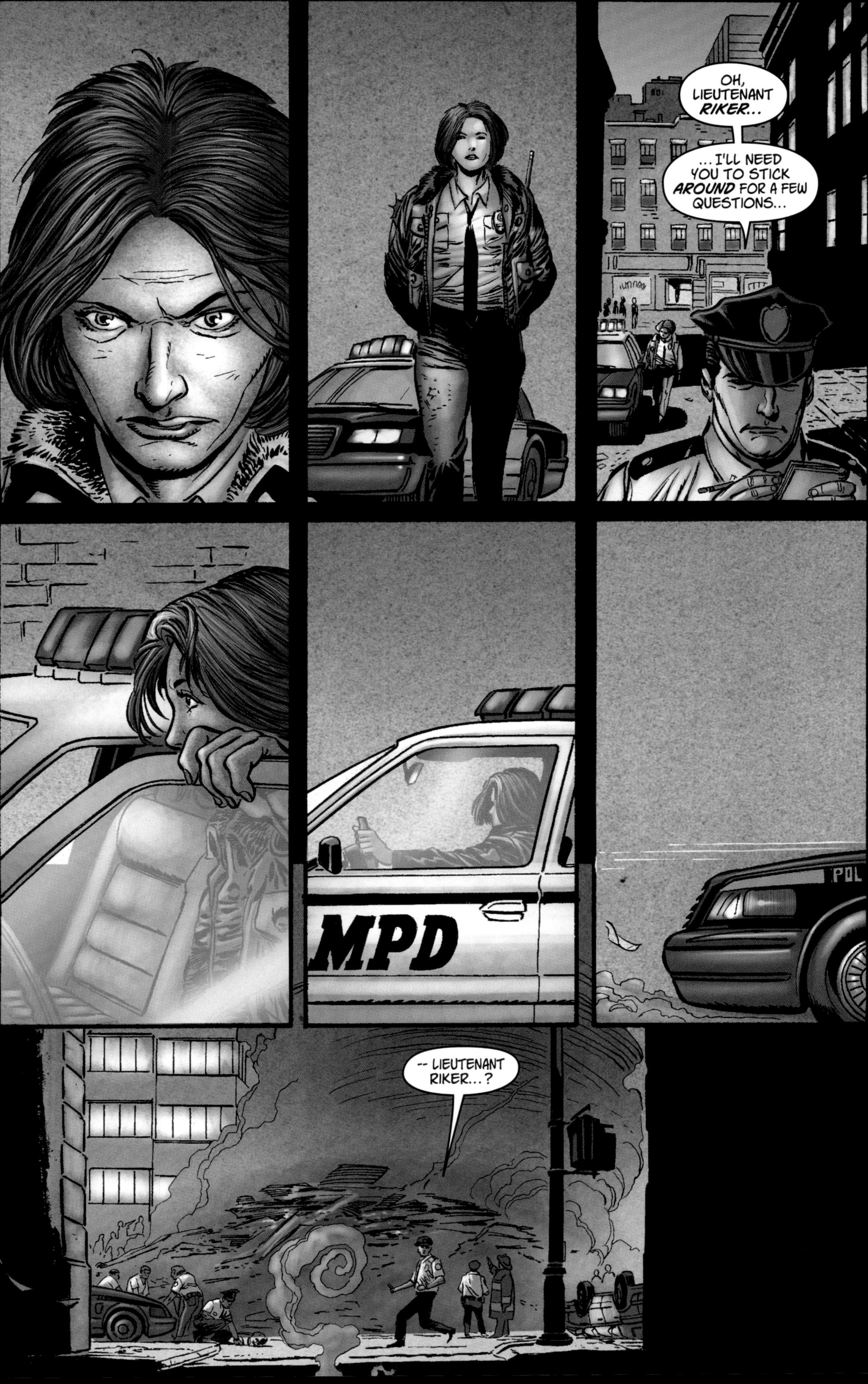
OH, LIEUTENANT RIKER...
...I'LL NEED YOU TO STICK AROUND FOR A FEW QUESTIONS...
MPD
POL
-- LIEUTENANT RIKER...?

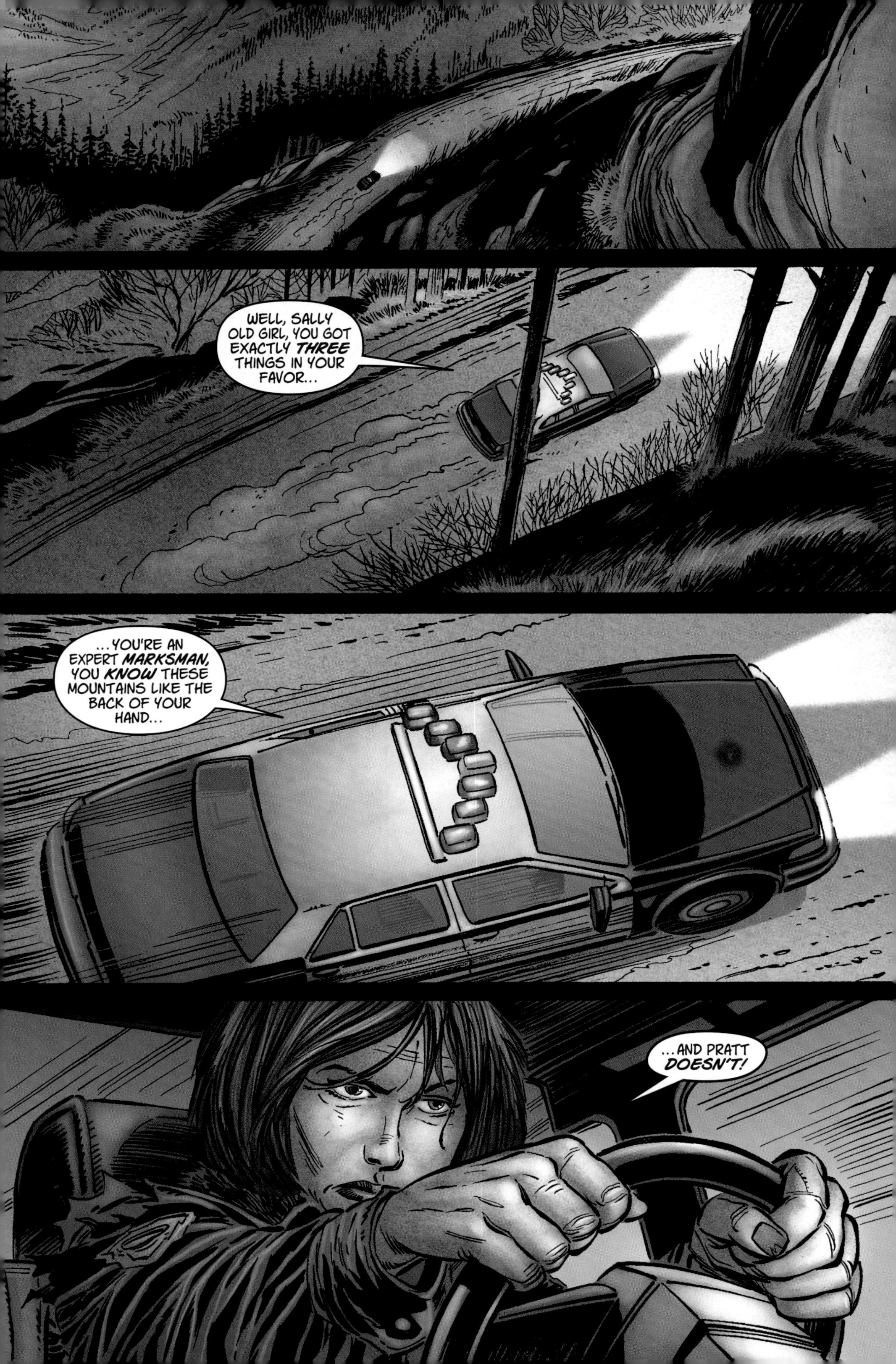
WELL, SALLY OLD GIRL, YOU GOT EXACTLY THREE THINGS IN YOUR FAVOR...
...YOU'RE AN EXPERT MARKSMAN, YOU KNOW THESE MOUNTAINS LIKE THE BACK OF YOUR HAND...
...AND PRATT DOESN'T!

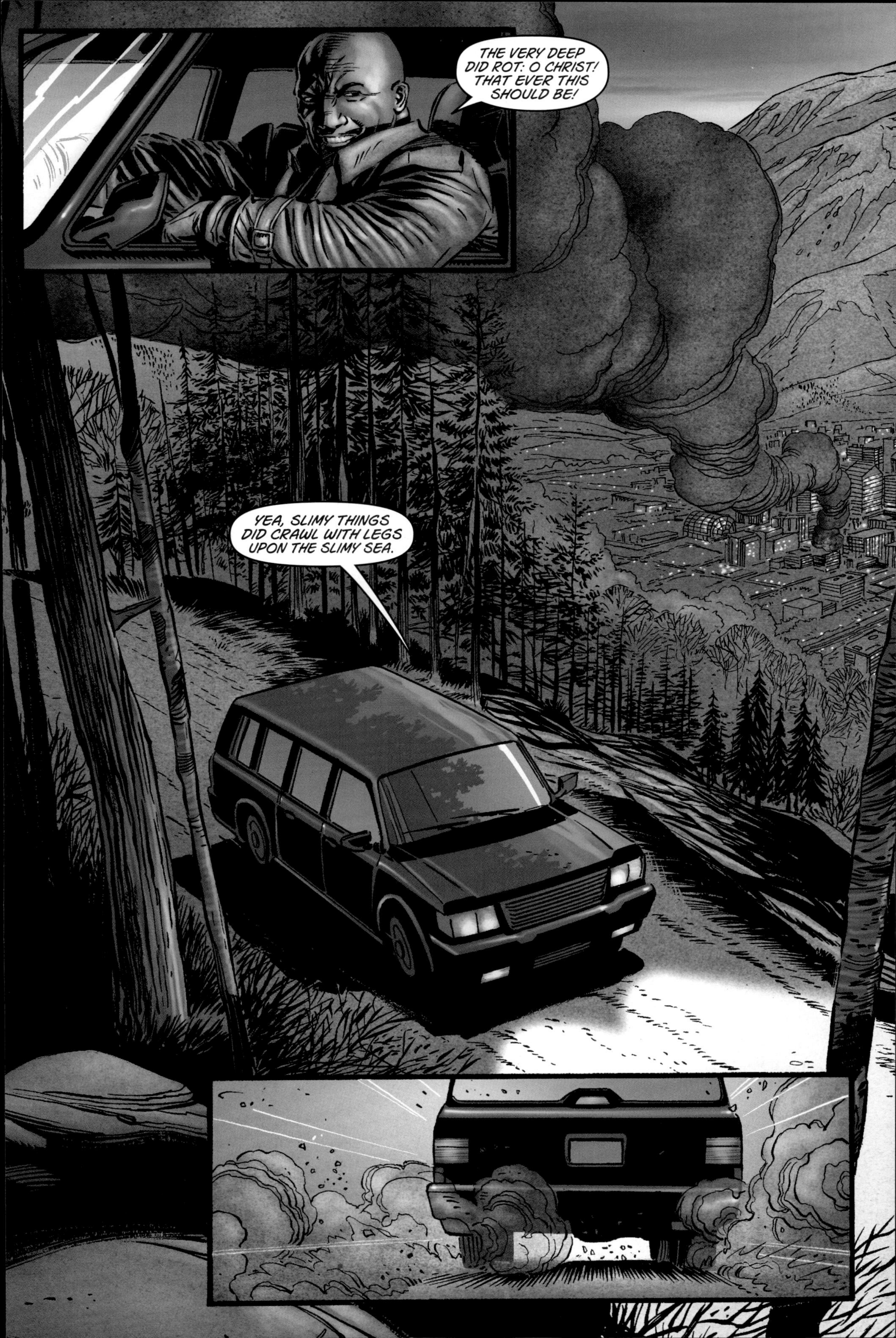
THE VERY DEEP DID ROT: O CHRIST! THAT EVER THIS SHOULD BE!
YEA, SLIMY THINGS DID CRAWL WITH LEGS UPON THE SLIMY SEA.

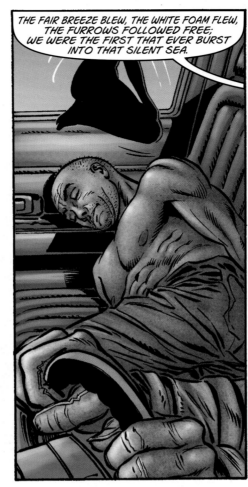

THE FAIR BREEZE BLEW, THE WHITE FOAM FLEW, THE FURROWS FOLLOWED FREE; WE WERE THE FIRST THAT EVER BURST INTO THAT SILENT SEA.

AH! YOU'RE AWAKE!

COLERIDGE, MISTER BANNER! READ HIM? VERY *VISUAL* WRITER.

YES...

...VERY.

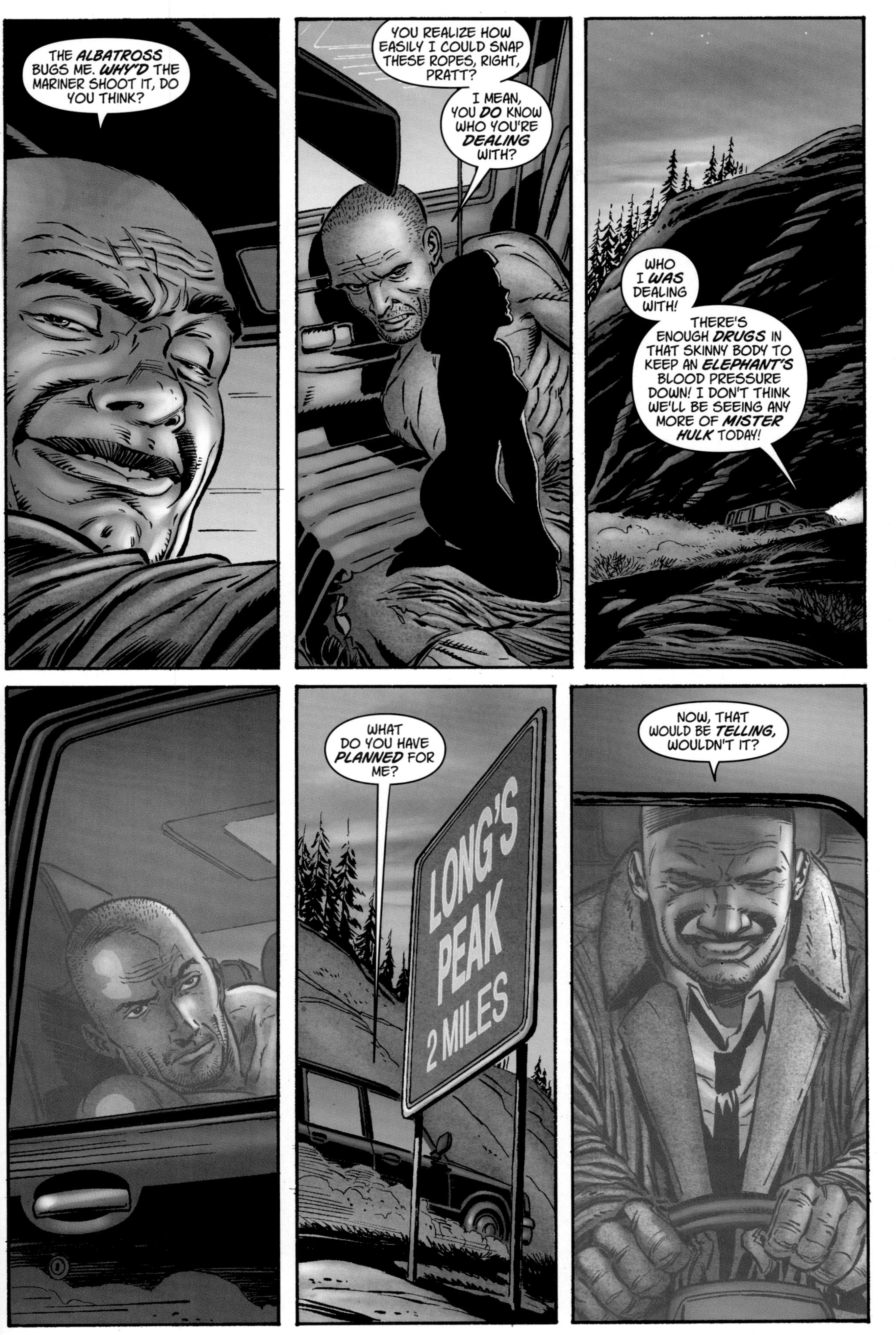
THE ALBATROSS BUGS ME. WHY'D THE MARINER SHOOT IT, DO YOU THINK?
YOU REALIZE HOW EASILY I COULD SNAP THESE ROPES, RIGHT, PRATT?
I MEAN, YOU DO KNOW WHO YOU'RE DEALING WITH?
WHO I WAS DEALING WITH!
THERE'S ENOUGH DRUGS IN THAT SKINNY BODY TO KEEP AN ELEPHANT'S BLOOD PRESSURE DOWN! I DON'T THINK WE'LL BE SEEING ANY MORE OF MISTER HULK TODAY!
WHAT DO YOU HAVE PLANNED FOR ME?
LONG'S PEAK 2 MILES
NOW, THAT WOULD BE TELLING, WOULDN'T IT?

INCREDIBLE HULK #43
Cover by Kaare Andrews

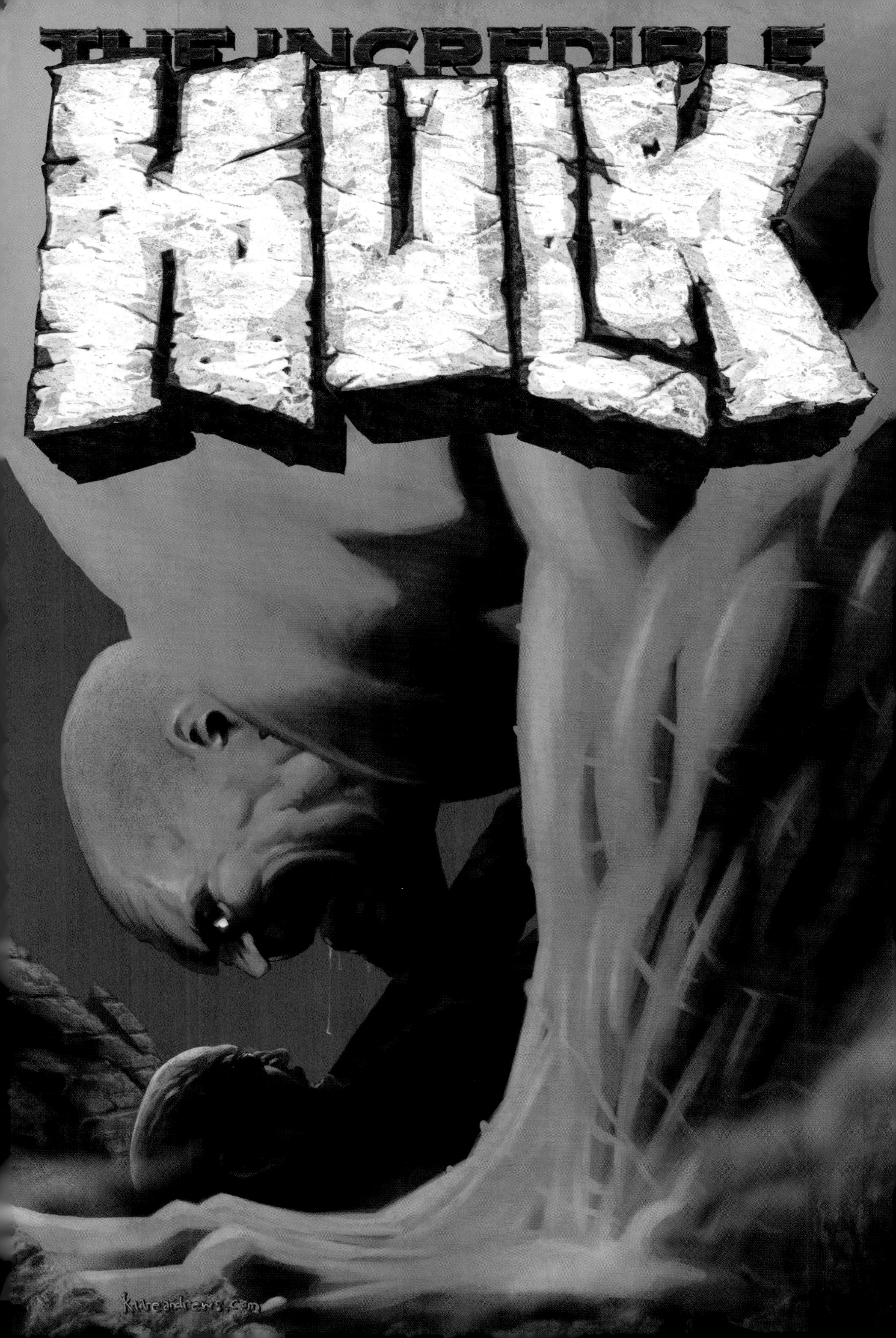
THE INCREDIBLE
HULK
kaareandrews.com

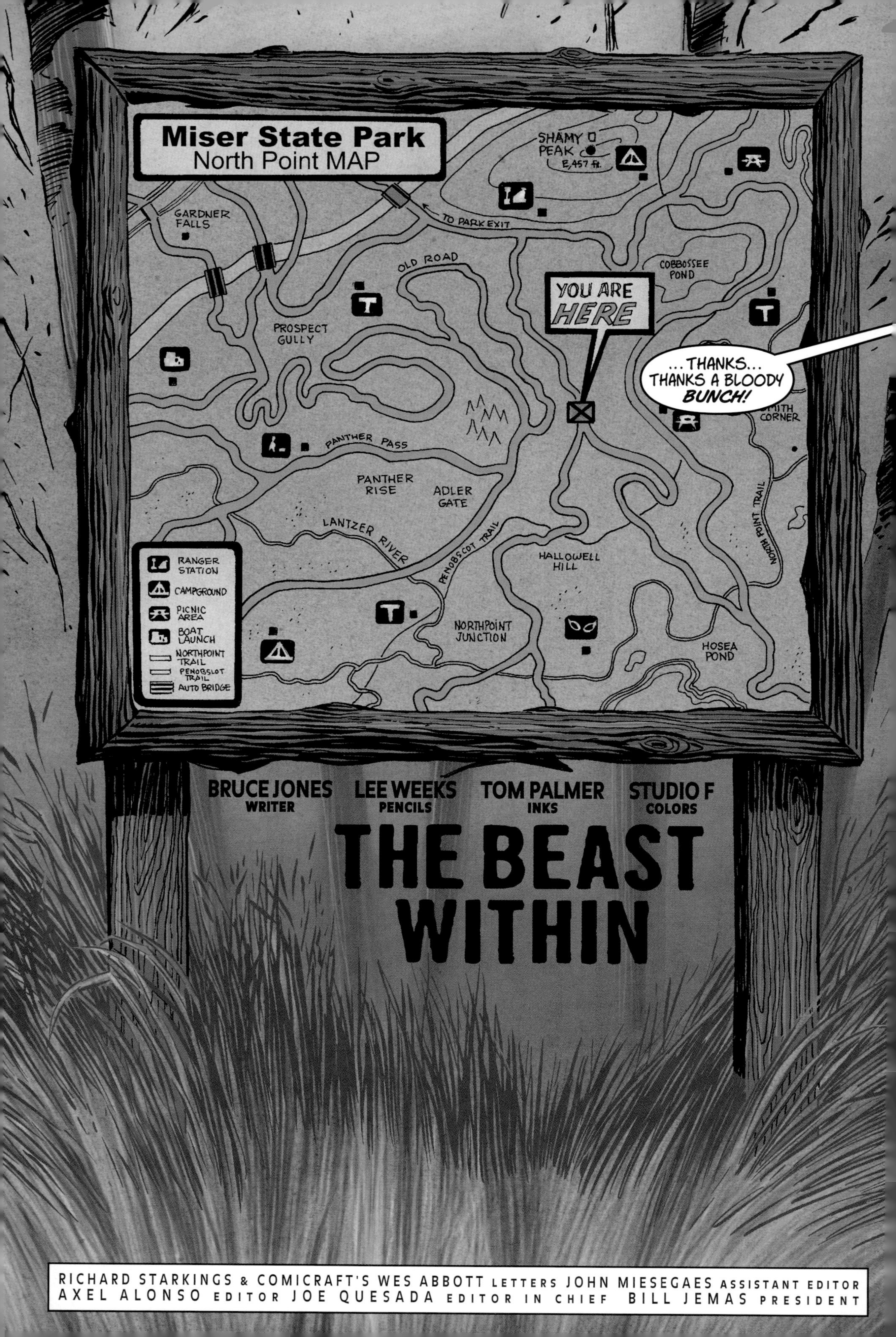

Miser State Park
North Point MAP
SHAMY PEAK
E,457 ft.
GARDNER FALLS
TO PARK EXIT
OLD ROAD
COBBOSSEE POND
YOU ARE HERE
PROSPECT GULLY
...THANKS... THANKS A BLOODY BUNCH!
SMITH CORNER
PANTHER PASS
PANTHER RISE
ADLER GATE
LANTZER RIVER
PENOBSCOT TRAIL
NORTH POINT TRAIL
HALLOWELL HILL
NORTHPOINT JUNCTION
HOSEA POND
RANGER STATION
CAMPGROUND
PICNIC AREA
BOAT LAUNCH
NORTHPOINT TRAIL
PENOBSLOT TRAIL
AUTO BRIDGE
BRUCE JONES WRITER
LEE WEEKS PENCILS
TOM PALMER INKS
STUDIO F COLORS
THE BEAST WITHIN
RICHARD STARKINGS & COMICRAFT'S WES ABBOTT LETTERS JOHN MIESEGAES ASSISTANT EDITOR
AXEL ALONSO EDITOR JOE QUESADA EDITOR IN CHIEF BILL JEMAS PRESIDENT

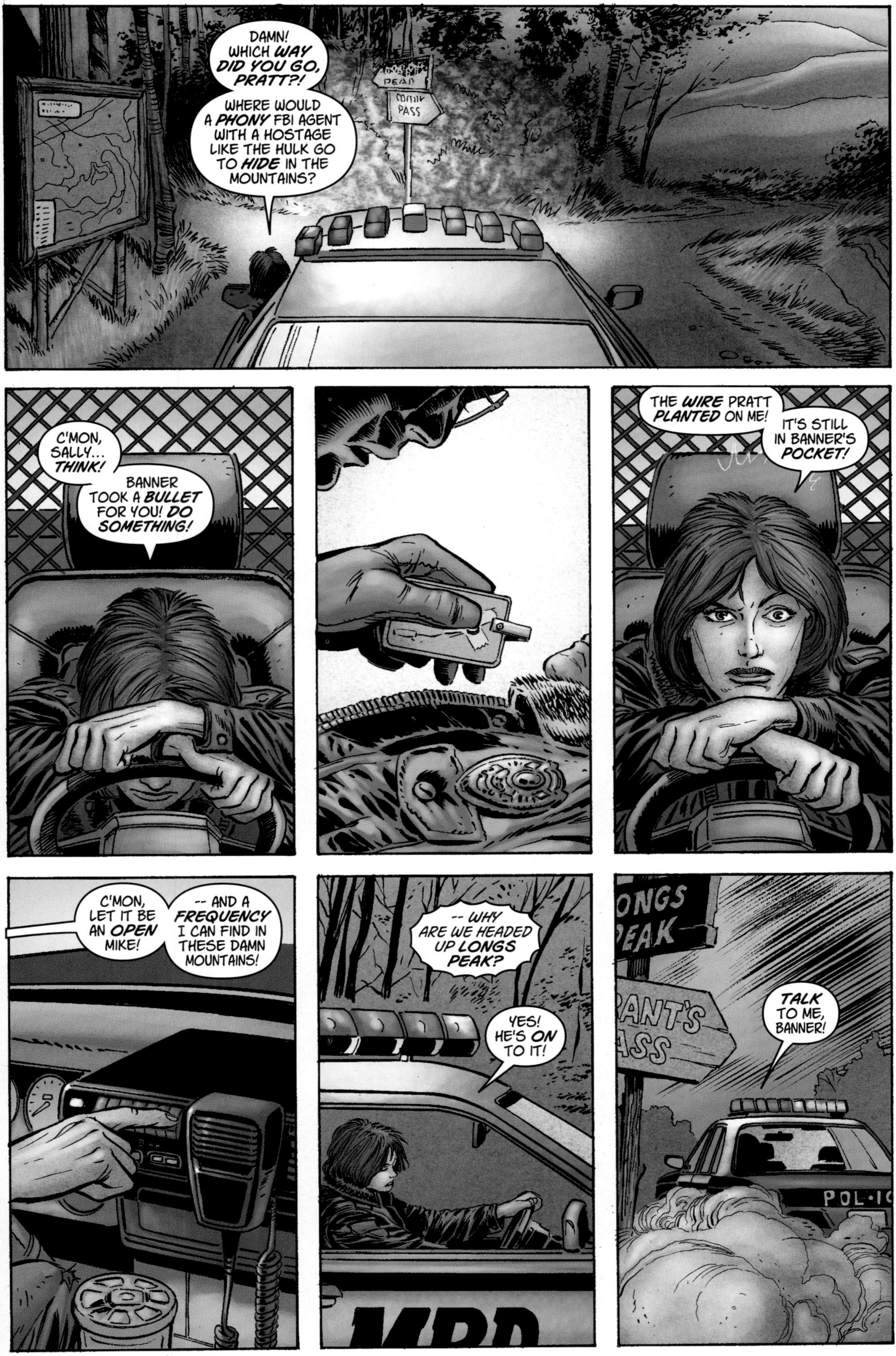
DAMN! WHICH WAY DID YOU GO, PRATT?!
WHERE WOULD A PHONY FBI AGENT WITH A HOSTAGE LIKE THE HULK GO TO HIDE IN THE MOUNTAINS?
C'MON, SALLY... THINK!
BANNER TOOK A BULLET FOR YOU! DO SOMETHING!
THE WIRE PRATT PLANTED ON ME!
IT'S STILL IN BANNER'S POCKET!
C'MON, LET IT BE AN OPEN MIKE!
-- AND A FREQUENCY I CAN FIND IN THESE DAMN MOUNTAINS!
-- WHY ARE WE HEADED UP LONGS PEAK?
YES! HE'S ON TO IT!
TALK TO ME, BANNER!

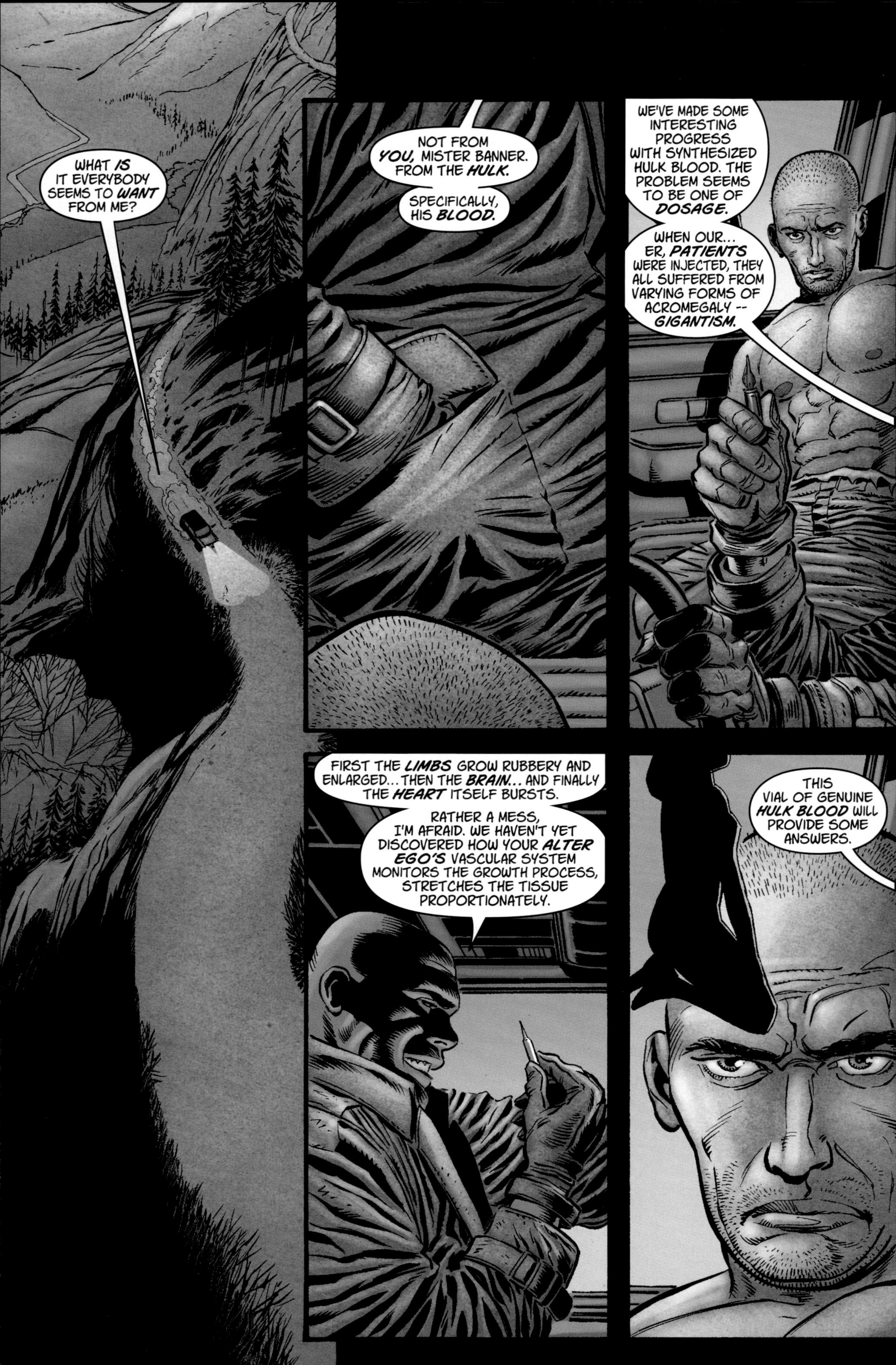
WHAT *IS* IT EVERYBODY SEEMS TO *WANT* FROM ME?
NOT FROM *YOU,* MISTER BANNER. FROM THE *HULK.*
SPECIFICALLY, HIS *BLOOD.*
WE'VE MADE SOME INTERESTING PROGRESS WITH SYNTHESIZED HULK BLOOD. THE PROBLEM SEEMS TO BE ONE OF *DOSAGE.*
WHEN OUR... ER, *PATIENTS* WERE INJECTED, THEY ALL SUFFERED FROM VARYING FORMS OF ACROMEGALY -- *GIGANTISM.*
FIRST THE *LIMBS* GROW RUBBERY AND ENLARGED... THEN THE *BRAIN...* AND FINALLY THE *HEART* ITSELF BURSTS.
RATHER A MESS, I'M AFRAID. WE HAVEN'T YET DISCOVERED HOW YOUR *ALTER EGO'S* VASCULAR SYSTEM MONITORS THE GROWTH PROCESS, STRETCHES THE TISSUE PROPORTIONATELY.
THIS VIAL OF GENUINE *HULK BLOOD* WILL PROVIDE SOME ANSWERS.

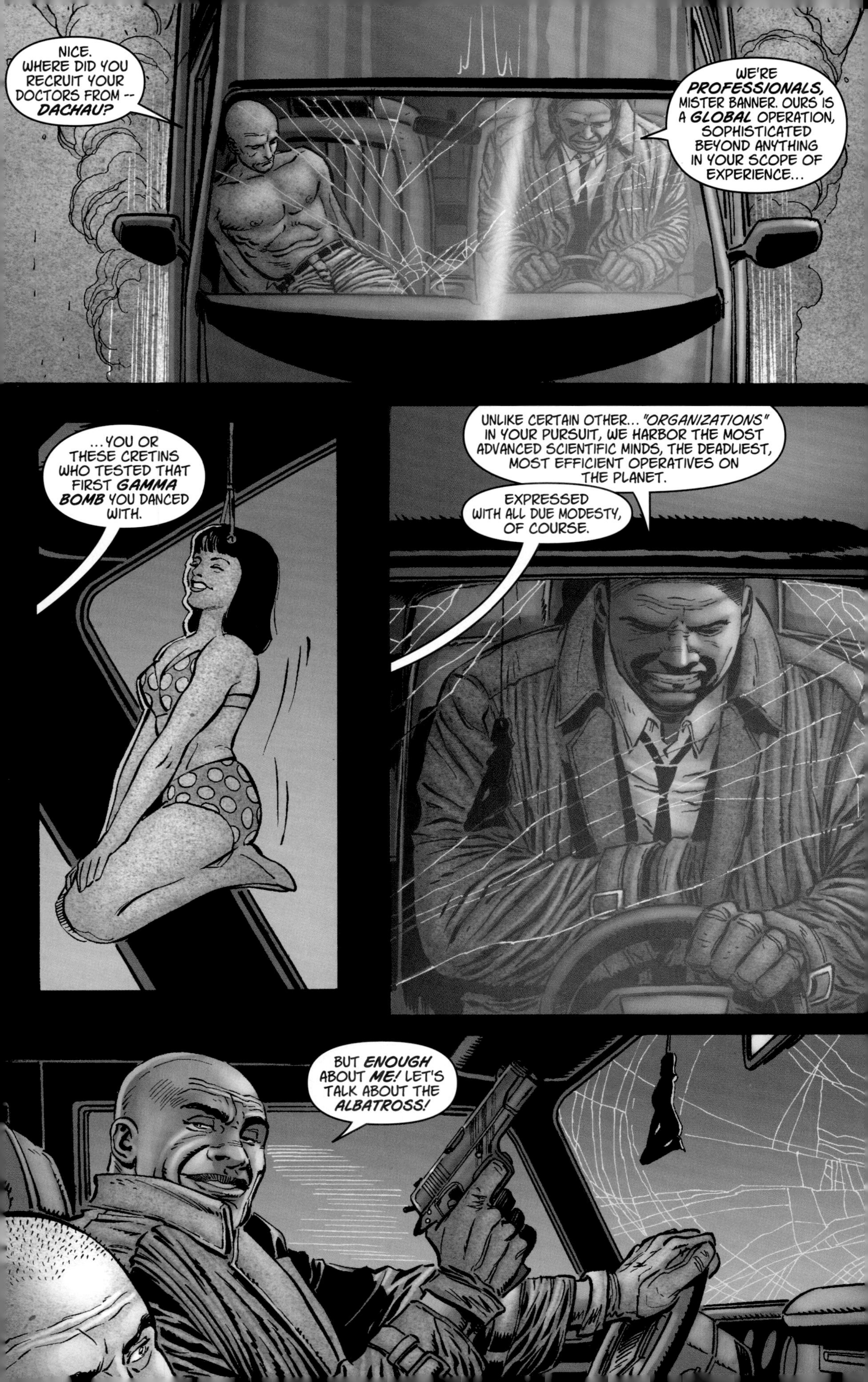
NICE. WHERE DID YOU RECRUIT YOUR DOCTORS FROM -- *DACHAU?*
WE'RE *PROFESSIONALS,* MISTER BANNER. OURS IS A *GLOBAL* OPERATION, SOPHISTICATED BEYOND ANYTHING IN YOUR SCOPE OF EXPERIENCE...
...YOU OR THESE CRETINS WHO TESTED THAT FIRST *GAMMA BOMB* YOU DANCED WITH.
UNLIKE CERTAIN OTHER... *"ORGANIZATIONS"* IN YOUR PURSUIT, WE HARBOR THE MOST ADVANCED SCIENTIFIC MINDS, THE DEADLIEST, MOST EFFICIENT OPERATIVES ON THE PLANET.
EXPRESSED WITH ALL DUE MODESTY, OF COURSE.
BUT *ENOUGH* ABOUT *ME!* LET'S TALK ABOUT THE *ALBATROSS!*

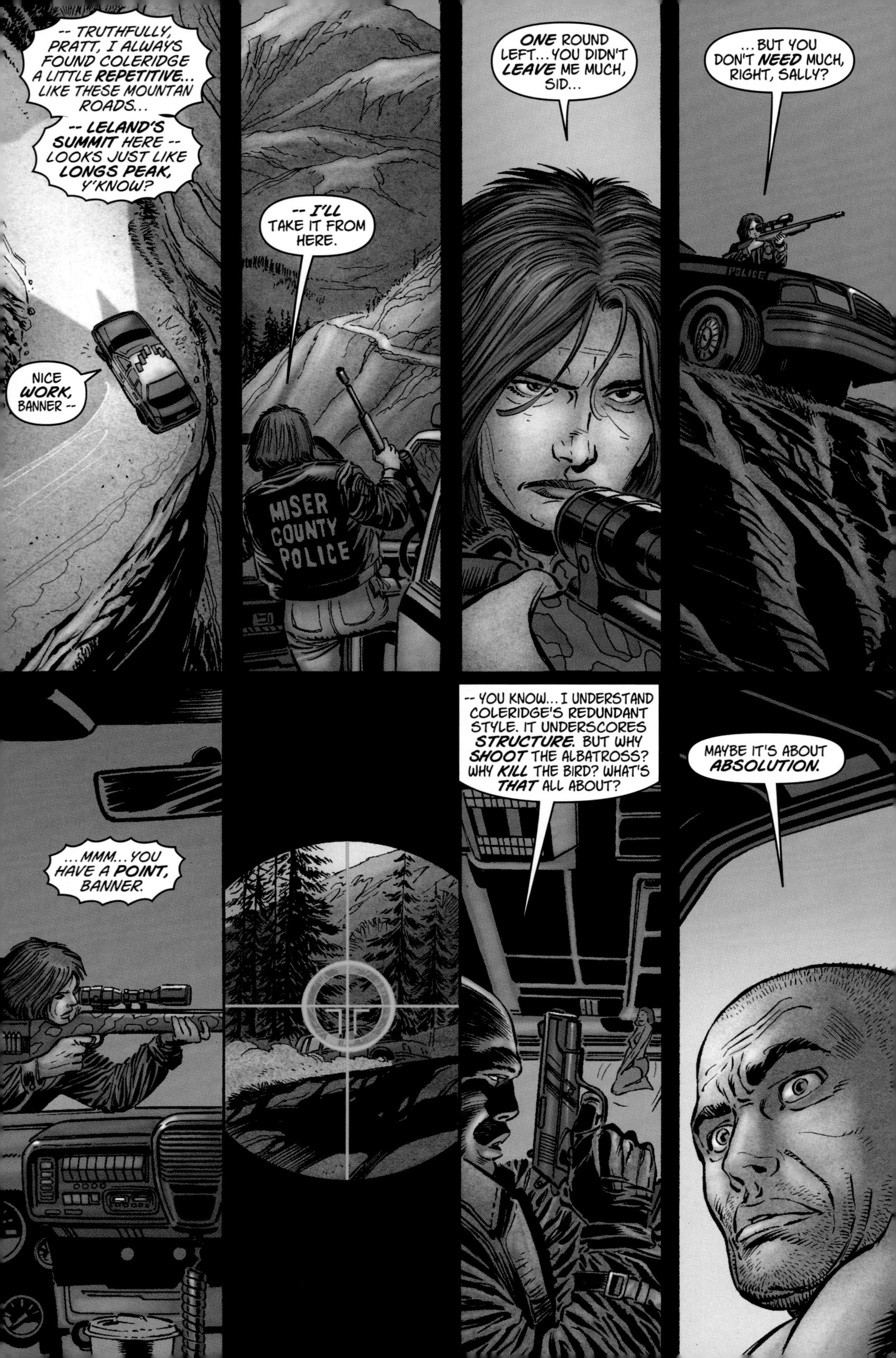
-- TRUTHFULLY, PRATT, I ALWAYS FOUND COLERIDGE A LITTLE REPETITIVE... LIKE THESE MOUNTAN ROADS...
-- LELAND'S SUMMIT HERE -- LOOKS JUST LIKE LONGS PEAK, Y'KNOW?
NICE WORK, BANNER --
-- I'LL TAKE IT FROM HERE.
MISER COUNTY POLICE
ONE ROUND LEFT... YOU DIDN'T LEAVE ME MUCH, SID...
... BUT YOU DON'T NEED MUCH, RIGHT, SALLY?
POLICE
...MMM... YOU HAVE A POINT, BANNER.
-- YOU KNOW... I UNDERSTAND COLERIDGE'S REDUNDANT STYLE. IT UNDERSCORES STRUCTURE. BUT WHY SHOOT THE ALBATROSS? WHY KILL THE BIRD? WHAT'S THAT ALL ABOUT?
MAYBE IT'S ABOUT ABSOLUTION.

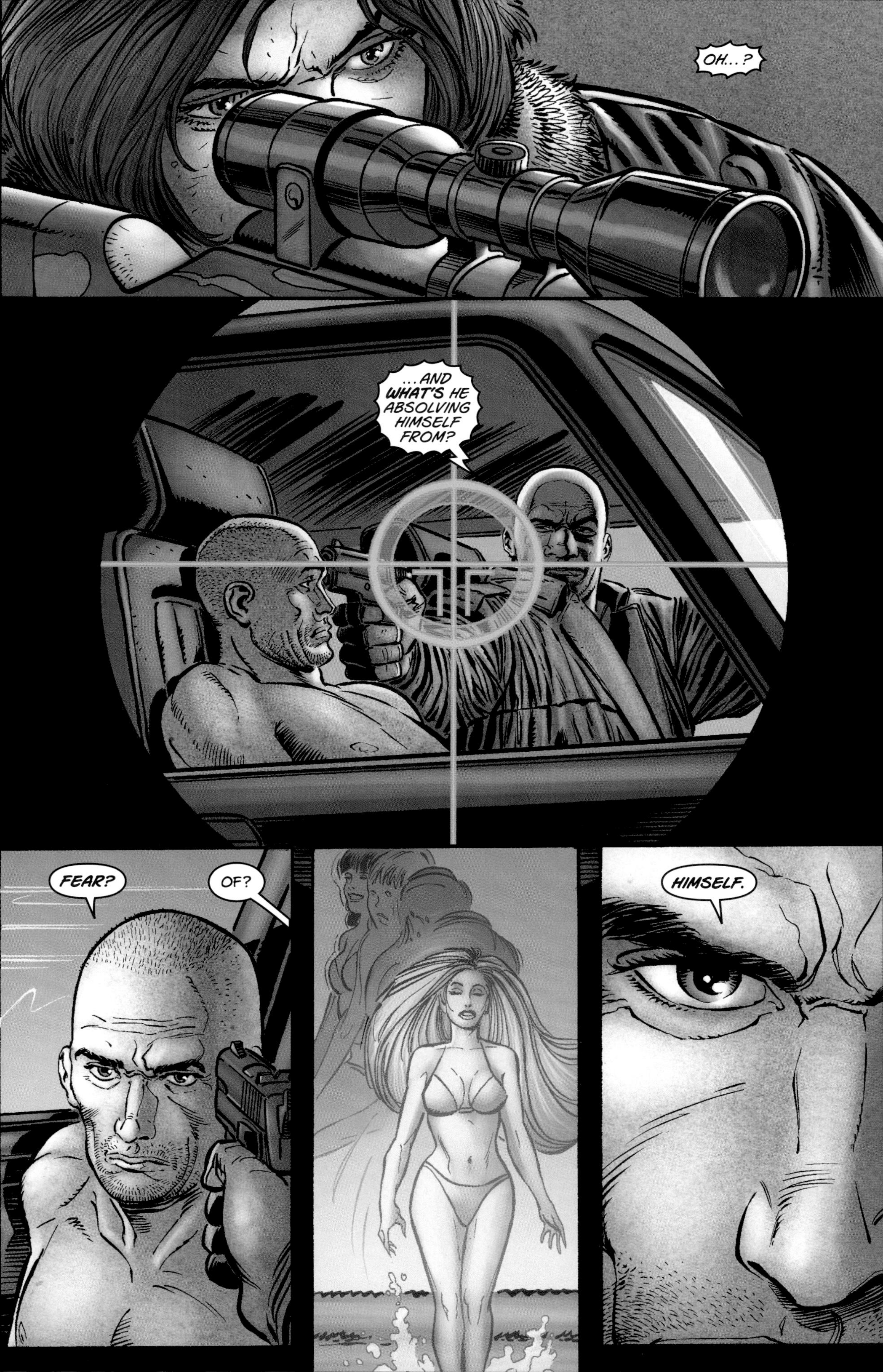
OH...?
...AND WHAT'S HE ABSOLVING HIMSELF FROM?
FEAR?
OF?
HIMSELF.

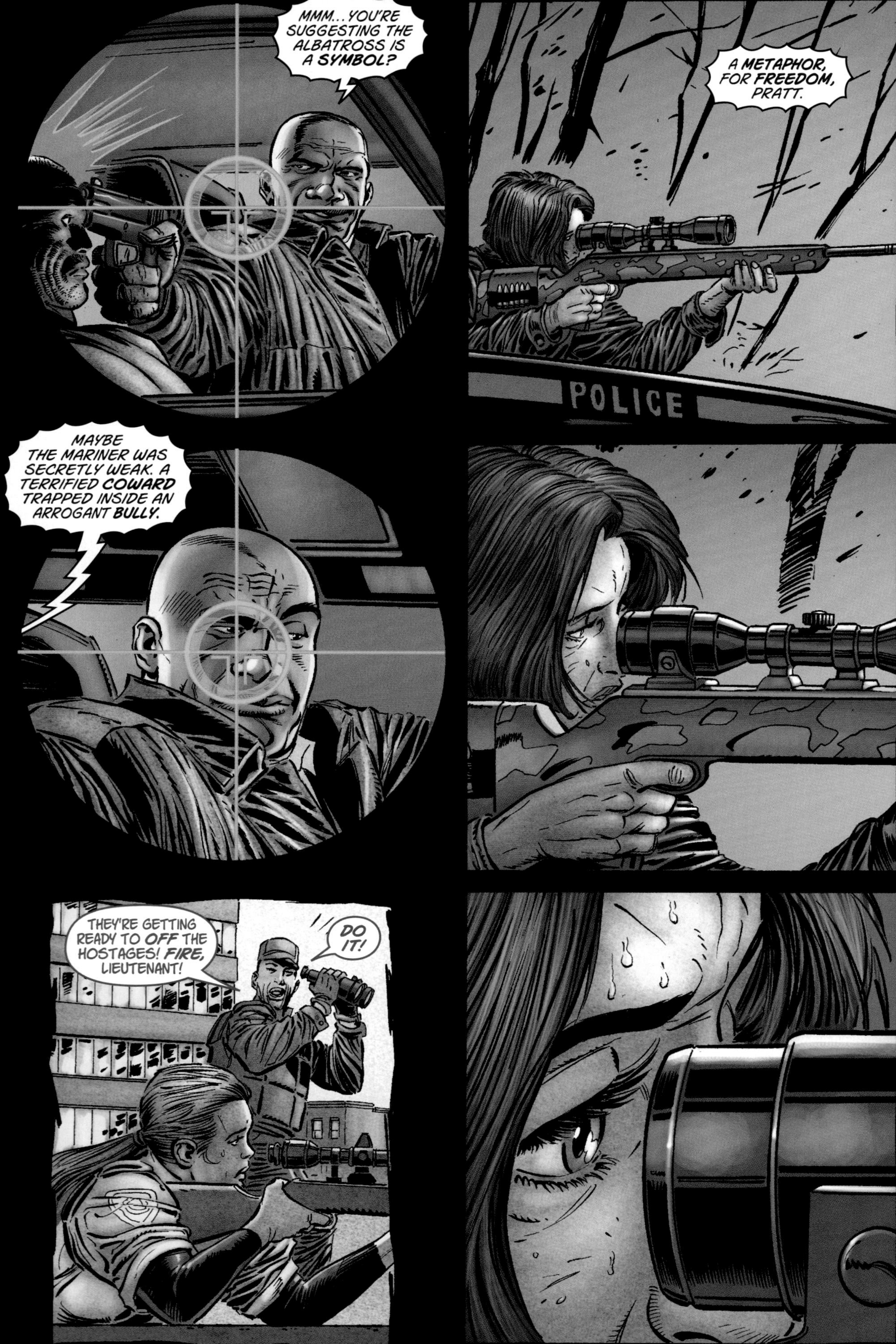
MMM...YOU'RE SUGGESTING THE ALBATROSS IS A SYMBOL?
A METAPHOR, FOR FREEDOM, PRATT.
POLICE
MAYBE THE MARINER WAS SECRETLY WEAK. A TERRIFIED COWARD TRAPPED INSIDE AN ARROGANT BULLY.
THEY'RE GETTING READY TO OFF THE HOSTAGES! FIRE, LIEUTENANT!
DO IT!

"TERRIFIED COWARD." THAT'S CUTE, BANNER. I LIKE THAT.

AND I'M THE MARINER, OF COURSE.

NO, PRATT. I'M THE MARINER...

"...YOU'RE THE ALBATROSS."

"HER LIPS WERE RED, HER LOOKS WERE FREE, HER LOCKS WERE YELLOW AS GOLD...

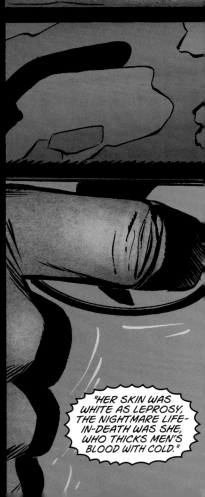

"HER SKIN WAS WHITE AS LEPROSY, THE NIGHTMARE LIFE-IN-DEATH WAS SHE, WHO THICKS MEN'S BLOOD WITH COLD."

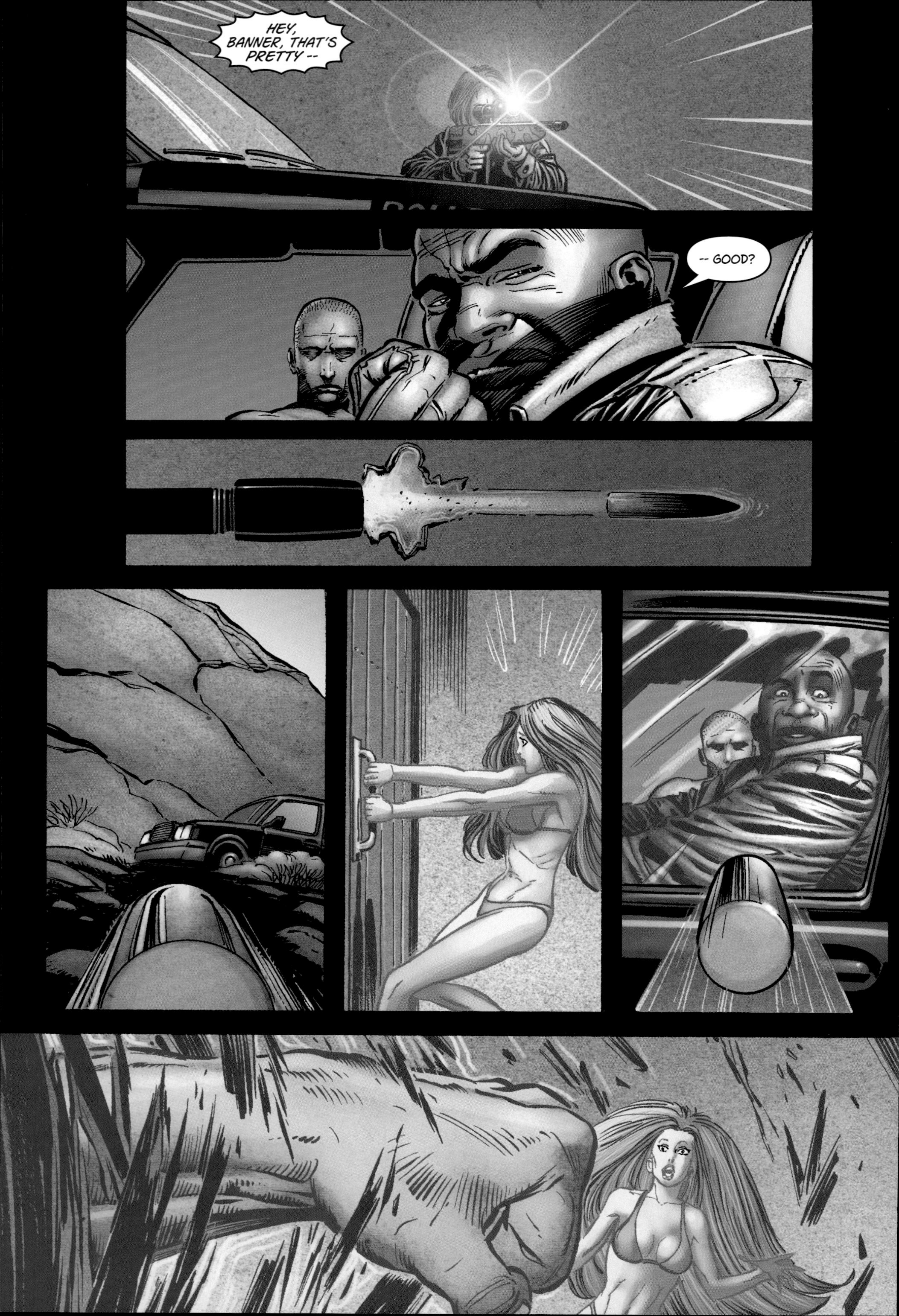
HEY, BANNER, THAT'S PRETTY --
-- GOOD?

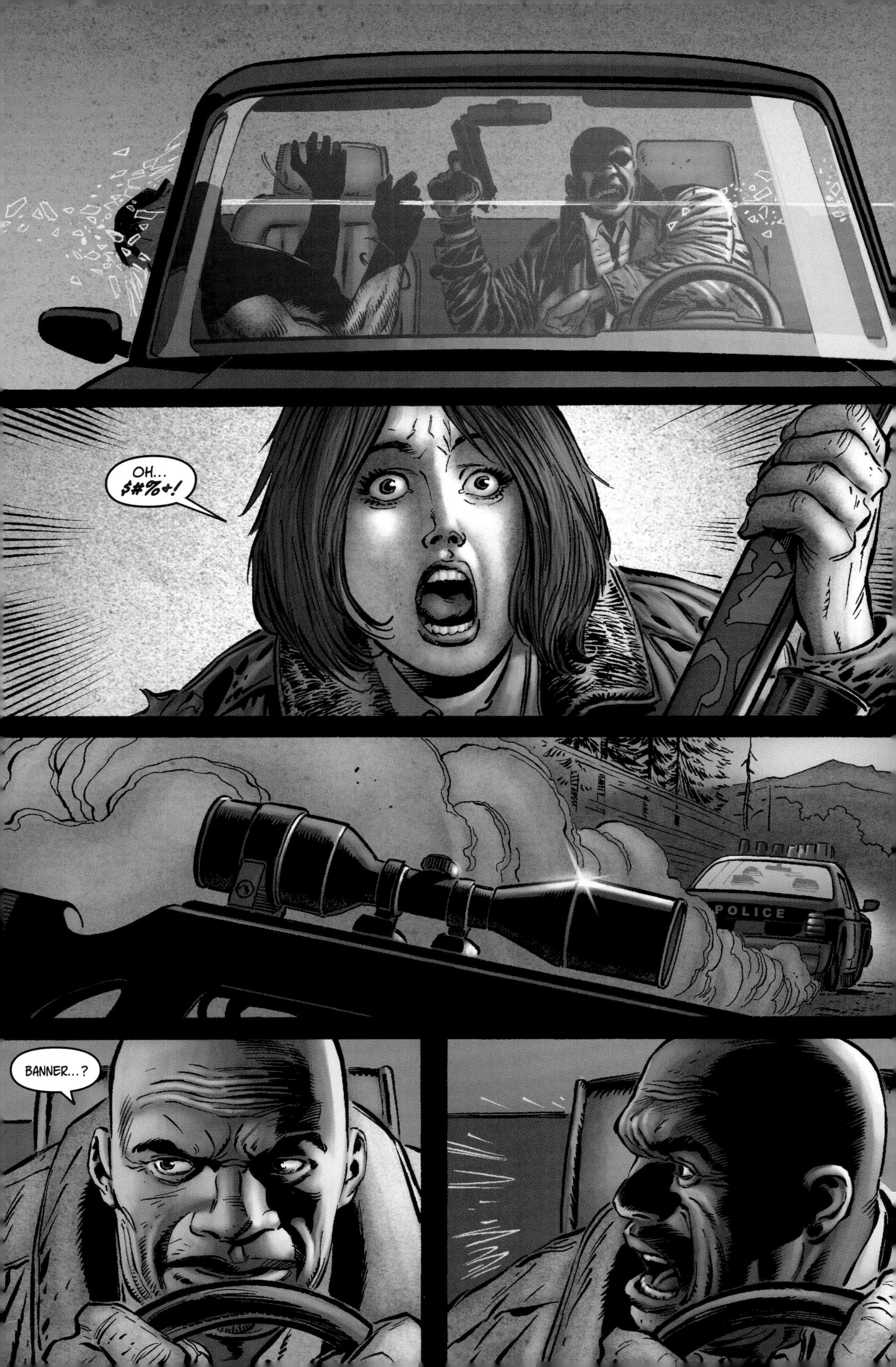
OH... $#%+!
POLICE
BANNER...?

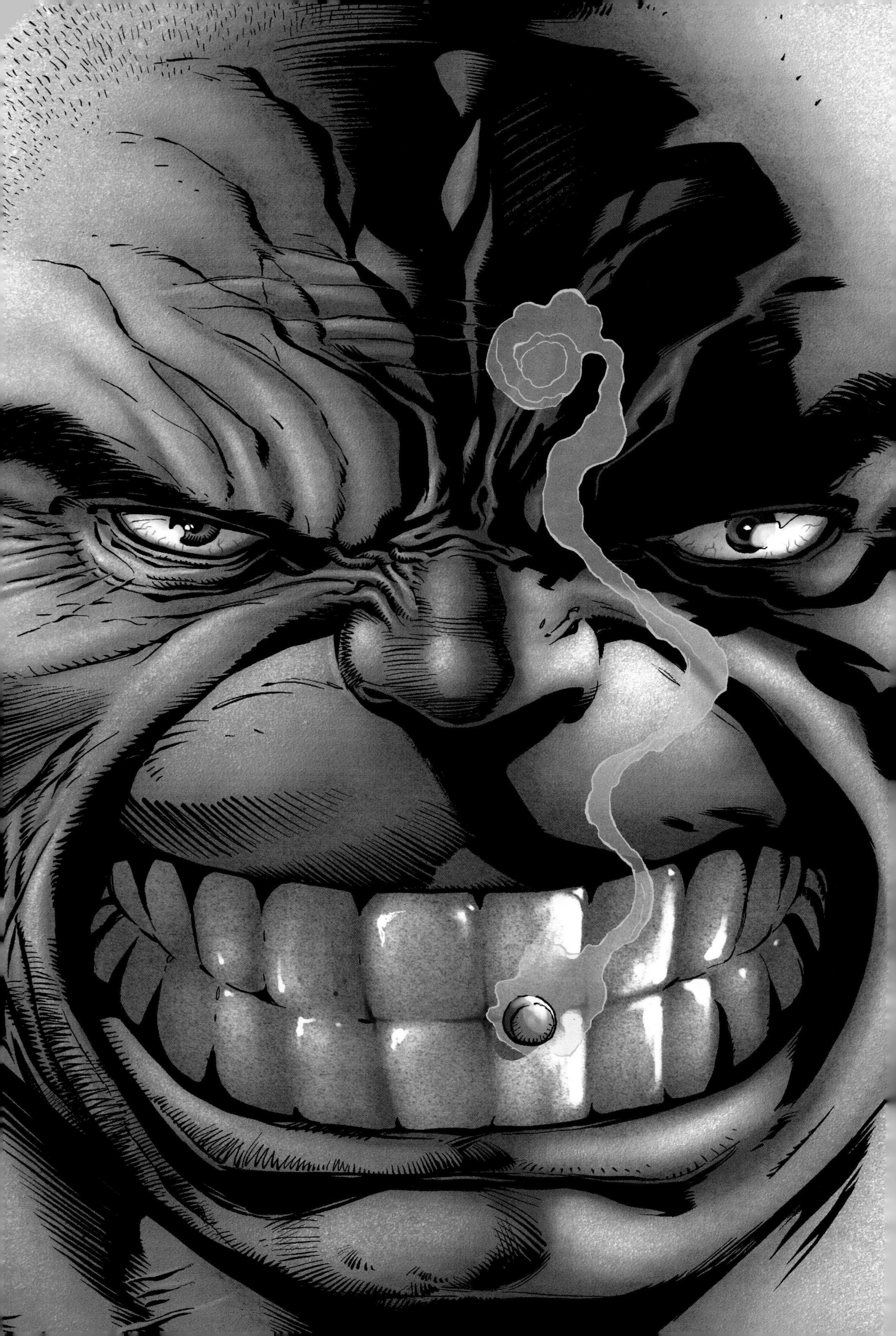

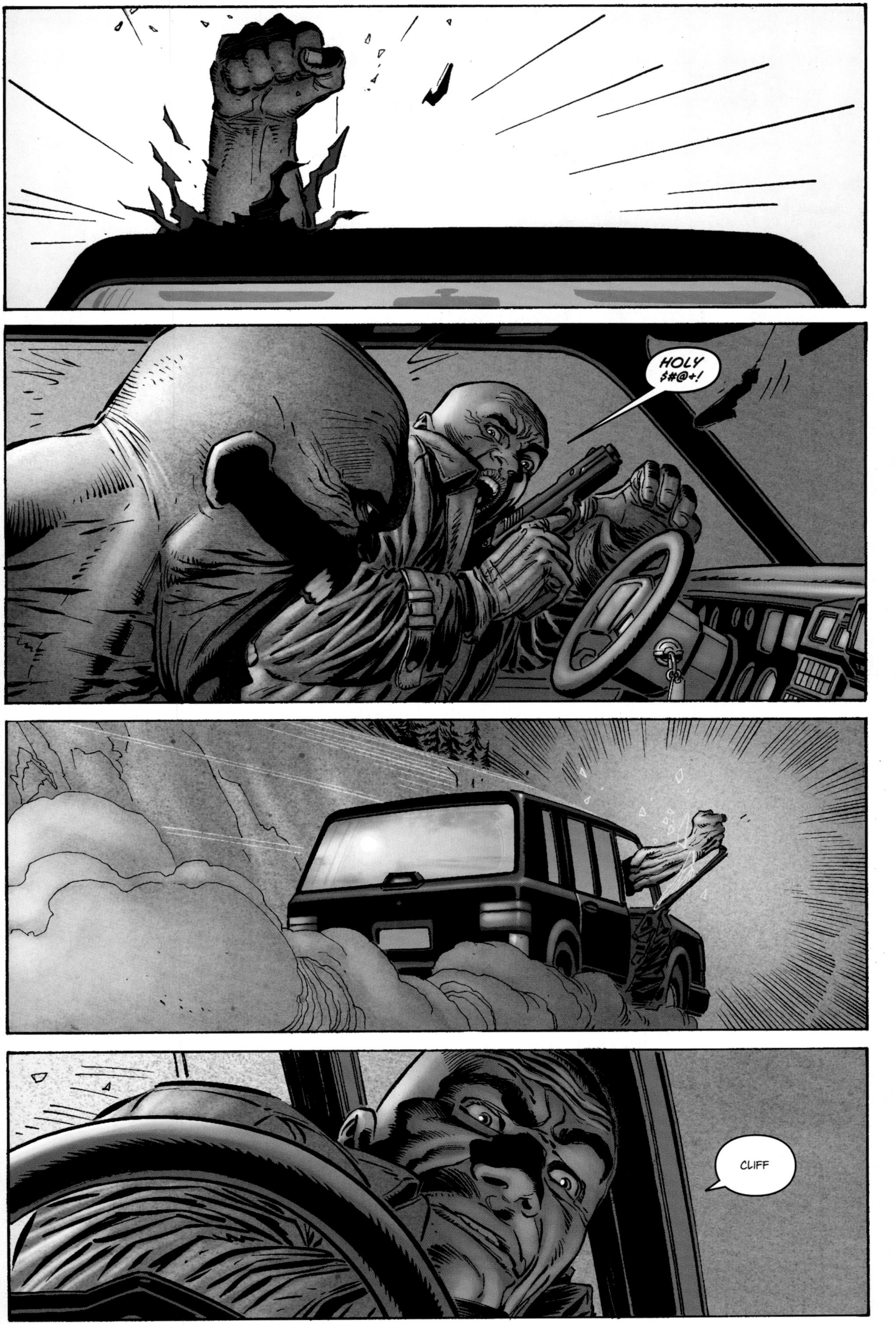
HOLY $#@+!
CLIFF

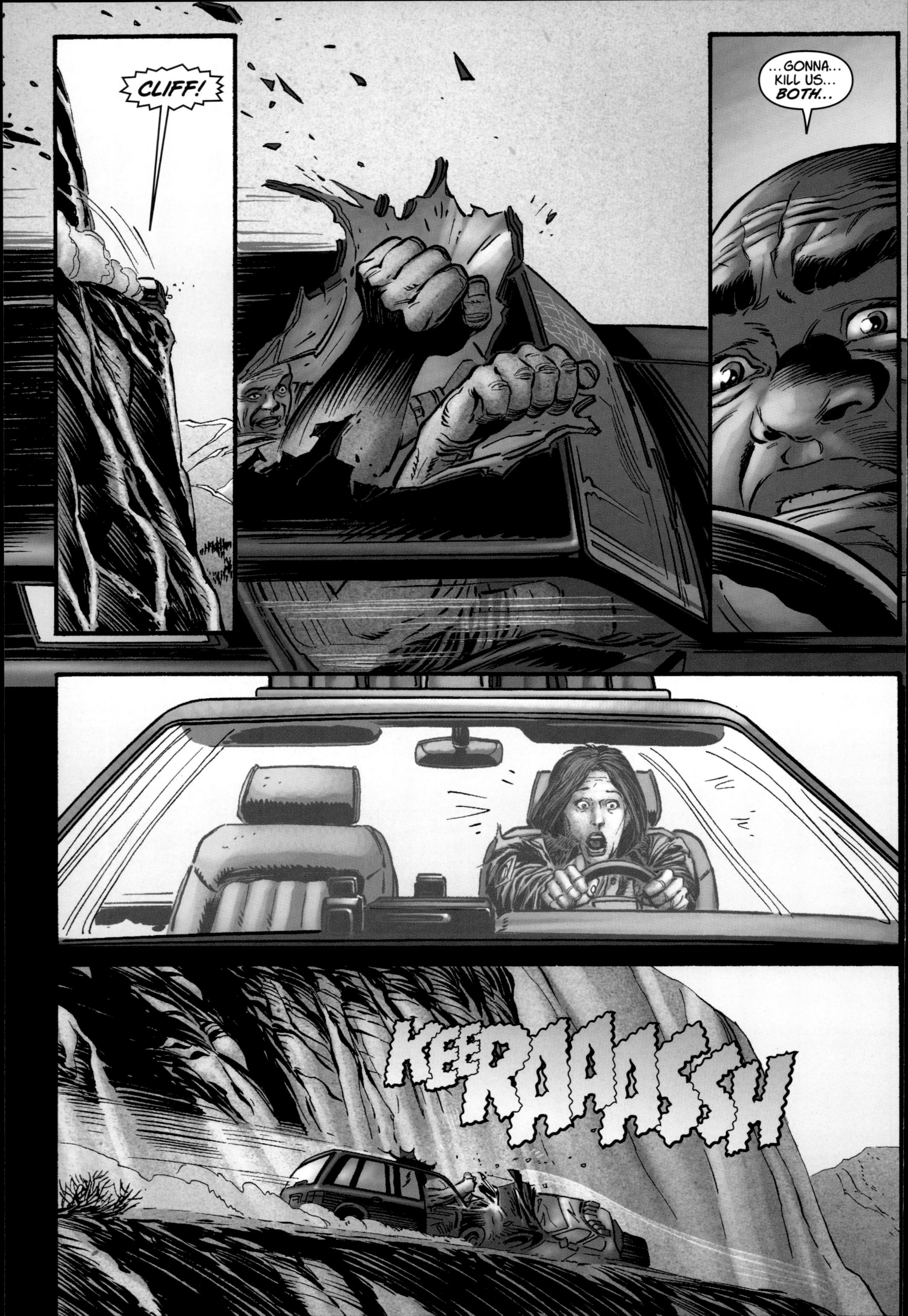
CLIFF!
...GONNA... KILL US... BOTH...
KEERAAASH

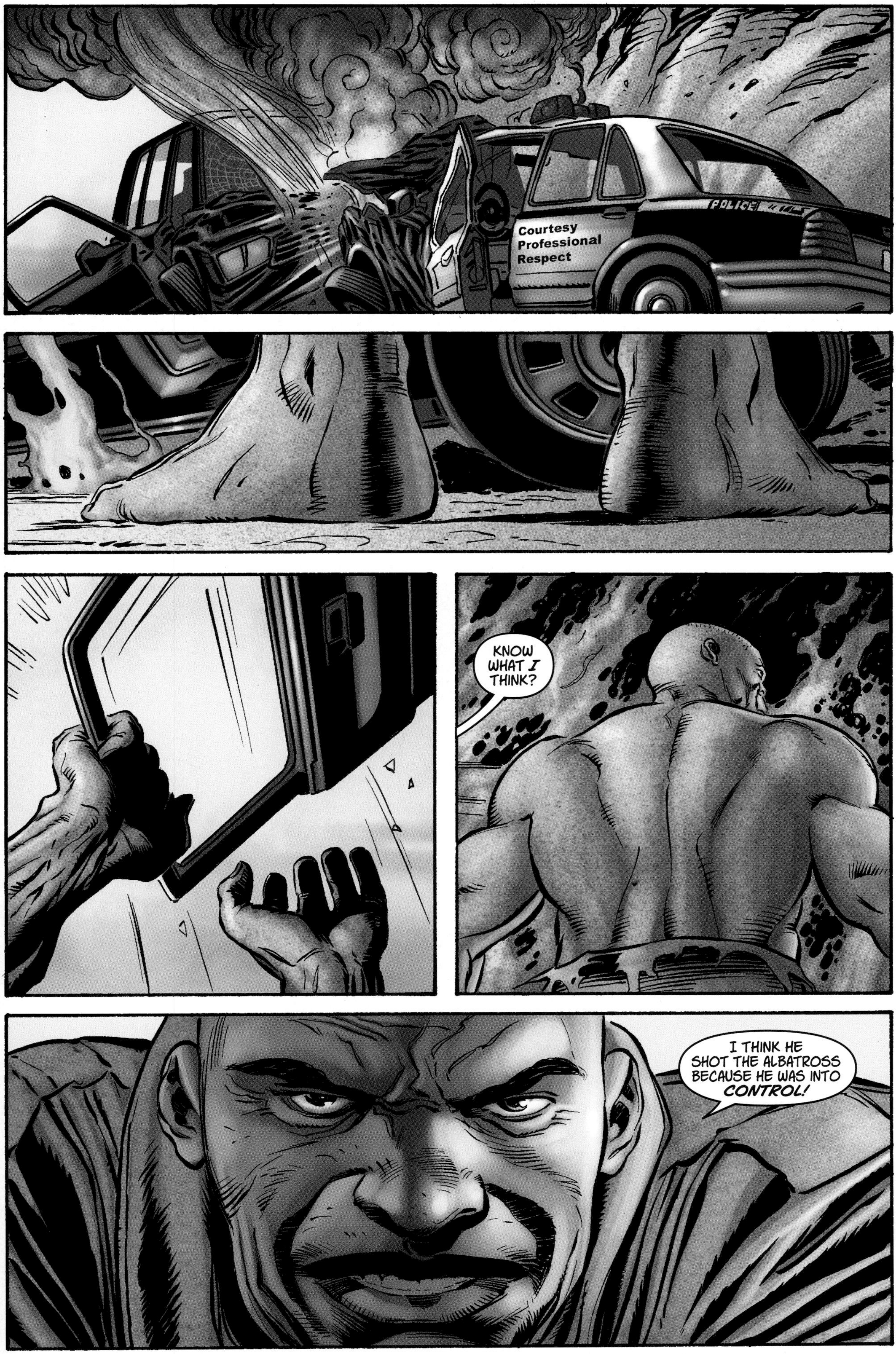
Courtesy
Professional
Respect
POLICE
KNOW WHAT I THINK?
I THINK HE SHOT THE ALBATROSS BECAUSE HE WAS INTO CONTROL!

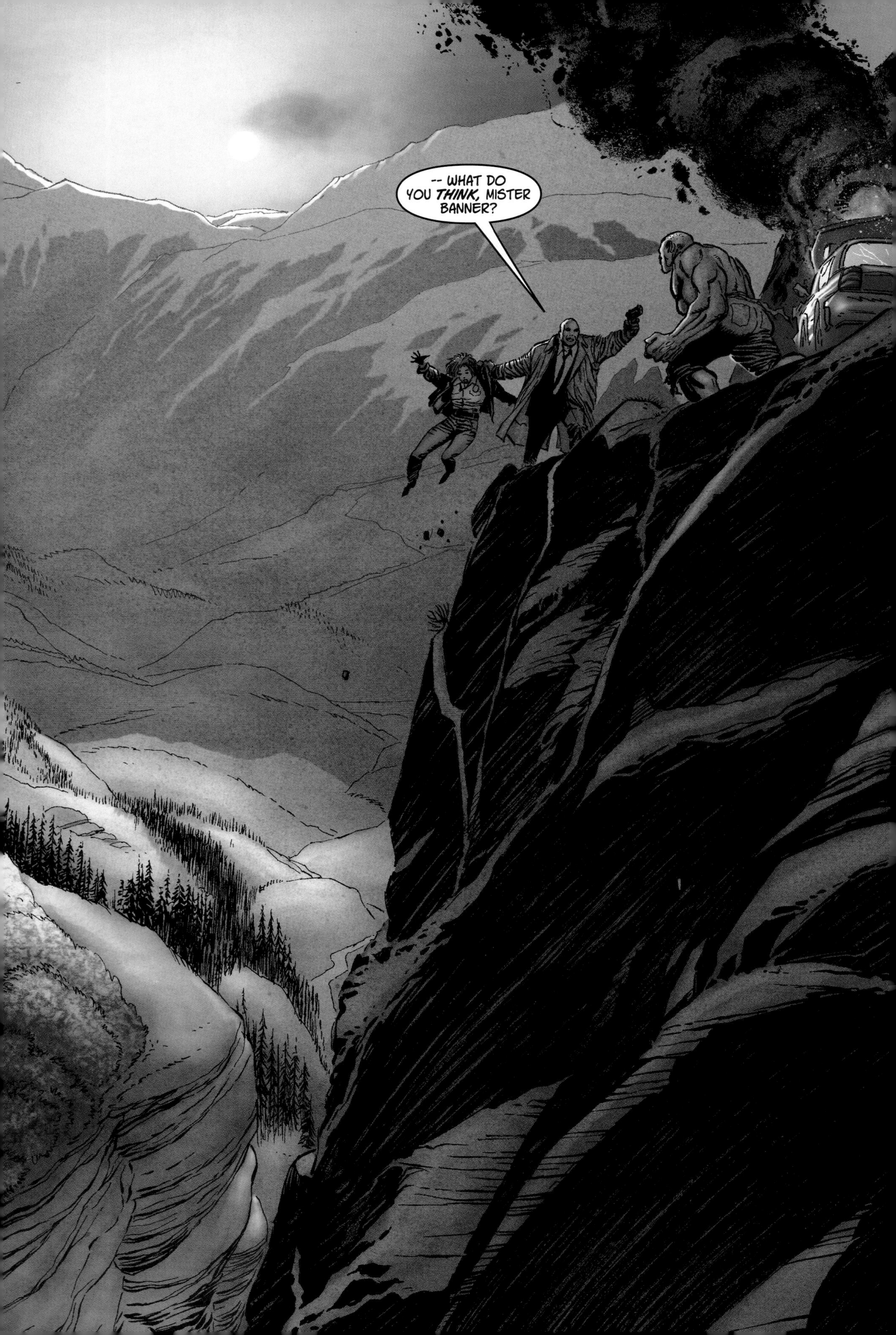
-- WHAT DO YOU THINK, MISTER BANNER?

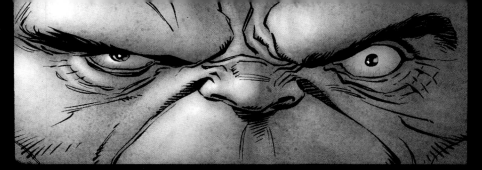

WELL DONE, BRUCIE, IF YOU'RE IN THERE *SOMEWHERE*. I DON'T KNOW *HOW* YOU DID IT, BUT MY COMPLIMENTS.

HERE'S MY *OFFER:* YOU MORPH BACK INTO THAT SLIMMER SHAPELIER YOU, AND *I* PROMISE NOT TO DROP HER...

WHAT DO YOU SAY? *QUID PRO QUO?*

DON'T DO IT, BRUCE. HE'LL *KILL* YOU.

IN YOUR PRESENT SITUATION, LIEUTENANT, I'D SUGGEST BEING SEEN AND NOT BEING HEARD, AS YOU'RE *HARDLY* IN A POSITION TO BARGAIN.

WHAT'S IT GOING TO *BE,* BRUCIE...?

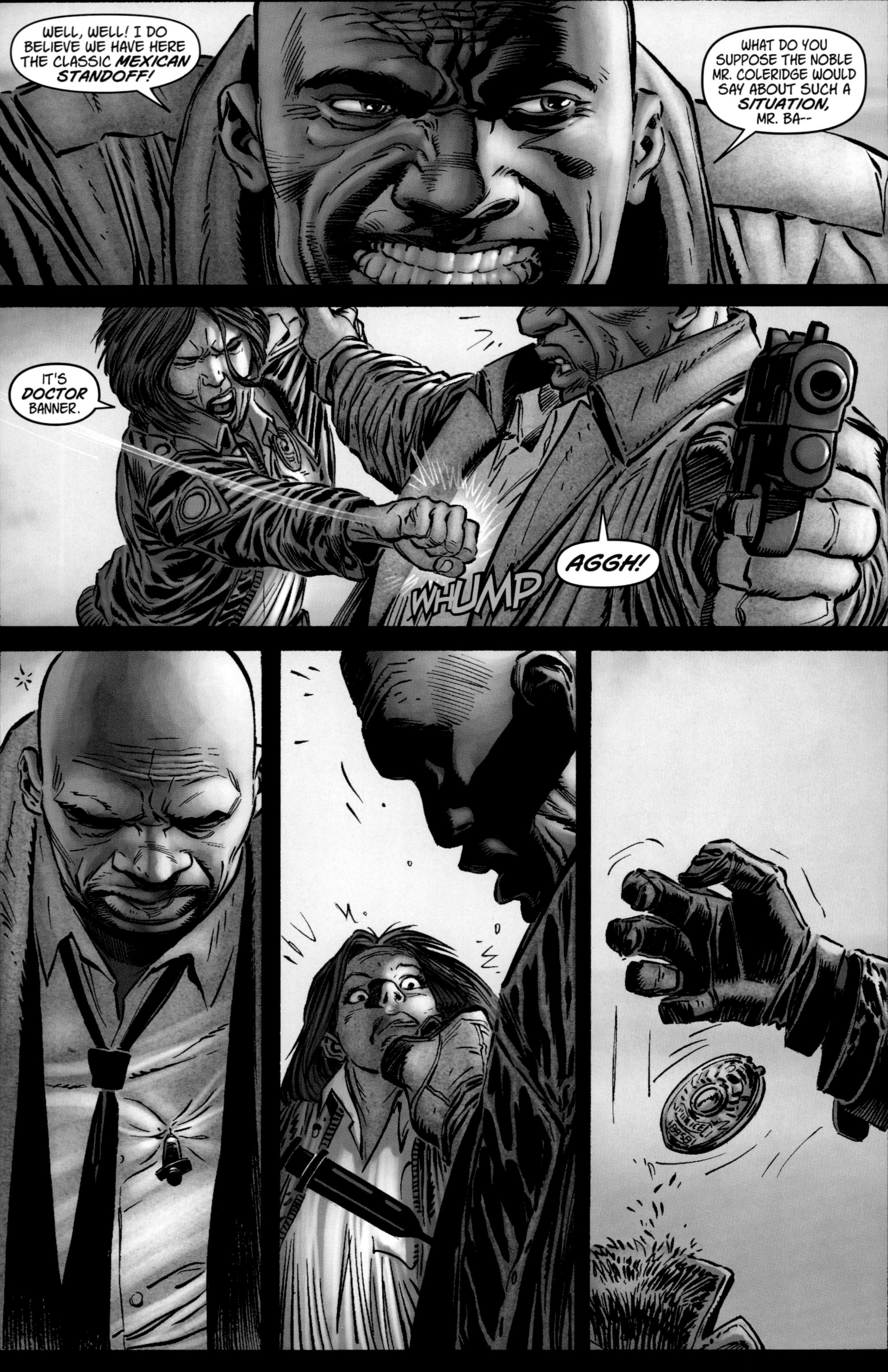
WELL, WELL! I DO BELIEVE WE HAVE HERE THE CLASSIC MEXICAN STANDOFF!
WHAT DO YOU SUPPOSE THE NOBLE MR. COLERIDGE WOULD SAY ABOUT SUCH A SITUATION, MR. BA--
IT'S DOCTOR BANNER.
AGGH!
WHUMP

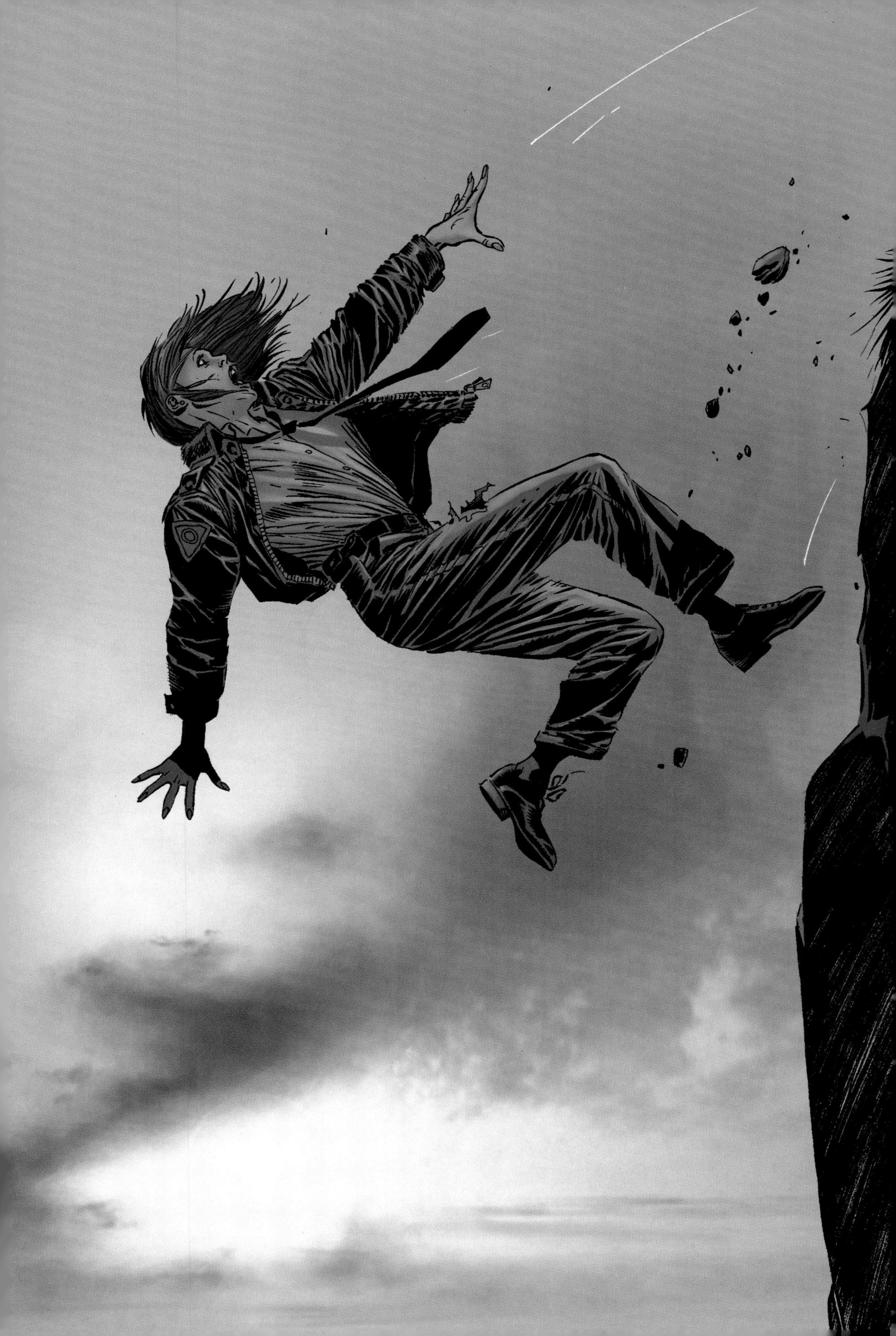

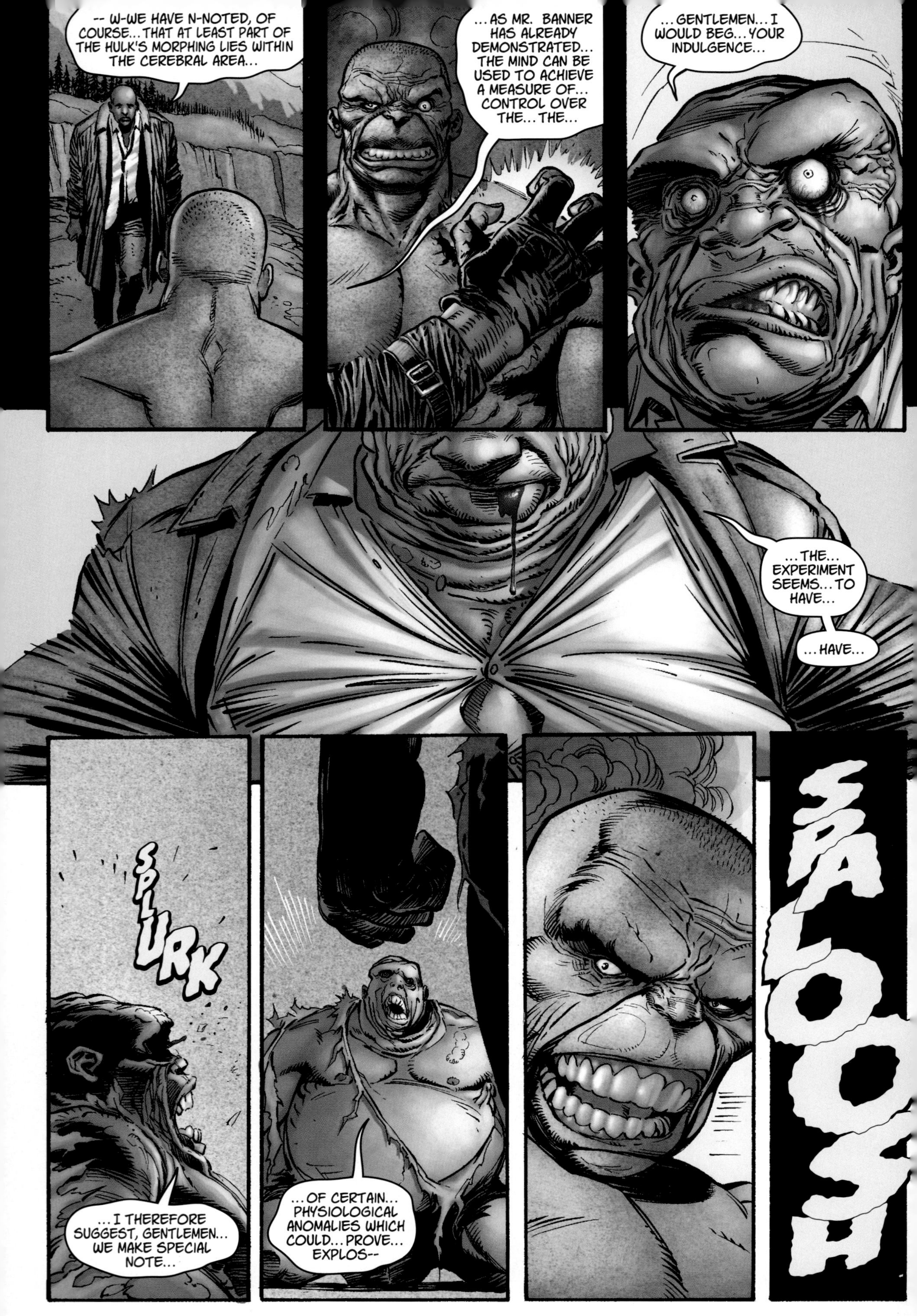
-- W-WE HAVE N-NOTED, OF COURSE... THAT AT LEAST PART OF THE HULK'S MORPHING LIES WITHIN THE CEREBRAL AREA...
...AS MR. BANNER HAS ALREADY DEMONSTRATED... THE MIND CAN BE USED TO ACHIEVE A MEASURE OF... CONTROL OVER THE... THE...
...GENTLEMEN... I WOULD BEG... YOUR INDULGENCE...
...THE... EXPERIMENT SEEMS... TO HAVE...
...HAVE...
SPLURK
...I THEREFORE SUGGEST, GENTLEMEN... WE MAKE SPECIAL NOTE...
...OF CERTAIN... PHYSIOLOGICAL ANOMALIES WHICH COULD... PROVE... EXPLOS--
SPALOOSH

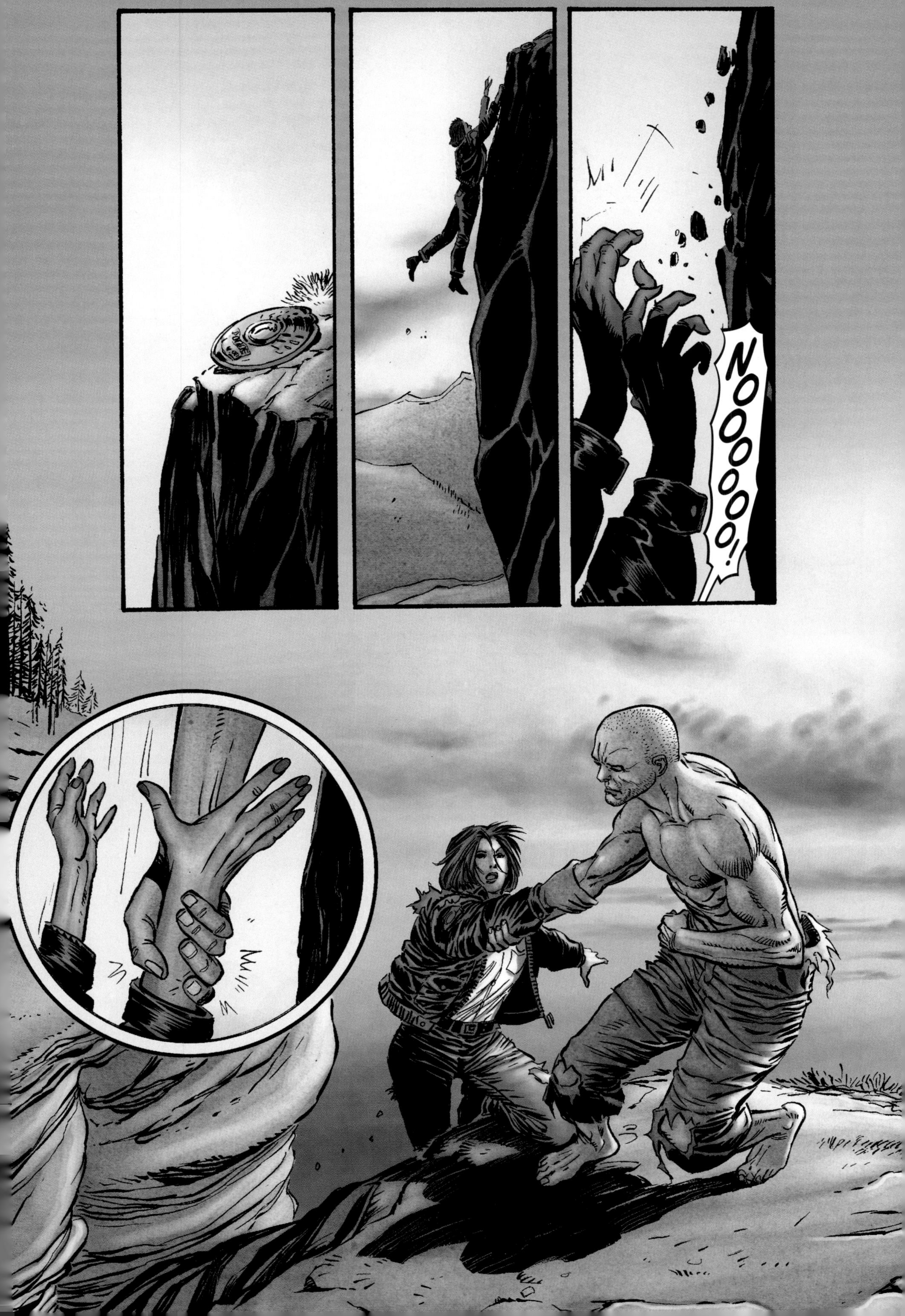
NOOOOOO!

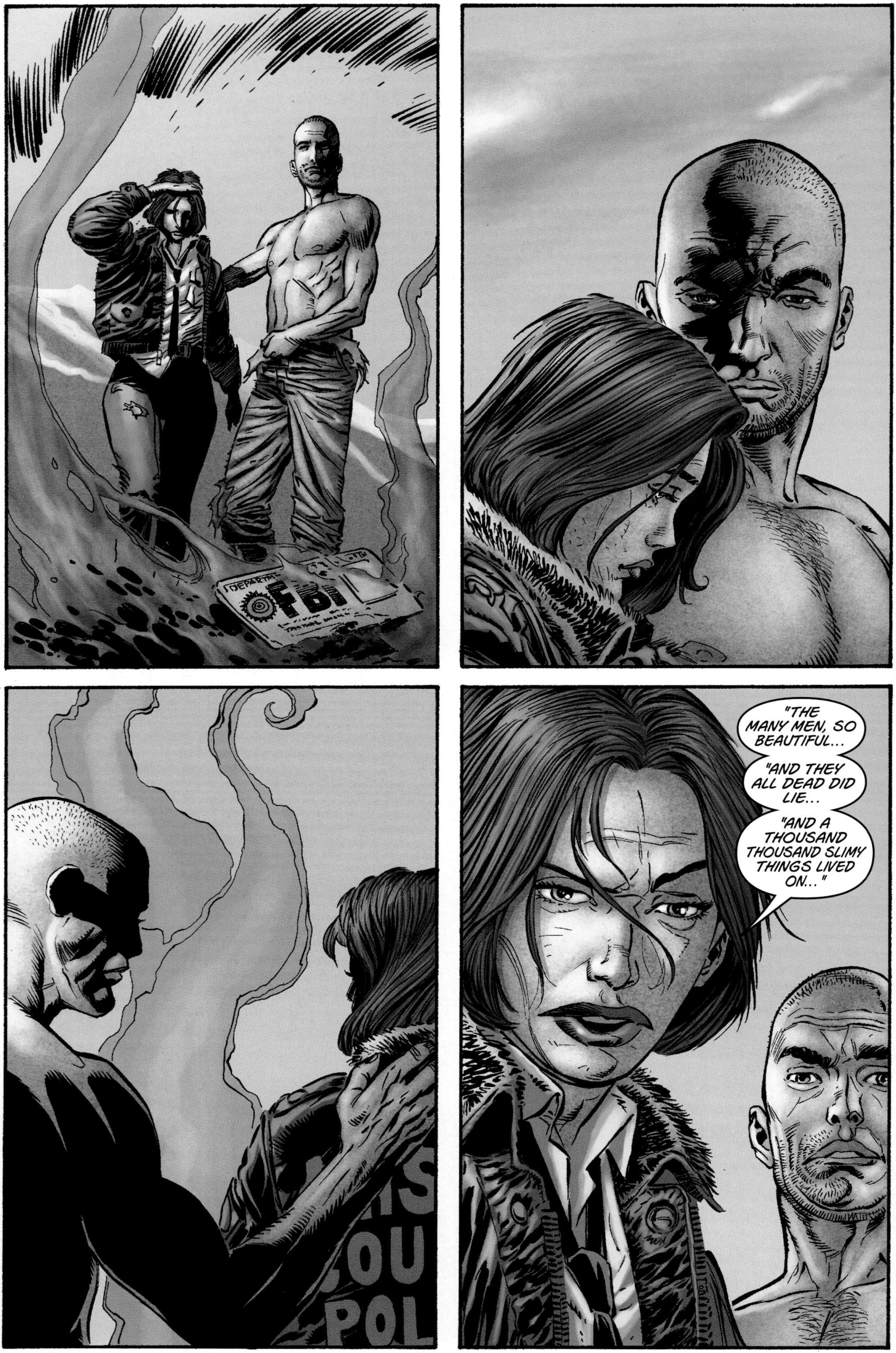
FBI
"THE MANY MEN, SO BEAUTIFUL...
"AND THEY ALL DEAD DID LIE...
"AND A THOUSAND THOUSAND SLIMY THINGS LIVED ON..."

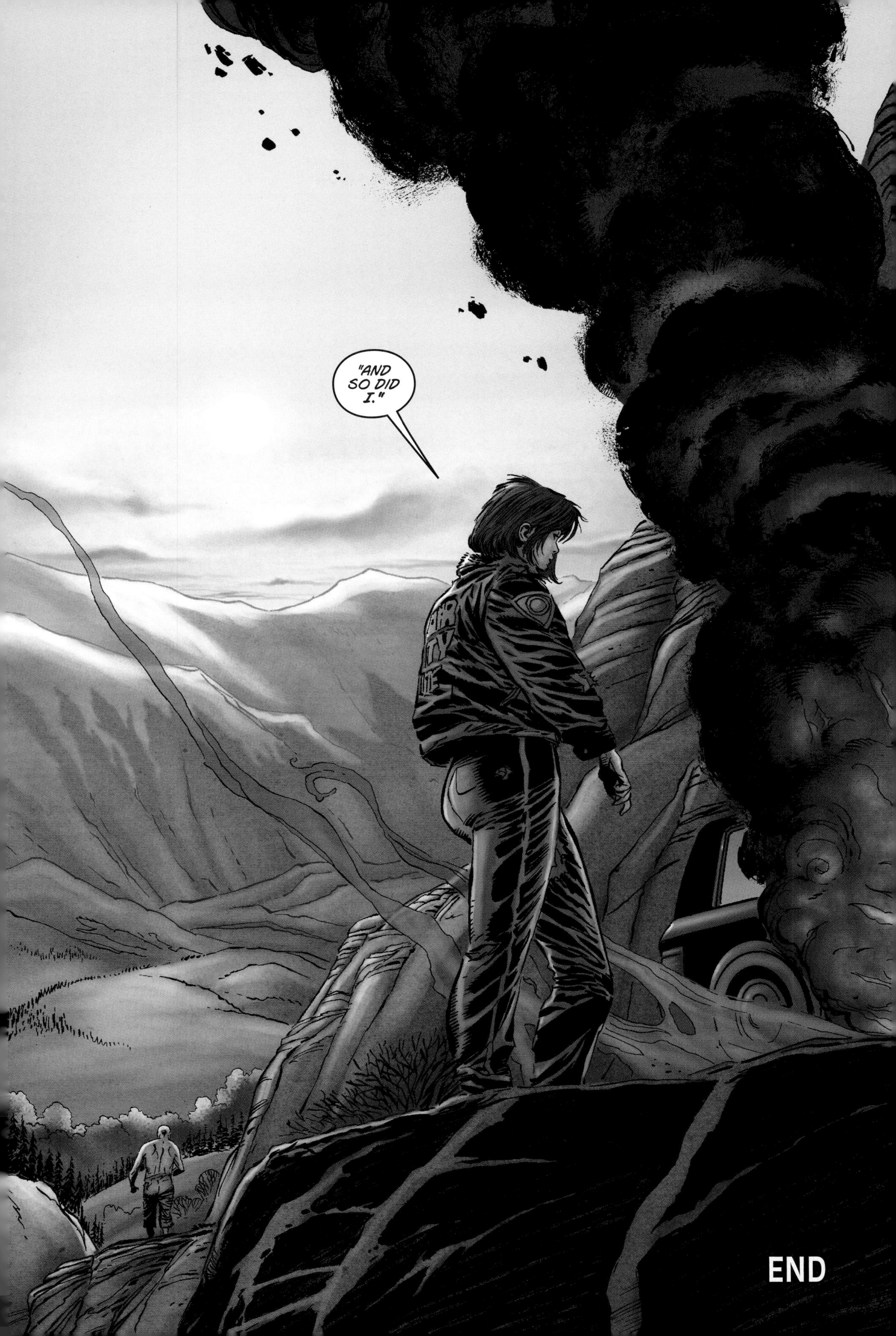
"AND SO DID I."
END

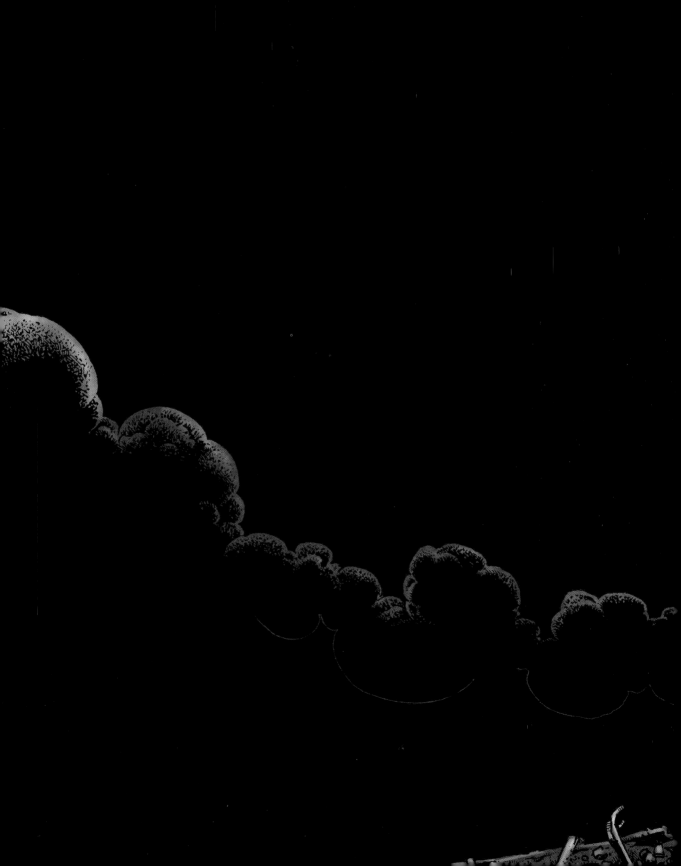

THAT is what iS ...
THiS is what COUlD HaVe BeeN ...

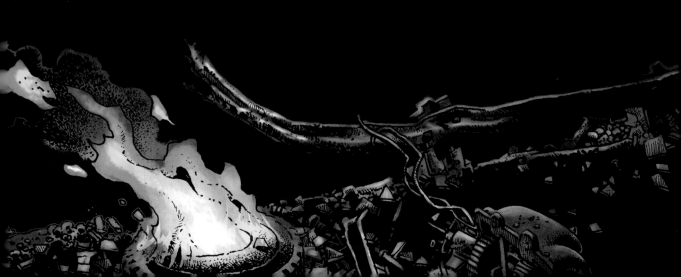

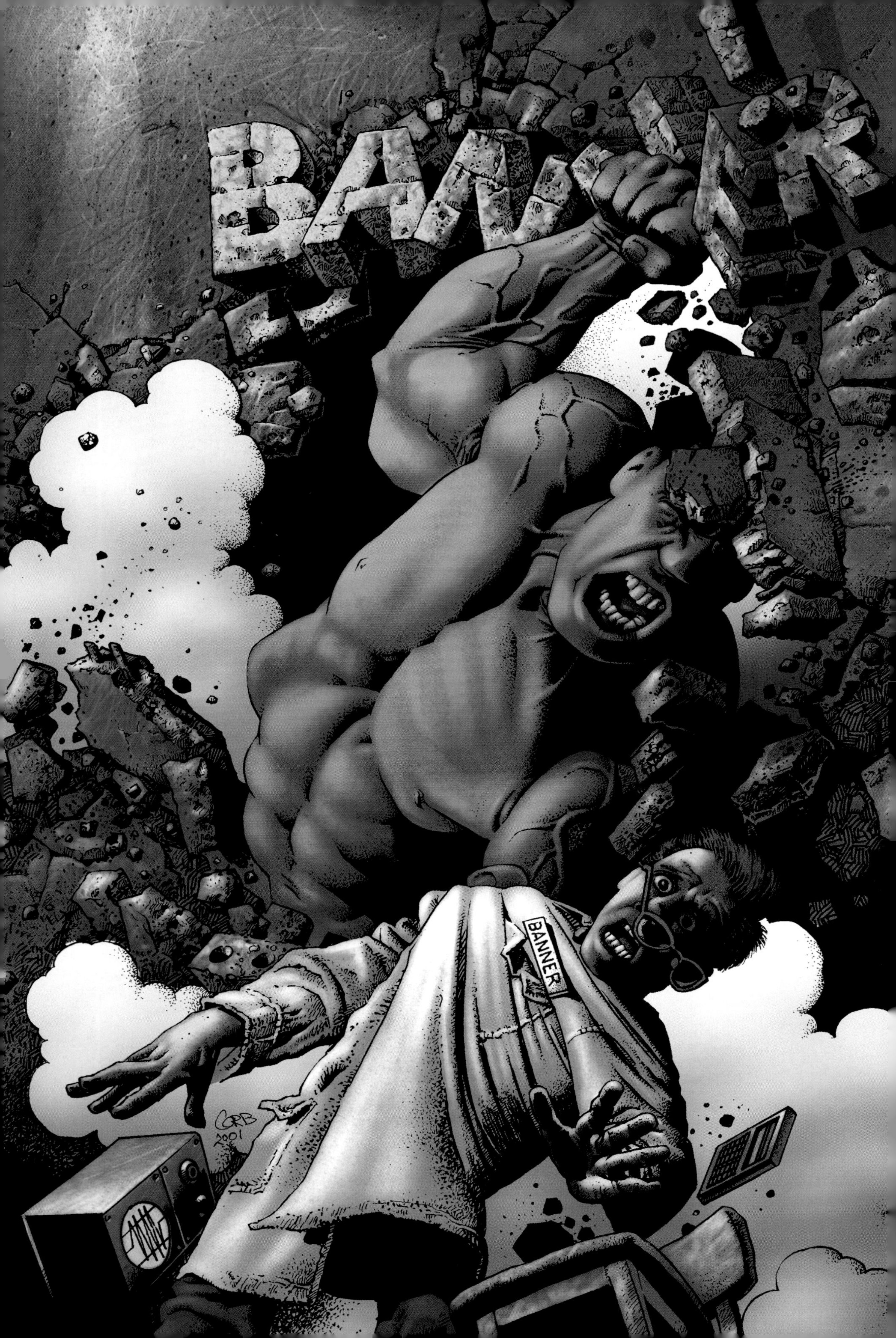

BANNER

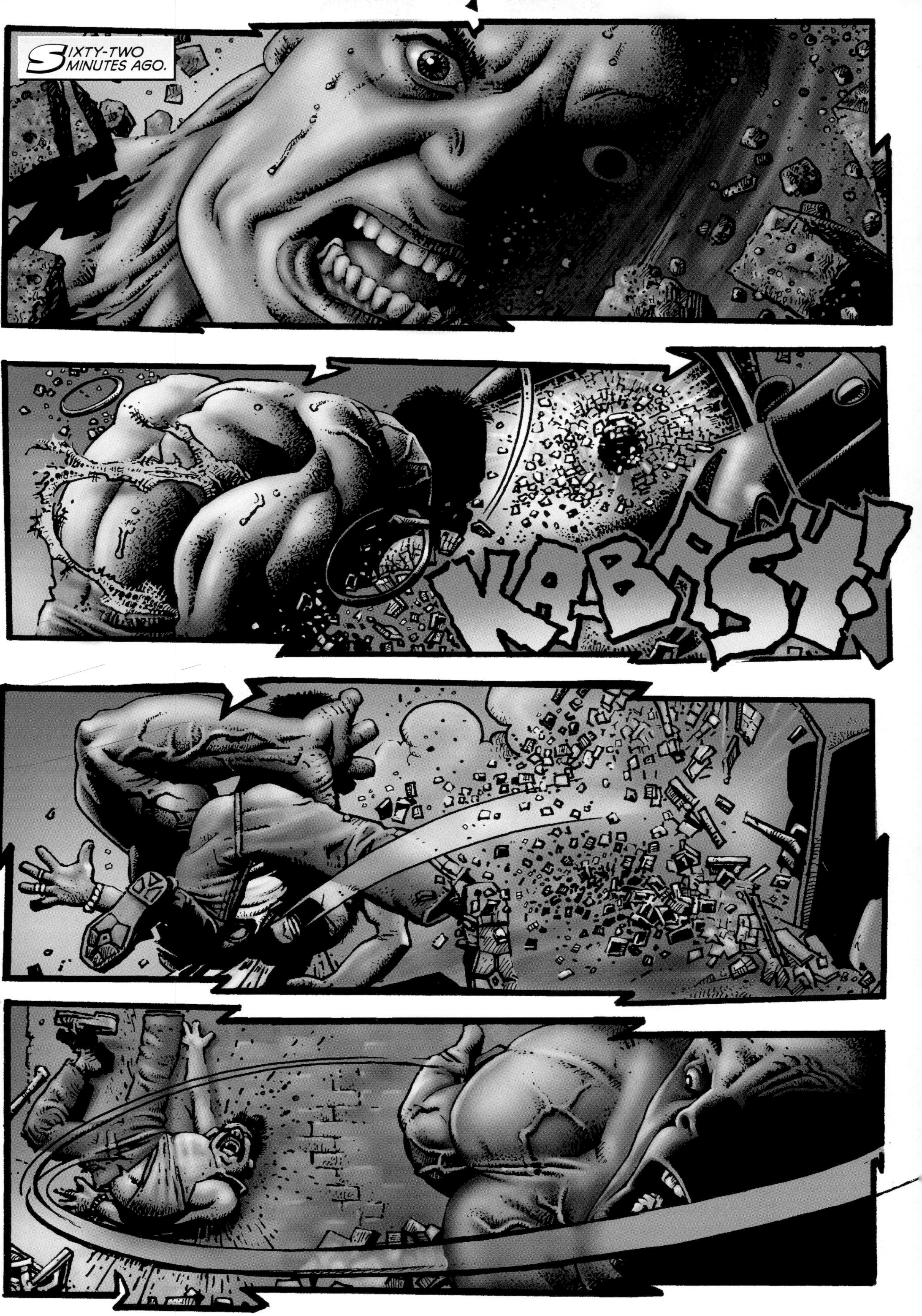
SIXTY-TWO MINUTES AGO.
KA-BASH!

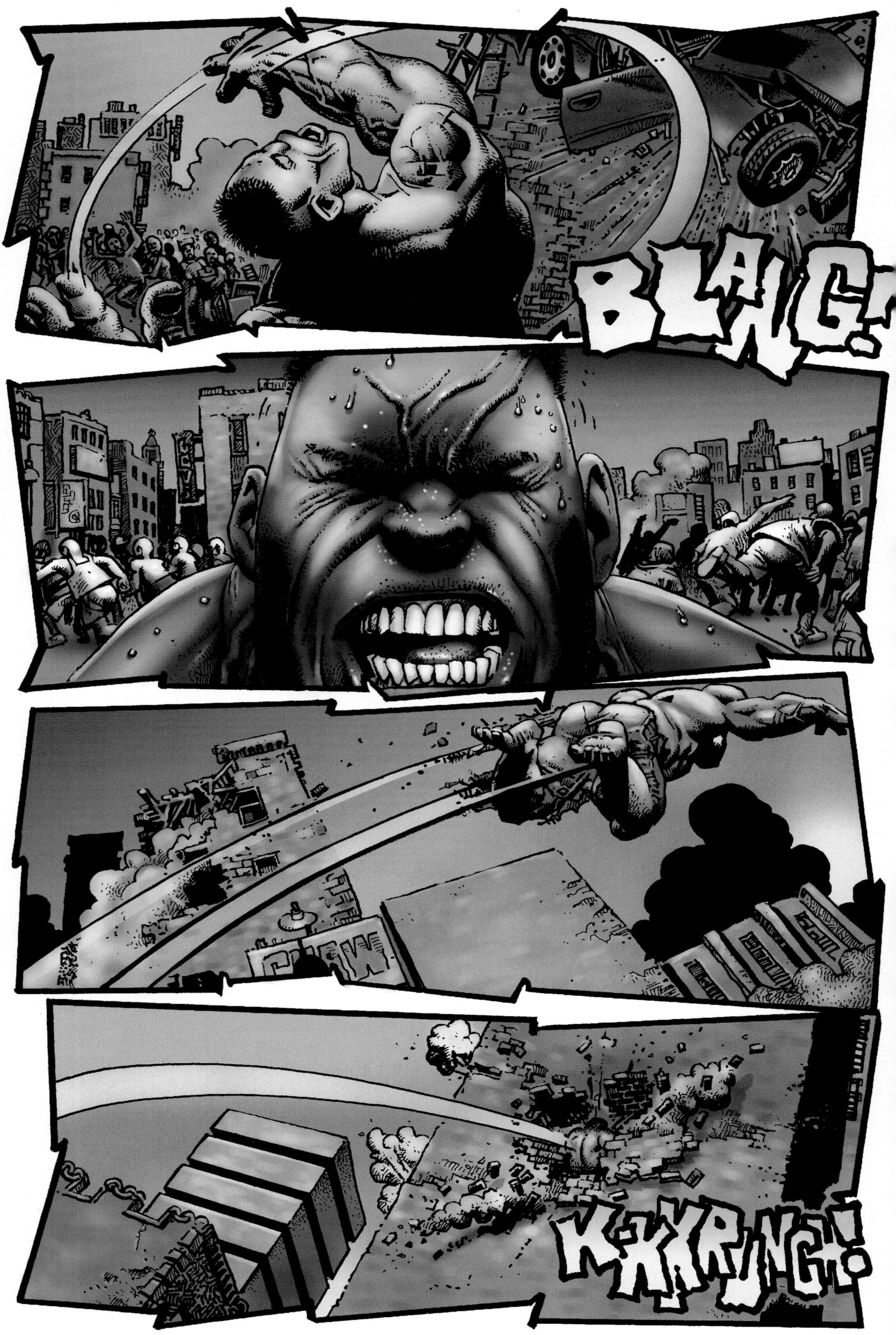
BLAG!
K-KRUNCH!

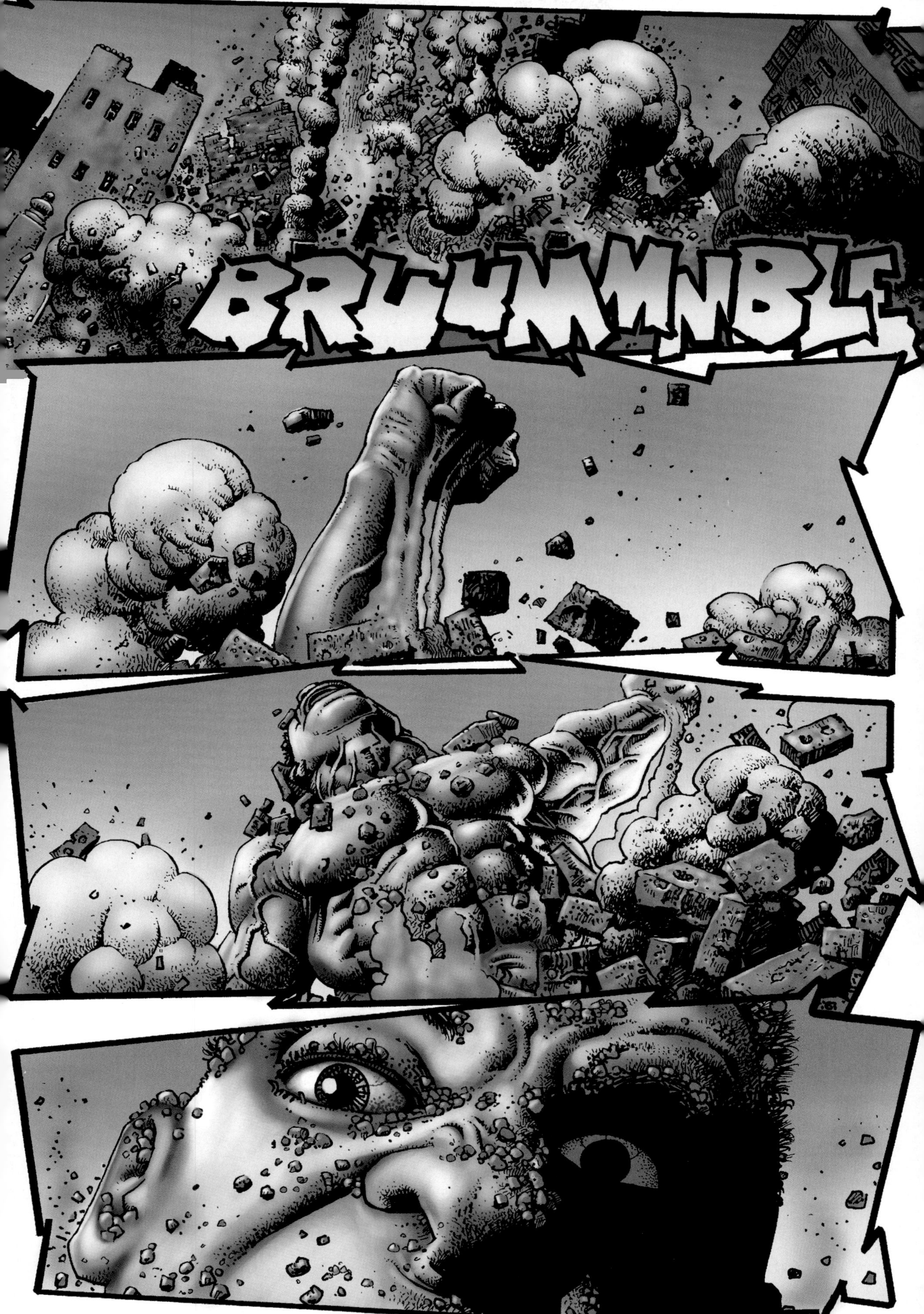
BRUMMMBLE

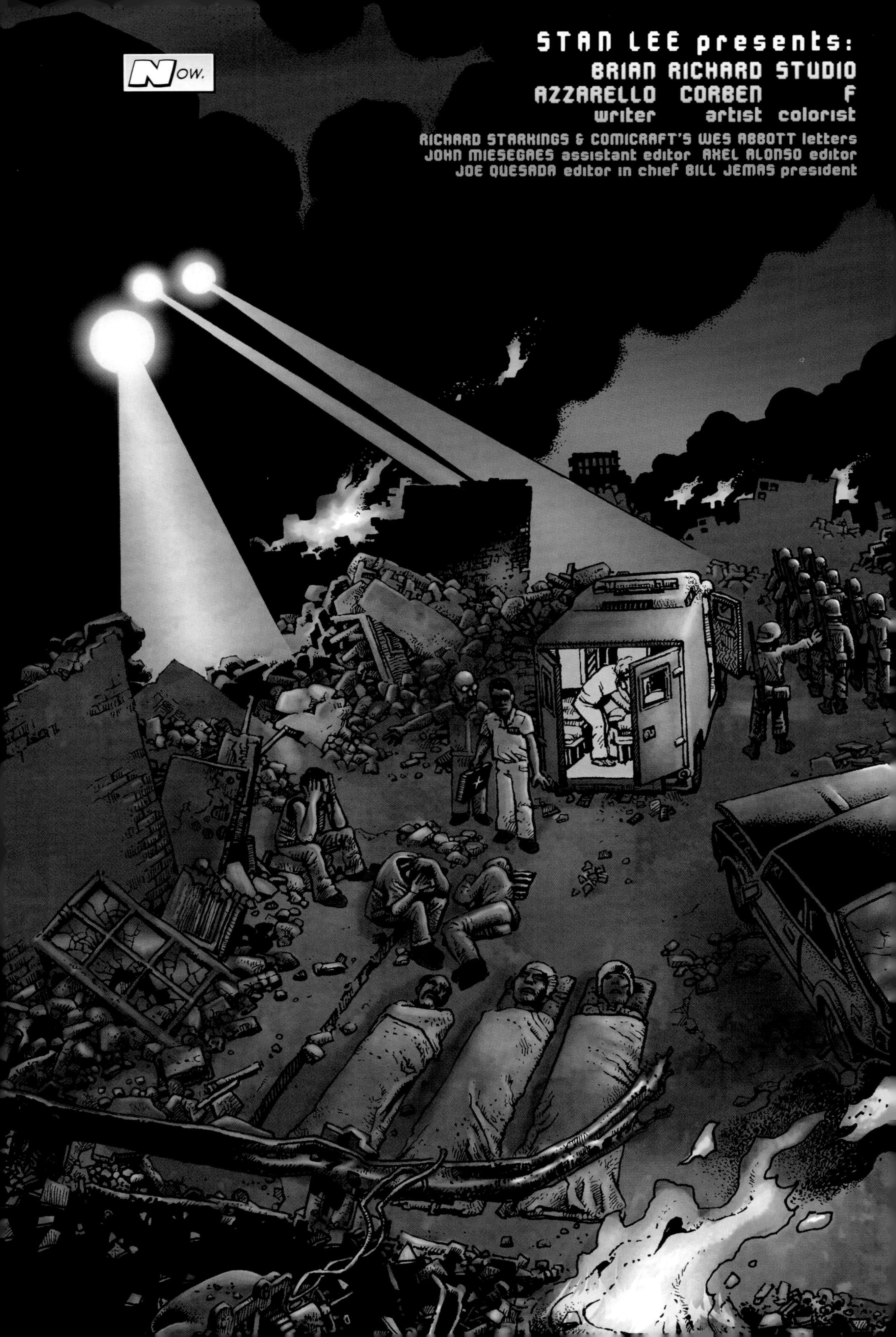
NOW.
STAN LEE presents:
BRIAN AZZARELLO writer
RICHARD CORBEN artist
STUDIO F colorist
RICHARD STARKINGS & COMICRAFT'S WES ABBOTT letters
JOHN MIESEGAES assistant editor AXEL ALONSO editor
JOE QUESADA editor in chief BILL JEMAS president

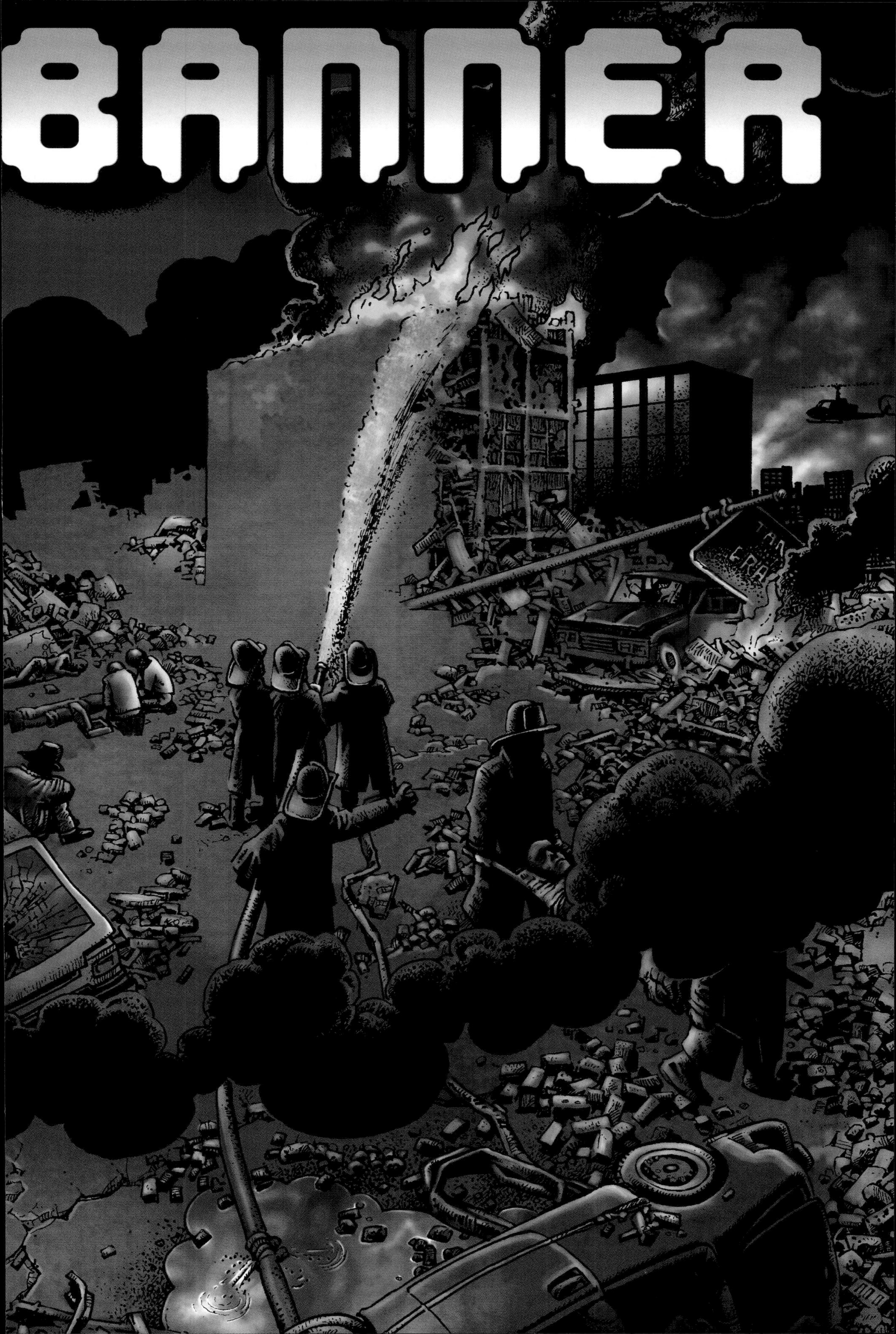
BANNER

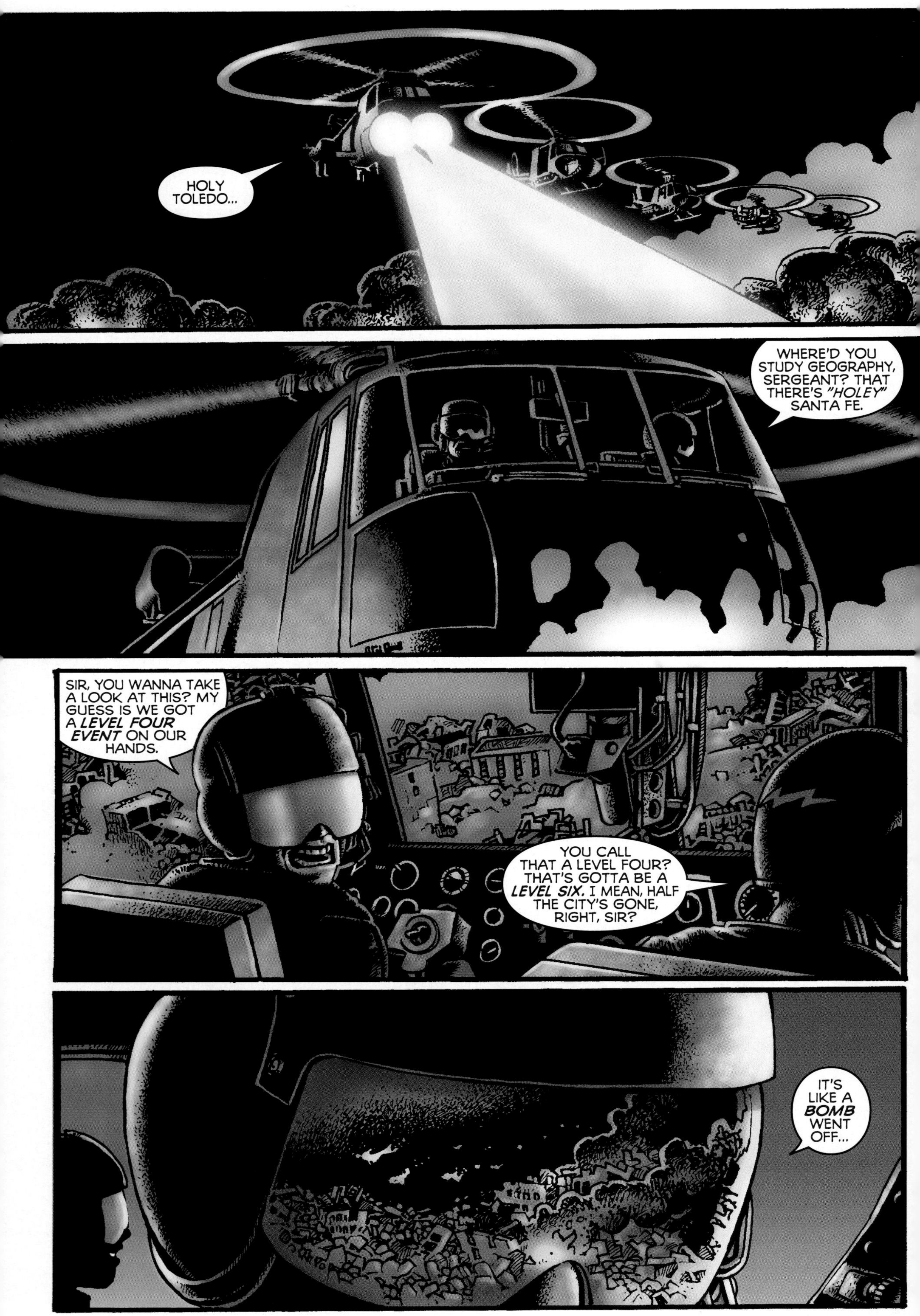
HOLY TOLEDO...
WHERE'D YOU STUDY GEOGRAPHY, SERGEANT? THAT THERE'S "HOLEY" SANTA FE.
SIR, YOU WANNA TAKE A LOOK AT THIS? MY GUESS IS WE GOT A ***LEVEL FOUR EVENT*** ON OUR HANDS.
YOU CALL THAT A LEVEL FOUR? THAT'S GOTTA BE A ***LEVEL SIX.*** I MEAN, HALF THE CITY'S GONE, RIGHT, SIR?
IT'S LIKE A ***BOMB*** WENT OFF...

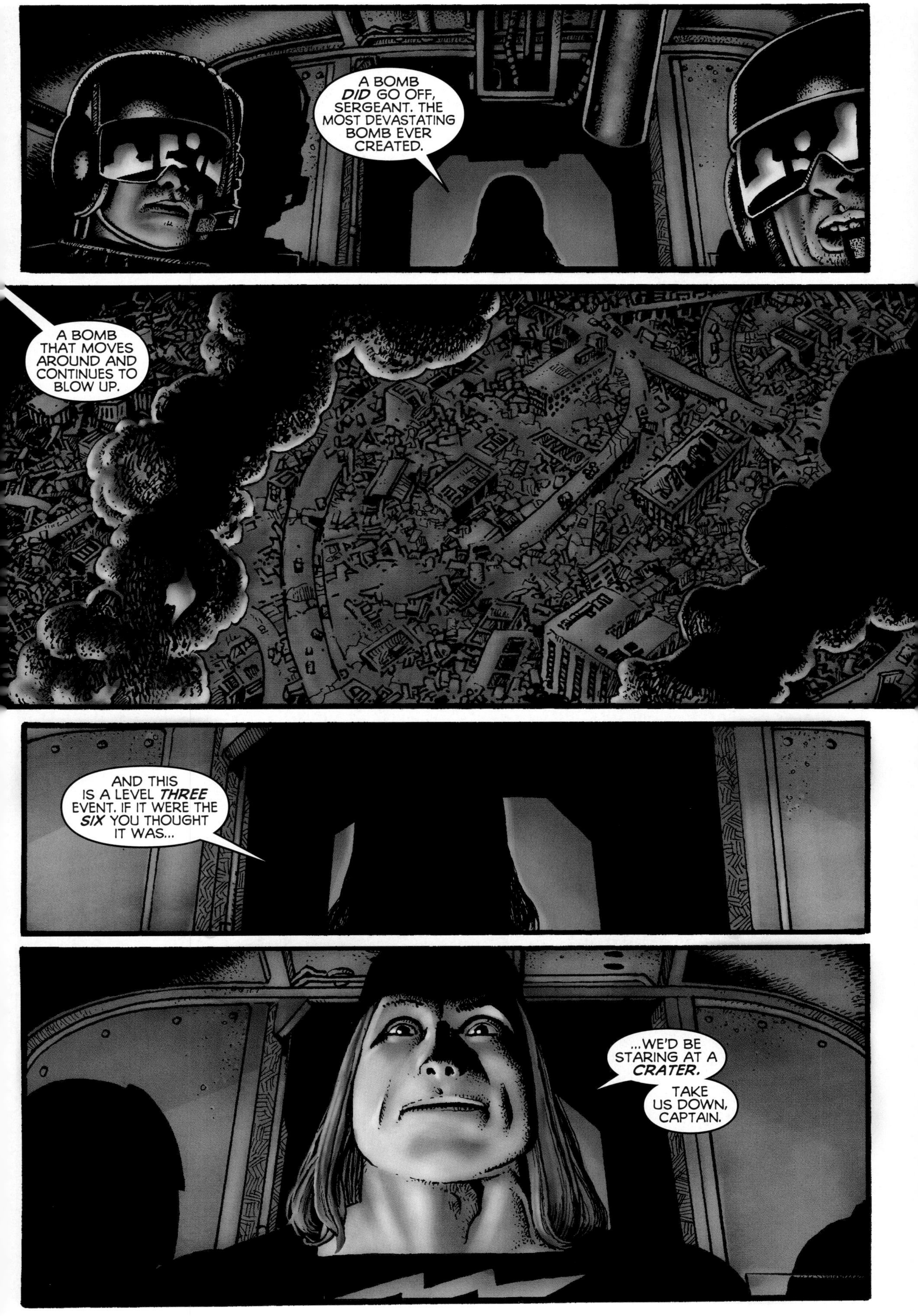
A BOMB DID GO OFF, SERGEANT. THE MOST DEVASTATING BOMB EVER CREATED.
A BOMB THAT MOVES AROUND AND CONTINUES TO BLOW UP.
AND THIS IS A LEVEL THREE EVENT. IF IT WERE THE SIX YOU THOUGHT IT WAS...
...WE'D BE STARING AT A CRATER.
TAKE US DOWN, CAPTAIN.

ALL RIGHT, MOVE! MOVE MOVE MOVE!

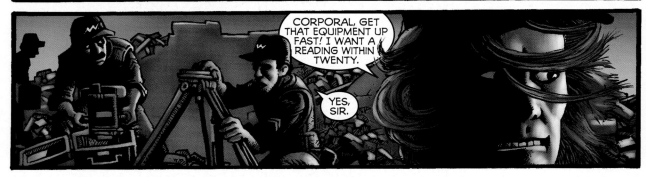

CORPORAL, GET THAT EQUIPMENT UP FAST! I WANT A READING WITHIN TWENTY.

YES, SIR.

DOCTOR SAMSON.

MAJOR. WHAT'S OUR SITUATION?

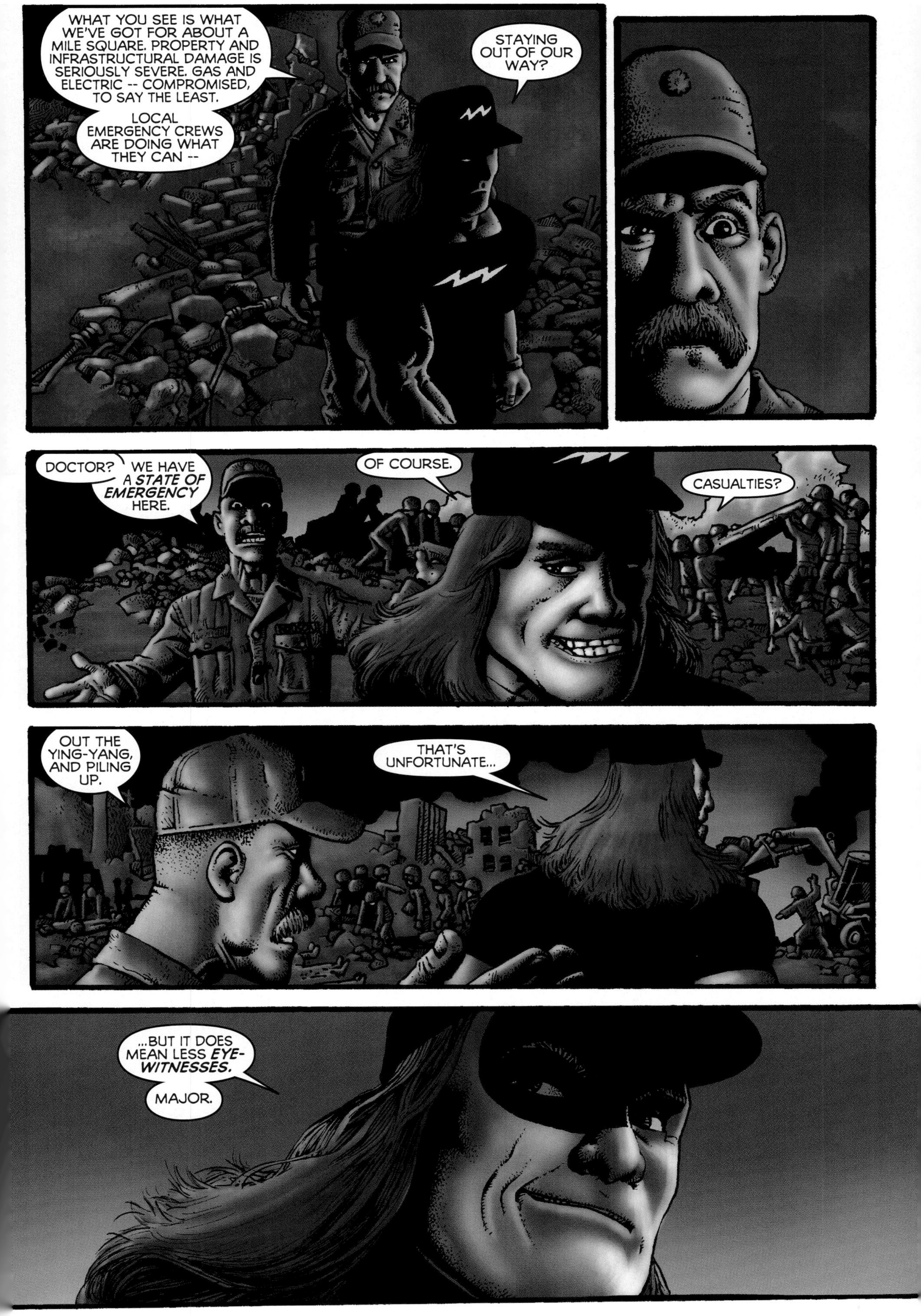
WHAT YOU SEE IS WHAT WE'VE GOT FOR ABOUT A MILE SQUARE. PROPERTY AND INFRASTRUCTURAL DAMAGE IS SERIOUSLY SEVERE. GAS AND ELECTRIC -- COMPROMISED, TO SAY THE LEAST.
LOCAL EMERGENCY CREWS ARE DOING WHAT THEY CAN --
STAYING OUT OF OUR WAY?
DOCTOR?
WE HAVE A *STATE OF EMERGENCY* HERE.
OF COURSE.
CASUALTIES?
OUT THE YING-YANG, AND PILING UP.
THAT'S UNFORTUNATE...
...BUT IT DOES MEAN LESS *EYE-WITNESSES.*
MAJOR.

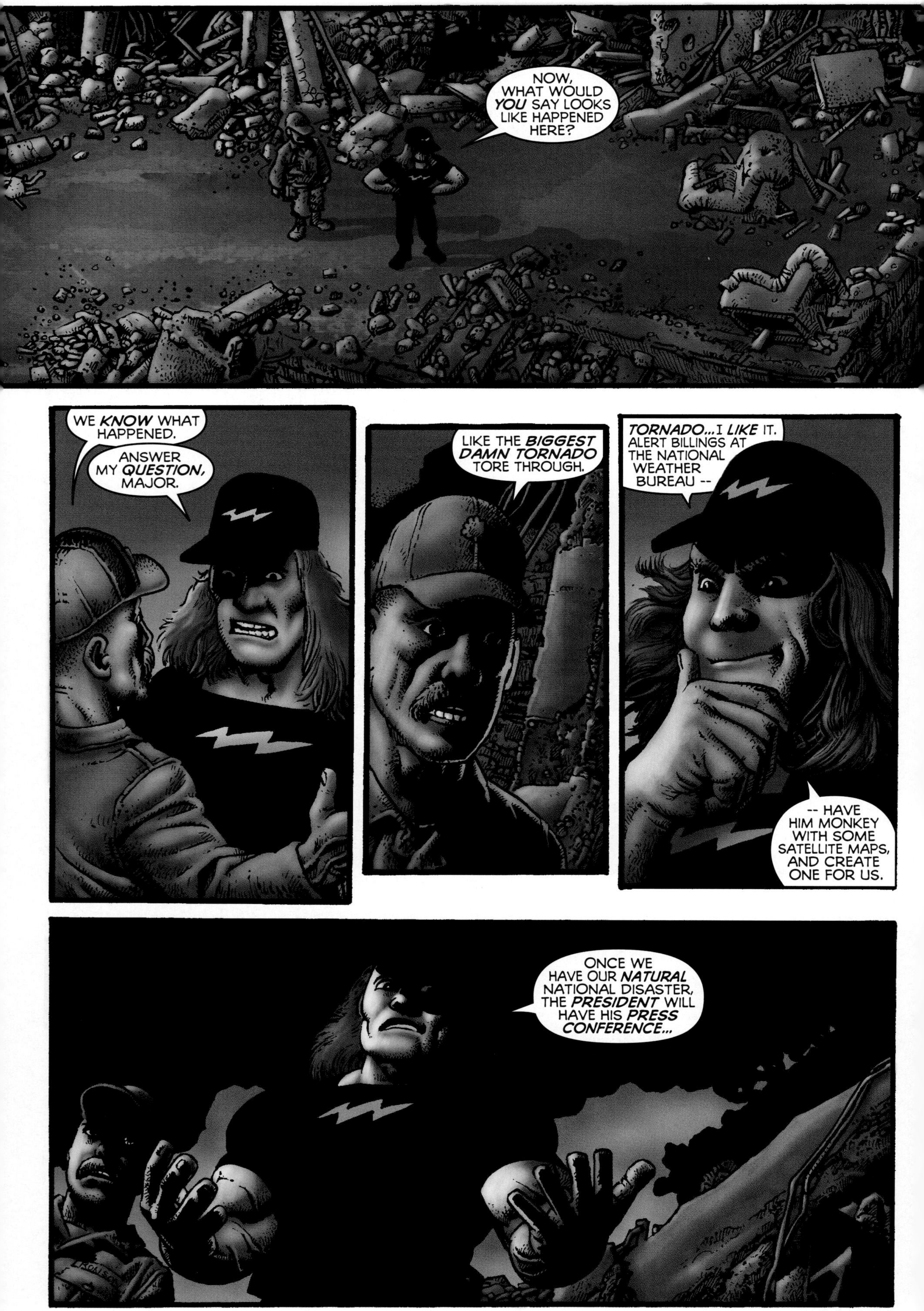
NOW, WHAT WOULD YOU SAY LOOKS LIKE HAPPENED HERE?
WE KNOW WHAT HAPPENED.
ANSWER MY QUESTION, MAJOR.
LIKE THE BIGGEST DAMN TORNADO TORE THROUGH.
TORNADO...I LIKE IT. ALERT BILLINGS AT THE NATIONAL WEATHER BUREAU --
-- HAVE HIM MONKEY WITH SOME SATELLITE MAPS, AND CREATE ONE FOR US.
ONCE WE HAVE OUR NATURAL NATIONAL DISASTER, THE PRESIDENT WILL HAVE HIS PRESS CONFERENCE...

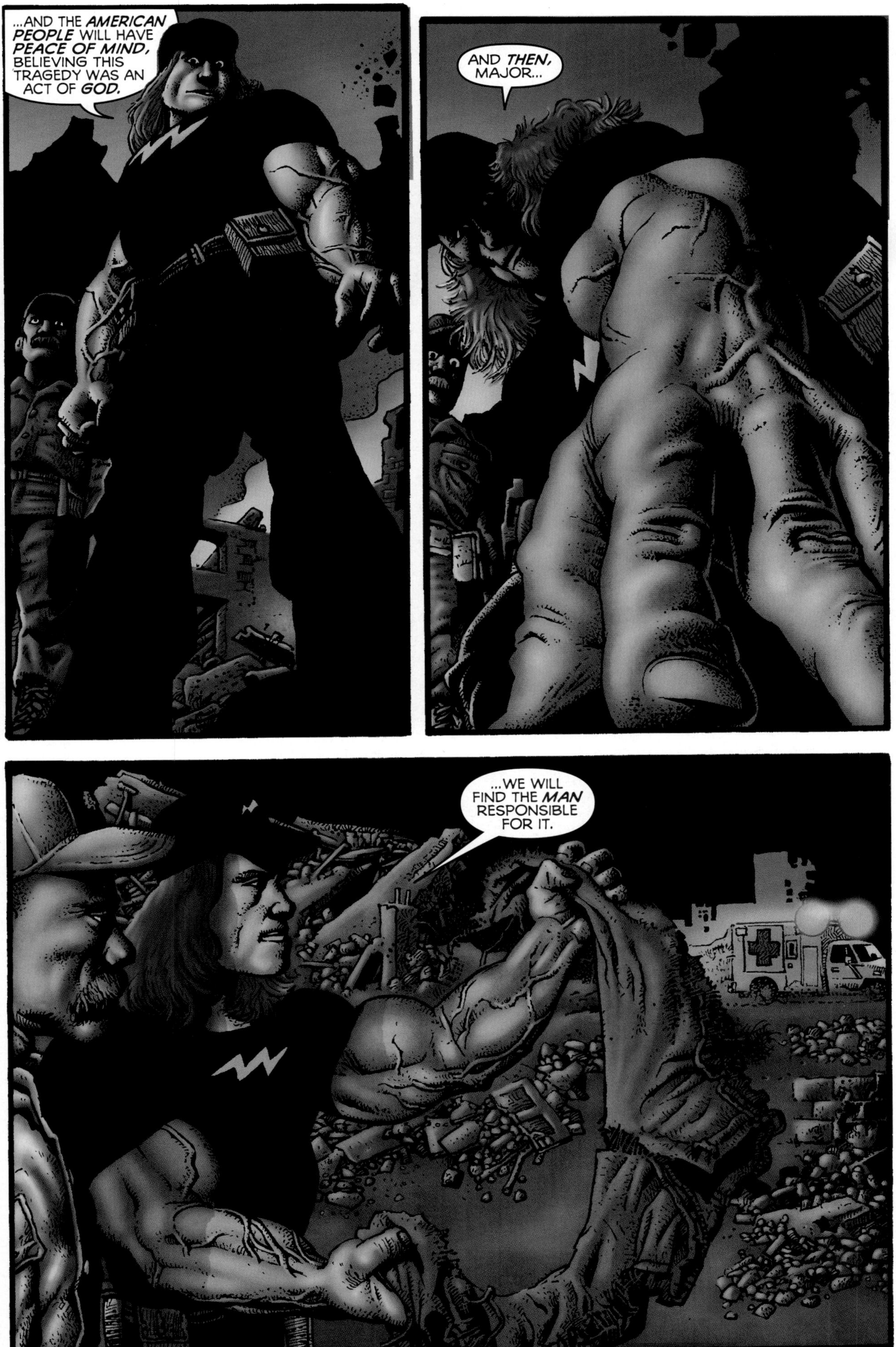
...AND THE *AMERICAN PEOPLE* WILL HAVE *PEACE OF MIND,* BELIEVING THIS TRAGEDY WAS AN ACT OF *GOD.*
AND *THEN,* MAJOR...
...WE WILL FIND THE *MAN* RESPONSIBLE FOR IT.

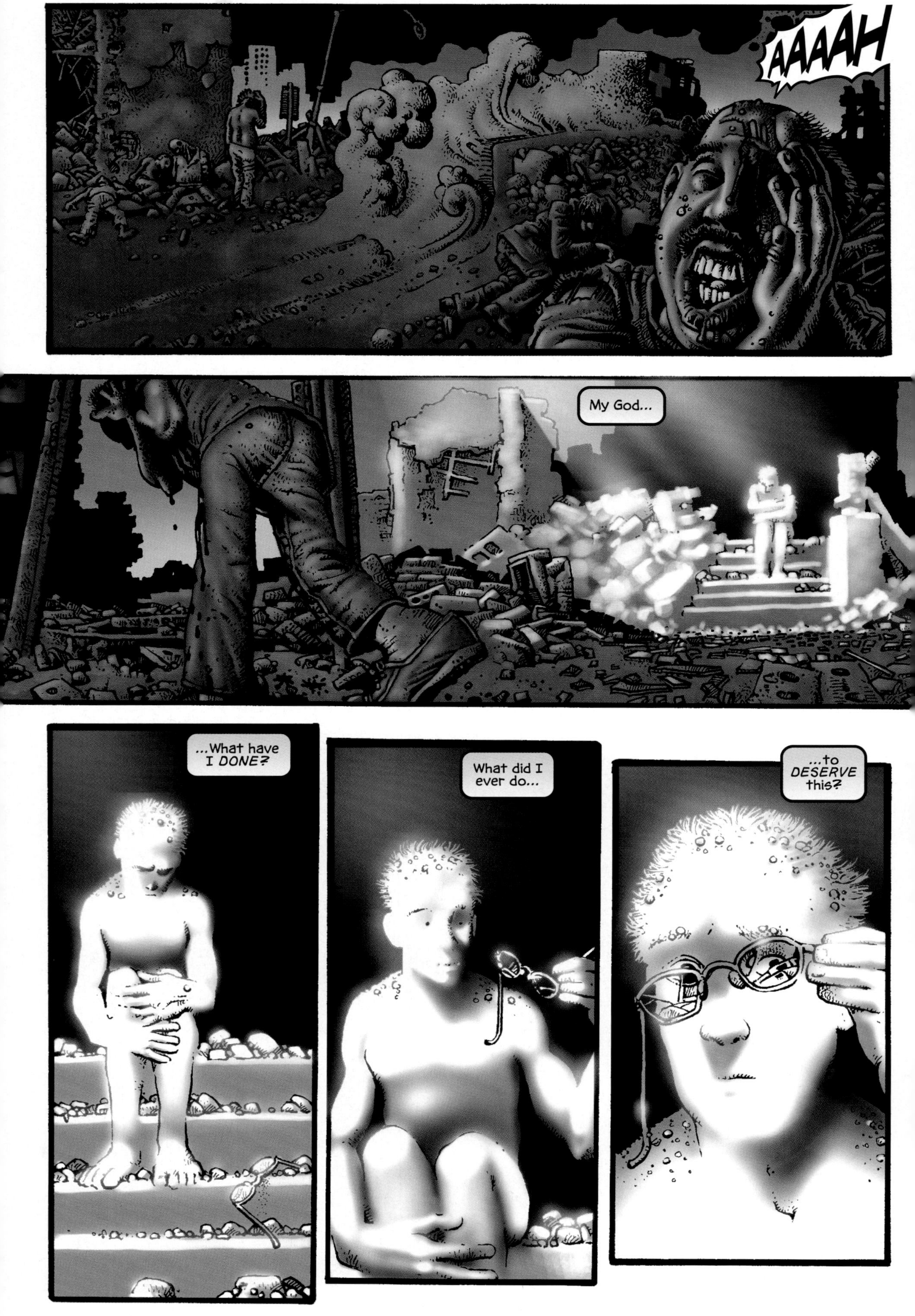
AAAAH
My God...
...What have I DONE?
What did I ever do...
...to DESERVE this?

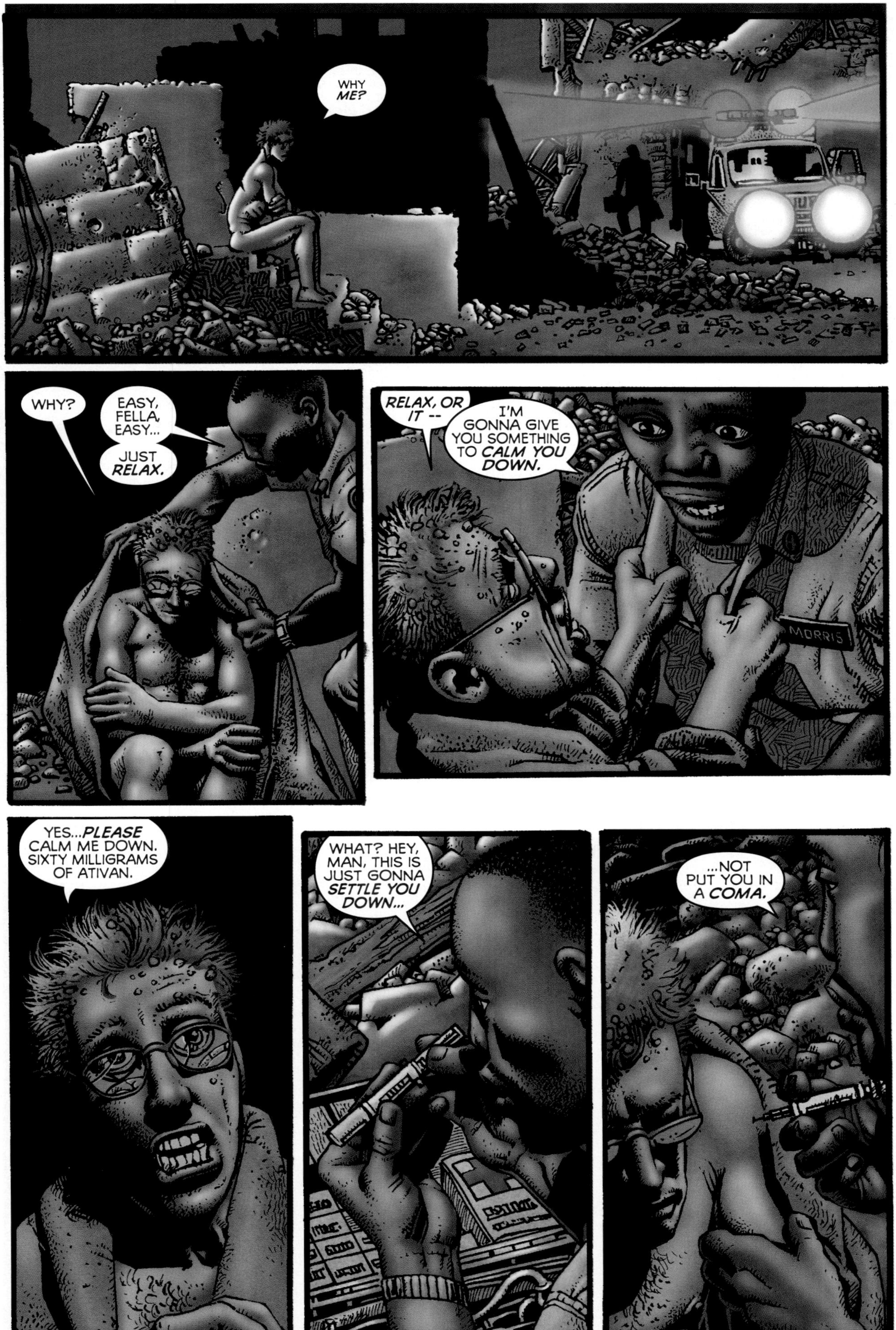
WHY ME?
WHY?
EASY, FELLA, EASY...
JUST RELAX.
RELAX, OR IT --
I'M GONNA GIVE YOU SOMETHING TO CALM YOU DOWN.
MORRIS
YES...PLEASE CALM ME DOWN. SIXTY MILLIGRAMS OF ATIVAN.
WHAT? HEY, MAN, THIS IS JUST GONNA SETTLE YOU DOWN...
...NOT PUT YOU IN A COMA.

Why me?
Why am *I* the cage?

A brittle cage, made of flesh and balsa wood, locked with rubber bands and emotions that can too easily snap?

WHY me?

Why am *I* responsible for this destruction -- this city, crumpled like some house of cards, these people that I...

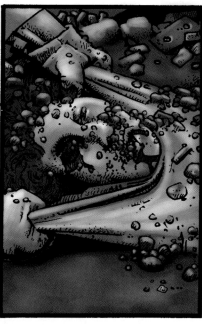

...I did this.

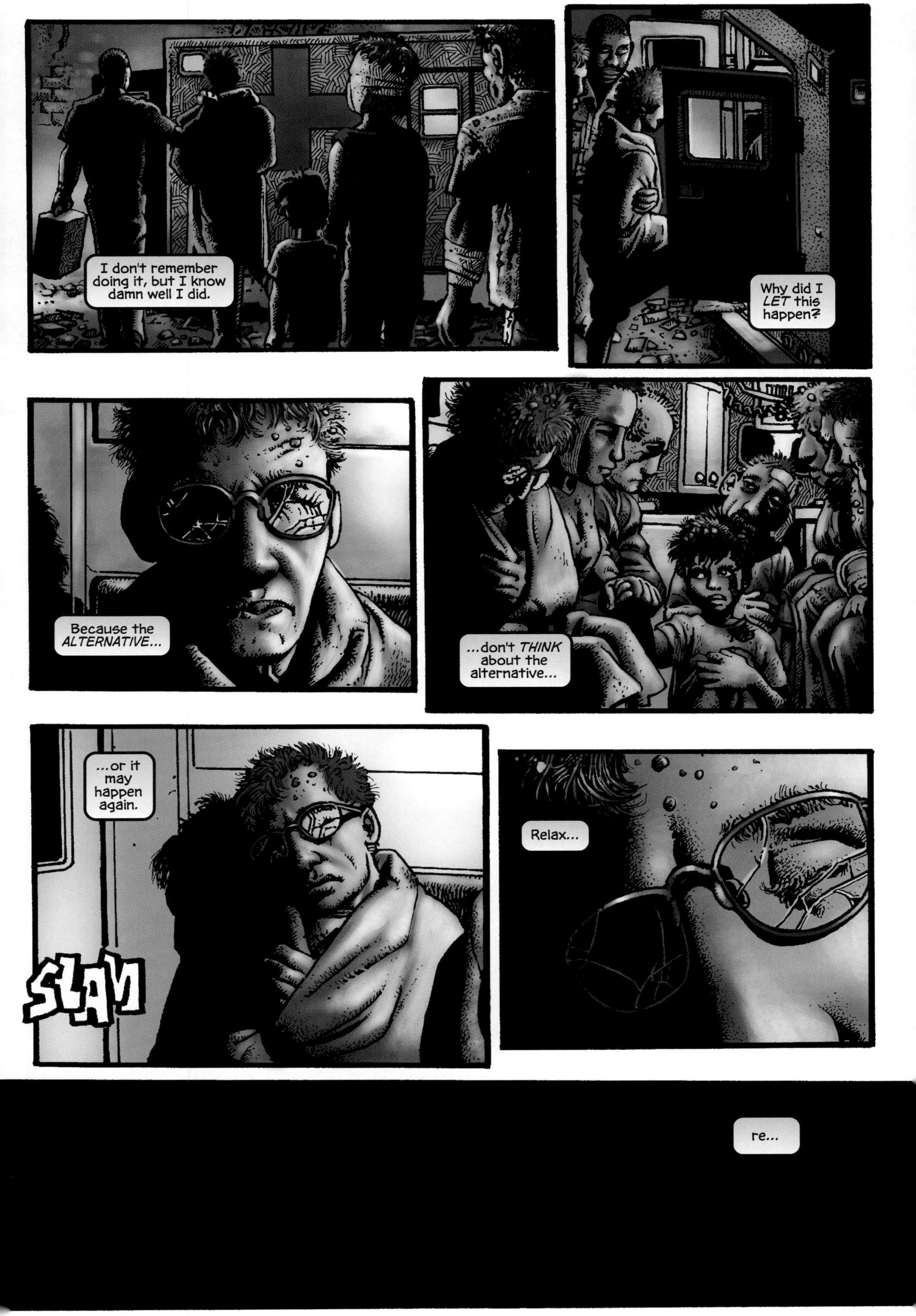
I don't remember doing it, but I know damn well I did.
Why did I LET this happen?
Because the ALTERNATIVE...
...don't THINK about the alternative...
...or it may happen again.
SLAM
Relax...
re...

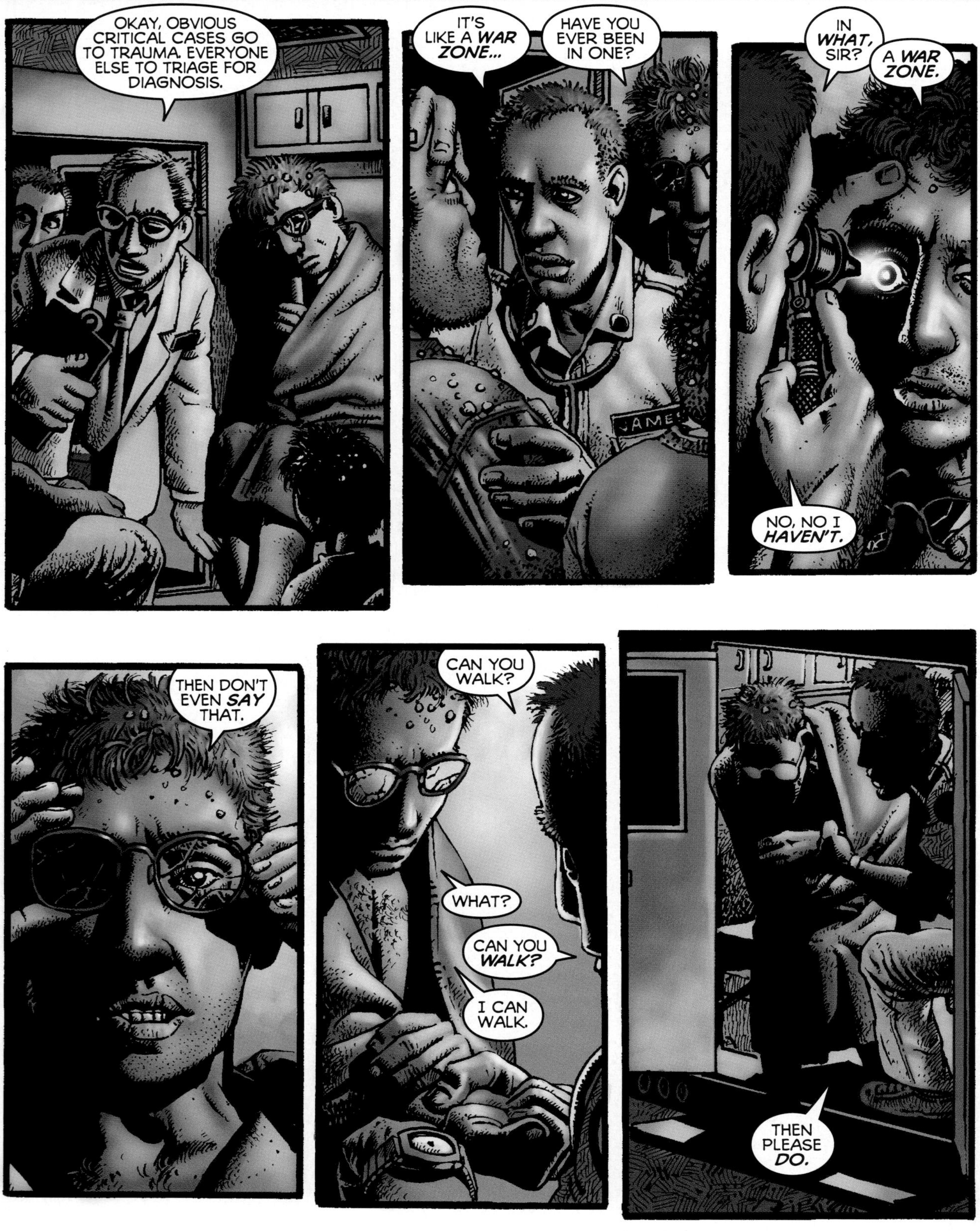
OKAY, OBVIOUS CRITICAL CASES GO TO TRAUMA. EVERYONE ELSE TO TRIAGE FOR DIAGNOSIS.
IT'S LIKE A *WAR ZONE...*
HAVE YOU EVER BEEN IN ONE?
IN *WHAT,* SIR?
A *WAR ZONE.*
NO, NO I *HAVEN'T.*
THEN DON'T EVEN *SAY* THAT.
CAN YOU WALK?
WHAT?
CAN YOU *WALK?*
I CAN WALK.
THEN PLEASE *DO.*

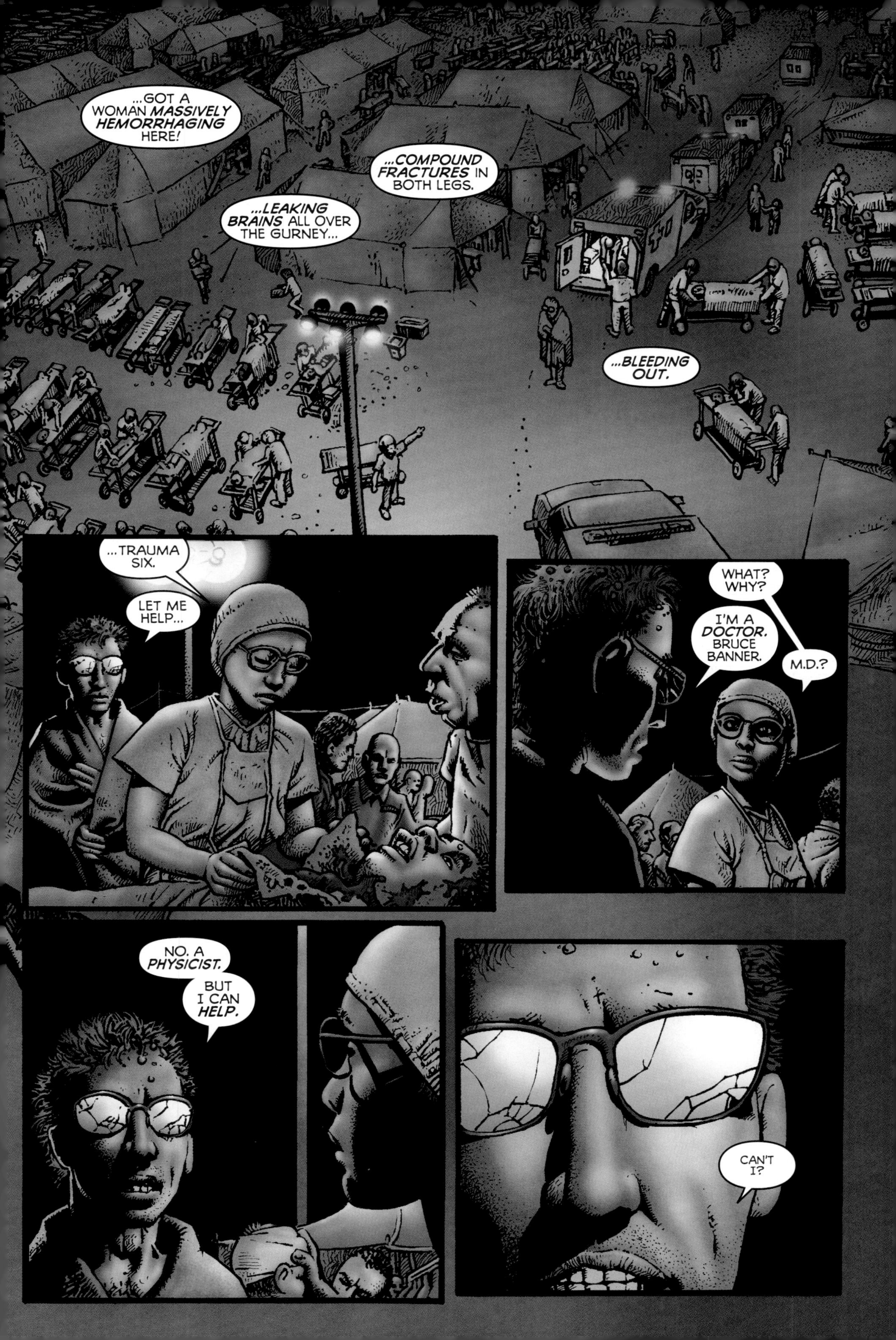
...GOT A WOMAN MASSIVELY HEMORRHAGING HERE!
...COMPOUND FRACTURES IN BOTH LEGS.
...LEAKING BRAINS ALL OVER THE GURNEY...
...BLEEDING OUT.
...TRAUMA SIX.
LET ME HELP...
WHAT? WHY?
I'M A DOCTOR. BRUCE BANNER.
M.D.?
NO. A PHYSICIST.
BUT I CAN HELP.
CAN'T I?

OVER *HERE.*

GOOD. HE'S STABLE.

FLAS...

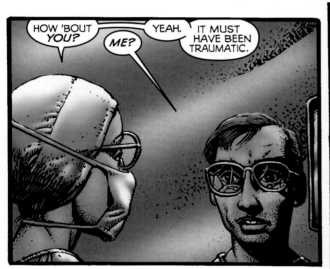

HOW 'BOUT *YOU?*

ME?

YEAH. IT MUST HAVE BEEN TRAUMATIC.

WHAT?

BEING CAUGHT IN A FREAK STORM LIKE THAT. THE *TORNADO.*

A FREAK STORM.

NEVER MISS A DIG, *DO* YOU, SAMSON?

SO *WHERE WERE YOU* WHEN IT HIT?

I...

"I WAS IN BED AT A FLOPHOUSE. I MUST'VE DOZED OFF. TWO MEN, I GUESS THEY WERE STAYING THERE AS WELL. THEY TRIED TO *ROB* ME, I THINK.

"I REMEMBER ONE OF THEM STANK LIKE SOUR MILK. I WAS GASPING FOR BREATH AND CHOKING AT THE SAME TIME. IT WAS ALMOST A RELIEF WHEN THE OTHER ONE PUT THAT PILLOW OVER MY FACE.

"THEN THERE WERE HANDS IN MY POCKETS...

"...HMM. MUST HAVE BEEN *THREE* MEN.

"ANYWAY, THE PILLOW; I COULDN'T *BREATHE.*

"THE MORE I STRUGGLED, THE TIGHTER THEY HELD ME DOWN.

"AND THEN...

"THEN..."

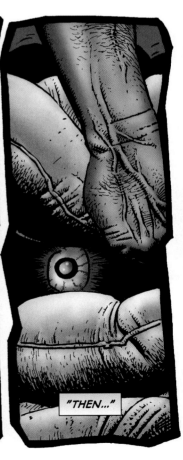

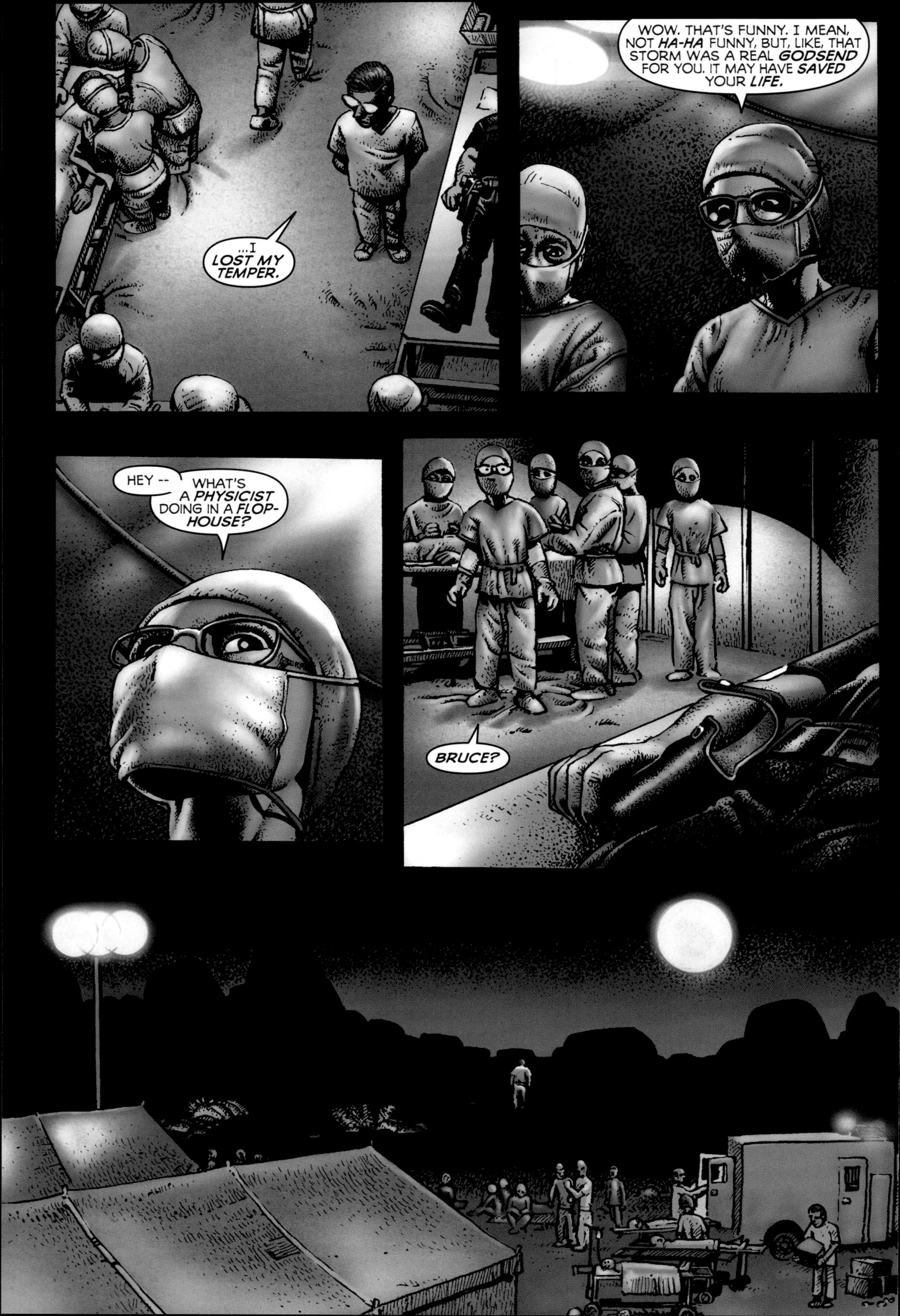
...I LOST MY TEMPER.
WOW. THAT'S FUNNY. I MEAN, NOT HA-HA FUNNY, BUT, LIKE, THAT STORM WAS A REAL GODSEND FOR YOU. IT MAY HAVE SAVED YOUR LIFE.
HEY --
WHAT'S A PHYSICIST DOING IN A FLOP-HOUSE?
BRUCE?

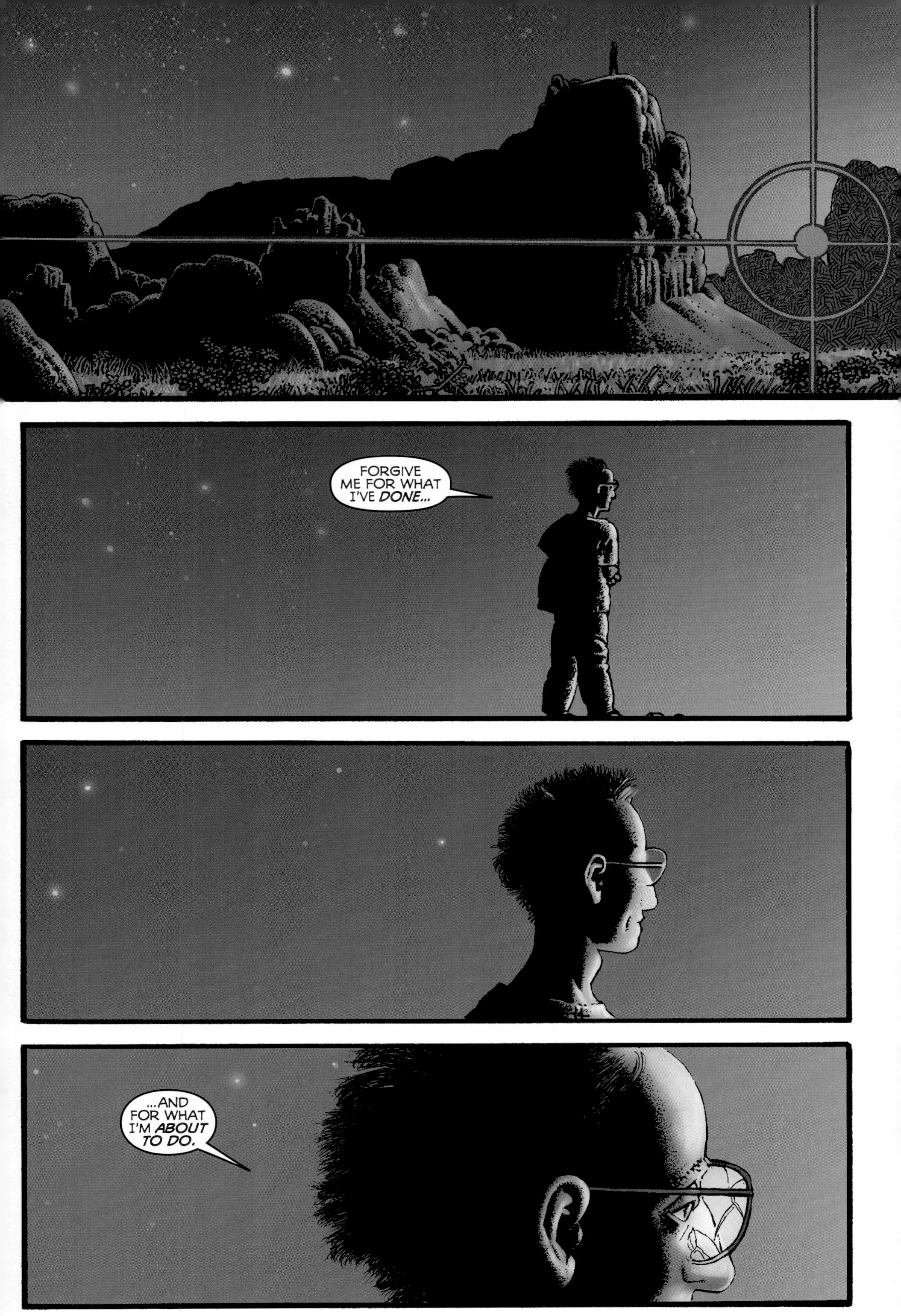
FORGIVE ME FOR WHAT I'VE DONE...
...AND FOR WHAT I'M ABOUT TO DO.

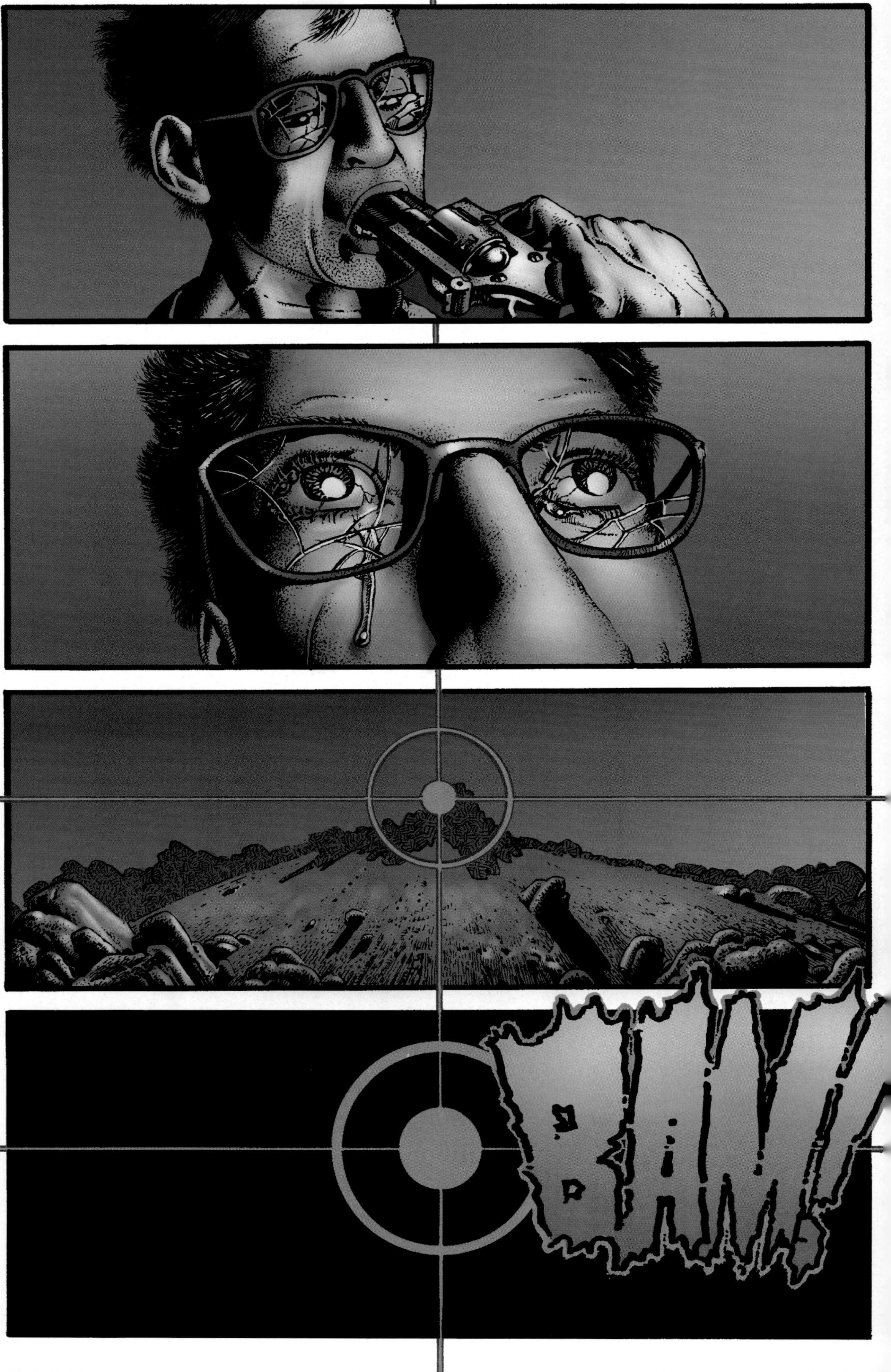
BAM!

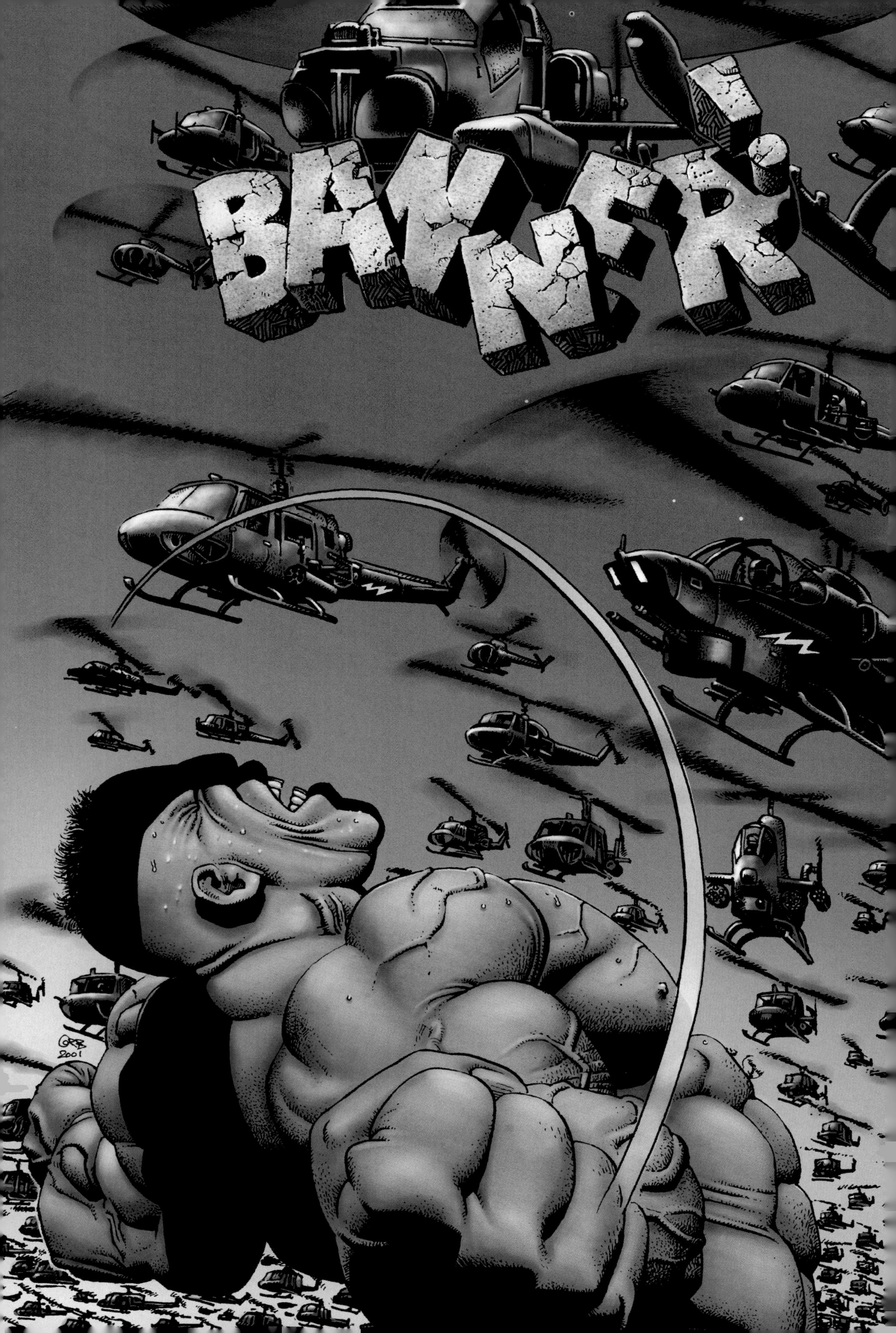
BANNER

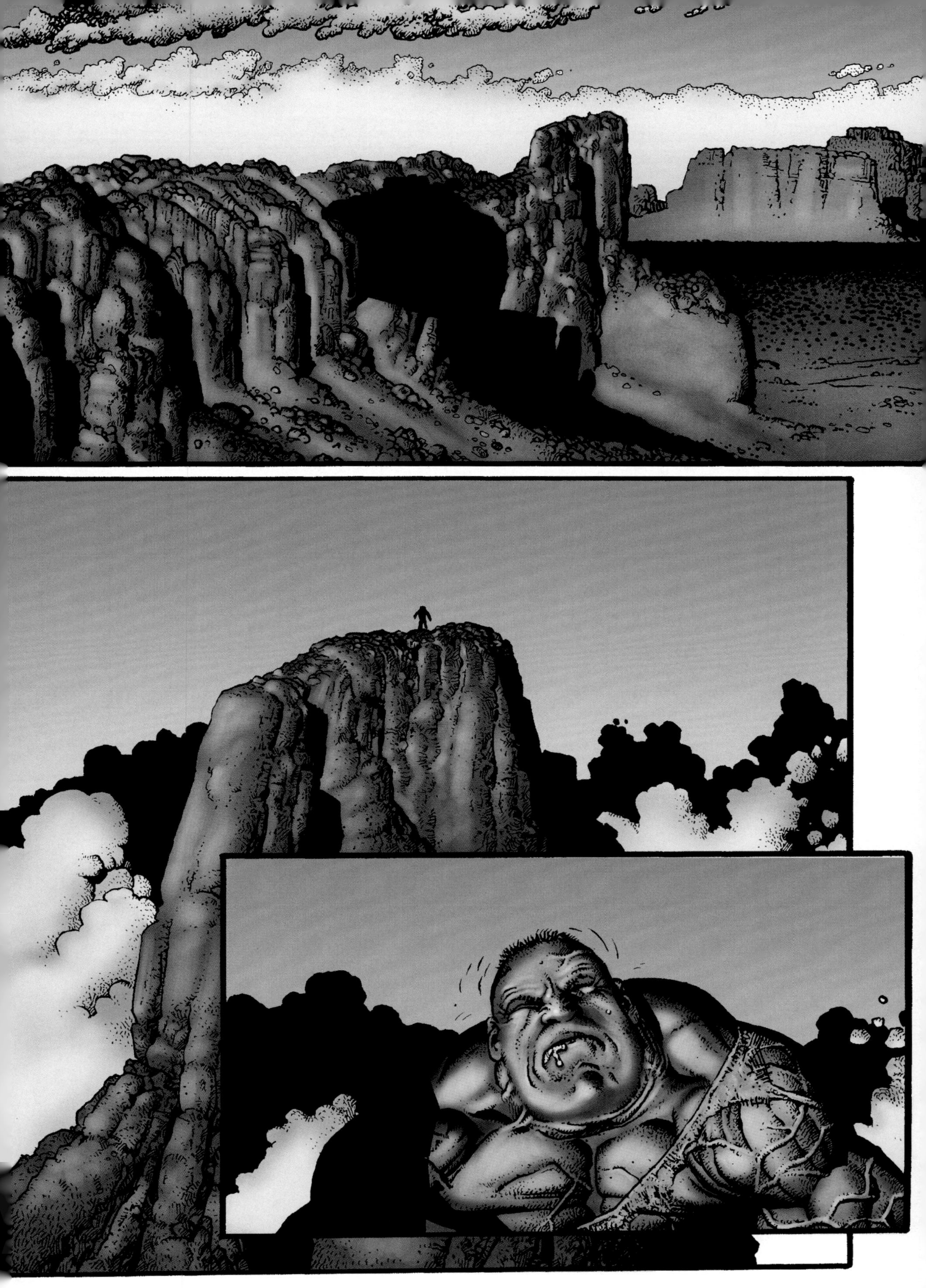

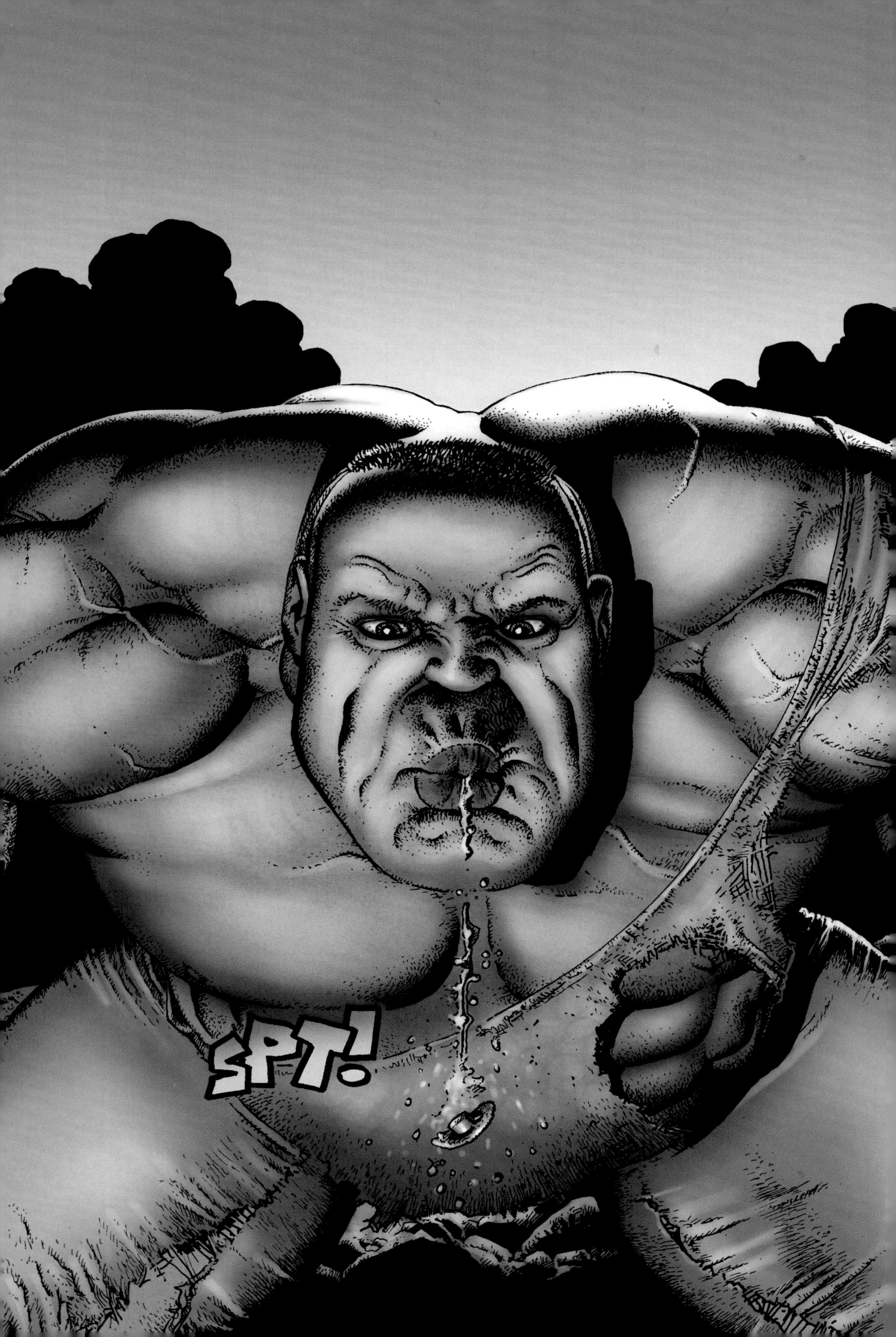
SPT!

BANNER?

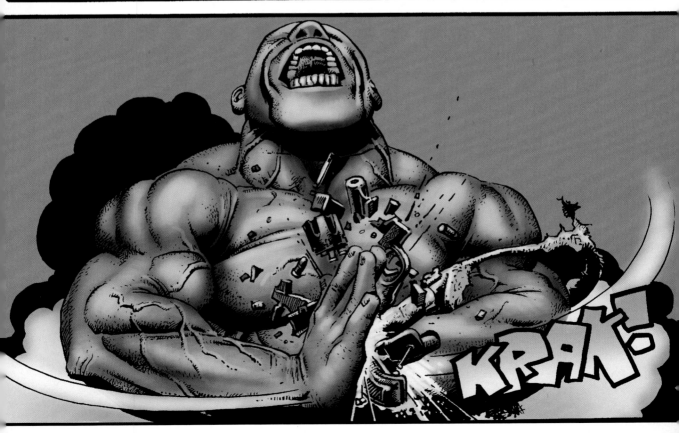

KRAK!

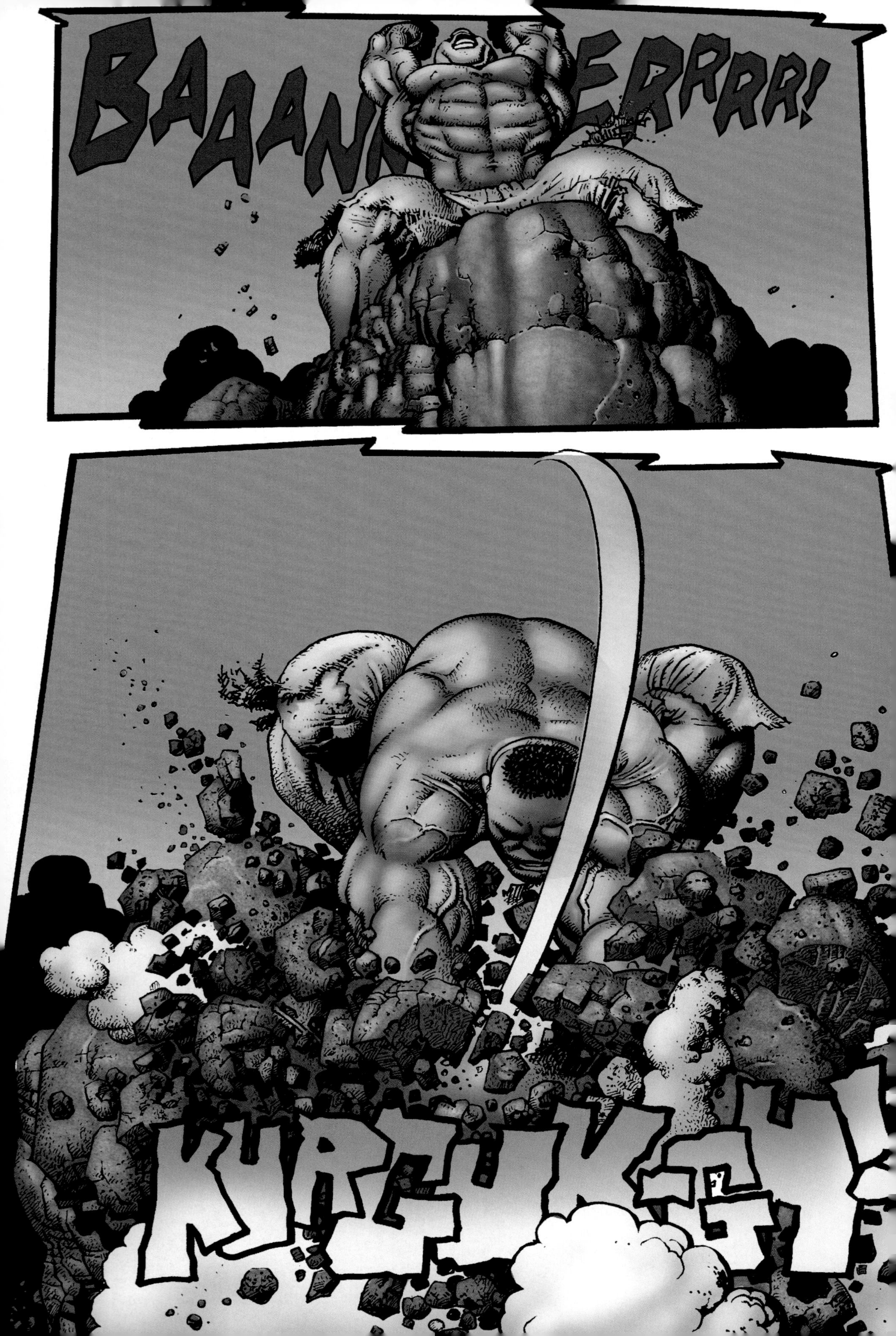
BAAANN
ERRRRR!

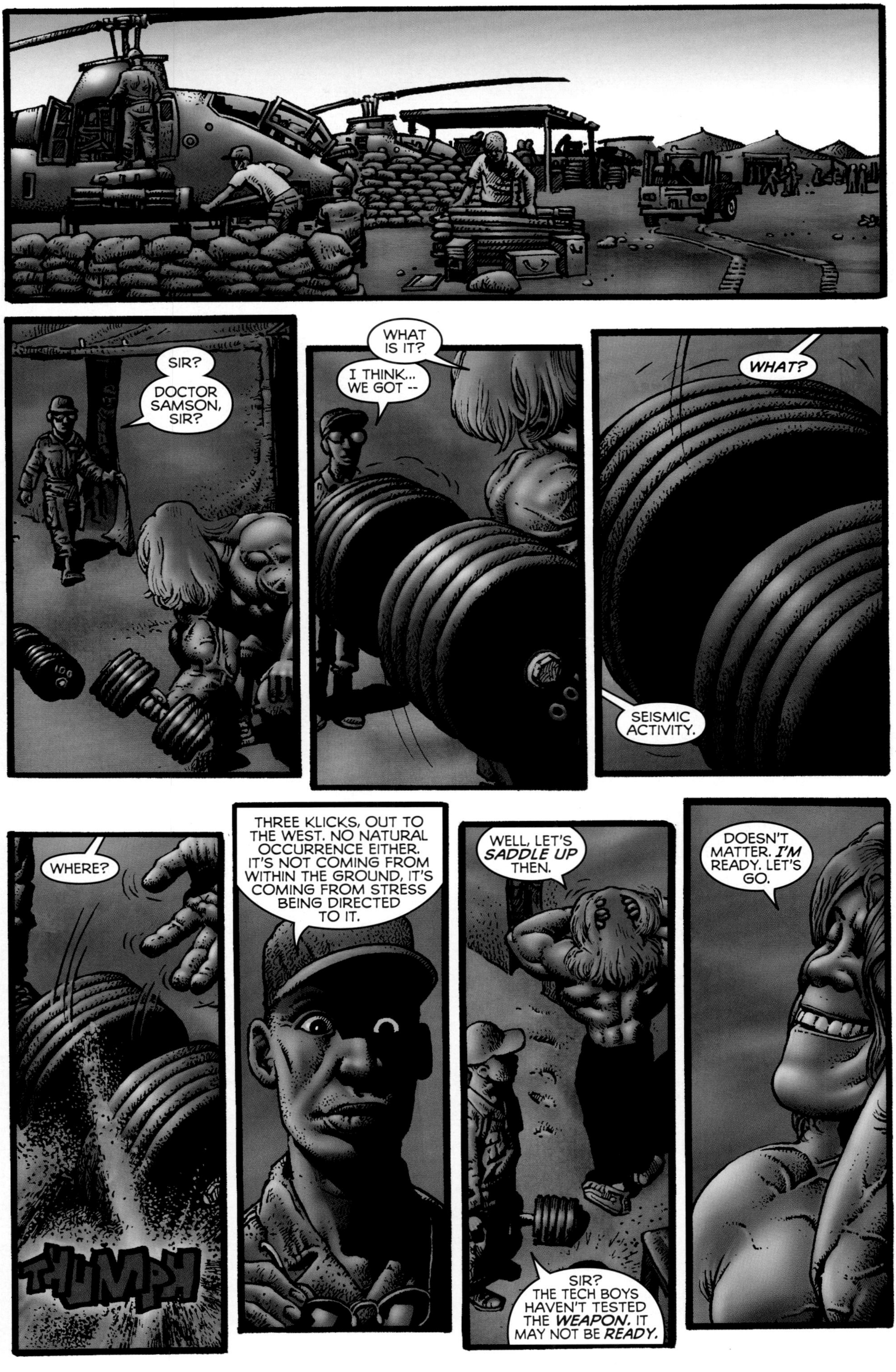
SIR?
DOCTOR SAMSON, SIR?
WHAT IS IT?
I THINK... WE GOT --
WHAT?
SEISMIC ACTIVITY.
WHERE?
THUMPH
THREE KLICKS, OUT TO THE WEST. NO NATURAL OCCURRENCE EITHER. IT'S NOT COMING FROM WITHIN THE GROUND, IT'S COMING FROM STRESS BEING DIRECTED TO IT.
WELL, LET'S *SADDLE UP* THEN.
SIR? THE TECH BOYS HAVEN'T TESTED THE *WEAPON.* IT MAY NOT BE *READY.*
DOESN'T MATTER. *I'M* READY. LET'S GO.

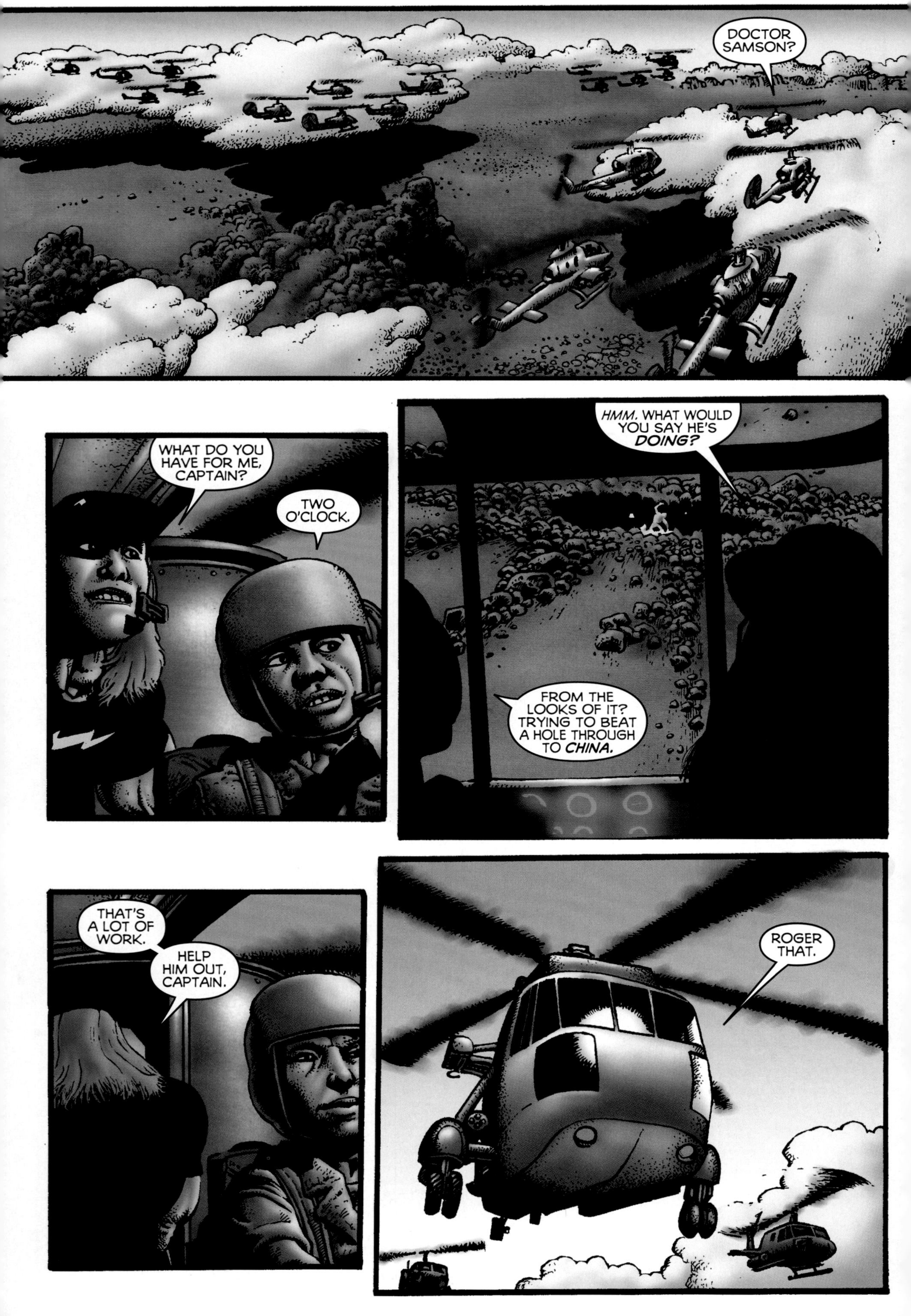
DOCTOR SAMSON?
WHAT DO YOU HAVE FOR ME, CAPTAIN?
TWO O'CLOCK.
HMM. WHAT WOULD YOU SAY HE'S DOING?
FROM THE LOOKS OF IT? TRYING TO BEAT A HOLE THROUGH TO CHINA.
THAT'S A LOT OF WORK.
HELP HIM OUT, CAPTAIN.
ROGER THAT.

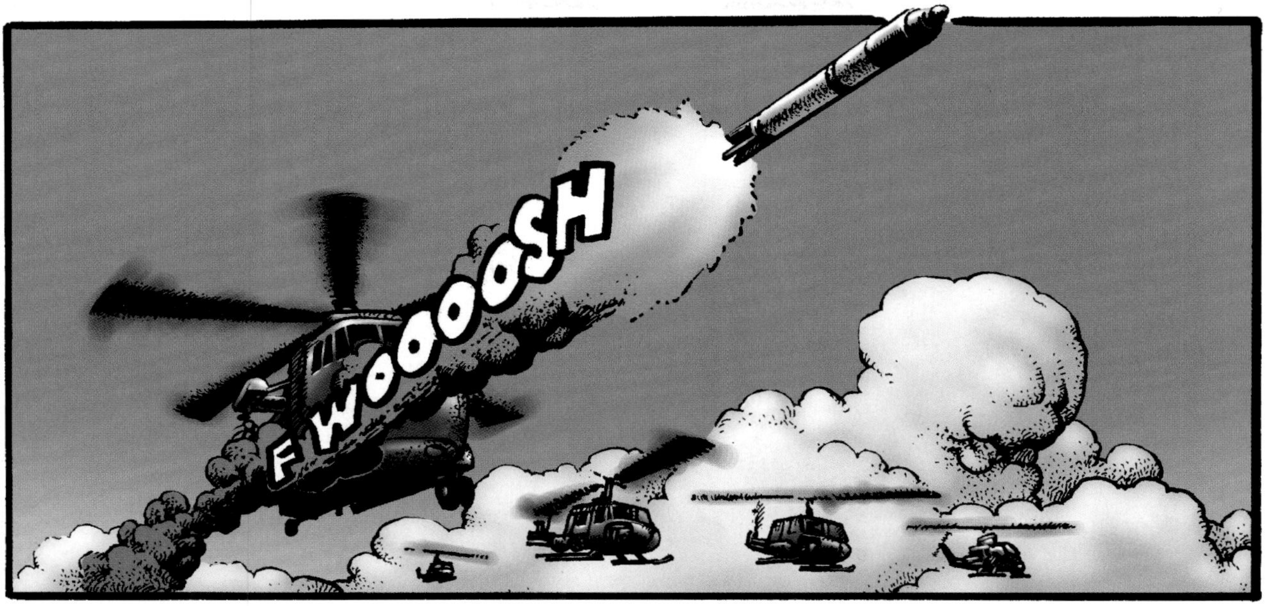
FWOOOOSH

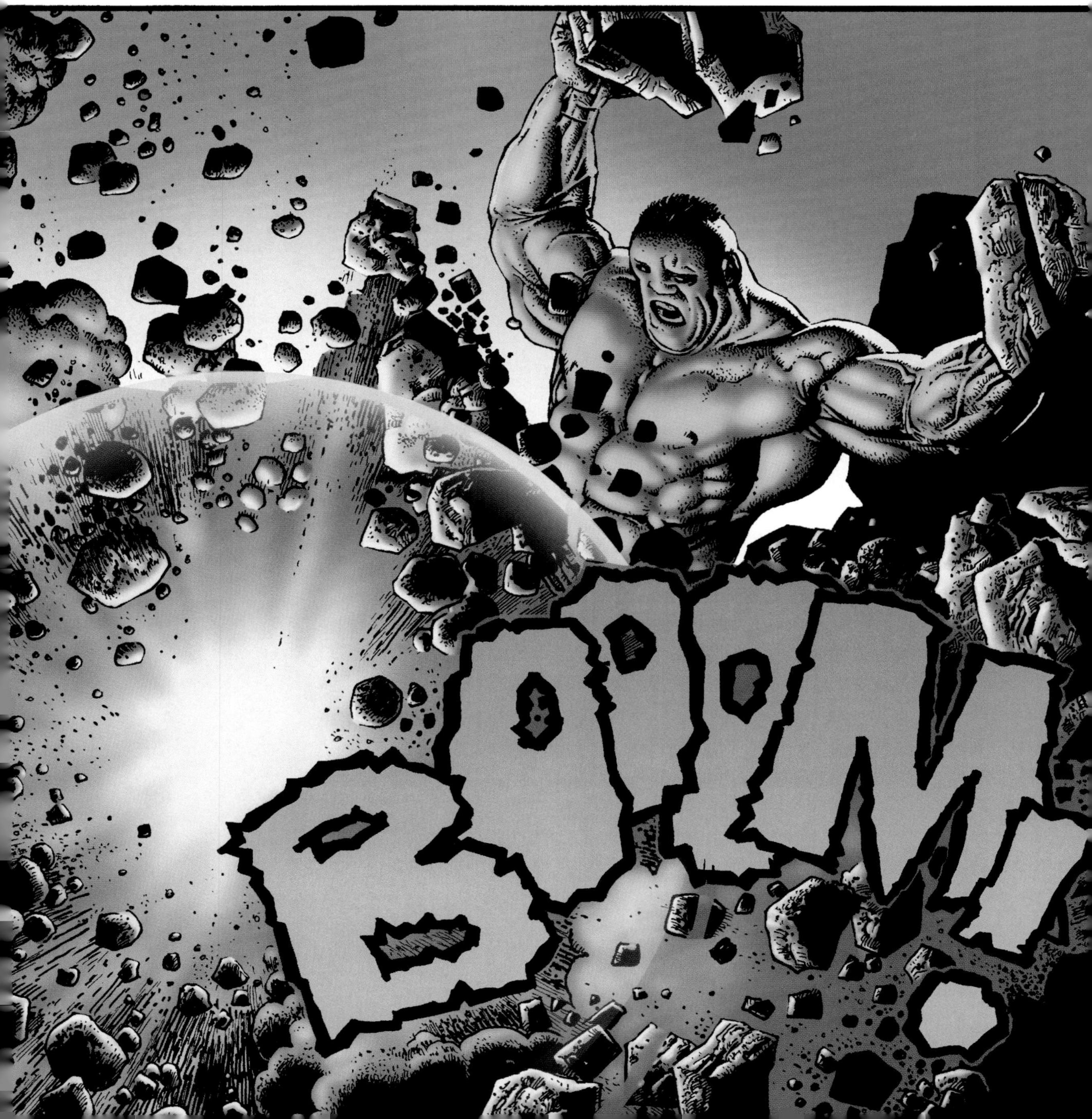

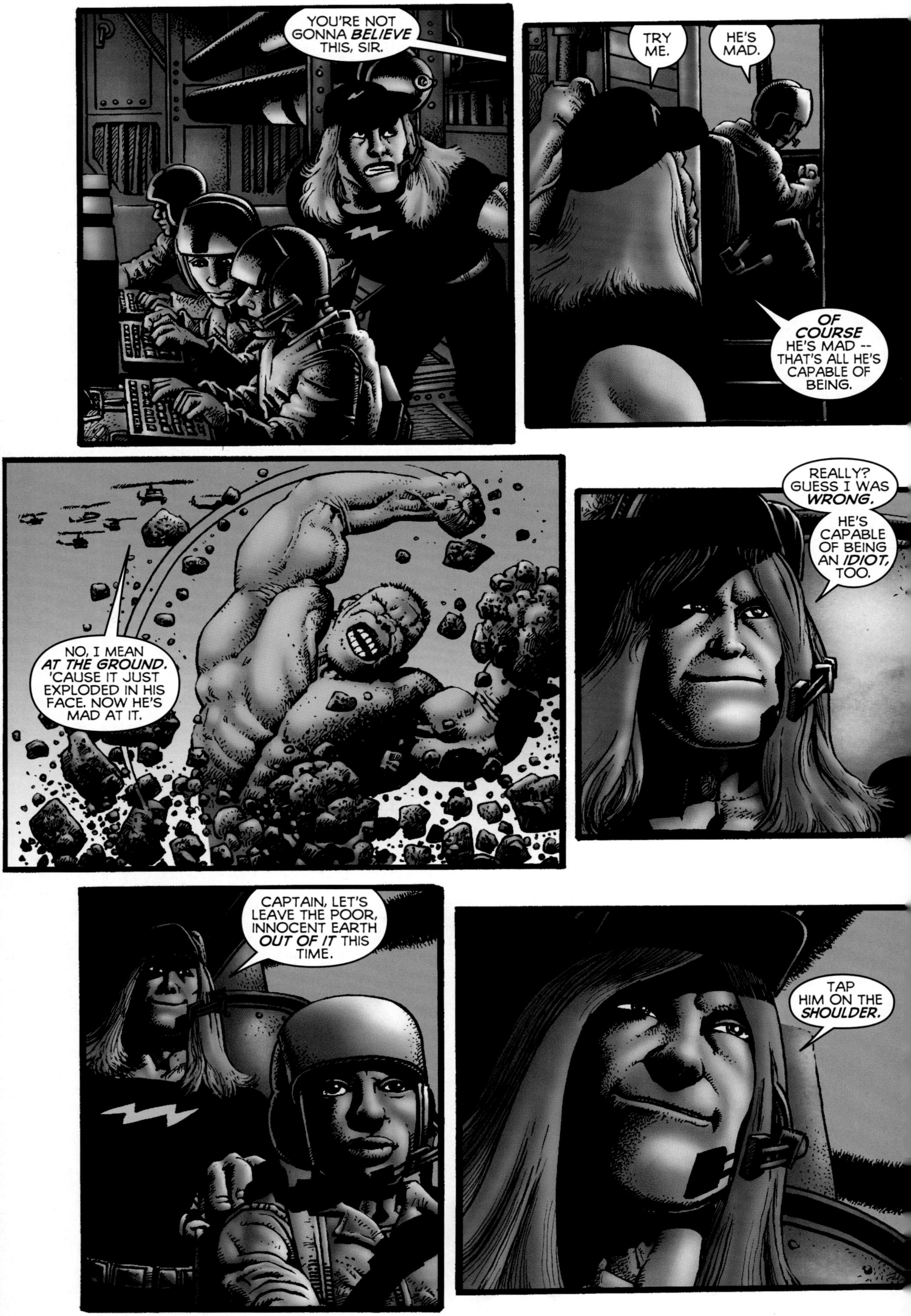
YOU'RE NOT GONNA BELIEVE THIS, SIR.
TRY ME.
HE'S MAD.
OF COURSE HE'S MAD -- THAT'S ALL HE'S CAPABLE OF BEING.
NO, I MEAN AT THE GROUND. 'CAUSE IT JUST EXPLODED IN HIS FACE. NOW HE'S MAD AT IT.
REALLY? GUESS I WAS WRONG.
HE'S CAPABLE OF BEING AN IDIOT, TOO.
CAPTAIN, LET'S LEAVE THE POOR, INNOCENT EARTH OUT OF IT THIS TIME.
TAP HIM ON THE SHOULDER.

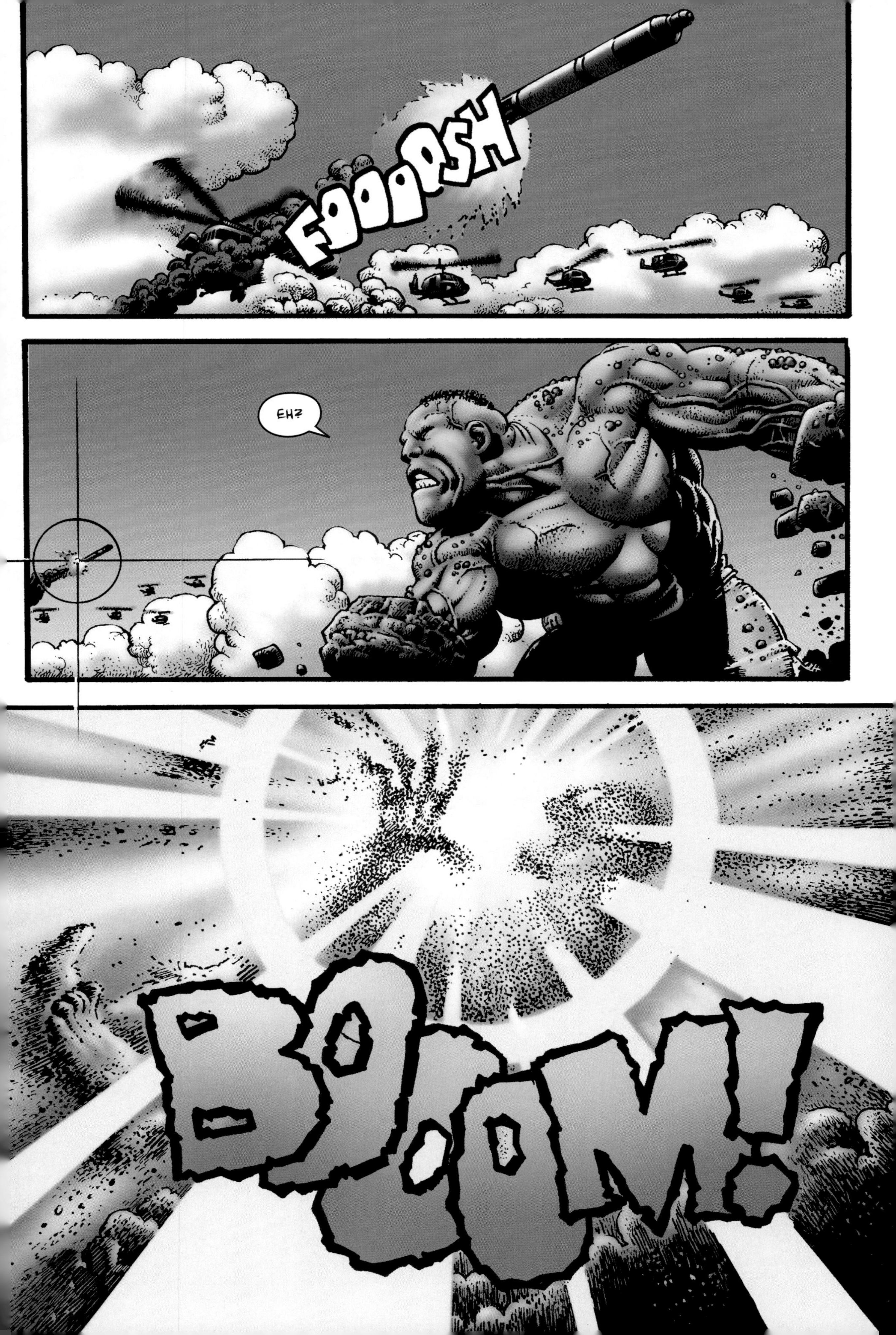
FOOOOSH
EH?
BOOOM!

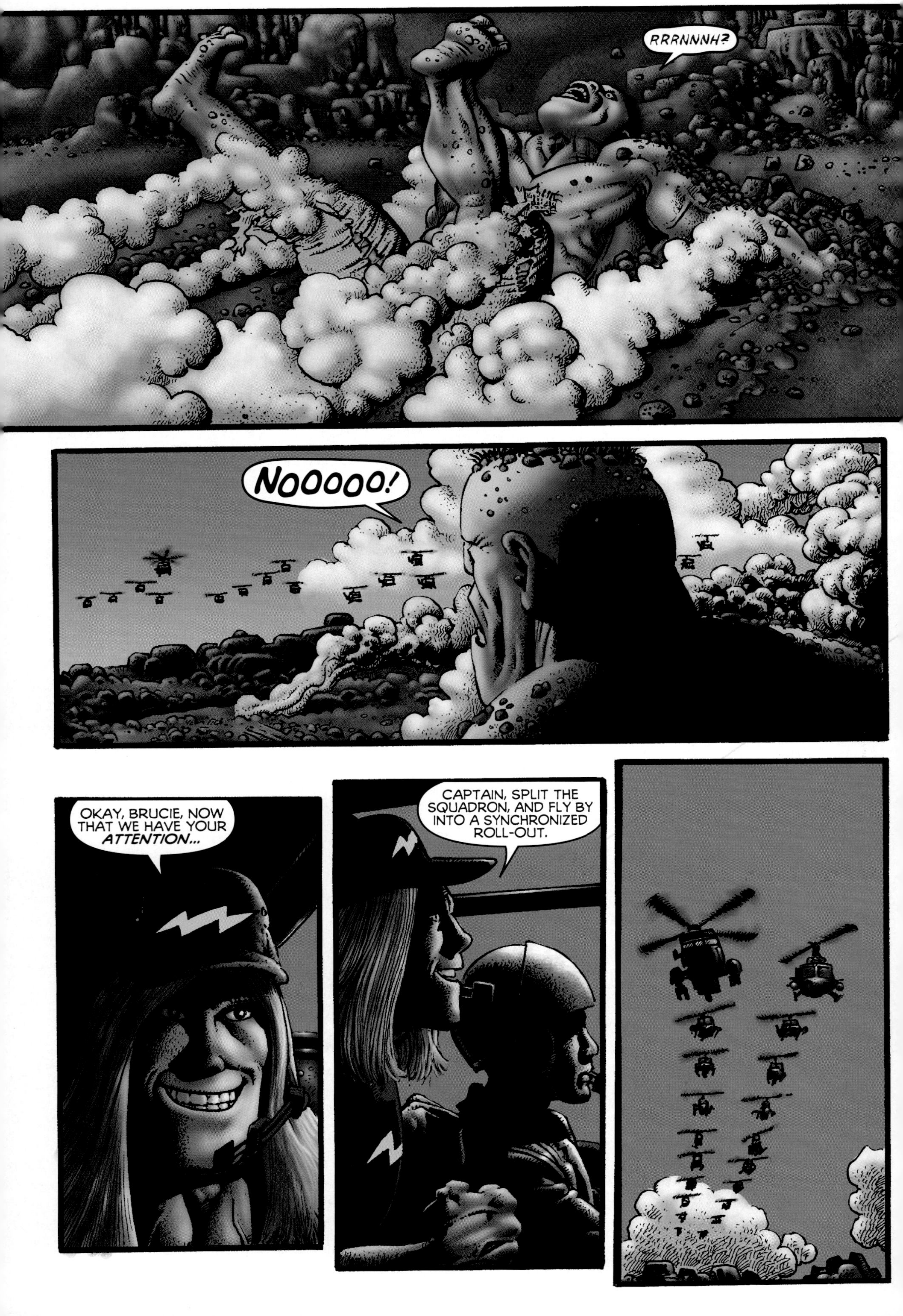
RRRNNNH?
NOOOOO!
OKAY, BRUCIE, NOW THAT WE HAVE YOUR ATTENTION...
CAPTAIN, SPLIT THE SQUADRON, AND FLY BY INTO A SYNCHRONIZED ROLL-OUT.

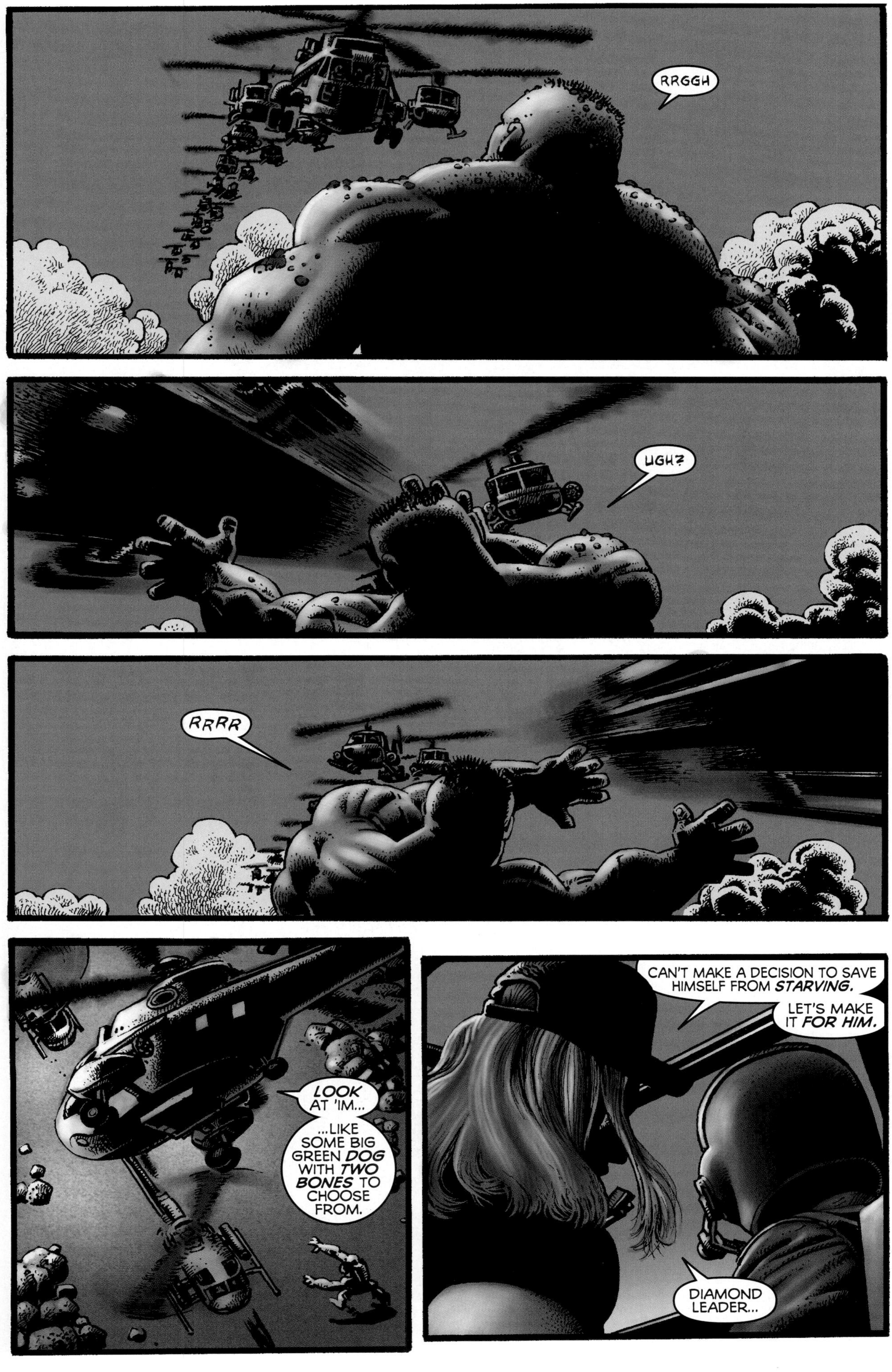
RRGGH
UGH?
RRRR
LOOK AT 'IM...
...LIKE SOME BIG GREEN DOG WITH TWO BONES TO CHOOSE FROM.
CAN'T MAKE A DECISION TO SAVE HIMSELF FROM STARVING.
LET'S MAKE IT FOR HIM.
DIAMOND LEADER...

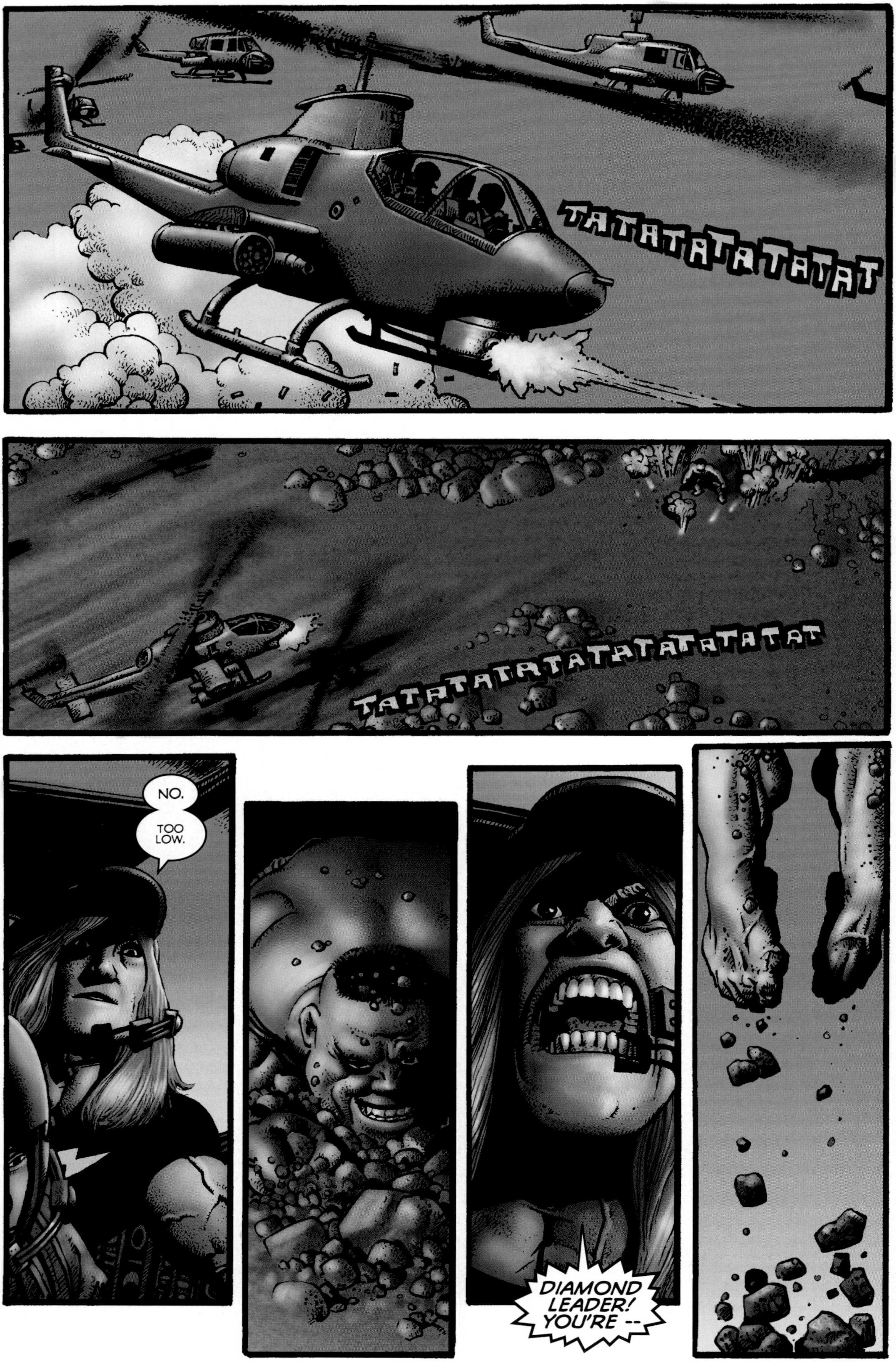
TATATATATATATAT
TATATATATATATATATATATAT
NO.
TOO LOW.
DIAMOND LEADER! YOU'RE --

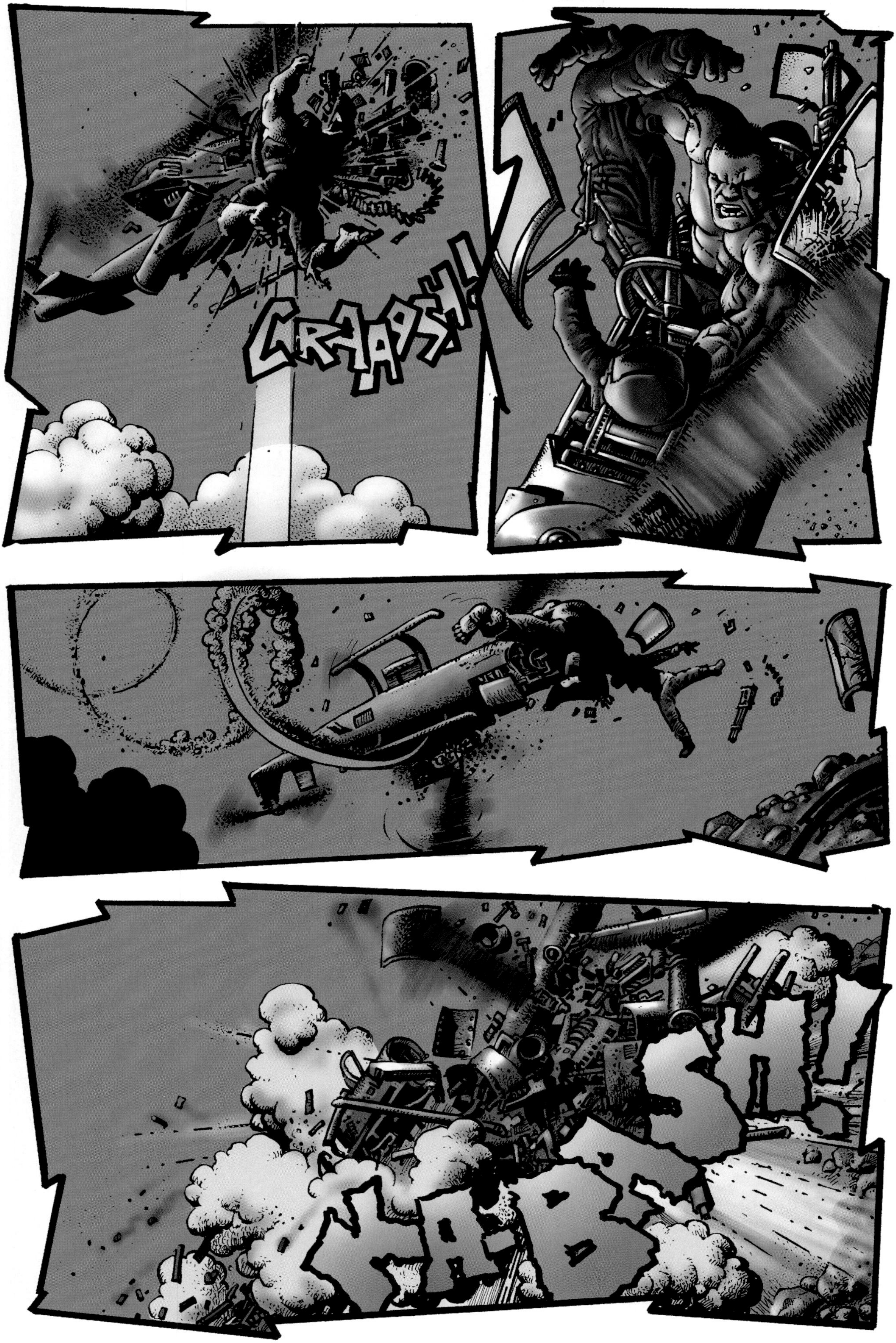
CRAAASH!

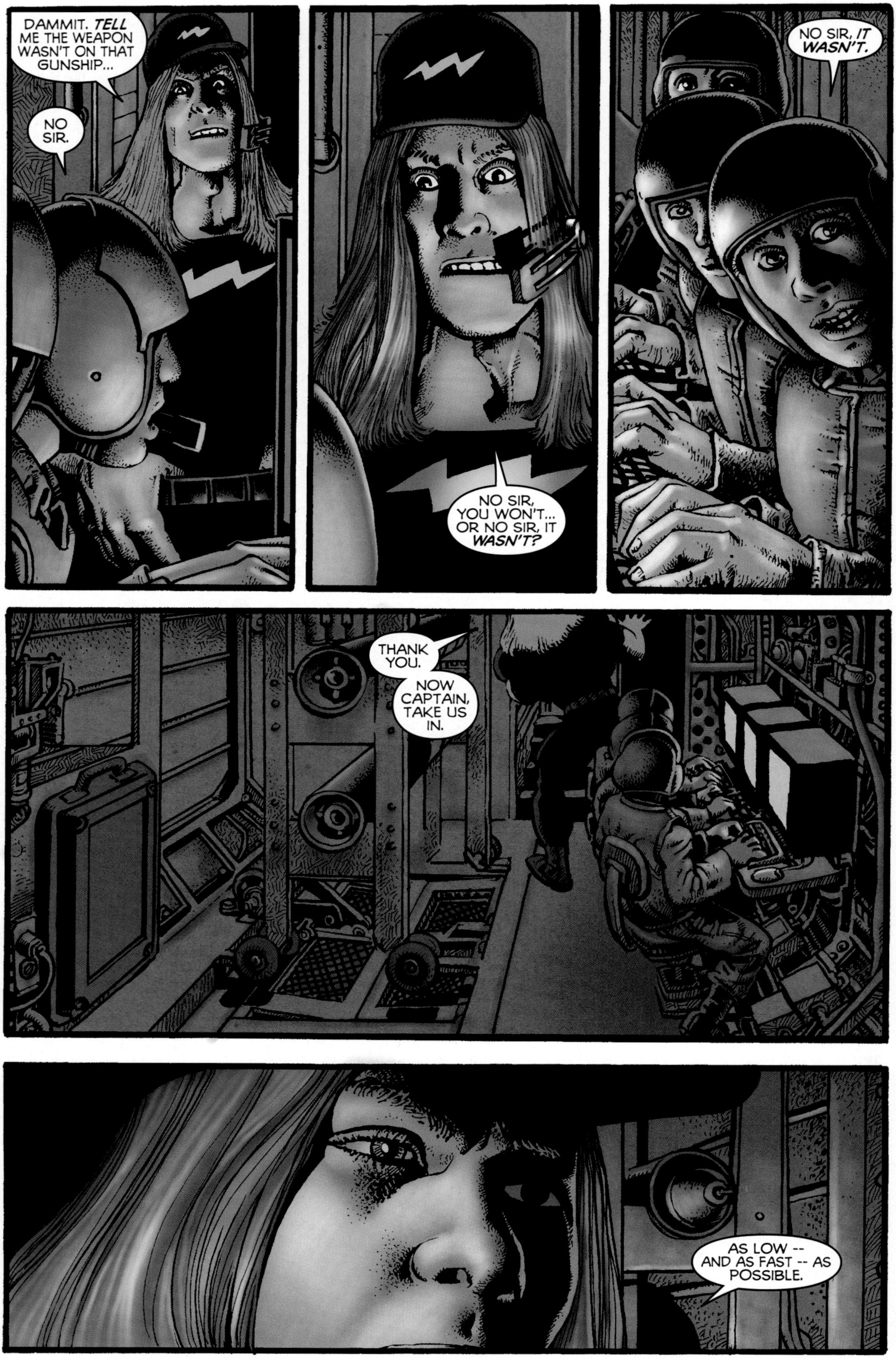
DAMMIT. TELL ME THE WEAPON WASN'T ON THAT GUNSHIP...
NO SIR.
NO SIR, YOU WON'T... OR NO SIR, IT WASN'T?
NO SIR, IT WASN'T.
THANK YOU.
NOW CAPTAIN, TAKE US IN.
AS LOW -- AND AS FAST -- AS POSSIBLE.

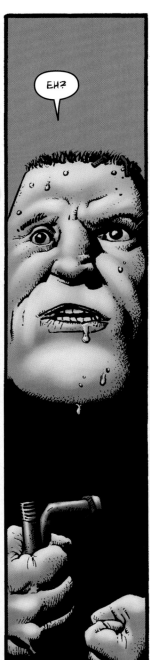

EH?

THAT'S *MY TOY*, YOU SON OF A --

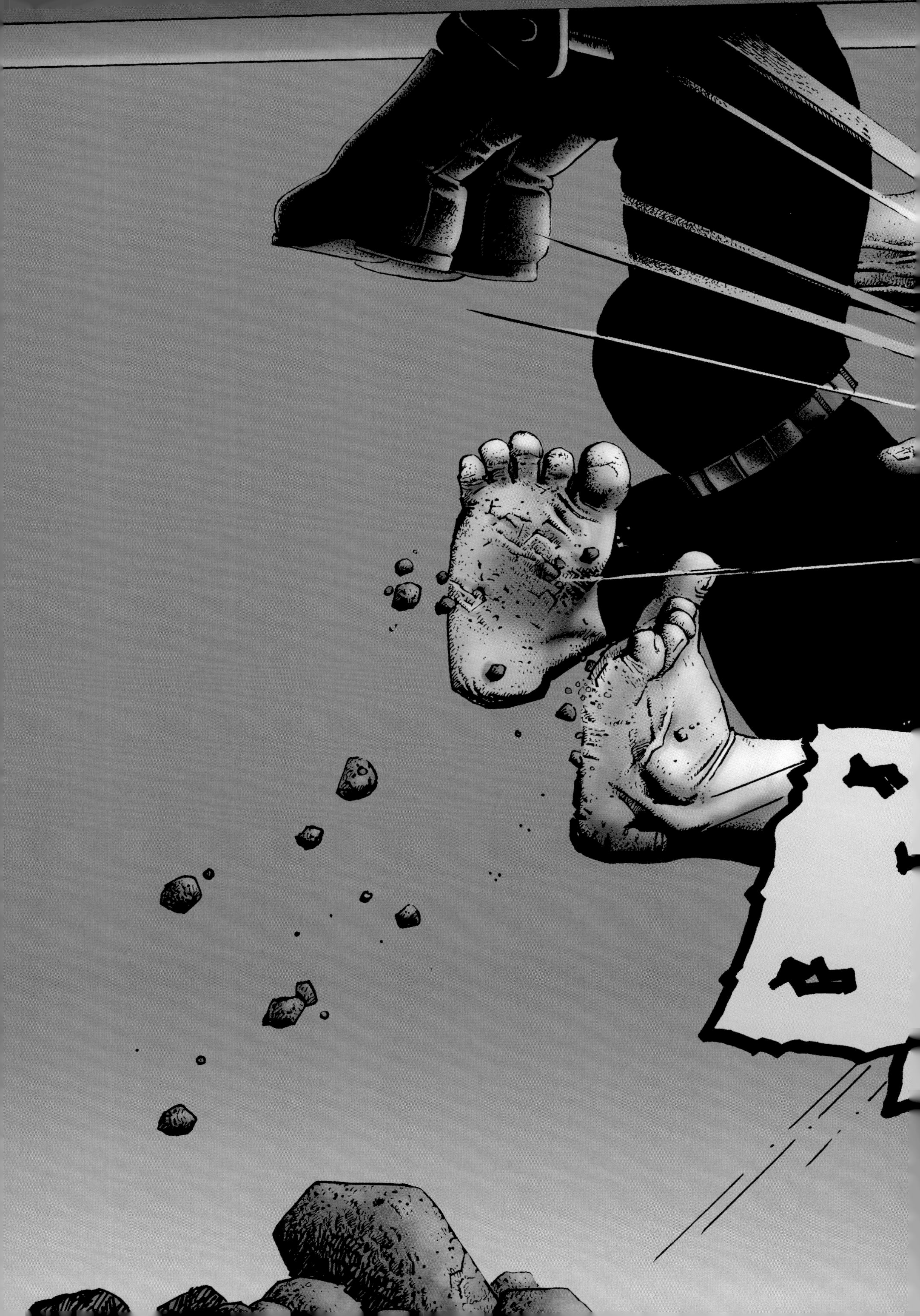

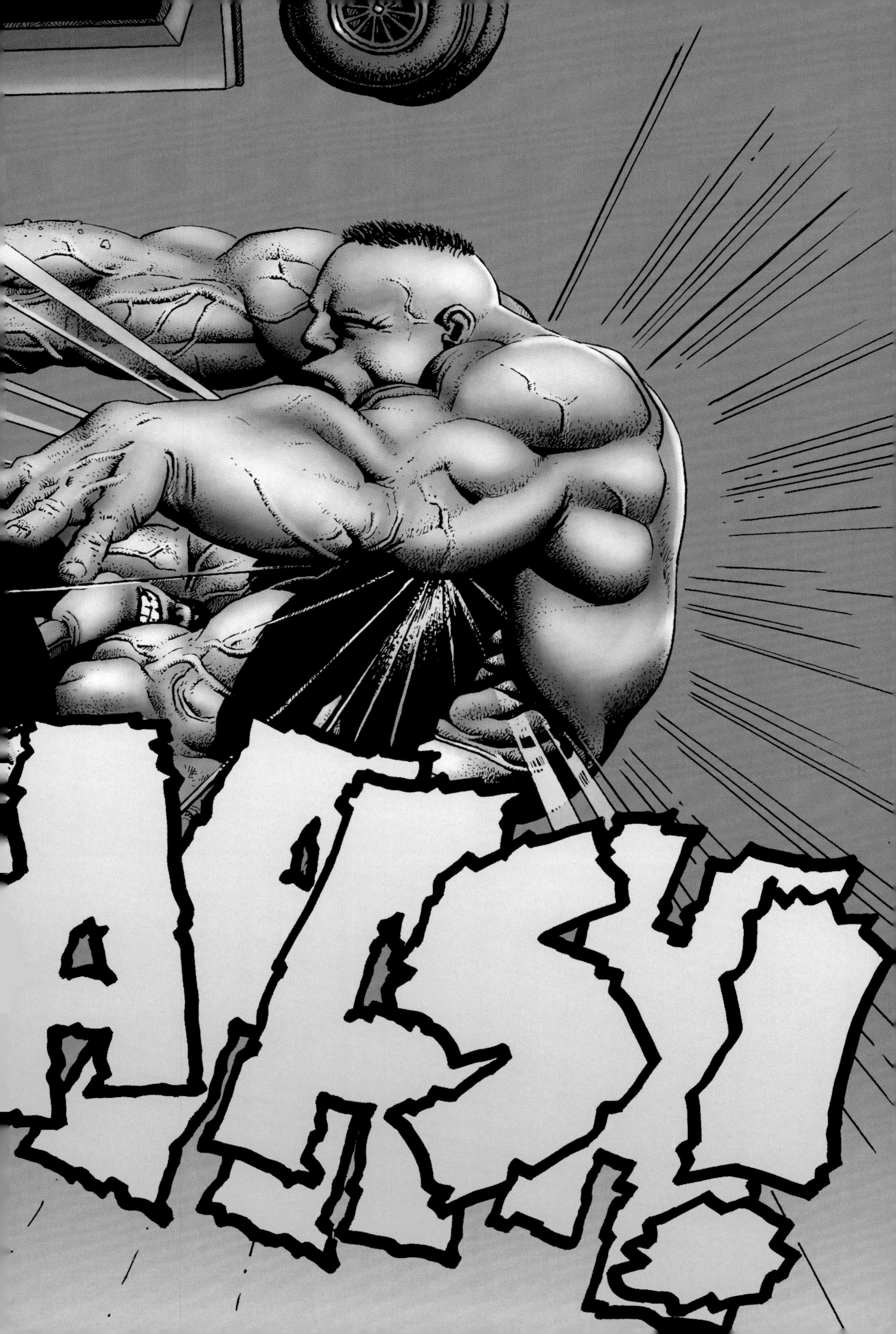

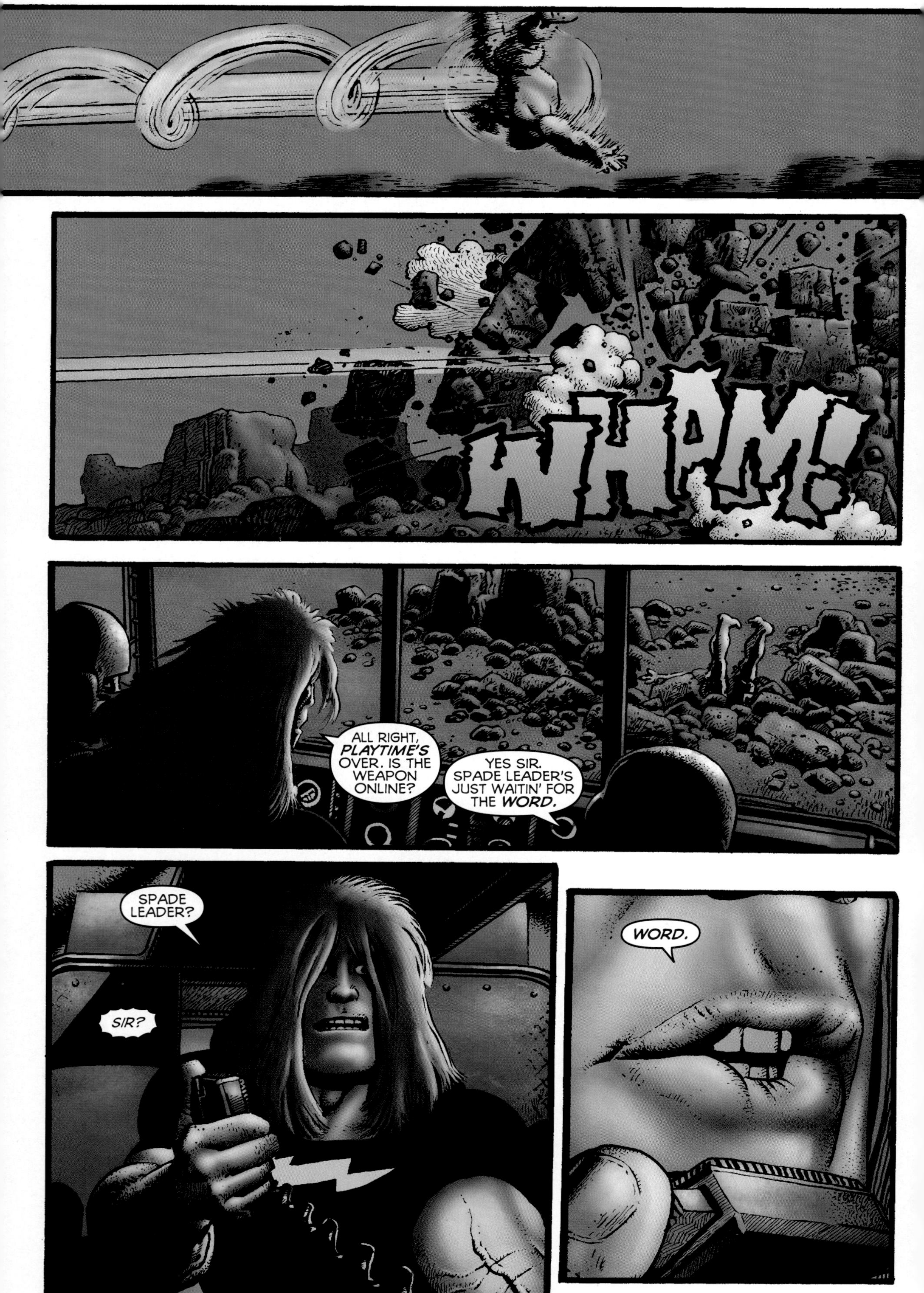
WHAM!
ALL RIGHT, PLAYTIME'S OVER. IS THE WEAPON ONLINE?
YES SIR. SPADE LEADER'S JUST WAITIN' FOR THE WORD.
SPADE LEADER?
SIR?
WORD.

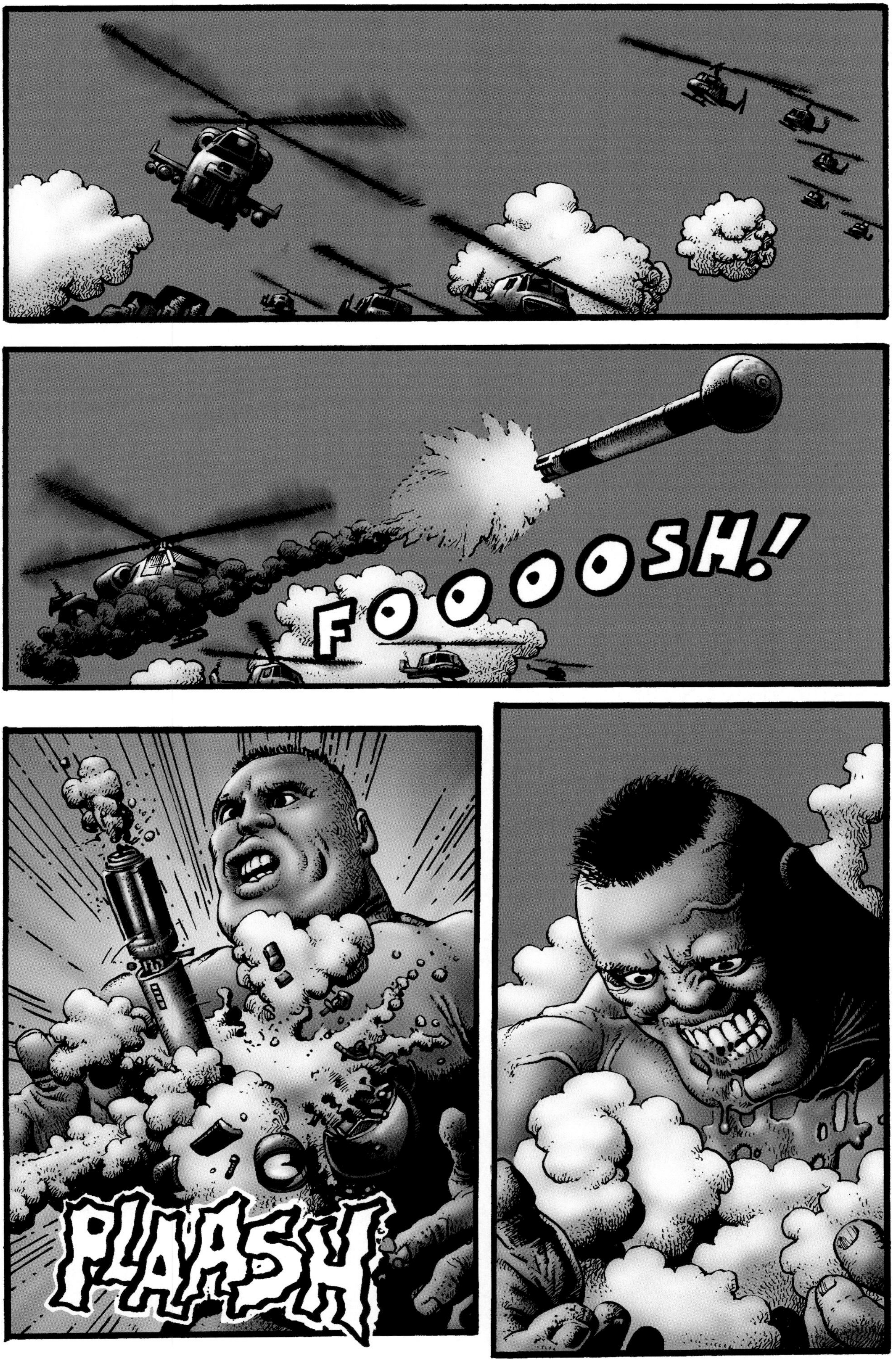
FOOOOSH!
PLAASH

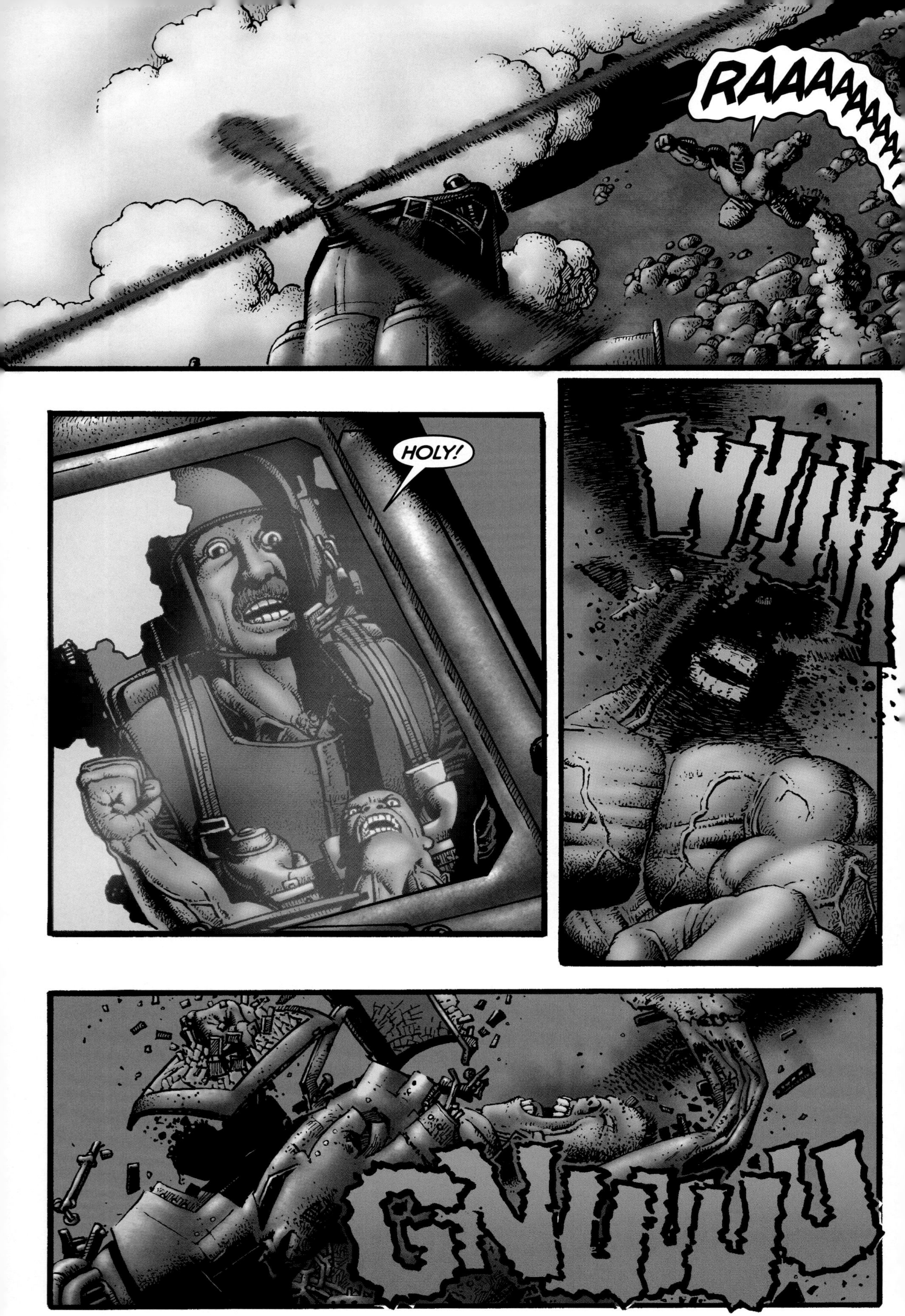
RAAAAAAAAA
HOLY!
WHUNK

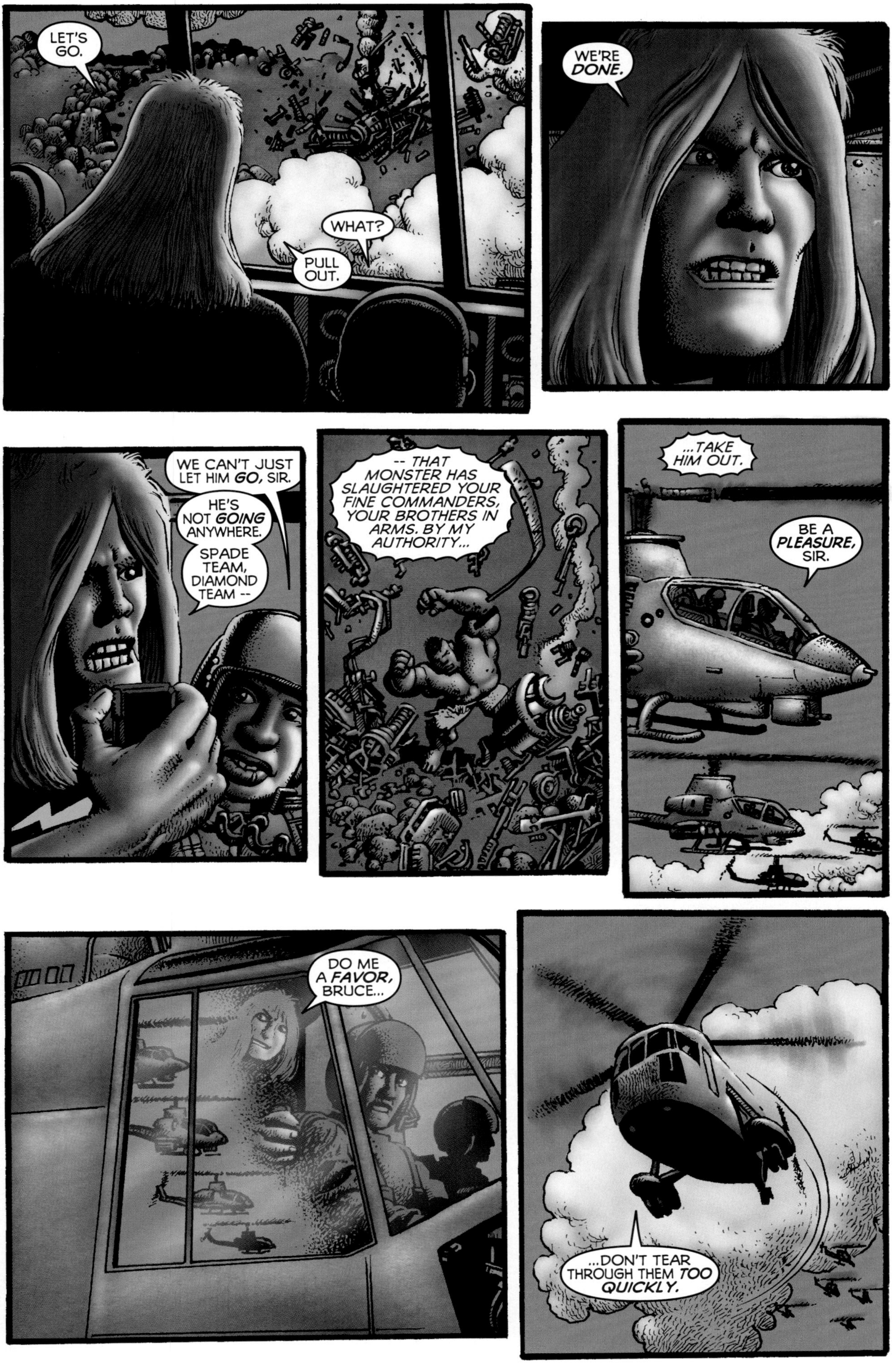
LET'S GO.
WHAT?
PULL OUT.
WE'RE DONE.
WE CAN'T JUST LET HIM GO, SIR.
HE'S NOT GOING ANYWHERE.
SPADE TEAM, DIAMOND TEAM --
-- THAT MONSTER HAS SLAUGHTERED YOUR FINE COMMANDERS, YOUR BROTHERS IN ARMS. BY MY AUTHORITY...
...TAKE HIM OUT.
BE A PLEASURE, SIR.
DO ME A FAVOR, BRUCE...
...DON'T TEAR THROUGH THEM TOO QUICKLY.

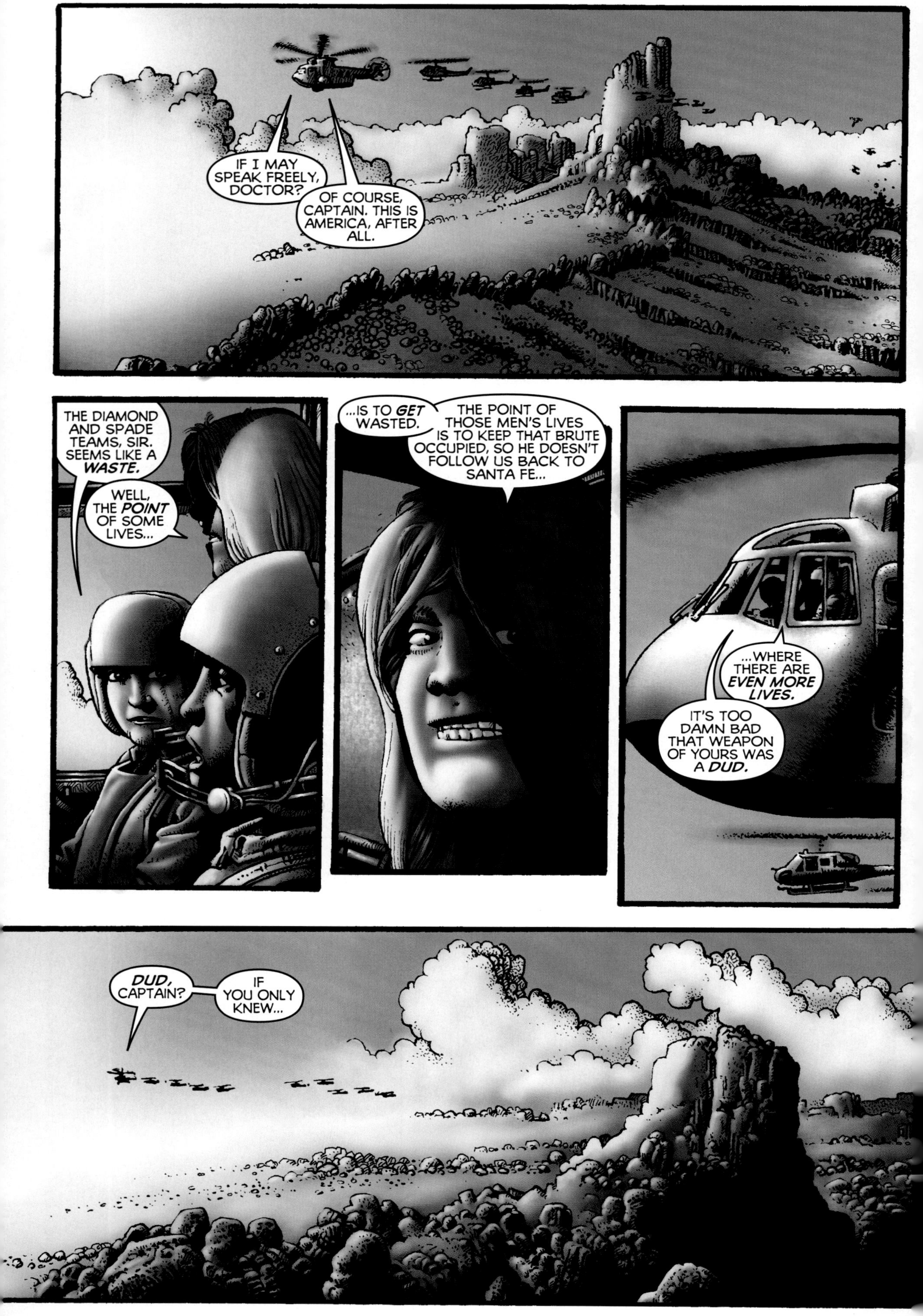
IF I MAY SPEAK FREELY, DOCTOR?
OF COURSE, CAPTAIN. THIS IS AMERICA, AFTER ALL.
THE DIAMOND AND SPADE TEAMS, SIR. SEEMS LIKE A WASTE.
WELL, THE POINT OF SOME LIVES...
...IS TO GET WASTED.
THE POINT OF THOSE MEN'S LIVES IS TO KEEP THAT BRUTE OCCUPIED, SO HE DOESN'T FOLLOW US BACK TO SANTA FE...
...WHERE THERE ARE EVEN MORE LIVES.
IT'S TOO DAMN BAD THAT WEAPON OF YOURS WAS A DUD.
DUD, CAPTAIN?
IF YOU ONLY KNEW...

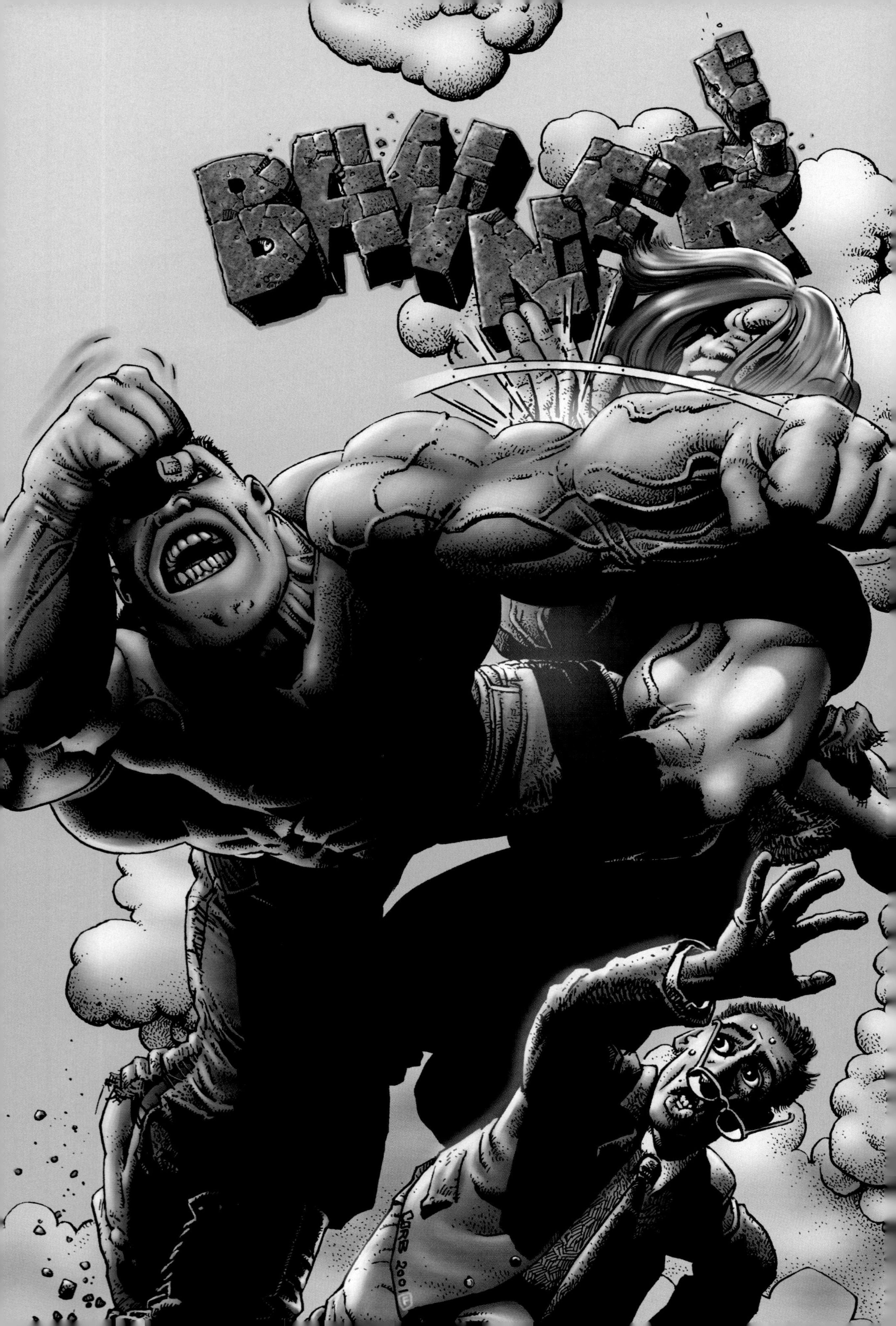

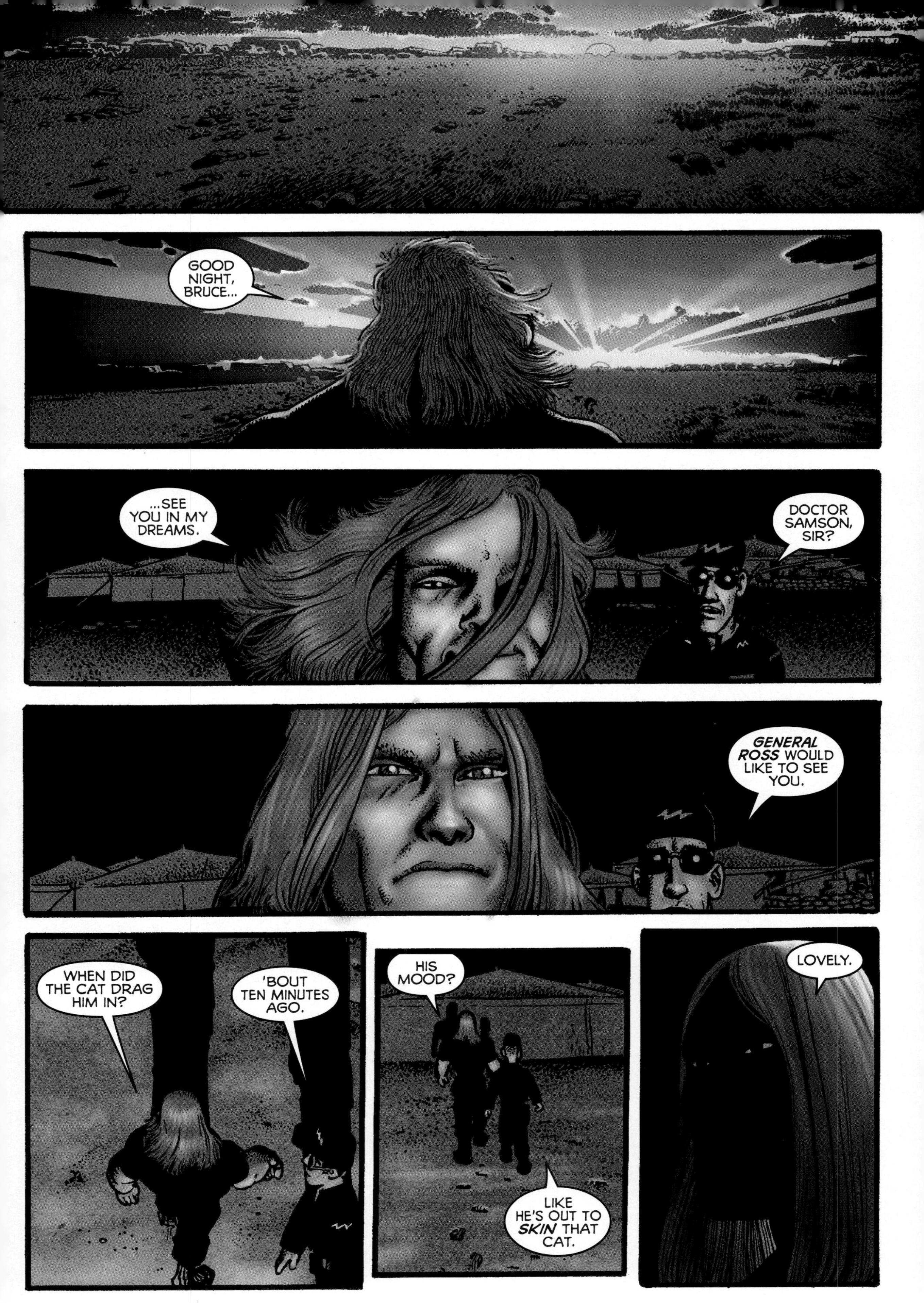
GOOD NIGHT, BRUCE...
...SEE YOU IN MY DREAMS.
DOCTOR SAMSON, SIR?
GENERAL ROSS WOULD LIKE TO SEE YOU.
WHEN DID THE CAT DRAG HIM IN?
'BOUT TEN MINUTES AGO.
HIS MOOD?
LIKE HE'S OUT TO SKIN THAT CAT.
LOVELY.

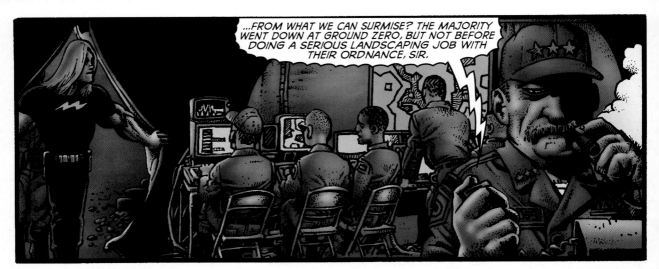

...FROM WHAT WE CAN SURMISE? THE MAJORITY WENT DOWN AT GROUND ZERO, BUT NOT BEFORE DOING A SERIOUS LANDSCAPING JOB WITH THEIR ORDNANCE, SIR.

IT THEN APPEARS *THREE* OF THE BIRDS TURNED TAIL AND HEADED OUT TOWARDS THE DESERT WITH THEIR ONE-TIME TARGET IN *HOT PURSUIT*.

...CAUGHT THE LAST ONE 'BOUT TWO AND A HALF KLIKS FROM ZERO. TORE THE SHIP UP LIKE IT WAS MADE OF *TIN-FOIL*.

NO SURVIVORS.

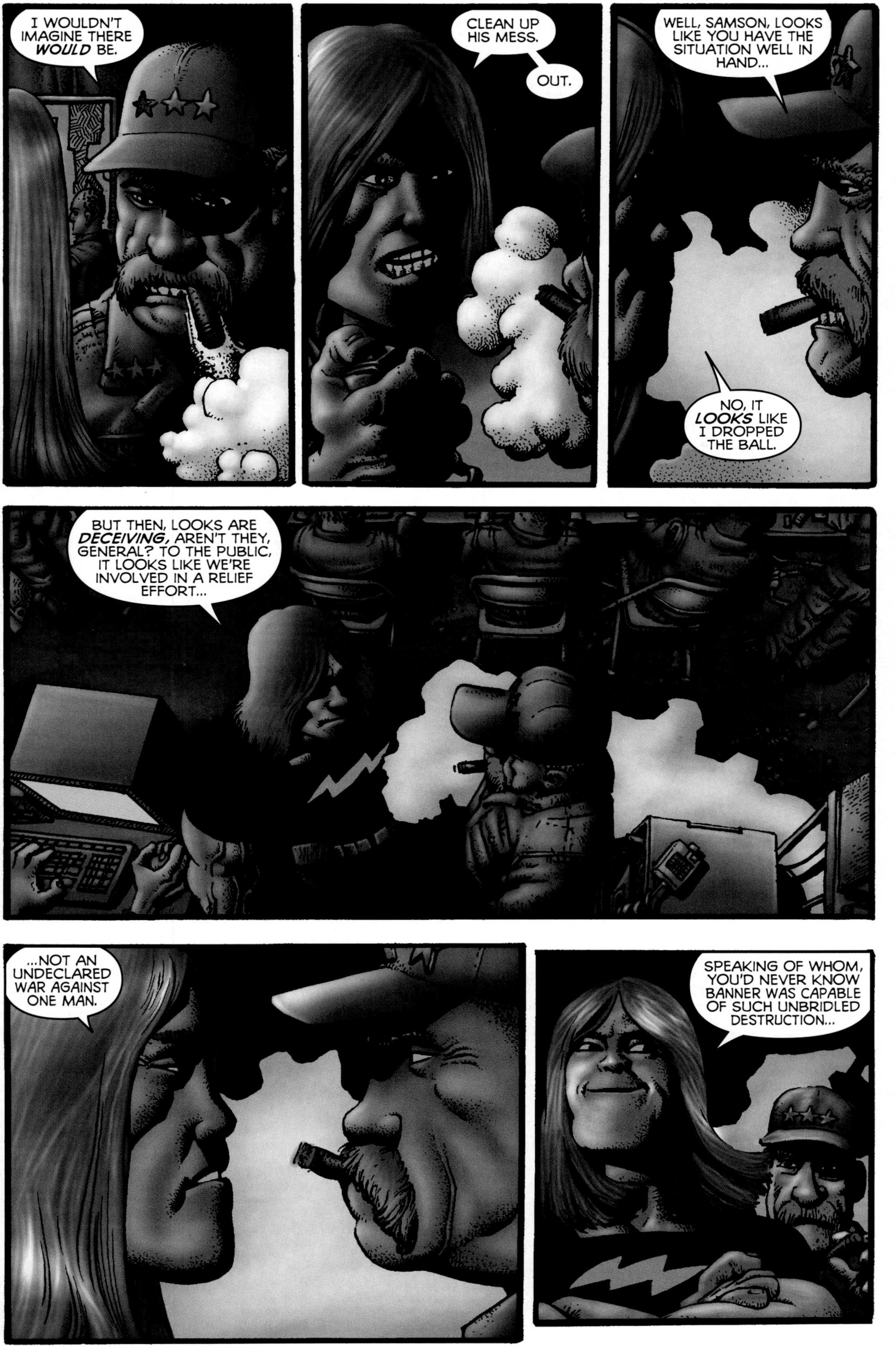
I WOULDN'T IMAGINE THERE *WOULD* BE.
CLEAN UP HIS MESS.
OUT.
WELL, SAMSON, LOOKS LIKE YOU HAVE THE SITUATION WELL IN HAND...
NO, IT *LOOKS* LIKE I DROPPED THE BALL.
BUT THEN, LOOKS ARE *DECEIVING,* AREN'T THEY, GENERAL? TO THE PUBLIC, IT LOOKS LIKE WE'RE INVOLVED IN A RELIEF EFFORT...
...NOT AN UNDECLARED WAR AGAINST ONE MAN.
SPEAKING OF WHOM, YOU'D NEVER KNOW BANNER WAS CAPABLE OF SUCH UNBRIDLED DESTRUCTION...

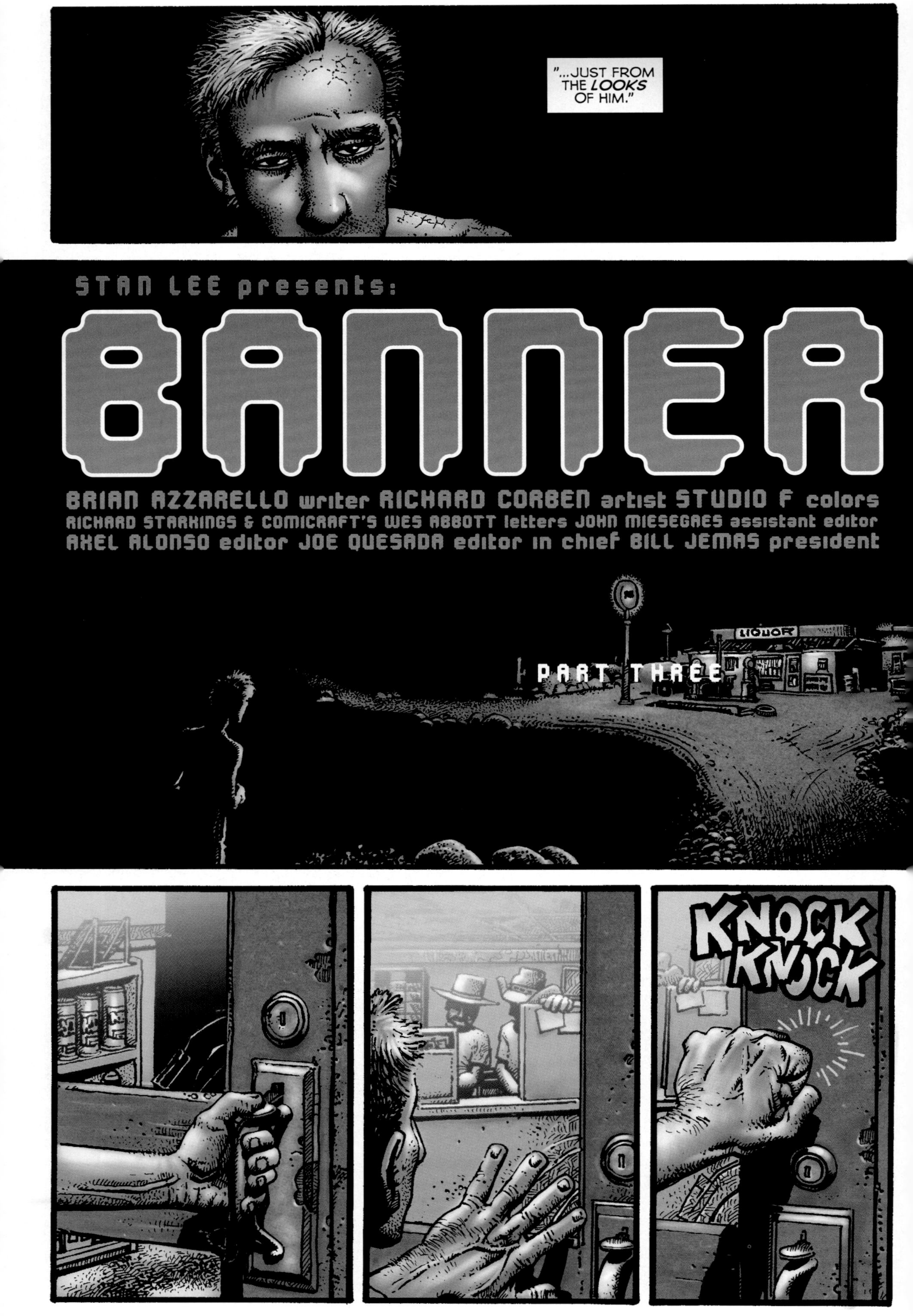
"...JUST FROM THE LOOKS OF HIM."
STAN LEE presents:
BANNER
BRIAN AZZARELLO writer RICHARD CORBEN artist STUDIO F colors
RICHARD STARKINGS & COMICRAFT'S WES ABBOTT letters JOHN MIESEGAES assistant editor
AXEL ALONSO editor JOE QUESADA editor in chief BILL JEMAS president
LIQUOR
PART THREE
KNOCK KNOCK

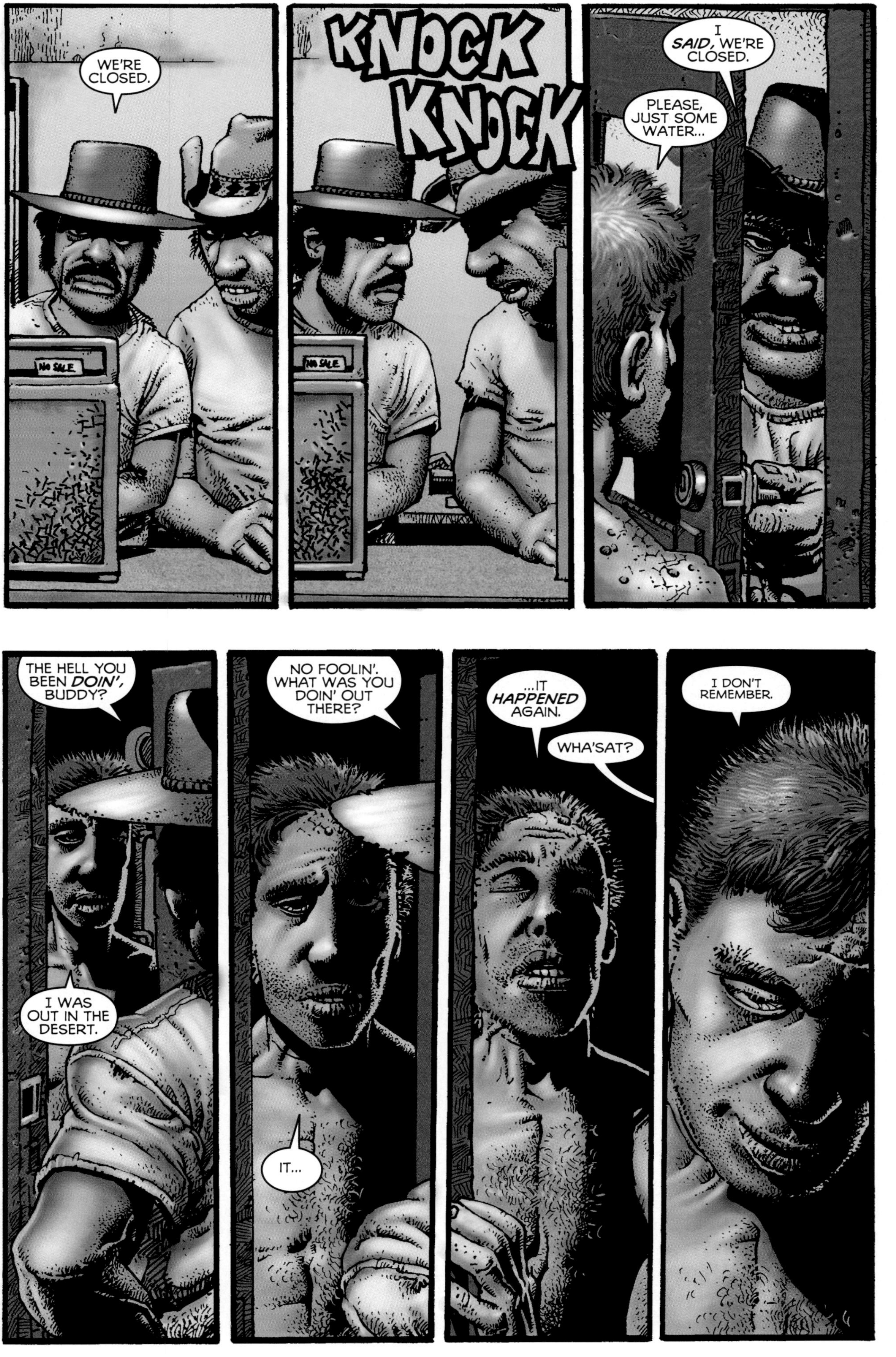
WE'RE CLOSED.
KNOCK KNOCK
I *SAID,* WE'RE CLOSED.
PLEASE, JUST SOME WATER...
THE HELL YOU BEEN *DOIN',* BUDDY?
I WAS OUT IN THE DESERT.
NO FOOLIN'. WHAT WAS YOU DOIN' OUT THERE?
IT...
...IT *HAPPENED* AGAIN.
WHA'SAT?
I DON'T REMEMBER.

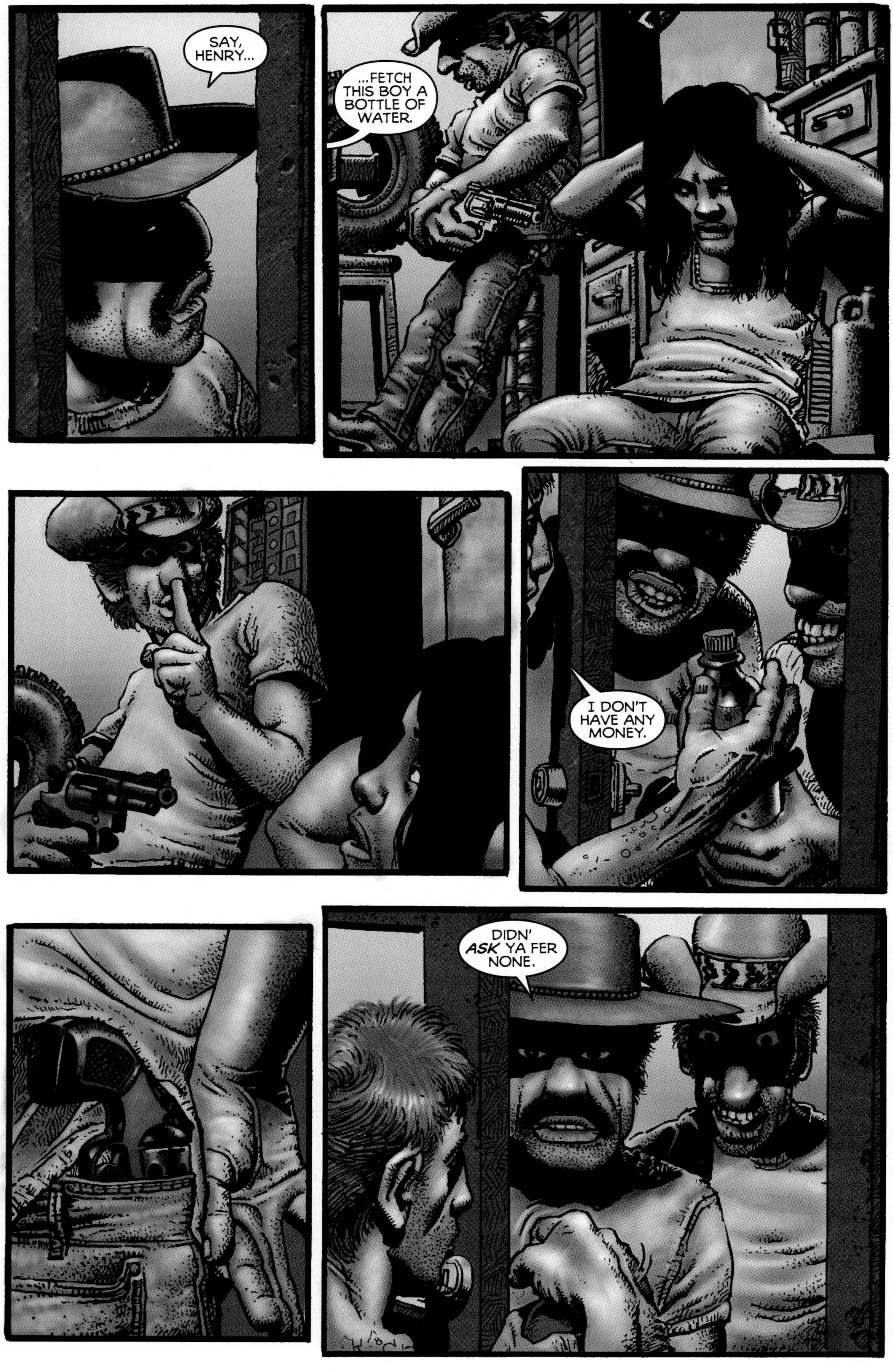
SAY, HENRY...
...FETCH THIS BOY A BOTTLE OF WATER.
I DON'T HAVE ANY MONEY.
DIDN' ASK YA FER NONE.

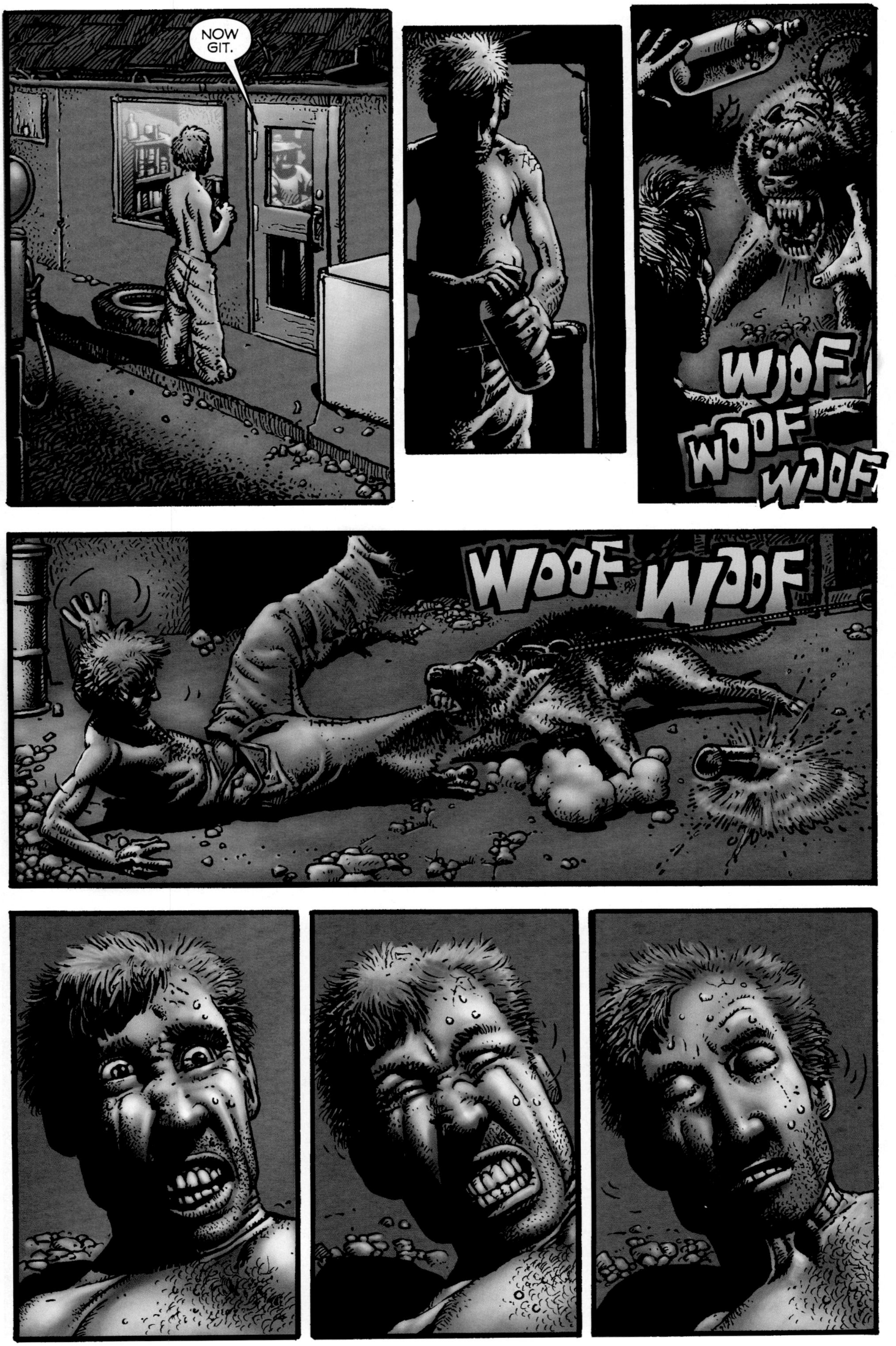
NOW GIT.
WOOF
WOOF
WOOF
WOOF WOOF

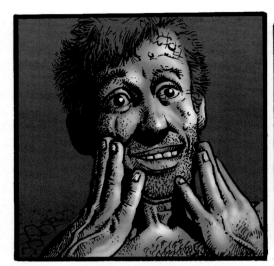

GRRRRRRR

FREEZE!

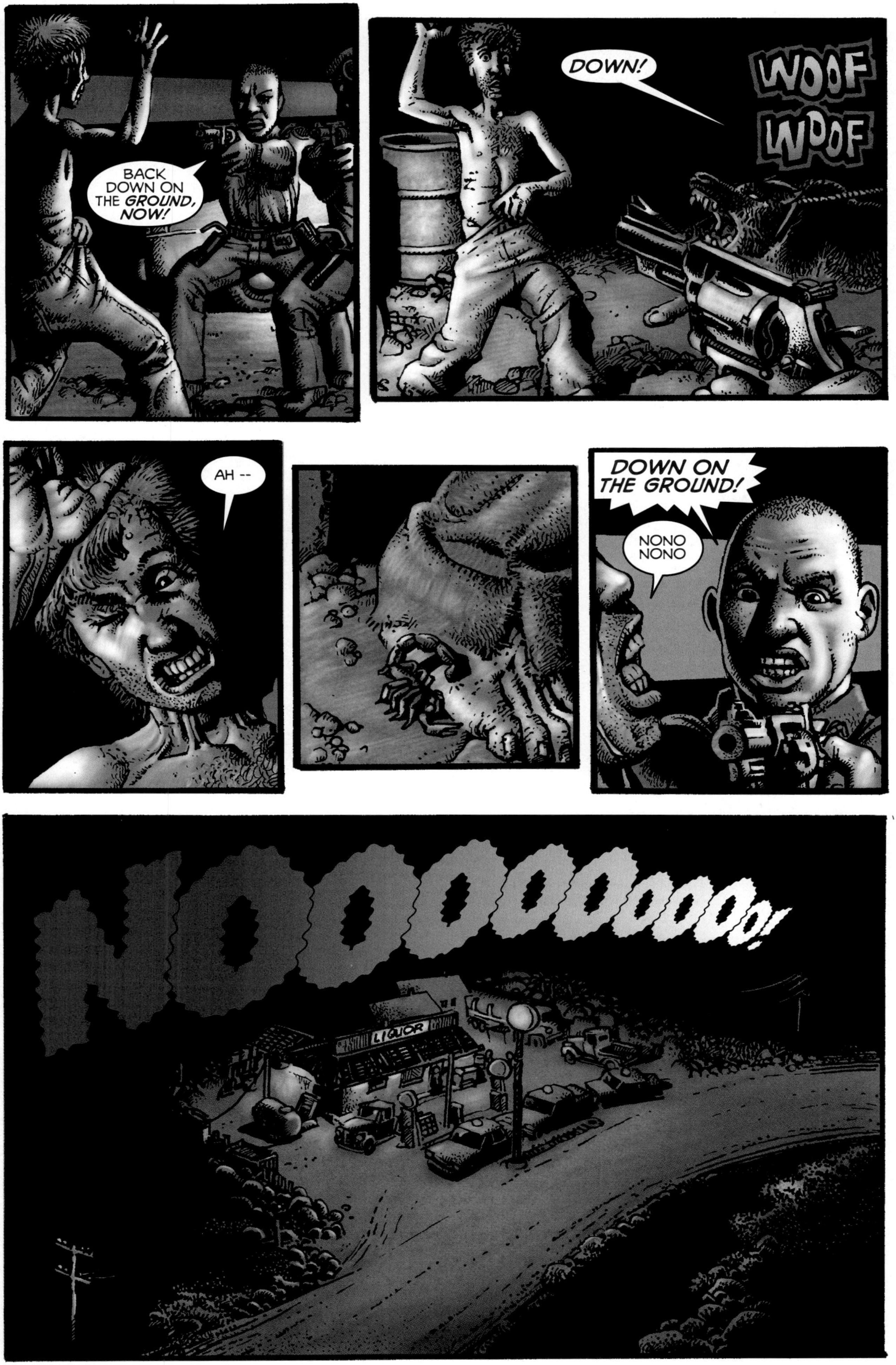
BACK DOWN ON THE GROUND, NOW!
DOWN!
WOOF WOOF
AH --
DOWN ON THE GROUND!
NONO NONO
NOOOOOOOOo!
LIQUOR

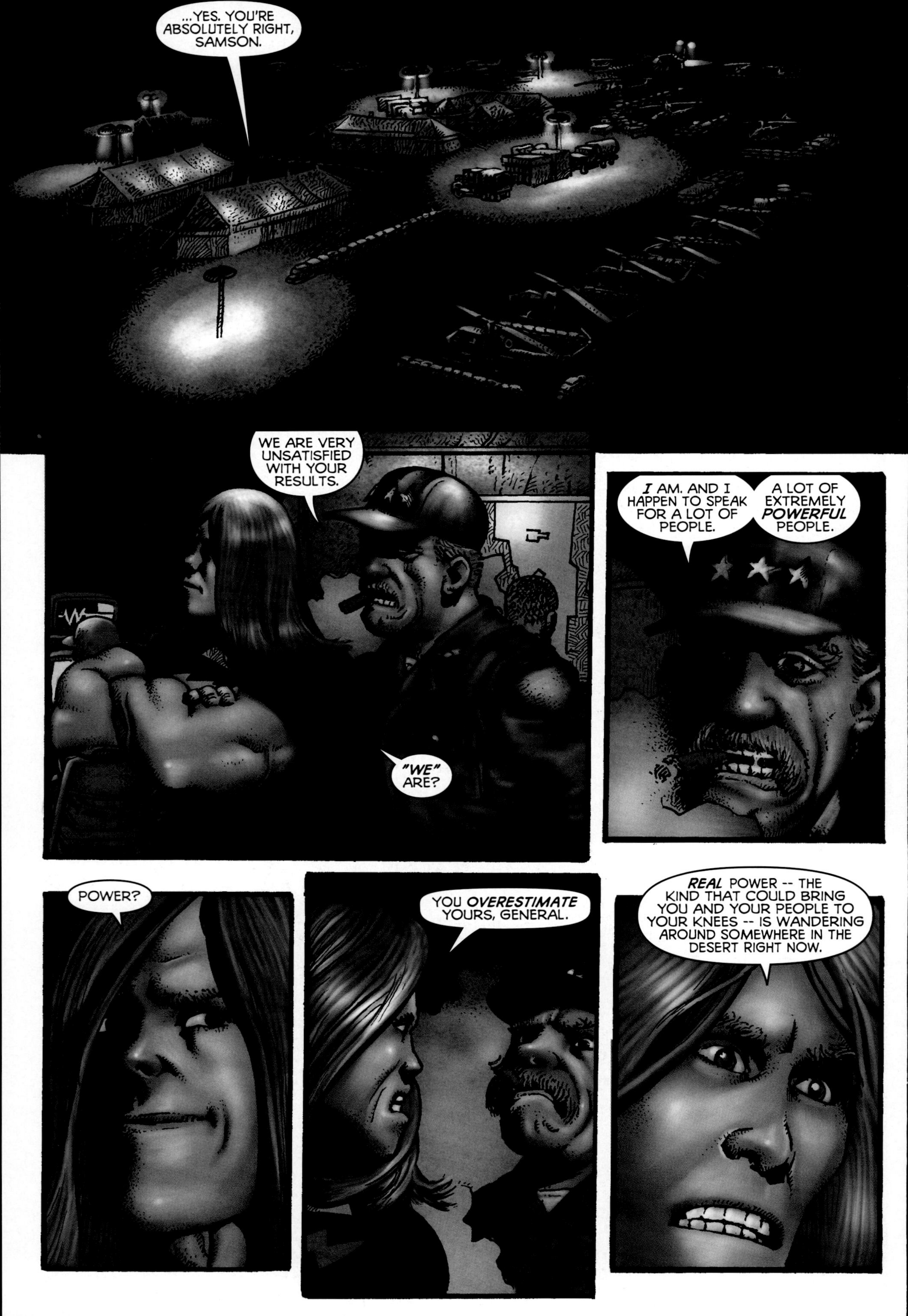
...YES. YOU'RE ABSOLUTELY RIGHT, SAMSON.
WE ARE VERY UNSATISFIED WITH YOUR RESULTS.
"WE" ARE?
I AM. AND I HAPPEN TO SPEAK FOR A LOT OF PEOPLE.
A LOT OF EXTREMELY POWERFUL PEOPLE.
POWER?
YOU OVERESTIMATE YOURS, GENERAL.
REAL POWER -- THE KIND THAT COULD BRING YOU AND YOUR PEOPLE TO YOUR KNEES -- IS WANDERING AROUND SOMEWHERE IN THE DESERT RIGHT NOW.

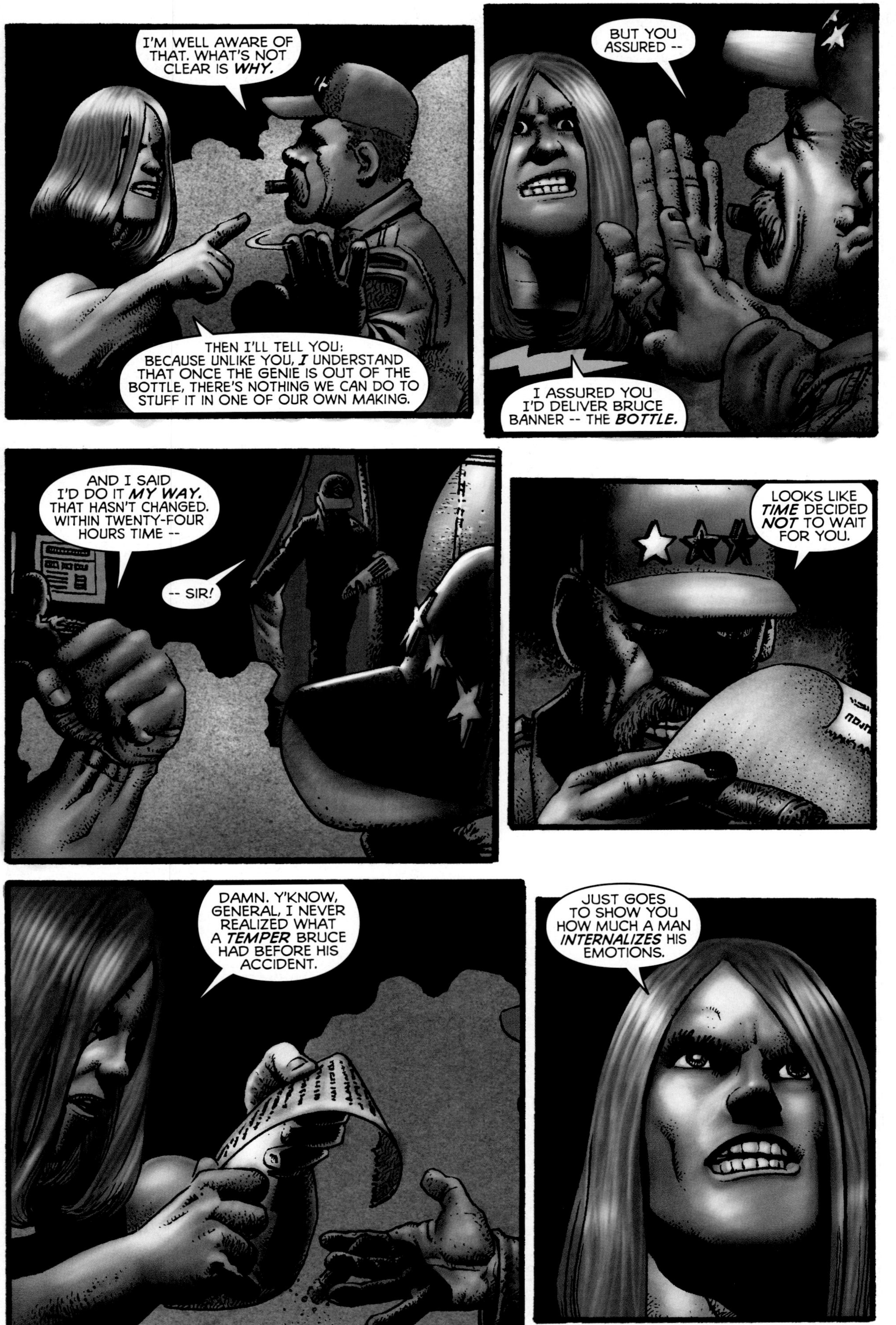

I'M WELL AWARE OF THAT. WHAT'S NOT CLEAR IS *WHY.*
THEN I'LL TELL YOU: BECAUSE UNLIKE YOU, *I* UNDERSTAND THAT ONCE THE GENIE IS OUT OF THE BOTTLE, THERE'S NOTHING WE CAN DO TO STUFF IT IN ONE OF OUR OWN MAKING.
BUT YOU ASSURED --
I ASSURED YOU I'D DELIVER BRUCE BANNER -- THE *BOTTLE.*
AND I SAID I'D DO IT *MY WAY.* THAT HASN'T CHANGED. WITHIN TWENTY-FOUR HOURS TIME --
-- SIR!
LOOKS LIKE *TIME* DECIDED *NOT* TO WAIT FOR YOU.
DAMN. Y'KNOW, GENERAL, I NEVER REALIZED WHAT A *TEMPER* BRUCE HAD BEFORE HIS ACCIDENT.
JUST GOES TO SHOW YOU HOW MUCH A MAN *INTERNALIZES* HIS EMOTIONS.

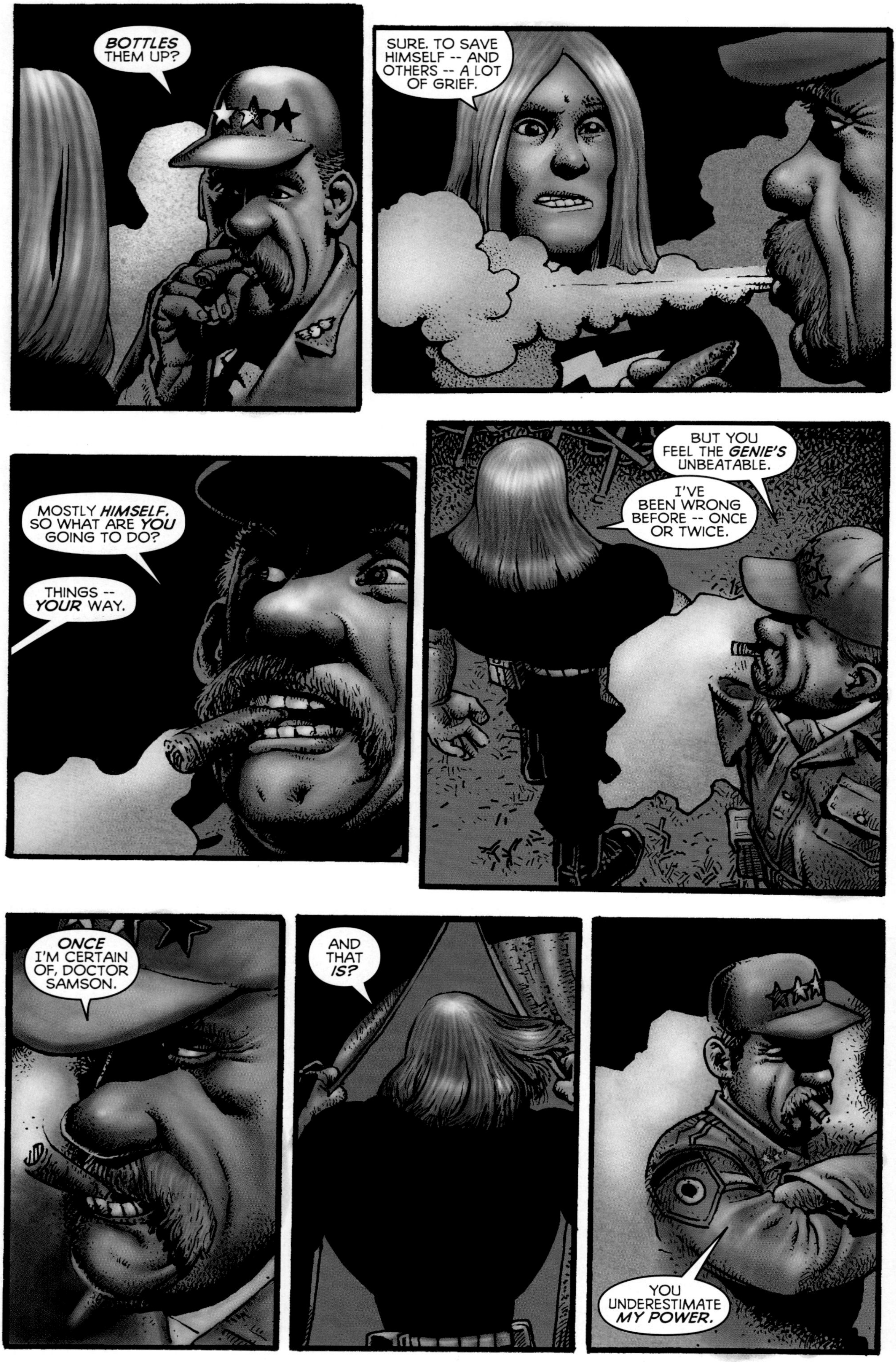
BOTTLES THEM UP?
SURE. TO SAVE HIMSELF -- AND OTHERS -- A LOT OF GRIEF.
MOSTLY HIMSELF. SO WHAT ARE YOU GOING TO DO?
THINGS -- YOUR WAY.
BUT YOU FEEL THE GENIE'S UNBEATABLE.
I'VE BEEN WRONG BEFORE -- ONCE OR TWICE.
ONCE I'M CERTAIN OF, DOCTOR SAMSON.
AND THAT IS?
YOU UNDERESTIMATE MY POWER.

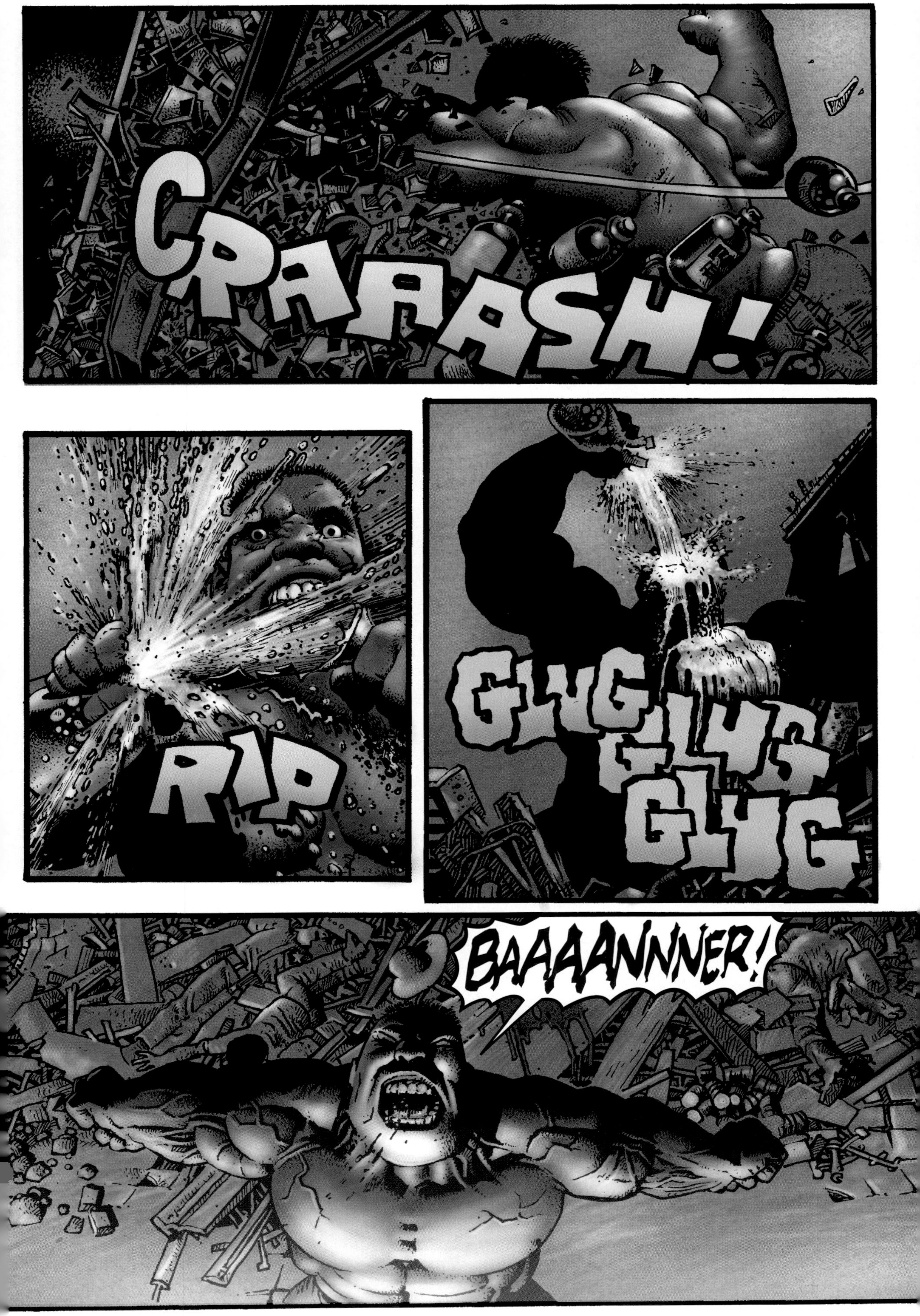
CRAAASH!
RIP
GLUG GLUG GLUG
BAAAANNNER!

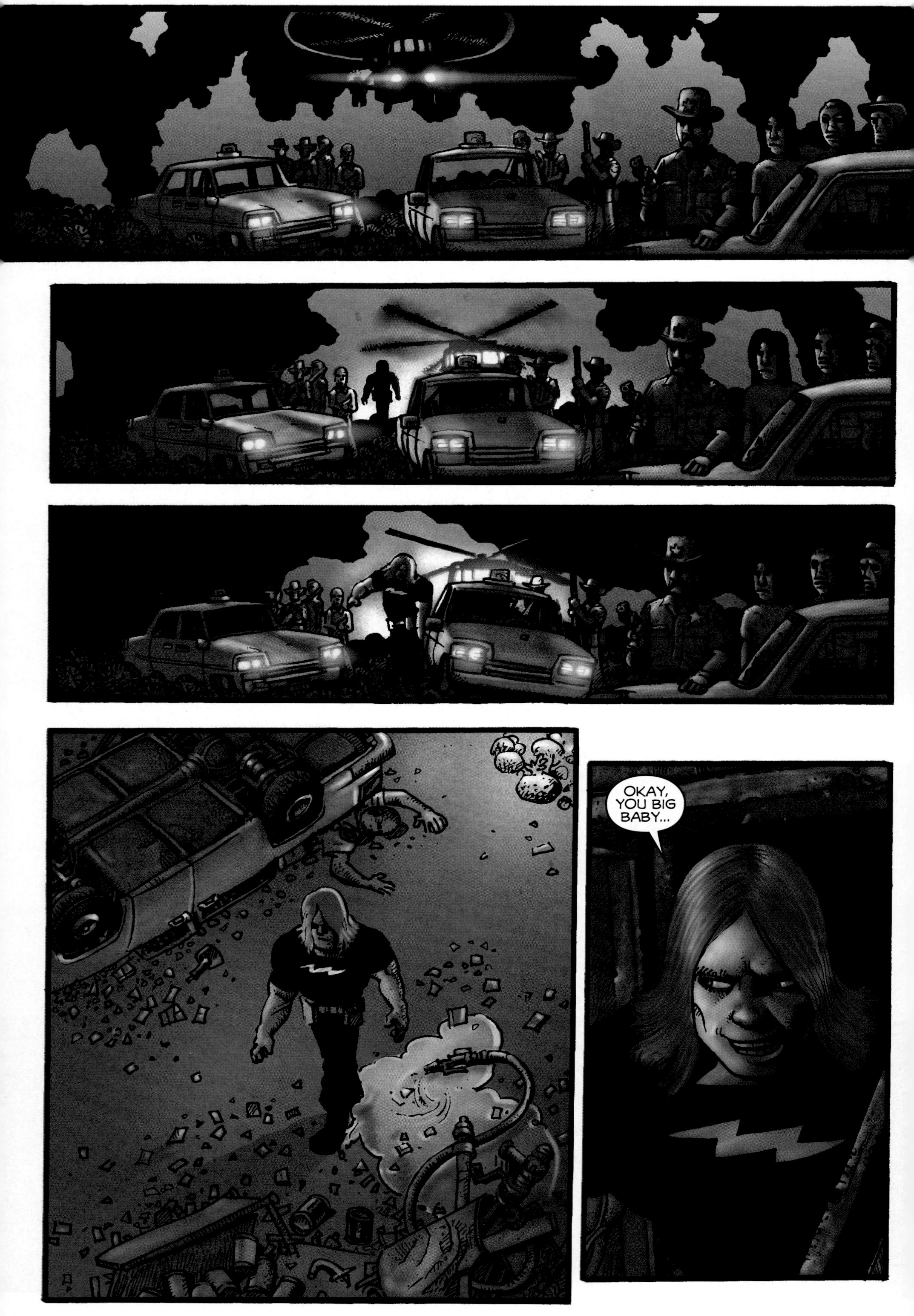
OKAY, YOU BIG BABY...

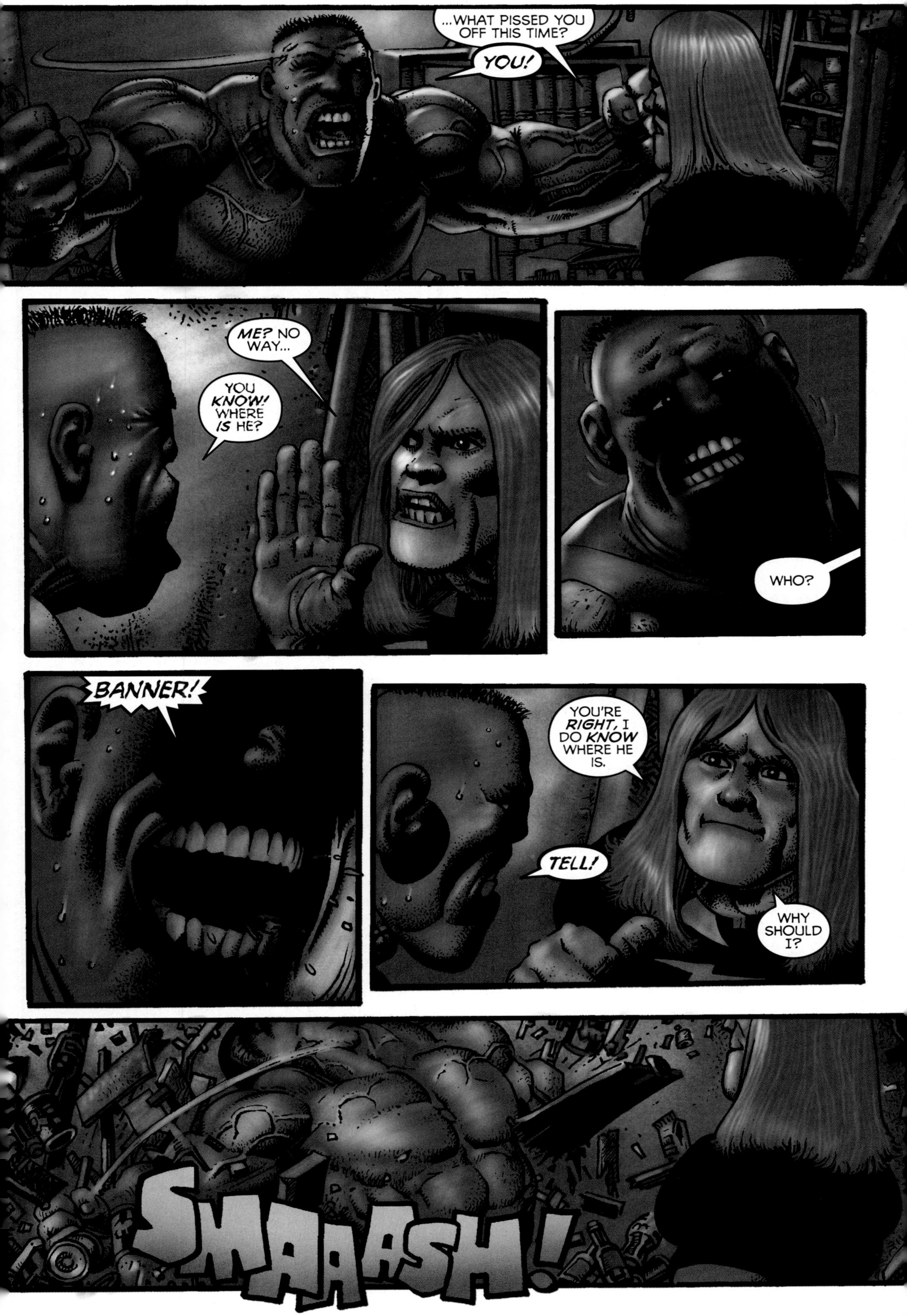
...WHAT PISSED YOU OFF THIS TIME?
YOU!
ME? NO WAY...
YOU KNOW! WHERE IS HE?
WHO?
BANNER!
YOU'RE RIGHT, I DO KNOW WHERE HE IS.
TELL!
WHY SHOULD I?
SMAAASH!

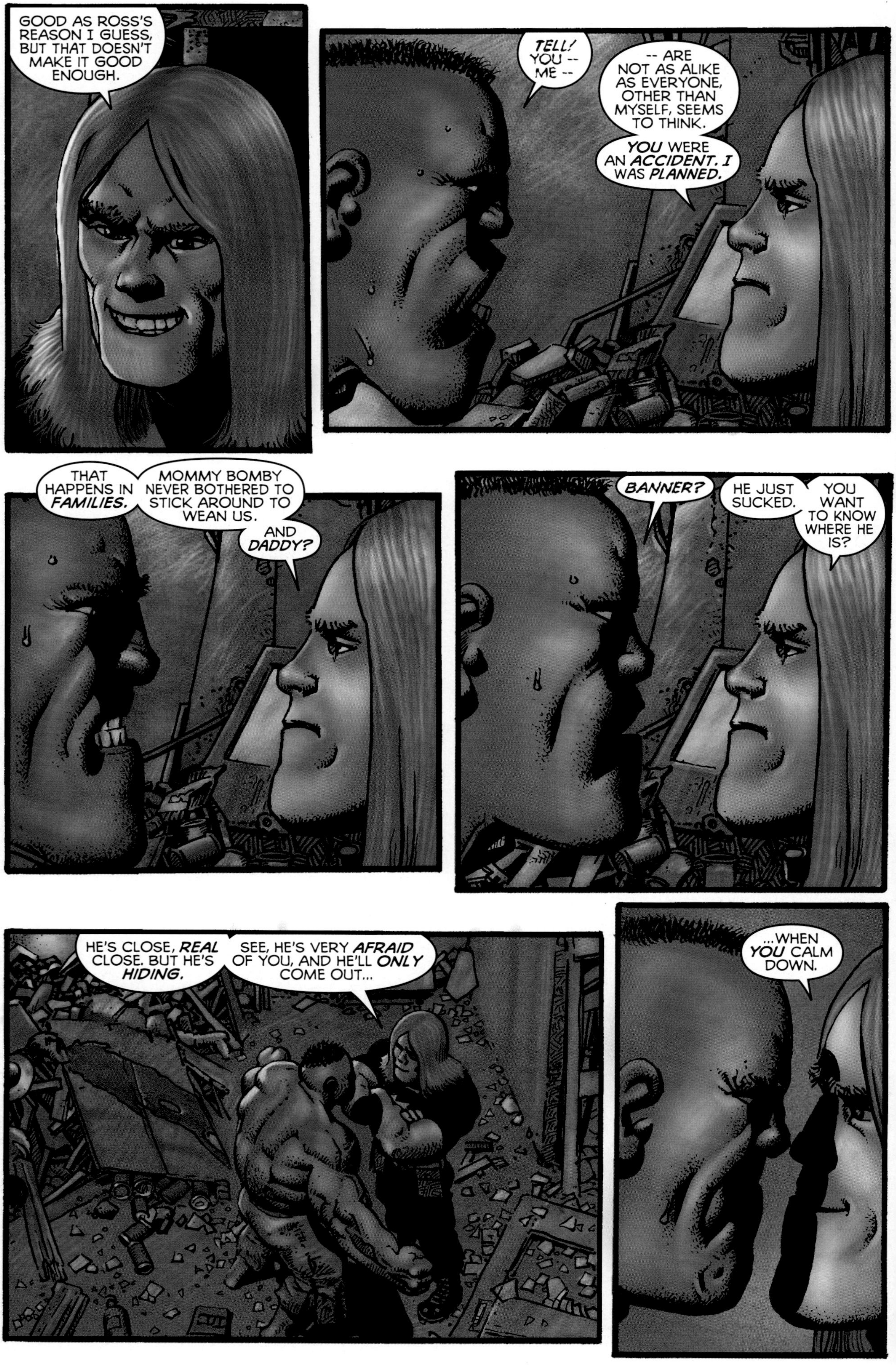
GOOD AS ROSS'S REASON I GUESS, BUT THAT DOESN'T MAKE IT GOOD ENOUGH.
TELL! YOU -- ME --
-- ARE NOT AS ALIKE AS EVERYONE, OTHER THAN MYSELF, SEEMS TO THINK.
YOU WERE AN ACCIDENT. I WAS PLANNED.
THAT HAPPENS IN FAMILIES.
MOMMY BOMBY NEVER BOTHERED TO STICK AROUND TO WEAN US.
AND DADDY?
BANNER?
HE JUST SUCKED.
YOU WANT TO KNOW WHERE HE IS?
HE'S CLOSE, REAL CLOSE. BUT HE'S HIDING.
SEE, HE'S VERY AFRAID OF YOU, AND HE'LL ONLY COME OUT...
...WHEN YOU CALM DOWN.

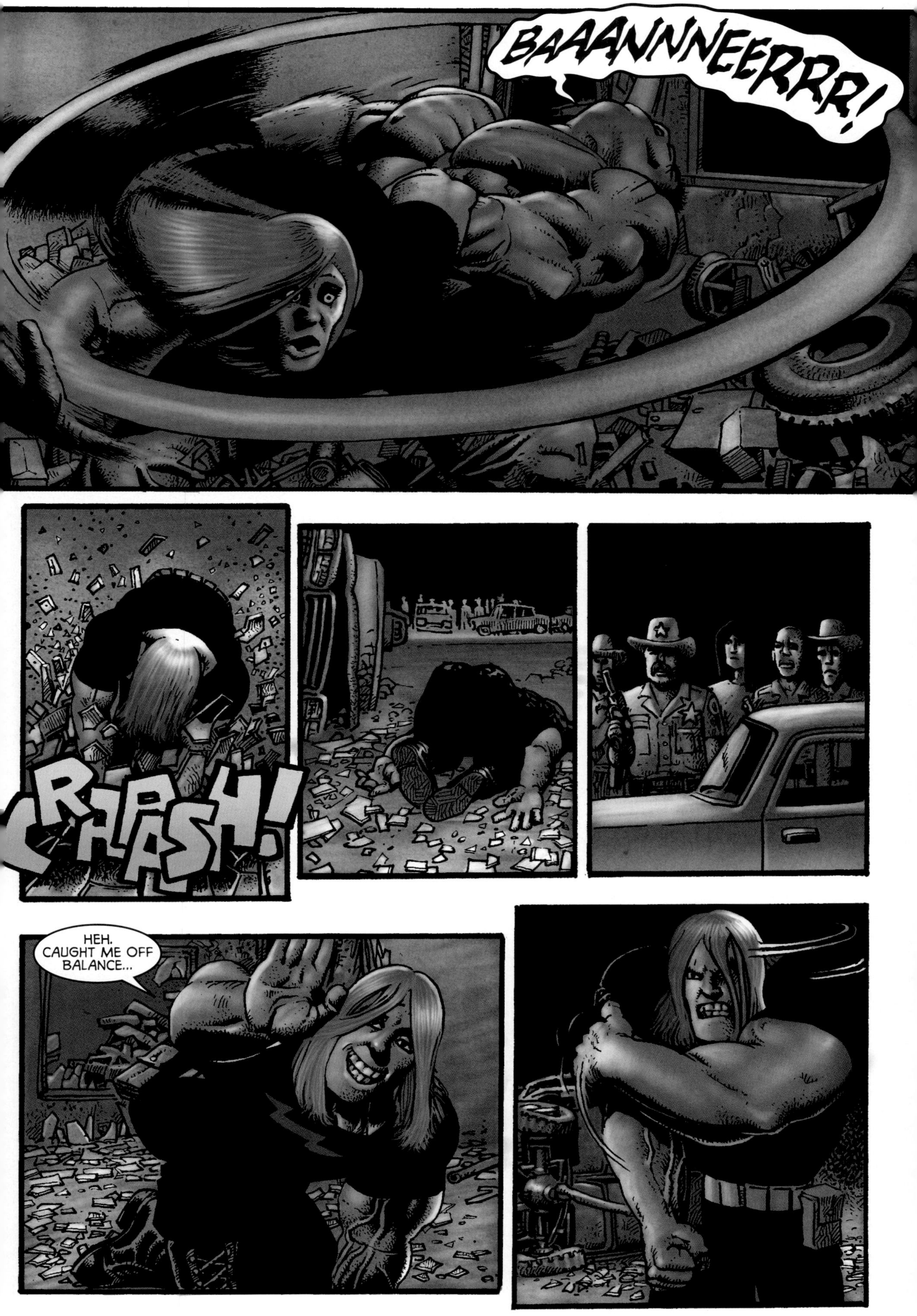
BAAANNNEERRR!
CRASH!
HEH. CAUGHT ME OFF BALANCE...

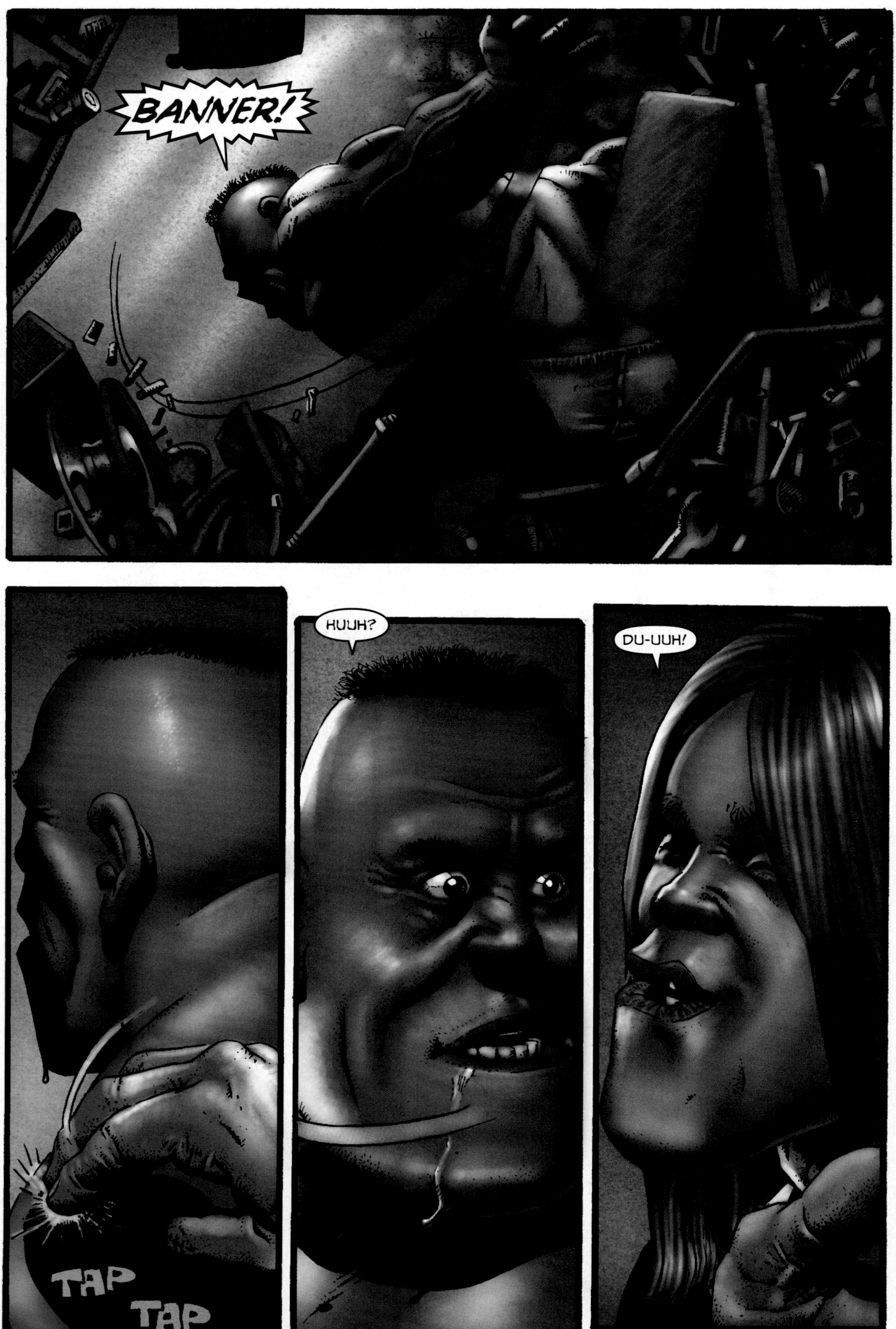
BANNER!
TAP
TAP
HUUH?
DU-UUH!

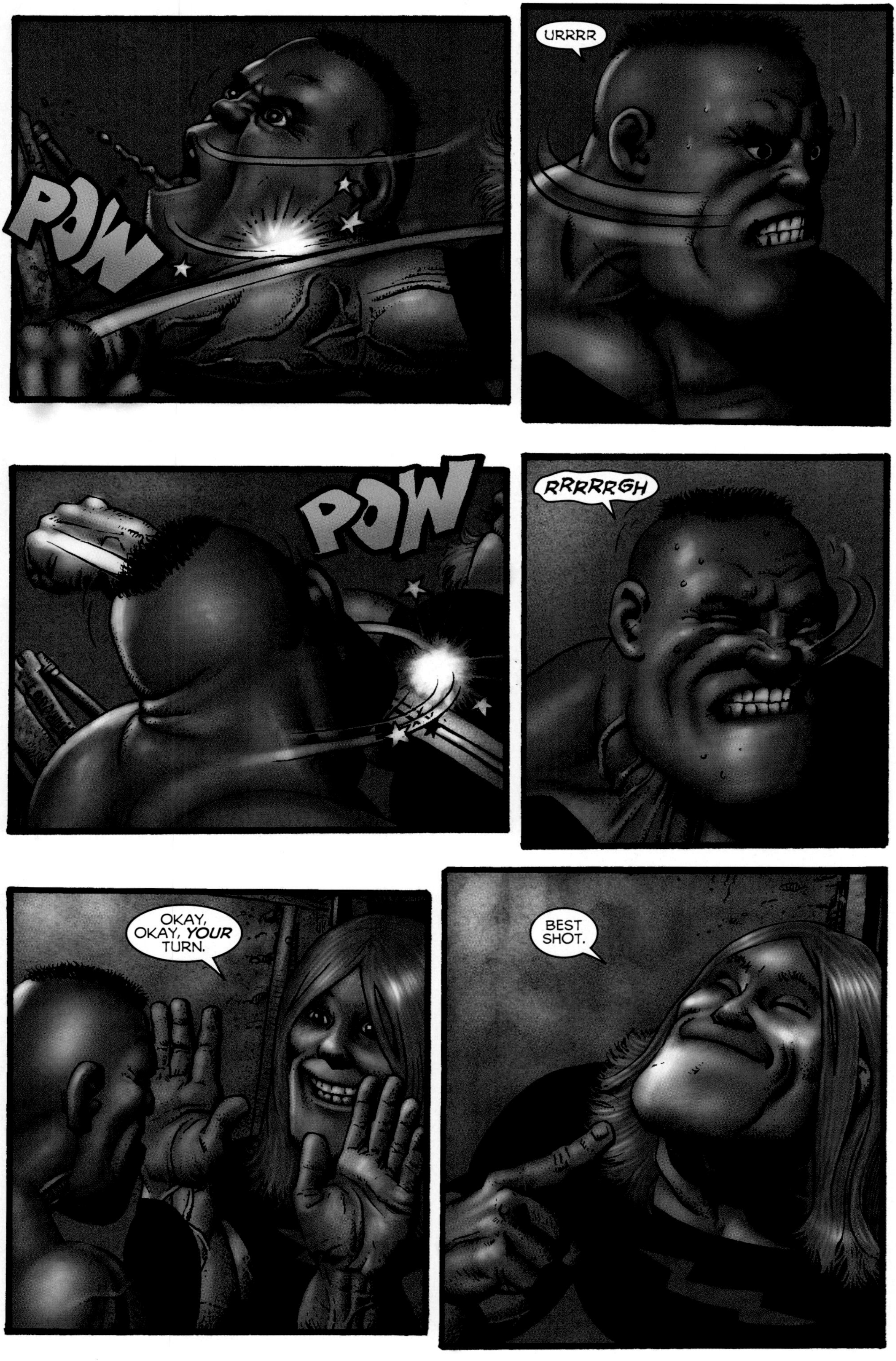
POW
URRRR
POW
RRRRRGH
OKAY, OKAY, YOUR TURN.
BEST SHOT.

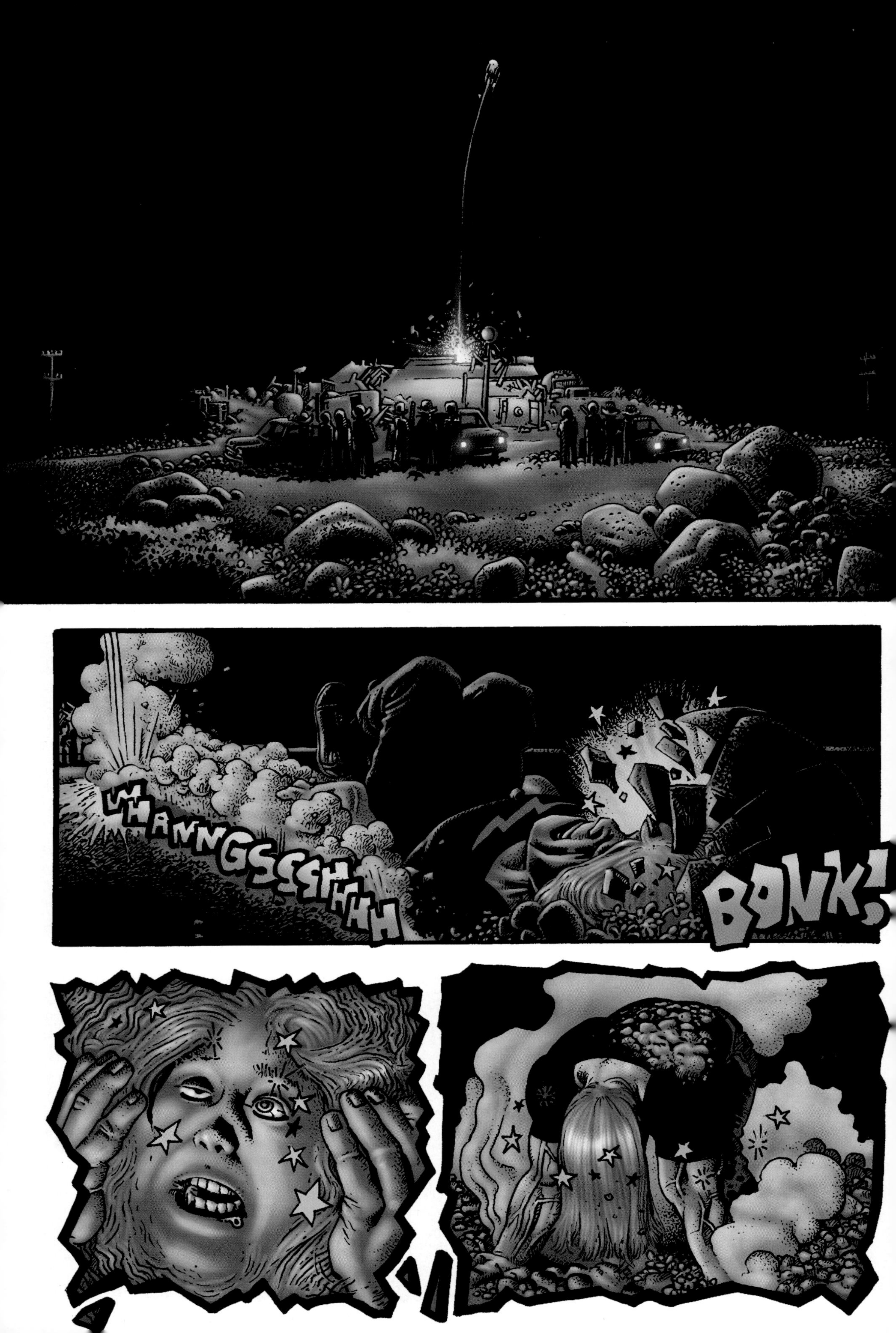
WHANNGSSSHHHH
BONK!

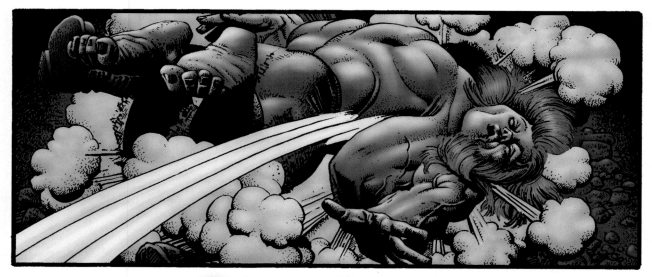

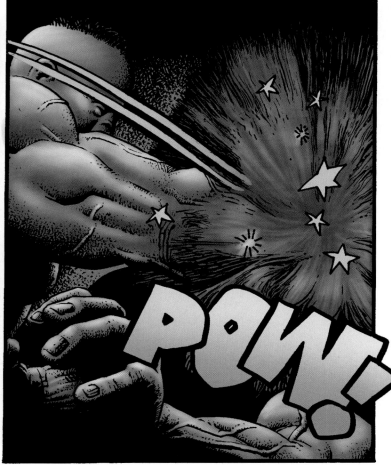

POW!

CRACK!

SMASH

AAAAAH!

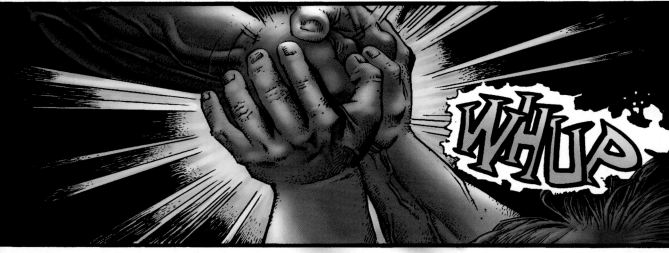

WHUP

I LIED.

BANNER'S *OUT THERE.*

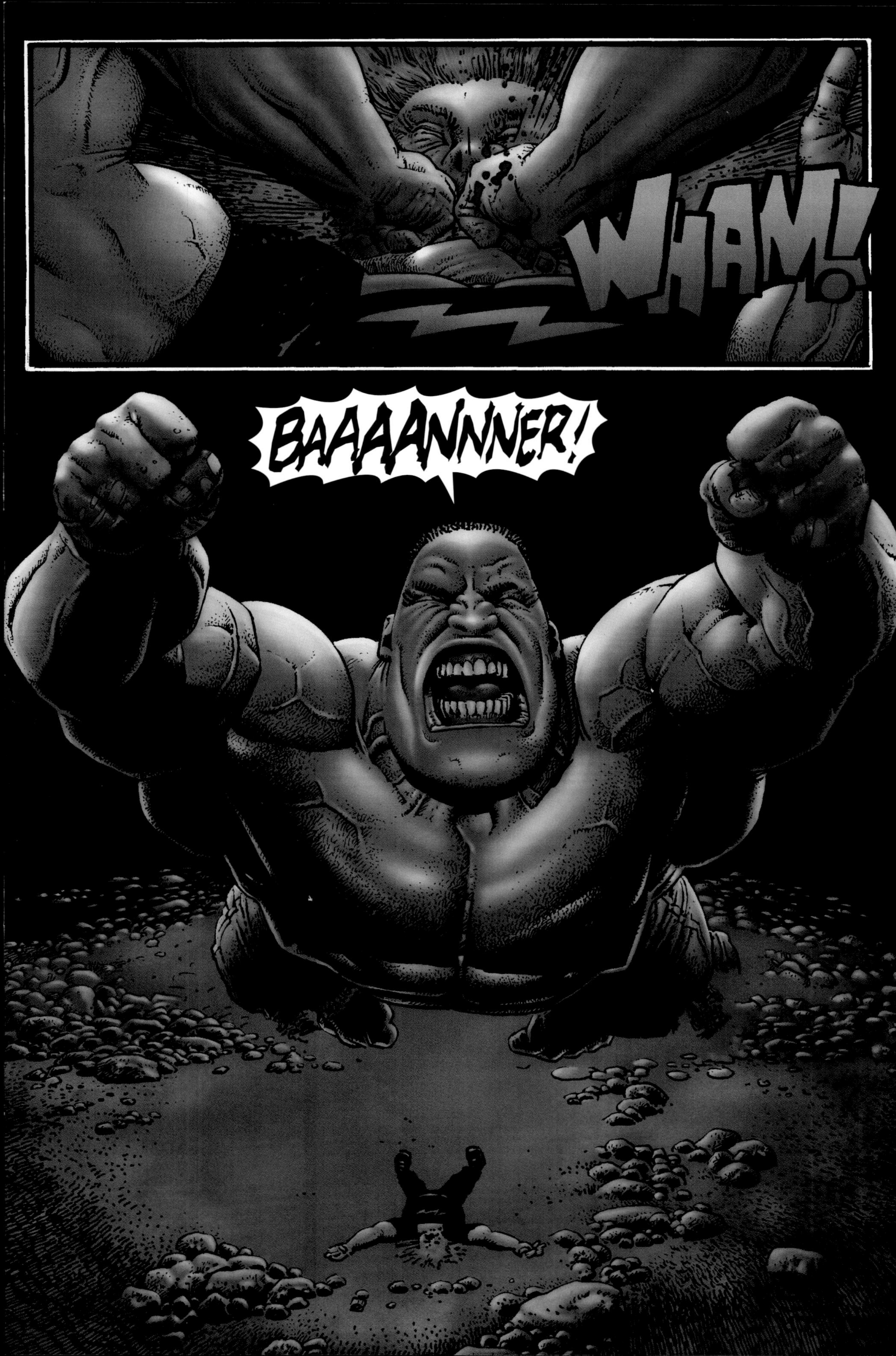
WHAM!
BAAAANNNER!

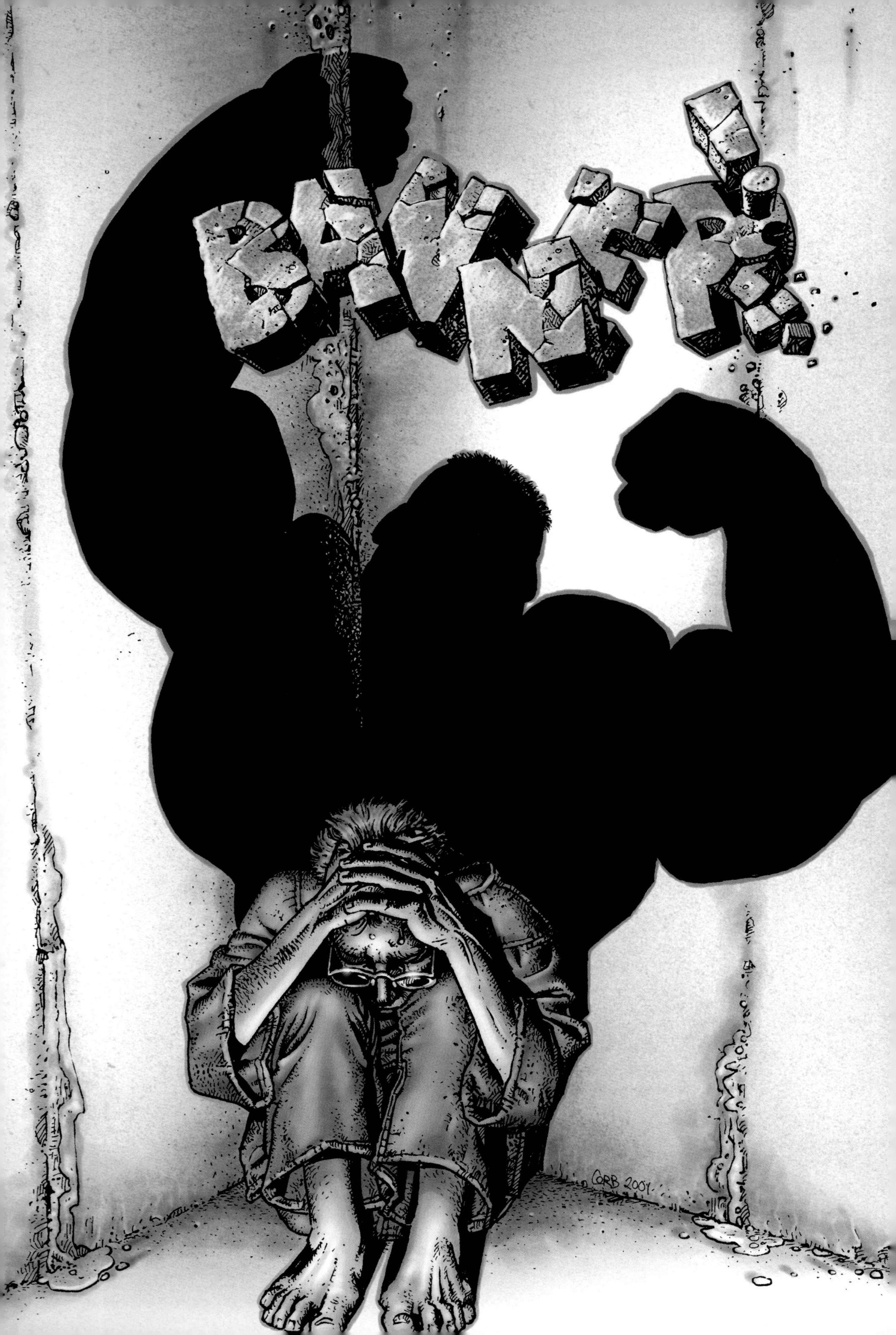
BANNER!
CORB 2001

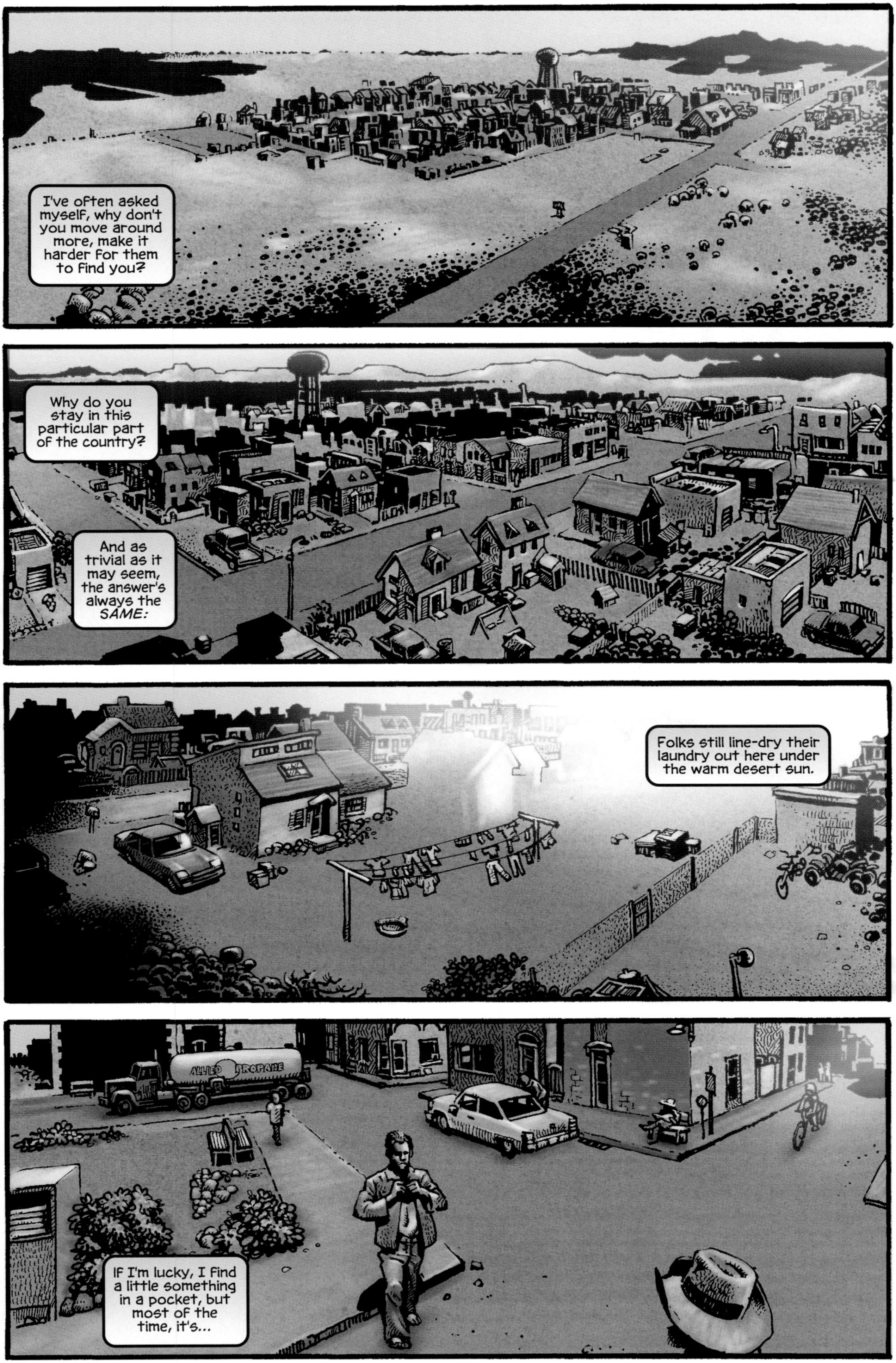
I've often asked myself, why don't you move around more, make it harder for them to find you?
Why do you stay in this particular part of the country?
And as trivial as it may seem, the answer's always the *SAME:*
Folks still line-dry their laundry out here under the warm desert sun.
ALLIED PROPANE
If I'm lucky, I find a little something in a pocket, but most of the time, it's...

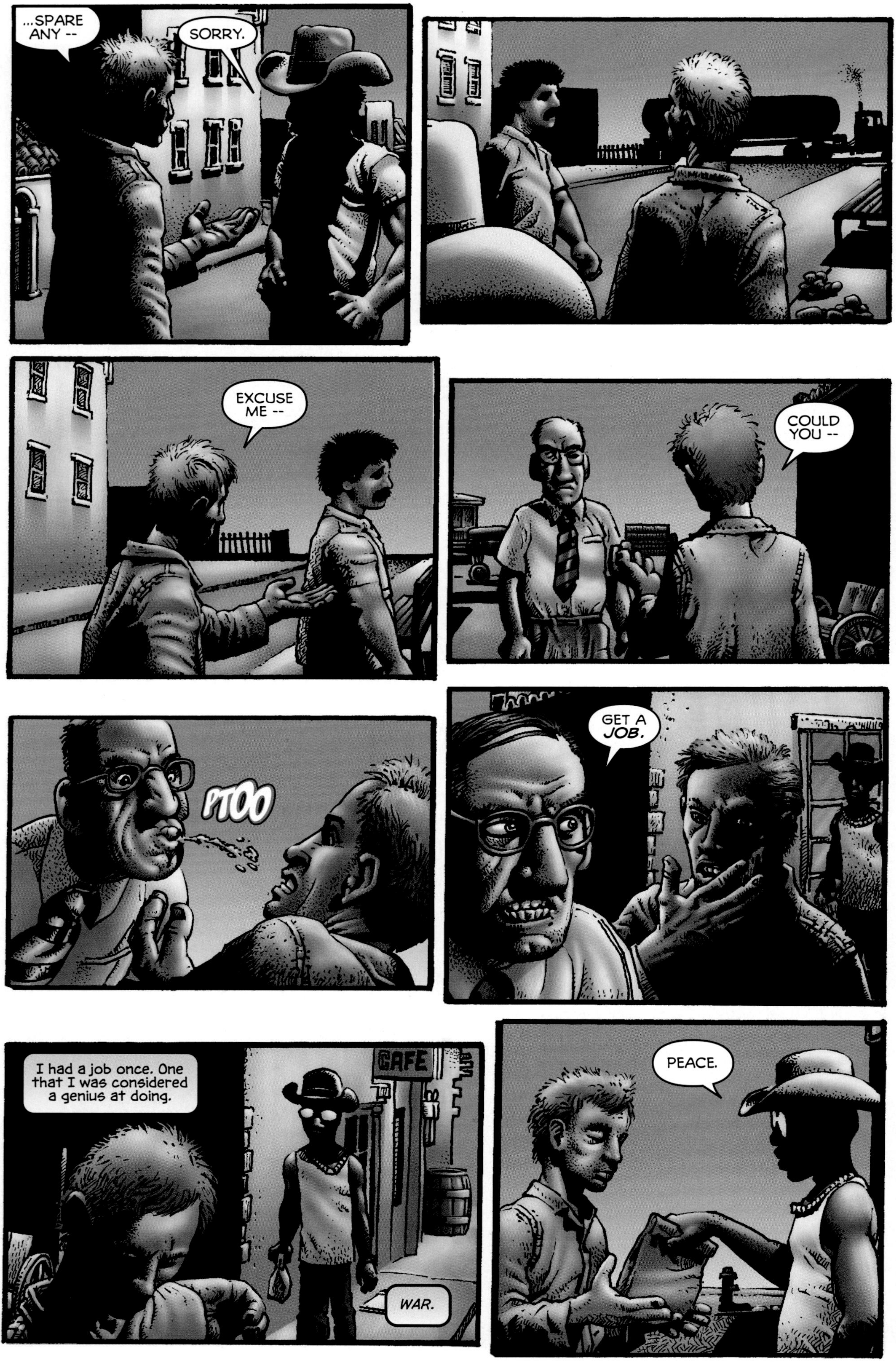
...SPARE ANY --
SORRY.
EXCUSE ME --
COULD YOU --
PTOO
GET A *JOB.*
I had a job once. One that I was considered a genius at doing.
WAR.
PEACE.
CAFE

I did this.

I think.

SERVICE STATION EXPLOSION LEAVES TWO DEAD

I don't know.

That's the worst part, the *GUILT* I feel for every damn headline I read that I might have caused.

I'm never mentioned -- they do a real bang-up job of too clearly stating that it was a mechanical failure or some natural disaster that was responsible for the catastrophe, but I can't help but feel I'm *THERE...*

...BETWEEN the lines.

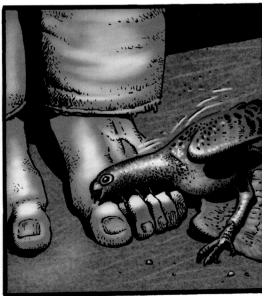

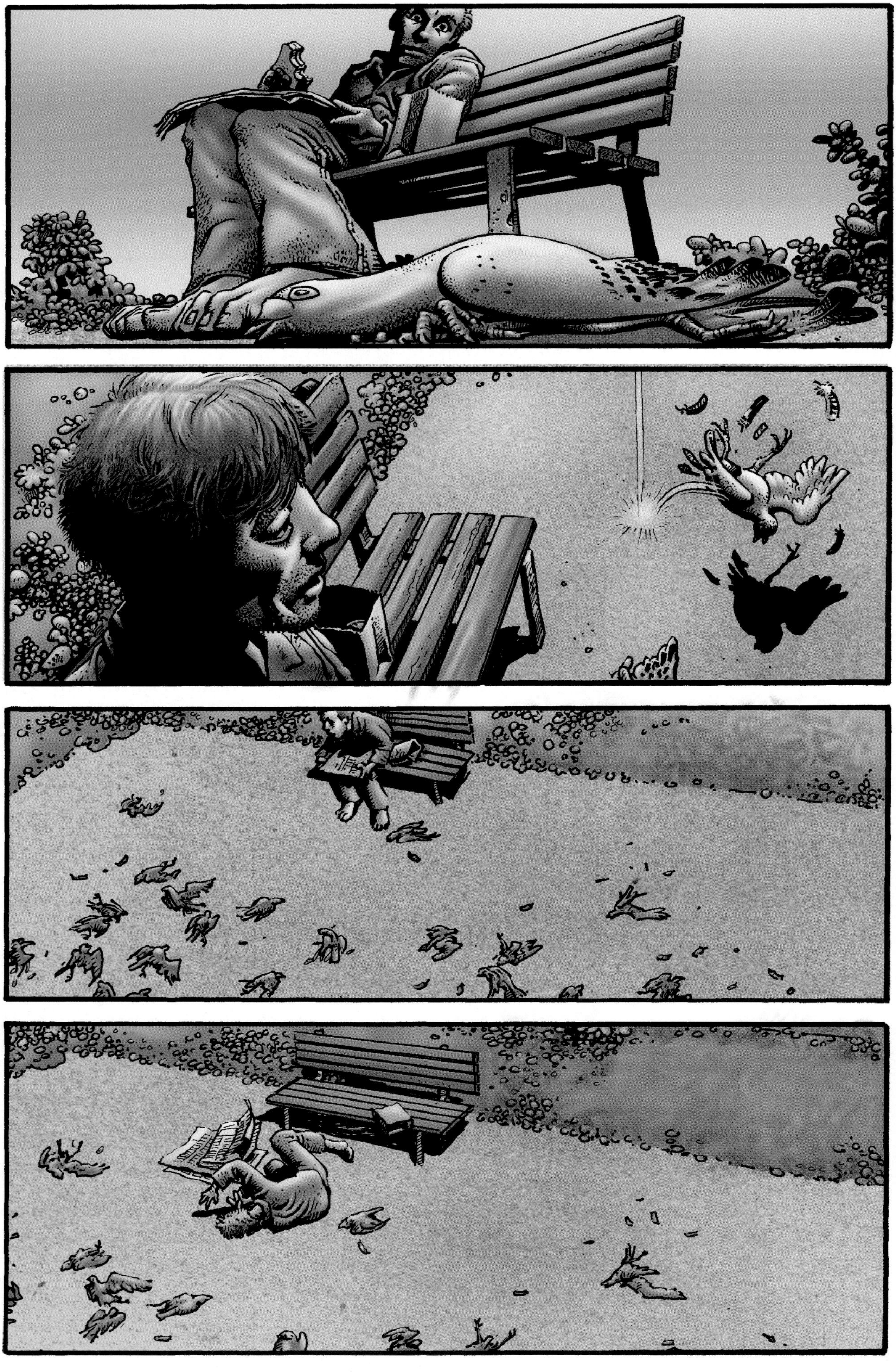

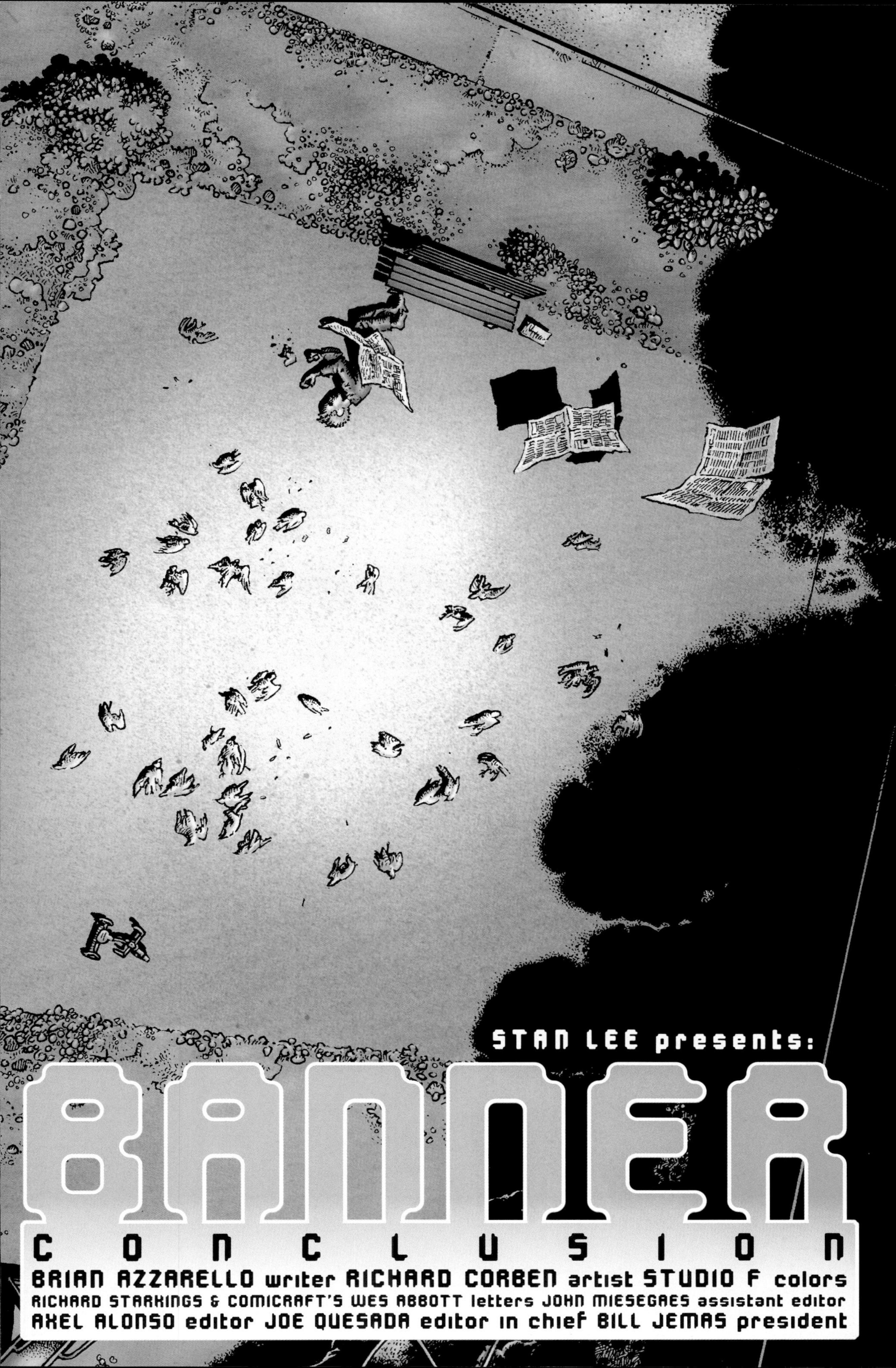
STAN LEE presents:
BANNER
CONCLUSION
BRIAN AZZARELLO writer RICHARD CORBEN artist STUDIO F colors
RICHARD STARKINGS & COMICRAFT'S WES ABBOTT letters JOHN MIESEGAES assistant editor
AXEL ALONSO editor JOE QUESADA editor in chief BILL JEMAS president

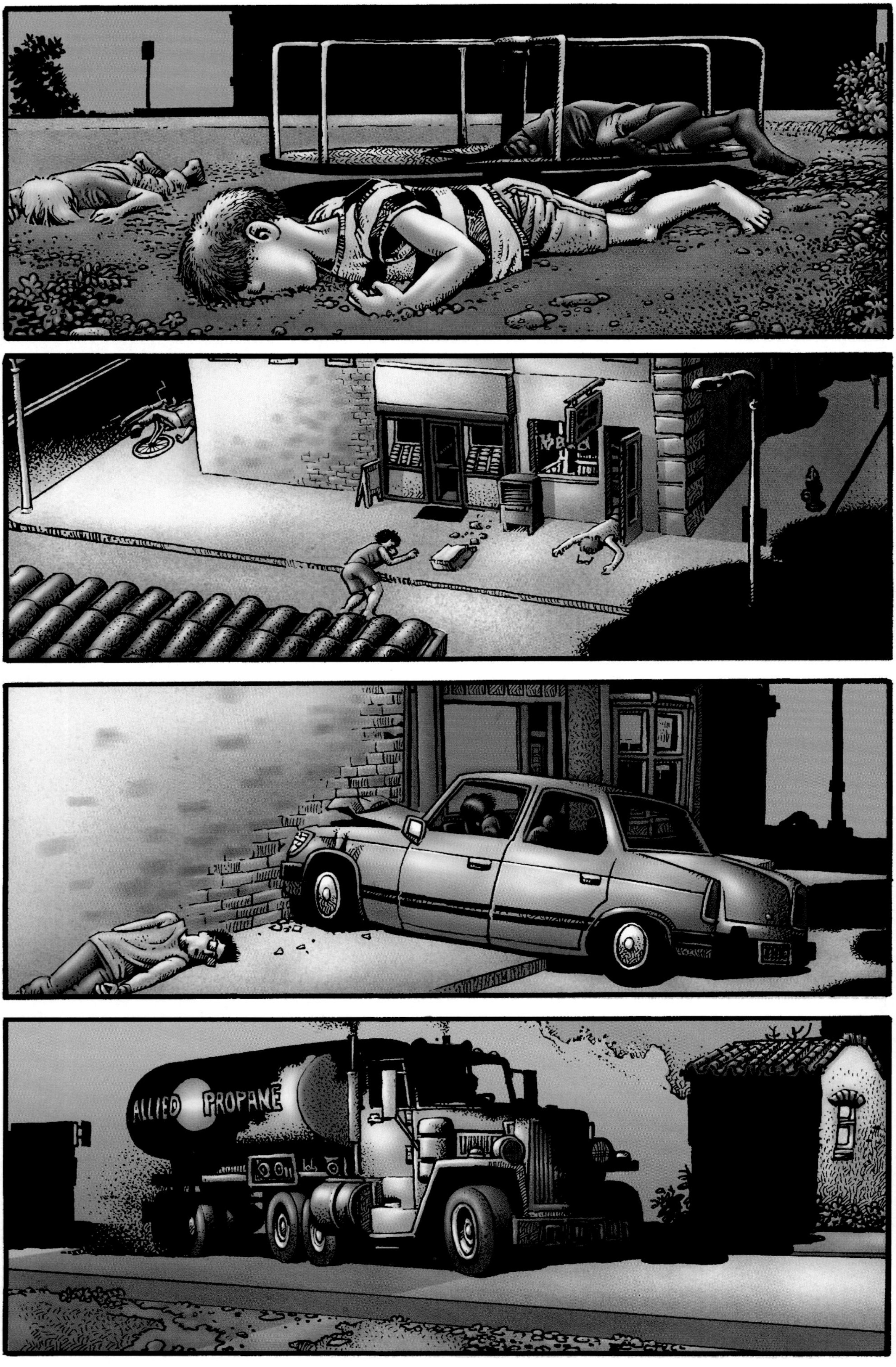
ALLIED PROPANE

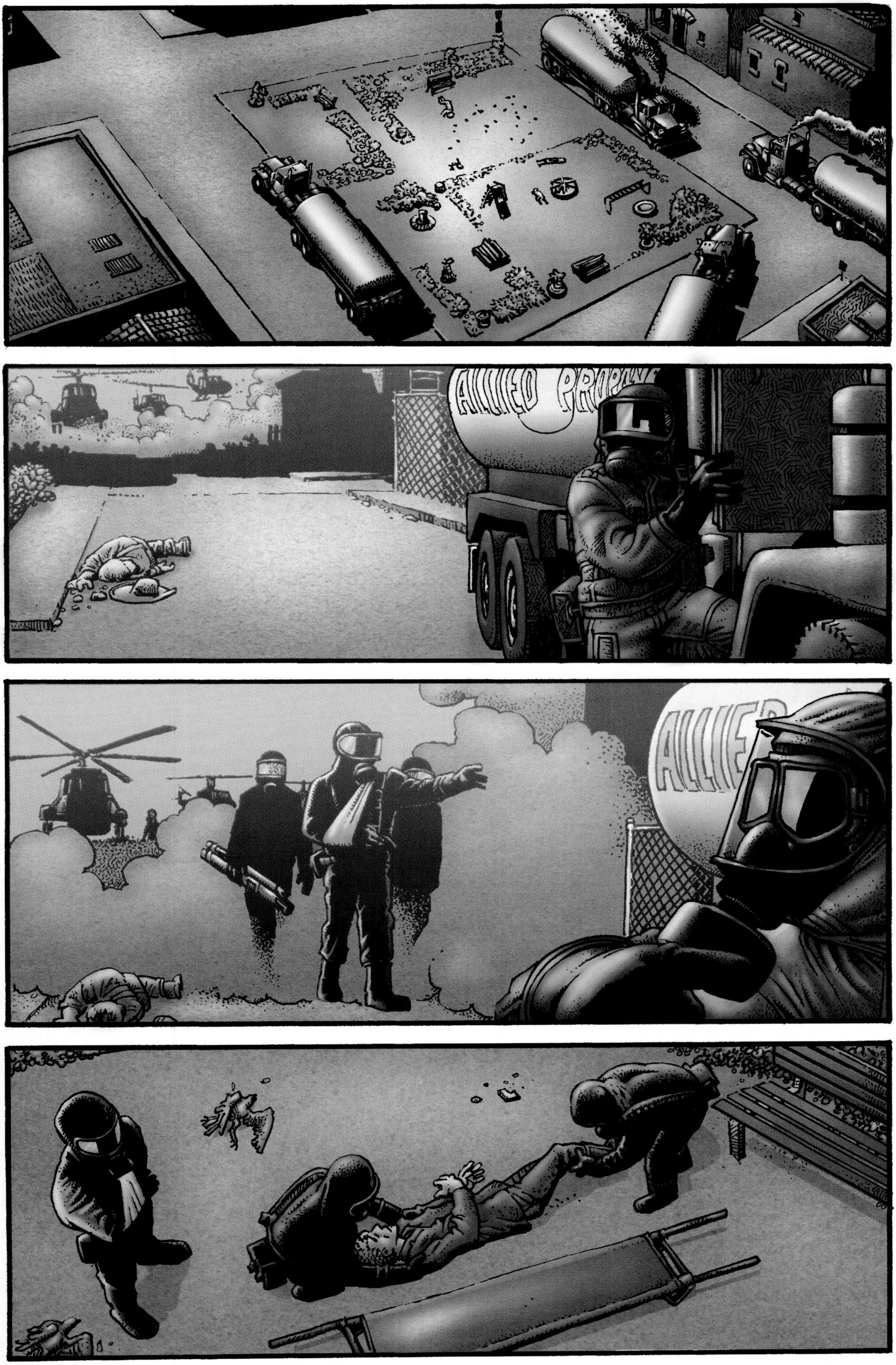
ALLIED
ALLIED

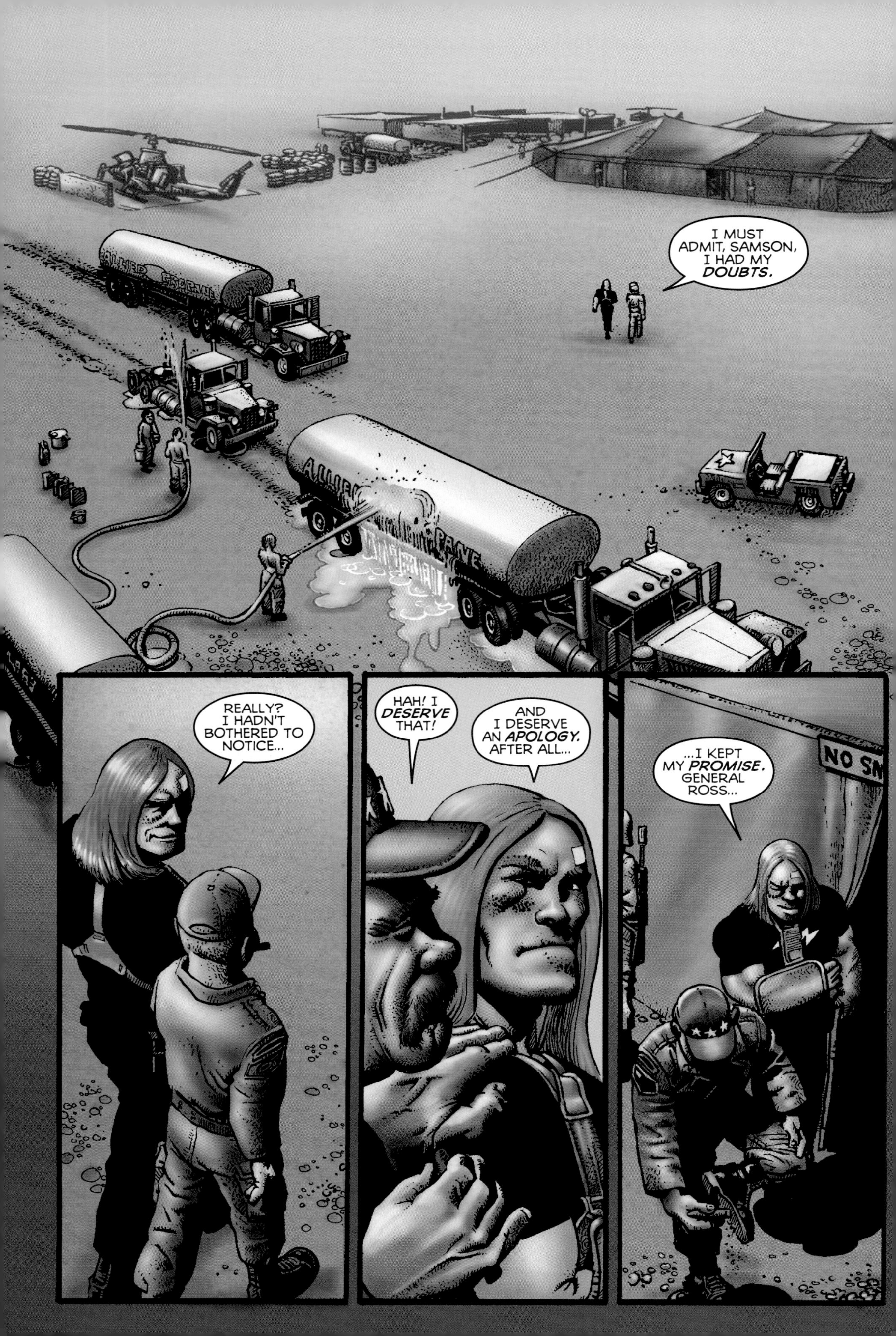
I MUST ADMIT, SAMSON, I HAD MY DOUBTS.
REALLY? I HADN'T BOTHERED TO NOTICE...
HAH! I DESERVE THAT!
AND I DESERVE AN APOLOGY. AFTER ALL...
...I KEPT MY PROMISE. GENERAL ROSS...
NO SM

...THE PRODIGAL SON.

HI.

DAMMIT, SAMSON --!

TAKE A CUE FROM BRUCE, AND *RELAX*, GENERAL. YOU'VE GOT NOTHING TO FEAR, THERE'S NO CHANCE HE CAN...

..."HULK OUT."

WHAT'S HE *BREATHING*?

OXYGEN

NITROGEN

YOU COULD BRING HIS MOTHER IN, PUT A GUN TO HER HEAD, AND FORCE HER TO DO A STRIPTEASE AND HE WOULDN'T GET ANGRY, *WOULD* YOU, BRUCIE?

I SAW MY MOTHER *NAKED* ONCE.

THAT'S MORE THAN WE'D LIKE TO KNOW.

I MEAN *I*. HATE TO SPEAK FOR YOU, GENERAL. SORRY.

THIS CONTAINMENT CELL IS BOTH AIR-TIGHT AND MOBILE, SO WE WON'T HAVE ANY --

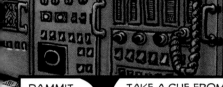

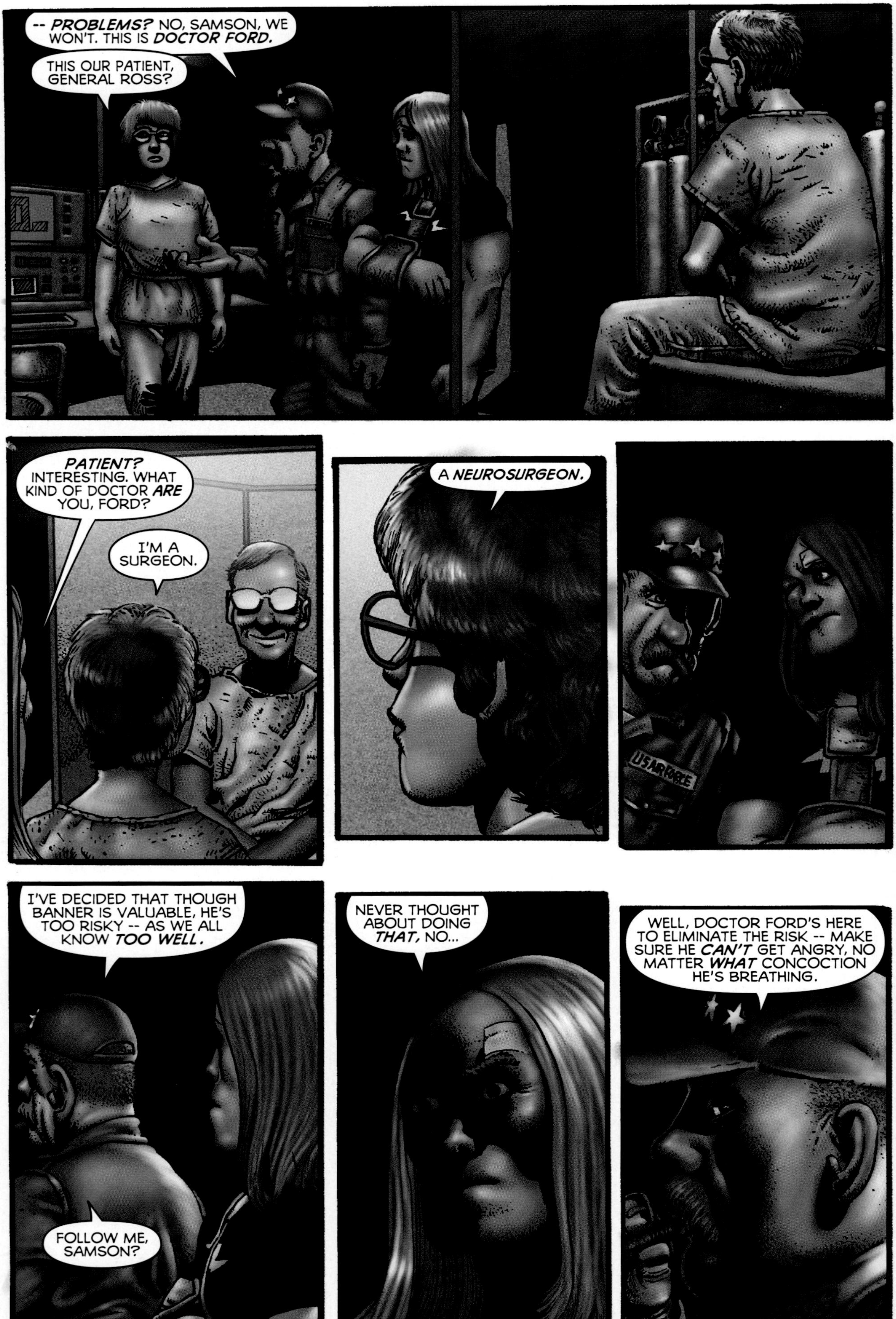
-- PROBLEMS? NO, SAMSON, WE WON'T. THIS IS DOCTOR FORD.
THIS OUR PATIENT, GENERAL ROSS?
PATIENT? INTERESTING. WHAT KIND OF DOCTOR ARE YOU, FORD?
I'M A SURGEON.
A NEUROSURGEON.
US AIR FORCE
I'VE DECIDED THAT THOUGH BANNER IS VALUABLE, HE'S TOO RISKY -- AS WE ALL KNOW TOO WELL.
FOLLOW ME, SAMSON?
NEVER THOUGHT ABOUT DOING THAT, NO...
WELL, DOCTOR FORD'S HERE TO ELIMINATE THE RISK -- MAKE SURE HE CAN'T GET ANGRY, NO MATTER WHAT CONCOCTION HE'S BREATHING.

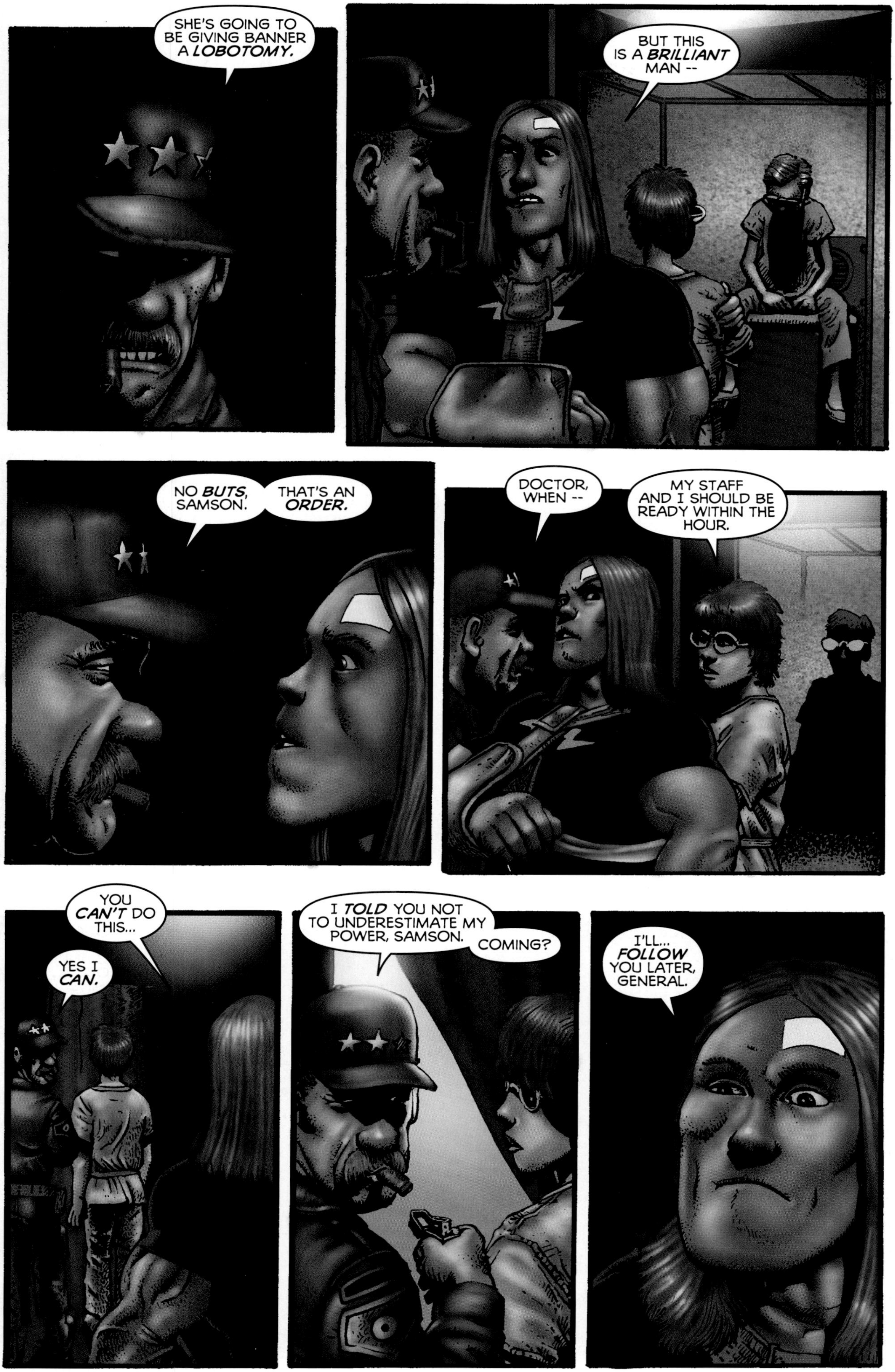
SHE'S GOING TO BE GIVING BANNER A *LOBOTOMY.*
BUT THIS IS A *BRILLIANT* MAN --
NO *BUTS,* SAMSON.
THAT'S AN *ORDER.*
DOCTOR, WHEN --
MY STAFF AND I SHOULD BE READY WITHIN THE HOUR.
YOU *CAN'T* DO THIS...
YES I *CAN.*
I *TOLD* YOU NOT TO UNDERESTIMATE MY POWER, SAMSON.
COMING?
I'LL... *FOLLOW* YOU LATER, GENERAL.

WHAT *HAPPENED* TO YOU?

YOU HAPPENED TO ME.

OH. SORRY. YOU MAD?

YOU SHOULD BE.

NO, THAT'S ONE THING I SHOULD *NEVER* BE.

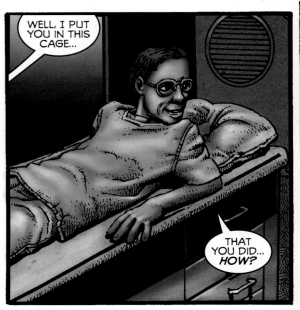

WELL, I PUT YOU IN THIS CAGE...

THAT YOU DID... *HOW?*

SIMPLE REALLY -- A SIMPLE ONE-CELL ORGANISM WE DEVELOPED THAT COULD SURVIVE THE GAMMA RADIATION YOUR BODY *"SWEATS"* DURING TRANSFORMATIONS.

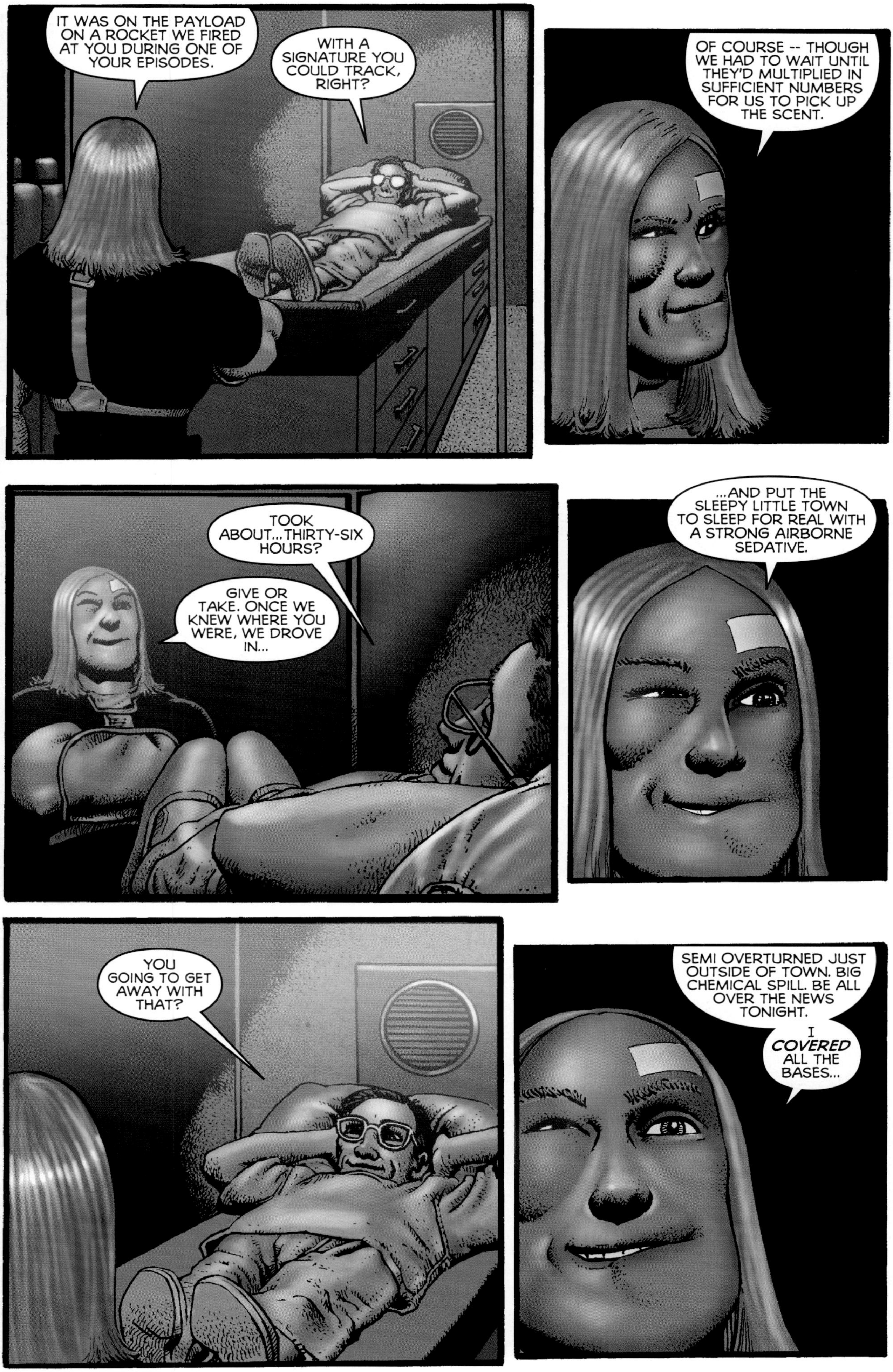
IT WAS ON THE PAYLOAD ON A ROCKET WE FIRED AT YOU DURING ONE OF YOUR EPISODES.
WITH A SIGNATURE YOU COULD TRACK, RIGHT?
OF COURSE -- THOUGH WE HAD TO WAIT UNTIL THEY'D MULTIPLIED IN SUFFICIENT NUMBERS FOR US TO PICK UP THE SCENT.
TOOK ABOUT...THIRTY-SIX HOURS?
GIVE OR TAKE. ONCE WE KNEW WHERE YOU WERE, WE DROVE IN...
...AND PUT THE SLEEPY LITTLE TOWN TO SLEEP FOR REAL WITH A STRONG AIRBORNE SEDATIVE.
YOU GOING TO GET AWAY WITH THAT?
SEMI OVERTURNED JUST OUTSIDE OF TOWN. BIG CHEMICAL SPILL. BE ALL OVER THE NEWS TONIGHT.
I *COVERED* ALL THE BASES...

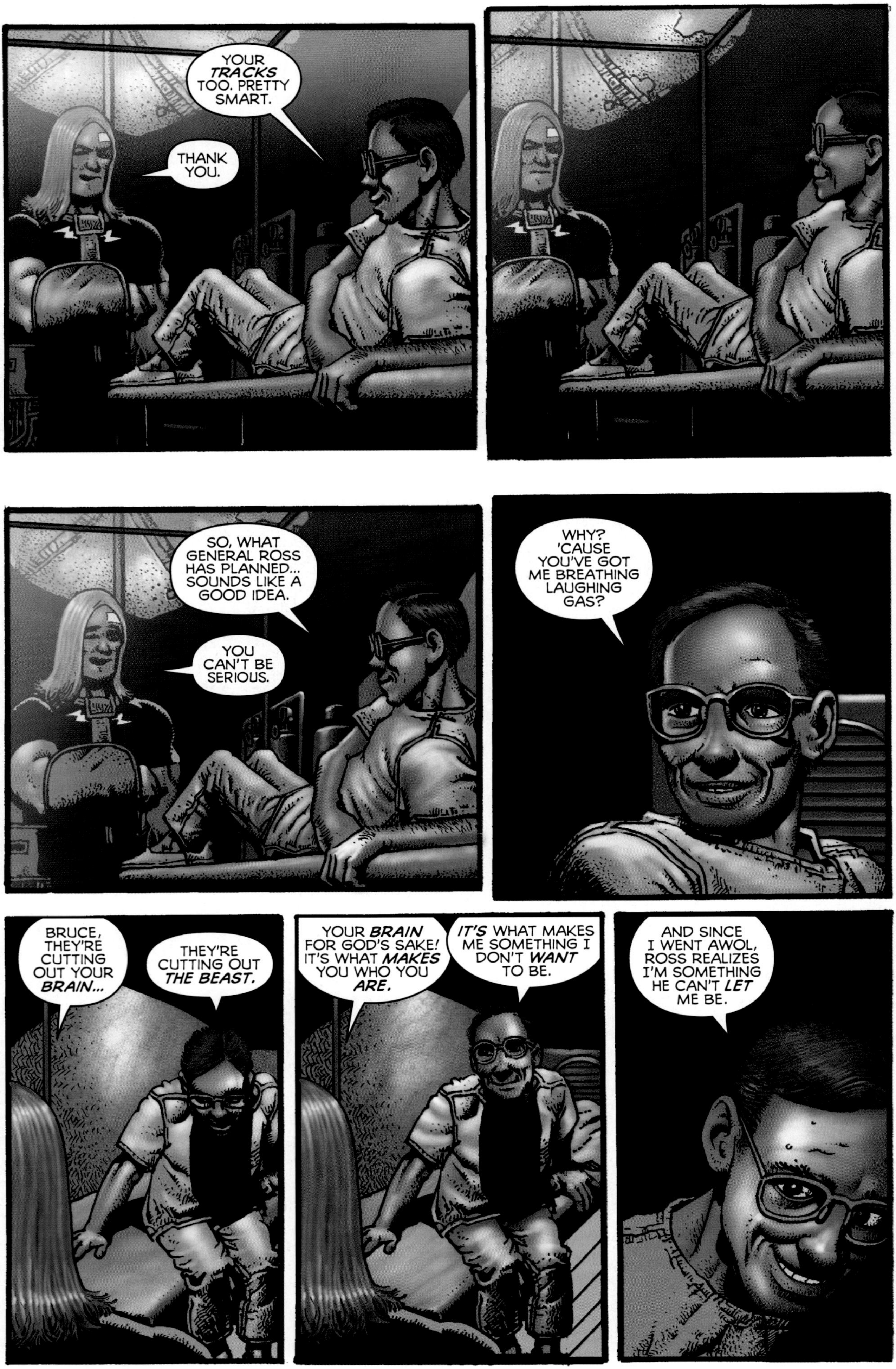
YOUR *TRACKS* TOO. PRETTY SMART.
THANK YOU.
SO, WHAT GENERAL ROSS HAS PLANNED... SOUNDS LIKE A GOOD IDEA.
YOU CAN'T BE SERIOUS.
WHY? 'CAUSE YOU'VE GOT ME BREATHING LAUGHING GAS?
BRUCE, THEY'RE CUTTING OUT YOUR *BRAIN...*
THEY'RE CUTTING OUT *THE BEAST.*
YOUR *BRAIN* FOR GOD'S SAKE! IT'S WHAT *MAKES* YOU WHO YOU *ARE.*
IT'S WHAT MAKES ME SOMETHING I DON'T *WANT* TO BE.
AND SINCE I WENT AWOL, ROSS REALIZES I'M SOMETHING HE CAN'T *LET* ME BE.

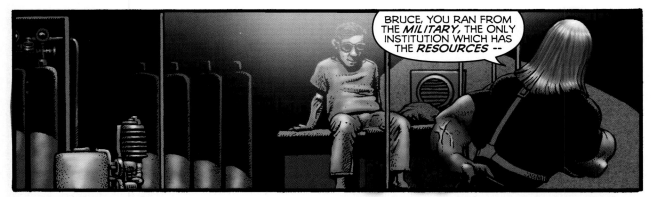

BRUCE, YOU RAN FROM THE *MILITARY*, THE ONLY INSTITUTION WHICH HAS THE *RESOURCES* --

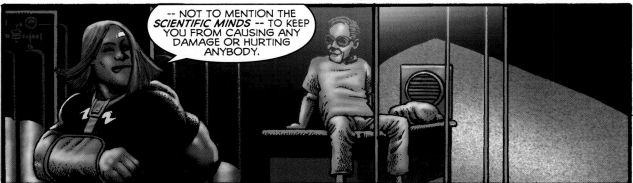

-- NOT TO MENTION THE *SCIENTIFIC MINDS* -- TO KEEP YOU FROM CAUSING ANY DAMAGE OR HURTING ANYBODY.

HURTING ANYBODY? I MADE *BOMBS.*

YOU CREATED THE *GAMMA BOMB* --

-- THE GAMMA BOMB CREATED *ME.*

AND YOU.

THAT WAS THE *POINT,* ALL ALONG.

AFTER MY ACCIDENT, I TOOK ALL THE DRUGS THEY PRESCRIBED TO KEEP MY...MOOD BALANCED. I COULD *FUNCTION.*

THEN ONE DAY, INSTEAD OF THE DRUGS...

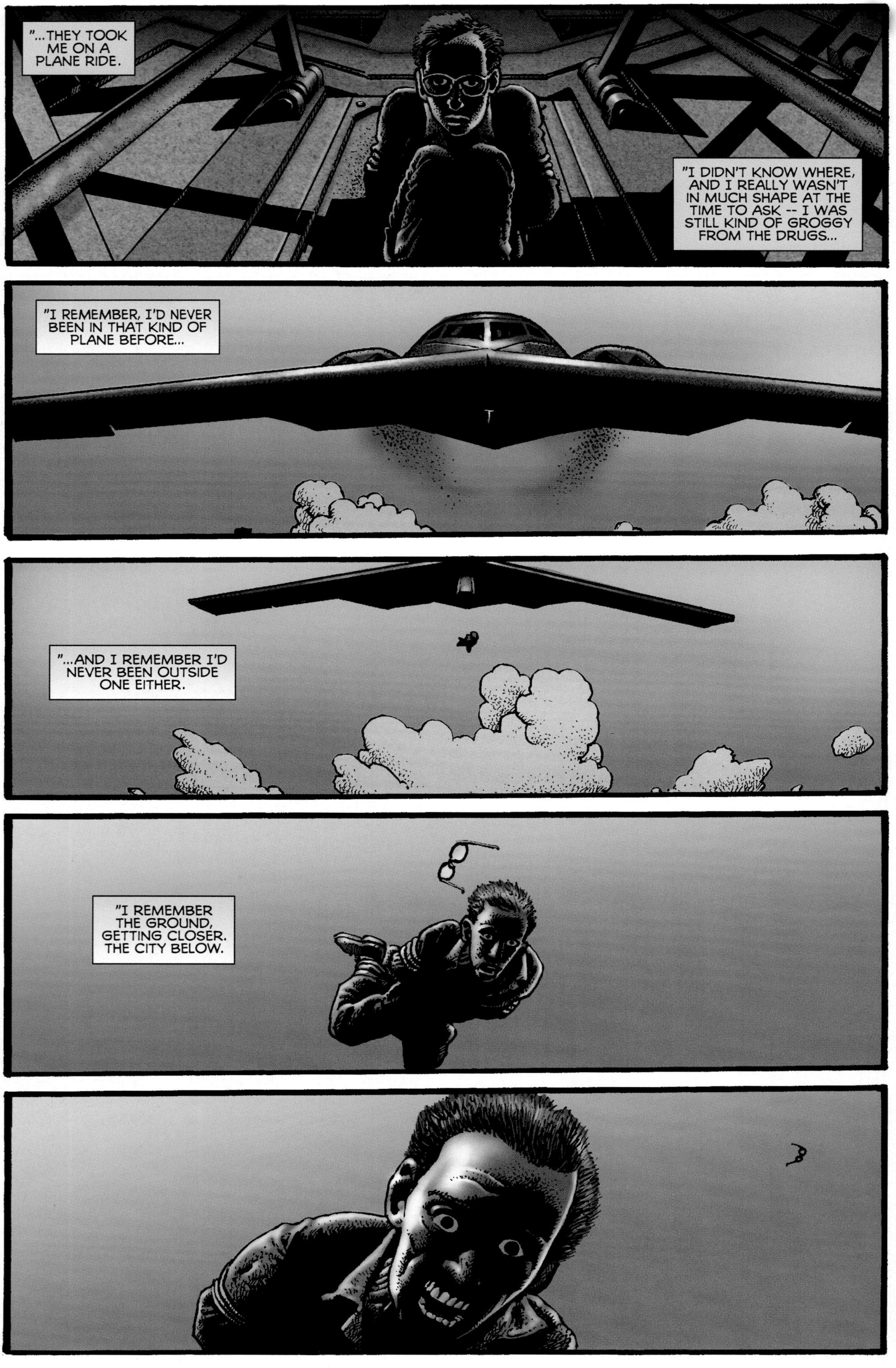
"...THEY TOOK ME ON A PLANE RIDE.
"I DIDN'T KNOW WHERE, AND I REALLY WASN'T IN MUCH SHAPE AT THE TIME TO ASK -- I WAS STILL KIND OF GROGGY FROM THE DRUGS...
"I REMEMBER, I'D NEVER BEEN IN THAT KIND OF PLANE BEFORE...
"...AND I REMEMBER I'D NEVER BEEN OUTSIDE ONE EITHER.
"I REMEMBER THE GROUND, GETTING CLOSER. THE CITY BELOW.

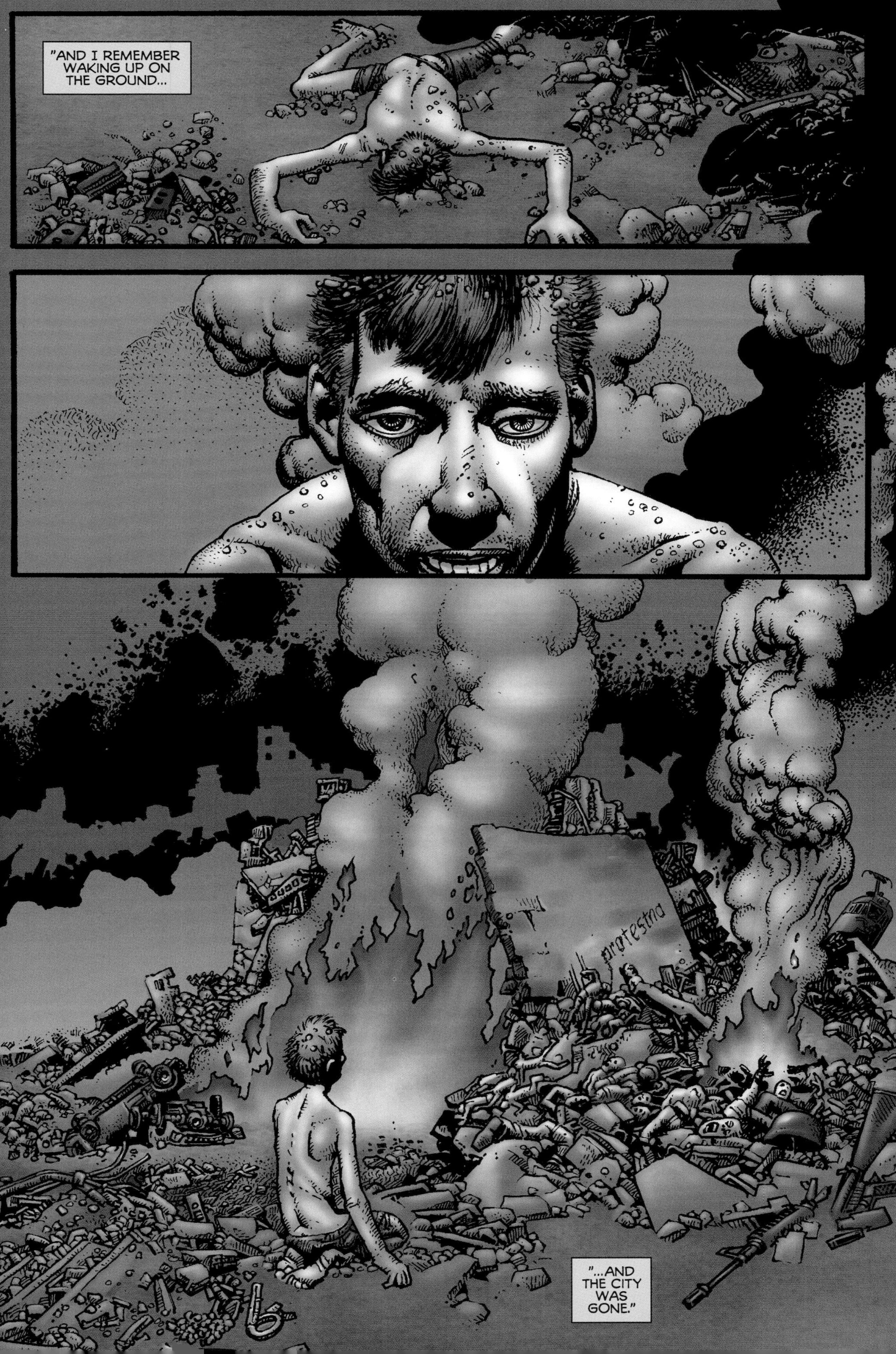
"AND I REMEMBER WAKING UP ON THE GROUND...
"...AND THE CITY WAS GONE."

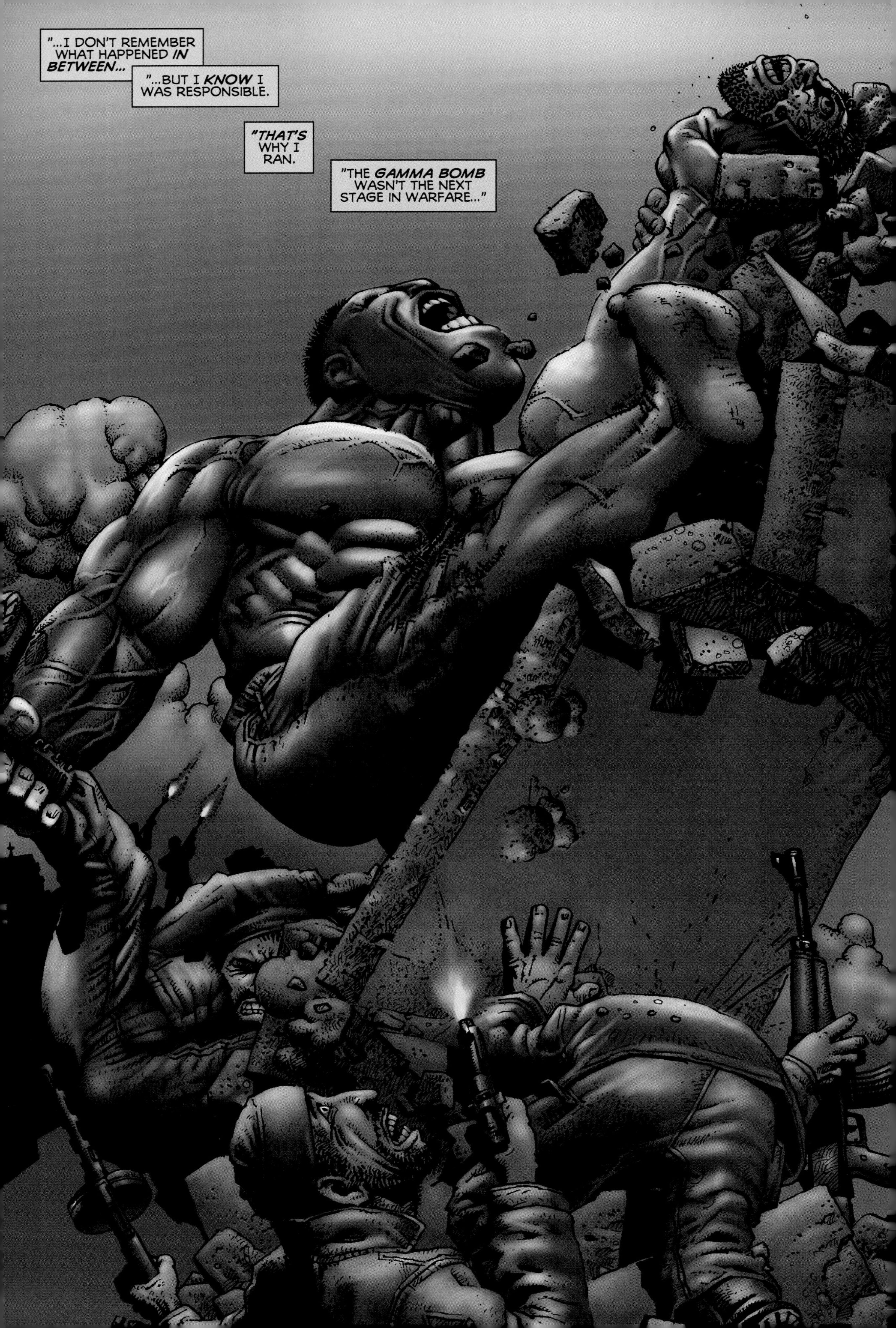
"...I DON'T REMEMBER WHAT HAPPENED *IN BETWEEN*...
"...BUT I *KNOW* I WAS RESPONSIBLE.
"THAT'S WHY I RAN.
"THE *GAMMA BOMB* WASN'T THE NEXT STAGE IN WARFARE..."

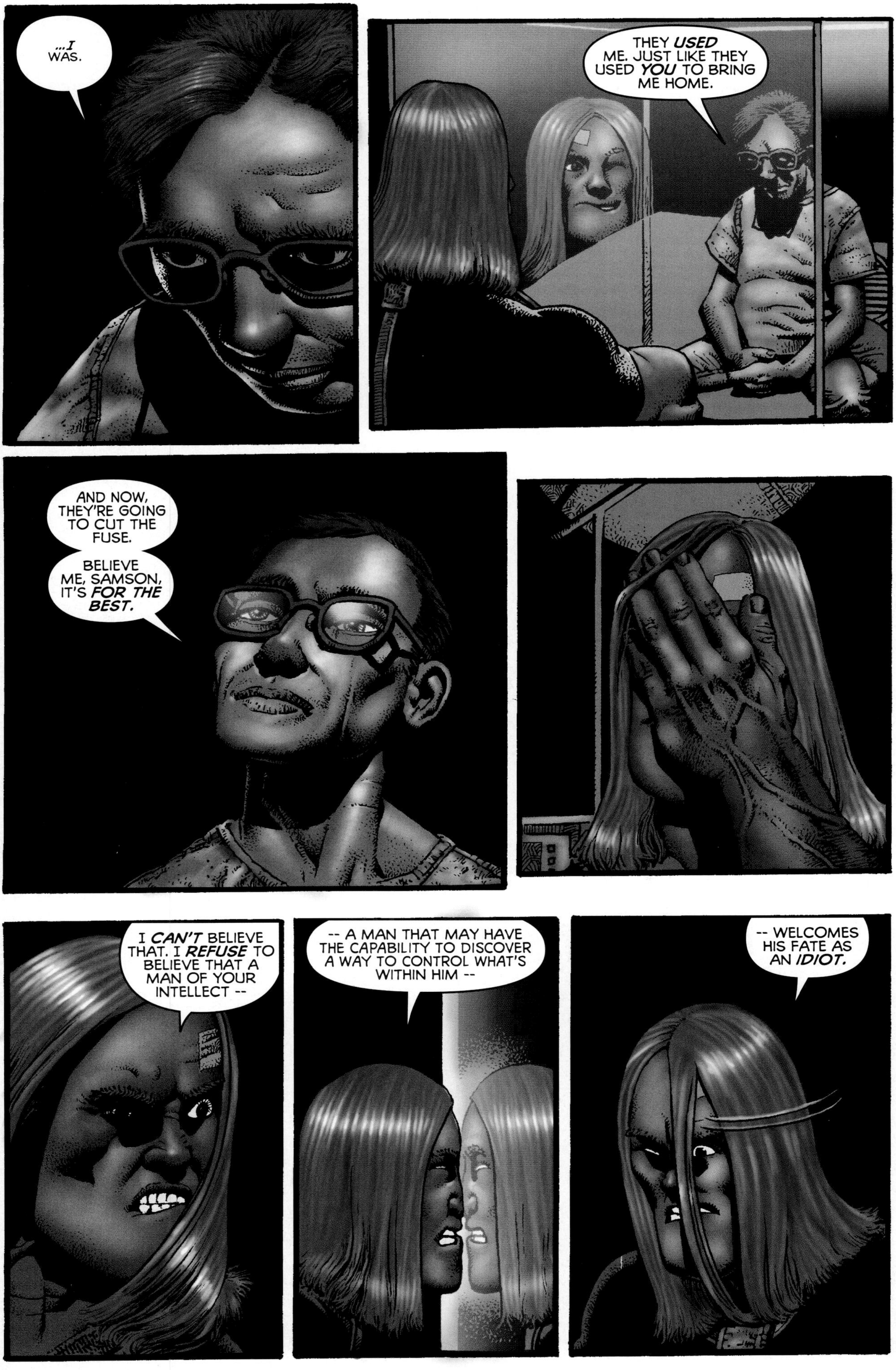
...I WAS.
THEY USED ME. JUST LIKE THEY USED YOU TO BRING ME HOME.
AND NOW, THEY'RE GOING TO CUT THE FUSE.
BELIEVE ME, SAMSON, IT'S FOR THE BEST.
I CAN'T BELIEVE THAT. I REFUSE TO BELIEVE THAT A MAN OF YOUR INTELLECT --
-- A MAN THAT MAY HAVE THE CAPABILITY TO DISCOVER A WAY TO CONTROL WHAT'S WITHIN HIM --
-- WELCOMES HIS FATE AS AN IDIOT.

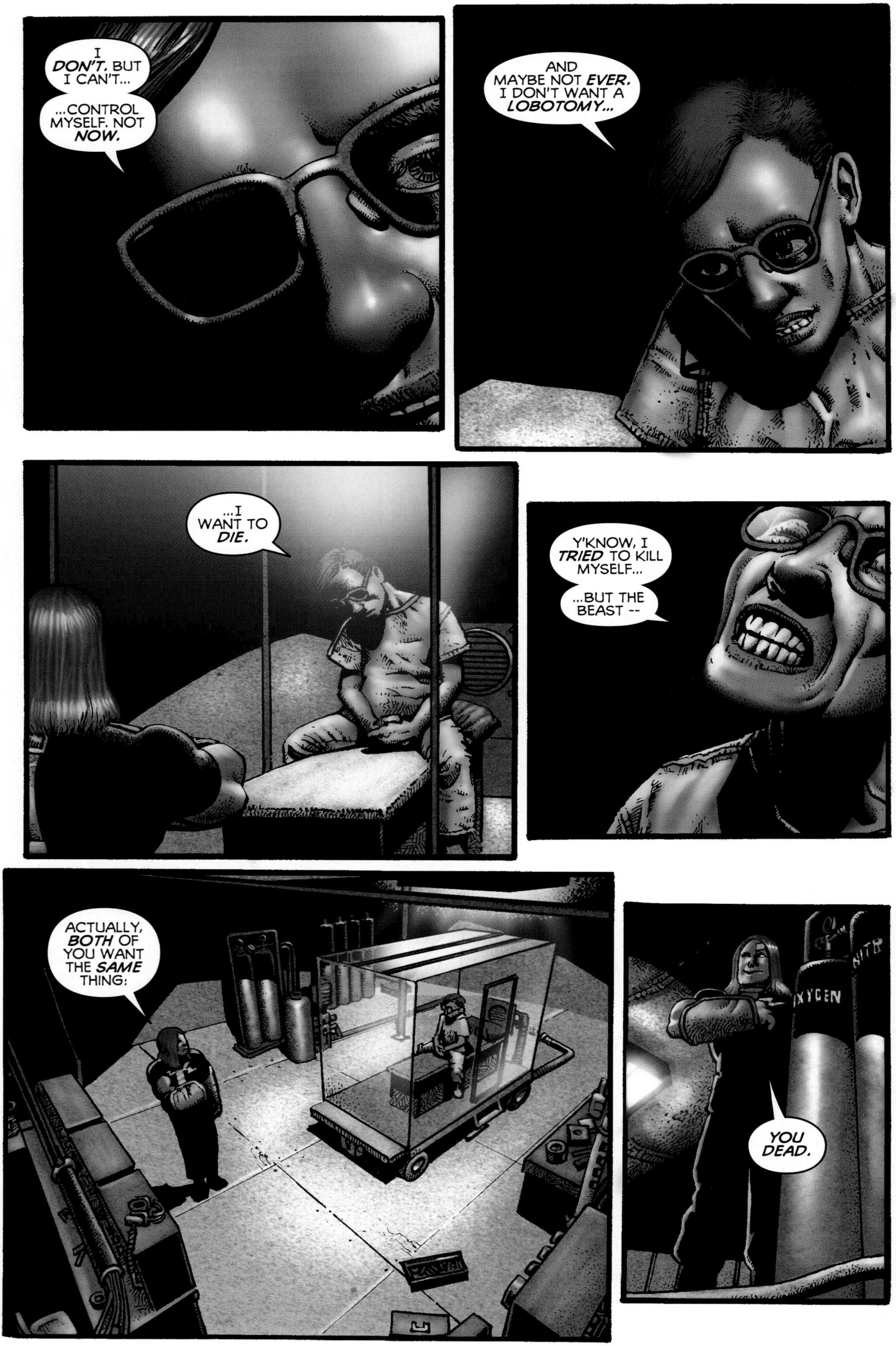
I DON'T. BUT I CAN'T...
...CONTROL MYSELF. NOT NOW.
AND MAYBE NOT EVER. I DON'T WANT A LOBOTOMY...
...I WANT TO DIE.
Y'KNOW, I TRIED TO KILL MYSELF...
...BUT THE BEAST --
ACTUALLY, BOTH OF YOU WANT THE SAME THING:
YOU DEAD.
OXYGEN

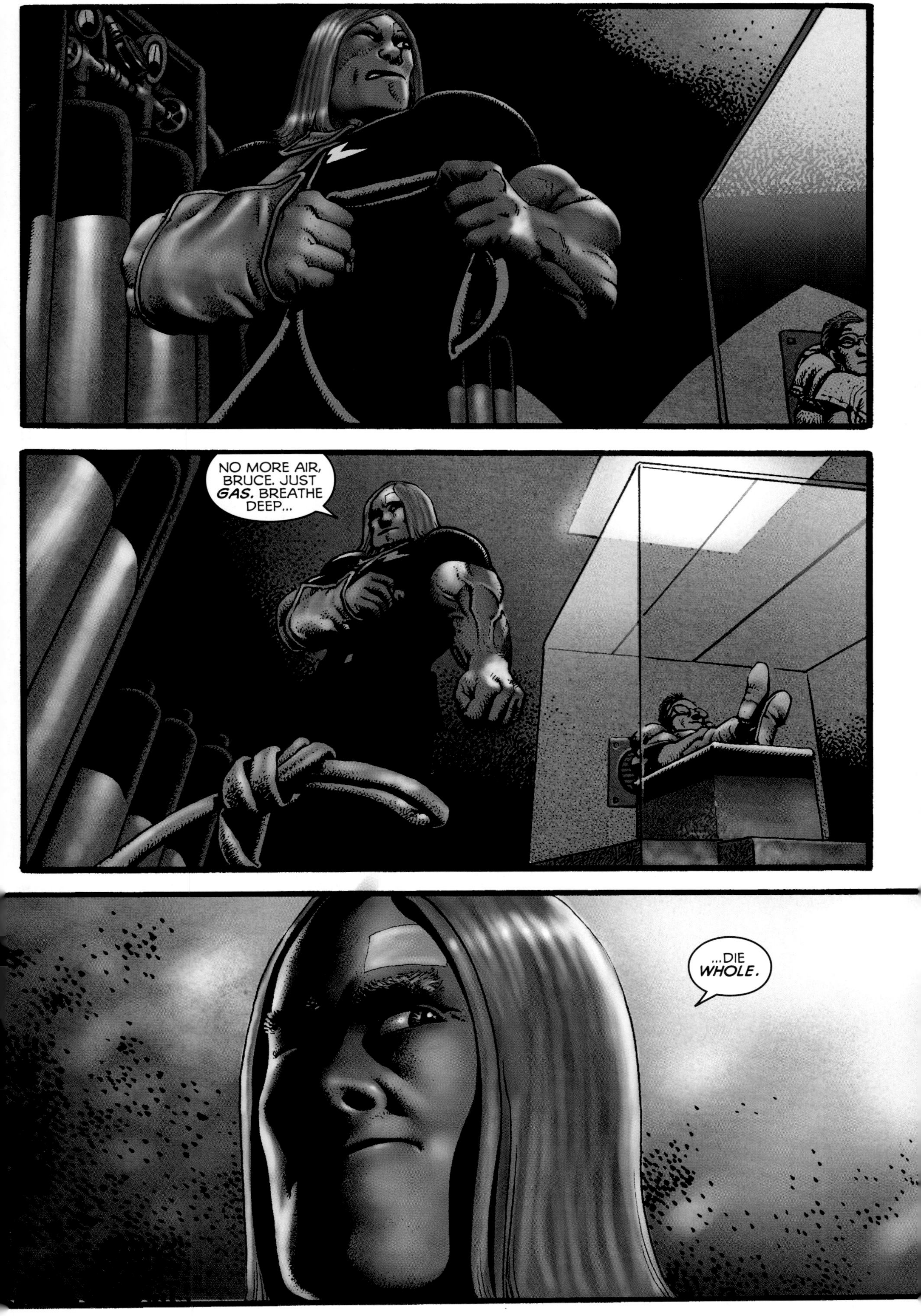
NO MORE AIR, BRUCE. JUST GAS. BREATHE DEEP...
...DIE WHOLE.

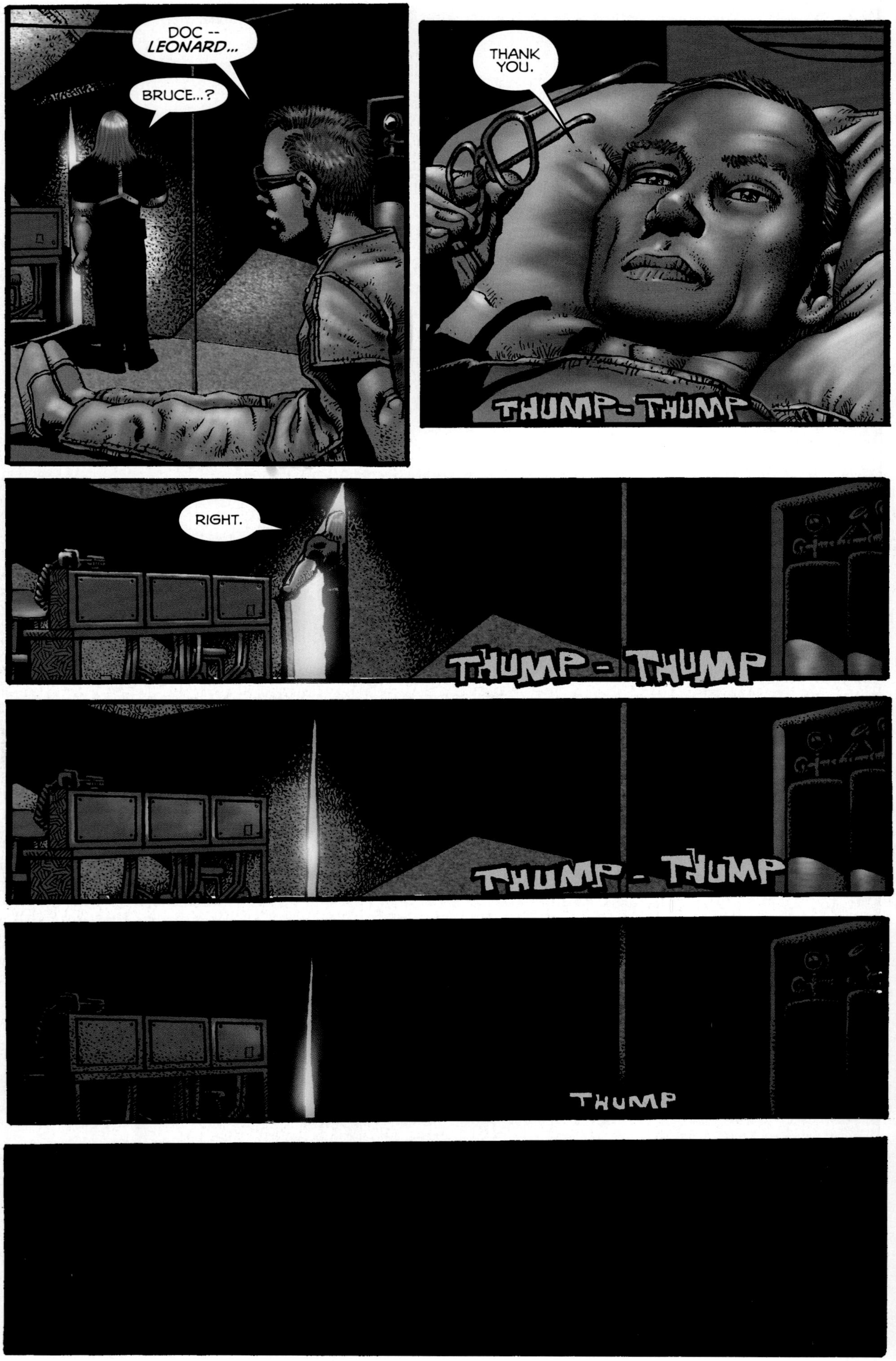
DOC -- LEONARD...
BRUCE...?
THANK YOU.
THUMP-THUMP
RIGHT.
THUMP-THUMP
THUMP-THUMP
THUMP

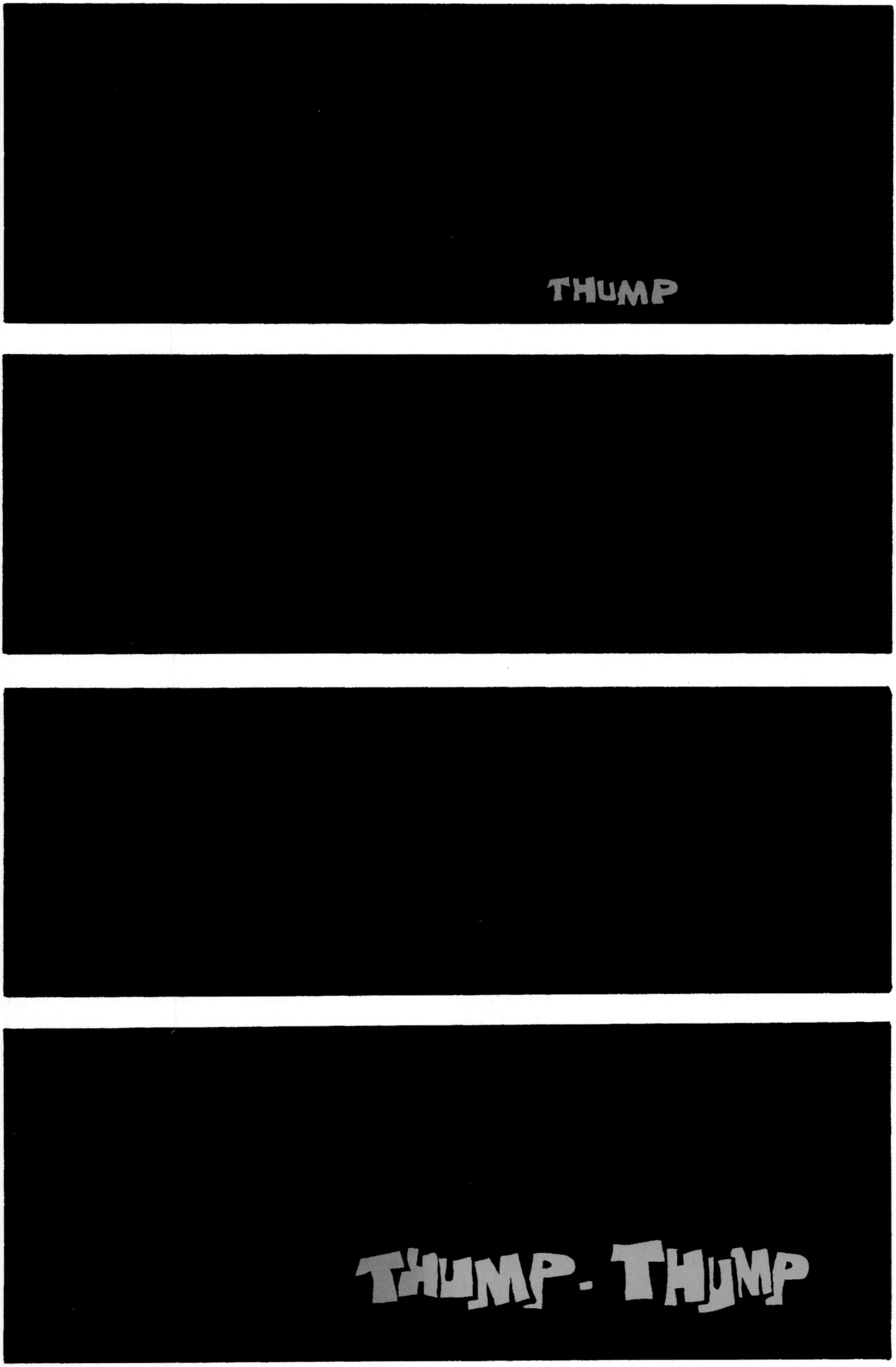
THUMP
THUMP - THUMP

Richard Corben Sketchbook

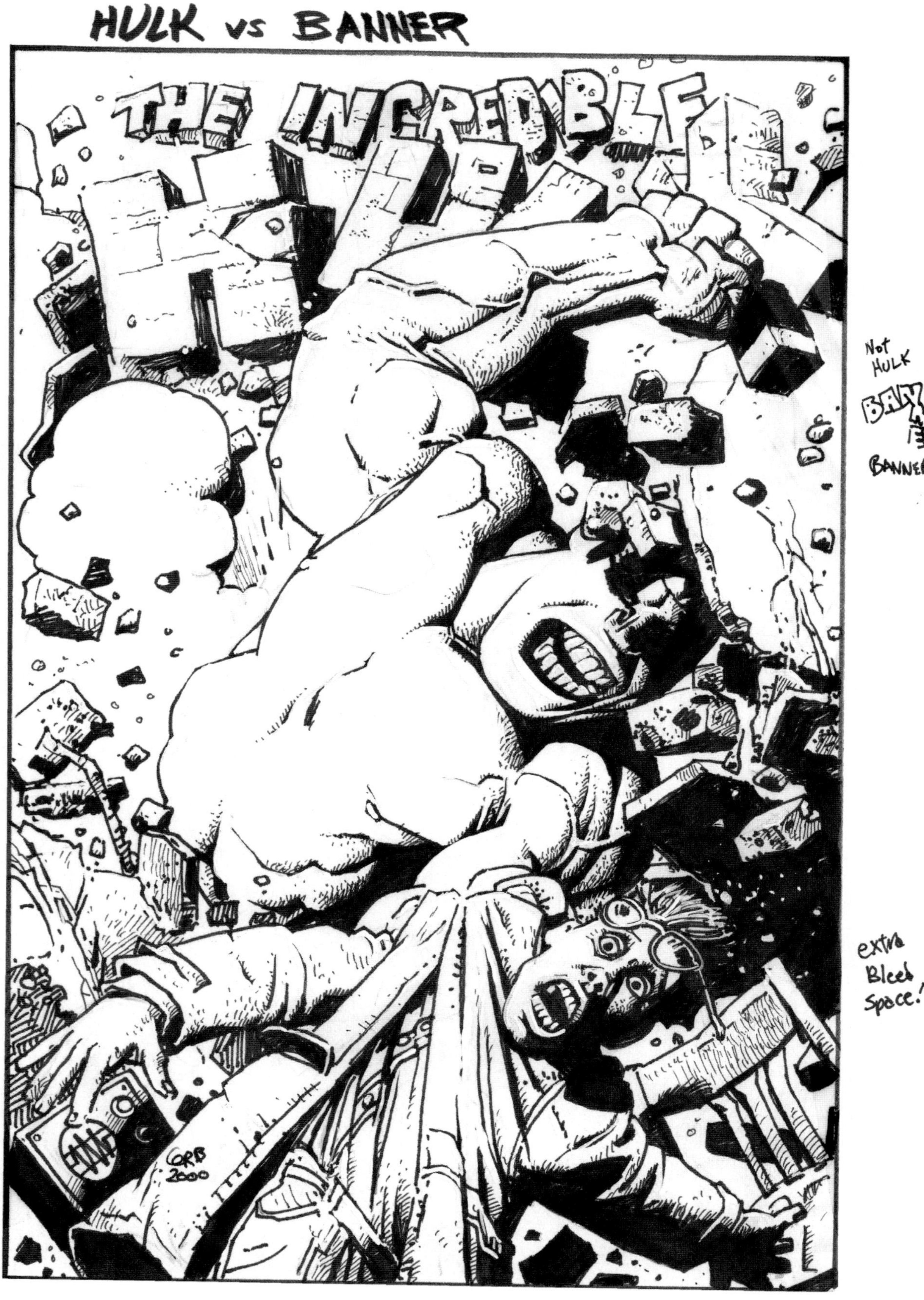
HULK vs BANNER
THE INCREDIBLE
CORB 2000
Not HULK
BANNER!
extra Bleed Space!

Banner #1 Cover Sketch

Banner Cover 2 sketch 2

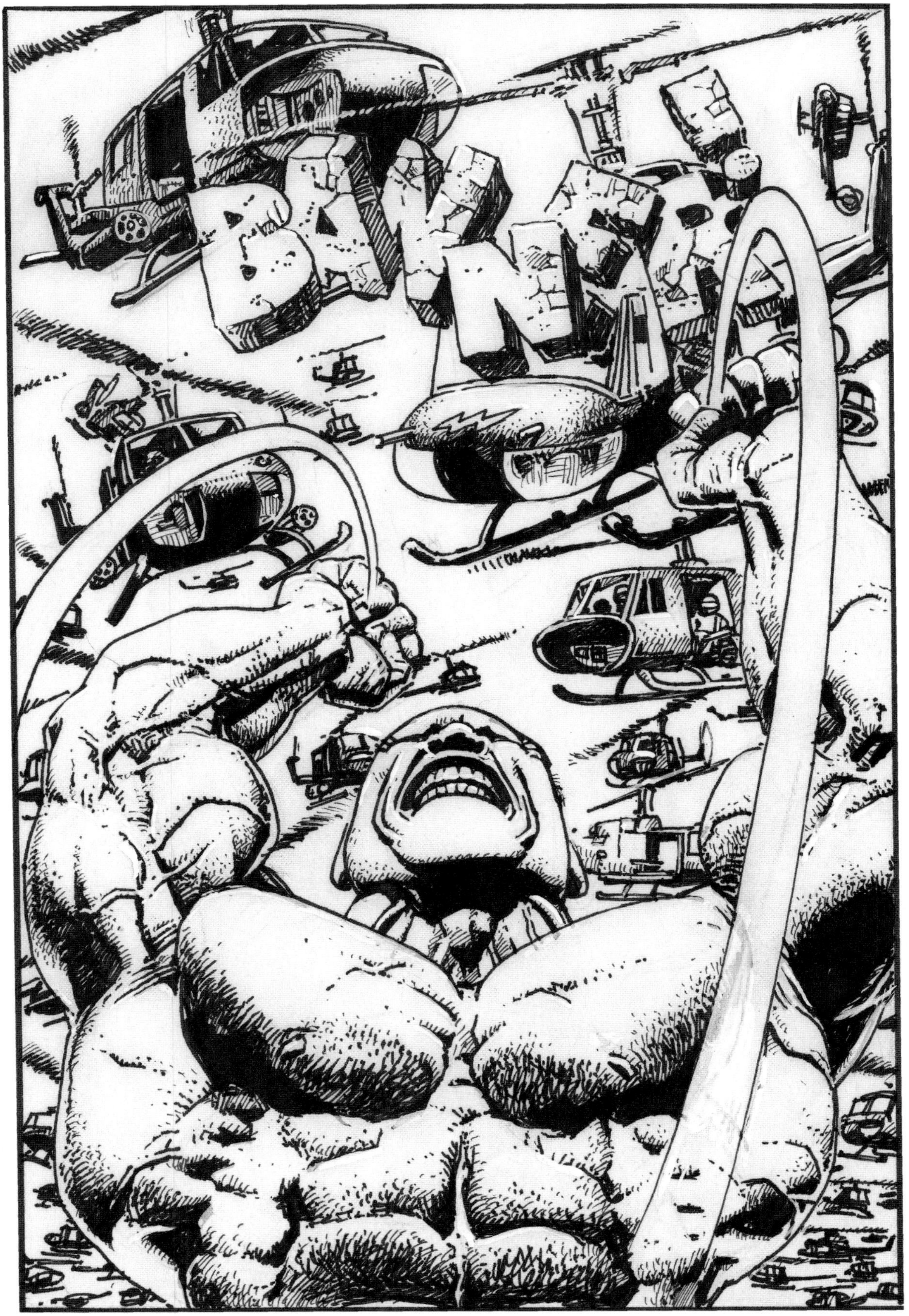

Banner #2 Preliminary Cover Sketch

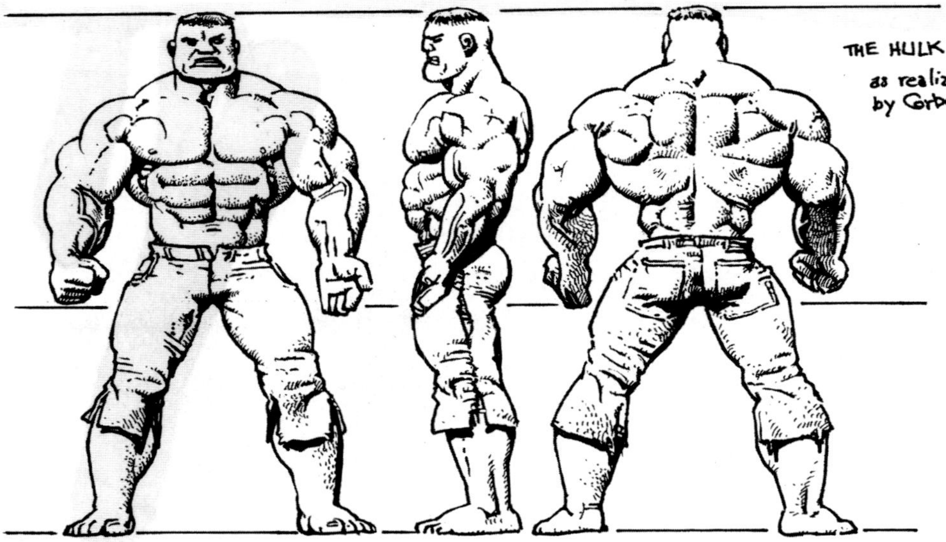

THE HULK
as realized
by Corben

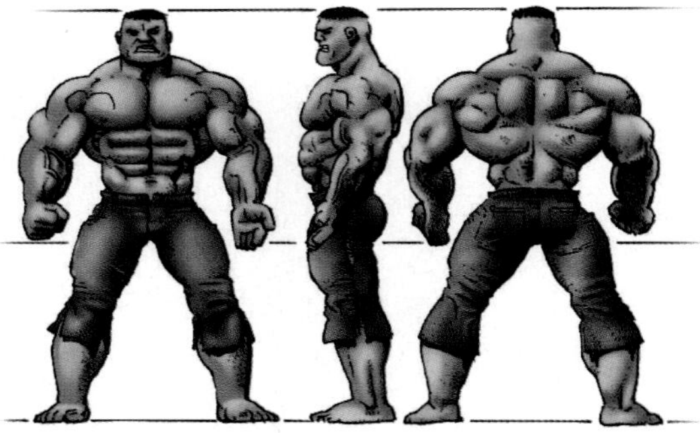

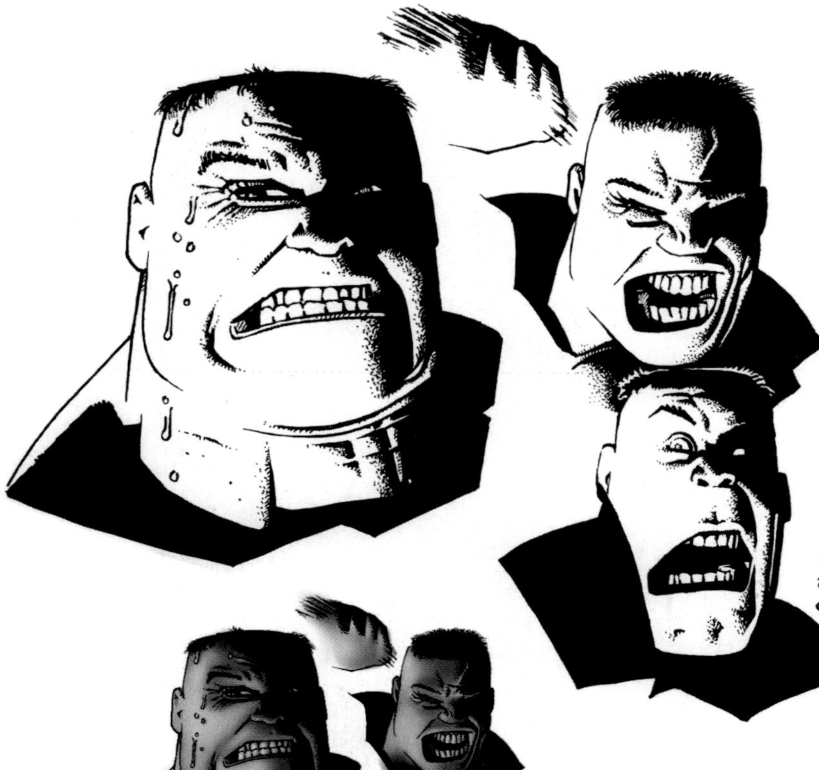

HULK
as drawn by
Corben

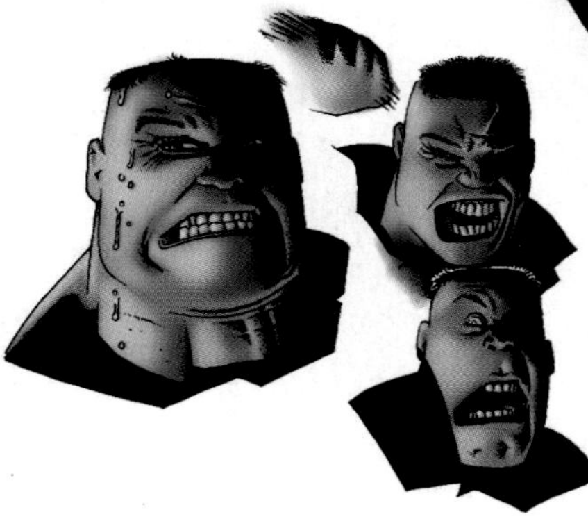